The
Judicial
Process

D1125043

The Judicial Process

An Introductory Analysis
of the Courts of the
United States, England,
and France

SIXTH EDITION

Henry J. Abraham
University of Virginia

New York   Oxford
Oxford University Press
1993

Oxford University Press

Oxford   New York   Toronto
Delhi   Bombay   Calcutta   Madras   Karachi
Kuala Lumpur   Singapore   Hong Kong   Tokyo
Nairobi   Dar es Salaam   Cape Town
Melbourne   Auckland   Madrid

and associated companies in
Berlin   Ibadan

Copyright © 1962, 1968, 1975, 1980, 1986,
1993 by Henry J. Abraham

Published by Oxford University Press, Inc.
200 Madison Avenue, New York, New York 10016

Oxford is a registered trademark of Oxford University Press.

All rights reserved. No part of this publication may be reproduced,
stored in a retrieval system, or transmitted, in any form or by any means,
electronic, mechanical, photocopying, recording, or otherwise,
without the prior permission of Oxford University Press.

Library of Congress Cataloging-in-Publication Data
Abraham, Henry Julian, 1921–
The judicial process : an introductory analysis of the courts
of the United States, England, and France / Henry J. Abraham. — 6th ed.
p. cm.   Includes bibliographical references and indexes.
ISBN 0-19-506801-7
1. Courts—United States.
2. Courts—Great Britain.
3. Courts—France.
4. Judicial process.
I. Title.
K2100.A725   1993   347'.01—dc20
[342.71]   92-8336

347.01
A159 j
1993

9   8   7   6   5   4   3   2   1

Printed in the United States of America
on acid-free paper

**To
Philip**

METHODIST COLLEGE LIBRARY
Fayetteville, N.C.

Preface

Initially published in 1962 and subsequently revised in 1968, 1975, 1980, and 1986, *The Judicial Process*'s continued popularity at home and abroad has justified a sixth edition. Indeed, the six years that have elapsed since the appearance of the fifth edition have borne witness to such major—in fact, dramatic—developmental changes in the nature and application of the judicial process, both domestic and foreign, that a new edition had become all but mandatory.

This latest edition has accordingly been thoroughly revised and updated through mid-summer 1992. Thus, the work of the Supreme Court of the United States is analyzed through its 1991–92 term (e.g., the impact of the four new Justices who have mounted the high tribunal since 1986: Antonin Scalia, Anthony M. Kennedy, David H. Souter, and Clarence Thomas; and the promotion of William H. Rehnquist to the center chair, succeeding Warren Earl Burger in 1986). Acceding to long-standing requests by the judicial branch, Congress provided significant changes in the jurisdiction of, and access to, the federal courts in 1988–89. Major changes in court personnel also naturally took effect during the six-year interim. These and a good many other apposite matters are fully addressed in this edition, resulting in a detailed revision of chapters 2, 3, 4, 5, 7, 8, and 9.

Significant political changes also necessarily affected those materials dealing with the judicial process in sister democracies abroad—especially England, Wales, and France—as well as in the special constitutional courts of Austria, Germany, and Italy; these developments are elucidated in chapters 2, 3, 6, and 7. One major excision was necessitated by the historic decline and dissolution of the Soviet Union. That cataclysmic event dictated the deletion of the section on the Soviet Union's judiciary that had been present in the first five editions.

The realities of economics and the availability of electronic data retrieval resulted in the reluctant decision to discontinue the bibliographical listings at the end of this book. It had become increasingly unwieldy, and since it was simply a vast compilation of publications rather than an annotated bibliography, both publisher and author agreed that it should be dropped in the present and future editions. In its place is a relatively brief annotated bibliography of key works in the constellation of the judicial process. The now familiar figures, tables, charts, graphs, and appendixes have all been retained and updated.

Once again I happily acknowledge my profound debt to a host of new and old colleagues—far too numerous to mention—who not only encouraged me to undertake this sixth edition but generously and readily provided expert assistance. I am especially beholden to two esteemed friends and colleagues—Margherita Rendel, Barrister at Law of the Institute of Education of the University of London, and Dr. Nicole de Montricher of the Observatoire Interrégional du Politique and the Fondation Nationale des Sciences Politiques in Paris—for their indispensable information on the many recent changes in their respective nations' judicial developments; and to two young associates—John C. Blakeman and Vincent Michelot—on the judiciaries of England and France, respectively. My fellow political scientists and devotees of the comparative judicial process, Professor Donald P. Kommers of the Notre Dame University and Professor Roberto Toniatti of the University of Bologna, provided generous and deeply appreciated assistance on the German and Italian judiciary, as did Mag. Jur. Helgar G. Schneider of Graz, Austria, on that nation's judicial structure. For particularly valued advice and counsel I wish to single out my colleagues David O'Brien of the University of Virginia, Barbara Ann Perry of Sweet Briar College, and Tinsley Eugene Yarbrough of East Carolina University, a trio on whom I could always count for objective critiques and suggestions.

The Mayer and Arlene Mitchell and Abraham A. Mitchell Fund of the Mobile Community Foundation provided much-appreciated financial support—as it has done so generously for decades. My research assistants, Kraig J. Powell and Mark D. Hall—with an assist from the Lynde and Harry Bradley Foundation—proved to be unfailingly good-natured and cooperative, and Russell DePalma compiled the index expertly. David Roll and Valerie Aubry of Oxford University Press were delightful editors. My students, of course, were an unceasing source of inspiration and resolve, and my wife, Mildred, and our son, Peter, and his wife, Anne, never failed to be both supportive and constructively critical.

When I wrote the first edition of this book more than thirty years ago, I dedicated it to our older son, Philip, then a four-year-old. Now a practicing attorney, married to Janet, and the proud father of their son, Benjamin, he remains a staunch fan of this book, which is rededicated to him with pride and love .

Charlottesville, Va.   H.J.A.
Summer 1992

Preface
to the
First Edition

When my *Courts and Judges: An Introduction to the Judicial Process* appeared in 1959, I began its preface by pointing to the general absence of even the most rudimentary knowledge of the judicial process on the part of the vast majority of students of political science entering elementary or even advanced courses and observed that equally striking was the unavailability of accessible materials providing basic data in the field. The measure of success my small book has enjoyed encouraged the writing of the present volume, which is far more ambitious in scope than its predecessor.

This new book is a selective comparative introduction to the judicial process and seeks to analyze and evaluate the main institutions and considerations that affect the administration of justice under law. The rather extensive coverage of certain significant features and elements of comparative judicial processes was prompted not only by several helpful suggestions by users of the earlier book but by the continued neglect of these processes in basic textbooks.

An important segment of this work is thus devoted to the judicial process in England and Wales, France, and—to a necessarily considerably lesser extent in this context—the Soviet Union. Other states are included whenever appropriate, especially in connection with the doctrine and practice of judicial review. Nonetheless, over half of the material deals with the judicial process in the United States.

The detailed Contents obviates capsule explanations of the substance of each chapter in this volume. I have compiled numerous graphs, figures, and charts, all designed to facilitate comprehension. There are two indices—one general and one for cases. And there are four extensive bibliographies dealing with (1) works in general on American constitutional law, (2) biographies and autobiographies of and by Justices of the U.S. Supreme Court, (3) comparative constitutional law, and (4) civil liberties.

Although I have endeavored to be objective in analysis and presentation throughout, in some circumstances it is neither possible nor desirable to shun value judgments; I have thus stated frankly my own opinions where it seemed appropriate to do so.

Once again I express my profound appreciation to the many colleagues who stimulated and urged me on in the writing of this book and whose generous suggestions were so helpful. I am especially grateful to Professors William M. Beaney, David Fellman, Wallace Mendelson, Jewell Cass Phillips, and R. J. Tresolini. Above all, I owe a particular debt of gratitude to Mr. James Wellwood, M.A., of Gray's Inn, Barrister-at-Law, Lecturer in Law at King's College, University of London, for his unselfish counsel and essential criticism on the sections on England and Wales. As they have been throughout my pleasant association with Oxford University Press, Mr. Byron S. Holinshead, Jr., and Miss Leona Capeless have been delightful and invaluable co-workers. Mrs. Helen White performed the thankless but essential task of typing the entire manuscript cheerfully and efficiently. Whatever errors remain are mine. My wife, Mildred, gave me the kind of constant encouragement and confidence that only a devoted partner can provide.

And the book is happily dedicated to one who also helped in his own way.

Wynnewood, Pa.   H.J.A.
February 1962

Contents

Tables
Charts
and Figures

TABLES

CHARTS

FIGURES

The
Judicial
Process

1

Introduction: The Law and the Courts

Respect for the law is one of the select group of principles that we have come to regard as essential to the effective and equitable operation of popular government. As a democratic principle it is recognized as binding on both the governed and those who govern.

In fostering this principle the role of the judiciary is crucial, for, in the words of Mr. Justice Arthur T. Vanderbilt:

> it is in the courts and not in the legislature that our citizens primarily feel the keen, cutting edge of the law. If they have respect for the work of their courts, their respect for law will survive the shortcomings of every other branch of government; but if they lose their respect for the work of the courts, their respect for law and order will vanish with it to the great detriment of society.[1]

This is true whether the judicial branch be technically separated from the other two branches of government, as in the United States, partly fused with them, as in France, or largely fused, as in England. The law will be respected as long as it is interpreted and applied within the structures of justice as accepted by the majority of society—in the long run, if not always in the short. Law is, after all, the expressed will of those who rule society.

But the law, in its procedural as well as its substantive aspects, is essentially made and administered by persons whose views and interpretations are buffeted by the winds of change through the years, so that it has become a "truism that the quality of justice depends more on the quality of the [persons] who administer the law than on the content of the law they administer."[2] Judicial activity, observed

---

1. *The Challenge of Law Reform* (Princeton, NJ: Princeton University Press, 1955), pp. 4–5.
2. Evan Haynes, *The Selection and Tenure of Judges* (Newark, NJ: National Conference of Judicial Councils, 1944), p. 5.

Roscoe Pound in one of his lectures, is really the creative element in law. Accordingly, if humankind's great interest on earth is justice, as Daniel Webster put it, then perhaps a more immediate interest is the securing of the most highly qualified individuals to administer justice impartially with a minimum of chicanery and obfuscation. It follows logically that judges must be assured of an optimal degree of independence and relative freedom from prejudicial pressures from forces both inside and outside government. Moreover, they must be able to function in a hierarchical structure that is effectively conducive to the performance of the basic task at hand—the impartial administration of justice under law.

They pursue this task through the medium of a court, an institution of government. As Carl Brent Swisher noted concisely, along with such other characteristics as it may incidentally possess, a court

> determines the facts involved in particular controversies brought before it, relates the facts to the relevant law, settles the controversies in terms of the law, and more or less incidentally makes new law through the process of decision. Over the centuries of Anglo-American history our judiciary has been developed and geared to this process so that it has an integrity or integratedness peculiarly its own. In particular it has a mode of informing the minds of the responsible officers—in this instance the judges—which is unique and which must be kept in sharp focus in any attempt to estimate the capacity of a judiciary to perform competitively in the gray areas which lie between it and institutions which are primarily legislative or executive.[3]

THE NATURE OF LAW

For centuries humankind has discussed the nature of law. In one way or another, it touches every citizen of every nation. The contact may be pleasant or unpleasant, tangible or intangible, direct or indirect, but it is nonetheless a constant force in the lives of people everywhere on the globe. It is essential that we have some understanding of its nature and of the human beings who interpret and administer it.

"What is Law?" has been asked by priests and poets, philosophers and kings, by masses no less than by prophets. A host of answers might be given, yet the answer to the question remains one of the most persistent and elusive problems in the whole range of thought. For one may well view the entire gamut of human life, both in thought and in action, as being comprised within the concept Law[4] (although a legal system is in fact but part of a larger social order).

It may seem strange that the true essence of such a ubiquitous phenomenon as law should be beyond the grasp of general human understanding. Because law deals with human conduct, to grasp its nature it would appear necessary merely to distinguish it from the other factors relating to that conduct: religion, science, morals, ethics, customs. Yet herein lies the difficulty, so ably stated by James Coolidge Carter more than half a century ago:

---

3. Presidential Address, delivered before the American Political Science Association, New York City, September 8, 1960 (reprinted in 54 *American Political Science Review* 879–80, December 1960).
4. William A. Robson, *Civilization and the Growth of Law* (New York: Macmillan, 1935), p. 3.

Law, Custom, Conduct, Life—different names for almost the same thing—true names for different aspects of the same thing—are so inseparably blended together that one cannot even be thought of without the other. No improvement can be effected in one without improving the other, and no retrogression can take place in one without a corresponding decline in the other.[5]

There is little doubt that law has much in common with all these other aspects of human conduct, yet it is true that it also possesses at least one characteristic unique to it and lacking in all others: its sanction is applied exclusively by organized political government.

Three Historical Categories. Some kind of law has always existed[6]—however inadequate, or even entirely absent, both legal organization and enforcement machinery may have been. First came *primitive* law, based chiefly on primitive custom and lacking even rudimentary machinery and organization. Still prevailing among some of the aboriginal Native American, Oceanic, and Asiatic tribes, it has always been the law of those "preliterate" peoples who have recognized social rules and have discovered means of coping with social conflict.

Archaic law, featuring some manner of courts and officialdom—institutions that are basic to every legal system—and introducing certain codes of procedure and substance, arrived on the scene during the early days of Rome and among primitive Germanic and African tribes. However, Moses' *Pentateuch,* given in the fifteenth century B.C., may well lay an earlier claim. Certainly the *Great Sanhedrin,* the seventy-one-man supreme council of the Jewish nation in Greco-Roman days, prior to the destruction of the Temple in Jerusalem by Roman forces in A.D. 70, was a judicial body, headed by a chief justice, which enacted decrees of religious observance *and* interpreted the law of the Hebrews.

Mature law heralded the professionalization of the law. It fathered the law we know today. As Roman law it existed from the third century B.C. to the fall of Rome. As English law it appeared in the twelfth century.

POSITIVE AND NATURAL LAW

The three kinds of law cited earlier are prongs of *positive law,* the type of law with which we will be concerned throughout this book. It is held to derive from man for the purpose of ruling man; it is a command based on the relationship between ruler and ruled; its primary nature is that it is *man-made.* It springs from no source higher than the human will. This is what John Chipman Gray alluded to when he defined a man's legal rights as

> power which he has to make a person or persons do or refrain from doing a certain act or . . . acts, as far as the power arises from society.[7]

5. *Law: Its Origin, Growth and Function* (New York and London: Knickerbocker Press, 1907), p. 320.
6. The earliest known system of written law was the Code of Hammurabi, so named in honor of its founder, a king of Babylonia. It was promulgated about 2050 B.C.—there is considerable disagreement among scholars on the precise decade or even century (estimates vary from 2067 to 1662 B.C.)—and was the embodiment of the existing rules and customs of the land. It presented the idea that justice was humankind's inherent right, derived from supernatural forces rather than being given by royally bestowed favor.
7. *The Nature and Sources of Law* (New York: Columbia University Press, 1916), p. 19.

In other words, according to the tenets of positive law—as defined by John Austin, the English utilitarian jurist (1790–1859) who, inspired by the French social theorist Auguste Comte (1798–1857), became the founder of the analytical school of jurisprudence—law consists of definite rules of human conduct with appropriate sanctions for their enforcement, both of these being prescribed by duly constituted human authority.

Natural Law. But in the eyes of many there is another category of law, *natural law*, known also as "higher law" or "the law of nature." This is law that would be binding on human societies in the absence of, or as a supplement to, positive law. Witness, for example, its impact on the American Declaration of Independence and the Constitution,[8] its citation by conscientious objectors to military conscription, and its invocation by the civil rights movements of the 1950s and 1960s—for instance, by the Reverend Dr. Martin Luther King's exhortations to disobey "unjust" laws. The theory of natural law originated with the Stoics, by whom it was regarded as embodying those rules of justice discernible by right reason. This view was sometimes taken by Roman jurists; thus, the statesman and theorist Cicero (106–43 B.C.), in defining law, was explicit in stating his concept of its essence:

> Law is the highest reason, implanted in Nature, which commands what ought to be done and forbids the opposite . . . the origin of justice is to be found in law, for law is its natural force; it is the mind and reason of the intelligent man, the standards by which justice and injustice are measured.
>
> I shall seek the root of justice in nature. . . . [9]

Justinian (483–565) adopted Ulpian's (170–228) definition of natural law as that law which "nature has taught all living beings," thus forecasting the modern bionomic view. The Scholastics generally regarded natural law as that part of the divine law which is not directly revealed but is discernible to reason; and the Rationalists of the eighteenth century derived from their analysis of human societies certain *natural rights* as to life, liberty, and the pursuit of happiness—which they regarded as of prior validity to institutional law.[10] Hence, it is the thread of rationality that holds the system together and gives it a definite order:

> [T]he universe obeys God; seas and lands obey the universe, and human life is subject to the decree of supreme law.[11]

It would seem that natural law thus stands on two assumptions: first, the rationality and intelligence of man; second, the existence of a higher *rational* order of things. Because man is presumed to be intelligent, he can readily "find" the law— that is, understand the higher rational order.

8. Its classic exposition in that connection is Edward S. Corwin's superb *The Higher Law Background of American Constitutional Law* (Ithaca, NY: Cornell University Press, 1929), known to every student of constitutional law and the judicial process.
9. Cicero, "The Laws," in Francis William Coker, *Readings in Political Philosophy,* rev. ed. (New York: Macmillan, 1955), pp. 145–46.
10. Webster's *New International Dictionary of the English Language,* 3d ed., unabridged (Springfield, MA: G. & C. Merriam, 1966).
11. Cicero, op. cit., p. 151.

Without endeavoring to prove or disprove this theory and estimate of man, his history at least places the issue in doubt. At best, it appears that man is as capable of capricious action based on passion as he is of rational action based on intelligence. If man's intelligence is placed in doubt, so is his ability to understand a higher rational order. Indeed, it is difficult for man to believe in a higher order or a universal law of justice because of what he sees in real life—as Carneades pointed out so many years ago. Oliver Wendell Holmes, Jr., who rejected natural law with vehemence and sarcasm—for which he was scathingly attacked in word and in print by, among others, prominent Jesuit law professors—regarded it as "mystic overlaw" and the "product of wishful thinking."[12]

Nonetheless, today natural law is identifiable with the abiding sense of justice that pervades the community of man—regardless of its changing substance—a sense of justice based on a body of rules and customs that the general development of mankind shows to be essential to human society. But it is the positive law that finally governs us as law-abiding members of organized society. And, as we shall presently see, although natural law, like equity, has had a marked influence on the English common law, "it is not the same as common law and has never absorbed it."[13]

COMMON LAW AND STATUTORY LAW

For our purposes, then, law, broadly speaking, represents the rules of conduct that pertain to a given political order of society, rules that are backed by the organized force of the community. As it has evolved through the centuries, law either has been made by the political representatives of the people—sometimes rather inaccurately styled "bar-made" law—or has been "bench-made" by judges and justices. The former type is generally known as *statutory law*, the latter as *common law*. Both will bear close examination, but, at the risk of some oversimplification, the crucial distinction between the two is that between codified written law and unwritten law based on custom and tradition. (The terms *bar-made* and *bench-made* are never used in England; there they are called *statutory* and *judge-made*.)

COMMON LAW

Utilized by most English-speaking states, *common law* is variously known also as *English, Anglo-Saxon,* or *Anglo-American law*. Despite its conceptualization by Lord Coke as "the perfection of reason," it is indeed a vast and complex instrument of justice. Although at first glance it may well seem chaotic and abstruse, on closer examination its many diverse components can readily be discerned to be logical, bound into a comprehensive and comprehensible entity.[14]

Common law is judge-made, bench-made law rather than a fixed body of defi-

12. See Francis Biddle, *Justice Holmes, Natural Law, and the Supreme Court* (New York: Macmillan, 1961), especially ch. 2, "The Attack on Justice Holmes."

13. Ibid., p. 31.

14. For an excellent description see F. H. Lawson, *The Rational Strength of English Law* (London: Stevens, 1951).

nite rules such as the modern civil law codes. In Roscoe Pound's words, it is a "mode of judicial and juristic thinking, a mode of treating legal problems."[15] He might well have added "a mood." Often based on precedents, common law embodies continuity in that it binds the present with the past. Since it thus necessarily grew, and still grows, by virtue of judicial decisions, it is best to explain and analyze it historically.

Historical Background. With the growth of Christianity and Christian philosophy came the decline and fall of Rome. The concept of the state as the highest form of society began to be questioned with the rise of the Christian Church. With the Norman invasion of the British Isles in 1066, precise and orderly methods were introduced into the government and law of England. Thus began, under the Norman and Angevin monarchs of the eleventh and twelfth centuries, the gradual growth of a central administration and the development of the courts of law. The term *common law* was used for the law developed in the Kings's Courts and was generally employed to distinguish between this law and that of the ecclesiastical courts. In effect, the concept of common law was adopted from the *canon law* of the Christian Church, which was the common law of Christendom. Thus, the common law came into use in the reign of Edward I (1272–1307) or just shortly thereafter. It meant "general" as opposed to "special" law; the law common to the whole land; unenacted law as distinguished from statutes and ordinances; the law of the temporal as opposed to the ecclesiastical courts. Later, common law came to be contrasted with equity.[16] The common law of the King's Courts was made by the royal justices from the mass of customary law of the realm and became the common law of England.

There were three great courts of common law: *King's Bench, Exchequer,* and *Common Pleas.* As the routine of these royal courts was firmly established, it became possible to forecast their decisions in terms of similar cases decided by them in the past. However, according to Theodore F. T. Plucknett,[17] the practice of basing decisions on precedent did not come about because it was the best rule to follow in decision making, but because it enabled all existing courts to function with a minimum of trouble.

In at least some respects the common law reflects the feudal structure from which it was derived. Over a period of centuries the law defining the relationship between the Anglo-Norman monarchs and their tenants-in-chief became the law that was applicable to all Englishmen. At first this dealt solely with private law, but it was gradually extended to cover public law as well. The core of the feudal law was the concept of fealty, which long prevailed after the passing of feudalism. Ruler as well as subject was bound—there were well-defined rights and obligations to be adhered to by all parties. Private rights of freemen were not subject to arbitrary change, and the primary task of the monarch was to preserve and protect the law.

15. Roscoe Pound, *The Spirit of the Common Law* (Boston: Little, Brown, 1921), p. 1.
16. "Equity" is discussed on pp. 12–14, *infra.* For an expert analysis of the genesis and concept of common law, see F. W. Maitland, *The Constitutional History of England,* ed. by H. A. L. Fisher (Cambridge: Cambridge University Press, 1961).
17. Theodore F. T. Plucknett, *A Concise History of the Common Law,* 5th ed. (Boston: Little, Brown, 1956), p. 342.

But the groups whose rights the monarch had to acknowledge were limited to the nobility, the landed gentry, and some segments of the rising bourgeoisie. Hence it is hardly astonishing that the common law—which was essentially a law of property, in particular landed property—was "regarded by the politically influential class . . . as its shield."[18] During the twelfth and thirteenth centuries, however, the practice of issuing *royal writs* was introduced—although they were then practically confined to a few classes of civil cases. But early in the reign of Henry II (1154–89)—often termed the Father of the Common Law, though some would credit Henry I (1100–35) with that title—an ordinance proclaiming that no man could be denied his freehold without a royal writ rendered centralization in a royal court inevitable. This was followed by several writs that continued the trend and culminated in the *Assize of Novel Disseisin of 1166*, ordaining that anyone who was denied his freehold could seek immediate remedy in the King's Court. (The Assize also provided for a jury of one's neighbors in questions of fact.) Thus, by 1166 the King was firmly established as the protector of the freehold.

By 1178 the work of the King's Court had become more than King and Council could handle, and five full-time judges were appointed, some of whom would travel about the countryside, settling disputes in each locality according to prevailing custom. They attended to the bulk of the cases, although the monarch and his Council still disposed of "novel and difficult" matters. This arrangement ultimately led to the schema of legal proceedings based on writs, which were issued in ever-increasing numbers and for a fixed price. Until the middle of the thirteenth century the King issued new writs to deal with a host of new problems. However, the barons became increasingly jealous of his power to make law, and in 1258 the King was forbidden to issue writs without the specific consent of his Council. As a result of that restriction, the thirty or forty writs then extant were often interpreted and stretched to deal with problems they were not designed to handle.[19]

With the founding of the Inns of Court as legal "guilds" in the latter half of the thirteenth century (see chapter 2), unofficial reports of cases commenced to be published in annual *Year Books*. These books were records of court proceedings dealing mainly with procedural points for the benefit of practitioners rather than full reports of "casebook law" in the modern sense. Nevertheless, they quite naturally came to serve as a source of gradually mounting precedents and were frequently referred to by those practitioners in the courts. *Stare decisis et non quieta movere*— stand by past decisions and do not disturb things at rest—began to have genuine meaning as a judicial policy. According to Charles Ogilvie, the first inkling of the future English system of case law may be found in the *Dialogus de Scaccario*, written by Richard Fitz-Nigel between 1177 and 1179:

> There are cases where the courses of events, and the reasons for decisions are obscure; and in these it is enough to cite precedents.[20]

Thus were laid the bases on which the common law rests. As society became more complex, so did law. At first it was made by the royal courts, but from the

18. Sir Charles Ogilvie, *The King's Government and the Common Law: 1471–1641* (Oxford: Basil Blackwell, 1958), p. 6.
19. Ibid., p. 13.
20. Ibid., p. 17.

thirteenth century on it was always accepted as the supreme and fundamental law of the land. (The Divine Right of Kings was a sixteenth-century idea, not a medieval one—indeed, the second sentence of the Preface to the *Dialogus* had admonished "there is no power but of God.") Bracton or Henry of Bratton (1216–68), a judge of the King's Bench under Henry III (1207–72)—and without equal as a judicial writer until Blackstone came along five centuries later—stated in his *De Legibus* that the King was "under God and the Law . . . for the Law made the King." He was seconded in 1442 by Sir John Fortescue (1394–1476), Chief Justice of the King's Bench, in his remarkable treatise, *De Laudibus Legum Angliae*, and by Sir Edmund Plowden (1518–85), chief builder of Middle Temple Hall, who was probably the foremost common law sage, commentator, and interpreter of his time. And the great Sir Edward (later Lord) Coke (1552–1634)—Attorney General, Member of Parliament, and Chief Justice of the Court of Common Pleas—when called before his King, James I (1603–25), echoed his three famed predecessors in declaring that the monarch should also be bound by law. When the King told him that he could not be subject "to any man," Coke replied that, agreed, the King "is not subject to any man, but to God and the law." It was Lord Coke who, more than any other man of his time, compiled and analyzed precedents of common law and who was largely responsible for the increasingly accepted practice of reporting cases fully. From these he drew a set of maxims and rules, later to be amplified and explained precisely by Sir William Blackstone (1723–80). The latter's monumental four-volume work, *Commentaries on the Law of England* (1765–69) was long the bible of legal training in both England and America. Its basic principles remain useful pillars of English and American law.

Any notion that judges are to serve the popular majority was and is utterly wrong. For while the common law recognized the authority of King and Parliament, it required all men to bow to the law and act within its limits. England's judges have ever abided by their judicial oath to "administer the law without fear or favor." Over the years common law was exported to many countries—among them Canada, Australia, New Zealand, India, Pakistan, Israel, and the thirteen colonies that would become the United States. (Scotland, although itself a member of the United Kingdom, is an interesting exception: its existing legal system was derived from Roman law, as were the Continental systems; but it has been greatly influenced by the common law.) It is, of course, important to recognize that ultimately statutory law is supreme. The judges are bound to give effect to an Act of Parliament. Thus, many statutes have modified the common law (e.g., the doctrine of common employment) or have codified it (e.g., the Sale of Goods Act).

Characteristics. As has already been pointed out, common law is predominantly *judge-made law*. Under it the judge is the creator, interpreter, and modifier of laws. Even when he merely "interprets" law, he may well be creating it. To that extent, statutory law, the law enacted by legislative bodies, is tentative. Discussing the benefits of judge-made law, Justice Benjamin N. Cardozo pointed out that the judge can use "free scientific research" when analyzing a problem. By "free" he meant that to a very real extent the common law removes the judge from action by positive authority; by "scientific" he meant that there is an objective element in the judge's decision. Thus, the judge may come closer to the just and the true, for law under the common law system develops by "judicial experience in the decision of cases."[21] For example, in 1972 the U.S. Supreme Court, invoking the ancient common law of nuisance, declared unanimously that federal district courts may order polluters to stop fouling the environment.[22]

Another significant characteristic of common law is the doctrine of *precedent*, under which the judges refer to a previous decision or decisions in order to adjudicate the case at issue. The importance of precedent varies with individual judges, for although common law normally recognizes precedent as binding, judges not only may occasionally depart from precedent when it "appears right to do so," but may distinguish between various precedents in evolving the new law. Moreover, times and conditions change with changing society, and "every age should be mistress of its own law"—an era should not be hampered by outdated law. "It is revolting," wrote Justice Holmes in characteristically forthright language, "to have no better reason for a rule of law than that it was so laid down in the time of Henry IV [1367–1413]. It is still more revolting if the grounds upon which it was laid down have vanished long since, and the rule simply persists from blind imitation of the past."[23] It is the readiness of the common law judges to discard that which does not serve the public that has contributed to the survival and adoption of common law,[24] wholly or partly, in so many lands. Nevertheless, although Justice Cardozo applauded this, he cautioned that while a judge may discard the old and adopt the new, he must remember that the past is often a reflection of the present and must know and understand it, "for the depths are the foundation of the heights."[25] And although Britain's House of Lords, its highest law court, announced in 1966 that it would henceforth no longer consider itself bound by its own precedents, as it had previously, all judges of first instance are bound by the decisions of higher courts, that is, the Court of Appeal or the House of Lords (and the Court of Appeal is bound by the decisions of the House of Lords).[26]

Because common law as such is uncodified, it is generally described as *unwritten law*. However, case precedents really are not unwritten; they are derived from the principles of law embodied in the judgments of cases that are decided and reported. Presumably most courts keep records, although they are not all required to do so—for example, some Justices of the Peace in certain of the constituent states of the United States who are not regarded as "courts of record."

In summary, the common law appears to have three distinct characteristics that together have enabled the system to develop and expand. First is its *vitality and capability to sustain change*. It does not impress its own peculiarities on any other law; it only aids in the systematic development of a richer and presumably more just law. Second is its *practical quality*. It is unwilling to accept anything a priori and follows the notion that ideally all laws ought to be tested in the courts. Thus,

21. Pound, op. cit., p. 216.
22. *Illinois v. Milwaukee*, 406 U.S. 91.
23. From an 1897 address, reprinted in his *Collected Legal Papers* (Boston: A. Harcourt, 1920), p. 187.
24. See ch. 8, *infra*, pp. 324–32, for a more detailed discussion of precedent.
25. Margaret E. Hall (ed.), *Selected Writings of Benjamin Nathan Cardozo* (New York: Fallon Law Book Company, 1948), p. 78.
26. See ch. 6, *infra*, for a description of the British judicial system.

rules and regulations are treated as working hypotheses, continually retested in what Munroe Smith called "those great laboratories of the law, the courts of justice."[27] Third is its *rendition of law as a moral obligation to be obeyed.* The results of the laboratory tests of the law are accepted as valid and everyone is obliged to obey them. After all, in the famous words of Justice Oliver Wendell Holmes, Jr.:

> The common law is not a brooding omnipresence in the sky, but the articulate voice of some sovereign or quasi-sovereign that can be identified.[28]

And as the great jurist put it so well and so hauntingly in his majestic *The Common Law:*

> The life of the law has not been logic; it has been experience. The felt necessities of the time, the prevalent moral and political theories, intuitions of public policy, avowed or unconscious, even the prejudices which judges share with their fellowmen, have had a good deal more to do than syllogism in determining the rules by which men should be governed. The law embodies the story of a nation's development through many centuries, and it cannot be dealt with as if it contained only the axioms and corollaries of a book of mathematics. In order to know what it is, we must know what it has been, and what it tends to become. . . . The very considerations which judges most rarely mention, and always with an apology, are the secret root from which the law draws all the juices of life. I mean, of course, considerations of what is expedient for the community concerned.[29]

Some three decades later Holmes emphasized this ever-recurring theme in his opinion for the Supreme Court of the United States in *Gompers v. United States:*

> The provisions of the Constitution are not mathematical formulas having their essence in their form; they are organic living institutions transplanted from English soil. Their significance is vital not formal; it is to be gathered not simply by taking the words and a dictionary, but by considering their origin and the line of their growth.[30]

EQUITY

A branch of Anglo-American jurisprudence, born hundreds of years ago—in fact, it was Aristotle (although some contend it was Plato) who first articulated the idea of juridical equity—and closely related to the common law, *equity* is actually a supplement to the common law.[31] Although the *Court of Chancery* did not appear until the fifteenth century, equity courts arose in England in the fourteenth— apparently as early as 1340—as a result of a practice that permitted a disappointed litigant at common law to lay his plight before his sovereign. That is, he could petition the King to "do right for the love of God and by way of charity," the King being empowered to mold the law for the sake of "justice," to grant the relief

---

27. Quoted by Benjamin N. Cardozo, *The Nature of the Judicial Process* (New Haven, CT: Yale University Press, 1921), p. 23.
28. *Southern Pacific Co. v. Jensen,* 244 U.S. 205 (1916), at 222.
29. Oliver Wendell Holmes, Jr., *The Common Law* (Boston: Little, Brown, 1881), pp. 1–2.
30. 233 U.S. 604 (1914), at 610.
31. Note equity's development in the jurisprudential works of Coke, Hobbes, Blackstone, and Story.

prayed for as an act of grace, when the common law gave no remedy, or no adequate remedy.

Chancellor and Chancery. The monarch, on the other hand, habitually referred these petitions to his Chancellor. This member of his Council, who until the Reformation was always a cleric, became known as the "Keeper of the King's Conscience." He was the Council's most important member and the Keeper of the Great Seal, an office to which considerable powers were attached. It was he who could, for example, issue a writ of *subpoena,* commanding a person to appear before a duly constituted legal authority. From many points of view the Chancellor was second in power only to his monarch. Ultimately, the volume of these petitions brought about the establishment of a separate court, the *Court of Chancery.* This was the early court of equity. It maintained its separate existence until 1875, when it was merged in the *Supreme Court of Judicature* by the Judicature Acts of 1873–75. Today, its jurisdiction is exercised mainly by the Chancery Division of the High Court of Justice. But all courts now administer both common law and equity, equity prevailing in cases of conflict between them; statutes (acts of Parliament) are supreme, however.

The United States of America never had *separate* courts of equity on the federal level. Yet several states retain such separate courts. In others, the same jurist doubles as law judge and equity judge, sitting one day as the former and one as the latter! In still others, no separate equity courts exist at all—the same courts that decide matters of common and statutory law also administer equity.

Defining Equity. But what is equity? We noted that it is a "supplement" to the common law, thus apparently the "conscience" of the law. It is a supplement to the common law in the sense that the principles of equity—which are now part of the fabric of the common law—were developed by the Court of Chancery as an addition to the principles of the medieval common law. Equity began where the law ended, and it is in that role that we know it today. Thus, it created and continues to create precedents. It takes the form of a *judicial decree*—including, since 1875, the award of damages, if deemed appropriate—not of a judgment of "yes" or "no." Equity leaves the judge reasonably free to order *preventive* measures— and under some circumstances even *remedial* ones—usually in the form of a writ, such as an *injunction,* or restraining order, designed to afford a remedy not otherwise obtainable, and traditionally given upon a showing of peril. The judge in the original Court of Chancery exercised his discretion, since remedies in equity were discretionary—and so they are today.

For instance, in equity an injunction may be issued by a judge to prevent members of a local of the United Steel Workers of America from going out on strike without having banked the furnaces of the Jones and Laughlin Steel Corporation, despite the inapplicability of the permissive injunctive provisions of the Norris–LaGuardia Act in this case, and despite the fact that the union had given due notice to strike in accordance with the requirements of the Taft–Hartley Act. True, the steel firm involved could probably recover monetary compensation for resultant damages from its insurance company, or from the USW if it should be found that a contractual provision had been violated by the action of the workers.

However, the company here is not interested in such money; its sole aim is to prevent its furnaces from the certain destruction that would result from a failure to bank them. Hence the demand for an equity decree in the form of an injunction against the union.

Another illustration, although considerably less in the realm of immediate peril, might be John Miller's lovely old copper beech on the edge of his private property, directly in the path of a future highway to be built by the Commonwealth of Pennsylvania. The state has every right to chop down the tree under its power of *eminent domain*, provided only that it does so for a public purpose, which a state public highway certainly is, and that it grant just compensation, which it usually does quite liberally in these circumstances. But Mr. Miller is not interested in financial compensation. He wants to continue to enjoy the beauty and shade of the magnificent tree, and the sentimental attachments that go with it—he proposed to his wife under it; his children and grandchildren climbed it with relish for years. Thus, he, too, may appeal to the courts for equity. His chances for success are undoubtedly considerably less than were those of the steel firm mentioned earlier, but judges are human beings as well.

An interesting and troubling question regarding the contemporarily expansive use of equity by American courts, particularly on the egalitarian front, has become whether equitable relief ought to be confined to *pro*scription or whether it may also be *pre*scriptive, as it has been judicially applied more and more of late. The issue is a volatile one: in fine, it comes down to the core of the parameters of appropriate judicial power and its exercise.[32] The authors of the Constitution did extend the latter to all cases in law and equity. Unfortunately, they failed to distinguish procedurally between the two. Congress has the power to create that distinction, but it is unlikely to do so.

STATUTORY LAW

Despite the origin of the concept of *statutory law*—variously known as *code, written, Neo-Roman* or *Roman,* or *civil law*—in ancient Rome, its broad application is essentially a modern one. Whereas the common law has dealt traditionally with matters of a private character, with the relations between individuals, statutory law is more frequently concerned with society as a whole. It is law that originates with specifically designated, authoritative lawmaking bodies—presumably legislatures but also executive-administrative decrees and ordinances, treaties, and protocols, all of which are committed to paper.

Historical Background. Although arguably traceable to the far-distant times of Moses, Manu, and Hammurabi, statutory law as we now conceive of it developed in and from the homogeneous city-state, exemplified by the Codes of Emperor Justinian I (527–65), the *Corpus Juris Civilis,* which was promulgated about A.D. 535. Hence it is frequently referred to as Roman law and, to confuse teachers and

---

32. For a thoughtful analysis of the problem, see Gary L. McDowell, *Equity and the Constitution: The Supreme Court, Equitable Relief, and Public Policy* (Chicago: University of Chicago Press, 1981). For a contrary point of view, see Peter Charles Hoffer, *The Law's Conscience: Equitable Constitutionalism in America* (Chapel Hill: University of North Carolina Press, 1990).

students alike, as *civil* law—which has nothing whatever to do with civil jurisdiction.[33] In contrast to diversified England, with its manifold customs that veritably seemed to cry out for some sort of common law, Rome lent itself ideally to the development of a statutory system, one that could be readily written down or codified. Statutory law had—and has, of course—the advantages of preciseness, simplicity, and clear-cut applicability, although it still remains subject to interpretation by administrators as well as judges.

Enacted by legislative and/or executive-administrative bodies of government, codified and spelled out in writing by the legal profession, clearly and readily available for all to see, statutory law has survived as the generally accepted law for most of the states of continental Europe, Russia, Latin America, and many of the newly emergent African nations. Justinian's Code had been initially introduced into Western Europe in 544 when the Eastern Empire reconquered Italy. But it did not assume genuine significance for the West until the systematic study of Roman law was revived at the Italian universities in the twelfth century.[34] One of the most famous codifiers was Emperor Napoleon I (1804–15), whose Civil Code was published in 1804, his Code of Civil Procedure in 1807, and other codes subsequently. Indeed, the *Code Napoleon* has been far more enduring than most of the colorful Emperor's military triumphs. Its first major change did not take place until the Gaullist reforms of 1959 that accorded France's married women increased property rights.

"MIXING" COMMON AND STATUTORY LAW

England and the United States today have legal systems based on the common law that readily and naturally found its way across the Atlantic Ocean from the Mother Country to the Colonies. But although it must be categorized as a common law system, the Anglo-American legal framework in effect now consists of a mixture of common *and* statutory law. A great deal of contemporary law is necessarily statutory; it is coded. However, notwithstanding the great Magna Carta of 1215, this is a relatively recent development, for although statutes as a basis of Anglo-American law were not unknown, they played a subsidiary role until the second quarter of the nineteenth century.

The mixture came into its own largely, although certainly not exclusively, as a result of the perpetuating conservatism of the common law, particularly in the realm of the sanctity of private property, based on the overriding concept of economic *laissez faire*. With the advent of a rising spirit of common social consciousness and responsibility, and a gradual movement toward the service or welfare state on both sides of the ocean, legislative bodies everywhere—but considerably more slowly in the United States than in the United Kingdom—commenced to change or even displace the age-old concepts and practices of the common law in favor of what were viewed as primary considerations of necessary public interest.

Nonetheless, common law remained an important basis of legislative motivations and actions, and often an enacted statute would—as indeed it still does

33. See p. 21, *infra*.
34. A. T. von Mehren, *The Civil Law System* (Englewood Cliffs, NJ: Prentice-Hall, 1957), p. 6.

today—simply spell out certain aspects of the grand sweep of common law. Furthermore, no legislative body—and sometimes not even the executive—is consistently, or even largely, capable of pinpointing in writing all the aspects and ramifications of a statute or order, nor would that necessarily be desirable even if it were possible. The result is interpretation, usually first by administrative units, then often by the courts, and, as we shall have ample opportunity to observe,[35] when courts interpret, they cause statutes to grow or contract. This interpretation becomes part of the statutes and orders, thus giving them meaning in the spirit and application of the common law. Truly, England and America resort to a framework of law that is a generally wholesome blend of common, statutory, and equity law.

Of course, there are certain areas of statutory law in which little, if any, discretionary elements remain for the judge. The U. S. Criminal Code, for example, represents a compendium of laws that prescribes what shall constitute a crime and what the penalties shall be. A judge may have a modicum of leeway regarding the former, but the sole substantive discretion left to him in the realm of the latter is one reflected in the provision of the code. Thus, a particular law may conceivably permit him to exercise his considered judgment as to the severity of a sentence he is called upon to impose for a given criminal infraction, but this discretion will necessarily be limited by the minimum and maximum penalties as provided in it. Moreover, it may well be limited by the nature of the verdict of the jury. Indeed, *criminal law* is more and more codified everywhere among the common law lands and hence is becoming statutory. The same applies to *public law* generally, although the great bulk of *private law* is still *common law*.

SOME ADDITIONAL LEGAL DEFINITIONS AND CONCEPTS

A few terms and concepts related to notions that play a part in these pages must be elaborated on here, however briefly. A host of others will be treated throughout the book.[36] We begin with a distinction between the two types of law into which *municipal law*—the law that applies within a state—is normally divided, namely, *private* and *public* law.

Private law governs the relationship between private citizens or persons; that is, it regulates the relations of individuals with each other. It is concerned with the definition, regulation, and enforcement of rights in cases in which both the person[37] in whom the right inheres and the person on whom the obligation devolves are private individuals. Obvious examples of private law are the law governing contracts between individuals or corporations and that pertaining to marriage and

35. See chapters 5–9, *infra*. For the clash between statutory and common law in the eighteenth century, which defined British legal arrangements to date (i.e., Parliamentary sovereignty), see David Lieberman, *The Province of Legislation Determined* (Cambridge: Cambridge University Press, 1989).

36. A standard legal dictionary, e.g., *Black's Law Dictionary*, will readily supply answers to any other questions regarding terms that may occur to the inquiring reader. The definitions used in this section are based in part on its 4th ed. (St. Paul: West Publishing, 1957), pp. 1394, 1359, 385, and 67.

37. In 1886 the Supreme Court declared corporations to be legal "persons" under the Constitution. (see p. 364, *infra*.) Yet in 1973 it ruled that human fetuses are *not* "persons" thereunder. (See *Roe v. Wade* and *Doe v. Bolton*, 410 U.S. 113 and 410 U.S. 179, resp.)

divorce. In the sense that infractions of the legal obligations inherent in these areas are subject to adjudication by courts, the state is involved, of course, but it is neither the subject of the right nor the object of the duty.

Public law, on the other hand, is a branch or department of law that is very much concerned with the state in its political or sovereign capacities—including the two important subheadings of administrative and constitutional law (to be described presently). Public law deals with the definition, regulation, and enforcement of rights in those cases in which the state *is* viewed as the subject of the right or the object of the duty, including criminal law and criminal procedure. In other words, it is that portion of law which is concerned with political conditions and situations—with the powers, rights, duties, capacities, and incapacities that are characteristic of and peculiar to both supreme and subordinate political authority.

Public law applies to and affects the entire people of a nation or state that adopts or enacts it—in contrast with private law, which affects and applies to only one or a few individuals—for public law regulates both the relations between individuals and the state and the relations between the branches of the government. Thus, the vast majority of legislation enacted by Congress is in the category of public law—and its statutes are codified, preceded by the term "Public Law ____ [Number]." Social welfare, defense appropriations, subversive activities control, farm subsidies—all these areas of legislation constitute illustrations of the vast, diversified content of public law.

Administrative law, which has quite naturally achieved ever-increasing prominence over the past few decades, consists of those rules and regulations that are promulgated by the sundry administrative agencies of government that have been empowered to deal with the operation of government under the delegated rule-making authority of the legislative body. That branch of public law prescribes in detail the activities of the agencies involved, such as those concerned with the collection of revenue, regulation of competitive practices, coinage, public health, welfare, safety, and morals, sanitation, and regulation of the armed forces. In the United Kingdom, for example, administrative law has developed greatly as a means of controlling, supervising, and sometimes enforcing administrative decisions and actions by the use of prerogative writs.[38]

Constitutional law is the other great branch of public law. It determines the political organization of a state and its powers while also setting certain substantive and procedural limitations on the exercise of governing power. Because of its position and nature it stands legally above all other types of municipal law, public as well as private. In the United States, with its written Constitution, constitutional law consists of the application of fundamental principles of law based on that document, as finally interpreted by its highest judicial organ, the Supreme Court of the United States. A contemporary example is the famous *Steel Seizure case.*[39] Believ-

---

38. "Prerogative writs" include such essential safeguards as the writs of *habeas corpus, certiorari, prohibition mandamus,* and *quo warranto,* (to be described *infra*).

39. *Youngstown Sheet and Tube Co. v. Sawyer,* 343 U.S. 579 (1952). See the excellent book by Maeva Marcus, *Truman and the Steel Seizure Case: The Limits of Presidential Power* (New York: Columbia University Press, 1977). The dramatic July 1974 decision in *United States v. Nixon,* 417 U.S. 683, is, of course, another pertinent illustration (see pp. 163, 188, 208 *infra*).

ing himself invested with the power to act in his capacity as Commander in Chief and endowed with what he and his advisers viewed as "inherent authority," President Truman seized the steel mills on April 8, 1952, in order to forestall a nationwide strike in the midst of the Korean War. The owners filed for a writ to enjoin him, charging the absence of both constitutional and legislative authority for his actions. After a series of dramatic skirmishes in the lower federal courts, the U.S. Supreme Court received the case for adjudication—clearly a matter in the realm of constitutional law. On June 2, 1952, the Court rendered its decision, featured by seven different opinions! But six of the nine Justices did agree on *one* crucial point: President Truman had violated the Constitution by *usurping legislative power*; therefore, the seizure of the steel mills was *ultra vires*—particularly so since Congress had expressly refused to enact a suggested amendment to the Taft–Hartley Act authorizing such governmental seizures in an emergency.[40]

In brief, constitutional law prescribes generally the plan and method under which the public business of the political organ, known as the state, is conducted. And it differs further from the other types of law described in that it is both enacted and changed either in an extraordinary manner by an ordinary legislative body, or by an extraordinary body—such as a constitutional convention—constituted especially for that purpose.

In the United States changes in the letter of the fundamental document are based on the special constitutional amendment provisions of its Article V, which combine extraordinary federal with extraordinary state action. In the United Kingdom, where no formal written constitution and no power of judicial review exist in the sense of striking down legislative or executive action, Parliament is supreme and may effect changes in the constitutional law of the land by ordinary legislation. But, notwithstanding the powerful potential of normally very strict Parliamentary party discipline (used persuasively by the Thatcher government, for one), it is unlikely to tamper with the great cornerstones of its unwritten Constitution—that intriguing British concept consisting of the heritage of the common law, great statutes, important documents, decisions of the courts (other than judicial review), autonomy of local elected authorities, and customs and conventions that combined constitute the very life blood of the realm. The prerogative writs (noted earlier) do provide wide powers of "judicial review," but it is a review quite different from that extant in the United States. In France the written Constitution of the Fifth Republic may be altered only by extraordinary action of Parliament with the cooperation of the President of France, either with or without ratification by a popular

40. Quipped *The Economist* (May 10, 1952) as the case was about to reach the Supreme Court: "At the first sound of a new argument over the United States Constitution and its interpretation, the hearts of Americans leap with a fearful joy. The blood stirs powerfully in their veins and a new lustre brightens their eyes. Like King Harry's men before Harfleur, they stand like greyhounds in the slips, straining upon the start. Last week, the old bugle-note rang out, clear and thrilling, calling Americans to a fresh debate on the Constitution." *The Economist* had an even better time with *United States v. Nixon* in 1974 (January 19 and 26, 1974, pp. 47 and 23, resp.; March 2, 9, and 23, 1974, pp. 49, 58, and 49, resp.; April 20, 1974, p. 63; May 4 and 11, 1974, pp. 53 and 49, resp.; June 15, 1974, p. 49; July 13 and 27, 1974, pp. 45 and 13, resp.; and August 3, 1974, p. 11).

referendum, depending on the procedure invoked by the President in the course of the initiating stages. And in Switzerland, not only do constitutional alterations by the government call for mandatory ratification by popular referenda, but the Swiss citizens may take the initiative directly by drawing up a proposed constitutional amendment and submitting it for direct popular referendum approval.

CIVIL AND CRIMINAL LAW

Another basic distinction of considerable importance that confronts the observer of the judicial and legal process is that between *civil law* and *criminal law*. (The former is not to be equated with the concept of "civil law" used as a synonym for statutory or Roman law; here the term is used in connection with the *subject matter* governing a particular case.) Whether a particular offense is of a civil or criminal nature determines not only the severity of the legal sanction that may be invoked but frequently the type of tribunal before which the case will be heard. As we shall see in subsequent chapters, some courts are empowered to hear cases involving *both* types of law, as are all three major federal constitutional courts of the United States. But in many instances the judicial hierarchy provides for a separate set of criminal and civil courts, as is the case, to a greater or lesser extent, in both England and France—although many of the English judges are used interchangeably.

Civil Law. A case at *civil law* is normally one between private persons and/or private organizations, for civil law governs the relations between individuals and defines their legal rights. A party bringing suit under it seeks legal redress in a *personal* interest, such as for a breach of contract, a divorce action, a defamation of character, or the use of a copyrighted story without permission. Yet although suits at civil law far more often than not are suits among private persons, the government, too, may conceivably be involved. For example, under the Sherman Anti-Trust Act of 1890, as amended, the federal government of the United States is empowered to bring either civil or criminal action, or both, against an alleged offender. It has much more frequently brought civil than criminal actions under that statute, probably because the former are not as difficult to win and cause less of an uproar in the interested community.

Criminal Law. A case at *criminal law* is invariably brought by and in the name of the legally constituted government, no matter at what level—national, state, or local—it may arise. Almost wholly statutory in the United States, criminal law defines crimes against the public order and provides for appropriate punishment. Prosecution brought under it by the proper governmental authority involves an accusation that the defendant has violated a specific provision of a law, an infraction for which a penalty has normally been provided by statute. Criminal cases comprise such felonies or major crimes as homicide, espionage, sabotage, rape, and perjury, to name but a few. The coverage is as extensive as the lawmakers choose to make it. Because the prosecuting authority in a criminal case is necessarily an agent of the sovereign, the latter's name appears in its title. Hence, assuming one Brown's indictment for murder in Virginia, the case would be docketed for trial as either *The Commonwealth of Virginia v. Brown* or *People v. Brown.* Moving to the federal level, one of the cases brought under the Smith Act of 1940 was entitled

United States v. Scales.[41] However, by far the largest volume of criminal law is still enacted at the state level in the United States and thus is enforced by state officials under state law. Countries with a unitary structure, such as France and the United Kingdom,[42] are not confronted with that jurisdictional problem.

But in all cases and at all levels it is the jurists who render the decisions. Alexis de Tocqueville put it lastingly well when he observed that hardly any question arises in the United States that is not resolved sooner or later into a judicial question. To the jurists, then, their fascinating and significant tasks, and the hierarchical framework in which they perform their duties, we now turn.

---

41. 367 U.S. 203 (1961).

42. As noted on p. 10 *supra* (and p. 31 *infra*), Scotland differs from England and Wales because it follows Roman or civil (statutory) law rather than common law as a guide in private law. However, Scotland *is* subject to Parliamentary legislation, which is statutory. The House of Lords (its Law Lords), as the highest court of civil appeals in the United Kingdom, sits as a Scottish court when considering civil appeals from Scotland. It adopts Scottish methods of legal reasoning (e.g., *Cantiere San Rocco v. Clyde Shipbuilding Co.,* 1923 S.C. [H.L.] 105). This means that for guidance the judges refer to accepted repositories or institutions of Roman law—which some Scottish lawyers claim to have been too much influenced by English law. See generally, David M. Wilker, *The Scottish Legal System* (Edinburgh: W. Green and Son, 1981). (Northern Ireland, too, adheres to a different legal system from that of England and Wales.)

2

Staffing
the Courts

SELECTION

What principles should govern the selection of the men and women who dispense justice? To raise this question brings us face to face with moral as well as political questions of the greatest importance. However awe-inspiring their functions may be, our judges are still human beings. As such they make the ultimate decisions in the judicial process. In essence, there are just two basic methods of selection: *appointment* and *election*—no matter who does the actual appointing or electing—although, as we shall see, a compromise between the two modes has been devised and is practiced on certain levels of the judiciary in a good many jurisdictions. A collateral question is whether judges should be members of a career service as in France, chosen from a special group of lawyers as in England (for its above-magistrate–level jurists), or selected through appointments from the legal profession generally as in the United States. Practices of selection differ in large measure in accordance with the traditions and needs of the country concerned. A crucial consideration here is the very position of the judiciary in the framework of government that provides the rationale for the particular mode adopted and practiced. Under the Roman law tradition of the Continent, the judiciary is a part of the overall administrative hierarchy and, as such, represents a position and profession other than that of the ordinary lawyer. Under the common law system, on the other hand, the judges are drawn exclusively from the ranks of the legal profession,[1]

---

1. Justice Black often suggested that at least one non-lawyer be appointed to the U.S. Supreme Court, and other observers of the judiciary—e.g., Arthur Selwyn Miller—have raised the persistent issue of enabling non-lawyers to serve as judges. In 1976 the U.S. Supreme Court in a Kentucky case, *North v. Russell*, 427 U.S. 328, challenging the use of non-lawyer jurists in jail-carrying criminal trials, ruled 6:2 that the practice was constitutional, provided the defendant be given the opportunity through an appeal to obtain a second trial, *de novo*, before a judge who *is* legally trained. Kentucky soon adopted a constitutional amendment requiring all judges to be lawyers (except juvenile court "trial commissioners").

except for certain jurists on the state or local level in the United States. Nevertheless, the guiding principles for the selection and tenure of the judiciary in the three nations that concern us most here—England, France, and the United States—display a commonly held ideal: judges are expected to be impartial and hence must be given assurance of independence, security, and dignity of tenure. When these requirements are present, the fact that different techniques govern selection in those lands is hardly of great significance. Nevertheless, the techniques must be studied and understood. The process of selection is assuredly more complicated than might be inferred from the otherwise trenchant observation of W. Curtis Bok's imaginary Judge Ulen, who quipped, "A judge is a member of the bar who once knew a Governor."[2]

THE TWO CHIEF METHODS

The fifty American states (and their local subdivisions) employ at least six diverse types of recruitment systems for their circa 35,000 (1992) judges: partisan election, nonpartisan election, merit selection at one or more levels of the judicial system, gubernatorial appointment, legislative election, and selection by sitting judges.[3] But the *appointive* method is used *exclusively* at the *federal* level of the U.S. government, regardless of whether a tribunal concerned is a constitutional or legislative court (a distinction that will be described in detail in chapter 4). Britain and France use appointment exclusively at all levels.

   Appointment. In the *United States* all of the approximately, 1,000 (1992)[4] federal judges are appointed by the President, subject to confirmation by simple majority vote of the Senate.[5] Depending on the Chief Executive involved, the President's

---

2. *Backbone of the Herring* (New York: Alfred A. Knopf, 1941), p. 3. H. L. Mencken once observed that "a judge is a law student who marks his own exams" (press conference, Philadelphia, Pa., July 27, 1948).

3. In 1990, the fifty states picked their Supreme Court (or its equivalent) judges as follows: partisan election (ten); nonpartisan election (thirteen); appointment (twenty-seven).

4. This figure does not include the 243 federal "bankruptcy judges" (formerly called "referees") who serve in the ninety-four federal judicial districts. As a result of major revamping legislation enacted in 1984 amid bitter controversy, they are now appointed for fourteen-year terms by the regional U.S. Courts of Appeals (the law is silent on renewability), are removable by the judicial councils of each circuit, and are paid $119,140 per annum (1992). Nor does the figure 1,800 include the now (1992) approximately 1,200 federal "administrative law judges" (formerly known as "trial examiners") who are appointed directly by the heads of, and serve in, twenty-eight separate federal administrative departments and agencies. These judges dispose of some 150,000 "cases" annually before administrative bodies and can impose penalties of up to $100,000. See the informative article by Thomas O'Toole, "Administrative Law Judge: Opinions Means Dollars," *The Washington Post,* September 13, 1980, p. A3. See also the special issue of of 65 *Judicature* 5 (November 1981), which is devoted exclusively to administrative law judges, and Paul W. Parmele, "Preserving the Judicial Independence of Administrative Law Judges: Are Existing Protections Sufficient?," 4 *The Journal of Law and Politics* 1 (Summer 1987). The figure 1,000 also does not include federal commissioners or magistrates.

5. Joe Dolan, Assistant and Deputy Attorney General under Presidents Kennedy and Johnson, told an American Bar Association meeting in 1977 that the Constitution "reads backwards" and that it should say: "The Senators shall nominate and by and with the consent of the President, appoint judges. . . . " (As reported by James Goodman, "The Politics of Picking Federal Judges," *Juris Doctor,* June 1977, p. 20.) The Carter reforms (see pp. 29ff.) and subsequent experiments with merit selection in the states altered that fact of judicio-political life to some extent, but hardly conclusively.

responsibility (a heavy one) has often been largely delegated to the Attorney General and the Deputy Attorney General. This was noticeably true during the later years of the administration of President Eisenhower, when the selection of members of the federal judiciary was left almost exclusively to Attorney General William P. Rogers and Deputy Attorney General Lawrence E. Walsh. On the other hand, President Lyndon B. Johnson gave Chairman John C. Macy, Jr., of the U.S. Civil Service Commission, a trusted fellow Texan, *the* crucial role in the judicial selection process in preference to his Justice Department.[6] In the Reagan Administration a formal committee was established under the chairmanship of the President's Counsel, Fred F. Fielding, including the Attorney General plus seven other high officials of the Department of Justice and the White House.[7] That Committee reviewed recommendations for vacancies, submitted these to checks by the FBI and judgments by the ABA (see later), and then forwarded its recommendation to the President. Yet whatever mode is employed, three other crucial factors enter here.

The *first* factor is the obvious need for consultation with the U.S. senator(s) and/or other seats of political power in the home state of the candidate for judicial office, provided these political figures are of the same party as the appointing authority. Thus, care must be taken that the appointee is not "personally obnoxious" to a home-state senator, on pain of having the latter invoke the age-old, almost invariably honored, custom of "senatorial courtesy"[8]—an almost certain death knell to confirmation by the Senate. The custom is based on the assumption that the President will, as a matter of political patronage, practice, and courtesy, engage in such consultation prior to the nominee's designation—provided that the senator is a member of the President's party. If the President fails to adhere to this custom, the aggrieved senator's colleagues will almost certainly support him or her on the call for the nominee's defeat as a matter of fraternal *quid pro quo* courtesy.

Until the incoming chairman of the Senate Judiciary Committee, Senator Edward M. Kennedy (D.-Mass.), announced early in 1979 that he would not "unilaterally" table a nomination simply because a "blue slip" was not returned by a colleague, the so-called blue slip system had more or less institutionalized senatorial courtesy *cum* patronage. It proceeded as follows: Once the President formally nominated someone, the Senate Judiciary Committee sent to each of the nomi-

6. See Neil D. McFeeley, *Appointment of Judges: The Johnson Presidency* (Austin: University of Texas Press, 1987).

7. The Deputy Attorney General, the Assistant Attorney General for Legal Policy, the Associate Attorney General, the Chief of Staff for the White House, the Assistant to the President for Congressional Relations, the Assistant to the President for Personnel, and, on some occasions, the Assistant to the President for Political Affairs. See "A Look at Fred F. Fielding," 8 *District Lawyer* 2 (November–December 1983), p. 46. This system was generally continued in the Bush Administration.

8. It dates back to the first years of the Republic, when the Senate recognized the need for solidarity to prevent a President from appointing a senator's political adversary to high office. Actually, it began in the very first session of Congress in 1789, when George Washington nominated Benjamin Fishbourn as a naval officer in the Port of Savannah, Georgia. Although qualified, Fishbourn was opposed by Georgia's two senators, and Washington withdrew his nomination when it was apparent that the Senate would side with its Georgia colleagues. Subsequently, Washington nominated someone favored by the two legislators.

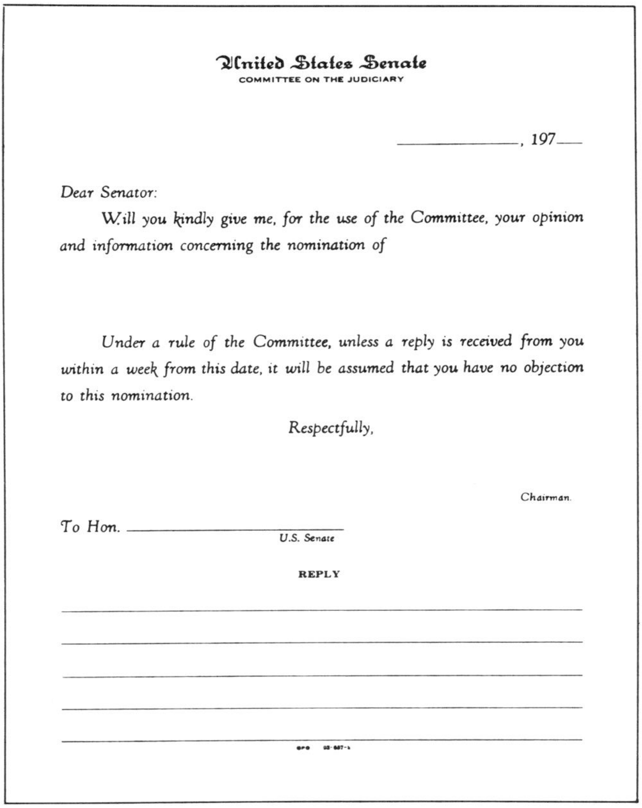

United States Senate
COMMITTEE ON THE JUDICIARY

__________, 197__

Dear Senator:

Will you kindly give me, for the use of the Committee, your opinion and information concerning the nomination of

Under a rule of the Committee, unless a reply is received from you within a week from this date, it will be assumed that you have no objection to this nomination.

Respectfully,

Chairman.

To Hon. __________
U.S. Senate

REPLY

Figure 1. The Senate's blue slip

nee's home-state senators a blue sheet of paper, asking his or her "opinion and information concerning the nomination." In fact, the blue slip asked whether the Chief Executive's formal choice was either the person the senator wanted or someone he or she could accept. If the senator approved, he or she returned the blue slip; if not, the senator retained the slip. If the senator was from the President's own party, a withheld blue slip amounted to a "one-person veto," terminating the nominee's chances. Senator Kennedy's bold effort to end this system met with considerable condemnation by a number of his committee colleagues. When he succeeded to the committee chairmanship in 1981, Senator Strom Thurmond (R.-S.C.) was at first inclined to reinstitute it, but he apparently decided not to do so.[9] His 1987 successor, Senator Joseph R. Biden (D.-Del.), announced a new policy under which failure to consult with the home-state senator, combined with a negative blue slip, would kill a nomination.

9. For at least some evidence of Thurmond's reluctance, see Sheldon Goldman, "Reagan's Judicial Appointments at Mid-Term: Shaping the Bench in His Own Image," 66 *Judicature* 8 (March 1983), p. 347 and n. 15.

Whatever the future may hold, however, let it be said at once that, as a practical matter of the political process—and regardless of the recent innovations explained later—it is simply not possible for the President to select a candidate for the bench and see that candidate confirmed without at least the grudging approval of his or her home-state senators. And some powerful senators of the President's political party will insist not only on the right of prior approval of the presidential choice but also on the right to have particular candidates of their own designated. This proved to be the case with Senator Lowell P. Weicker, Jr.'s (R.-Conn.), insistence on the nomination of Connecticut's ex-Governor Thomas J. Meskill to the federal appellate bench in 1974–75, resulting in the latter's ultimate approval by the Senate, 54:36, despite the American Bar Association's unanimous NQ (Not Qualified)[10] rating. On the other hand, following the establishment of President Carter's Circuit Judge Nomination Commission in 1977,[11] and spurred by the President's constant prodding, coupled with his Executive Order 12097 of November 8, 1978, which established guidelines and stipulated standards of candidate qualification, the late 1970s began to witness a burgeoning system of U.S. senator-created merit advisory groups and commissions, charged with recommending nominees for the federal bench to the senators (e.g., Virginia, Pennsylvania, Iowa, Georgia, Florida, Colorado, and New York). By early 1984, fifty senators in thirty-five states had thus agreed to choose federal district judges on a merit basis only, aided by commission recommendations. Others, however, had categorically declined to do so, among them Democrats Adlai E. Stevenson (Illinois), Thomas F. Eagleton (Missouri), Paul S. Sarbanes (Maryland), and Lloyd M. Bentsen (Texas), the latter announcing, "I am the merit commission for Texas."[12] Yet more than one-half of Reagan's 290 U.S. District Court appointees emerged from selection panels voluntarily sponsored by senators.

The *second* factor that has played an increasingly significant role in the appointive process of the federal judiciary in the United States, especially since the latter months of the Truman Administration, is the American Bar Association's fifteen-member[13] Committee on Federal Judiciary, established in 1946. That Committee was widely utilized thereafter at the preformal nomination stage during President Eisenhower's term of office, a practice continued under all subsequent Presidents,

10. See p. 28, *infra.*
11. Ibid.
12. *The Washington Post*, November 15, 1978, p. 4A. See the article by ex-Senator Joseph W. Tydings, "Merit Selection for Federal Judges," 61 *Judicature* 3 (September 1977).
13. Initially twelve, it had risen to thirteen as of September 1976, with the addition of the first black lawyer ever to be a member of the group in the person of Charles Z. Smith, associate dean of the University of Washington School of Law. It went to fourteen in August 1977 when the large Fifth and Ninth Circuits were assigned two members each (Washington being the Ninth). Each of the other circuits was assigned one member, with a separate slot for a chairman. Members serve for three years, with one possible renewal. In 1980, the Committee, for the first time, named a woman as its head—Brooksley E. Landau Born (of the prestigious Washington law firm of Porter & Arnold, formerly Porter, Fortas, & Arnold). When the 1981–82 circuit court organization acts provided for two new circuits, the Eleventh (created by splitting the Fifth) and the Thirteenth— known as the U.S. Court of Appeals for the Federal Circuit—both received a "representative" on the Committee, thus totaling fifteen. The number of members stood at fifteen as of mid-1992, the Ninth still having two, twelve circuits having one each, and a "member at large."

although President Nixon, following the Committee's disapproval of his 1970–71 list of putative candidates, refused to submit names to it until *after* he had already selected and publicized them.[14] The Committee's work has generally produced good results and is understandably popular with the legal profession, although there is no unanimity on that evaluation. There are those who believe deeply that the selection of the members of the judicial branch of the government must rest, in fact as well as in name, with the executive branch, its head being specifically charged to do so under Article III of the Constitution, and that the apparent delegation of important aspects of that authority (i.e., approval of, or at least judgment on, selectees) to a private body—one that is in fact monopolistic—no matter how qualified and how representative—a crucial point—is at best questionable, and at worst a dereliction of duty. Nor is the bar free from political or personal biases, as the contrast between the Committee's handling of the Fortas and the Haynsworth cases in 1969 and that of Bork in 1987 demonstrated. To cite an earlier case in point, had President Wilson heeded the advice of the ABA, Justice Brandeis would never have been nominated. Furthermore, as an intriguing book-length study of the committee's activities over a period of two decades demonstrated rather convincingly,[15] its membership was initially dominated by the "legal establishment." Until the 1970s, almost all of its members were successful lawyers, older, experienced men, partners in large, big-city firms, and veterans of local bar association politics. Of the relatively few lawyers the Committee had asked to give an evaluation of judicial candidates twenty years ago, 70 percent were officers of local bar associations and 80 percent were senior partners in "respectable" law firms. A genuine and broadly based measure of diversification has demonstrably set in, however,[16] and may confidently be expected to continue.[17] Indeed, there are now complaints that the pendulum has swung too far.

Whatever the merit of demurrers, the committee has become a powerful and respected vehicle in the vital initial stages of the nominating process. It does not generate names for judicial vacancies, but it evaluates the qualifications of "persons considered for appointment to the Supreme Court of the United States, Circuit Courts of Appeals, District Courts and the Court of International Trade."[18] After

---

14. ———the A.B.A.!," exclaimed Mr. Nixon, in ordering this future policy of nonsubmittal of Supreme Court nominees *prior* to formal selection in 1971 (as reported by Goodman, op. cit., p. 26).

15. Joel B. Grossman, *Lawyers and Judges: The Politics of Judicial Selection* (New York: John Wiley & Sons, 1965), especially pp. 87–92.

16. Thus, Professors Richard G. Watson, Rondal G. Downing, and Frederick G. Spiegel, in an article concerned with the members of Missouri's Bar, contend that the notation that the Bar is inevitably conservative is disproved by the Missouri experience. See "Bar Politics, Judicial Selection and the Representation of Social Interests," 61 *American Political Science Review* 54 (March 1967). Contemporary developments amply bear out that judgment.

17. See Elliot E. Slotnick, "The ABA's Standing Committee on Federal Judiciary: A Contemporary Assessment," in 66 *Judicature* 8, 9 (March–April 1983).

18. For a formal, recently updated description of the Committee's procedures, see *The ABA's Standing Committee on Federal Judiciary: What It Is and How It Works* (Chicago: American Bar Association, 1991).

an investigation, customarily lasting from six to eight weeks,[19] it reports to the Justice Department on the qualifications of the prospective nominee and rates him or her in one of three ways: Well Qualified (WQ), Qualified (Q), or Not Qualified (NQ).[20] In a number of cases the consideration of nominees for the federal bench was dropped after the ABA's Committee found them less qualified than others; thus, no NQs were approved between 1965 and 1975 (until the instance of the Meskill nomination approval in the latter year—see notes 19 and 23). Moreover, its reports have enabled the Justice Department to rule out certain names recommended by the home-state senator(s), though "senatorial courtesy" may prevail in the end. It should be noted that the Committee also sends its ratings *independently* to the Senate Judiciary Committee. Its final report is a one-sentence judgment by the full membership.

To illustrate the Committee's role, in September 1961 the Senate confirmed sixty lower court federal judges nominated by President Kennedy, fifty-two of whom had been rated by the ABA. Nine had been rated Exceptionally Well Qualified (a category then in use but abandoned in 1989), twenty-seven Well Qualified, fourteen Qualified, and two Not Qualified. Yet the two rated Not Qualified— James R. Browning, then the clerk of the U.S. Supreme Court, and Luther Bohanan, an Oklahoman—had sufficiently powerful support to gain confirmation, the latter from that state's powerful Democratic U.S. Senator "Bob" Kerr, the chairman of the Senate Finance Committee. However, a finding of NQ is not necessarily a reflection on a nominee's character or ability. Until 1981 the ABA's Committee would not approve anyone who had reached the age of sixty-four, and no one older than sixty unless he or she was ratable at least WQ. President Kennedy's

19. The investigation is based in part on the candidate's responses to a lengthy, detailed questionnaire, one question of which asks about the ten most significant cases the candidate has handled. (In his response, former Governor Thomas Meskill (R.-Conn.) included three grotesquely insignificant cases that dealt with civil negligence suits.) In its own decision-making process the Senate's Committee on the Judiciary also uses a questionnaire to elicit a candidate's qualifications. The ABA Committee conducts a great many interviews, looks at the nominee's briefs, and consults sitting jurists. The initial burden falls on the appropriate circuit-representative committee member, who ultimately sends a draft report to the Chairman. The latter then convenes the entire Committee for a vote. If requested by the Senate Judiciary Committee, the former's Chairman or individual members may testify in confirmation hearings (as was true in the 1986 nominations of William H. Rehnquist and Antonin Scalia).

20. These categories—which, until 1989 also included an Exceptionally Well Qualified (EWQ) rating—are not applicable to Supreme Court nominees, however, who began to be rated only as of the 1956 Brennan appointment and then simply as Q or NQ to the Senate Judiciary Committee. But after the Haynsworth and Carswell debacles, the Committee, as of the Blackmun nomination, adopted the following Supreme Court rankings: (a) "high standards of integrity, judicial temperament, and professional competence," (b) "not opposed," (c) "not qualified." As of the 1986 Rehnquist and Scalia nominations by President Reagan, the Committee adopted yet another standard or nomenclature for *Supreme Court* nominees only: (a) "well qualified," (b) "qualified," (c) "not qualified." Both nominees received the highest qualification unanimously. For the Robert H. Bork nomination in 1987 it employed still another trichotomy: (a) "well qualified," (b) "not opposed," and (c) "not qualified." Its vote was 10:1:4. The Scalia standards were applied to Clarence Thomas; the Committee's vote was 0:12:2 and one abstention.

selection of Sarah T. Hughes of Texas[21] to be a federal district court judge was disapproved on the former ground, but she was confirmed. In the case of a sitting judge the Committee would approve *promotion* up to age sixty-eight. The Committee is loath to recommend lawyers without trial experience—which was true of both Browning and Bohanan—and it generally insists on fifteen years of experience in "the rough and tumble of legal practice"[22] or at least twelve "in substantial trial work"—although it adopted a policy of making numerous exceptions on both counts in the instances of women and minorities as of the mid-to-late 1970s.

Considerably more will be said on the point later, but it should be reemphasized here that no alert and prudent Chief Executive of the United States would nowadays attempt to designate members of the judiciary *purely* on the basis of political considerations. Too much is at stake in matters of policy and public awareness, and the American Bar Association is a powerful factor in the selection process. Yet, granted the various needs and drives for appointments on the basis of overall merit and excellence, the political pressures must nevertheless be reckoned with and are disregarded only at the appointing authority's peril.[23] Moreover, a federal judgeship is viewed as a "plum" by all concerned, in that it represents a potent patronage whip in the hands of the executive vis-à-vis state politicians as well as Congress.

Both the continuing problem and its flavor are suggested nicely and candidly by this passage in Senator Joseph S. Clark's newsletter of August 11, 1961, to his constituents in Pennsylvania:

> I have forwarded to the Attorney General recommendations to fill additional Judgeships recently authorized by Congress in the United States District Courts in Penn-

---

21. Judge Hughes swore in Lyndon B. Johnson in the presidential plane *Air Force 1* after President Kennedy's assassination on November 22, 1963. In "age disqualification" characterizations, the ABA Committee used to issue a rating of "Not Qualified by Reason of Age" (NQ-A). But, in response to mounting criticism, it resolved to discontinue this age barrier classification as of January 1, 1981.
22. Committee member Robert Trescher, personal communication to me, December 9, 1971.
23. Nixon and then President Ford pushed Senator Lowell P. Weicker, Jr.'s (R.-Conn.), insisted-upon nomination of the professionally potentially unqualified ex-Governor Thomas J. Meskill for a vacancy on the U.S. Court of Appeals for the Second Circuit. Senator Weicker had the crucial support of Connecticut's senior Senator, Democrat Abraham Ribicoff. But it was not until eight months after the Senate received the nomination that it reluctantly confirmed Mr. Meskill by the less than impressive margin of 54:36 in April 1975 (see Jerry Landauer, "How Not to Pick a Judge," The *Wall Street Journal*, April 10, 1975, p. 4). In late 1978, the Senate confirmed the U.S. District Court nomination of Donald E. O'Brien of Iowa despite the ABA Committee's 14:0 NQ rating. It ought to be noted that Judge Meskill has served ably. Indeed, he received the Association of Trial Lawyers of America's 1983 Outstanding Federal Appellate Judge Award (*The Washington Post*, July 19, 1983, p. C3). In 1980, the Senate's Judiciary Committee rejected the U.S. District Court judgeship nomination of Charles H. Winberry, campaign manager of U.S. Senator Robert Morgan (D.-N.C.), after the ABA's Committee had ranked him NQ (having reversed its initial Q verdict). But shortly thereafter that same Committee approved the nomination of U. W. Clemon, a black Alabama legislator, notwithstanding the ABA's NQ rating. In mid-1986 the Senate Judiciary Committee, on a 9:9 tie vote, refused to send President Reagan's nomination of Jefferson B. Sessions of Alabama to its U.S. District Court to the floor, despite the ABA's "Q" imprimatur. At the same time, and on the same tie vote, it did, however, clear the Controversial "Q" approval of Daniel A. Manion to the U.S. District Court of Indiana for floor action. He was confirmed by a mere one-vote margin after a bitter battle.

sylvania, and one vacancy in the Court of Appeals for the Third Circuit. I regret that, by custom, Senators have the obligation of making these recommendations after appropriate consultation with their State political leaders. I believe the selection of judges should be entirely nonpartisan and should be made by the Attorney General and the President without Senatorial intervention [a proposal backed unsuccessfully by Attorney General Elliot L. Richardson during his brief tenure under President Nixon in 1973]. Nevertheless, I must live with the rules as they exist until they are changed. After consultations with [Democratic] Governor Lawrence, Democratic State Chairman Otis Morse II, [Democratic] Congressman William J. Green, Jr., and others, I am satisfied that the recommendations made for existing vacancies are men of ability and integrity. The Attorney General and the President will make the final decisions on these Judgeships of course, and may disregard our recommendations if they wish.

But there was a very real possibility of a major change, indeed conceivably a revolutionary development, on February 14, 1977, when President Carter, having been in office only one month, issued Executive Order 11972 establishing "The United States Circuit Judge Nominating Commission" to make recommendations, based on "merit"—a major 1976 campaign promise—for *all* future judgeship nominations at the level of the U.S. Circuit Courts of Appeals. He noted that he would have preferred to embrace federal district court judgeships under the same order, but, reading the political signs, determined to postpone any such endeavor to a future day. The new commission consisted of thirteen separate eleven-member panels—one for each circuit, two each for the big Fifth and Ninth—that under its order's initial terms were to be composed roughly of one-half lawyers and one-half non-lawyers, and, specifically required the inclusion of both men and women as well as members of minority groups. The panels were designed to be *ad hoc* in nature, with each appointment's terminating thirty days after the submittal of each panel's report to the President, unless the latter chose to extend its life. Each panel was expected to forward to the President within sixty days those five names it considered most qualified on the basis of "character, experience, ability, and commitment to equal justice under law" to fill the particular vacancy of which it had been apprised by the Chief Executive (via the Attorney General).

After the first set of President Carter–appointed panels, the sex distribution varied from eight men and three women on the First Circuit's panel to six women and five men on the Southern Fifth and Western Ninth; that of lawyers to non-lawyers from 7:4 to 4:7; all panels now had group representation, an overall pattern that continued apace. No judges were among the lawyers who had been appointed to any of the set of 1977, 1978, 1979, and 1980 panels.[24] On May 11, 1978, President Carter promulgated the amendatory Executive Order 12059, that, together with accompanying supplemental instructions, made several important changes in the Commission's composition and procedures. Specifically, panel membership was no

24. See Dorothy W. Nelson, "Carter's Merit Plan: A Good First Step," 61 *Judicature* 3 (September 1977); Sheldon Goldman, "A Profile of Carter's Judicial Nominees," 62 *Judicature* (November 1978); Susan Carbon, "The U.S. Circuit Judge Nomination Commission," ibid.; and Elliot E. Slotnick, "What Panelists Are Saying about the Circuit Judge Nomination Commission," ibid. (February 1979).

longer limited to eleven; there could be more or fewer. Also, panels were no longer required to be composed of approximately equal numbers of lawyers and nonlawyers. Finally, whereas the 1977 order had required that each state within a panel's circuit be represented by at least one "resident," that of 1978 specified one "lawyer." Moreover, there was now no longer a sixty-day completion-of-operation requirement; the new order neither limited nor required the panel to submit five names, merely calling for a list of "persons . . . best qualified . . . "; and the panel was no longer mandated to report the names of its potential nominees to the President "in confidence."

That the Commission's work and the results thereof had a mixed reception is not surprising, especially since a number of the panels found themselves in heated controversies over charges that in selecting nominees they were more concerned with "group," "sex," and "race" representativeness than with merit. Further, 87 percent of all commissioners were Democrats; 50 percent had supported the Carter campaign; and 33 percent were Democratic officeholders.[25] What is clear, however, is that as a result of the new lower federal court staffing policies developed by the Carter Administration, the Circuit and District Court levels witnessed a very marked increase—indeed, a dramatic one—in the number of both women and minority selectees and nominees, as the President and the Department of Justice categorically insisted on that aspect of "affirmative action." By late 1980, with the Carter Administration's nearing its end, fully one-half of those chosen under the new system were female, black, or of Hispanic origin. Questioned by both friendly and inquisitive members of the Senate Judiciary Committee on the matter, Attorney General Griffin Bell had testified earlier that "Mr. Carter was prepared to appoint to the Federal bench a black, Hispanic, or woman lawyer who was found to be *less qualified* than a white male so long as the appointee was found qualified."[26] And in a December 7, 1978, press conference, President Carter had stated, "If I didn't have to get Senate confirmation of appointees, I could tell you flatly that 12% of my appointees would be blacks and 3% would be Spanish-speaking and 40% would be women and so forth."[27] The Carter Commission system was abolished by President Reagan early in 1981.

There is a *third* factor: the increasing evidence of the unquestionably significant influence that sitting and retired members of the Court itself, especially the Chief Justice, have on nominations by consulting with and being consulted by the President and the Attorney General in the selection process of a new Supreme Court

25. Larry C. Berkson and Susan B. Carbon, *The United States Circuit Judge Nominating Commission: Its Members, Procedures, and Candidates* (Chicago: American Judicature Society, 1980), at p. 49.
26. *The New York Times*, February 13, 1979, p. A16. As of November 1979, President Carter had an option to select a female or a black in 67 percent of the nomination suggestions submitted to him. He selected a woman or a black in each instance (Larry E. Berkson, "Equal Justice under Law," Paper delivered at the Southern Political Science Association Annual Meeting, Gatlinburg, Tennessee, November 3, 1979). By October 1980, President Carter had appointed 45 women and 55 minorities, far more than all his predecessors combined! (When he took office, there were but nineteen blacks, five females, and five Hispanics on the federal benches.)
27. The White House, Washington, D.C.

Justice.[28] Among a good many others, Chief Justices Taft, Hughes, Stone, Vinson, Warren, and Burger and Associate Justices Harlan I, Miller, Van Devanter, Brandeis, and Frankfurter have thus all been involved—Taft more openly and actively than anyone else on the high bench, followed at some distance by Stone, Hughes, Harlan I, and Miller, in that order.[29] Taft's role in Harding's nomination of Butler is a classic example. In fact, Harding's Attorney General, Harry M. Daugherty, told Henry Taft (William's brother) that "the President would not approve anybody for appointment who was not approved by the Chief Justice."[30] It is entirely possible to make a good case for the practice, but within limits.

In *Britain*—we are here again concerned almost exclusively with England and Wales (for convenience hereafter referred to as England), because Scotland and Northern Ireland, the two other members of the United Kingdom of Great Britain and Northern Ireland, operate separate court systems—judges are designated by the Crown with little direct surrender to politics. Practically speaking, they are made by, or on the advice of, the Lord High Chancellor of Great Britain, the senior law member of the government, who is the Queen's chief adviser on the selection. Because the Lord Chancellor, who is a political appointee and a member of the Cabinet, is chosen by the Prime Minister, the latter does have an indirect voice in the highly secretive process of selection of judges, however truly small and inaudible that voice is, especially on the middle and higher levels. Among these are the Lords of Appeal in Ordinary (the Law Lords), the Lord Chief Justice, the Master of the Rolls, the President of the Family Division of the High Court of Justice, and the Lord Justices of the Court of Appeal. In the cases of the Lord Chief Justice and the Master of the Rolls, the highest ranking judicial offices, the Prime Minister in effect designates the appointees but acts on the advice of the Lord Chancellor. But it is the Queen who actually issues the commission of appointment.

The Lord Chancellor himself, however, is the politically designated head of the judicial hierarchy of the United Kingdom. In addition, he advises on all appointments to judicial office from the rank of Justice of the Peace to the higher offices of the English Judiciary. As Speaker of the House of Lords he presides from the Woolsack (a bright red padded bench, its name signifying how important the wool trade was to the British economy in earlier centuries); he is a member of the Cab-

28. See Henry J. Abraham and Bruce A. Murphy, "The Influence of Sitting and Retired Justices on Presidential Supreme Court Nominations," 3 *Hastings Constitutional Law Quarterly* 37 (Winter 1976). The data in the article, plus the subsequent O'Connor, Scalia, Kennedy, Souter, and Thomas appointments, in 1981, 1986, 1987, 1990, and 1991, demonstrate that of the 106 individuals who had sat on the Court as of early 1992, 50 had exerted ascertainable pressure in a total of 97 separate instances involving 46 vacancies.

29. For a good description of Taft's role in Harding's designation of Pierce Butler, see David Danelski, *A Supreme Court Justice Is Appointed* (New York: Random House, 1964). See also Alpheus T. Mason, *William Howard Taft: Chief Justice* (New York: Simon and Schuster, 1965) and *Harlan Fiske Stone: Pillar of the Law* (New York: Viking Press, 1956). For a full-scale study of *all* nominations and appointments to the Supreme Court through 1990, see my *Justices and Presidents: A Political History of Appointments to the United States Supreme Court*, 3d ed. (New York: Oxford University Press., 1992).

30. Quoted by Mason, *Taft*, loc. cit., p. 173.

inet; and, as head of the Judiciary, he combines in his person the threefold function of executive, legislator, and jurist—a complete refutation of the principle of separation of powers so dear to Montesquieu. His office, which pays (1992) a total of £104,750, is older than that of Prime Minister (whose salary is the same; high jurists receive more). Because the group of lawyers from whose ranks the Lord Chancellor[31] chooses England's and Wales's approximately five hundred and fifty full-time judges (1992)—not counting the circa 1200 Recorders and Assistant Recorders—is comparatively small and select, he may know some of them; when members of the Opposition in government show promise as competent judges, he will certainly not hesitate to cross party lines to make appointments. If he does not personally know, or know of, a candidate, he will probably consult a senior judge or judges and obtain their views—but *not* their prior approval. Incidentally, barristers must leave the bar when they go on the bench.

No letters of recommendation are accepted, and efforts to put political pressure on the Lord Chancellor are scouted strongly. Since the early 1980s it has been the "L.C.'s" practice to appoint and promote to full-time office only those who have served satisfactorily in relevant part-time appointments. The L.C.'s Department also reviews each year the careers of *all* practicing barristers under fifty to see who might receive appointments.[32] R. M. Jackson, professor of public law and administration at the University of Cambridge, in his excellent study on the machinery of justice in England,[33] contends—although a good many would voice doubts—that political considerations have hardly entered the process of judicial selection since 1907, while they died a slower death in the selection of Lord Chief Justice; he also insists that, as a consequence, there has been no apparent connection between the "political antecedents" of the judges and their decisions for more than a century. On their resignation, however, members of the House of Commons may be appointed to county court judgeships and also to the High Court.[34]

It ought to be noted that there has been mounting criticism of the selection process, because of the all but total absence of women and minorities among the high judges. Thus, in late 1991 there was no woman among the Law Lords, only one on the Court of Appeal and three on the High Court. Tony Scrivener, QC, Chairman of the Bar, promised to endeavor to alleviate that condition and also to advance the candidacies of more liberal members of the profession to judgeships.[35]

---

31. On two occasions the title was held by men who were later sainted—Thomas à Becket and Sir Thomas More. In 1991 some 4 percent of the full-time judges and 6 percent of the Recorders and Assistant Recorders were women—a total that is bound to increase. See Sally Hughes, "The Circuit Bench—A Woman's Place," *The Law Society*, London, April 1991.

32. See S. A. de Smith, *Judicial Appointments* (London: Her Majesty's Stationery Office, 1986), pp. 373ff.

33. Richard M. Jackson, *The Machinery of Justice in England*, 7th ed. (Cambridge: Cambridge University Press, 1977), p. 469. See also the 8th ed., revised by J. R. Spencer (1989).

34. For example, in 1962 two of the members of the High Court were from the House of Commons, and the then-new president of its Probate, Divorce, and Admiralty Division (now called the Family Division) was the former Solicitor-General, a member of the House.

35. See *The Guardian*, September 28, 1991, Law 25, "Writ Large," by Marcel Berlins. Courtesy of Dr. Margherita Rendel, Barrister at Law, Reader in Human Rights and Education, University of London.

In France, and in many other countries on the Continent, the trained judges are appointed to, rise in, and are promoted from a type of career service that is an adjunct of the general civil service. The de Gaulle Constitution of 1958 specifically makes a point of the time-honored concept that an ideal judge is an impartial judge. There is a Ministry of Justice, but the judges of France (numbering circa 5,500 in 1984, one-fourth of them women) do not really feel its authority, although the Minister is part of the appointing process. Political patronage plays only a small role in their selections. They all have either been schooled as judges for a minimum of twenty-eight months by the *École Nationale de la Magistrature* in Bordeaux (established in 1959) or had experience as judges, and they enter the judicial service on the basis of passing competitive examinations.

Theoretically, the President of the Republic, who is charged by the Constitution to be "the guarantor of the independence of judicial authority,"[36] selects the judges; actually, they are chosen either by the eleven-member *Conseil Supérieur de la Magistrature* (High Council of the Judiciary) in the case of the *Cour d'Appel* and the *Cour de Cassation,* or by the Minister of Justice, who may consult with, or receive advice from, the High Council, in the case of the lower courts. The High Council consists of the President of the Republic (as *le président*), the Minister of Justice (as vice-president), and nine persons with legal background chosen by the President for a once-renewable term of four years, partly on the recommendation of the *Cour de Cassation* and the *Conseil d'État*, as follows: one from the latter, three from the former, three from other courts, and two selected for their general competence ("leurs competences"). In any event, the selecting authorities have little choice—considerably less than in England and infinitely less, of course, than in the United States.

The assets and liabilities of the appointive versus the elective method are rather obvious. In general the main argument in favor of appointment hinges on the contention that a candidate for a judicial post who is obliged to run on a partisan ballot cannot possibly serve as an *impartial* judge, and that he is selected, as Al Smith once put it, "by an electorate who are not really in a position to pass upon the legal and other abilities of the individual."[37] On the other hand, the champions of election on a partisan ballot argue that appointment by a political executive contains even worse features of political beholdenness than election. As is so often the case, neither side of the argument is *ipso facto* correct on all counts; both contain some merit, and it is easy to oversimplify. Someone, however, has to assume responsibility for staffing the courts; it might as well be the executive, who not only possesses the expertise and has access to all pertinent data but also is fairly well known to the populace at large on almost all levels and, in fact, is usually the sole officer of government with an all-embracing constituency. In a free society, the people, at least in theory, are always in a position to hold him or her accountable. Making the executive responsible for unfortunate judicial appointments is more meaningful and more palatable to the electorate than any arrangement that requires the

---

36. Title VIII, Article 64.
37. As quoted by Arthur T. Vanderbilt, "Brief for a Better Court System," *The New York Times Magazine,* May 5, 1957, p. 9.

voters not only to submerge judges into the political arena but also to become intimately familiar with their adjudicatory record. Whatever the ramifications of this balancing of scales, executive appointment of judges—however it may be subject to input and influence by other sources, private as well as public—has proved to be the preferred method of selection in the United States (with notable state-level exceptions), England and Wales, and France. Although compromise arrangements of the type illustrated later may well move onto the scene here and there, there is no chance that election will supplant appointment for the selective process of judges in the vast majority of countries in the free world.[38]

Election. Nevertheless, election of members of that branch of the government is not unknown, even at the national or federal level of governments. In Switzerland, a major exception to the *federal* appointment principle, judges are elected by the two federal chambers—the *Nationalrat* and the *Ständerat*—sitting jointly as the *Bundesversammlung* (National Assembly) to ensure that German-, French-, and Italian-speaking members are appropriately distributed on the bench. However, reelection is so usual that for all intents and purposes permanent tenure of office is the result.

Election of judges is still widespread in a majority of the states in America, where as recently as 1970 fully 82 percent[39] of the nation's state and local judges ran on various election ballots. Only eight states did not have elections for judges at any level in 1991.[40] Thus, judges may be elected by the electorate (e.g., Arkansas and Alabama) or by the legislature (e.g., South Carolina and Virginia). They may run on partisan tickets (e.g., West Virginia and New Mexico) or on nonpartisan ones (e.g., Washington and Michigan) on occasion, but loyal service in partisan politics normally tends to be a prerequisite for nomination—in line with Jacksonian tradition. Also, although the term of office for most elected judges is on the average six to ten years, for some it extends to fifteen years (e.g., in Maryland). In a few states the concept of supporting the sitting judge has been adopted when he or she is up for reelection,[41] but this theoretically laudatory practice has been ignored

---

38. In Israel, recommendations for judicial appointments are made to the government by an Appointments Committee, consisting of the President of the Supreme Court, two judges from the court containing the vacancy who are chosen by its members, two Bar Association–selected lawyers, the Minister of Justice, and two members selected by the *Knesset* (Parliament). Nominees must come from the ranks of experienced judges, advocates, or legal academicians.

39. *Time* Magazine, March 30, 1970, p. 48. But *real* contests are relatively rare, and active politicking by judges is usually, although by no means always, regarded as demeaning.

40. *The Book of the States, 1990–1991.* (Lexington, Ky.: Council of State Governments), pp. 210–12. They were Delaware, Hawaii, Massachusetts, New Hampshire, New Jersey, Rhode Island, Vermont, and Virginia. Three other states (Connecticut, Maine, and South Carolina) elect *only* probate judges.

41. Thus, New York State Court of Appeals Associate Judge Stanley H. Fuld, who had demonstrated great talent in twenty years of service on that tribunal, was nominated for the post of Chief Justice on the November 8, 1966, ballot by all four political parties: Republican, Democratic, Liberal, and Conservative. However, New York moved to the appointive method for that tribunal as a result of a popular referendum-approved constitutional amendment in 1978.

almost as much as it has been observed. Moreover, the mitigating factors that are inherent in the deviations from the straight, partisan, short-term ballot election are found in but a few states, and even in these they are usually confined to the upper echelon of the judiciary.

Other practices worthy of note in this general consideration of selection are those of at least some judges by gubernatorial appointment subject to legislative consent (e.g., New Jersey and Maine) and appointment of some, either temporary or permanent, by courts (e.g., Alaska and Louisiana). Massachusetts's commission-selected, gubernatorially appointed judges, except justices of the peace, serve for life, "conditioned upon good behavior"; those of New Jersey, strictly gubernatorially selected, serve for seven years and then, if reappointed, for life terms "during good behavior."

A COMPROMISE?

An intriguing attempt at a compromise between the elective and appointive methods of choosing state judges in America has been advanced and popularized in somewhat different versions by a number of states at some or all appellate and/or trial court levels. This is the case (1992) in Georgia, Hawaii, South Dakota, California, Maryland, Idaho, Missouri, Alaska, Kansas, Colorado, Iowa, Arizona, New York, Oklahoma, Indiana, Nebraska, Utah, Florida, Tennessee, Wyoming, Montana, Illinois, New Mexico, and Vermont. This compromise is designed to minimize political influence and provide a degree of security of tenure while retaining an element of popular control. Repeatedly and even enthusiastically supported by leading spokespersons of the legal profession and by knowledgeable laypersons alike, it has been widely adopted; its chief obstacle is powerful political opposition, which views this compromise as a genuine threat to the patronage aspects of judicial selection, as well it might be. California and Missouri, the pioneers in the compromise movement, deserve special discussion.

The California Plan. The first well-known original attempt at a solution to the vexatious problem of judicial selection was the *California Plan*, adopted by a voter initiative and referendum in 1934. Proposed originally in 1912 by the Commonwealth Club of San Francisco, the plan's ratification was assiduously supported by the California State Bar Association, encouraged by its national parent body. The State Bar Association was also closely allied with the California Chamber of Commerce. Both of these powerful state groups had become convinced of the inadequacy of the system under which California then operated—judicial appointment by the governor with subsequent popular approval, which in their eyes constituted little more than public rubber-stamping of the appointing authority's rank political designations.

Under the California Plan, which applies to the judges of the Supreme Court and Courts of Appeal only (trial court appointments are at the governor's discretion), the governor nominates *one* person to the Commission on Judicial Appointments. The latter is composed of the Chief Justice of the State Supreme Court, the Presiding Judge of the Court of Appeals of the area concerned, and the Attorney General.[42] If the commission approves the governor's nominee[43]—and only one has been rejected to date (late 1991)[44]—he or she is deemed appointed *only* until the next general election (but not for less than one year). At the end of that period the nominee stands for popular election for the full twelve-year term of office that is statutorily assigned to each slot on the tribunal, or to whatever number of years remains in the twelve-year cycle. His or her name is the only one on the nonpartisan ballot. The sole question appearing on the ballot in connection with the nominee's candidacy is "Shall —— be elected to the office for the term prescribed by law?" There are no limits on the number of terms to which a successful candidate may aspire. Should the electorate's response to the question on the ballot be in the negative, the governor will designate a successor in the same manner, who ultimately will go before the electorate as well. In any event, the burden of approval is on the people, who must familiarize themselves with the candidate's record—or at least they ought to do so.

The first test of the plan returned the sitting judges by a 2:1 affirmative vote, a margin of approval that has steadily widened since that time. Until the retention elections of November 1986 *no* California jurist running for election under the retention plan had been rejected by the electorate. But that election featured the rejection of Chief Justice Rose Elizabeth Bird[45] and Associate Justices Cruse Reynoso and Joseph Grodin by the decisive margins of 66.2, 60.2, and 56.6, respectively.[46] Appraisals of the California Plan have generally been favorable, although some have criticized as inadequate what they view as the essentially negative restriction placed on the Governor's power by the Commission. To refuse to confirm a gubernatorial appointment takes a certain amount of courage, which has not inevitably been demonstrated by the Commission. Doubts have also been voiced concerning the wisdom of placing a measure of control over judicial appointments, however negative, into the hands of the chief law officer of the state, the Attorney General. Nonetheless, the plan has worked well and has been favorably received by the vast majority of those concerned.

The Missouri Plan. Desirous of adopting a modified version of the California Plan—a more clearly merit-selected one—and learning a tactical lesson from its

---

42. Since 1980 all nominees have also been submitted to the California Bar's twenty-five-member Committee on Judicial Nominees Evaluation for a "ranking" (from "excellent" down to "unqualified").

43. Thus, the first female Chief Justice of the California Supreme Court, Rose Elizabeth Bird, nominated in early 1977 for the post by Governor Edmund G. ("Jerry") Brown, Jr., was approved by the Commission by a 2:1 vote; Attorney General Evelle Younger cast the decisive vote in her favor. It proved to be a highly controversial choice: in the confirmation election of November 1978, she won by a mere 51.7 percent of the votes cast—the closest margin to date (mid-1991) in the history of California's judicial races. See Preble Stolz, *Judging the Judges: The Investigations of Rose Bird and the California Supreme Court* (New York: The Free Press, 1981). She was defeated in her quest for another term in late 1986. (See text, *infra.*)

44. In 1940, Governor Clubert Olson's nomination of Max Radin, a "liberal" Berkeley professor of law, was defeated by a 2:1 commission vote. From 1934 to 1984 a mere twenty dissenting votes were cast by commission members on some two hundred nominees to the two tiers of appellate courts.

45. She had voted to overturn lower courts' death sentences in *all* of the 61 cases that had come before her since her appointment as Chief Justice in 1977.

46. See the special issue of 70 *Judicature*, April–May 1987, pp. 340–69.

defeat in popular referenda in 1938 in both Ohio and Michigan, the supporters of the *Missouri Plan* waged a vigorous and enlightened campaign, headed by both professional and lay groups. The movement for its adoption was spearheaded by the Missouri Institute for the Administration of Justice, an educational corporation composed of one-third lawyers and two-thirds laypersons, who successfully enlisted the active support of civic, labor, farm, and business organizations. They explained to the electorate the true purpose of the plan: to secure an intelligent and impartial selection of personnel for the bench, to eliminate as much as possible the haphazard results of the elective system, and to relieve the judges of the pressures of political campaigning. And the supporters of the plan pointed out shrewdly that neither the California nor the Missouri Plan was designed to supplant entirely the elective method—this was clearly a compromise between appointment and election. Characterized by the American Bar Association as the "most acceptable substitute available for direct election of judges," the plan became law in the form of an amendment to Missouri's Constitution in 1940.

The Missouri Plan is mandatory for the judges of the Missouri Supreme Court, the state's other appellate courts, the circuit and probate courts in St. Louis and in Jackson County, and the St. Louis Court of Corrections. It is optional, subject to popular referenda, in the thirty-eight other circuits of the state. Thus, judges of a number of courts, especially those of the lower levels, may well remain outside the compromise plan, as do the judges in California. Under the Missouri version, nonpartisan nominating boards known as the Missouri Appellate Commissions, operating on different court levels, select *three* candidates for every vacant judgeship. For the Supreme Court and the appellate courts, the Commission consists of the Chief Justice of the State Supreme Court, the chairman; three lawyers, elected by the state Bar, one from each of the three courts of appeals; and three citizens who are *not* members of the Bar, appointed by the Governor, again on the basis of one from each of the three appellate districts. The commissions for the circuit and other lower court judges comprise the presiding judge of the court of appeals district in which the circuit happens to be situated, two members of the Bar elected by its own members residing in the circuit involved, and two similarly resident non-Bar citizens appointed by the Governor. The members of all these nonsalaried commissions are designated for staggered six-year terms of office, with changes taking effect in alternate years. Because the Governor has a four-year term and can succeed to the office but once, it is unlikely that he or she would appoint *all* of the lay members. To ensure an additional degree of impartiality, commissioners are permitted to hold neither public office nor an official position in a political party.

The Governor of Missouri is obliged to choose *one* of the three individuals selected by the Appellate Commission and appoint him or her until the next general election but not for less than one year, similar to the California Plan. After this probationary period, the appointee must be approved by the electorate for a full twelve-year term in the appellate courts or for a lesser term in the trial courts, running unopposed on a separate, nonpartisan judicial ballot at the time of the general election. The question on the ballot, similar to that of California, is "Shall Judge —— of the —— Court be retained in office? Yes ( ) No ( ) (Scratch one)."

Generally deemed to be the most adult and most attractive system of judicial selection extant in the various states, the Missouri Plan embraces a number of commendable features. It combines the democratic notion of accountability to the electorate with an intelligent method of selecting qualified candidates for judicial office. The necessity of facing the electorate on the record provides the judge with an incentive of judiciousness; and the fact that he or she runs on a personal record rather than against that of an opponent allied with a specific political party goes far toward taking the courts out of the more crass aspects of politics. On the other hand, a case could be made for the contention that the awareness of establishing a "good record" for the electorate's eyes and ears may lead to timid and/or "popular" judgments. The results of the Missouri Plan in action, however, do not generally support that theory.

An examination of the election returns for a number of years demonstrates the overall acceptance of the plan by Missouri's electorate. In 1942 the state went Republican, but two judges of the Supreme Court, both Democrats, were retained by a favorable vote of 2:1; six circuit court judges in St. Louis were similarly returned for new full terms in that same election. In 1944 Missouri went Democratic, yet two judges of the Supreme Court, one a Republican and one a Democrat, received the same proportion of the popular vote. In 1946 St. Louis went Republican but retained its ten circuit judges, all Democrats, seven of those rolling up 4:1 majorities. In 1948 the state went Democratic, yet of the two judges retained by Kansas City by an identical vote of 5:1, one was a Democrat and one a Republican. In St. Louis, in the same general election, five Democratic circuit judges and one Republican circuit judge were returned for full terms of office, the Republican and two Democrats receiving 4:1 votes and the other three Democrats 3:1 votes.

From 1940 through 1970, 179 judicial elections under the plan were held in Missouri: *only one* of these saw a judge rejected by the vote of the people, and he received 46.4 percent affirmative votes;[47] none has been defeated there since (as of mid-1992). (In marked contrast, six Missouri circuit court judges running on *partisan* ballots were defeated in November 1976.) The political parties have respected the plan and, by and large, have made no effort to influence elections under it. The Missouri Plan has also been strongly defended by the judges, who find themselves in a position to attend to their court dockets free from worries and pressures about forthcoming political campaigns. It is thus not at all astonishing that almost one-half of the states have now (1992) adopted the Missouri Plan or variations thereof,[48] including a number of states that had defeated the California Plan some years ear-

---

47. He was Marian Waltner, a circuit judge, prominently identified with the discredited Pendergast machine. See Richard A. Watson, a leading expert on the Missouri Plan, "Choosing the Judges," 53 *Judicature* 289 (February 1970). In 1976, only 3 of 353 judges on retention ballots throughout the nation were rejected.

48. See p. 35, *supra*, for a full list (as of mid-1992). Alaska adopted an interesting variation in 1975, under which the Nominating Commission—called the Judicial Council there—is now required to "conduct an evaluation" of each judge or justice before the retention election and to provide the public with "information about the candidate." In the first "adverse" example of the new system, the individual rated "unqualified" was reelected by the voters with an overwhelming majority!

lier. Given such continuing retention statistics as those of 1978, for example, in which only 13 of 486(!) judges on retention ballots were rejected—and 2 of the 13 under extenuating circumstances—it is not astonishing that now the question "Retention Elections: Who Wins When No One Loses?" should be asked more frequently.[49] Indeed, in the first fifty-seven years of all of the California–Missouri type of retention elections, only 36 judges were not retained.[50] Of these, 35 were ousted after 1960.

The two leading plans described represent what is probably a happy compromise between the appointive and elective systems of selection, and they have deservedly engendered considerable support among professionals and laypersons. Yet most students of the political scene are inclined to agree that in a representative democracy the appointive system is the more desirable one for the judiciary, provided it is backed up by long—preferably life—tenure and it possessses a genuine degree of independence.[51] Even when one constructs a pattern based on party allegiance, it becomes evident that *appointed* judges are *much* more willing to "vote" against "their" party on the bench than are elected judges.[52] The appointing authority is not beyond accountability, and there is no meaningful substitute for effectively lodged governmental responsibility in a free society.[53] As has been well said elsewhere, "on balance our judicial system still represents primarily a compromise between representativeness and neutral competence."[54]

---

49. See the article of that title by William Jenkins, Jr., 61 *Judicature* 2 (August 1977), pp. 79–86. The retention vote percentages averaged 72.1 for all appelate court judges and 74.7 for all trial court judges. Of the thirteen rejectees, one was an appellate judge and twelve were trial judges. For detailed up-to-date statistics, see Kenyon N. Griffin and Michael J. Horan, "Merit Retention Elections: What Influences the Voters?" 63 *Judicature* 78 (August 1979).
50. Susan B. Carbon, "Judicial Retention Elections: Are They Serving Their Intended Purpose?" 64 *Judicature* 5 (November 1980), plus subsequent updating.
51. There are notable exceptions: Stuart Nagel, for example, argued in an interesting article, "Political Party Affiliation and Judges' Decisions," 60 *American Political Science Review* 850 (December 1961), that "if judges should have value positions that are representative of the public at large, then is seems arguable that judges (at least on the higher court levels) should be elected, since presumably a judge elected at large will tend to have more representative values than a judge chosen in another manner." Philip L. Dubois, in his *From Ballot to Bench: Elections and the Quest for Accountability* (Austin: University of Texas Press, 1980), argues that, at least on the state appellate level, partisan elections are superior to nonpartisan methods as instruments for obtaining accountability.
52. Nagel, op. cit., pp. 848–49.
53. See Justice Byron R. White's 1987 ABA Convention speech, strongly critical of the election of judges: Forcing jurists to run for election poses "serious problems" of interfering with judicial independence, he warned (*The Washington Post*, August 11, 1987, p. A5).
54. Herbert Kaufman, *Politics and Policies in State and Local Governments* (Englewood Cliffs, NJ: Prentice-Hall, 1963). p. 60. An intriguing proposal was advanced by Harold W. Chase in his *Federal Judges: The Appointing Process* (Minneapolis: University of Minnesota Press, 1972), pp. 205ff., in which he called for appointment of all *lower federal* judges by the nine Justices of the Supreme Court of the United States alone. When polled informally, the Justices rejected the suggestion unanimously. Alternative suggestions abound, a good many among these propounding the creation of more or less autonomous judicial selection commissions, composed of lay as well as professional members.

TENURE OF OFFICE

Essential to the independence of the judiciary is the security of tenure, particularly in the case of appointed judges—our main concern here. Without a lengthy term of office, preferably life, adequate remuneration, and stringent constitutional and/ or statutory safeguards against removal, the concept of judicial independence becomes a mockery. The record of the three major Western democracies in this regard has been laudatory generally; their practices at the level of the national judicial hierarchies are relatively similar.

THE UNITED STATES

At the *federal* level in the United States of America, all judges of the *constitutional* courts—those appointed under the provisions of Article III of the Constitution (the judicial article)—hold their position during "good behavior," which in effect means for life or until they choose to retire. The other federal judges—those of the *legislative* courts, created under the provisions of Article I of the Constitution (the legislative article)—occupy their positions for whatever period Congress may have prescribed at the time of its establishment of the court or in subsequent legislation. In some instances this has meant "good behavior" tenure for them too, or, frequently, terms of office ranging between four and fifteen years. The constitutional judges have the additional safeguard, stated in Article III, that their " . . . compensation . . . shall not be diminished during their continuance in office." Hence, although their salaries may be increased during their incumbency, they may not be lowered, short of constitutional amendment of the section concerned. Were a judge of a constitutional court to be removed from office other than in the manner expressly permitted by the Constitution, his salary would indeed be rather drastically "diminished."[55]

Although arguably far from commensurate with the responsibilities and prestige of their office, and often lower than comparable positions in private enterprise, judicial salaries are adequate. In 1992 the annual salary range on the federal level, as will be discussed in more detail in chapters 4 and 5, was from $129,500 for judges of the U.S. District Court to $166,200 for the Chief Justice of the U.S. Supreme Court; his associates receive $7,200 less. But it is hardly for financial gain that a person would aspire to high judicial office. (Compared with those of federal judges, the salaries of state judges are suprisingly good, ranging from a 1992 *average of*

---

55. In 1976 a group of 140 federal district and appellate judges entered litigation, alleging that, as a result of inflation, their constitutional guarantee (Article III, Section 1) against reduction in salary during their tenure of office had been violated. The U.S. Court of Claims, in which the suit was begun, disagreed, 4:2, in *Atkins v. United States*, 556 F.2d 1028 (1977), and the Supreme Court denied review a few months later (429 U.S. 939). But in 1980, following renewed litigation, the latter now ruled 8:0 that two statutes of 1977 and 1980, which had revoked salary increases of 4.8 and 12.9 percent, respectively, in judges' compensation *after* those laws had taken effect, constituted a violation of the Compensation Clause of Article III of the Constitution. On the other hand, the Court held that the "Compensation Clause" did *not* apply to the merely *promised*, but not enacted, 1978 and 1979 increases, which Congress had canceled *before* they went into effect. (*United States v. Will*, 499 U.S. 200; Chief Justice Burger wrote the opinion for his Court.)

$87,693 for the highest appellate judges, $85,622 for intermediate, and $78,723 for trial court judges—New York paid as much as $115,000 to the justices in its highest court; Alaska $105,872 ($103,600 for trial judges); and California $121,207 ($99,297 for trial judges).[56]

Partly to enable aging jurists to step down from the bench with dignity, and concurrently to render their replacement with younger personnel more palatable, Congress enacted a vastly improved retirement statute in 1937. Under its provisions, federal judges may retire outright on full pay equal to their last year's salary at the age of seventy after having served ten years on the federal bench, or at sixty-five after having served fifteen years.[57] These requirements are waived in the presence of physical disability, in which case retirement pay is computed in accordance with length of service. A more financially advantageous arrangement, of which many retirees have availed themselves, is to opt for a "senior judge" status upon retirement. That status assumes availability for service, when called upon (although only about 20 to 25 percent actually do serve), but it also means an increase in their pension whenever the sitting members of the Court receive a raise. Widows and dependents receive an annual purse equivalent to 37.5 percent of the judge's average salary—if the jurists elected to participate in a contributory "judicial survivors annuity plan."

Despite the liberal provisions of the act, the average federal judge—in particular, the average Justice of the Supreme Court (if there is such)—is reluctant to leave active service. More vacancies occur as a result of death in harness, particularly at the higher levels, than in any other way. Of the one hundred Supreme Court vacancies between 1789 and 1991, death in office was responsible for forty-eight—although, since the passage of the 1937 statute, retirement was responsible for fifteen of twenty-five vacancies, resignation or disability for ten. In the entire twentieth century to date only seven Justices have stepped down from the high bench for reasons other than ill health or advanced age: Hughes (to run for President in 1916), Clarke (in 1922, to work for world peace), Byrnes (in 1943, to become F. D. R.'s "Assistant President for Domestic Affairs"), Goldberg (in 1965, to succeed Adlai E. Stevenson at the UN), Tom Clark (in 1967, because his son, Ramsey, had become U.S. Attorney General), Fortas (in 1969, as a result of disclosures of off-

---

56. Figures compiled by the National Center for State Courts, Williamsburg, Va., "Survey of Judicial Salaries," July 1991, as amended.

57. More than half of the Justices have served fifteen years or more on the highest bench. (Indeed, the members of the U.S. Supreme Court have enjoyed significantly greater longevity than men in the general population. See *Statistical Bulletin*, October 1977, p. 3.) An official example of an assignment order directed to a "retired" member of the Court is the following, issued by Chief Justice Warren to retired Associate Justice Stanley Reed. "Assignment Order: An order of the Chief Justice designating and assigning Mr. Justice Reed (retired) to perform judicial duties in the United States Court of Claims beginning November 1, 1965, and ending June 30, 1966, and for such further time as may be required to complete unfinished business, pursuant to 28 U.S.C. Section 294 (A), is ordered entered on the minutes of this court, pursuant to 28 U.S.C. Section 295." (Quoted as it was published in *The New York Times*, October 19, 1965.) A somewhat different order saw Chief Justice Warren assign Justice Tom C. Clark (retired) to service in the U.S. District Court for Northern California in June 1970. Late in 1965 *retired* Justice Charles E. Whittaker submitted his *resignation* in order to accept a legal position with the General Motors Corporation.

Court involvements with financier Louis Wolfson—the first Supreme Court Justice to resign after allegations of misconduct in office), and Potter Stewart (in 1981, simply because he wanted to return to private life). It is human to cling to power and influence, and it is particularly human to enjoy a role of such significance and nationwide esteem.[58]

Removal. The removal of federal judges who wish to remain on the bench can be effected only by the process of impeachment and conviction. However, not only has it evidently been legal for some time for the Judicial Council of a U.S. Circuit to discipline one of its federal judges by stripping him or her of duties and authority while permitting the retention of both title and salary,[59] in 1980 Congress enacted legislation, The Judicial Councils Reform and Judicial Conduct and Disability Act, creating authority in the judicial councils of the (now thirteen) judicial circuits to *discipline*, but not to remove, for misconduct all federal judges except those of the Supreme Court.[60] In accordance with constitutional requirements, impeachment for "Treason, Bribery, or other high Crimes and Misdemeanors"[61] may be voted by a simple majority of the members of the House of Representatives, there being a quorum on the floor. Trial is then held in the Senate, which may convict by a vote of two-thirds of the members of the Senate present and voting, if a quorum is present.

Considerable controversy exists as to the exact meaning intended by the framers of Article II, Section 4, when they spoke of "other high Crimes and Misdemeanors." Some—Gerald Ford, for one—have contended that an impeachable offense is whatever a majority of the House views as such (although he came to insist that he referred only to the appointed members of the judicial branch, not to the elected President). Others, among them the followers of James Madison and Alexander Hamilton, insist, with those Founding Fathers, that the concept of "misdemeanor" is broad enough to encompass "any offense against society" and/ or any offense "against the state" committed by a public official, be it criminal or

58. Thus, Chief Justice Taft: "As long as things continue as they are, and I am able to answer in their place, I must stay in the Court in order to prevent the Bolsheviki from gaining control. . . . " (as quoted in C. Herman Pritchett, *The Roosevelt Court* [New York: The Macmillan Co., 1948], p. 18). Justices Grier, Field, and McKenna, all three in various stages of senility after lengthy service, had to be coaxed off the bench by their colleagues, who were driven to resort to some ingenious devices. See also the California Commission on Judicial Performance's removal for "senility" of Supreme Court Justice Marshall F. McComb in 1977.

59. This was done by the Tenth Circuit's Judicial Council in the case of U.S. District Court Judge Stephen S. Chandler of Oklahoma in 1966. He appealed unsuccessfully to the Supreme Court for review (*Chandler v. Judicial Council of the Tenth Circuit*, 382 U.S. 1003 [1966]). A related matter concerns the power of an upper court (here a six-member tribunal of Court Judge Miles W. Lord of Minnesota) for "great bias" and "substantial disregard for the mandate of this court." (*The New York Times*, January 7, 1976, p. 1).

60. For a detailed description of the new statute's provisions, see 2 *Judicial Conduct Reporter* 3 (Fall 1980). For a comparison of the several circuits' rules and guidelines, see, ibid., No. 1 (Spring 1980). And for updated explications as well as analyses, of the Judicial Councils Reform and Judicial Conduct and Disability Act of 1980, see "The Federal Judicial Discipline Act: Is Decentralized Self-Regulation Working?" by Stephen B. Burbank, who provides an inconclusive response (67 *Judicature* 4 [October 1983]) and "How the Federal Judicial Discipline Act Works," a thorough description of the statute, in 71 *Judicature* 1 (June–July 1987), pp. 15ff.

61. Article II, Section 4.

not. Still others, President Nixon's defense team, for example, claimed that there can be no impeachment in the absence of a criminal act and that that act, moreover, would have to be an *indictable* offense, while, in the same breath, they insisted that no President can be indicted while in office. A close reading of the Constitution and the works of its framers and a careful study of the publications of such leading constitutional experts as Harvard legal scholar Raoul Berger, The Committee on Federal Legislation of the Bar Association of the City of New York, and other legal bodies lead to the considered conclusion that neither a criminal act nor an indictment is a necessary requirement for a vote of impeachment by the House—which should not, however, drive us to embracing the Ford statement as a guide to a proper course of action. The Committee on the Judiciary of the House of Representatives, which voted three articles of impeachment against President Nixon in July 1974, clearly did not.

To date (mid-1992) the House of Representatives has initiated a total of sixteen impeachment proceedings, of which thirteen were directed against federal judges (nine other judges resigned before formal charges were lodged against them[62]); one, in 1798, against U.S. Senator William Blount of Tennessee (charges against him were dismissed by the Senate by a 14:11 vote early in 1799 for want of jurisdiction, that body having already voted 25:1 to expel him six months earlier, on grounds of conspiracy to seize Spanish Florida and Louisiana with British and Indian help); one, in 1868, against President Andrew Johnson (who was acquitted by the margin of one courageous vote, 35:19, the House having charged him 126:47); and one, in 1876, against Secretary of War William Belknap (who was subsequently acquitted, 37:25, of taking kickbacks in office). President Nixon *resigned* on August 9, 1974, *before* the House of Representatives took a formal vote on the three counts of impeachment placed against him by its Committee on the Judiciary on July 27, 29, and 30 by votes, respectively, of 27:11 (for obstruction of justice), 28:10 (for unconstitutional abuse of power), and 21:17 (for failure to comply with a subpoena for tapes as evidence). However, after Nixon's public admission that he had withheld pertinent evidence, and his subsequent resignation, the Committee sent to the House a now *unanimous* report, charging that he had engaged in "deliberate, repeated, and continued deception of the American people" about the Watergate case. The House took no stand on its Committee's conclusions but officially voted to "accept" its report, 412:3.[63]

---

62. The last one was Seventh U.S. Court of Appeals Judge Otto Kerner, former Governor of Illinois, who resigned on July 24, 1974, having been only the second federal judge ever to be convicted of a felony (bribery). (The first was Second Court of Appeals Judge Martin Manton, also for bribery, in 1939.) Kerner had served seven months of a three-year sentence when he was found to have lung cancer. Paroled, he underwent surgery; he died on May 9, 1976. The first *sitting* federal judge to go to prison was U.S. District Court Judge Harry Claiborne of Nevada in 1986. He was sentenced to two years for a 1984 conviction for federal income tax violations. The U.S. Supreme Court denied his appeal (*Claiborne v. United States*, 54 LW 3697 [1986]). He was impeached and convicted that October.

63. The negative votes were cast by Representatives Earl Landgrebe (R.-Ind.), G. V. Montgomery (D.-Miss.), and Otto Passman (D.-La.). Landgrebe told a news conference that he would not vote for impeachment, even if Nixon were to defy the Court: "I believe in the man and I'm thankful for what he's done for America. I say praise Nixon and Praise America" (*The New York Times*, July 25, 1974, p. C23).

Of the thirteen impeachment proceedings involving federal judges, eleven went to trial, with four resulting in acquittals and seven in actual removals: one, U.S. District Court Judge Mark H. Delahay, who had been impeached by voice vote, resigned in 1873 before the articles of impeachment were prepared for Senate action; and another, George W. English, resigned in 1926 before the Senate could vote. The four that ended in acquittal, briefly sketched in the following paragraphs, are headed, both chronologically and in importance, by the only impeachment trial to date that had involved a Justice of the Supreme Court, that of Associate Justice Samuel Chase.

1. *Samuel Chase* was a staunch and partisan convert to the Federalist cause, and one of President Washington's last appointments to the Supreme Court. Justice Chase was impeached by the House in March 1804 by a vote of 72:32. He had made himself obnoxious to the Jeffersonians and others by a long series of injudicious and often outrageous partisan attacks against them, both on and off the bench; by his "tyrannical trials [of opponents] under the Alien and Sedition Law [of 1798]"; by his obvious favoritism toward Federalists; and by his cavalier approach to the concept of impartial juries. His judicial posture was certainly not a happy one, but he had probably not committed any impeachable offense per se. Even so, the Senate tried him amid great ceremony. Vice-President Aaron Burr presided, and Chief Justice Marshall was an important defense witness. Chase was justly acquitted in March 1805, the Senate's failing to attain the required two-thirds majority for a conviction on any of the eight charges: with twenty-three votes needed for removal, the largest total attained against Chase on any count was nineteen. The result was a signal victory not only for the narrow interpretation of the impeachment process but also for the principle of an independent judiciary. Chase, somewhat contrite, remained on the highest bench until his death in 1811.[64]

2. *James H. Peck*, a judge of the U.S. District Court for the District of Missouri, impeached 123:49 in April 1830 for "misconduct in office by misuse of contempt power," was acquitted in January 1831 by a vote of 22:21.

3. *Charles Swayne*, a judge of the U.S. District Court for the Northern District of Florida, was impeached by voice vote in December 1904 on twelve charges of "padding expense accounts, using railroad property in receivership for his personal benefit; and misusing contempt of power," he was acquitted in February 1905 on all counts by varying votes.

4. *Harold Louderback*, a judge of the U.S. District Court for the Northern District of California, impeached in February 1933 by a vote of 183:142 on five charges of "appointing incompetent receivers and allowing them excessive fees," was acquitted in May 1933 on all counts by diverse votes.

Of the seven impeachment trials that resulted in conviction, the first was probably unconstitutional as well as unjust, the second was questionable, all the others were justified:

---

64. For an authoritative commentary and interpretation, see Richard Tillich, "The Chase Impeachment," 4 *American Journal of Legal History* 49 (1960). See also Philip G. Henderson, "Marshall v. Jefferson: Politics and the Federal Judiciary in the Early Republic," 11 *Michigan Journal of Political Science* 2 (1983), pp. 54–55.

1. *John Pickering*, a judge of the U.S. District Court for the District of New Hampshire, who was known to be medically insane at the time, was impeached by the House in December 1803 on four counts of "irregular judicial proceedings, loose morals, and drunkenness" by a vote of 45:8. In March 1804 the Senate removed him from office by identical 19:7 votes on each of the articles. John Adams characterized the Pickering removal as "an infamous and certainly an illegal conviction." The unfortunate Pickering had been hopelessly insane and an alcoholic for three years, but he had committed no "high crimes and misdemeanors."

2. *West H. Humphreys*, a judge of the U.S. District Court for the Middle, Eastern, and Western Districts of Tennessee, was impeached by voice vote in May 1862 on seven counts of "support of secession and holding Confederate office." In a one-day trial, on June 26, the Senate convicted Humphreys on all charges but one, removing him from office by a 38:0 vote and disqualifying him from holding any further office by a 36:0 vote.

3. *Robert W. Archbald*, an associate judge of the U.S. Commerce Court, which was abolished in 1915, was impeached in July 1912 by a 223:1 vote on thirteen serious charges of misconduct in office. The Senate removed him in January 1913 by voice vote after he had been convicted on five of the articles of impeachment. He was then disqualified from holding any further office by a 39:35 vote.

4. *Halsted L. Ritter*, a judge of the U.S. District Court for the Southern District of Florida, was impeached by the House, 181:146, in March 1936 on seven counts of "bringing his court into scandal and disrepute," for actions including receipt of corrupt payments, practicing law while on the bench, and falsifying income tax returns. That April the Senate acquitted him on six of the counts but found him guilty on the seventh, 56:28. A motion to disqualify him from holding any further office lost by 76:0, however.[65]

5. *Harry E. Claiborne*, a judge of the U.S. District Court for Nevada—who had been convicted and imprisoned on two felony counts of tax evasion in 1984 and entered prison in May 1986—was impeached on four counts by unanimous vote of the House (413:0) and convicted of three and thus removed by the Senate in October 1986 by the overwhelming margins of 87:10 (failure to report income); 90:7 (concealing income); and 89:8 (betraying his trust and "bringing disrepute" on the federal courts). No vote was taken on disqualifying him from holding any further office. After having served seventeen months in prison and a halfway house Claiborne was discharged in November 1987. He was subsequently authorized by the Supreme Court of Nevada to resume the private practice of law.

6. *Alcee L. Hastings*, a judge of the U.S. District Court for the Southern District of Florida—and the state's first black judge—was impeached by the House on a 413:3 vote on August 3, 1988. He had been found impeachable on seventeen counts of conspiracy to receive a bribe in a 1981 criminal case; making false statements during his 1983 trial on conspiracy and obstruction of justice charges; and disclosing confidential information from an F.B.I. wiretap. The sole dissenting

---

65. When the U.S. Court of Claims refused to take jurisdiction in the Ritter case, Ritter appealed to the U.S. Supreme Court, which denied certiorari (*Ritter v. United States*, 300 U.S. 368, [1937]).

votes were cast by Representatives Gus Savage (D.-Ill.) and Mervyn M. Dymally and Edward R. Royball (both D.-Calif.). Hastings was convicted by the Senate 69:26 on October 10, 1989, for engaging in a "corrupt conspiracy" to extort a $150,000 bribe. In toto, the Senate convicted him of eight of the eleven articles of impeachment of the total of seventeen in which it voted, finding him guilty of the conspiracy as well as repeatedly lying under oath at his trial and forging letters in order to win acquittal.

7. *Walter L. Nixon, Jr.*, a judge of the U.S. District Court for the Southern District of Mississippi, was impeached by the House on May 10, 1989, by the unanimous vote of 417:0. He had been convicted on February 9, 1986, of two counts of perjury for lying to investigators and to a special federal grand jury in Hattiesburg, Mississippi, about his relationship with Hattiesburg businessman Wiley Fairchild, whose son was being prosecuted for drug smuggling. The impeachment resolution charged that Judge Nixon "consciously and repeatedly gave false and misleading information" about whether he had discussed the case with the local district attorney and had attempted to influence its outcome. Nixon was sentenced to jail for five years for perjury; the Senate convicted him on two counts and removed him from office on November 3, 1989, by 89:8 and 79:18 votes. Eighteen days later he was paroled from a New Orleans halfway house after having served twenty months of his sentence.

The arguably fortunate failure of most impeachment attempts is not an indication of any lack of verbal efforts by legislators who, partly sincerely and partly for constituent consumption, are eager to "get" federal judges—in particular, the Justices of the Supreme Court—usually for decisions that the congresspersons have found repugnant for a variety of reasons. To cite but one modern example: In June 1953 a special subcommittee of five members was created by the House of Representatives to consider the impeachment of Supreme Court Justice William O. Douglas. The resolution for impeachment, which was brought to the House by Congressman W. M. Wheeler (D-Ga.), charged the jurist with "high crimes and misdemeanors in office," Douglas having granted a brief stay of the scheduled execution of convicted spies Julius and Ethel Rosenberg—a stay that had been set aside by the full Court almost at once. Nothing came of Mr. Wheeler's efforts.[66] (In fact, the attempt would be all but forgotten today were it not for a statement made by Gerald Ford on the floor of the House: "An impeachable offense is whatever a majority of the House of Representatives considers it to be at a given moment in history." Mr. Ford, then a Representative from Michigan, came to regret that assertion two decades later.) Such efforts are not confined to the people's representatives. In February 1957 a group of some two dozen men and women filed with the Clerk of the House Representatives a petition demand-

---

66. In July 1966 Rep. George W. Andrews (D.-Ala.) introduced another unsuccessful impeachment resolution against Douglas, this one on the ground of his "character," in view of the then sixty-seven-year-old Justice's fourth marriage. (His new wife was twenty-three.) Andrews was joined by Reps. Paul Findley (R.-Ill.) and Thomas G. Abernathy (D.-Miss.). And in 1970 Douglas's congressional enemies—led by Gerald Ford, who by then had become Republican Floor Leader—tried again to impeach him, and again failed.

ing that the House impeach the entire membership of the Supreme Court. It con-
sisted of foot-long pages headed "Impeach Warren," a battle cry that was taken
up with a vengeance by the John Birch Society, which widely advertised "The
Warren Impeachment Packet" (obtainable for "One Dollar, Post-paid"). And the
Georgia State Assembly, in a colorful brochure decorated with the state flag, distributed "A Resolution Requesting Impeachment of Six Members of the United
States Supreme Court"—Justices Warren, Black, Reed, Frankfurter, Douglas, and
Clark (Burton, Harlan, and Brennan escaped their wrath, somehow). The main
charge: "Unconstitutional . . . pro-Communist racial integration policies."[67]

The majority of the states—in all but one of which judicial terms were fixed as
of 1984—used to follow the federal pattern regarding removal of their appointed
judges with lengthy tenure: impeachment and conviction was the normal process.[68]
Among the few states that had found it necessary to resort to it in the past were
Tennessee, in the case of Criminal Court Judge Raulston Schoolfield, for "corrupt
and injudicious conduct," in 1958, and Oklahoma, in that of its Supreme Court
Justice, Napoleon Bonaparte Johnson, in 1965. But since the early 1970s most
states have turned to other modes of removal, usually by resort to "commissions
on judicial qualifications," "commissions on judicial performance," or "commissions on judicial disability and tenure." These commissions, composed frequently
of both lawyers and nonlawyers,[69] serve as adjudicatory bodies; the ultimate
removal power normally is vested in the highest court of the state, generally its
Supreme Court.[70] In a few states, for example, Alabama, Delaware, Illinois, and
Kentucky, special courts or commissions are provided to serve both as the adjudicating and the removing body. Tennessee and West Virginia still cling to the
impeachment process. New York has used three methods: prior to 1948 its legislature held judicial removal power; from 1948 through 1977 a special removal

---

67. H. R. No. 174, "A Resolution," adopted on February 22, 1957, pp. 3–12.
68. In 1991 the U.S. Supreme Court ruled 7:2 that states have the power to force judges to retire when
they reach a certain age (Gregory v. Ashcroft, 59 LW 4714).
69. As of late 1991, there were forty-nine state plus several federal-level jurisdictions within the United
States (e.g., the District of Columbia and Puerto Rico) that had boards, commissions, or courts
charged in one fashion or another with the process of judicial discipline. In the spring of 1976 a total
of 362 persons served on these bodies; of them 93 were nonlawyers, 153 judges, and 116 lawyers
who were not judges (see Frank Greenberg, "The Task of Judging the Judges," 59 *Judicature* 10,
[March 1976], pp. 458ff). The District of Columbia established a seven-member "Commission of
Judicial Disability and Tenure" under its 1975 reorganization statute. Its first challenge was an
attempt to block the reappointment of District of Columbia Superior Court Judge Charles W. Hal-
leck, who had come under attack because of his conduct in forty specific cases during his controversial first decade on that bench.
70. Thus, in November 1970 the Louisiana Supreme Court, acting on the recommendation of the State
Judicial Commission, removed from office, by a 6:1 vote, Judge Edward A. Haggerty, Jr., who had
been arrested in a vice squad raid on a "stag party" in a local motel a year earlier (*in re Judge Edward
A. Haggerty, Jr.*, La. 241 So. 2d 469). The dissenting judge could see no connection between Mr.
Haggerty's personal and judicial conduct. In 1980 the Wisconsin Supreme Court suspended Circuit
Judge Christ T. Seraphim for three years for "major violations of the Code of Judicial Ethics,"
including "gross personal misconduct with six women . . . that constituted unprivileged and non-
consensual physical conduct with offensive sexual overtones."

court, the now abolished *Court on the Judiciary*,[71] possessed that authority; and, as a result of a constitutional amendment, 1978 saw the beginning of the utilization of the 1975-established eleven-member *Commission on Judicial Conduct*, which hears all complaints against judges, conducts the trial, and imposes sanctions, subject to de novo review by the Court of Appeals, New York's highest tribunal. In several western states, sitting judges may be recalled from office by popular vote— an intriguing and controversial manifestation of "direct democracy" of which the referendum and the initiative are illustrations along with the recall.[72]

BRITAIN

The British have come a long way since the days of James I (1603–25) and Charles I (1625–49), when the English judges held their office *durante bene placito nostro* ("according to our good pleasure"). Most, but not all, English judges today, very much like their cousins in the United States, enjoy what to all intents and purposes is tenure for life. But since the Courts Act of 1971, "the Lord Chancellor may remove a circuit judge from office on the ground of incapacity or misbehavior."[73] Recorders—lower judges—are removable for "failure to comply with any requirements" of their appointment. The custom of appointing judges for indefinite terms of office during their "good behavior" dates back to the Act of Settlement of 1701, which provided that judges' "commissions" be made *quam dim se bene gesserint* ("as long as they will have performed well"). One significant recent change must

71. That tribunal heard its first case in 1959, at which time it considered the removal of two Kings County jurists, Nathan R. Sobel and Samuel S. Liebowitz. It voted not to remove them, although it did "censure" them both for their public demeanor. In 1963, however, it did oust Supreme Court Justice Louis L. Friedman and Claim Court Judge Melvin H. Osterman in two separate actions: Friedman was removed on a vote of 4:2 for having engaged in "unethical judicial conduct" and having violated the "concept, spirit, and letter" of the canons of judicial ethics. He unsuccessfully appealed for U.S. Supreme Court review (*Friedman v. Court on the Judiciary*, 375 U.S. 10 [1963], *certiorari* denied). Osterman was removed on a 6:0 vote for his refusal to sign a waiver of immunity and answer questions before a New York grand jury investigating the 1963 New York State Liquor License Board scandals. His appeal to the U.S. Supreme Court also met with a terse "*certiorari* denied" response (*Osterman v. Court on the Judiciary*, 376 U.S. 914 [1964]). Two other jurists, Michael M. D'Auria and Mitchell D. Schweitzer, resigned in 1971 and 1972, respectively, rather than face action by the Court on the Judiciary. In 1973, the latter removed Supreme Court Justice Joseph P. Pfingst, who had been under suspension for having been convicted of concealing a monetary conflict of interest. Pfingst, too, appealed his ousting to the U.S. Supreme Court, which once again sided with the Court of the Judiciary (*Pfingst v. Court on the Judiciary*, 412 U.S. 941 [1973]). And in late 1975 the now-defunct New York tribunal "censured," but did not remove, Supreme Court Justice Wilfred A. Waltemade. Between 1978 and the spring of 1984 the Commission had removed seven full-time and thirty-five part-time judges (not counting four who were "saved" on appeal). In two instances the Court of Appeals ordered removal when the commission had failed to do so, recently in April 1984 in the case of Buffalo City Court Judge Barbara M. Sims.
72. Thus, in 1977 Wisconsin Dane County Judge Archie E. Simonson lost a recall election, initiated by voters' petition, caused by his public statement in the case of a fifteen-year-old youth who had raped a sixteen-year-old girl, suggesting that rape was a "normal reaction" in a permissive society. Setting the boy free on probation, Simonson explained his soft sentence as a "message " to women to "stop teasing." He lost the resultant recall election handily to a woman, Moira Krueger, a local feminist attorney, by a vote of 27,244 to 18,435.
73. Sec. 17 (4) and Sec. 21 (6), respectively.

be noted, however. As a result of the mandate of the Judicial Pensions Act of 1959 and the Courts Act of 1970 a seventy-two-year retirement limit for judges of the superior and circuit courts has been adopted for all appointments at that level, with a possible three-year extension. Recorders retire at seventy-two, but Higher Court judges may stay until seventy-five. Retirement pensions are paid on a graduated scale that rises from one-quarter of basic salary after five years of service to a maximum of half of the annual salary after fifteen years.

For practical purposes, the English judges, notably those of the superior courts, are irremovable, as the Judicature Act of 1925 provides that all judges except the Lord Chancellor hold office "during good behaviour subject to a power of removal by His [now Her] Majesty on an address presented to His [now Her] Majesty by both Houses of Parliament.[74] However, the judges of the county courts are deemed to be removable at the insistence of the Lord Chancellor for "inability" and "misbehaviour" under various statutes, such as the County Courts Act of 1959. The justices of the peace are also removable for similar reasons of "misconduct" or "proved incapacity." In fact, the English judges are not protected in any way from a change by statute; Parliament retains its fundamental power to alter their tenure and emoluments of office. Suffice it to say that it is highly unlikely to do so in a detrimental sense. In any event, a dismissal of a judge for political reasons is impossible today for all practical purposes. Indeed, since the Act of Settlement of 1701, *only one* judge has been removed on any grounds (although official complaints have been lodged against seventeen). That single removal took place in 1830, when Sir Jonah Barrington, a superior judge—a judge in admiralty—was deprived of his office by petition of both houses of Parliament as a result of an inquiry into the Irish courts of justice carried out during that year. It is fair to observe that, on balance, disciplinary procedures are not enforced with élan or strictness—which is not a phenomenon unique to the British judiciary.

The salaries of the judges (late 1991 and April 1992), £61,600 (for Circuit Judges), £50,500 (for Stipendiary Magistrates and District Judges), £84,250 (for High Court Judges), £106,750 (for the Lord Chancellor, which includes a salary payable to the L.C. as Speaker of the House of Lords), and £104,750 (for the Lord Chief Justice of England), are set by an Act of Parliament,[75] but are, in effect, determined by the Lord Chancellor with the consent of the Prime Minister and the Chancellor of the Exchequer after a thorough discussion in Cabinet. The executive branch may not move to reduce these while the recipients hold office, and the legislature is similarly enjoined since judicial salaries do not even come up for parliamentary review. A further indication of effective judicial independence is the parliamentary custom that no questions at all may be asked about the conduct of courts in particular cases. Moreover, according to two court rulings now firmly regarded as *res judicata* in England,[76] a judge may not be held for civil or criminal

---

74. Sec. 12 (1) of 15 & 16 G.O., ch. 49.
75. See Sec. 1 (2) of the Ministerial and Other Salaries Act of 1972, N. B. Whittaker's *Almanac* for 1983, the Supreme Court Act of 1981, and subsequent amendments thereto. Further increases took effect in April 1992.
76. *Anderson v. Gorrie* 91 L.J.K.B. 897 (1922) and *Heddon v. Evans*, 35 T.L.R. 642 (1919). See also *Sirros v. Moore*, Q.B. 118 (1975).

proceeding because of anything he may have said or done in his judicial capacity, even if it is alleged to have been malicious or in bad faith. Given these cherished safeguards of judicial strength and independence, the English bench has recipro-cated in full measure with a record of efficiency and impartiality not likely to be readily matched anywhere in the free world today. That is not to say, however, that criticism does not abound. Indeed, it has been mounting of late, especially on procedural grounds. Accordingly, a Royal Commission was established in 1991 to review procedures, particularly with regard to evidentiary review in the Court of Appeal.[77]

FRANCE

The career judges of the Fifth French Republic who, as we have seen, compose a branch of the national civil service, also have life tenure. There is no doubt that they are at least as secure today as are their English and American counterparts. But it took a considerable while to attain that cherished goal. During the *ancien régime* judicial office went customarily to the favorites of the monarch, and espe-cially to those who could afford to pay for it. *La révolution* replaced that interesting system of patronage *cum* purchase with popular election of judges, which was not much of an improvement, if any. Napoleon Bonaparte grandly eliminated that method and announced the principle of "irremovability," which, in practice, meant rather complete dependency on him. A period of minor changes and ame-liorations was effected by the institutions and individuals that succeeded the col-orful Corsican until the days of the Third Republic, just a bit more than a century ago, when the status of the French judges improved—without, however, reaching a truly separate status.

Irremovability as an avowed policy for the career judiciary was resuscitated by a proclamation of the Provisional Government a few days after V-E Day in 1945. It was made a part of the basic document of the de Gaulle Republic by the specific verbiage of the Constitution of 1958, which asserts that these judges are "irremov-able." Actually, that is technically incorrect, for they are removable, but solely for "misconduct in office," and then only on the recommendation of the High Council of the Judiciary, which acts as a disciplinary court for judges. When the council sits as such, the President of the *Cour de Cassation* is its presiding officer.

The judges of France are not quite as well paid as those across the Channel,[78] but there is no evidence that they are in any sense significantly more susceptible to corruption of injudiciousness than their English counterparts. Strengthened even more by the specific proviso of the de Gaulle Constitution making the Pres-ident of the Republic the "guarantor of the independence of the judicial author-ity," and by the genuine protective power of the High Council of the Judiciary, they enjoy an extensive degree of both professional freedom and authority, not-

77. See J. R. Spencer, op. cit., p. 33, n. 31, passim.
78. The average annual salaries of the French judges in 1984 ranged from approximately $24,000 for the lowest echelon to $40,000 for the highest, *not* counting certain allowances that might add up to 20 percent (data provided by M. Raymond Exertier of the French Ministry of Justice, November 21, 1984).

withstanding sporadic criticism of their labors—especially by lower-level judges, who were widely thought to be, and expected to be, subservient to government.

QUALIFICATIONS AND MOTIVATIONS: THE UNITED STATES

Although attitudes and practices regarding tenure of office do not differ significantly among the American, British, and French judiciaries, substantial, indeed, crucial, distinctions become immediately apparent in any consideration of the qualifications—background, experience, and training—of the judges in these countries. They represent distinctions that flow rather logically from different traditions and theories regarding the role of government in society, and they are attuned to what, for better or for worse, are deemed to be the needs and experiences of each land. With these thoughts in mind we turn to a consideration of the problem of judicial qualifications in the United States.

BASIC PREREQUISITES

In contrast to the specialized requirements that obtain in Britain and France, there is but one standardized prerequisite for qualification as a U.S. *federal* judge today—the LL.B. or J.D. degree of the aspirant or, as was still true of seven states in 1990,[79] the completion of several years (usually three or four) of reading law or a combination of the latter plus a reduced attendance requirement in law school. The possession of these requirements is neither a constitutional nor a statutory requirement for appointment, yet custom would automatically exclude from consideration anyone who did not have them. Moreover, the legal profession, which, as already noted, has a very real voice in today's appointive process, would remonstrate so determinedly that the political powers of the government involved would assuredly acquiesce. (Still, at the state and local levels not even a law degree is necessary in at least some instances.[80]) It is of at least historical interest that only 59 of the 106 Justices on the U.S. Supreme Court attended law school. Indeed, it was not until 1922 that a majority of the sitting Justices was composed of law school graduates, and not until 1957 that every Justice then sitting was a law school graduate!

Theoretically, any graduate of an accredited bona fide school of law with his or her eye on a federal judgeship may thus look forward to an appointment to the coveted niche—provided that he or she is politically "available" *and* acceptable to the executive, legislative, and private forces that, in the order enumerated, constitute the powers-that-be underlying the paths of selection, nomination, and appointment in the judicial process. In the final analysis, of course, it is the President and his immediate advisers concerned—here usually the Attorney General and his or her Deputy—who take the crucial step of submitting the nominee to the Senate. Thus, all of America's chief executives except William Henry Harrison, Zachary Taylor, Andrew Johnson, and Jimmy Carter have succeeded in seeing at least one nominee attain membership on the highest court of the land—our

---

79. California, Maine, New York, Vermont, Virginia, Washington, and Wyoming. Alaska merely required "completion of certified clerkship."
80. See ch. 4, *infra*, pp. 138–43 and nn. 6–8.

chief concern in these particular pages. Of the four exceptions, the first two were removed too quickly by death; Johnson was the victim of congressional machinations that successfully prevented him from filling several Supreme Court vacancies; and fate simply never presented Carter with an opportunity. Table 1 illustrates the number of Justices each President appointed and who *actually served*, including those not ultimately confirmed by the Senate. An example of the latter is John Rutledge, who was designated Chief Justice by President Washington in 1795, although the Senate, by a vote of 10:14, refused to confirm him. The Senate had approved Rutledge as Associate Justice in 1789; but he had resigned that post less than two years later without ever sitting—although he had served on circuit duty—in order to accept the post of Chief Justice of the Supreme Court of South Carolina (and hence is listed as only one Washington appointment). Counting Justice Rutledge thus only once, and Justices E. D. White, Hughes, Stone, and Rehnquist twice—since those four all actually served both as Associate Justice *and* as Chief Justice and were appointed by a *different* President in each instance—the 106 individual Justices who had served on the Court as of the end of the 1991–92 term provided thirty-six Presidents (counting Cleveland only once) with 110 successful appointments.

JUDICIAL EXPERIENCE AND ITS ABSENCE

In view of the minimal basic need of the LL.B, or J.D., it is hardly astonishing that many a newly appointed U.S. jurist lacks practical judicial experience.[81] Among the appellate courts, this has been especially true of U.S. Supreme Court designees; those of the court level immediately below, the U.S. (Circuit) Court of Appeals, have often had some lower court experience on the U.S. District Court—the federal trial court. Among the 106 individual Justices who served on the Supreme Court between 1789 and the end of 1991, only twenty-four (not counting prior on–Supreme Court service in the cases of the promoted-to-Chief Justice from Associate Justice E. D. White, Hughes, Stone, and Rehnquist) had had ten or more years of previous judicial experience on any lower level, federal or state, at the time of their appointment, and forty-two had no judicial experience whatsoever. Yet, as Table 2 demonstrates, the list of the totally inexperienced contains many of the greatest and most illustrious names in America's judicial history. Among them are five of the sixteen Chief Justices—Taney, S. P. Chase, Waite, Fuller, and Warren—and Associate Justices Story, Miller, Bradley, Brandeis, Douglas, Frankfurter, and Powell, to name a few. (John Marshall had a mere three years in the very minor local Richmond, Virginia, City Hustings Court, 1785–88.)

In a learned essay calling for selection of Supreme Court justices "wholly on the basis of functional fitness," Justice Frankfurter argued keenly that neither judicial experience nor political affiliation nor geographic considerations ought to play a significant role in the appointment of these highest jurists, whose job he viewed as

---

81. By way of contrast, in addition to other requirements, nominees to the intermediate appellate judiciary in Pakistan, for example, must have a minimum of ten years of judicial experience, and they need fifteen years (including five years at the intermediate appellate level) for appointment to the Pakistan Supreme Court.

Table 1. Number of Presidential Appointments of U.S. Supreme Court Justices Who Actually Served on the Court (Arranged Chronologically)

President	Dates in Office	Number of Appointments
Washington	1789–1797	10
J. Adams	1797–1801	3
Jefferson	1801–1809	3
Madison	1809–1817	2
Monroe	1817–1825	1
J. Q. Adams	1825–1829	1
Jackson	1829–1837	6 (5)[a]
Van Buren	1837–1841	2 (3)[a]
W. H. Harrison	1841	0
Tyler	1841–1845	1
Polk	1845–1849	2
Taylor	1849–1850	0
Fillmore	1850–1853	1
Pierce	1853–1857	1
Buchanan	1857–1861	1
Lincoln	1861–1865	5
A. Johnson	1865–1869	0
Grant	1869–1877	4
Hayes	1877–1881	2
Garfield	1881	1
Arthur	1881–1885	2
Cleveland	1885–1889; 1893–1897	4[b]
B. Harrison	1889–1893	4
McKinley	1897–1901	1
T. Roosevelt	1901–1909	3
Taft	1909–1913	6
Wilson	1913–1921	3
Harding	1921–1923	4
Coolidge	1923–1929	1
Hoover	1929–1933	3
F. D. Roosevelt	1933–1945	9
Truman	1945–1953	4
Eisenhower	1953–1961	5
Kennedy	1961–1963	2
L. B. Johnson	1963–1969	2
Nixon	1969–1974	4
Ford	1974–1977	1
Carter	1977–1981	0
Reagan	1981–1989	4
Bush	1989–	2
		110

[a] Jackson had nominated Catron, but the latter was not confirmed until Van Buren had taken over.
[b] Two in each of his two terms, which were split by Harrison's single term.

Table 2. Prior Judicial Experience of U.S. Supreme Court Justices and Their Subsequent Service

Justice	Year Appointed[a]	Number of Years of Prior Judicial Experience			Years of Service on Supreme Court[b]
		Federal	State	Total	
Jay[c]	1789	0	2	2	6
J. Rutledge[c,d]	1789 and 1795[c]	0	6	6	2
Cushing	1789	0	29	29	21
Wilson	1789	0	0	0	9
Blair	1789	0	11	11	7
Iredell	1790	0	½	½	9
T. Johnson	1791	0	1½	1½	2
Paterson	1793	0	0	0	13½
S. Chase	1796	0	8	8	15
Ellsworth[c]	1796	0	5	5	4
Washington	1798	0	0	0	31
Moore	1799	0	1	1	5
J. Marshall[c]	1801	0	3	3	34½
W. Johnson	1804	0	6	6	30
Livingston	1806	0	0	0	16
Todd	1807	0	6	6	19
Story	1811	0	0	0	34
Duval	1811	0	6	6	24
Thompson	1823	0	16	16	20
Trimble	1826	9	2	11	2
McLean	1829	0	6	6	32
Baldwin	1830	0	0	0	14
Wayne	1835	0	5	5	32
Taney[c]	1836	0	0	0	28
Barbour	1836	6	2	8	5
Catron	1837	0	10	10	28
McKinley	1837	0	0	0	15
Daniel	1841	4	0	0	19
Nelson	1845	0	22	22	27
Woodbury	1845	0	6	6	6
Grier	1846	0	13	13	23
Curtis	1851	0	0	0	6
Campbell	1853	0	0	0	8
Clifford	1858	0	0	0	23
Swayne	1862	0	0	0	19
Miller	1862	0	0	0	28
Davis	1862	0	14	14	15
Field	1863	0	6	6	34¾
S. P. Chase[c]	1864	0	0	0	8½
Strong	1870	0	11	11	10¾
Bradley	1870	0	0	0	22
Hunt	1872	0	8	8	10
Waite[c]	1874	0	0	0	14

Justice	Year Appointed[a]	Number of Years of Prior Judicial Experience			Years of Service on Supreme Court[b]
		Federal	State	Total	
Harlan I	1877	0	1	1	34
Woods	1880	12	0	12	6½
Matthews	1881	0	4	4	8
Gray	1881	0	18	18	21
Blatchford	1882	15	0	15	11
L. Q. C. Lamar	1888	0	0	0	5
Fuller[c]	1888	0	0	0	22
Brewer	1889	5	14	19	20
Brown	1890	16	0	16	16
Shiras	1892	0	0	0	11
H. E. Jackson	1893	7	0	7	2½
E. D. White[c]	1894 and 1910[c]	0	1½	1½	27
Peckham	1895	0	9	9	14
McKenna	1898	5	0	5	27
Holmes	1902	0	20	20	30
Day	1903	4	3	7	19
Moody	1906	0	0	0	4
Lurton	1909	16	10	26	4½
Hughes[c]	1910 and 1930[c]	0	0	0	17
Van Devanter	1910	7	1	8	27
J. R. Lamar	1910	0	2	2	5
Pitney	1912	0	11	11	10
McReynolds	1914	0	0	0	27
Brandeis	1916	0	0	0	23
Clarke	1916	2	0	2	6
Taft[c]	1921	8	5	13	9
Sutherland	1922	0	0	0	16
Butler	1922	0	0	0	17
Sanford	1923	14	0	14	7
Stone[c,e]	1923 and 1941[c]	0	0	0	21
Roberts	1930	0	0	0	15
Cardozo	1932	0	18	18	6
Black	1937	0	1½	1½	34
Reed	1937	0	0	0	19
Frankfurter	1939	0	0	0	23
Douglas	1939	0	0	0	36½
Murphy	1940	0	7	7	9
Byrnes	1941	0	0	0	1
R. H. Jackson	1941	0	0	0	13
W. B. Rutledge	1943	4	0	4	6½
Burton	1945	0	0	0	13
Vinson[c]	1946	5	0	5	7

Table 2. Continued

Justice	Year Appointed[a]	Number of Years of Prior Judicial Experience			Years of Service on Supreme Court[b]
		Federal	State	Total	
Clark	1949	0	0	0	18
Minton	1949	8	0	8	7
Warren[c]	1953	0	0	0	16
Harlan II	1955	1	0	1	16
Brennan	1956	0	7	7	34
Whittaker	1957	3	0	3	5
Stewart	1958	4	0	4	22¾
B. R. White	1962	0	0	0	
Goldberg	1962	0	0	0	2¾
Fortas	1965	0	0	0	3½
T. Marshall	1967	3¾	0	3¾	
Burger[c]	1969	13	0	13	18
Blackmun	1970	11	0	11	
Powell	1971	0	0	0	16½
Rehnquist[c]	1971 and 1986[c]	0	0	0	
Stevens	1975	5	0	5	
O'Connor	1981	0	6½	6½	
Scalia	1986	4	0	4	
Kennedy	1988	12½	0	12½	
Souter	1990	½	12	12⅛	
Thomas	1991	1½	0	1½	

[a] May be earlier than the date on which the successful nominee took the oath of office (e.g., Cushing, 1790, and Blair, 1790).
[b] Counted as of date of receipt of commission, following Senate confirmation.
[c] Indicates Chief Justice and date of appointment and/or promotion.
[d] Rutledge's nomination as Chief Justice was rejected by the Senate, but he did serve in the post as a recess appointee for four months.
[e] Had no judicial experience when appointed as Associate Justice.

necessarily requiring the qualities of *philosopher* ("but not too philosophical," commented his student Paul A. Freund), *historian, and prophet.*[82] Or, in the words of Justice Holmes, the judge should be a "combination of Justinian, Jesus Christ, and John Marshall."[83] Even though ill-equipped to do so (the task requires "poetic sensibilities" and the "gift of imagination"), the jurist must "pierce the curtain of the future . . . give shape and visage to mysteries still in the womb of time,"[84] must

82. To which, in a conversation with me in May 1964, Justice Brennan added "inordinate patience."
83. As quoted by Judge Irving R. Kaufman, "Charting a Judicial Pedigree," *The New York Times,* January 24, 1981, p. 23.
84. Charles Evans Hughes, who missed the presidency of the United States by a mere 3,000 California votes in 1916, described what he would have looked for as nominator of Supreme Court Justices, in the following order of priority: "strength of character, courage of convictions, sound learning, exact knowledge, painstaking study" (as quoted in *The New York Times,* February 22, 1970, p. 13).

"have antennae registering feeling and judgment beyond logical, let alone quantitative proof."[85] Thus, Felix Frankfurter asserted:

> One is entitled to say without qualification that the *correlation between prior judicial experience and fitness for the Supreme Court is zero.* The significance of the greatest among the Justices who had such experience, Holmes and Cardozo, derived not from that judicial experience but from the fact that they were Holmes and Cardozo. They were thinkers, and more particularly, legal philosophers.[86]

And on this point Justice Frankfurter was fond of quoting the distinguished Judge Learned Hand, who for so many years rendered outstanding service on the U.S. Court of Appeals for the Second Circuit (New York, Connecticut, and Vermont) but who never attained his richly merited promotion to the Supreme Court:

> I venture to believe that it is as important to a judge called upon to pass on a question of constitutional law, to have a bowing acquaintance with Acton and Maitland, with Thucydides, Gibbon and Carlyle, with Homer, Dante, Shakespeare and Milton, with Machiavelli, Montaigne, and Rabelais, with Plato, Bacon, Hume, and Kant as with books which have been specifically written on the subject. For in such matters everything turns upon the spirit in which he approaches the questions before him. The words he must construe are empty vessels into which he can pour nearly everything he will. Men do not gather figs or thistles, nor supply institutions from judges whose outlook is limited by parish or class. They must be aware that there are before them more than verbal problems; more than final solutions cast in generalizations of universal applicability. They must be aware of the changing social tensions in every society which make it an organism; which demand new schemata of adaptation; which will disrupt it, if rigidly confined.[87]

Attitudes toward Experience. Yet the experience factor for Supreme Court Justices,[88] although more or less dormant during some administrations, such as those of President Franklin D. Roosevelt, is sometimes revitalized by others, as it was by that of President Eisenhower. Roosevelt paid little, if any, heed to it, whereas Eisenhower, after his initial appointment of Chief Justice Warren, insisted that his nominees have at least *some* judicial experience, no matter how slight. Of the nine men who sat on the Court as a result of President Roosevelt's appointments (or promotion to Chief Justice in the case of Stone), neither Chief Justice Stone nor Associate Justices Reed, Frankfurter, Douglas, Byrnes, and Jackson had any judicial experience whatsoever, while Justice Rutledge served on the Court of Appeals for the District of Columbia for four years and Justice Black saw one-and-a-half and Justice Murphy seven years, respectively, on state tribunals.

85. Felix Frankfurter, *Of Law and Men* (New York: Harcourt, Brace, 1956), p. 39.
86. "The Supreme Court in the Mirror of Justices," 105 *University of Pennsylvania Law Review* 781 (1957) (italics supplied). "A copy of your lecture," wrote Sherman Minton, a recently retired colleague, to Frankfurter, "should be sent to each member of Congress. Your statement explodes entirely the myth of prior judicial experience. I am a living example that judicial experience [he had eight years on lower federal benches before coming to the Court] doesn't make one prescient" (letter, dated April 18, 1957, Frankfurter Papers, Library of Congress).
87. As quoted in *The New York Times Magazine*, November, 28, 1954, p. 14.
88. One of the reviewers of my *Justices and Presidents*, op. cit., found that the twelve Justices rated "great" had a total of 40½ years of judicial experience prior to attaining the Supreme Court (Holmes and Cardozo 28 of them!) while the fourteen rated as "failures" or "below average" had 64⅓ years!

President Truman followed his predecessor's habit of ignoring judicial background: of his four appointees, Associate Justices Burton and Clark had none at all; Chief Justice Vinson and Associate Justice Minton had five years and eight years, respectively, of prior service on the lower federal bench. President Eisenhower's four appointees subsequent to that of the Chief Justice—Associate Justices Harlan, Brennan, Whittaker, and Stewart—all had seen some prior service, although the total number of years for the four was but fifteen. Neither Associate Justices White and Goldberg, appointed by President Kennedy, nor Fortas, appointed by President Lyndon B. Johnson, had had any judicial experience, whereas Johnson's other appointee, Thurgood Marshall, had spent three and a half years on the federal bench below the Supreme Court. President Nixon's first two appointees, Chief Justice Burger and Associate Justice Blackmun, had served thirteen and eleven years, respectively, on lower federal benches, but Associate Justices Powell and Rehnquist had had no prior judicial experience at all when nominated. President Ford's sole appointee, Associate Justice John Paul Stevens, had seen five years of service on the U.S. Court of Appeals, and President Reagan's Associate Justice appointees, Sandra Day O'Connor, Antonin Scalia, and Anthony Kennedy, had served six and a half, four, and twelve and a half years on lower benches, respectively. President Bush's first selectee, David Souter, had seen twelve and a half years of service below, all but one-half on New Hampshire tribunals.

Congress, too, is hardly of one mind on the matter of the necessity or even the desirability of judicial experience as a prerequisite for appointment to the highest court in the land. Bills are continually introduced that would require future nominees to the Supreme Court to have upward of five years of experience on lower court benches. In the 89th Congress, and again in the 91st, for example, thirteen bills of this type were sponsored by members on both sides of the aisle in both houses of Congress. But all of these measures have failed of enactment. Moreover, many legislators agree with what is clearly a majority of the closest observers of the Supreme Court, as well as with the thesis of Justice Frankfurter, that judicial experience, because of the special nature of that Court's work, is not essential. The Supreme Court is not a trial court in the sense that the federal district courts below are, nor is it called on to deal with a particular judicial constituency as are these courts of first instance and, to a considerably lesser extent, the federal courts of appeals that lie immediately above the district courts in the judicial hierarchy. Further, there is very little transition or connection between the experience in the lower federal constitutional courts and that of the highest—the procedural and jurisdictional frameworks are quite different. The type of private litigation at common law, so prevalent below, is practically extinct at the bar of today's Supreme Court; the highest Court is almost exclusively occupied with questions of public law, led by cases at constitutional law or with constitutional overtones, review of administrative actions, and other related questions. Experience on the courts below may well be theoretically desirable, although there are some observers who would not even grant that much, but it should not become a *requirement* for qualification for the Supreme Court. Again returning to Justice Frankfurter and Judge Learned Hand, the business of the Supreme Court today is "with the application of rather fundamental aspirations," what Judge Hand called *moods*, that are embodied in constitutional provisions such as the due process of law clauses of the Fifth and Fourteenth Amendments and the latter's equal protection of the laws mandate—clauses and concepts that were quite evidently deliberately designed "not to be precise and positive directions for rules of action." In the words of Justice Frankfurter:

> The judicial process in applying them involves a *judgment on the process of government*. The Court sits in judgment, that is, on the views of the direct representatives of the people in meeting the needs of society, on the views of Presidents and Governors, and by their construction of the will of legislatures *the Court breathes life, feeble or strong, into the inert pages of the Constitution and the statute books*.[89]

Small wonder that this function calls for a combination of philosopher, historian, and prophet.

A Case Study. A brief survey of the judicial experience of the members of the 1985–86 Supreme Court may aid in demonstrating that even if that specific qualification is largely, or even wholly, absent in many instances, experience in other relevant areas of public service is often abundantly present. On that Court, which began its term on October 7, 1985, only five had past judicial experience, and in all but two or at most three of these cases it was rather negligible: as already noted, Chief Justice Burger had served thirteen years on the U.S. Court of Appeals for the District of Columbia, and Justice Blackmun eleven on the U.S. Court of Appeals for the Eighth Court. Justice Brennan had seen seven years of service on New Jersey state courts, Justice O'Connor six and a half on Arizona's. But Justices Stevens and Marshall had had a mere five and three and a half years on the U.S. Court of Appeals for the Seventh and Second Circuit, respectively, and Justices White, Powell, and Rehnquist came to the Court without any prior judicial service.

Yet *all* of the members of the 1985–86 Court had a record of considerable experience in *public life*, frequently of an administrative nature, in addition to or in place of whatever judicial experience they might have had. Thus, in 1969, on his designation as Chief Justice at the age of sixty-one, Warren Earl Burger had practiced law for twenty-three years; had been mildly politically active in his native Minnesota; and for three years had been Assistant Attorney General, leading the civil division of the U.S. Department of Justice. William J. Brennan, Jr., had practiced law for fifteen years, was a decorated army officer during World War II, and had served the State of New Jersey when Governor Driscoll appointed him, at the youthful age of forty-three, to the state bench in 1949. Byron R. White (known as

---

89. Frankfurter, "The Supreme Court in the Mirror of Justices," op. cit., 793 (italics supplied). In an address at the University of Virginia a few years earlier, "F. F." had spelled out what he considered "essential" to service on the Court, as follows: "[Justices must] bring to their task, first and foremost, humility and an understanding of the range of the problems and of their own inadequacy in dealing with them; disinterestedness, allegiance to nothing except the search, amid tangled words, amid limited insights, loyalty and allegiance to nothing except the effort to find their path through precedent, through policy, through history, through their own gifts of insight to the best judgment that poor fallible creatures can arrive at in that most difficult of all tasks, the adjudication between man and man, between man and state, through reason called law" (as quoted in *The Washington Post*, September 27, 1971, p. A20).

"Whizzer" White)—that rare phenomenon of both Rhodes Scholar and professional athlete—had practiced law for fourteen years and was U.S. Deputy Attorney General when his wartime friend President Kennedy sent him to the highest bench in 1962. White was then forty-five, one of the younger appointees in the Court's history (Douglas was a mere forty-one when F.D.R. sent him to the highest bench in 1941). President Johnson's second appointment, Thurgood Marshall—the first black to reach the highest Court—had practiced law for three decades, much of it constitutional law at the bar of the Court he was destined to join, had been a nationally known leader in the civil rights movement; had served on the Second Circuit Court of Appeals from 1962 to 1965, and was the U.S. Solicitor General when the President thus honored him in 1967, at the age of fifty-nine. Harry A. Blackmun, President Nixon's second appointee, had practiced law in a Minneapolis firm for sixteen years and had served as general counsel to the Mayo Clinic in Rochester, Minnesota, for nine when he was named to the U.S. Court of Appeals for the Eighth Circuit by President Eisenhower in 1959, at the age of fifty-one. Lewis F. Powell, the third Nixon appointment (made late in 1971), sixty-four years old, had a long and distinguished career as a legal practitioner and civic leader in Virginia, including the chairmanship of the Richmond Public School Board in the late 1950s, and had been President of the American Bar Association. Nixon's fourth appointee, William H. Rehnquist, a youngish forty-seven when he was sent to the Court concurrently with Powell, had clerked for Justice Robert H. Jackson, had practiced law and been active in Arizona politics for a good many years, and was serving as U.S. Assistant Attorney General in charge of the Office of Legal Counsel at the time of his appointment to the Court. John Paul Stevens, fifty-five, the sole Ford appointee, had clerked for Justice Wiley Rutledge and practiced pri-

Table 3. Occupations[a] of the 110 U.S. Supreme Court Designees at Time of Appointment[b]

Judge of inferior federal court	26
Federal officeholder in executive branch	22
Judge of state court	22
Private practice of law	18
U.S. senator	8
U.S. representative	4
Associate Justice of U.S. Supreme Court[c]	3
Professor of law	3
State governor	3
Justice of the Permanent Court of International Justice	1

[a]Many of the appointees had held a variety of federal or state offices, or even both, prior to their selection.

[b]In general, the appointments from state office are clustered at the beginning of the Court's existence; those from federal office are more recent.

[c]Justices E. D. White, Stone, and Rehnquist, who were *promoted* to the Chief Justiceship in 1910, 1930, and 1986, respectively.

vate law, specializing in antitrust matters, when he was appointed to the Circuit Court of Appeals for the Seventh Circuit in 1970, five years antecedent to coming to the Supreme Court. Sandra Day O'Connor, the first woman to reach the highest bench in the land, had seen service as a Deputy County Prosecutor in California, and as Assistant Attorney General of Arizona, had practiced private law, was active in Republican politics, served in the Arizona State Senate—where, as the first woman in the nation to hold such a post, she was elected as majority leader— and at fifty-one was in her seventh year on Arizona courts in 1981 when President Reagan's call came.

If, for the sake of argument, one were to grant the wisdom of judicial experience as a pertinent requirement for Supreme Court nominees, a background rich in non-judicial experience, such as those just described, does not compensate in and of itself for the lack of actual experience on a lower bench. However, it does indicate that those—until Sandra Day O'Connor there were no women on a federal court level *higher than* the Court of Appeals (the first at that was Judge Florence Allen of the Sixth Circuit[90])—who come to the Supreme Court of the United States, and for that matter to the lower federal courts, have had lengthy *legal* experience. Moreover *all* of the 106 individuals who have actually *sat* on the highest bench, except Justice George Shiras (1892–1903), had engaged in at least *some* public service at various levels of government, often elective, or had participated in political activity. Nevertheless, unlike the jurists of France, for example, who are schooled and trained as jurists, a great many of the judges of the major courts in the United States have no *judicial* background—as distinguished from a *legal* one. England relies on still another system, to be discussed presently. Table 3 indicates the occupations of the Justices (using the full figure of 110 here) at the time of their appointment to, or promotion on, the Supreme Court.

THE JUSTICES IN COMPOSITE

Whatever individual exceptions may be applicable, and keeping in mind the subjective attitude many an observer brings to bear on the qualifications and performance of the Justices of the Supreme Court of the United States, the caliber of that select group has been all but universally high. Indeed, no other unit of American

90. It was not until 1979 that every state bench had at least one female judge. Of the 738 active and senior federal judgeships extant as of June 1979, twenty (six circuit and fourteen district) were held by women. (The first female federal judge was the Coolidge-appointed Genevieve R. Cline to the U.S. Customs Court in New York in 1928.) Judge Allen was appointed to the Sixth Circuit by President Roosevelt in 1934 from her position as the first woman on the Ohio State Supreme Court. She became Chief Judge of the Circuit in 1958—another "woman's first"—and retired from the bench at the age of seventy-five in 1959. She died in 1966. Her earliest trail-blazing feat as a woman was her service on the Cleveland (Ohio) Court of Common Pleas from 1920 to 1922, from which she was elected to the seven-member Ohio Supreme Court. She had served for two six-year terms when F. D. R.'s call to the federal bench came. President Carter tripled the number of women on the federal bench. See the special issue of *Judicature*, "Women in the Judiciary," Vol. 65, No. 6 (December–January 1982). By late 1990 there were 165 women on the *federal* bench (approximately 12 percent of the latter).

METHODIST COLLEGE LIBRARY
Fayetteville, N.C.

government can readily match its general record of demonstrable competence and achievement. An overall analysis of the background and characteristics of the Justices to date (1991–92 term) would produce the following composite:

> Native-born (only six exceptions, most recent Justices Sutherland [England] and Frankfurter [Austria]), male (only one woman to date—late-1991), Caucasian (the first black was appointed in 1967),[91] generally Protestant (eight Catholic and five Jewish Justices), fifty to fifty-five years of age at the time of appointment, first-born (fifty-six, or 62 percent), of Anglo-Saxon ethnic stock (all except fifteen), of upper-middle to high social status, reared in a nonrural but not necessarily urban environment, civic-minded and politically active or at least politically aware, from an economically comfortable family, with a B.A. and LL.B or J.D. degrees (one-third from "Ivy League" institutions),[92] having held some type of public office.[93]

MOTIVES THAT UNDERLIE APPOINTMENTS[94]

The only person who knows with certainty why a particular individual is appointed to the Supreme Court is the President of the United States. However, historians and students of the judicial process can come close to the truth by interpreting the facts at their disposal: thus, a study of the records of the thirty-six Presidents who have fashioned members of the Supreme Court—an evaluation of their reasons for making the choices they did—points to several criteria that have been predominant in influencing presidential decisions. The following four have probably been the most important: (1) objective merit, (2) personal friendship, (3) balancing "representation or representativeness" on the Court, and (4) political and ideological compatibility.

When a President considers the objective merit of a candidate, he attempts to determine whether he or she possesses the ability and background requisite for a mastery of the vital and complicated issues that reach the Supreme Court. To achieve that end, the Chief Executive might look to the candidate's basic intellectual acumen; reputation for legal scholarship; competence in a particular area of the law; experience as a judge, lawyer, legislator, or executive; integrity and morals; judicial temperament; and work habits. Even age may be relevant. If the nominee

---

91. In mid-1992 there were 995 black state and federal judges among the nation's 13,000—a number that had initially accelerated dramatically with the enactment of the Omnibus Judgeship Bill of 1978, coupled with President Carter's previously described policies of pronounced affirmative action vis-à-vis appointments of females and minorities to federal judgeships.

92. Of the 1991–92 Court, all except Justices O'Connor and Thomas were members of Phi Beta Kappa. Although the percentage began to decline in the late 1970s, Ivy League degrees still predominated on the high bench.

93. For studies corroborating this "composite," see John R. Schmidhauser, "The Justices of the Supreme Court: A Collective Portrait," 3 *Midwest Journal of Political Science* 1 (1959); his *The Supreme Court: Its Politics, Personalities and Procedures* (New York: Holt, Rinehart and Winston, 1960), ch. 3, passim; and his *Judges and Justices: The Federal Appellate Judiciary* (Boston: Little, Brown, 1979), chs. 3 and 4, passim. See also my *Justices and Presidents*, op cit., especially chs. 3 and 4.

94. Much of the material in this section and in that on the role of the Senate is derived from chs. 1–4 of my *Justices and Presidents*, op. cit., nn. 28, 85, and 90.

is too young, he or she may be lacking in judgment, wisdom, and experience; if too old, retirement, illness, or death may intervene.

Personal friendship is difficult to measure, but assuredly it has influenced a considerable number of nominations. In Taft's choice of Horace H. Lurton, in Wilson's of Louis D. Brandeis, in Truman's of Harold H. Burton, and in Kennedy's of Byron R. White, to cite some obvious illustrations, personal friendship figured prominently. Other examples are Truman's appointments of Chief Justice Fred M. Vinson and Associate Justices Tom C. Clark and Sherman Minton. It was probably the crucial consideration in the case of Minton, although the Indianan was a good Democrat and had seen eight years of service, however colorless, on the federal appellate bench. The most obvious and most discussed case in recent years was Lyndon Johnson's choice of Abe Fortas. Long Fortas's intimate personal friend, L.B.J. time and again urged him to accept a vacancy. Perhaps intuitively, Fortas was demonstrably reluctant. But he ultimately bowed to the President's entreaties and, with considerable lack of enthusiasm, accepted appointment to the seat vacated by Justice Goldberg when the latter resigned to become U.S. Ambassador to the United Nations in 1965.

Balancing "representation" on bases of religion, geography, race, and sex has also played a major role in presidential choice of Supreme Court nominees. Yet of the four key general factors that influence presidential selections, that of "representativeness" is arguably the least defensible and the most emotion-charged. No matter how controversial it may be in theoretical terms, however, it is not only here to stay in its long-established religion and geography components but, considering present-day group consciousness, it will very likely be markedly exacerbated by insistent demands for "representation" on the basis of both sex and race—demands avowedly championed by President Carter, for one.[95]

The widespread notion that all sections of the land should be represented on the bench—to date the Justices have come from thirty-one of the fifty states—cannot be dismissed readily (see Table 4). It has considerable appeal as a matter of political equity. It was a primary consideration among almost all of the nineteenth-century Presidents; hence, Lincoln's successful search for "an outstanding trans-Mississippi lawyer" (Samuel F. Miller) and a Californian (Steven J. Field, a Democrat) and Cleveland's insistence on geographic appropriateness, best exemplified by his choice of a Chief Justice (Melvin Fuller). Among recent Presidents strongly influenced by the "geography factor" Richard Nixon stands out. Yet after the Haynsworth and Carswell rejections, he abandoned his much-publicized quest for a "Southern strict-constructionist" by choosing Judge Harry A. Blackmun, long time Minnesotan—an old and close friend of Chief Justice Burger, who was not only a Northerner but a resident of a state already "represented" twice on the Court.

95. In 1985, Britain's senior legal figure, Lord Hailsham, the Lord Chancellor, voiced disagreement. Ruling out any "affirmative action" program in making judicial appointments, he announced, "No considerations of party politics, sex, religion or race must enter into my calculations (for appointments) and they do not" (*The Los Angeles Times*, February 20, 1985, p. 1).

Table 4. The 31 States from Which the 110 U.S. Supreme Court Appointments Were Made[a]

New York	15	Iowa	2
Virginia	10	Louisiana	2
Ohio	9	Michigan	2
Massachusetts	8	Minnesota	2
Pennsylvania	6	New Hampshire	2
Tennessee	6	North Carolina	2
Kentucky	5	Arizona	2
California	4	Colorado	1
Illinois	4	Indiana	1
Maryland	4	Kansas	1
New Jersey	4	Maine	1
Alabama	3	Mississippi	1
Connecticut	3	Missouri	1
Georgia	3	Texas	1
South Carolina	3	Utah	1
		Wyoming	1

[a]The state where the appointee *then* resided, not necessarily the state of his birth.

On the other hand, a determined President will not permit geography to stand in the path of a desired appointment. Woodrow Wilson proved this with his insistence on the confirmation of Brandeis, notwithstanding the presence on the bench of Holmes, a fellow citizen of Massachusetts; so did Hoover when he finally appointed Cardozo in the face of the Court presence of fellow New Yorkers Stone and Hughes.

The religious factor is based on the notion that there should be a "Roman Catholic seat" and a "Jewish seat" on the Supreme Court. A development of questionable communal wisdom, the concept of religious-group representation has become one of the characteristics of contemporary American political and judicial life (see Table 5)—one clearly here to stay.

Eight men have occupied the "Catholic seat" to date: Chief Justice Roger B. Taney (Jackson, 1835), and Associate Justices Edward D. White (Cleveland, 1894—he was promoted to Chief Justice by Taft, 1910), Joseph McKenna (McKinley, 1898), Pierce Butler (Harding, 1922), Frank Murphy (Roosevelt, 1940), Wil-

Table 5. Acknowledged Religion of the 106 Individual Justices of the U.S. Supreme Court at Time of Appointment

Episcopalian	29	Jewish	5
Unspecified Protestant	25	Methodist	4
Presbyterian	17	Congregationalist	3
Roman Catholic	8	Disciples of Christ	2
Unitarian	6	Lutheran	1
Baptist	5	Quaker	1

liam J. Brennan (Eisenhower, 1956), Antonin Scalia (Reagan, 1986), and Anthony M. Kennedy (1987). With the exception of the seven years between Justice Frank Murphy's death in 1949 (when President Truman deliberately ignored the unwritten rule of the "reserved" seat—"if he has the qualification, I do not care if he is a Protestant, Catholic or Jew" [*The New York Times*, July 29, 1949, p. 1]—and nominated Protestant Tom C. Clark to the vacancy created by Murphy's death), and Justice Anthony M. Kennedy's nomination in 1988, a Roman Catholic has been on the Supreme Court continuously since the 1894 E. D. White appointment.

The "Jewish seat" was established in 1916 with the appointment of Louis D. Brandeis. (Actually, President Fillmore had offered an appointment to Judah P. Benjamin of Louisiana in 1853, but the latter preferred to be in the U.S. Senate and declined. Brandeis was next, sixty-three years later.) That tradition, too, was broken when, in 1969, President Nixon successively nominated three Protestants (Haynsworth, Carswell, and Blackmun) to succeed Fortas. In 1971 Nixon had two opportunities to "atone" for this, but he again nominated two more Protestants, Lewis F. Powell, Jr., and William H. Rehnquist. Questioned on the continued "oversight" at one of his infrequent news conferences, Nixon gave the logical response: that merit, rather than religion, should and must govern—a laudable aim, provided it is in fact invoked. The five occupants of the "Jewish seat" to date have been Louis D. Brandeis (Wilson, 1916), Benjamin N. Cardozo (Hoover, 1932), Felix Frankfurter (Franklin D. Roosevelt, 1939), Arthur J. Goldberg (Kennedy, 1962), and Abe Fortas (Johnson, 1965).

On June 14, 1967, Lyndon Johnson designated Thurgood Marshall, the first black ever to be nominated to the Supreme Court. The President, leaving no doubt that the nominee's race was probably the major factor in his decision, told the country in a major news conference on that historic day, "I believe it is the right thing to do, the right time to do it, the right man and the right place." It is fair to conjecture that there now exists a "black seat" on the bench that is more secure than the Catholic and the Jewish seats.[96] It is also all but certain that a permanent "woman's seat" will be established. The presidential campaign of 1972 had featured public assurances by both candidates that a woman would be appointed: George McGovern promising that "the next vacancy" would go to a woman, and Richard Nixon, already on record with his abortive trial balloon Mildred Lillie nomination, speaking often of his desire to nominate "a qualified woman." Successful 1976 candidate Jimmy Carter repeatedly promised to send a woman to the Court at the first opportunity. He never had one, but Ronald Reagan

96. Felix Frankfurter, himself a Jew, had little patience with these "requirements": "*Tempore* Taft, his Secretary of War, one Stimson, told me that the President was desirous of putting a Jew on the federal bench in New York and has asked that I make a suggestion to that end. I told Stimson that racial and religious considerations seemed to me not only irrelevant in appointments to the bench but mischievously irrelevant. And that to appoint men for racial or religious reasons was playing with fire. Therefore, I would have no truck with it and I begged to be excused for what I regarded a highly indefensible and dangerous procedure" (letter to Frank Buxton, Editor-in-Chief of the *Boston Herald*, Box 39, Manuscripts, National Archives). See also Bruce A. Murphy, "A Supreme Court Justice as Politician: Felix Frankfurter and Federal Court Appointments," 21 *The American Journal of Legal History* 316–34 (1977), at 328.

did and appointed a woman as soon as the initial opportunity presented itself in mid-1981.

Political and ideological compatibility often go hand in hand in influencing presidential choices for the Supreme Court. Among the points a President is almost certain to consider are whether or not (1) his choice will render him more popular among influential interest groups, (2) the nominee has been a loyal member of the President's party, (3) the nominee favors presidential programs and policies, (4) the nominee is acceptable, or at least not "personally obnoxious," to his home-state senators, (5) the nominee's judicial record, if any, meets the incumbent president's criteria of constitutional construction, (6) the President is indebted to the nominee for past political services, and (7) he feels "good" or "comfortable" about his choice.

It is an unwritten law of the judicial nominating process that the President will not normally select an individual from the ranks of the political opposition. To lessen charges of "court-packing," however, this rule is purposely relaxed now and then, but only within "political reason"—which seems to have meant roughly to the tune of 10 percent of all appointments to district and appellate tribunals and 15 percent to the Supreme Court. In at least thirteen instances of the latter, including two promotions to the post of Chief Justice, the appointee came from a political party other than that of the President. Thus, Whig President John Tyler appointed a Democrat, Samuel Nelson, and Republican Presidents Abraham Lincoln, Benjamin Harrison, William H. Taft, Warren G. Harding, Herbert Hoover, Dwight D. Eisenhower, and Richard M. Nixon appointed nine Democrats. Taft alone appointed three! The nine Justices and their nominators were Stephen J. Field (Lincoln), Howell E. Jackson (Benjamin Harrison); Horace H. Lurton, Edward D. White (to Chief Justice), and Joseph R. Lamar (Taft); Pierce Butler (Harding); Benjamin N. Cardozo (Hoover); William J. Brennan (Eisenhower); and Lewis F. Powell, Jr. (Nixon). And Democratic Presidents Woodrow Wilson, Franklin D. Roosevelt, and Harry S. Truman appointed three Republicans: Louis D. Brandeis (Wilson), Harlan F. Stone to Chief Justice (F. D. R.), and Harold D. Burton (Truman). Some would add, as a fourteenth case, F. D. R.'s selection of Felix Frankfurter, who labeled himself an Independent. What accounted for these thirteen or fourteen appointments from the ranks of "the other" party?

Crossing Party Lines. The naming of *Nelson* by President Tyler came after Tyler had been defeated by Democrat James K. Polk in the election of 1844. Eager to have history show at least one of his own nominees attain the Supreme Court, the "lame duck" Tyler—after three of his four first Whig choices had to be withdrawn because of obviously decisive opposition, and the fourth one, John Spencer of New York, was rejected by the Senate 26:1—then designated Nelson, who had not been an active political figure.

In 1863 *Field,* who was to serve on the Court longer (34¾ years) than anyone to date but Douglas (36½ years), was chosen by Lincoln largely for three reasons. First, Field came from California, a part of the country not then represented on the Court—in fact, Congress created a tenth seat for that purpose—and even though he had been a Buchanan Democrat as late as 1861, Lincoln felt his nominee would help to "fuse" the Northern cause by preserving the loyalty of California and strengthening its political ties. Second, Field's many influential friends, including California's Governor Leland Stanford, put considerable pressure on the President. Third, Field's brother, David Dudley Field, a bitter and vocal opponent of slavery, had played a considerable role both in the organization of the Republican party and in Lincoln's nomination as its standard-bearer in 1860.

Harrison's choice of *Jackson* was motivated by reasons similar to those that governed the Tyler-Nelson case. Cleveland had already defeated Harrison when the vacancy on the Court occurred, the Democratic Senate was in no mood to confirm the Republican lame duck President's partisan choice, and happily, Harrison and Jackson, who had served in the Senate together, were close friends, as were their wives.

The Taft appointments of *Lurton* and *Lamar* and his promotion of *White*, all three Southern Democrats appointed by a good Republican, are attributable to a combination of personal friendship or esteem, ideological kinship, and politicosectional expediency. Taft and Lurton had served together for eight years on the U.S. Circuit Court of Appeals for the Sixth Circuit, where they had become fast friends. Taft, who had been its Chief Judge, was very much impressed with the legal and judicial ability of the Tennessee Democrat who had succeeded him as Chief Judge when the future President went to the Philippine Islands. Conservative kinsmen, they were usually at one in their opinions from the bench and in their general philosophy of government. Taft called the nomination of his friend Lurton "the chief pleasure of my administration."[97] Although Joseph R. Lamar of Georgia was not as close to Taft personally as Lurton, he readily met Taft's standards of conservatism and his general ideological bent. For example, the two men saw eye to eye on the tariff—a matter of the utmost importance to the President. And Taft perceived in the appointment of the Confederate Army veteran an additional opportunity for strengthening his position among Southern political leaders who, if they would not vote for him at election time, would at least help him with his legislative program. He promoted White—then in his seventeenth year on the Court—in part because he considered him the ablest administrator among the Justices on the bench; in part because his fellow Justices apparently had petitioned the President to designate him rather than Hughes,[98] who had seemed to have the proverbial inside track ("White, Not Hughes, for Chief Justice," was the December 12, 1910, front-page headline in *The New York Times* when the announcement was made); in large part because in Taft's eyes he had voted "right" on the bench—among his votes there was one to uphold a military tariff in the Philippine Islands at the time Taft was governor there[99]—and, because of Taft's never-ceasing hopes of some day attaining that so ardently desired Center Chair, the sixty-five-year-old White was distinctly a more promising occupant than the forty-eight-year-old Hughes. Taft's shrewd gamble paid off in 1921.

Wilson's hotly contested nomination of *Brandeis*, a registered Massachusetts

97. Silas Bent, *Justice Oliver Wendell Holmes* (New York: Garden City Publishing, 1932), p. 248.
98. George Shiras III, *Justice George Shiras* (Pittsburgh: University of Pittsburgh Press, 1953), p. 130.
99. Cf. William Howard Taft, *Our Chief Magistrate and His Power* (New York: Columbia University Press, 1916), pp. 99–102.

Republican, was confirmed by the Senate by a vote margin of forty-seven to twenty-two after a delay of more than four months. Of the forty-seven affirmative votes, forty-four were cast from the forty-five Democratic senators present and voting; the three Republican votes in favor came from Senator Robert M. La Follette (Wisc.), George W. Norris (Neb.), and Miles Poindexter (Wash.). Twenty-one of the twenty-two negative votes came from the Republican senators present and voting.[100] The lone Democratic negative vote was cast by Senator Francis G. Newlands of Nevada. Twenty-seven senators, including the influential Borah, did not vote at all.[101] Brandeis, the famed "People's Lawyer," as Wilson was fond of calling him, was a personal friend of the President and a close ideological ally—a political and social liberal who shared Wilson's philosophy of life and government and who had worked hard for him in the 1912 campaign. It was primarily these two factors and his great regard for Brandeis's character and ability that prompted Wilson to ignore the sectional factor (Massachusetts was then already "represented" by Holmes); possible repercussions because of the nominee's religion (he was the first Jewish person to reach the Supreme Court); and the danger during the 1916 election year of designating a controversial personage such as Brandeis in the face of the violent opposition of the most influential segment of the bar and the business community, particularly in his New England home base. Ironically, despite his convictions regarding the "curse of bigness," Justice Brandeis never wrote an opinion in favor of the government in an antitrust case!

Harding's choice of *Butler*—vigorously promoted by the now Chief Justice Taft—had three motives. First, the President liked his record of almost four decades of service in the law and in public life; second, and probably most important, Harding found Butler's ideological ultraconservatism to be entirely sympathetic (he became one of the two leading avowed reactionaries on the bench); and third, the President deemed it politically advantageous to appoint a man who combined what would seem to be the desirable factor of being a "safe" Democrat—most Democrats refused to regard Butler as one of their number in roughly the same fashion as the Republicans did Brandeis—with that of being a member of an "unrepresented" minority religion (Roman Catholic) and a native Minnesotan, only the second nominee born west of the Mississippi to reach the bench. Initially rejected by the Senate, Butler was renominated by Harding on the following day and ultimately won confirmation easily, though he was veritably scorched by large segments of the public press.

The *Cardozo* appointment was almost literally forced on President Hoover by the country, despite the fact—conceivably detrimental or even fatal in the case of other nominees, depending on circumstances—that the nominee came from New York, already "represented" on the bench at that time by Chief Justice Hughes

100. Among these were illustrious and powerful men such as Henry A. du Pont, Henry Cabot Lodge, George Sutherland (a future colleague of the nominee), Warren G. Harding, and Albert B. Fall. The remaining twenty-seven Senators did not vote; but twelve—all Republicans—were paired *against*, and twelve—ten Democrats and two Republicans (Moses E. Clapp of Minnesota and Asle J. Grenna of North Dakota)—*for*; three senators were absent and were not recorded at all.

101. For a fascinating account of the Brandeis nomination and confirmation battle, see A. L. Todd's *Justice on Trial: The Case of Louis D. Brandeis* (New York: McGraw-Hill Book, 1964).

and Justice Stone, and that he was Jewish, a religion already "represented" by Justice Brandeis. Hoover raised these points during a command visit by Republican Senator Borah of Idaho, chairman of the Committee on Foreign Relations, who had been very vocal in urging the Cardozo appointment, along with many others, including Justice Stone. (Stone, who was to play a major role in persuading the President to designate the man whom he had introduced to him initially, even offered to resign his own seat on the Court if that was what it would take to see his fellow New Yorker nominated.) Hoover handed Senator Borah a list of the names of several prominent individuals he was considering for the vacancy on the Court left by Justice Holmes's resignation. The last name on the list was that of the Chief Judge of the New York State Court of Appeals, Benjamin N. Cardozo. "Your list is all right," commented Senator Borah, "but you handed it to me upside down![102] When the President then strongly urged that his visitor consider the geographical situation involved and mentioned "possible religious and sectarian repercussions," Senator Borah told him in no uncertain terms that "Cardozo belongs as much to Idaho as to New York" and that geography should no more bar him than the presence of two Virginians on the high bench—John Blair and Bushrod Washington—should have prevented President John Adams from naming John Marshall Chief Justice.[103] Furthermore, Borah told Hoover, " . . . anyone who raises the question of race [*sic*] is unfit to advise you concerning so important a matter."[104] When the President bowed to what was all but unanimous professional as well as popular clamor for the Cardozo appointment—which the Senate would confirm "in ten seconds"[105]—he became the recipient of much praise, typical of which was Senator Clarence Dill of Washington's remark that " . . . when President Hoover appointed Judge Cardozo . . . he performed the finest act of his career as President."[106]

President Franklin D. Roosevelt promoted *Stone*—who had been one of his professors at Columbia University Law School—largely as a manifestation of unity in the face of the incipient war crisis. When Chief Justice Hughes announced his intention to retire, speculation as to his successor revolved around Stone and then Attorney General Robert H. Jackson. Roosevelt's heart was on the side of Jackson, who desperately craved the Chief Justiceship, but he deemed it wiser and more politically astute and appropriate at this turbulent juncture of history to name Stone. In fact, he discussed the matter with Jackson, who agreed heavyheartedly and later, having become an Associate Justice of the Court, wrote that the need for judicial leadership and the "desirability for a symbol of stability as well as of progress" were evidently the reasons for Stone's elevation "in the interest of the [fostering of the] judiciary as an institution."[107] Moreover, the retiring Chief Justice himself had strongly urged Stone's elevation on the basis of his record and had

---

102. Claudius O. Johnson, *Borah of Idaho* (New York: Longman's Green, 1936), p. 452.
103. *The New York Times*, January 30, 1932.
104. Johnson, loc. cit., p. 453.
105. *The New York Times*, July 10, 1938, p. 30.
106. *The New York Times*, March 2, 1932, p. 13.
107. Mason, *Harlan Fiske Stone*, op. cit., p. 573.

suggested that Roosevelt consult Justice Frankfurter, Jackson's close friend, in the matter. "F.F." told the President:

> when war does come, the country should feel you are a national, the Nation's President, and not a partisan President . . . [to bolster this assessment] you [should] name a Republican, who has the profession's confidence, as Chief Justice.[108]

President Truman's nomination of *Burton*—the first of his four—is far too readily dismissed merely as a reward to an old Senate crony. The Republican senator from Ohio and mayor of Cleveland had served well and closely with the then Senator Truman on the latter's Special Committee to Investigate the National Defense Program (the "Truman Committee"). Unquestionably, Truman's personal affection for Burton was a factor in the appointment. But there were assuredly others: the advice given to the President that he designate a Republican to replace the retiring Justice Roberts, a Republican; Chief Justice Stone's advance approval of the nominee because of his valuable legislative experience; Truman's belief in Burton's judicial temperament; the absence of anyone from Ohio on the bench; the assumption that the nominee's Senate seat would be filled by a Democrat, as indeed it subsequently was, by incumbent Governor Frank Lausche (though he was a rather unpredictable Democrat); plus the faithful support Burton had given to the Democratic party on foreign policy, and even on some domestic policy, throughout his tenure in the Senate.

President Eisenhower chose New Jersey Democrat *Brennan* for a variety of reasons. The President's initial choice had been that state's able Chief Justice, Arthur T. Vanderbilt, who had achieved an outstanding national reputation as head of the then recently reorganized New Jersey court system. Because of his advanced age and failing health (he died in 1957), Vanderbilt declined the appointment but he highly recommended the nomination of his colleague and protégé, Associate Justice Brennan of the State Supreme Court. This recommendation was strengthened by the support of Secretary of Labor James Mitchell, a New Jersey Republican; the two Republican senators from New Jersey, Clifford P. Case and Alexander H. Smith; and Democratic Governor Robert B. Meyner. Moreover, it was the very eve of the 1956 election, and the choice of a Roman Catholic from the metropolitan East would hardly hurt the President in the impending campaign. With only Republican Senator Joseph R. McCarthy of Wisconsin voting "no," the Brennan nomination was confirmed by the Senate in March 1957.

The most recent selection of a Supreme Court nominee from the opposition party is President Nixon's late 1971 choice of nominal Democrat Lewis F. Powell, Jr. Yet that distinguished Virginia ideological conservative seemed ideally fitted for the President's expressed qualifying criteria of "a philosophy for the Constitution similar to my own"—which he was fond of styling, not overly helpfully, as "strict construction." Powell did not meet the Nixon guidelines of "right age" (at sixty-four he was some ten years older than the preferred age) nor of "broad experience as an appeals judge" (he had no judicial experience whatsoever). But Powell came from a milieu sympathetic to the President both politically and personally:

---

108. Ibid., p. 567.

Table 6. Avowed Political Affiliation of the 110 U.S. Supreme Court Justices at Time of Selection

Federalists	13	Republicans	46
Whig	1	Independent	1
Democrats	49		

he was a recognized, visible leader of the Virginia Bar; he had seen important local and state civic service; he was a recent past president of the American Bar Association; and his writings in the "law-and-order" sector could not have been more pleasing to Mr. Nixon. Hence his professed formal party allegiance on the Democratic side was of small moment. Justice Powell's subsequent service on the Court proved the President's judgment of his third appointee's jurisprudential philosophy to be generally sound—but not without at least some "disappointments," such as the Justice's authorship of a unanimous opinion by the high bench (Justice Rehnquist not participating) clearly and unequivocally denying the existence of any "inherent" independent presidential power to wiretap in instances of suspected subversive *domestic* elements.[109]

There will always be some crossing of party lines, particularly at the lower court levels, in order to maintain at least the appearance of nonpartisanship in the judicial process and to placate the opposition, but the practice may be safely viewed as the exception rather than the rule (as Table 6 and the following statistics indicate). Many a President has been told by his political advisers to stay on his side of the fence, where surely there are just as many qualified and deserving lawyers as on the other side. "Think Republican," Republican National Chairman Rogers C. B. Morton frankly urged President Nixon when the latter was presented with his initial opportunity to fill two seats on the Supreme Court in the spring of 1969.[110] As Table 7 amply demonstrates, Morton's sentiments are not confined to *his* political party! After a consistent 1976 campaign promise of substituting "merit" for "politics" in nominating federal judges, President Carter had amassed a higher partisan percentage by late 1980 than any other President except Woodrow Wilson. If the percentage of "other party" Supreme Court appointees has been larger than that of the lower federal courts, it is because the President recognizes that what matters more than anything else is the ideological compatibility of the candidate—what Teddy Roosevelt referred to as the nominee's "real" politics.

"PACKING THE COURT" AND THE NOMINEES' "REAL" POLITICS

Whatever the merits of the other criteria attending presidential motivations in appointments may be, what must be of overriding concern to any nominator is his

109. *United States v. United States District Court for the Eastern District of Michigan,* 407 U.S. 297 (1972).
110. *The New York Times,* May 17, 1969, p. 1. "That's the name of the game," Morton continued, "[t]his is our opportunity and we ought to take it."

Table 7. Percentages of Federal Judicial Appointments Adhering to the Same Political Party as the President, 1884–1985

President	Party	Percentage
Cleveland	Democratic	97.3
B. Harrison	Republican	87.9
McKinley	Republican	95.7
T. Roosevelt	Republican	95.8
Taft	Republican	82.2
Wilson	Democratic	98.6
Harding	Republican	97.7
Coolidge	Republican	94.1
Hoover	Republican	85.7
F. D. Roosevelt	Democratic	96.4
Truman	Democratic	93.1
Eisenhower	Republican	95.1
Kennedy	Democratic	90.9
L. B. Johnson	Democratic	95.2
Nixon	Republican	93.7
Ford	Republican	81.2
Carter	Democratic	98.4
Reagan	Republican	94.4
Bush	Republican	93.5[a]

[a](as of mid-1992)

perception of the candidate's "real" politics. The Chief Executive's crucial predictive judgment concerns itself with the nominee's likely future voting pattern on the bench, based on his or her past stance and commitment on matters of public policy, insofar as they are reliably discernible.[111] All Presidents have tried to thus "pack" the bench to a greater or lesser extent.

In the public eye Court-packing has been most closely associated with Franklin D. Roosevelt. Having had not a single opportunity to fill a Court vacancy in his first term (1933–37) and seeing his domestic programs consistently battered by the Court, the frustrated President attempted to get his way all at once. His "Court-packing bill," however, died a deserved death in the Senate.

111. An illuminating illustration is President Kennedy's selection of his long-time friend and ideological kinsman, Deputy Attorney General Byron J. White, to fill the first vacancy on the Court during his brief administration. As *Washington Star* reporter James E. Clayton reported the decision: "Thinking back on the process months later, the Attorney General [Robert F. Kennedy] tilted back his chair and said [to his brother, the President]: 'You wanted someone who generally agreed with you on what role government should play in American life, what role the individual in society should have. You didn't think about how he would vote in a reapportionment case or a criminal case. You wanted someone who, in the long run, you could believe would be doing what you thought was best. You wanted someone who agreed generally with your views of the country.' Both he and the President believed that White and Arthur J. Goldberg met that test. They could not be as sure of the others on the list [Paul A. Freund of Harvard University and Judge William H. Hastie of the U.S. Court of Appeals for the Third Circuit]" (as quoted in James E. Clayton's *The Making of Justice: The Supreme Court in Action* [New York: E. P. Dutton, 1964], p. 52).

It is not surprising that Court packing and the name of President Roosevelt have become synonymous. Yet even such popular heroes as Jefferson, Jackson, and Lincoln followed similar courses of action in the face of what they considered "judicial intransigence and defiance." Their approach was not as radical as Roosevelt's, but they very likely would have been sympathetic to his efforts. George Washington, though broadly regarded as far removed from "politics," had insisted that his fourteen nominees to the Court meet a veritable smorgasbord of qualifications.[112] In fact, every President who has made nominations to the Supreme Court has been guilty of Court packing in some measure. It is entirely understandable that a President will choose people who will share his own philosophy of government and politics, at least to the extent of giving him a sympathetic hearing. Theodore Roosevelt, for example, in discussing the potential candidacy of Horace H. Lurton with Henry Cabot Lodge, put the issue well:

> The nominal politics of the man has nothing to do with his actions on the bench. His real politics are all important. . . . He is right on the Negro question; he is right on the power of the federal government; he is right on the Insular business; he is right about corporations, and he is right about labor. On every question that would come before the bench, he has so far shown himself to be in much closer touch with the policies in which you and I believe than even [Associate Justice Edward D.] White because he has been right about corporations where White has been wrong.[113]

Lodge concurred in substance, but he replied that he could see no reason "why Republicans cannot be found who hold those opinions as well as Democrats."[114] Consequently, he strongly urged the candidacy of a Republican, whom T. R. then duly nominated—William H. Moody, Attorney General of Massachusetts.

Thus, concern with a nominee's real politics is a fundamental issue, and examples abound. It prompted Republican Taft to give half of his six appointments to Democrats who were kindred souls, Republican Nixon to appoint Democrat Powell, Democrat Roosevelt to promote Republican Stone, and Democrat Truman to appoint Republican Burton. Yet there is no guarantee that what a President perceives as real politics will not fade into a mirage. Hence Charles Warren, eminent chronicler of the Court, observed that

> nothing is more striking in the history of the Court than the manner in which the hopes of those who expected a judge to follow the political views of the President appointing him are disappointed.[115]

Few have felt the truth of that statement more keenly than Teddy Roosevelt did with Oliver Wendell Holmes, Jr., whose early "antiadministration" opinions in antitrust cases (notably in *Northern Securities v. United States*)[116] were entirely unexpected. A bare 5:4 majority in that case upheld the government's order, under

---

112. Seven, to be exact (see my *Justices and Presidents*, op. cit., pp. 71–72). Of Washington's fourteen nominees, thirteen were acted upon by the Senate, twelve were confirmed, but only ten served.

113. Henry Cabot Lodge, *Selections from the Correspondence of Theodore Roosevelt and Henry Cabot Lodge, 1884–1918* (New York: Charles Scribner's Sons, 1925), 2, pp. 228, 230, 241.

114. Ibid., p. 229.

115. *The Supreme Court in United States History*, rev. ed. (Boston: Little, Brown, 1926), 2, p. 22.

116. 193 U.S. 197 (1904).

the Sherman Anti-Trust Act, dissolving the Northern Securities Company, brain-child of E. H. Harriman and J. J. Hill, the wealthy and powerful owners of competing railroads who had organized the company in order to secure a terminal line into Chicago. Roosevelt had won that important litigaton, but he was furious about his recent appointee's "anti-anti-trust" vote in the case. He stormed: "I could carve out of a banana a Judge with more backbone than that!"[117] Holmes reportedly merely smiled when told the President's remark, commented that the President was burdened by a shallow intellect, and noted his intention to "call the shots as I see them in terms of the legal and constitutional setting." Later, during T. R.'s second term of office (1905–9) Holmes expressed his sentiments to a labor leader at a White House dinner: "What you want is favor, not justice. But when I am on my job, I don't give a damn what you or Mr. Roosevelt want."[118]

James Madison, having refused to heed his political mentor, Thomas Jefferson, was similarly chagrined with his appointment of Justice Joseph Story. Jefferson had warned him that Story was an inveterate Tory who would become a rabid supporter of Chief Justice Marshall, and he was right: Story not only instantly joined Marshall's approach to constitutional adjudication and interpretation, but he even out-Marshalled Marshall in his nationalism. Perhaps even more chagrined was Woodrow Wilson when his appointee James C. McReynolds proved himself at once to be the antithesis of almost everything his nominator stood for and believed in.

More recently, Harry Truman observed that " . . . packing the Supreme Court simply can't be done. . . . I've tried and it won't work. . . . Whenever you put a man on the Supreme Court he ceases to be your friend. I'm sure of that."[119] Future Presidents may be well advised to heed the admonition of Zechariah Chafee, Harvard's famed expert on the judicial process, who contended that in order to forecast the behavior of a future jurist it is wiser to consider the books in his library than the list of clients in his office.

There is indeed a considerable element of unpredictability in the judicial appointing process. To the often-heard "Does a person become any different when he puts on a gown?" Justice Frankfurter's sharp retort was always, "If he is any good, he does!" In the words of Alexander M. Bickel, "You shoot an arrow into a far-distant future when you appoint a Justice and not the man himself can tell you what he will think about some of the problems that he will face."[120] And late in 1969, reflecting on his sixteen years as Chief Justice of the United States, Earl Warren pointed out that he, for one, did not "see how a man could be on the Court and not change his views substantially over a period of years . . . for change you must if you are to do your duty on the Supreme Court."[121] It is a duty that, in many ways, represents the most hallowed in the governmental process of the United States.

117. As quoted by James E. Clayton, op. cit., n. 71, p. 47.
118. As quoted by Arthur Krock, *The New York Times,* October 19, 1971, p. 431.
119. Lecture at Columbia University, New York City, April 28, 1959.
120. As quoted in *Time Magazine,* May 23, 1969, p. 24.
121. Comment to Anthony Lewis, "A Talk with Warren on Crime, the Court, the Country," *The New York Times Magazine,* October 19, 1969, pp. 128–29.

ON THE ROLE OF THE U.S. SENATE

That the Senate takes its confirmation role seriously is documented by its refusal to confirm 30 of the 143 Supreme Court nominees forwarded to it in the two centuries plus of our history. (Eleven were not rejected per se but were not acted upon.) True, even when counting the Senate's refusal to vote in the Fortas promotion, only five have been voted down during the present century (and two others not acted upon); but, as the experiences of the Nixon Administration demonstrate, the possibility is ever present. Yet a return to the nineteenth-century record of one rejection or refusal to act for every three nominees would appear to be highly unlikely nowadays.

Just why were the thirty turned down? Among the more prominent reasons have been (1) opposition to the nominating President, not necessarily to the nominee; (2) the nominee's involvement with a visible or contentious issue of public policy (i.e., "politics"); (3) opposition to the record of the incumbent Court, which the nominee was presumed, rightly or wrongly, to have supported; (4) senatorial courtesy (closely linked to the consultative nominating process); (5) a perceived "political unreliability" of the nominee; (6) the evident lack of qualifications or limited ability of the nominee; (7) concern about sustained opposition by interest or pressure group; (8) fear that the nominee would dramatically alter the Court's jurisprudential "lineup." Usually several of these reasons figure in the rejection of a nominee, not one alone; the purpose of the previous list is merely to suggest some applicable prototypes.

Thus, a number of candidates were rejected because of Senate opposition to the nominating Chief Executive. For example, John Quincy Adams's nomination of John J. Crittenden in 1828 was "postponed" by the Senate in a strictly partisan vote of 17:23 two months after the nomination. The "loyalist" Democrats in the Senate thereby foiled Adams's last-minute Whig appointment and preserved the vacancy so that it could be filled instead by the President-elect, strong-party Democrat Andrew Jackson. In 1844 Whig President John Tyler sent six nominations to the upper house—which disapproved five and confirmed but one, the outstandingly qualified Chief Justice Samuel Nelson of New York's highest court. Of the former, John C. Spencer, an erstwhile Whig who had accepted high cabinet posts under Tyler and whom the "loyalist" Whig followers of Henry Clay regarded as a traitor, was rejected by a formal roll call vote of 21:26; and action regarding Edward King, who was nominated twice, Ruben H. Walworth, and John M. Read was postponed by the Senate chiefly because of the mistaken expectation of the Clay Whigs that their leader would defeat James K. Polk in the presidential election of 1844. In 1852 action on George E. Badger, one of Whig President Millard F. Fillmore's nominees was postponed indefinitely—despite the fact that Badger was then a U.S. senator (Whig) from North Carolina—and no action at all was taken on his two others, Edward A. Bradford and William E. Micou. The purpose of the anti-Fillmore maneuvers was to preserve court vacancies for incoming Democratic President Franklin Pierce, yet Pierce succeeded in filling only one of them, as he too fell victim to similar Senate tactics. Democrat James Buchanan's nomination of Jeremiah S. Black in December 1860, one month before his term ended, fell 25:26, chiefly because Republican senators wanted to hold the seat for Abraham

Lincoln to fill. In 1866 Union President Andrew Johnson nominated his gifted Attorney General, Henry Stanberry, but the Senate's hostility to Lincoln's successor was such as to frustrate every attempt he made to fill a Supreme Court vacancy. Congress even went so far as to *abolish* the vacancy (thus "icing" Johnson's nominating impotence). A century later, in 1968, the Senate refused to approve Lyndon B. Johnson's attempt simultaneously to promote Abe Fortas to Chief Justice and to replace him with Judge Homer Thornberry of the U.S. Court of Appeals for the Fifth Circuit. Johnson failed largely because most members of the Senate "had had it" with the lame-duck President's nominations. Victory-scenting Republicans also wanted such plums as Supreme Court appointments for themselves; they had not had an opportunity to fill a vacancy on the bench since President Eisenhower's appointment of Justice Potter Stewart ten years earlier.

A good many illustrations are on record in which nominees failed to receive senatorial confirmation because of their involvement with public issues. Thus, in 1795 the Senate rejected John Rutledge as Chief Justice by a vote of 10:14 even though he had been serving as such for four months on a recess appointment, when Congress was not in session. On John Jay's resignation from the Chief Justiceship Rutledge had asked Washington for the appointment, but he now found his fellow Federalists voting against him because of his vigorous opposition to the Jay Treaty of 1794. The Federalist senators refused to confirm a public figure who actively opposed the Treaty they had championed so ardently—even though he was able to meet Washington's stiff criteria for service on the highest bench. Their cause was aided by an all-but-unanimous denunciation by the Northern Federalist press. In 1811, James Madison's nomination of Alexander Wolcott fell 9:24 because the Federalist senators, eagerly backed by the press, opposed Wolcott's vigorous enforcement of the embargo and nonintercourse acts when he was U.S. Collector of Customs in Connecticut. There was, however, also some genuine question as to Wolcott's legal qualifications.

The rejection of President Polk's nomination in 1845 of fellow Democrat George W. Woodward of Pennsylvania, although in part due to the opposition of Pennsylvania's Independent Senator Simon Cameron on the basis of "senatorial courtesy," was largely a result of what was termed Woodward's "gross nativist American sentiments." Chiefly because of these alleged sentiments, which were particularly offensive to Irish Americans, five Democratic senators joined Cameron and a phalanx of Whigs to defeat the nomination by a vote of 20:29. The President, however, saw the action as a power play calculated to weaken his Administration at its very outset. On December 15, 1869, Republican President Ulysses S. Grant nominated his eminently qualified and popular Attorney General Ebenezer R. Hoar. The debate over his nomination dragged on for seven weeks, until February 3, 1873, when Hoar was finally rejected by a vote of 24:33. Hoar had antagonized most of the Senators by his consistent refusal to back senatorial nominations for judgeships, by his publicly uncompromising insistence on "nonpolitical" appointments throughout the government, and by his early championship of civil service reform. Moreover, he had made enemies of fellow Republicans by his outspoken opposition to the proposed impeachment of President Andrew Johnson. Few professional politicians appreciated Judge Hoar's high standards of excellence and assertive political independence, and the Court was deprived of an unusually promising candidate.

Another issue-oriented rejection was that of John J. Parker, Chief Judge of the U.S. Fourth Circuit Court of Appeals (Hoover, 1930). A prominent and distinguished Republican leader in North Carolina for many years and an outstanding jurist, Judge Parker fell victim to the sustained opposition of the American Federation of Labor and the National Association for the Advancement of Colored People. Still, the Senate would not have had the votes to defeat the nomination—Parker lost by a two-vote margin, 39:41—had they not been aided by anti-Hoover Progressive Republicans, including such prominent and influential senators as Hiram Johnson of California, Robert M. La Follette, Jr., of Wisconsin, George W. Norris of Nebraska, and such powerful mavericks as William Borah of Idaho. The AFL's chief grudge against the nominee stemmed from the impression that he was "unfriendly" to labor and that it was he who had handed down an opinion affirming a lower court decision upholding "yellow dog" contracts in the "Red Jacket" case.[122] However, a close reading of Judge Parker's opinion in the case indicates neither approval nor disapproval of "yellow dog" contracts; rather, it reflects the jurist's belief that he was bound by a U.S. Supreme Court precedent.[123] Yet the impression of antilabor bias lingered, fostered by AFL President William Green and other influential labor spokesmen, who, on the other hand, did concede that Judge Parker's integrity, high standards, and professional qualifications were not in question. The NAACP contended that the nominee was opposed generally to black participation in politics and especially to black suffrage. Thus, Walter White of the NAACP leadership pointed out that Judge Parker, while stumping North Carolina as a gubernatorial candidate in 1920, had made an unfortunate remark: "The participation of the Negro in politics is a source of evil and danger to both races and is not desired by the wise men in either race or by the Republican Party of North Carolina."[124] Parker had uttered the statement in response to repeated taunts and charges by his Democratic opponents that he intended to enfranchise blacks and to alter the North Carolina Constitution to accommodate "them." Ironically, it was Judge Parker—he continued to sit on the Fourth Circuit bench after his rejection—who would write some of the earliest and most significant pro-black opinions on desegregation. Among them was *Rice v. Elmore* (1947), in which he sustained U.S. District Court Judge J. W. Waring's outlawing of South Carolina's machinations to bar blacks from primary elections.[125]

The next outright rejections were Judges Clement F. Haynsworth, Jr., and G. Harrold Carswell, both Nixon nominees, almost forty years later. Although their involvement with civil rights did play a considerable role in their rejection, especially in that of Carswell, the overriding and ultimately decisive margin of defeat

122. *United Mine Workers v. Red Jacket Consolidated Coal and Coke Co.*, 18 F. 839 (1927).
123. *Hitchman Coal and Coke Co. v. Mitchell*, 245 U.S. 229 (1917).
124. *Hearings Before the Subcommittee of the Committee on the Judiciary, U.S. Senate, on the Confirmation of John J. Parker to Be an Associate Justice of the Supreme Court of the United States*, 71st Cong., 2d sess., 1930, p. 74.
125. 165 F. 2d 387. (It sustained 72 F. Supp. 516, also decided in 1947.)

lay elsewhere: in Haynsworth's case it was the question of judicial ethics; in Carswell's case it was lack of professional qualification. To his basic specifications Mr. Nixon had added a desire to choose a Southern jurist of conservative judicial bent. Of course, the Court already had at least one Southern strict constructionist, indeed, a constitutional literalist of the first magnitude, in the person of the distinguished Justice Hugo Lafayette Black of Alabama, but that was not exactly what the President had in mind. Haynsworth, a native of South Carolina and a Harvard Law School alumnus, a relatively able jurist meriting a "B" or "B-minus" grade in the minds of most Court watchers, fit all of the President's specifications—and, perhaps even more significantly, those of such influential Southern senators as Strom Thurmond (R.-S.C.), James O. Eastland (D.-Miss.), and John L. McClellan (D.-Ark.). He was also supported by the Attorney General, John N. Mitchell.

Most of the Senate seemed disposed to confirm Judge Haynsworth for the Fortas vacancy. But to the President's anger, frustration, and embarrassment, the hearings of the Senate Committee on the Judiciary provided clear evidence of the nominee's patent insensitivity to financial and conflict-of-interest improprieties. Apparently, as with Fortas, no actual legal infractions had taken place—but how could the Senate confirm Haynsworth when it had played such an activist role in causing Fortas's resignation? It could not, and among those who vocally opposed the South Carolinian and voted against his confirmation were such anti-Fortas, "strict constructionist" leaders as Senators Robert Griffin (R.-Mich.) and Jack Miller (R.-Iowa). Down went the Haynsworth nomination by a vote of 55:45 on November 21, 1969—largely for the reasons indicated, although he had also drawn considerable labor and minority-group fire for allegedly anti–civil libertarian and anti–civil rights stands. The livid President Nixon, however, chose to lay the blame for his nominee's defeat on "anti-Southern, anticonservative, and anti–strict-constructionist" prejudice, and he vowed to select another "worthy and distinguished protagonist" of Southern, conservative, and strict constructionist persuasion.[126]

To the dismay of those senators who had counseled confirmation of Judge Haynsworth lest a successor-nominee be even less worthy of the high post, the President, again on the recommendation of Attorney General Mitchell, quickly countered by nominating Judge G. Harrold Carswell of Florida, a little-known and little-distinguished ex-U.S. District Judge with only six months of experience on the U.S. Court of Appeals for the Fifth Circuit. "He is almost too good to be true," Mr. Mitchell was reported to have said.[127] The appointment was an act of vengeance—one intended to teach the Senate a lesson and to downgrade the Court. The Senate, intimidated by the President and the Attorney General, was disposed to confirm him. But suspicious reporters and researchers soon cast serious doubt on that "almost too good to be true" classification of the nominee. Immediately damaging was the discovery of a statement Carswell had made to a meeting of the American Legion on August 2, 1948, while he was running for a seat in the legislature of his native Georgia. "I yield to no man as a fellow candidate or as a fellow

---

126. *The New York Times*, November 22, 1969, p. 20.
127. Richard Harris, *Decision* (New York: E. P. Dutton, 1971), p. 11.

citizen in the firm, vigorous belief in the principles of White Supremacy, and I shall always be so governed."[128] To be sure, the nominee, pointing to his youth and inexperience (he was twenty-eight at the time), now disavowed that statement and any racism as well. But an examination of his record on the bench did more than cast further doubt on his objectivity in racial matters: While serving as U.S. Attorney in Florida, Carswell had been involved in the transfer of a public, municipally owned Tallahassee golf course—built with $35,000 of federal funds—to the status of a private club. It was a move obviously designed to circumvent a contemporary Supreme Court decision proscribing segregation in municipal recreation facilities.

Still, the administration appeared to have the votes for Senate confirmation, given the vivid memories of the Haynsworth battle, the intensive wooing of doubtful senators by the White House and the Justice Department, and the natural predisposition to give the President his choice, all things being equal. But things were far from equal, for as the Carswell opponents continued their attack it became apparent that, quite apart from the controversy surrounding his civil rights record, the candidate was patently inferior, simply on the basis of fundamental juridical and legal qualifications. If Judge Haynsworth had merited a "B" or "B-minus" grade, Judge Carswell scarcely merited a "D" on the scale of relevant ability. Senator Roman Hruska (R.-Neb.), the President's floor manager of the nomination, made a fumbling, pathetic attempt to convert the candidate's mediocrity into an asset: "Even if he is mediocre there are a lot of mediocre judges and people and lawyers. They are entitled to a little representation, aren't they, and a little chance? We can't have all Brandeises, Cardozos, and Frankfurters, and stuff like that there."[129] Hruska's remarkable assertion was seconded by Carswell-supporter Senator Russell Long (D.-La.), who intoned:

> Does it not seem . . . that we have had enough of those upside down, corkscrew thinkers? Would it not appear that it might be well to take a B student or a C student who was able to think straight, compared to one of those A students who are [sic] capable of the kind of thinking that winds up getting us a 100-percent increase in crime in this country?[130]

This line of argument failed to convince the doubtful senators. Instead, they became increasingly aware of the lack of ability of the nominee, who among other debilitating features, held the dubious record of having been reversed by appellate courts more than any of the other federal jurists then sitting except eight! Yale Law School Dean Louis H. Pollak styled the Carswell nomination as one of "more slender credentials than any Supreme Court nominee put forth in this century."[131] Perhaps even more tellingly, the distinguished William Van Alstyne, professor of law at Duke University, opposed the nomination. Van Alstyne, an ardent and vocal backer of the Haynsworth nomination, now testified: "There is, in candor, nothing in the quality of the nominee's work to warrant any expectation whatever, that he

---

128. As quoted by Harris, op. cit., pp. 15–16; in *The New York Times*, January 23, 1970, p. 16; and by Senator Birch Bayh (D.-Ind.) in *Congressional Record*, Vol. 116, p. 6, p. 7498, 91st Cong., 2nd sess.
129. As quoted by Harris, op. cit., p. 110.
130. *Congressional Record*, op. cit., p. 7487.
131. Harris, loc. cit.

could serve with distinction on the Supreme Court of the United States."[132] When the final vote on confirmation came on April 9, 1970—three months after the nomination—the President's choice went down by a vote of 51:45. Among the "no's" were such significant Republican votes as those of Margaret Chase Smith of Maine, Winston L. Prouty of Vermont, Marlow W. Cook of Kentucky, and Richard S. Schweiker of Pennsylvania.

It was indeed a bitter defeat for the President. Not only had he seen two nominees rejected within less than five months, but his carefully devised "Southern strategy" had suffered a serious blow. His reaction was swift and vitriolic. Conveniently ignoring the basic issues for his candidates' defeats, he blamed them instead on sectional prejudice, abject politics, and philosophical negations, and told the country:

> I have reluctantly concluded that—with the Senate as presently constituted—I cannot successfully nominate to the Supreme Court any federal appellate judge from the South who believes as I do in the strict construction of the Constitution. . . . Judges Carswell and Haynsworth have endured with admirable dignity vicious assaults on their intelligence, their honesty, and their character. . . . When all the hypocrisy is stripped away, the real issue was their philosophy of strict construction of the Constitution—a philosophy that I share. . . .[133]

Quite to the contrary, several distinguished federal jurists in the South were eminently qualified to serve, jurists who indeed shared the President's philosophy of government and politics and whom the Senate assuredly would have confirmed. It could not, in good conscience, given the Fortas precedent, the public concern, and the nature and role of the Supreme Court, have confirmed Haynsworth or Carswell, especially not Carswell. The latter, ironically, was soon to be defeated by his constituents in the Florida senatorial primary, during which he was photographed with a lettered sign around his neck reading "Heah Come 'de Judge." It is an intriguing thought that had Haynsworth been nominated *after* Carswell, he might well have been confirmed.

President Nixon followed up his blast against the rejections with the petulant suggestion in a well-publicized letter to Senator Wiliam B. Saxbe (R.-Ohio) that the Senate had denied him the right to see his choices appointed. The right, he insisted, had been accorded all previous Presidents—a patently false statement, in the face of twenty-seven rejections of nominees to the Court on record. Moreover, the President's collateral suggestion to Saxbe and the nation, that senatorial advice and consent to nominations (which is *expressly* provided for in Article II, Section II, Clause 2, of the Constitution) is merely a *pro forma* requirement, is utterly incorrect with regard to nominations to the judiciary in general and the Supreme Court in particular. Mr. Nixon, fully familiar with the contrary judgment of practically all students of constitutional law and history, as well as with Hamilton's equally contrary assertions in *The Federal Papers* (Nos. 76 and 77), must have been aware of how wrong he was. His anger and frustration were understandable, but his historical misstatement was a distinct disservice to Country, Constitution, and Court.

132. As quoted by Harris, op. cit., p. 56.
133. From the President's nationwide television address of April 9, 1970, as quoted in *The New York Times*, April 10, 1970, p. 1, and in *Time Magazine*, April 20, 1970, p. 9.

The Senate's 45:43 refusal to accept cloture in 1968 in order that the senators might vote on the promotion of Justice Fortas—no such vote was ever taken—has been variously attributed to his "record" on the high bench on such contentious issues as obscenity and criminal justice. In fact, although those issues were dramatically vocalized by such powerful and committed opponents to the nomination as Senators Strom Thurmond (R.-S.C.) and John L. McClellan (D.-Ark.), they were not an important reason for the nomination's failure. It was fought with such ardor largely because of deep-seated opposition to the jurisprudential philosophy of the "Warren Court," whose approach to constitutional interpretation had resulted in the inevitable disaffection of numerous groups and individuals, both public and private. The Court's stance and record of "judicial activism" on such emotion-charged issues as desegregation, reapportionment and redistricting, criminal justice, separation of church and state, civil disobedience, and freedom of expression were bound to offend as well as to please.

Coming, as it did conveniently, at the close of the Johnson Administration, the Fortas nomination readily served as target and symbol of the pent-up frustrations against the Warren Court—but against the Court as a unit rather than against the individual Justices. One of the famous episodes surrounding the attacks against Fortas occurred early in the hearings on the nomination by the Senate Judiciary Committee, when Senator Thurmond shouted at Fortas: "Mallory! Mallory! I want that name to ring in your ears!" Thurmond's reference was to Andrew Mallory, a nineteen-year-old black from South Carolina who was arrested in 1954 on a charge of choking and raping a thirty-eight-year old Washington woman while she was doing her laundry. After a seven-hour interrogation by the police *prior* to his arraignment, Mallory had confessed. The trial was delayed for a year because doubts had been raised that he understood the proceedings against him, but ultimately Mallory was sentenced to the electric chair. He appealed to the Supreme Court on the grounds of coerced confession. In 1957, in what became the celebrated case of *Mallory v. United States*,[134] the Court unanimously reversed Mallory's conviction on the ground that the failure of the police to bring him before a magistrate "forthwith" constituted an "unnecessary delay," in violation of (congressionally sanctioned) federal rules of criminal law procedure, thereby giving "opportunity for the extraction of a confession." Released, Mallory resumed a life of drifting and crime that culminated in his 1960 arrest in Philadelphia and his subsequent apprehension for burglary, assault, and rape. He was convicted on the assault count, served eleven years in jail, and barely six months after his release in 1971 attacked and robbed a couple in a Philadelphia park. When discovered by two policemen, he aimed a gun at one and was killed by the other. It was the so-called Mallory Rule, as pronounced by the Supreme Court in 1957, that Senator Thurmond referred to in his outburst at Justice Fortas. Yet Fortas had never been connected with the case and had not even been appointed to the Court until 1965, eight years after the Mallory decision! (The Mallory Rule itself was modified by Congress in the Omnibus Crime Control Act of 1968.) Other charges were leveled at the nominee, some of them concerning decisions in obscenity cases rendered long before Fortas ever sat. The 1987 rejection of Judge Robert H. Bork, whom

---

134. 354 U.S. 449.

the Senate had approved unanimously to the U.S. Court of Appeals just a few years earlier, was based overridingly on his perceived jurisprudence.

Senatorial courtesy, the fourth in our list of reasons for Senate refusal of Supreme Court nominations, has already been discussed. A fifth is broadly styled "political unreliability," as perceived by the Senate. Perhaps the most obvious example of the application of this reason is another among the several unsuccessful Grant nominations—that of former Attorney General Caleb Cushing, who was the President's choice to assume the Chief Justiceship in 1874, following the death of Salmon P. Chase. Cushing's age—seventy-four—was noted prominently during debate, but the real reason for his rejection was the Senate's not-entirely-erroneous belief that Grant's close personal friend was a political chameleon. Indeed, Cushing had been in turn a Regular Whig, a Tyler Whig, a Democrat, a Johnson Constitutional Conservative, and, at last, a Republican. He had proved himself a first-rate practitioner and scholar; nevertheless, with opposition from almost all political factions growing daily, Grant withdrew Cushing from consideration.

A sixth reason for Senate refusal of a nominee is simply real or apparent lack of qualification to sit on the Supreme Court. Of course, the concepts of "quality" and "ability" are subject to diverse analysis, yet a number of ascertainable standards and guidelines clearly exist; a nominee's age, experience, and record in and out of public life are all available guidelines. Ulysses S. Grant, in choosing his Attorney General George H. Williams to fill the vacancy caused by the death of Chief Justice Chase, thus evoked an entirely justifiable storm of adverse reactions. Williams had seen service in the Senate and had been territorial governor of Oregon, but his record as Attorney General was undistinguished and his talents as a lawyer were clearly mediocre. (It was alleged that he had unnecessarily lost several important cases in private as well as public litigation.) Both the bar and the press were severely critical of his achievements and his promise. Stunned and hurt by this reaction, and despairing of a lengthy confirmation battle, Williams asked President Grant to withdraw his nomination in early January 1874.

It is fair to conclude that Presidents have avoided nominating patently unqualified individuals to the high tribunal, although a number of rather weak nominations have slipped past the Senate, such as James C. McReynolds (Wilson), Pierce Butler (Harding), Sherman Minton (Truman), and Charles E. Whittaker (Eisenhower).[135] The one nominee on whose lack of qualifications almost all fair-minded observers now agree is G. Harrold Carswell. With the calm hindsight of history President Nixon's choice still merits the characterization of a spite nomination. It is fortunate that the Senate simply would not accept Carswell.

Seventh, sustained, concerted opposition by interest or pressure groups to a particular nominee may well be a major contributing factor in a nominee's defeat. That of the Bork nomination in 1987 is a classic case in point. Although it was neither the sole nor, arguably, the most important reason for Bork's rejection by the Senate—the latter's capture by the Democrats in the 1986 midterm elections

---

135. For a ranking of all Justices through Thurgood Marshall (1967), based on a poll conducted by sixty-five experts in 1970, plus some subsequent ones, see Appendix A in my *Justices and Presidents*, op. cit.

probably was *the* decisive one—there is no doubt that the expertly orchestrated, well-organized, heavily financed galaxy of political interest groups, such as People for the American Way, the Leadership Conference on Civil Rights, and a plethora of Hollywood activists, were profoundly influential in Bork's dramatic rejection.

The eighth, and for these purposes final, reason for the rejection of a presidential nominee is fear that the proposed nominee would decisively alter the Court's jurisprudential "lineup" as it existed at the time of the nomination. Again, the Bork case is illustrative here: the outspoken, brilliant lower court federal judge would have replaced the Court's leading centrist and "swing" vote, Lewis F. Powell, Jr., who had retired from the Court at the end of its 1986–87 term. But Judge Bork's copious scholarly writings, which would have been an enviable asset in any academic setting, and his lucidly crafted, elegantly penned opinions on the appellate bench contained attacks on Warren and Burger Court precedents that played directly into the hands of hostile interest group and Senate opponents, the latter effectively led by Edward M. ("Ted") Kennedy (D.-Mass.). Bork's intellectual commitment to a jurisprudence of original intent appeared rigid and was fair game for being portrayed as beyond the "mainstream" of contemporary judicial philosophy. President Reagan's eleventh-hour attempt to sell his nominee as the logical heir to the Powell legacy could not overcome the simple truth that Robert Bork did not qualify as a Powell clone. The distinguished jurist's potent opponents were unwilling to take a chance on what they viewed as Bork's certain vote on the "right" of the then closely divided 4:4 tribunal in "liberal"-"conservative" contemplation on crucial issues.

Would any of the twenty-eight who failed in being confirmed have been approved if they had been members of the Senate at the time of their nomination? The evidence is persuasive that they would have: the Senate almost invariably treats as a *cas d'honneur* the presidential designation of a sitting member—and, normally, although not as predictably, of a past colleague in good standing. Among the many illustrations are Senators James F. Byrnes (D.-S.C.) and Harold H. Burton (R.-Ohio). Byrnes, highly respected and very much a member of the Senate's "inner club," was confirmed unanimously without even being scrutinized by the Committee on the Judiciary when President Roosevelt nominated him in 1941. (After barely fifteen months, Byrnes resigned eagerly, happy to become F. D. R.'s "Assistant President for Domestic Affairs.") Burton's nomination, although that of a Republican by a Democratic President (Truman), was unanimously confirmed in 1945 on the same day it reached the Senate, which was then controlled by a Democratic majority.

That the special treatment accorded senatorial colleague-nominees is normally reserved for then sitting members is demonstrated by the case of ex-Senator Sherman Minton of Indiana. Minton, who had been defeated for reelection in 1940, largely because of his ardent espousal of the New Deal, was serving as a judge on the U.S. Court of Appeals for the Seventh Circuit when President Truman selected him for the Supreme Court in 1949. In part because of his support of the "Court-packing bill," the Senate Judiciary Committee voted 5:4 to ask him to testify before it. Minton refused, pointing to his position as a jurist and questioning the propriety of testifying lest conflicts arise concerning pending litigation. The

Committee relented and reported his nomination favorably, 9:2. But the Senate, led by prominent Republicans, took a formal vote on a motion to recommit Minton's nomination. It lost 45:21; thereafter he obtained quick confirmation, 48:16.

A notable exception to the unwritten rule of the all but automatic approval of sitting senatorial colleagues was Franklin D. Roosevelt's controversial nomination of Senator Hugo LaFayette Black (D.-Ala.) in August 1937. Black's nomination was referred to the Judiciary Committee for full hearings, an action not taken on a fellow-senator since 1888. The initial reasons for that move, over the strong objections by the Chairman of the Committee, Senator Henry Ashurst (D.-Ariz.), were Black's strong support of the President's 1937 "Court-packing bill," his ardent New Deal partisanship, and his ruthless public investigations of the utility lobby. The attempt to increase the size of the Court was anathema to a majority of the Senate and the bar. And the controversy was compounded and exacerbated by rumors that Black had once been—and some alleged still was—a member of the Ku Klux Klan in his native Alabama. Even so, the Committee ultimately approved the nomination by a vote of 13:4 (two Democrats, King of Utah and Burke of Nebraska, and two Republicans, Austin of Vermont and Steiwer of Oregon, voted against him), and the Senate confirmed him 63:16; ten Republicans and six Democrats voted "nay."[136] Meanwhile, reporter Ray Sprigle of the *Pittsburgh Post-Gazette* came up with evidence that Black had indeed belonged to the KKK. Black, however, faced the charges squarely, and in a candid, dramatic broadcast to the American people admitted a two-year KKK membership in the mid-1920s but pointed to his established liberal record and vowed to be a fair and impartial jurist. During his tenure on the Court, which lasted more than a third of a century, he kept his word.

The last test of the Senate's refusal to refer nominations of incumbent senators to the Judiciary Committee came with Burton in 1945, but no senator has since been nominated. It was precisely the recognition of that rule which prompted leading supporters of President Nixon to urge him to nominate a senator after Judge Haynsworth's rejection in 1969. Evidently the President briefly toyed with the idea of selecting John Stennis (D.-Miss.) or Sam Ervin (D.-N.C.), both Southern Senators generally supportive of his "strict construction" views; yet in his determination to "teach the Senate a lesson" he chose Carswell. But it will be recalled that one of "The Six" he had under consideration for the Black and Harlan vacancies in 1971 was Senator Robert C. Byrd (D.-W. Va.), a man arguably less qualified to serve on the Court than his colleagues Stennis and Ervin. Whether or not Nixon seriously contemplated the Byrd nomination, there is but scant doubt that his colleagues would have given their approval. Those same colleagues would have been far less likely, however, to approve someone of equally marginal qualifications from outside the halls of the Senate.

In general, opposition to the confirmation of a Supreme Court Justice seems to reflect the existence of deep-seated concern in the nation. In the early years of the Court's history, relatively little interest was shown in the potentially "unfortunate

---

136. The six Democrats were Byrd (Va.), Glass (Va.), Copeland (N.Y.), Gerry (R.I.), Burke (Neb.), and King (Utah). The ten Republicans: Austin (Vt.), Borah (Id.), Bridges (N.H.), Davis (Pa.), Hale (Me.), Johnson (Calif.), Lodge (Mass.), Steiwer (Ore.), Townsend (Del.), and White (Me.).

effects" of Justices of uncertain, or certain, convictions. It became more frequent and noticeable as the influence of the Court became more apparent. At the present time, when there are so many issues in which large numbers of people are deeply concerned, almost every nominee is made to run the gauntlet; he or she may even feel slighted if the appointment is unopposed! The nomination and confirmation procedure has become one more battleground on which large issues are fought out before the public eye.

QUALIFICATIONS AND EXPERIENCE: THE SPECIAL CASES OF ENGLAND AND FRANCE

In endeavoring to explain and analyze the staffing of the courts of England[137] and France, and in comparing their respective judiciaries, it is necessary to remain cognizant of the two different types of law that govern the systems concerned—the common or Anglo-Saxon law in England and the civil or Roman law in France. There are fundamental differences between the laws of the two countries—and far greater ones become apparent, of course, in contrasting one or both with the prevalent norms and practices in the United States. But it is above all the very position of the judiciary that provides the key to these differences. Under the Roman law tradition of the Continent, the judiciary is a part of the administrative-executive hierarchy (as will be explained in considerable detail in chapter 6) and it constitutes a *profession* distinctly separate from that of the practicing lawyer. Where the common law tradition holds, however, the legal profession is practically an autonomous body, the judges' being drawn from its ranks—not withstanding the different mode and mood of selection that governs in England compared with that of the United States, where the common law tradition also holds.

Nevertheless, we have already observed that a common ideal, that of impartiality of the appointees, is held by all three lands for both selection and tenure of their judiciaries and that each is therefore willing, as it must be, to protect its independence and provide a large measure of immunity in order to achieve it. But the techniques of training and selecting judges and ensuring their impartiality differ widely.

ENGLAND

Unlike the United States, England divides its legal profession into two major groups—the *solicitors* and the *barristers*—and it is impossible to be both concurrently. The former deal mainly with the general public; they conduct about 95 percent of the ordinary legal business of the country, leaving the remaining highly important work of pleading and advocacy in the courts to the barristers, who see the layperson only when so instructed by a solicitor. The best analogy of the difference between the two groups is found in medicine: the difference between the general practitioner and the consultant and specialist. Barristers are consultants for the solicitors—the latter do all the ordinary work of the law and call in the barristers when they need or desire their services, either for advice or for conducting a case in court.

137. The reader is reminded that "England," as understood for the purposes of this book, includes Wales (but *not* Scotland or Northern Ireland).

The Solicitors. The "office lawyers" of the legal structure, the solicitors are obviously its workhorses. It is they who deal directly with the clients, who do the routine legal office work, and who prepare the spadework for cases to be argued at the bar of the higher courts by the barristers. But they also enjoy the right of audience in the magistrates and county courts and, at the discretion or "direction" of the Lord Chancellor, under section 12 of the Courts Act of 1971, at certain limited proceedings, in the Crown Court; in fact, they practice a great deal of advocacy in these several courts. However, they are still not allowed to appear in the higher courts. They handle practically all of the drawing up of legal documents, such as transfers of property. In short, the 62,000 practicing solicitors (1992) do the bulk of England's ordinary legal work. Having determined to become a solicitor on the conclusion of his or her educational career, and having undergone additional legal training,[138] the aspirant then takes a number of special professional examinations. Passing these, he or she becomes a "Solicitor of the Supreme Court" and commences a career. The solicitor will also probably join the Law Society, a voluntary association of solicitors with certain statutory powers. Every *practicing* solicitor must become a member of this society. Incidentally, university training is not an absolute requirement—over half of the solicitors are not university products.

The Barristers. It is the 5,500 practicing barristers (1992) who constitute England's *best-known* legal talent. Their chief function is to render legal advice to clients (in the great majority of cases, on instructions given to them by solicitors), either generally or in preparation for trial, and, of course, to conduct cases, both civil and criminal. Thus, they argue all cases in the higher courts—cases that, by custom and tradition, are almost always given to them directly by the solicitors, who have processed them in a preliminary manner, rather than by the clients themselves. The barristers are professionally specialized and usually, although not inevitably, highly experienced members of the legal profession. Their specialization may lead them to practice in limited and specialized fields, such as Chancery, Common, or Criminal law, and Commercial law including Admiralty. It is from the ranks of the barristers that the Lord Chancellor normally selects the judges on behalf of the Crown. Indeed, with the exception of justices of the peace, the English and Welsh judges were always appointed from the ranks of practicing barristers until the passage of the Court Act of 1971, when solicitors became eligible for the posts of Recorder or Circuit Judge.[139]

The barristers are divided into two groups, or ranks: junior barristers and Queen's Counsel. The latter are referred to colloquially as "silks" because they are entitled to wear a silk gown instead of the "stuff" gown worn by the junior barristers. The two gowns are different in style also: those worn by the Juniors are like academic gowns with flowing sleeves; those of the silks have simpler lines. One becomes a silk upon the recommendation of the Lord Chancellor, on reaching top status in the profession, seldom until the completion of ten years' successful prac-

---

138. See further description, *infra*, p. 88.
139. A Recorder must now be a barrister or solicitor of at least ten years' standing; a Circuit Judge must be a barrister of at least ten years' standing or a Recorder who has held that judicial office for at least five years. A County Judge, however, must have been a barrister for at least seven years, a High Court Judge for at least ten, and a Lord Chief Justice of Appeal for at least fifteen.

tice, although it should be noted that some very distinguished lawyers never "take silk." Successful juniors usually apply for silk in their forties or fifties. In consultation with senior judges, the Lord Chancellor chooses between 40 and 50 names each year from the 180 or so who apply. The silks, who comprise 10 percent of the bar, constitute the elite among the barristers, and they generally receive higher fees than the junior barristers. Their main tasks include appearances in court, where they are usually accompanied by a junior. It is from the ranks of Queen's Counsel that judges are mainly chosen. Yet sometimes it is possible to become a judge without being a "Q.C."—for example, Lord Chief Justice Parker was made a judge as a junior. He had been junior counsel to the Treasury, the government advocate for Crown business in the High Court. Normally those who have taken silk for at least seven years, and, in the cases of the higher courts, for at least ten years, may expect to be considered for a judgeship in the event of a vacancy. But the number of superior court judges is low, and when one of the promotions does come it is viewed with a certain awe and respect by the legal profession and the public at large. Judges of the High Court are *invited* to become such by the Lord Chancellor— that is, they do not solicit the post—whereas those of the County Court are appointed from the ranks of those who have *applied* to the Lord Chancellor for consideration of appointment.[140]

All barristers are members of one of the four historic *Inns of Court* in London: Lincoln's Inn, Gray's Inn, Inner Temple, and Middle Temple.[141] In effect, they constitute both a "law school" and a corporate professional organization. Separate colleges, each with its own hall, chapel—except that the Inner and Middle Temple share the Round Church—and library, they arose as a result of the lawyers' custom of living together during terms. Self-governing, historic organizations, officially dating back roughly to the time of Edward I, "Longshanks" (1272–1307), the Inns of Court have different histories, but they were generally modeled on the old trade guilds, to which they owe their origin. An Inn of Court was not so much a school of law as a school for Englishmen (as Sir John Fortescue so well described it in his

---

140. In mid-1984, successful Q.C.s averaged around £60,000 a year. A handful of specialists—especially those in tax and company work—grossed over £200,000. Most established juniors ranged between £15,000 and £35,000, roughly at the same earning level as the average solicitor. But partners in the central London solicitors' firms (barristers may not engage in partnerships) average more than £40,000, and senior partners in top firms, very much like their counterparts in America, can earn in six figures annually, whereas those in small firms in poor areas of England and Wales may have to struggle to earn £12,000 (see "The Two Legal Professions," Part 2 of "English Justice," *The Economist*, August 6, 1983, pp. 46–47).

141. The Inner and Middle Temples derive their names from the Round Church, which was built by the Knights Templar in 1160 and stood, despite being widely damaged—as were the other two Inns—in the 1941 London blitz, between the Strand and the Thames. They were faithfully restored (and the church was rededicated) in the early 1960s. What is now known as the Inner Temple covers what used to be the consecrated portion of the grounds surrounding the Temple Church. The Middle Temple covers what used to be the unconsecrated part. Gray's Inn derives its name from Reginald de Gray, Justician of Chester, who lived there in the thirteenth century. (Sir Francis Bacon, one of Gray's Inn's most famous members, planned and planted its beautiful gardens, where he loved to walk and talk with such statesmen as Sir Walter Raleigh). Lincoln's Inn, whose records are continuous from 1492, owes its name to the Earl of Lincoln, who was a member of the King's Council, also in the thirteenth century.

epic *De Laudibus Legum Angliae*). The outlook developed in a university (Oxford and Cambridge) was purely scholastic; that in an Inn of Court was eminently national. In an Inn of Court the students lived together as one community. Fortescue describes the Inns of his time (fifteenth century) as not merely places for the students of the law, but as universities or schools of all commendable qualities. There, students as well as members of the bar would study, live, work, eat, and pray. But now they are no longer residences in the full sense of the term, although quite a few barristers still do live there, sometimes with their families.

Legal Education. In the past, under the tutelage of barristers, England's future lawyers were thus trained in the Inns rather than in a university law school, where Roman or civil law and canon law, as opposed to the common law, were taught. Today, these students may attend the lectures of the Council of Legal Education, a joint committee for education from the four Inns of Court. They are tested by examiners of the council, and on passing the examination and having kept their "dining terms," they apply to the "Benchers," the governing body of the Inn, for admission as barristers. This "dining term" rule is a relic of the days when students of the common law lived in the Inns of Court and had to frequent the hall of their Inn for dinner, for the exercises in "mooting," and for other forms of learning before becoming barristers. To this day they must dine in the hall on three nights in each dining term.

Once admitted to the bar, the young barrister remains under the general jurisdiction of his or her Inn of Court throughout his or her career—in fact, for life—and it is his or her Inn that constitutes both his professional protector and his disciplinarian. A full measure of *esprit de corps* flows naturally from life and membership in the Inn. Disciplinary problems are further under the supervision of the General Council of the Bar, a special body elected by the members of the Bar to act for it in a wide range of matters. Authority to expel a barrister for misconduct is given to the "Benchers" of the Inn of which he or she is a member. Disciplinary and other matters affecting the Bar generally also now come under the jurisdiction of the Senate of the Four Inns of Court, which has representative members of the four Inns and of the Bar Council.

The legal education provided by the Law Society for solicitors, who may have offices at the Inns but do not study there, differs from that given to the barristers. It is based on intensive courses, practical training, and a year's compulsory attendance at a recognized law school. The future barrister, on the other hand, must pass the bar examinations, which involve a background in general legal principles, although he or she may not have had specific training in these; often does not attend the elaborate series of lectures provided by the Council of Legal Education; and is not required to have practical training. However, recently a pledge has been exacted from candidates to spend six months as pupils in chambers.

The reason the future solicitor is given a thorough practical training in a solicitor's office by being apprenticed to the latter for three years if a university product, and five years if not, is that solicitors are entitled to practice from the moment they are admitted and can do legal work of practically any kind *at once* for the general public. But a barrister is never employed directly by a member of the public; he or she is employed, or instructed, by a solicitor and in practice is a highly trained lawyer before being given work of any importance from a solicitor.

Even given the possibility of a judicial appointment, his or her attractive social status, and the "psychic income" he or she may receive from membership in the profession, the future of the barrister's branch of that profession is nevertheless undergoing some examination. One of the considerations is the relatively low income of many barristers, although big incomes are earned by those at the top of the profession. As of late 1991, the number of practicing barristers was 6,000. The former total represents a 70 percent increase since 1970, due in not inconsiderable measure to the rising legal aid work in Law Centres by barristers in both criminal and civil law—not necessarily their most desired type of practice.

Both solicitors and the Bar are now graduate professions. That is to say people who were nongraduates in the past and have qualified will obviously stay, but all those entering from some time in the 1980s have had to have university degrees, although there is a possibility of admitting those who have had exceptional experience. For solicitors there is another route via qualifying as a legal executive in the first instance. This is an extremely long route and is tantamount to having to earn a law degree part-time while working as a "legal executive." *Legal executive* is the new term for what used to be clerks in solicitors' offices.

Yet whatever the problems of the profession may be—and they have been exaggerated at times—the English judges are very likely the most highly esteemed, the most independent, and, relatively speaking, the most generously paid in the West. There is little doubt that these three factors account in considerable degree for the generally higher quality of British justice, properly so often cited and envied by much of the rest of the world—which does not mean that the British judiciary does not have its detractors, a factor that has begun to witness a drive for the consideration of European law in relation to the law of the United Kingdom (and other European countries, both EEC and Council of Europe). Thus, the European Court of Justice, which sits at Luxembourg, has power to strike down legislation that is contrary to EC directives.

THE COURTS AND LEGAL SERVICES ACT OF 1990

In 1989, the Thatcher Government issued a Green Paper concerning proposed reforms of the legal profession. The Government's objective was to "see that the public has the best possible access to legal services and that those services are of the right quality for the particular needs of the client."[142] The Government's reform recommendations relied on a market ideology which would allow legal services to operate freely and efficiently. Ultimately, in order for the marketplace to govern the legal profession, *the distinction between barristers and solicitors had to be removed.* In this respect, the most controversial provision was to give solicitors rights of audience in the High Courts. (They had a limited right of audience in the lower magistrate and county courts prior to the Green Papers.)

The response from the Bar was wide ranging and was directed against the reforms defined by the Government. Specifically, the Bar put forward many arguments as to why the status quo should not be changed.[143] Ultimately, the Bar was

142. *The Work and Organisation of the Legal Profession*, Lord Chancellor's Dept., HMSO, January 1989, p. 1.
143. For these arguments see *Quality of Justice: The Bar's Response* (London: Butterworths, 1989).

able to forestall many of the Government's proposed reforms when the final bill was passed. The Government submitted the Courts and Legal Services Bill to the House of Lords first. The debate in the Lords was long-winded and many of the Government's proposals were "watered down." One should also note that the Lords certainly has a stronger connection to the Bar than does the Commons.

Eventually, the final Courts and Legal Services Bill became the Courts and Legal Services Act of 1990. The Government abandoned its "blueprint for the future" by removing language stressing the importance of free competition in the legal profession. Instead it only established the machinery which would enable evolutionary changes to the legal profession and courts system to be effected.[144]

The most important provisions of the Courts and Legal Services Act of 1990 concern this "machinery" established by the Government: One provision is that the Lord Chancellor may change the jurisdiction between the High Court and county courts, thus in effect giving county courts jurisdiction over many matters which are now the province of the High Court. The Lord Chancellor is also empowered to set up a corporate body known as the "Lord Chancellor's Advisory Committee on Legal Education and Conduct," which will "assist in the maintenance and development of standards in the education, training, and conduct of those offering legal services." Rights of Audience are also covered by the Act, and it is the primary duty of the Advisory Committee on Legal Education to determine the necessary qualifications for the right of audience. However, this will not automatically erase the bar's monopoly on rights of audience, because the Act is qualified by two points:

> 27 (4)Nothing in this section [27] affects the power of any court in any proceedings to refuse to hear a person (for reasons which apply to him as an individual) who would otherwise have a right of audience before the court in relation to those proceedings.
> 27 (5)Where a court refuses to hear a person as mentioned in subsection (4) it shall give its reasons for refusing.

Therefore, even though the Lord Chancellor's Department now has more control over the jurisdiction of the county courts and High Courts and over standards governing the legal profession, it is still the province of judges to determine who has the right to argue in that specific court concerning that specific case. Considering the close links between the judiciary and the bar, it is quite evident how these reforms will progress.

FRANCE

The Republic of France, together with several other states on the continent of Europe, goes considerably further than Britain in distinguishing between judges, public prosecutors, and officials of the powerful Ministry of Justice, on the one hand, and privately practicing lawyers on the other. Although there is a clear-cut distinction between the British solicitor and the barrister, both are nonetheless

---

144. See "Reform of the Legal Profession," by Lord Donaldson of Lymington in *Current Legal Problems, 1990* (London: Sweet and Maxwell/Stevens, 1990), p. 3.

members of the legal profession and may commence their advanced legal training together. In France, however, the bench is a separate career; it is not viewed as a reward for legal excellence or renown as it is in both Britain and in the United States.

A French student of the law must decide after his or her schooling whether to become either a private lawyer or a judge or prosecutor or go to the Justice Ministry. If the former, he or she chooses among six available specialties: *avocat*, roughly akin to the British barrister; *avoué*, the approximate equivalent of the British solicitor; *agrée*, who specializes in pleading before certain commercial tribunals, although these three specialties were, in effect, gradually being fused as of September 1972;[145] *conseiller fiscal*, who is trained in drafting and registering of legal papers, related in name only to the American notary public, who need not be a lawyer; *fiduciaire*, who specializes in tax matters; or *conseiller juridique*, who gives general legal advice. These six groups, including some 30,000 persons in 1984, constitute the French *legal*, not *judicial*, profession. The French law student desirous of becoming a judge of the lower or appellate courts or a public prosecutor or member of the Ministry of Justice follows a totally separate path of training, for—as has been explained earlier—the judiciary of France is, in effect, a branch of the government, a part of the civil service.

Training for a Judgeship. Until the judicial reforms of 1958–59 took place, after finishing law school prospective members of the judiciary would initially gather some experience, a sort of apprenticeship, in a law office. From there they usually moved on to a minor office in a local court while awaiting appointment. In the meantime, when they deemed themselves sufficiently qualified, they would take an examination and, if successful, could then anticipate placement in the judicial system. It was common practice to be first assigned to a position as public prosecutor and then gradually effect promotion to a judgeship.

However, since 1959, as a result of a governmental decree designed to broaden and further professionalize their background, experience, and training, all potential applicants for judgeships as well as for legal posts in the executive branch are required to take a national competitive examination in order to attend the post-graduate (post–law school) level École Nationale de la Magistrature (National School for Jurists) for twenty-eight months: the first eleven of these are spent at the school's Bordeaux site in seminars, lectures, extrajudicial training (e.g., forensic medicine and criminology); in the next seventeen months the applicants gain practical experience in Paris and in the provinces. Now having selected their careers, the candidates conclude their education with a special two-month preappointment training period. Those who wish to become matriculants of the École Nationale are selected on the basis of competitive examinations, in both legal subjects and the general liberal arts. Its students, who are paid by the government for attending the École Nationale, must have finished law school and generally, although not always, be under twenty-seven years of age. Graduates are then assigned to one of the courts of first instance, the *tribunaux d'instance*, in accordance with their class

---

145. Pierre Drai, "Les 'Gens' de Justice," *Les Cahiers Français*, 156–57, September–December 1972 (*La Documentation Française*, Paris 1972).

standing—assuming they wish to become judges. But they are also eligible for the *parquet* (the office of the public prosecutor) or for service in the Ministry of Justice. The National School for Jurists was purposely designed to do for the judiciary what the National School of Administration (*École Nationale d'Administration*) has done so well for the upper echelons of the general civil service (and the members of the *Conseil d'État*, [see chapter 3], some of whom at least think of themselves as judges): to create a competent, reputable, and esteemed group of public servants.

In the United States[146] and, to a more modified extent, in England, selection of a lawyer as a judge customarily represents the culmination of a long and quite frequently distinguished career in the law—subject to certain obvious political contingencies in the United States. But in France the judge is chosen from the *judicial profession*, for which he or she is prepared by special schooling and examination[147]—a profession just as medicine, teaching, and the law are. We shall now see it in action on the bench.

146. Early in 1967 the American Bar Association endorsed, and Congress enacted into law that December, President Johnson's plan to establish a Federal Judicial Center in the Administrative Office of the U.S. Courts (see ch. 4, *infra*) with the Chief Justice of the United States as chairman of its independent board (Act of December 20, 1967, 81 Stat. 664). Its purpose is "to further the development and adoption of improved judicial administration in the courts of the United States," as well as to train federal court employees, including federal judges, and to foster programs of continuing education for them. Other tasks of the Center, which is now quite properly regarded as the "research and development arm" of the federal judiciary, include keeping abreast of computer technology, conducting and stimulating research on methods to speed the handling of cases, and reducing case backlogs. In addition to the Chief Justice, the Center's membership consists of two circuit court judges and three district court judges, elected by the Judicial Conference of the United States and the Director of the Administrative Office of the U.S. Courts. The Center had a staff of 122 in late 1991.

147. The education and training of the judges of the Federal Republic of Germany are again different from those discussed in the preceding pages. Whatever legal or judicial career may ultimately be pursued by a future member of the legal profession, the *same* preparation is followed, consisting of a two-stage process. The first is formal university study, lasting approximately five years (the minimum is three and a half in some thirty German universities with faculties of law). At the end of this formal educational stage, the student takes the "first state examination" and, if successful, is designated as *Referendar*, who is now ready to commence the second stage, a two-year period of practical training. During that period, the *Referendar* must work in five areas: in civil courts, in a criminal court or a prosecutor's office, in an administrative office, in a private law office, and in one other approved legal or governmental activity. In each of these five areas the *Referendar* will spend from three to nine months. Regarded now as a temporary civil servant, the *Referendar* receives a government salary. At the end of the two-year practical period the difficult "second state examination" must be taken. Consisting of several days of written parts, it is followed by an oral examination, conducted by four individuals for different segments of the legal profession. If the *Referendar* passes, he or she now becomes an *Assessor*—eligible to enter any one of the five basic career branches of the law: judge (*Richter*); prosecuting attorney *(Staatsanwalt)*—upper-level bureaucratic post; private practice attorney *(Rechtsanwalt)*; private commercial enterprise or financial institution legal position. (*Additional* advanced university training would open the door for a sixth possibility, an academic career.) This disciplined, thorough composite of university education and practical training emphasizes a sameness of experience that has resulted in a highly professionalized career, one that other nations might well ponder. (Much of the above data is drawn from Daniel J. Meador, "German Appellate Judges: Career Patterns and American-English Comparisons," 67 *Judicature* 1 (June–July 1983).

3

Courts Courtrooms and Juries

TYPES OF COURTS: TRIAL AND APPELLATE

Each of the countries discussed in this book has a system of courts designed to serve its own needs and choice. Some have similar features, but no two are truly alike. Speaking broadly, however, each of these systems—and in fact practically every known judicial system in the world—has endeavored to separate the jurisdiction of *trial* (first instance) and *appellate* (review) courts. Some courts do fulfill both functions, but in that event, if justice is to have any meaning at all, they will at the very least separate dockets for each area. This applies, for example, to the English Crown Court and the French *Cour d'Assise*. In a rather limited sense, the Supreme Court of the United States is also constitutionally empowered to exercise jurisdiction in the trial as well as in the appellate area—termed *original* and *appellate* by Article III of the Constitution, in which these designations are found. However, that high tribunal's original jurisdiction docket is usually empty; seldom, if ever, has it exceeded more than a fraction of 1 percent of the volume of cases handled by the Court. The overwhelming number of cases and controversies that reach the highest tribunal in the American judicial hierarchy do so under its appellate jurisdiction. In fact, as will be explained in more detail in chapter 5, the Supreme Court may, except in the instance of litigation involving two or more of the fifty states, share its original jurisdiction with courts below—that is, its original jurisdiction is thus *concurrent* with them—which, in effect, means that seldom, if ever, will the Supreme Court decide such a case in its role of a trial court.

TRIAL COURTS

Trial courts perform the function their title clearly implies: they *try* cases in the first instance, as tribunals of original jurisdiction. Cases commence there because they are statutorily required to do so. More often than not they are also completed there upon the pronouncement of the verdict of guilt or acquittal, which may or may not, depending on organizational requirements and choice, have resulted from a trial by jury. Rather obvious illustrations of trial courts of varied jurisdiction are a U.S. District Court, a Court of Common Pleas in the Commonwealth of Pennsylvania, a French *Tribunal de Grande Instance*, and the Queen's Bench Division of the High Court of Justice of England and Wales.

Again depending somewhat on the law of the land and governmental subdivision concerned, both law and fact are taken into account at the bar of a trial court, and both parties to the litigation (plaintiff as well as defendant) are presumably accorded a full opportunity to present their respective sides of the case or controversy. In common law countries, such as most of the English-speaking lands, a single judge customarily, but by no means always, presides over a trial alone; in statutory law systems, such as those found in most continental European states, normally two or more judges sit *en banc*—sometimes joined by a plurality of laypersons, such as the *rådmän* in Sweden.[1] When a jury sits in a case, the judge *charges* (instructs) it at the conclusion of the presentation of pertinent evidence in the law and in the procedures attendant upon the case. The jury then returns a verdict on completion of its deliberations, which may last from a few hours to several days.

APPELLATE COURTS

The raison d'être of a court of appeals is to provide a forum for review of decisions rendered in trial court. Such appeals are presumably limited to questions of law at issue in the litigation below, but in some circumstances they may also deal with questions of fact, either collaterally or on their own merits. In any event, it is often extremely difficult to separate categorically matters of law and fact, and the final word on such a distinction, if it is crucial to the question of the grant of the petition for review, will necessarily lodge in the appellate tribunal itself. In large measure, this decision depends on the tribunal's statutory authority and the extent and nature of the discretionary review powers given to it. Some appellate courts *must* accept all cases properly presented to them for review, such as the U.S. (Circuit) Court of Appeals (assuming the presence of appropriate jurisdiction), which has no effective discretionary power to decline to accept appellate petitions. Others—for example, the U.S. Supreme Court—possess all but complete *discretionary* authority as to whether or not to accept a case brought for review from below, although in theory there are *some* cases of mandatory review (as will be shown in chapter 5). Still other appellate tribunals, the British House of Lords for one (see chapter 6), have discretionary power to accept or reject cases, but are guided to a considerable degree by certification from the court below (here the Court of Appeal). Courts of appeals are usually multiple-member bodies; commonly, but not inevitably, at least three judges sit *en banc* to hear the appeal without a jury.

1. The trial court jury that found Carl Christer Petterson, the alleged assassin of Sweden's Prime Minister Olof Palme in 1986, guilty 6:2 of murder three years later, consisted of two professional judges and six laypersons. Petterson appealed his conviction to a seven-member appeals court, consisting of four professional jurists and three laypersons: it reversed the lower court and freed the accused.

A well-known appellate court, in addition to those already named, is England and Wales's important Court of Appeal (for civil and criminal cases). That court is empowered to *retry* a case, a departure from the normal role of appellate tribunals—but solely on the ground of fresh evidence having become available, and subject to the court's judgment that a retrial is indeed appropriate in the interests of justice. It thus retries cases but rarely. Indeed, it is only in exceptional cases that fresh evidence is admitted in the Court of Appeal.[2] In order to appeal from the Court of Appeal it is necessary to ask for leave to do so; if this is refused, the appellant may apply to the House of Lords for leave to appeal. In criminal cases this would only be granted if a very significant point of criminal law were raised by the case. The criteria are rather broader in civil cases. The House of Lords Law Lords do not enjoy the all but absolute discretion of the Supreme Court of the United States to reject appeals. The *Cour de Cassation*, at the apex of the regular French judicial system, is another example of a court of appeals. In some appellate courts, such as the criminal division of the English Court of Appeals, appeals may be instituted only by the defendant. In the United States, although the federal government may usually appeal an adverse decision of a trial court on a point of *law*, unless it involves "double jeopardy," it is barred from appealing on a point of *fact*; this means that, in effect, the government cannot appeal an adverse verdict in a criminal proceeding on the basis of the factual evidence presented in court on pain of violating the double jeopardy safeguards of the Fifth Amendment to the U.S. Constitution (although, since a 1981 decision, it is permitted to appeal the length or brevity of certain sentences).[3] Until the Supreme Court so ruled in 1969, that Bill of Rights provision had not automatically applied to the states.[4]

COURTROOM PROCEDURE: GENERAL

There are essentially two methods by which society, through its judicial and legal organs, may approach a member of its body politic accused of an offense—either by presuming his or her innocence until it has effectively succeeded in proving guilt under due process of law, or, in effect if not in theory, by presuming the accused's guilt unless he or she successfully disproves that assumption under similar processes.

2. See *Ladd v. Marshall* 1956 1 W.C.R.1489. This description of the legal system is confined to the formal courts. However, there are also various series of tribunals, such as the Industrial Tribunals, which deal with a whole range of employment cases: race and sex discrimination, redundancy, unfair dismissal, and some other matters. The Appeal Tribunal is called the Employment Appeal Tribunal and has the same standing as a division of the High Court. The Council of Tribunals acts as a proverbial watchdog over these tribunals.

3. Based on a provision contained in the Organized Crime Control Act of 1970 and here upheld 5:4 in an opinion written by Justice Blackmun (*United States v. DiFrancesco*, 449 U.S. 117).

4. *Benton v. Maryland*, 395 U.S. 784. The 1960s had witnessed an increasing number of "applications," "absorptions," or "incorporations" of provisions of the Bill of Rights, by virtue of a series of landmark rulings of the Supreme Court. For a full discussion of this intriguing constitutional problem, see my *Freedom and the Court: Civil Rights and Liberties in the United States*, 5th ed. (New York: Oxford University Press, 1988), ch 3, "The Applicability of the Bill of Rights to the States."

"INNOCENT UNTIL PROVED GUILTY": THE ACCUSATORIAL PROCEDURE

It is a cornerstone of Anglo-Saxon justice that an accused is presumed innocent unless and until proved guilty beyond a reasonable doubt. Few, if any, concepts are more deeply rooted in our traditions. Admittedly, that principle has been violated from time to time, especially during periods of war and other emergencies when an occasional departure from it has been justified on the grounds of constitutionally sanctionable expediency, however distasteful. Thus, writing painfully for a divided (6:3) bench that "hardships are part of war, and war is an aggregation of hardships. . . ." Justice Black, one of the foremost civil libertarians in the life of the Supreme Court of the United States, upheld the compulsory evacuation of 112,000 persons of Japanese ancestry from their homes on the West Coast— among them some 77,000 native-born American citizens, none of whom had been *specifically accused* of disloyalty.[5] On the whole, however, the record of the common law countries, such as Britain and the United States, has been good in this regard. The layperson may quite naturally be quick to adjudge an accused guilty in his or her own mind and be sometimes joined by the press, particularly in America, but the Anglo-Saxon legal profession on both sides of the Atlantic Ocean, and throughout the English-speaking world, has done its best to adhere to the time-honored principle that an accused person is presumed to be innocent until proved otherwise beyond a reasonable doubt by due process of law. As Justice Brennan wrote for the Supreme Court in a decision highly unpopular with Congress and the public at large, in which the Court by a vote of 7:1 reversed the conviction of one Clinton Jencks, a suspected Communist perjurer who had not been permitted to attempt to impeach testimony given to the Federal Bureau of Investigation on the basis of which he had been convicted in the trial court: "[T]he interest of the United States in a criminal prosecution . . . is not that it shall win a case, but that justice shall be done."[6] And, in the words of Justice Frankfurter's majority opinion in a coerced confession case in 1961, "[O]urs is an accusatorial and not an inquisitorial system—a system in which the State must establish guilt by evidence independently and freely secured and may not by coercion prove its charge against an accused out of his own mouth."[7] Of course, this jurisprudential posture applies equally to any civil proceeding, whether or not the government is a party to it. In the gravamen of one of Justice Robert H. Jackson's opinions concerning one attorney's right to compel another to disclose certain papers involved in the litigation concerned, "A *common law* trial is and always should be an adversary proceeding."[8]

Thus, the presumption of the innocence of the accused is transformed into courtroom procedure in the Anglo-Saxon countries. Essential to it are the ancient, basic safeguards inherent in that philosophy of the law, safeguards which, to a greater or lesser degree, are fundamental to the notions of liberty and justice that pervade the political system of the liberal democratic West. Among these are the

---

5. *Korematsu v. United States*, 323 U.S. 214 (1944).
6. *Jencks v. United States*, 353 U.S. 657 (1957), at 668. With some paraphrasing, he in effect was quoting Justice Sutherland's opinion in *Berger v. United States*, 295 U.S. 78 (1935), at 88.
7. *Rogers v. Richmond*, 365 U.S. 534, at 540–41.
8. *Hickman v. Taylor*, 329 U.S. 495, at 516 (1946) (italics supplied).

privilege against compulsory self-incrimination; the right to cross-examine witnesses; the writ of *habeas corpus*—perhaps the most basic right of all—and many others in the same general category.

The Judge's Role. An important feature of the accusatorial type of procedure is that the judge does *not* normally—except as noted later, and in rare instances in order to call forth certain types of evidence, usually of a technical nature—insert himself or herself into the substantive questioning during the trial, although the English trial judge is decidedly more interventionist than the American. Quite naturally, he or she does, indeed must, hand down rulings on various motions, points of order, and other problems that may arise during the course of the trial. The judge is, or certainly is expected to be, in complete charge of courtroom procedure, and as such possesses a considerable residue of what in legal parlance is termed *judicial discretion*. In this connection, that intriguing compound noun demands an application

> enlightened by intelligence and learning, controlled by sound principles of law, of firm courage combined with the calmness of a cool mind, free from partiality, not swayed by sympathy nor warped by prejudice nor moved by any kind of influence save alone the overwhelming passion to do that which is just. . . . [9]

In that discretion, the judge will question a witness only to avert grave injustice, not to advance the case for either side. He or she is not in any sense an active elicitor of truth regarding the testimony presented unless becoming convinced, as did U.S. District Court Judge John J. Sirica in the initial "Watergate" trial, that there were gross prevarications. (His tactics were subsequently challenged in, but upheld by, the U.S. Court of Appeals.[10]) In essence, the judge is an independent arbiter between the state and the individual or between the litigating parties. This is a concept basic to the common law adversary proceeding mentioned by Justice Jackson, a system that "sets the parties fighting." According to Professor Max Radin, one of the giant interpreters of jurisprudential theory and practice, that system has been in vogue since its adoption in Rome in the fourth or fifth century B.C., when—for better or for worse, and quite conceivably the latter—the judge's task changed from determining the truth to the umpiring of a competition.[11] There is little doubt that many, probably most, of today's lawyers would have great difficulty in conceiving of a trial as anything else. It is thus often viewed, not at all inaccurately, as a grim game.

"GUILTY UNTIL PROVED INNOCENT": THE INQUISITORIAL PROCEDURE

In France, to use the most obvious example, a different philosophy regarding the legal process obtains. For while in England and the United States the basic question is whether or not the accused can be proved guilty, in France it is simply to determine "who did it." Not independent arbiters, the French judges are part of

---

9. *Davis v. Boston Elevated Railway*, 235 Mass. 482, at 496–97. Quoted by Felix Frankfurter, *The Case of Sacco and Vanzetti* (Boston: Little, Brown, 1927), pp. 90–91.
10. *Nixon v. Sirica*, 487 F. 2d 700 (1973). See the illuminating article by Robert M. Smith, "T-R-U-T-H or T-R-I-A-L," *The New York Times*, November 4, 1973, p. C37.
11. Max Radin, "The Permanent Problems of the Law," 15 *Cornell Law Quarterly* 10–11 (1929).

the machinery of the state, and courtroom procedure in criminal trials is charac-terized by the *inquisitorial* method, known as the *enquête*. Here the presumption may almost be regarded as implicitly one of guilt, although it is doubtful that any civilized land actually proceeds on such an assumption. Indeed, Radin refers to the notion of presumption of guilt as a "curiously persistent calumny," and views the presumption of innocence as "inherent in the French Declaration of the Rights of Man and the Citizen."[12] Still, so much painstakingly accumulated preliminary investigation by a professional judge—the *juge d'instruction* (examining magis-trate)—has already preceded the courtroom trial that the French judge or judges presiding at the trial may well all but presume the defendant to be guilty of the offense charged. Nonetheless, the presiding judges—who are quite different actors in the judicial process from the *juges d'instruction*—actively, often vehemently and acidly, participate in the courtroom questioning of witnesses as well as of the accused—who, incidentally, cannot invoke the Anglo-Saxon privilege of refusing to take the stand on grounds of possible self-incrimination. Yet had the investigat-ing judge been unable to find any evidence of apparent guilt, the accused would very likely never have been brought to trial regardless of the police's wishes. In a sense, this preliminary "investigation" (the *enquête*) is an advanced, combined form of grand jury investigation and indictment, still so prevalent in the American courts, but with the significant distinction that whereas the *enquête* in France is conducted by professional magistrates the American grand jury is composed entirely of laypersons.

The Juge d'Instruction *and the* Enquête. The office of the *juge d'instruction*—which is not a uniquely French institution—combines the powers of prosecutor and magistrate, but the *juge d'instruction* is not a member of the prosecution per se. His or her function—altered to be a joint three-member venture, rather than a single one, as of 1988, at least in terms of the overall responsibility of whether or not to arrest a suspect under *enquête* investigation—is to determine the truth on behalf of the state, with the aid of the police. Yet the *juge* may commence an investigation only upon notification by a member of the *parquet*, that is, the public prosecutor (*procureur*),[13] who must have been advised of the crime by the police, which will have begun its own investigation. The powers of the *juge d'instruction* are awesome indeed: he or she may call witnesses and question them intensely, ask

12. *The Law and You* (New York: Mentor M34, 1948), p. 99. Prof. Radin took specific and strong excep-tion to my characterization in an interview shortly before his death on June 22, 1950. Going beyond his written statement, he insisted that the presumption of innocence may be regarded as guaranteed by the Declaration in express terms. His view was also propounded by Professor Margherita Rendel of the University of London Institute of Education, a specialist in the French judiciary, in a letter to me, August 8, 1984 and by Dr. Nicole de Montricher of the Observatoire Interregional du Poli-tique, Paris, on February 25, 1992. In a further communication (October 31, 1991), Dr. Rendel called my attention to the specific verbiage of Article 9 of the Declaration of the Rights of Man and of the Citizen, which reads, "Every man being counted innocent "(*Tout homme étant présumé inno-cent. . . .*") until he has been convicted, whenever his arrest becomes indispensable, all vigour more than is necessary to secure his person ought to be severely provided against by law." The reader's verdict of these pages may well vary in analysis and interpretation.

13. The role of *parquet* is roughly similar to that of the U.S. Attorney General and his associates when they act as public prosecutors.

suspects to reenact the alleged crime, open mail and tap telephone wires, even keep people in jail indefinitely (although since 1974, those accused of committing "minor transgressions" can be jailed for only six months without being brought before a *juge*)[14]; the revered Anglo-Saxon institution of the writ of *habeas corpus* is unknown in France. The *juge* may commission experts to investigate and report on special aspects. But perhaps the most potent weapon in the *juge d'instruction's* considerable arsenal is the famous *confrontation de témoins* (confrontation of witnesses), which is unlike anything in Anglo-American legal procedure. When two or more witnesses tell contradictory stories, they are called into the *juge d'instruction's* office for a confrontation. There, under watchful and experienced eyes and ears, and in the presence of a court official who writes down every uttered syllable, each witness is quoted repeatedly, with the other(s) invited to point out "errors" or "discrepancies" in his or her testimony. The questioning of witnesses may of course proceed after the *confrontation*—presumably it also took place before— with a witness's lawyer present in all instances. As a result of the *confrontation*, perjured testimony in criminal cases has been almost eradicated.

When all the evidence, including that obtained by the police on its own, has been procured in a case, and both the defense and prosecution lawyers —the latter headed by the *procureur*—have had access to the complete *dossier*, the *juge d'instruction*, who will usually consult the *procureur*, can now send the case to trial on his or her own authority. Because that is highly unlikely unless he or she is convinced of the presence of guilt, the resultant trial itself turns largely into a public verification of the accumulated record, *including* any previous criminal record. In the event of a statutorily designated *serious* crime, the entire record of the investigation must be reviewed before it is admitted to trial by a *chambre d'accusation*, a judicial body at the appellate court level. (There were 678 *juges d'instruction* in 1988.)

Although the broad powers accorded to the *juge d'instruction* are sometimes criticized even by French legal scholars as being akin to a "star chamber" proceeding, that charge is grossly exaggerated. The *juge d'instruction* operates in a system that simply refuses to concede to the contending parties control over the presentation of evidence—either its submission or its impeachment by cross-examination. During the trial such control becomes the duty of the presiding judge. In the absence of cross-examination, the data procured by the *enquête* are necessary to ensure the accuracy of testimony. However "tough" it may be, the *enquête* is characterized by a patient, painstaking discovery procedure, one that has presumably solved mysteries and eliminated discrepancies in testimony. All the evidence is recorded in the *dossier*, enabling the *juge d'instruction* and the *procureur* to build the case against the accused. But it does more: it permits the presiding judge to conduct the trial free from the many "games" inherent in the adversary process, especially as it is so frequently practiced in American courtrooms.

In its final impact, the French system of the *enquête* would appear to be at least

---

14. According to Articles 64 and 65 of the Penal Code, the police must bring an arrestee before a judge within forty-eight hours, after which the suspect must be taken before a *juge d'instruction* within a further forty-eight hour period.

as effective as the Anglo-American accusational method, in which all the evidence is brought out for the first time, in the manner of a contest, by testimony and cross-examination in open court before trial judge and jury. A grand jury indictment, after all, requires only a *prima facie* case. One may well contend that a criminal trial in a French court is truly a *bona fide* investigation, rather than the characteristic American battle between two opposing platoons of learned counsel—a "sporting theory" battle that, in the words of one legal authority, denotes "a bitter adversary duel" rather than a disinterested investigation—in which the duelers indulge in trickery and fight with "make believe" evidence that often bears scant relation to the facts at issue.[15]

VOX DEI OR VOX POPULI IN ACTION: THE JURIES

There is no doubt that the institution of the jury is at once one of the most fascinating and one of the most controversial aspects of the judicial process and that justice in the West owes a great debt to the jury system. Sundry types of juries exist; but in essence a jury is a group of ordinary citizens of predetermined number whom a duly constituted public official has called together for the purpose of answering a question. Used in Athens as long ago as five or six centuries before the birth of Christ, they appeared in Rome some ten centuries later and in France in the ninth century. The modern Western world traces their origin to the England of some eight hundred years ago, where, in the early stages, they were regarded simply as a body of men to aid the monarch in dispensing justice by attesting to certain facts—that is, the jurors did not determine guilt or innocence but instead were *witnesses*. Whatever their age, juries have been praised and attacked ever since. Although many countries, not necessarily excluding dictatorships, still resort to juries—apart from English-speaking lands they exist today largely in Austria, Belgium, Denmark,[16] Greece, Norway, some Latin American countries, and some Swiss cantons—the institution has clearly declined. This is more true of the *grand jury* than it is of the *trial (petit) jury*, but use of both types has decreased, especially in England and Wales, where the grand jury was abolished by the Administration of Justice (Miscellaneous Provisions) Act of 1933, and where the use of the trial jury in civil cases was seriously curtailed by the same law. Today, the latter jury is used in fewer than 5 percent of all cases in the British Isles (to be exact, juries serve in fewer than 1 percent of *civil* cases, but they *are* used in all "grave" *criminal* ones—approximately 4 percent of the total—in which there is a plea of "not guilty"). In France, of course, the grand jury is not employed at all, because of the role of the *juge d'instruction*. Juries are still generally widely prevalent in the United States. In many of the fifty states, however, juries, notably grand juries, have fallen into at least partial disuse. Indeed, more and more trials everywhere are decided by judges sitting without a jury, sometimes as a result of statutory or constitutional provisions, sometimes by the agreed-upon choice of the parties to the suit. Today it seems almost unbelievable that the courts of Athens in the fifth

15. See James Marshall, *Law and Psychology in Conflict* (Garden City, N.Y.: Doubleday, 1969), p. 7.
16. Iceland, although still essentially adhering to the Danish judicial system, uses *no* juries at all.

century B.C. were composed of a jury only—there was no judge at all! Moreover, the more significant the nature of the case was, the more jurors there were. Thus, Socrates was tried by a panel of 501 in the fourth century B.C., and Alcibiades's trial on charges of treason in the fifth featured 1,501 jurors. These able Attics were drawn from all over the Athenian communities by a complicated but apparently popular lot system.[17]

The foundation of the English jury system is traceable to the French empire under the Carolingian kings. As part of their successful attempt to unite their empire, a procedure called the *inquisition,* or *inquest,* was devised. Carried out by representatives of the monarch, its purpose was to call together various bodies of neighbors to ask questions and explain the sovereign's "immemorial" rights. The Norman conquerors subsequently carried the concept of the inquest to England, where they used it first in the compilation of the 1086 *Domesday Book.*[18] This tome, which listed the ownership of all English land, was compiled from data obtained from royal administrators who gathered neighbors together in various parts of the country and used them as their source of information. This served to establish the right of the state to obtain data from its citizenry, and thus furthered the concept of the jury system (which many insist is thus essentially Anglo-Saxon in origin).

The first true juries were used to discover facts under the various writs of the *Possessory Assizes;* for example, litigant neighbors decided who was dispossessed— which, in most instances, they already knew—and who owned a certain piece of land under the writ of *Novel Disseisin* ("newly dispossessed"). Thus, trial by jury was closely linked with the protection of possessions; indeed, Norman dukes and English kings sometimes specifically granted, both to private persons and to churches, the privilege of having their rights ascertained by this method. However, these juries merely filled a particular need at a particular moment in English history; they were permitted to die out and are hence not the bona fide predecessor of the modern English jury. The latter institution, initially used for civil cases only, was founded under King Henry II in the sixth decade of the twelfth century. Today, it would look strange in its original form, for then it represented what in effect was a combination grand jury and trial jury that enabled the accusing body (the modern *grand* jury) also to pass judgment on the guilt of the accused (the modern *trial* jury). Ultimately these two functions were separated, heralding the now axiomatic difference between them.[19]

---

17. See Charles P. Curtis, *It's Your Law* (Cambridge: Harvard University Press, 1954), p. 102.
18. *Doom* is an Anglo-Saxon word, whereas *law* is derived from the Danish *lov.* The *Domesday (Doomsday) Book* was ordered compiled by William the Conqueror. It provides massive information, covering not only the ownership and rights of use in relation to the land but also the nature of the land, i.e., whether it was agricultural, meadow, forest, etc., and the livestock, cattle, sheep, and pigs, as well as the inhabitants and their status. It provides a very full account of the state of a country during that period.
19. See Frederick G. Kempin, Jr., *Development of the Common Law* (Philadelphia: Lecture Note Fund, University of Pennsylvania, 1959), I-3-2 and I-3-7. For an excellent source on the origin and history of the jury, see F. W. Maitland, *The Constitutional History of England* (Cambridge: Cambridge University Press, 1979 [a reprint of the 1908 ed.]).

THE GRAND JURY

The chief distinction between a grand jury and a petit (trial) jury is that the former does not decide a defendant's innocence or guilt. The grand jury merely determines whether or not, in its considered judgment, sufficient evidence exists or has been brought to its attention to justify a trial on criminal charges. (Grand juries do not ordinarily sit in civil charges.) A trial jury, on the other hand, determines whether to convict or acquit—although a handful of states in the United States (e.g., Virginia, Alabama, Kentucky, Missouri, Oklahoma, and Texas) allow trial juries to determine sentences as well as guilt or innocence; a number of other states authorize jury sentencing only in capital murder cases. Hence a grand jury does not return a verdict; it listens to a bill of evidence presented by the legal representative of the prosecuting authority, who must draw up the formal written accusation, and who almost invariably dominates its deliberations—given the absence of a judge or other "neutral" in the grand jury room. The grand jury then decides whether or not the evidence warrants an *indictment*, also known as a *true bill*, which it returns in approximately ninety-five out of one hundred instances. In effect, an indictment thus charges one or more persons with having committed a crime—be it a felony or misdemeanor. The party called before the grand jury does not actually have an opportunity to give his or her full story; if indicted, that day will come in the courtroom in the event of a trial. Nor may counsel be brought into the jury room (except in a handful of states, including New York), though the respondent may return to an antechamber to consult with counsel. He or she is entitled to know the names of, yet not confront, let alone cross-examine, witnesses that have appeared before the grand jury, but little else—except, of course, the evidence presented at the preliminary hearing before the committing magistrate.[20] There is no *right* to appear before the grand jury; one is invited or ordered to come before it—and there is no right to advance notice of the nature and scope of the crime being investigated. When the grand jury does not find sufficient evidence, it issues what is known as an *ignoramus*, or a *no bill*, in which case the would-be-defendant is not brought to trial.

By most accounts, the institution of the grand jury antedates the Magna Carta of 1215, but its origin is a source of considerable disagreement. Some have claimed to find its traces among the Athenians, but Athenian history, though mentioning the trial jury repeatedly, is quite silent on any body of citizens whose duty it was merely to accuse. The first grand jury, then called a *presenting jury*, was created

---

20. In 1977, the U.S. Supreme Court handed down two rulings by the decisive margins of 9:0 and 7:2, respectively, reaffirming that grand juries are not trial juries and that those who appear before them have but limited procedural rights. In the first case (*United States v. Wong*, 431 U.S. 174), it held that a suspect under investigation, who is indicted for perjury on the basis of statements to a grand jury, may not have the grand jury testimony excluded from evidence at the trial stage simply because of the lack of an effective notice of the Fifth Amendment privilege of remaining silent to avoid self-incrimination. In the second case (*United States v. Washington*, 431 U.S. 181) the Court held that testimony given by a grand jury witness suspected of wrongdoing *could* be used against him in a later prosecution for a substantive criminal offense, even though he had not been warned in advance of his testimony that he was a potential defendant in danger of indictment. Nor are prosecutors obliged to present evidence favorable to defendants (*United States v. Williams*, 1992).

by the Assize of Clarendon in 1166 under King Henry II as an accusatory body composed of twelve knights or twelve "good and lawful men" in each community. It provided

> that inquiry be made in each county and in each hundred, by twelve lawful men of the hundred and four lawful men of every township—who are sworn to say truly whether in their hundred or township there is a man accused of being or notorious as a robber, or a murderer or a thief, or anybody who is a harborer of robbers, or murderers, or thieves, since the king began to reign. And this let the justice and sheriffs inquire, each before himself.

Interestingly enough, this provision was not included to protect the liberties of freemen, but rather to protect the King's interests. By 1352, in the reign of Edward III, the principle that a man's indictors were not to serve both as grand and trial jurors was firmly established. The modern concept of the grand jury dates from 1368, when Edward III impaneled twenty-four men to act as county inquisitorial boards. It was not until three centuries later, however, that a grand jury became truly independent: in two successive cases—*Colledge's Case* and *Earl of Shaftesbury's Case*[21]—it for the first time refused to return an indictment on the grounds of *ignoramus*, that it "knew nothing." According to at least one historian, the immediate reason for the *ignoramus* in one of the cases was that the sheriff and many of the grand jurors were friends of the Earl of Shaftesbury![22]

Information. In England and Wales, where the grand jury was abolished as a result of the aforementioned statute of 1933 after a century of decreasing use, and in many parts of the United States, the fast and easy method of *information* has been adopted in its place. This is a simple and efficacious device whereby the public prosecutor merely submits his charges in the form of an affidavit of evidence, supported by sworn statements, to a court of original jurisdiction.[23] Usually a preliminary hearing has been held before a committing magistrate here, too, and after these brief procedures the accused is ready to stand trial. In France, the *enquête* by a professional judge performs—in addition to collateral duties—the functions of the grand jury. Only in the United States is the common law heritage of that body still relatively popular.

The documented history of the process of information is not nearly as complete as that of the grand jury and the trial jury. However, Blackstone noted in his *Commentaries* that "there can be no doubt that this mode of prosecutions by information filed on record by the King's Attorney General, or by his coroner or master of the crown office in the court of the King's bench . . . is as ancient as the common law itself."[24] Although its usage lagged until the twentieth century, the process did figure prominently in the famous case of Peter Zenger, commonly recalled as a

21. 8 How St. Tr. 550 (1681) and 8 How St. Tr. 759 (1681).

22. George J. Edwards, Jr., *The Grand Jury* (Philadelphia: George T. Bisel, 1906), p. 29.

23. "Iran-Contra" Independent Counsel Lawrence E. Walsh utilized a four-count *information* in the case of Robert McFarlane, one-time national security adviser to President Reagan. McFarlane had waived indictment by the grand jury and, instead, entered a guilty plea before U.S. District Court Judge Aubrey E. Robinson, Jr.

24. IV *Commentaries on the Laws of England* 309, (ch. 23, "Of the Several Modes of Prosecution").

milestone in the battle against press censorship. In 1735 an attempt was made to indict that courageous editor of the *New-York Weekly Journal* for libel against the conduct of the royal government, as personified by Governor William Cosby. When the grand jury—symbolizing its independence in North America—ignored the bill of charges against him, Zenger was then held on the basis of an information filed by the attorney general of the province. After a celebrated trial in which he was ably defended by famed Philadelphia attorney Andrew Hamilton, Zenger was acquitted. It was the English settlers—many of whom came in quest of freedom of conscience as well as economic bounty—who had brought the grand jury with them from their native land, together with all of the other civil rights they had enjoyed there. America's revolutionaries thought of it later as a means to prevent political prosecutions.

Grand Jury Guarantees Today. The opening sentence of the Fifth Amendment to the Constitution of the United States in effect guarantees grand jury action on the *federal* level. Exempting members of the armed forces, it specifies that no person may be held for a "capital, or otherwise infamous crime," unless on a presentment or indictment of a grand jury. But the grand jury provision of the Fifth Amendment is not applicable to the *states*, the Supreme Court of the United States having held repeatedly and consistently that its absence in these constituent parts of the nation does not in itself violate those "fundamental principles of liberty and justice which lie at the base of all our civil and political institutions."[25] Indeed, fewer than one-half of the fifty states—twenty as of late 1991—still retain the grand jury system, and some of these use it solely to investigate crime and corruption among public officials in a limited number of cases, such as homicide and treason. The balance of the states have replaced it with the device of "information," which may also be employed by the federal government in noncapital cases at the district court level, as it was in the 1972–74 Watergate scandals in the instance of one-time counsel to President Nixon, John W. Dean III, and, generally, in civil cases, a famous early example of which is the 1886 case of *Boyd v. United States.*[26]

Today's *federal* grand jury consists of a panel of twenty-three members, chosen at random from registered voters, followed by questioning by a judge and the U.S. Attorney. *State* grand juries range the proverbial gamut from five to seven (Virginia) to twenty-three (Maryland, Massachusetts, New Hampshire, and New Jersey). The selection process varies, but it is usually at random from the local register of voters. The appropriate judge selects the foreman and the deputy. Unlike the trial jury, the grand jury need not be unanimous even at the federal level, but an average minimum of twelve jurors—ranging from a low of five (Virginia) to sixteen (Minnesota) must agree on an indictment or an *ignoramus*; on the federal level, sixteen constitute a quorum and twelve are needed to indict. A grand jury is usually impaneled for a period of three to eighteen months at a time, unless it is discharged

25. *Palko v. Connecticut*, 302 U.S. 319 (1937). See also *Hurtado v. California*, 110 U.S. 516 (1884). The Supreme Court again refused to consider its "incorporation" in 1968 (*Gyuro v. Connecticut*, 393 U.S. 937).
26. 116 U.S. 616.

earlier by the judge to whom it reports,[27] and it is called together (and paid $40.00 a day plus 25¢ a mile at the federal level in 1991) during that time whenever need for its services arises, usually a few days each week. Because no one is being "tried," its proceedings are secret—all witnesses are heard *in camera*—and may not be released to the public. The latter *caveat*, which is protective of both the accused and the grand jurors, is an essential and traditional aspect of the grand jury system, which, unfortunately, has not been demonstrably foolproof.[28] With but a number of exceptions, such as New York since 1978, as already explained, not only are no defense attorneys allowed to be present, not even a judge is permitted *inside* the grand jury chamber. All witnesses thus testify alone. The grand jury normally deliberates with remarkable speed: the prosecutor appears before it; briefly outlines the government's case, and asks for an indictment, almost always succeeding in getting it. A contemporary example is the eight-count indictment of Washington, D.C., Mayor Marion S. Barry, Jr., handed up by a federal grand jury in 1990.

Presentments. Grand juries may do considerably more than determine the sufficiency or lack of evidence submitted to them; they may also, and often do, conduct certain types of public investigations, enabling them to hand up a finding known as a *presentment*. Such an action represents a formal accusation against one or more individuals, made on the grand jury's own motion, calling attention to alleged illegal or improper activities—but *not* including an indictment.[29] The first presentment on record came in England in 1683; it charged certain Whigs, including the Earl of Macclesfield, with disloyal and seditious conduct. The accused brought an action for libel, but the court held for the grand jury, thus establishing the propriety of its report.[30]

---

27. But the "Watergate" grand jury, impaneled by Judge Sirica, served for two and a half years—with Congress's statutorily extending its term from the usual maximum of eighteen months. (It disbanded in a brief ceremony on December 5, 1976, a grand jury that will go down in history as having rendered important service to government and society.)

28. See the troubling account by Ronald J. Ostrow, "Disclosures from Grand Juries Rampant," *The Virginian-Pilot*, October 24, 1980, p. A9.

29. Thus, in early 1975 a Manhattan grand jury, while returning an *ignoramus* on criminal charges in a 1973 hotel collapse, (1) called for a change in New York City's laws to require thorough annual inspections of all buildings constructed before 1901 and (2) urged other steps designed to avert disasters in old buildings, including speedier processing by city agencies of hazardous building violations and jail sentences rather than merely fines where building laws and regulations are violated (*The New York Times*, January 24, 1975, p. M29). In 1980 a special grand jury, looking into an unsolved murder of a policeman in a Harlem mosque in 1972, charged that the New York City Police Department's own investigation of the death "was curtailed in deference to fears of civil unrest in the black community" (*The New York Times*, January 24, 1980, p. B3). None of the police or other public officials who were criticized in the report were named, however, because a state law forbids (see p. 106, *infra*) grand juries to criticize publicly an identified or identifiable person, except under specified "special circumstances." See also the actions recommended in a 1989 report by a grand jury that investigated how lawyer Joel B. Steinberg had managed to obtain the little girl he was subsequently convicted of killing. It called, among other recommendations, for the establishment of a confidential state registry, listing the identity of all mothers contemplating the giving up of their children for adoption as well as the names of all prospective adoptive couples.

30. 10 How St. Tr. 1330 (1684).

Presentments have a habit of stirring up the public as well as the bar, quite frequently giving rise to general anguish. Thus, when a New York grand jury during the "quiz-show" scandals in 1959 on its own initiative handed up a presentment highly critical of the television and radio industry, General Sessions Court Judge Mitchell D. Schweitzer impounded and permanently sealed it. He declared that no grand jury had a right to return a report dealing with the activities or morals of a *private* individual or corporation. A bill designed to embody Judge Schweitzer's position in a law subsequently failed to pass the New York State legislature.[31] However, the matter was reopened tangentially two years thereafter, when the New York State Court of Appeals ruled 4:3 in the *Wood case* that a grand jury has the following choices: return an indictment, dismiss the charge, or remain silent.[32] Because this case involved *public* officials only, the ban seemed to have been extended to all elements of the citizenry. The action in the suit was brought by one James F. Wood, the foreman of a Schenectady county grand jury, to compel Judge Charles M. Hughes of the New York Supreme Court to make public a report the jury had filed on its own motion regarding the county highway department.

The narrowly decided *Wood* case, which overruled a prerogative in existence since 1688, put the role of the grand jury and its problems into closer focus. The majority decision, written by Judge Stanley H. Fuld—and applauded by most of the lawyers' associations of the State of New York—declared that the jury involved made an inquiry that, by its own admission, failed to find "willful and corrupt conduct" by a public official. The phrase quoted came from the statute under which the jury had been impaneled and charged, yet the jurors had simply decided to chart a course of action on their own, one that was both unauthorized and publicly deprecatory of reputations. The dissenters, on the other hand, urged that such action by the grand jury was simply a reaffirmation of a basic American principle under common law and of considerations of ethics in government— namely, that an authorized body of citizens may, indeed must, take appropriate action to counter the suppression or burial of evidence of "tyranny and corruption in public office." In April 1961 Judge Schweitzer augmented his earlier action by expressly warning four grand juries he impaneled that "under no circumstanes" were they to submit a presentment to his court. And the New Jersey State Supreme Court ruled that presentments must not be used to rebuke individuals in the absence of conclusive proof of wrongdoing. On the other hand, Philadelphia Common Pleas Court Judge Joseph E. Gold permitted a 1962 special grand jury charged to investigate municipal corruption in Philadelphia to hand up a stinging presentment in 1963, publicly naming individuals as well as organizations.[33] When, in 1964, the New York legislature finally agreed on a bill to deal with grand jury

---

31. A similar bill, but one which outlawed *all* presentments, had passed in 1946 but was vetoed by Governor Dewey. But note the 1964 statute.
32. *Wood v. Hughes*, 212 N.Y.S. 2d 33 (1961).
33. For details of the presentment, see *The Philadelphia Inquirer*, March 9, 1963, p. 1. The most celebrated "runaway" grand jury is the one that, in 1935, requested Governor Herbert Lehman of New York to supersede the District Attorney, who, the jury said, was trying to hamstring its investigation into organized vice and racketeering. The governor responded by naming Thomas E. Dewey as special prosecutor, and indictments and convictions followed.

presentments, it turned out to be a compromise: under it a grand jury is empowered to criticize a public official or employee, but *only* if its main purpose is to recommend remedial administrative or legislative action. And U.S. District Judge John J. Sirica agonized for two weeks in early 1974 before he forwarded his sealed Watergate Grand Jury's presentment regarding President Nixon's involvement in the case to the U.S. House of Representative's Committee on the Judiciary for its consideration in weighing impeachment charges against the President. No wonder he agonized! It was later revealed that the Grand Jury in that presentment had cited Nixon, 19:0, as an "unindicted co-conspirator." It had refrained from indicting him only because Special Prosecutor Leon Jaworski had expressed the arguable opinion that a President was not indictable—an issue the Supreme Court pointedly refused to address in its momentous 8:0 "tapes" decision against the President late in July 1974 (*United States v. Nixon* and *Nixon and Nixon v. United States*[34]).

Whatever one's judgment of the merits of these developments may be, there is little doubt that although grand juries have traditionally been vested with broad powers to investigate crimes, such powers are not, and cannot be, either unlimited or unbridled. Grand juries are not powers unto themselves, but are essentially lay bodies whose actions are subject to judicial scrutiny and remedial relief. In that role grand juries have existed for such interesting and significant investigatory and stand-by purposes as juvenile delinquency, private adoption procedures, waterfront crime, narcotics traffic, subversive activities, quiz-show manipulation, official and private corruption, "kickbacks," tax evasion (e.g., the Agnew case in 1973), and the Watergate scandals of 1972–74.[35] Necessarily, grand juries became fairly well steeped in their particular area of jurisdiction. And they have often done a good job. The grand jury may well be cumbersome, amateurish, time-consuming, annoying, emotional, and a fifth wheel in the legal process, but on balance—as was well demonstrated by the persistent 1973–74 Watergate grand jury—it does appear to serve as a potentially powerful arm of direct democracy, if one is willing to accept the philosophy of the institution in the first place and if one has faith in the competence and intelligence of one's fellow citizens.[36]

34. 417 U.S. 683. (In that same eventful year the Court ruled in *United States v. Calandra*, 414 U.S. 338 that the contentious judge-made "exclusionary rule does not apply to grand jury proceedings.")
35. In a post-Watergate book-length study of the grand jury, *The Grand Jury: The Use and Abuse of Political Power* (New York: Quadrangle/New York Times Book, 1975), Leroy D. Clark proposes a number of reforms, including more protection for witnesses, making the grand jury independent of the prosecutor's office, and limiting its ability to examine news reporters, scholars, and government officials. See Congressman Joshuah Eilberg (D.-Pa), "A Proposal for Grand Jury Reform," in 60 *Judicature* 8 (March 1977), pp. 390–94, and the critical symposium, "The Grand Jury Under Examination: It Has Fallen on Hard Times," *The New York Times*, June 26, 1977, Sec. 4, p. E20. A highly negative view of grand juries is advanced by Judge Marvin E. Frankel and Gary P. Naftalis in their 1977 book, *The Grand Jury* (New York: Hill and Wang); a favorable one by Richard D. Younger, *The People's Panel: The Story of the Grand Jury* (Providence: Brown University Press, 1963).
36. A basic question that immediately arises in the face of the type of drastic reforms in the grand jury system advanced by such opponents as, for example, Messrs. Clark and Eilberg, is whether, in effect, their projected schema would not transform the grand jury into another layer of trial jury and thus further hinder the concept of a speedy and fair trial. Congressman Eilberg's bill to review grand juries (H.R. 94) died in the 95th Congress. (Its author, accused of a series of criminal infractions involving "kickbacks," was defeated for re-election that fall.)

THE TRIAL OR PETIT JURY

Normally, when the average person or the public press refers to a jury, he or she has the trial or petit jury in mind.[37] As has been indicated, the trial jury has suffered a decline in many parts of the world, but it is still a popular institution. In England and Wales it is employed mainly, but limitedly, in criminal cases, only very sparingly in civil cases; the same is true of France, possibly more so. In Switzerland only ten of the twenty-five cantons permit its use in criminal cases, none in civil cases. Its last important, and evidently secure, stronghold in the Western world is in the United States, where the concept of a trial by a jury of one's peers still thrives.

In England and Wales, where trial by jury, first for civil and later for criminal cases, effectively commenced during the reign of King Henry II (1154–89), the accused is still entitled—with some qualifications—to call for such a trial for all serious crimes and for a very limited number of substantial civil infractions, save in the highest and lowest courts, but the defendant may waive the privilege. Today fewer than 1 percent of all English civil cases are tried by juries—only those involving fraud and libel—and many of the erstwhile English-speaking colonies and possessions have either abolished the right to civil jury trial or have severely restricted it. However, at least in theory, a jury is always impaneled in criminal cases if the accused pleads not guilty to a serious offense. Still, as a result of the aforementioned 1933 statute, the English and Welsh courts have been given such wide discretion whether or not to call a jury even in a criminal case that it is hardly astonishing that jury impaneling has dramatically diminished. Indeed, 90 percent of criminal prosecutions are now decided by a judge or magistrate without a jury. However, if a trial jury is employed in a case, it is composed, as far as possible, of local people, and it consists of twelve persons (except ten to twelve in Coroner's Court). Their verdict of guilt or acquittal was, for seven hundred years, required to be unanimous, a stipulation that was discarded when Parliament enacted the Criminal Justice Act of 1967 and 1971 permitting trial juries to convict by 10:2, 10:1, or 9:1.[38] The trial jury declined in England and Wales for a number of reasons, among which the more important are that (1) a judge sitting alone was believed to be able to perform at least as well as, and usually better than, the jury; (2) a speedy trial was desired; (3) juries tended to award very high damages in personal injury cases; and (4) the litigants rather than Her Majesty's government pay the jurors' fees.

The French Republic resorts to jury trials solely at the level of the assizes, the courts of original jurisdiction for serious crimes. Trial by jury has no deep roots in France. Indeed, although it once did exist as part of customary procedure in some parts of the country in the fifteenth century, it disappeared during the reign of Charles VII, and was not reimported from England until the Revolution. Today,

37. In some areas, such as in parts of Pennsylvania, it is still known as the *traverse* jury, a term deriving from medieval days when Norman French was beginning to displace Latin as the official language of the Court of England.
38. In Scotland, where juries may consist of fifteen persons in some cases, a simple majority of 8:7 suffices to convict. There juries may also render a verdict of "not proven."

it consists of nine local *citoyens* (who sit with one or more judges): there is no una-nimity requirement, and frequently the verdict is rendered by a simple majority vote. The French have no great fondness for the jury system, and their adherence to the inquisitorial mode in the judicial process leaves little or no genuine purpose for a trial jury per se. In any event, they generally view the jury as an instrument designed to confuse the issues in a case.

But the United States, where a total of approximately 3 million jurors[39] serve in some 300,000 cases each year in the approximately 3,000 jury-employing federal and state courts, has remained broadly faithful to the concept of a trial by jury— although only one in ten of the cases on court calendars actually reaches the jury stage. Still, 85 percent of the world's criminal jury trials take place here. This is necessarily true at the level of the *federal* courts because of the express require-ments of the Sixth and Seventh Amendments to the Constitution. The Sixth ascer-tains a trial by jury in *all* federal criminal cases; the Seventh does the same for all civil cases in which the value of the controversy exceeds the sum of $20, which today means in practically every instance. Although all fifty states had also pro-vided for at least *some* type of trial by jury, the specific mandating guarantees of the federal Bill of Rights to a trial by jury did not automatically apply to them until the Supreme Court, in 1968, ruled that this procedural right was "implicit in the concept of ordered liberty."[40] The highest tribunal had long insisted that a defen-dant in a state proceeding be given a *fair trial*, on pain of a violation of the Four-teenth Amendment's due process of law and/or equal protection of the laws clauses. Among the several state practices affecting juries that had *inter alia* been held thus to constitute an *unfair* trial, are *systematic* exclusion of blacks from juries[41] and the labeling of black jurors with brown, and white jurors with white, selection tickets.[42]

However, because each of the states may prescribe its own brand of jury system, a variety of practices exists, and many of these would be unconstitutional if prac-ticed by the federal authorities. Thus, some states grant no jury trials in *civil* cases at all, others do in just a handful. The frequency of jury trials may thus vary widely—from only 11 per 100,000 accused in Wisconsin to 153 per 100,000 in the District of Columbia in 1983.[43] At the federal level, it is generally possible to *waive* a trial by jury, *provided* that common consent of the parties to the suit and of the

39. *Juror* is Latin for "to swear." A total of 667,264 *federal* jurors served in 1983–84.
40. *Duncan v. Louisiana*, 391 U.S. 145. But the Court ruled in 1970 that it does not reach crimes clas-sified by *states* as "misdemeanors" *if* the penalty therefore does *not* exceed six months' incarceration (*Baldwin v. Connecticut*, 399 U.S. 66).
41. *Norris v. Alabama*, 294 U.S. 587 (1935); *Hill v. Texas*, 316 U.S. 400 (1942); *Patton v. Mississippi*, 332 U.S. 463 (1947); *Whitus v. Georgia*, 385 U.S. 545 (1967).
42. *Avery v. Georgia*, 345 U.S. 559 (1953). On the other hand, if nonwhites in an assembled jury pool are excluded from jury duty on the basis of the use of intelligence tests administered equitably to all members in the pool, such exclusion is not *ipso facto* a prima facie denial of due process (see *Don-aldson v. California*, 404 U.S. 968, 1971, *certiorari* denied). Nor is the systematic exclusion of young people such a denial (*Ross v. United States*, 410 U.S. 990, 1973).
43. For statistics, see issues of the *State Court Journal*.

judge assigned to the case is obtained,[44] but many states will not permit such a waiver, especially in certain criminal cases.[45] Other significant procedural differences between federal and state practices pertain to the *size* of juries and the requirement of *unanimity*. As a result of a series of significant Supreme Court decisions in the 1960s and 1970s, the following constitutional posture has emerged: *Federal* juries must still render *unanimous verdicts* in both *civil*[46] and *criminal* cases, but the English common law tradition of having twelve jurors is no longer constitutionally required in *civil* cases;[47] indeed, all but nine of the ninety-four federal trial courts either permitted[48] six-member juries in *civil* cases or even required them as of 1984—a mere 2.9 percent of such cases having been tried by juries.[49] *State* juries were long ago deemed not to be controlled by the federal unanimity jury rule,[50] and the states had adopted a host of diverse numerical requirements in both civil *and* criminal cases which repeatedly passed judicial muster. They were again exempted from the rule by two 1972 Court decisions that specifically sanctioned a 10:2 Oregon criminal jury verdict[51] and a 9:3 Louisiana one,[52] with Justice White's opinion for the 5:4 majority holding that, in *noncapital* cases such as these, nonunanimous rulings could equally well serve "the interests of the defendant in having the judgment of his peers interposed between himself and the officers of the state who prosecute and judge him. . . ."[53] (But the Court hedged as to the precise cutoff point at which even lower numerical nonunanimity would constitute a denial of due process of law.) Juries of fewer than twelve on the state level had

---

44. In 1965, in *Singer v. United States*, 380 U.S. 24, the Supreme Court ruled unanimously that a defendant in a federal trial does *not* have a constitutional right to insist on trial by a judge rather than by a jury if the government insists on a jury.

45. According to the seminal study by Harry Kalven, Jr., and Hans Zeisel, *The American Jury* (Boston: Little, Brown, 1966), regional custom apparently determines whether or not a defendant will waive jury trial, with the percentage of jury waivers varying from a high of 79 percent in Wisconsin to 3 percent in the District of Columbia and to 0 percent in Montana. Also significant is the category of crime: jury waiver occurs in 70 percent of drug violation cases (in which the judge is presumed to be less emotionally involved than lay jurors), whereas the jury is waived in only 13 percent of homicide cases (pp. 20–26).

46. But note the 9:3 verdict permitted by U.S. District Judge Don J. Young in the "Kent State Victims" civil damage suit (*Krause and Scheuer, et al v. Rhodes and White, et al*, decided August 27, 1975). Apparently, that verdict was allowed because of a Rule 48 stipulation by both parties, given the nature of the case *(civil)* and the Court's approval of the use of six-member civil case juries in *Colgrove* (n. 47, *infra*).

47. *Colgrove v. Battin*, 413 U.S. 149 (1973).

48. *Reports* of the Administrative Office of the U.S. Court for 1979ff.

49. E.g., the U.S. District Court for the Southern District of New York, which mandated the six-member civil jury for all of its twenty-seven judges as of August 1, 1973 (see *The New York Times*, July 22, 1973, p. 16).

50. *Minneapolis & St. Louis Railroad Co. v. Bombolis*, 241 U.S. 211 (1916). In 1898 the Court had declared a constitutionally required standard of twelve-member *federal* juries in *Thompson v. Utah*, 170 U.S. 343, when Utah was still a federal territory. And just one year later it extended that requirement to federal civil trials as well (*Capital Traction Co. v. Hof*, 174 U.S. 1).

51. *Apodaca v. Oregon*, 406 U.S. 404 (1972). In murder cases, however, all twelve members must vote for conviction.

52. *Johnson v. Louisiana*, 406 U.S. 356 (1972).

53. *Apodaca v. Oregon*, loc. cit., at 411.

been Court-approved for some time—even as small a panel as Florida's six-member criminal trial jury,[54] one of which convicted, and another subsequently acquitted, Clarence Earl Gideon in his celebrated constitutional battle regarding the incorporation of the right to counsel in all criminal cases.[55] Today, approximately 80 percent of the states sanction jury verdicts by 75 percent of the jurors in civil cases, with 20 percent of the states extending this form of split verdict also to noncapital criminal cases. Three-fourths of the states now authorize various trials with juries of fewer than twelve members, often six,[56] but the Court specifically interdicted the use of juries of *fewer than six* in criminal cases in a unanimous, albeit badly split five-opinion, 1978 decision, striking down the use of *five-member* juries even if unanimous, in Georgia and in 1979 of a 5:1 split in a six-member Louisiana one.[57] The governing question concerning these state practices is not one of comparison or method but the essential one of whether or not the defendant received a fair trial under conditions of due process of law.

SELECTION AND IMPANELING OF JURIES

Since the enactment by Congress of the Jury Selection and Service Act of 1968—largely the work of Senator Joseph D. Tydings (D.-Md) and U.S. Court of Appeals Judge Irving R. Kaufman—federal grand and petit juries in the United States must be drawn by lot [58] from the "voter registration lists or the lists of actual voters" of the political subdivision's citizens by the jury clerk, who uses these names to form

---

54. *Williams v. Florida*, 399 U.S. 78 (1970). Justice White here again expressed his conviction—one he altered in 1978, however—that size has no bearing on the essential feature of a jury. He viewed the latter as the "interposition between the accused and the accuser of the common sense judgment of a group of laymen, and in the community participation and shared responsibility that results from that group's determination of guilt or innocence" (at 100). For a tentative conclusion that six-member juries convict *fewer* defendants than twelve-member juries, see 61 *Judicature* (September 1977), pp. 225–29; for one finding "no significant differences in conviction/acquittal rates or proportion of hung juries," see 62 *Judicature* (September 1978), pp. 153–54. But an extensive 1980 study of 110 juries, composed of nearly one thousand jurors, indicated that size does indeed affect a jury's behavior. See Robert T. Roper, "Jury Size and Verdict Consistency: 'A Line Has to Be Drawn Somewhere?'" 14 *Law and Society Review* (Summer 1980). Thus, he proves, for example, that twelve-member juries "hang" significantly more often than do smaller juries.
55. *Gideon v. Wainwright*, 372 U.S. 335 (1963). In 1976 the Connecticut Supreme Court upheld the constitutionality of a law reducing the size of Connecticut juries from twelve to six for all criminal cases except murder (*The New York Times*, August 11, 1976, p. C27). New Jersey has *mandated* six-member civil case juries unless the judge requests twelve members.
56. Why twelve was initially selected for a jury's composition remains a mystery. However, that number has been mathematically significant ever since the days of the Sumerians, 5000 B.C., and also has religious significance: twelve signs of the Zodiac, twelve tribes of Israel, twelve Christian apostles.
57. *Ballew v. Georgia*, 435 U.S. 223, and *Burch v. Louisiana*, 441 U.S. 130, respectively.
58. The statute speaks of "a master jury wheel (or a device similar in purpose and function)." In its broad statement of policy the statute proclaims: "It is the policy of the United States that all litigants in federal courts entitled to trial by jury shall have the right to grand and petit juries selected at random from a fair cross section of the community in the district or division wherein the court convenes" (28 U.S.C. 1861).

a jury panel or *venire*.[59] The statute, long requested by both public and private observers, became all but a foregone conclusion when a federal court of appeals ruled that a defendant's rights had been violated precisely because his jury had not been selected from "a cross section" of the community,[60] but under the so-called key man system.

That key man system, widely used until 1968 on the federal as well as the state level, still obtains in some of the latter jurisdictions, but it is dying out. Under it, the jury clerk asks "upstanding" citizens of the community to submit names of individuals whom *they* believe to be potentially qualified jurors, with the panel ultimately being selected by the clerk from these lists. A time-honored practice, it nonetheless lends itself to the possibility of considerable mischief as well as being unrepresentative, and the day may be close when the states too will either abandon it voluntarily or do so as a result of court "due process" requirements. The cross-section mandate requirement was buttressed with the enactment of the Jury Selection and Service Act of 1975. But neither by law nor by the terms of the Constitution does a jury need to be a microcosm of the larger community. *Systematic* exclusion is forbidden, but proportional representation is not required.

In England and Wales juries are selected by the sheriff from a list of householders compiled by local authorities; in France they are chosen from departmental lists of citizens of thirty years of age and over who possess all civic and political rights. In Switzerland juries sitting with the Criminal Chamber of the Federal Tribunal to try certain criminal cases are *elected* by the people for six-year terms on the basis of 1 juror for each 3,000 inhabitants. In Sweden they are elected by county councils for four-year periods. Happily, in more and more jurisdictions, notably in the United States, automation has entered, with electronic data-processing systems increasingly taking over the task of clerks who pick names from mahogany drums or glass jars to choose the jurors to be called for service, thus reducing to an average of twenty minutes a process that formerly took two days. Theoretically, any citizen of voting age is eligible for jury duty and may expect a call, unless he or she has served for more than a year in prison on a criminal charge and has not been pardoned for that offense.[61] This limiting proviso is statutorily applicable only to the

---

59. Two challenges to the confining of the lists to registered voters had been turned aside by the Court by 1975 (*Thompson v. Sheppard*, 420 U.S. 984 and *Bowman v. Presiding Judge of Superior Court*, 421 U.S. 1011, both *certiorari* denied). For a suggestion to combine voters and drivers as jury source lists, see Charles H. Logan and George F. Cole, "Reducing Bias in a Jury Source List by Combining Voters and Drivers," 67 *Judicature* (August 1983), pp. 87–94.

60. *Scott v. Walker*, 358 F.2d 561 (1966). Because he viewed the prospective jury list in Erie County, N.Y. (Buffalo), to be less than a true cross section, State Supreme Court Justice Edward Brovenzano discharged the entire list of 110,000 for the county in July 1974 (*The New York Times*, July 4, 1974, p. 1). The "cross-section" requirement was embraced by the Supreme Court in 1946 in *Thiel v. Southern Pacific Co.*, 329 U.S. 217. In 1985 Hamptom County, South Carolina, still resorted to a quaintly antique system in which a child under ten or a blind person sits in court and pulls the names of potential jurors from a metal box.

61. The official qualifications for *federal* jurors, which are similar to those in the several states, are (1) U.S. citizenship—aliens are ineligible, (2) attainment of at least eighteen years of age, (3) one year's residence in the district, (4) no prior conviction punishable for more than one year unless pardoned or amnestied, (5) ability to read, write, and understand English, and (6) no mental or physical disabilities that would hamper efficient jury service. In a 1976 holding the Court unanimously affirmed the exclusion of aliens from federal and/or state juries (*Perkins v. Smith*, 426 U.S. 913).

federal government, but most of the fifty states now have the same, or at least a similar, requirement. Although everyone else of voting age may thus expect to get a jury call at one time or another, not only is it relatively easy to avoid jury duty—which, incidentally, is one of the chief criticisms leveled against the jury system—but entire segments of the body politic are exempt either by permissible judicial rule, by law, or by custom. Among the occupational groups generally exempt in the vast majority of jurisdictions, especially in the United States, are professionals such as lawyers (a jury composed of arguing and advocating lawyers would indeed be an interesting, if hardly an edifying, experience!), licensed physicians and dentists (too busy to serve), members of the armed forces (often absent from the community), officials of all three branches of government (possible conflict of interest), police officers and fire fighters (indispensable professionally), clergy (a jury must deliberate, not pray), teachers (essential occupation). Other busy employed people can avoid jury service by submitting affidavits of indispensability from employers. Still others, such as nursing mothers and those with a large family of young children,[62] will normally have to do little more than write a letter to the court concerned to be excused by the judge.[63] But failure to do at least that much may conceivably result in a citation for contempt of court, which occurred in the case of one thirty-seven-year-old Waterloo, Iowa, mother who repeatedly flouted requests to serve on a criminal trial jury and finally found herself sentenced to be incarcerated for six months in Rockwell City Women's Reformatory, for criminal contempt of court.[64] Moreover, the U.S. Supreme Court ruled 8:1 in 1975 that *women* as a class can no longer be excluded or be given *automatic* exemption based *solely* on sex if the consequence is that criminal jury *venires* are almost totally male.[65]

If none of the reasons cited is acceptable to the court as a bona fide excuse, an irresponsible citizen can, of course, still evade this civic duty by confessing to one of the many otherwise validly disqualifying factors in jury impaneling (which, the

62. In 1975 the Supreme Court upheld a Florida law that, *on their request,* exempts pregnant women and mothers of children under eighteen (*Marshall v. Gavin,* 420 U.S. 907).
63. Under new rules adopted following the enactment of the 1968 statute, the U.S. District Court for the Southern District of New York (Manhattan) now excuses the following *on written request:* lawyers; persons over 70; actively engaged ministers and members of religious orders; women with children under ten; practicing physicians, dentists, and registered nurses; persons who have served on juries thirty days in the preceding two years; sole proprietors of businesses who have no help; teachers, supervisors, or administrators of schools; and anyone living more than fifty miles from the Foley Square Court House.
64. *The Philadelphia Inquirer,* May 18, 1952, p. 13. However, her conviction was reversed on procedural grounds on appeal by the Iowa Supreme Court (*Watson v. Charlton,* 50 N.W. 2d 605).
65. The White-authored ruling—which overturned a fourteen-year-old decision that had allowed states to excuse women from jury duty automatically *unless* they went to the courthouse and *volunteered* for such duty (*Hoyt v. Florida,* 368 U.S. 57)—struck down, with Justice Rehnquist in lone dissent, Louisiana's jury law that was a carbon copy of Florida's in terms of its "volunteer only" rule for women (*Taylor v. Louisiana,* 419 U.S. 522). Actually, all other states, including Florida, had repealed such laws in the interim between the *Hoyt* and *Taylor* decisions. However, the Court declined to make *Taylor* retroactive (*Daniel v. Louisiana,* 420 U.S. 31 [1975]). Early in 1979, with Justice Rehnquist again the sole dissenter, it went beyond the *Taylor* holding by ruling 8:1 that a state law allowing women to claim an automatic exemption from jury duty had deprived a murder defendant of his constitutional right to be tried by a jury composed of a cross section of the community (*Duren v. Missouri,* 439 U.S. 357). But see n. 62, *supra.*

Supreme Court ruled 9:0 in 1984, must be open to the public and the press).[66] Among these are confession of prejudice for or against one of the litigants (although in England there is no right to *examine* a jury for prejudice and, since a 1973 rule established by the Lord Chief Justice, jurors are not to be excused on such "general grounds" as race, religion, political beliefs, or occupation),[67] acquaintance with either party to the suit, however slight, allegation of sympathy with or opposition to certain pertinent philosophies of life involved in the case, no matter how tangentially, and so forth. However, only those who are really willing and able to serve will normally do so in the long run. On the other hand, in 1968 the Supreme Court ruled 6:3 that persons expressing general conscientious scruples against the death penalty could no longer *automatically* get off, or be kept off, juries in capital cases; consequently, no death sentence could stand if it had been propounded by a jury *purged* of all persons who said they opposed the death penalty or had conscientious scruples against it—absent a juror's expression of views that would "prevent or substantially impair the performance of his duties as a juror in accordance with his instructions or oath."[68]

Challenges. Jurors may naturally be removed from a panel for any of the preceding reasons or a myriad of others by the procedure of appropriate *challenges* (first given credence by Roman tribunals during the Empire's heyday, when one was allowed to object to a jury's trying any particular case), which are granted to both the defense and the prosecution as a matter of regular courtroom procedure in England and France as well as the United States, although the procedure is much more limited in the former two than in the last. Federal judges in the United States have clear authority to conduct all jury qualification questioning, as do the judges in one-half of the states, although judges may, and usually do, share that authority with the trial attorneys. In the other half of the states, however, the latter dominate the process.

Most frequently employed in the United States, challenges are essentially of two types, *peremptory* and *for cause*. They occur at the *voir dire* level of jury selection[69] and play a major role in the adversary process. A peremptory challenge entitles either party to the suit to request the removal of a would-be juror by *fiat*—

---

66. *Press Enterprise Co. v. Superior Court of California*, 52 LW 4113.

67. See John Baldwin and Michael McConville, "Does the Composition of an English Jury Affect Its Verdict?," 64 *Judicature* 3 (September 1980), p. 137. The authors demonstrate convincingly that English juries are not representative of the whole community, but that their verdicts generally do *not* reflect any imbalance (ibid., pp. 133ff.).

68. *Witherspoon v. Illinois*, 391, U.S. 510. While the *Witherspoon* holding was expanded in 1976 to cover even "just" exclusion (*Davis v. Georgia*, 429 U.S. 122) it was markedly narrowed in 1985 when the Court ruled 7:2 that a juror may be excluded if he expresses views that would "prevent or substantially impair the performance of his duties as a juror. . . ." (*Wainwright v. Witt*, 53 LW 4108). It was narrowed further in 1986 when the Court ruled 6:3 that "*committed*" opponents of the death penalty may indeed be "for cause" barred from juries in capital cases, regardless of whether or not this increases the likelihood of conviction (*Lockhart v. McCree*, 474 U.S. 816).

69. See Arthur J. Stanley, Jr., and Robert G. Gegam, "Who Should Conduct Voir Dire?," 61 *Judicature* 2 (August 1977), pp. 70–78. (Examination of jurors is governed by Rules 47(a) and 24(b) of the Federal Rules of Civil and Criminal Procedure, respectively, which are subject to amendment by the Supreme Court.)

no reason need be given: the mere request, whatever the motivation, will be honored. As the Supreme Court held in 1965, in a 6:3 decision written by Justice White that upheld, against equal protection challenges, the peremptory striking by the prosecution of all blacks remaining on the petit jury venire (after two had been excused "for cause"): "[T]he essential nature of the peremptory challenge is that it is one exercised without a reason stated, without inquiry, and without being subject to the court's control."[70] It is a critical, often crucial element in the lawyer's strategy, one that was consistently upheld without exceptions at the *federal* level (again in 1983). However, in 1986 prosecutorial racial striking was declared unconstitutional by the Court in a dramatic 7:2 overturning of its erstwhile holdings as a violation of the equal protection of the laws clause of the Fourteenth Amendment, as the author of the 1965 ruling, Justice White, concurred in Justice Powell's majority opinion: "The equal protection clause," wrote the latter, "forbids the prosecutor to challenge potential jurors solely on account of their race on the assumption that black jurors as a group will be unable impartially to consider the state's case against a black defendant."[71] In 1988, on the other hand, the Court denied review (7:2) in a case in which the *defense* had unsuccessfully pleaded for the same privilege as that accorded the *prosecution* one year earlier.[72] Yet when it addressed the merits involving white defendants in 1991, it ruled 7:2 that whites charged with crimes had the same right as black defendants had been accorded in the 1986 *Batson* decision.[73] But it must be noted that the justices had held in 1990, in a 5:4 opinion by Justice Scalia, that the Sixth Amendment requires "not a representative jury but an impartial jury," thereby upholding a prosecutor's right in a criminal case involving white defendants to utilize peremptory challenges to remove the only two potential jurors who were black from the panel at the *voir dire* stage.[74] At last the Court seemed to move toward coming full cycle in 1991 when it ruled 6:3, speaking through Justice Kennedy, that at least in *civil* cases potential jurors may not be excluded because of their race, *by either the prosecution or the defense.*[75]

At the *state* level (e.g., New York, California, Illinois, Massachusetts, and New

---

70. *Swain v. Alabama*, 380 U.S. 202, at 220. The Court reconfirmed the constitutionality of the practice of "group" or "class" striking by way of challenges in the instances of two 1975 decisions upholding the exclusion of women from a man's trial jury (*Lawson v. Edwards* and *Quick v. Harris*, 420 U.S. 907). The cases were decided after *Taylor v. Louisiana, supra,* n. 59. The 1983 case noted in the following text was *McCrary v. Abrams*, 461 U.S. 961, in which the Court (7:2) pointedly refused to reexamine its 1965 *Swain* decision. The two dissenters were Justices Brennan and Marshall. Justices Blackmun, Powell, and Stevens wrote separate concurring opinions supporting the states' prerogatives of "serving as laboratories" and backing the Court's vote to deny review in the case.

71. *Batson v. Kentucky*, 476 U.S. 79. Justice Marshall also penned a concurring opinion, pleading for a *total* ban on peremptory challenges. Justices Brennan, Blackmun, Stevens, and O'Connor joined in Justice Powell's controlling opinion, whereas Chief Justice Burger and Justice Rehnquist wrote separate dissenting opinions, each joining the other's. See David F. Breck, "Peremptory Strikes after *Batson v. Kentucky,*" *Journal of The American Bar Association*, April 1, 1988, pp. 54ff.

72. *Alabama v. Cox*, 488 U.S. 1018.

73. *Powers v. Ohio*, 59 LW 4268.

74. *Holland v. Illinois*, 58 LW 4162.

75. *Edmonson v. Leesville Concrete Co.*, 59 LW 4574. The Court extended *Batson* to *criminal* defendants' cases as well in 1992 (*Georgia v. McCollum*, 60 LW 4574).

Mexico) appellate courts had already begun approximately a decade earlier to dis-allow prosecutors' use of peremptory challenges to exclude arbitrarily all members of a race or other identifiable class from a jury.[76] What *is* normally subject to court control, however, is the *number* of these challenges granted—unless it has been predetermined by statute, as it often is. It is customary to permit the defense more peremptory challenges than the prosecution, but this is not inevitably the case. Thus, in federal trial courts, one to three such challenges per juror are customarily permitted each side, depending on the nature of the offense, and usually twenty to each side in capital offenses. Yet in the 1974 Mitchell–Stans trial for perjury, conspiracy, and obstruction of justice, which resulted in the defendants' acquittal, U.S. District Court Judge Lee P. Gagliardi, citing "acute pre-trial publicity," assigned twenty peremptory challenges to the defense but only eight to the pros-ecution. In Pennsylvania, the usual rule for murder cases is twenty for the defense and twenty for the prosecution. In the sensational trial of Richard Speck, who was ultimately convicted of the murder of eight student nurses in Chicago in 1966, Illinois Judge Herbert C. Paschen, endeavoring to be scrupulously fair and guard-ing against reversals on appeal, permitted the unprecedented total of 320 peremp-tory challenges! Each side was permitted twenty for *each* of the eight murder charges—and a grand total of 2,500 jurors were questioned in a *voir dire* proceed-ing that ran for twenty-seven days.[77] In the notorious Pontiac Ten trial, involving the killing of three prison guards in the Pontiac, Michigan, state prison riot of 1978, each side was given 120 peremptory challenges. (The Ten were all jury acquitted.) On the other hand, in the famed Pentagon Papers (espionage, theft, and conspir-acy) federal trial of Dr. Daniel Ellsberg and Anthony J. Russo in 1973, the defense was allowed a total of fourteen such challenges, the prosecution only six.

When a panelist is challenged for *cause*, however, the challenger must be in a position to advance a bona fide reason for his or her demand for the disqualification, and it will have to be one sufficiently related to the substantive or procedural aspects of the litigation involved in order to be acceptable in the eyes of the court. There are no limits to the *number* of challenges for cause, but, to point to one often-raised *quaere*, there is emphatically no constitutional or legal right to an all-black or all-white or all-male or all-female jury.

These challenges, whose procedures are regulated by the court concerned, fre-quently delay the impaneling of the trial jury for days, occasionally even for weeks. For instance, it took four months to select the twelve-member jury in the 1971 Connecticut murder trial of Bobby G. Seale—with a total of 1,550 jurors being called to the venire, 1,035 of whom were questioned.[78] And the arduous and deli-cate task of selecting a jury to sit in the trial of the eleven top-echelon members of the Communist Party-U.S.A. in Judge Harold Medina's U.S. District Court for the Southern District of New York in 1949 consumed a total of six weeks. Because of

76. See Angel Castillo, "Courts Using State Constitutions to Bar Biased Selections of Juries," *The New York Times*, March 9, 1981, p. B9.
77. See the accounts in *Time Magazine*, March 24 and April 7, 1967.
78. *The New York Times*, March 12, 1971, p. 43.

the nature of the charges of the case, which ultimately resulted in the conviction of all eleven (although with varying sentences),[79] both defense and prosecution were painstaking in their questioning of the prospective jurors, many of whom managed to extricate themselves from serving by simply acknowledging that they could not possibly have an open mind regarding the alleged guilt of the accused. Judge Gerrard L. Goettel impaneled 200 jury candidates in the sensational trial of the controversial South Korean evangelist Sun Myung Moon in federal district court in 1982. And U.S. District Court Judge Gerhard Gesell spent weeks until he succeeded in seating a panel of nine women and three men, all black, from 210 summoned potential jurors in the highly publicized trial of embattled national security official Oliver L. North in 1989.[80]

It is not astonishing, therefore, that jury selection has become not only an art but a game, albeit a grim one—one that often takes longer than the trial itself—in which defense and prosecution frequently go to extreme lengths to jockey for a jury panel favorable to their side. Thus, in 1972 defense attorneys employed psychologists and handwriting analysts to help select the Angela Davis jury which acquitted her. A team of social scientists went to Harrisburg, Pennsylvania, three months prior to the 1973 trial of Father Philip Berrigan—accused of plotting to raid draft boards, blow up heating tunnels in Washington, D.C., and kidnap Dr. Henry A. Kissinger—to help the defense in its efforts to get a "sympathetic" jury impaneled from the final venire of forty-six prospective jurors. Their suggested "ideal" was "a female Democrat with no religious preference and a white collar or skilled blue collar job."[81] The jury that tried Dr. Carl Coppolino for murder in New Jersey in 1966 was selected from a panel of 275 that had been the object of the closest professional scrutiny and weeks-long attention of experienced Asbury Park lawyer Joe Mattice, who had been hired by the crack defense attorney, F. Lee Bailey, "to pick the jury" that would acquit. It did.[82] A "jury and trial consultant," Houston-based Cathy E. Bennett—one of now more than one hundred professionals rendering similar services across the country—orchestrated the selection of the jury that stunned prosecutors and the public by declaring millionaire former automaker John Z. DeLorean not guilty of drug conspiracy charges, despite the patently demonstrable evidence of five hours of videotape of DeLorean discussing a cocaine deal with undercover agents. Ms. Bennett coached defense attorneys in their ultimately successful quest of attaining a panel of jurors of well-educated, talented, sensitive professionals, who responded sympathetically to the defense's

79. *United States v. Dennis*, 72 F. Supp. 417 (1949).
80. *The Washington Post*, March 22, 1982, p. A5, and ibid., February 10 and 21, pp. A4 and A9, respectively.
81. After some sixty hours of deliberations, the jury—nine women and three men—reported itself "hopelessly deadlocked" on all of the charges and found Father Berrigan and Sister Elizabeth McAllister guilty simply of "letter smuggling" (*The Philadelphia Bulletin*, May 6, 1973, pp. 10ff). For an account of the operation of the team of social scientists at work here (and in two other famous cases), see *Time* Magazine, January 28, 1974, p. 60, and "Recipe for a Jury," *Psychology Today*, May 1977, p. 40.
82. See the colorful report by Joe McGinnis in *The Philadelphia Inquirer*, December 19, 1966, p. 29.

hard-hitting allegations of government entrapment.[83] On the other hand, the jury that found would-be Reagan assassin John Hinckley "not guilty by reason of insanity" consisted of a wholly opposite educational and social profile. The five men and seven women were hardly Hinckley's peers, they included a janitor, a cafeteria worker, a garage attendant, a secretary, and only one of the twelve was white.[84] The Washington, D.C., jury that tried Mayor Marion S. Barry, Jr., was composed entirely of blacks—defense attorneys successfully managed to keep whites off. The aforementioned New York jury that acquitted Messrs. Mitchell and Stans was constructed with the professional aid of one Marty Herbst, the president of a self-styled "communications think tank," following a profile that called for blue-collar workers, primarily Roman Catholics, who earned an average of $8,000 to $10,000 annually and read the *Daily News*. The profile had no place for Jews (none was impaneled), nor for people with college degrees (none was impaneled, although one alternate, who ultimately served, did have one), nor for those whom Herbst called "limousine liberals" (there was none). As Herbst told Martin Arnold of *The New York Times*, "We wanted people who were home established, to the right, more concerned with inflation than Watergate"—jurors who would associate the dour John Mitchell with John Wayne.[85] It is no wonder that the prosecutor remarked bitterly after the acquittal that he had lost the case at the impaneling stage. He might have explained, too, that, although the defense had indeed employed its own impaneling tactics, the composition of the jury was also in no small measure determined by Judge Gagliardi, who eliminated an unusually large number of potential jurors at the *voir dire* "for possible prejudice" because they were "politically interested" and "better educated"! That kind of action taken by a trial judge, although a controversial practice, is neither uncommon nor illegal.[86] No wonder that, as Daniel Schorr commented on the jury selection system, "Jury service has tended to become an activity for those whose regular activities are not valued by society."[87] Or, as U.S. District Court Judge Gerard L. Goettel put it during his frustrating presiding over the difficult impaneling of a jury in the Reverend Sun Myung Moon tax evasion case of 1982, "The choice is being narrowed to those who don't read much, don't talk much, and don't know much."[88]

It will come as no surprise that jury selection in England differs dramatically from the American norm: Above all, it is quick. Frequently, the first twelve prospective jurors through the door end up as the jury. "Picking the jury here," in the words of one commentator, "requires about as much time as it takes twelve people

83. See Jay Mathews, "DeLorean Jury Selected with Expert Help," *The Washington Post*, August 17, 1984, p. A1.
84. See "Insane on All Counts," *Time* Magazine, July 5, 1982, pp. 17–20.
85. May 5, 1974, p. 1.
86. See the disturbing account in *The New York Times*, May 5, 1974, p. 1, in particular of the role played by an alternate juror, Andrew Choa, who had replaced a regular juror because of the latter's illness and became the most influential juror *cum persuador* in the case. See pp. 116, 118 *supra*.
87. *The New York Times*, April 25, 1974, p. C39.
88. *The Washington Post*, December 29, 1983, p. A16.

to swear an oath."[89] Neither the prosecution nor the defense can question potential jurors, and the number of candidates they can reject stood at three in 1990.

In a completely different vein, it has proved so difficult at times to impanel a jury that clerks of courts literally have had to stoop to grabbing people off the streets in search of a trial panel, under the traditional common law right of going to the streets "to impress citizens into duty"—which is what happened on two occasions to strolling unemployeds near City Hall in Philadelphia in 1965 and 1966, and to a UN delegate taking a walk in Paterson, New Jersey, in 1958. A judge in Kentucky, in an unsuccessful attempt to impanel jurors for a case involving the murder of two deputy sheriffs in 1962, sent out state troopers; New Jersey sheriffs collared seventeen Morristown residents for service within forty minutes on an October day in 1967; in 1981, in Prince Georges County, Maryland, a judge, impatient over a shortage of jurors, sent sheriff's deputies to scour the streets and shopping centers, causing twenty unhappy denizens to be dragged in for possible jury service; in 1985 a LaPorte, Indiana, judge used a state law to recruit unsuspecting passers-by from the courthouse square for jury duty.[90]

Blue Ribbon Juries. Among the charges voiced frequently against juries, both grand and petit, are that they merely give vent to the established community prejudices, that they are utterly unqualified to render judgment in other than simple, routine cases, and that, worse still, they are composed quite consistently of people who not only are uninformed in civic affairs, but are actually not interested. In Illinois, at least for a while, the names of those persons who consistently failed to vote were placed at the top of prospective jury lists. This interesting practice was apparently based on the assumption that nonvoters make excellent jurors! In large part to meet the general criticism of unsatisfactory juries, some states in America have statutorily adopted either a special jury test, or, more commonly, the *blue ribbon jury*. This device, as used at various times and in sundry jurisdictions of a quarter of the states,[91] sees judges of certain courts giving potential veniremen a series of test questions involving legal terminology that the jurors would almost certainly encounter. If an otherwise eligible juror misses more than one or two of these chiefly multiple-choice and matching questions, disqualification is almost certain.

Blue ribbon juries (then called *struck juries*) made their first appearance in England in 1730. They were employed solely at the level of the King's Bench and only for "trials of great consequence" or when the subject matter of the case was beyond "discussion of the ordinary freeholder." Court officials would choose forty-eight men who were "competent, intelligent, and less prejudiced than the ordinary juror." Somewhat later, the privilege to impanel such a blue ribbon or "special"

---

89. *The Los Angeles Times*, December 20, 1985, p. 1.
90. *The New York Times*, April 15, 1962; *The New York Times*, October 26, 1967; *Readers Digest*, April 1981, p. 126; *Time* Magazine, September 28, 1981, p. 45; and *The New York Times*, August 10, 1985, p. 46. (The second example cited was for the trial of LeRoi Jones, the black poet and playwright, and two others on a weapons charge following the bloody 1967 riots in Newark, New Jersey.)
91. E.g., Alabama, Delaware, Indiana, Michigan, New York, New Jersey, Tennessee, Vermont, Virginia, West Virginia.

jury was extended to all courts, who could authorize it for either of the two preceding reasons or, generally, when an ordinary jury "could not be impaneled." However, they were finally statutorily abolished in England in 1971.

It is hardly astonishing that the institution of the blue ribbon jury would ultimately face a test at the bar of the highest court of the United States.[92] It came in 1947 and 1948, in both instances not surprisingly involving the New York County special jury—which, in existence since the turn of the century, consisted of a "special jury" panel of some 3,000 eligibles out of a total pool of 60,000 veniremen, and it was closely followed barely one year later by a similar test. By the narrowest of margins, 5:4 in each case, the Supreme Court of the United States upheld the statute and the practice against the dual challenge that it violated both the due process of law and the equal protection of the law clauses of the Fourteenth Amendment to the Constitution. The majority of the Court contended that the professionals and white collar workers, so dominant on the jury, could well come from widely varying salary groups and that neither clause cited requires that a jury must represent all components of society. As Justice Jackson wrote for the Court in the first case: "Society also has a right to a fair trial. The defendant's right is a neutral jury. He has no constitutional right to friends on a jury."[93] Furthermore, the majority felt that a state might reasonably use blue ribbon juries as a means of rendering the administration of justice more efficient. But four Justices—Murphy, Black, Douglas, and Rutledge—dissented vigorously in an opinion written by Murphy, who had been President Franklin D. Roosevelt's Attorney General. He insisted that an accused person was entitled to be tried by a jury fairly drawn from a true cross section of the population, and that a blue ribbon jury simply could not be representative.

> One is constitutionally entitled to be judged by a fair sampling of all one's neighbors, . . . not merely those with superior intelligence or learning. . . . The vice lies in the very concept of "blue ribbon" panels—the systematic exclusion of all but the "best" or most learned or most intelligent of the general jurors. Such panels are completely at war with the democratic theory of our jury system, a theory formulated out of the experience of generations.[94]

The majority decision in that case has never been overruled and thus stands as *res judicata*. Yet its abolition on the *federal* level by the terms of the Jury Selection and Service Act of 1968 may well herald its demise in the states also—although, without a judicial decision to the contrary, its constitutionality prevails and its desirability in cases involving "highly technical" matters was specifically endorsed by Justice Powell as recently as 1981.[95] A blue ribbon jury may be both unfair and undemocratic, but these qualifications do not render it *ipso facto* unconstitutional.

92. *Fay v. New York*, 332 U.S. 261 (1947) and *Moore v. New York*, 333 U.S. 565 (1948).
93. *Fay v. New York*, loc. cit., at 288. Almost four decades later, the Supreme Court unanimously echoed Jackson's pertinent conclusion when it ruled 9:0, speaking through Justice Rehnquist, that a litigant "is entitled to a fair trial but not to a perfect one, for there are no perfect trials" (*McDonough Power Co. v. Greenwood*, 464 U.S. 548 [1984] at 553. Rehnquist quoted from *Brown v. United States*, 411 U.S. 223 (1973) at 231–32, which, in turn, had quoted from *Bruton v. United States*, 391 U.S. 123 (1968) at 135 and *Lutwak v. United States*, 344 U.S. 604 (1953) at 619.
94. *Moore v. New York*, loc. cit., at 570.
95. Interview, *The Cavalier Daily* (University of Virginia, Charlottesville), October 21, 1981, p.1.

Furthermore, it may be well to reiterate that the notion that juries should be composed of men and women from all walks of life is a relatively recent one. At its English origins, the jury was composed of favorites of the Crown, men of position, or men who were indebted to the Crown. In the early history of the jury in the United States, it comprised a handful of propertied men. Several decades passed before being male and owning property, to name but the two more obvious qualifications, were no longer prerequisites to participation in jury duty.

THE TRIAL JURY AT WORK

A trial jury (which always contains one or more alternates to guard against a case of sudden indisposition of a juror) sits en banc throughout the course of the trial. It does so no matter how long the trial may take, and the jurors are compensated, generally inadequately, on a daily fee basis.[96] Each of its members is presumed to listen impartially, attentively,[97] and with an open mind to both sides of the case; is not to discuss the trial with anyone, no matter how near or dear; and, at least in theory, is not permitted to read, view or hear any media of communication that might conceivably have some bearing on the ongoing trial. In fact, most judges ban resort to *any media whatsoever* during the trial. The latter requirement may well be an illusory one: there is every reason to believe that, regardless of a juror's conscientiousness and dedication, few public-spirited individuals would in fact literally deny themselves the news of the day. However, if either side in the litigation succeeds in presenting incontrovertible proof of such an aberration, it may move for a mistrial or even a directed verdict of acquittal. Until fairly recently (there were exceptions[98]) the jurors were not permitted to take notes, for they are expected to "register the evidence as it is given, on the tablets of (their) memory and not otherwise."[99] But by 1988 some twenty-two states had statutes or Supreme Court rules that explicitly allow juror note taking within the trial judge's discretion.[100] When

96. In 1991 the juror's fee on the federal level was $40 daily and 25¢ a mile. (If the trial lasts longer than thirty days, the trial judge may authorize an increase to $50 daily.) In 1974, U.S. Senator Gaylord Nelson (D.-Wisc.) unsuccessfully proposed that federal jurors' pay be raised to the equivalent of their "on-the-job" income (*The New York Times*, March 31, 1974, p. C17). One year later he introduced legislation to pay federal jurors as much as $100.00 per day "to offset hardship." On the latter issue, see "The Economic Hardship of Jury Duty," 58 *Judicature* 493–501 (1975). Senator Nelson, undaunted, tried again in 1977–78, once more *sans* success. In 1981 jury fees at the state level ranged from $45 a day in Kewannee County, Wisconsin, to $5 for civil cases in San Francisco (*Time Magazine*, September 28, 1981, p. 45).

97. See Lee Hockstader, "Sleepy Jurors Sorely Try Lawyers," *The Washington Post*, August 7, 1988, p. D1.

98. For example, Circuit Court Judge John C. Beatty, Jr., of Multnomah County, Oregon, has allowed the taking of notes as of 1970, and he even provided stenographic pads and pencils (see 64 *Judicature* 3 [September 1980], p. 3). And in two decisions in 1991 Connecticut's Supreme Court held that a jury verdict could not be overruled merely because the judge had allowed the jurors to take notes (*Wall Street Journal*, February 27, 1991). See *Esaw v. Friedman*, 586 AR2d 1164 (1991).

99. Indiana Supreme Court, as quoted by L. L. Bromberger, "Jurors Should Be Allowed to Take Notes," 32 *Journal of the American Judicature Society* 57–8 (1948). For a rather persuasive argument that jurors be permitted to take notes under carefully controlled guidelines, see Victor E. Flango, "Would Jurors Do a Better Job If They Could Take Notes?" 63 *Judicature* 9 (April 1980), pp. 436–43.

100. See Larry Hever, *Toward More Active Juries: Taking Notes and Asking Questions*, (Chicago: American Judicature Society, 1991), p. 6.

the presiding judge has delivered his charge (see later) to the jury at the end of the trial, the jury retires for its deliberation until it reaches a verdict—which, according to the findings of a host of knowledgeable students of the jury system, they may well have decided *prior* to their deliberations!

If the deliberative proceedings stretch into the night, the jury is locked up ("sequestered") in a nearby hotel and subsequently continues its work on the following day or days. According to the results of research on jury deliberations conducted by one expert, 50 percent of the average jury's deliberation time is spent exchanging "personal experiences," 25 percent on "procedural matters," 15 percent on reviewing facts, and exactly 8 percent on discussing the judge's instruction.[101] If, after a reasonable period of time and repeatedly unsuccessful balloting, a trial jury is unable to arrive at a verdict of guilt or acquittal, the judge will declare it to be a *hung jury*, dismiss it, and remit the case to the docket for a trial *de novo* before an entirely different judge and jury. *But* the average judge will battle hard to avoid a deadlock. Thus, U.S. District Judge Edward Weinfeld of New York declined to accept the request of a long-deadlocked jury in 1962, sending it back to a midtown hotel with orders to return to his court at 9 A.M. It did, redeliberated, and later that day returned a verdict of "guilty."

"Hung" Juries. A famous example of a hung jury was that of the first Alger Hiss case,[102] in which the jury deadlocked 8:4 for conviction after countless ballots, and U.S. District Judge Samuel Kauffman declared it hung. Not long thereafter, Hiss was convicted of perjury in a new trial and with a new jury before U.S. Judge Henry W. Goddard.[103] A sensationalized illustration of not just one but two hung juries in succession was the highly publicized Finch–Tregoff murder–conspiracy case in California. The first trial ended in a hung jury in March 1960, after thirteen weeks of courtroom action, with the jury hopelessly deadlocked after thirty-seven hours of deliberation. At that time it stood 10:2 for convicting Dr. R. Bernard Finch, but 8:4 for his mistress Carole Tregoff's acquittal. The retrial was completed in November 1960, and again ended in a hung jury, this time having lasted seventeen weeks, with the jury taking fifty-nine ballots during seventy full hours of active deliberation. Edwin Fry, foreman and the only male on the jury, reported that the twelve jurors had unanimously found Dr. Finch guilty of the murder of his wife, but were divided 9:3 on the degree of murder to be charged, three jurors stubbornly insisting on a second-degree finding. On Miss Tregoff the jury had split 9:3 on the degree as well as the guilt—and that same count held against both regarding the conspiracy charge. Another seemingly interminable trial finally resulted, ending the fiasco in March 1961 with a clear-cut verdict against the two defendants: Dr. Finch was convicted of first-degree murder and conspiracy to commit murder, Miss Tregoff of second-degree murder and conspiracy to commit murder. Both were given life sentences. She was out on parole in 1969, he in 1971, after having served eight and ten years, respectively. A contemporary example of three hung

---

101. Ibid., quoting Rita M. James, "Status and Competence of Jurors," 64 *American Journal of Sociology* 563 (1959).

102. *United States v. Hiss.* Jury hung in August 1949.

103. *United States v. Hiss,* 88 F. Supp. 559 (1950). See also *United States v. Hiss,* 107 F. Supp. 128 (1952).

juries in succession following an initial, reversed conviction—with the government then despairing of a fourth trial—was that of Black Panther co-founder Huey Newton, who had been charged with the killing of Oakland, California, policeman John Frey in a 1967 gun battle. Newton had been found guilty of manslaughter in his initial trial in 1968, but a new trial was ordered by the California Supreme Court because of judicial error in the charge to the first jury. In the first two subsequent trials the jury deadlocked, that is, was "hung" 6 : 6 and 11 : 1 for conviction; the third—which did not come until 1979—resulted in another hung jury, this time 10 : 2 for acquittal.

One determined juror can, of course, hang any jury that requires unanimity. This was demonstrated forcefully in 1979, when one elderly juror, proudly stipulating that Congressman Daniel Flood (D.-Pa.) was indeed guilty of bribery, conspiracy, and perjury as charged, *hung* the 11 : 1 for conviction jury because he considered the seventy-five-year-old Flood "too old" to pay for his crimes.[104] (Reference is sometimes made to a *hanging jury*, which is a *grand jury* that has earned a reputation for almost certain indictments.)

INSTRUCTING THE JURY: THE JUDGE'S CHARGE

One of the highlights of a trial in the pertinent federal and state courts of the United States, and a crucial point in its evolvement, is the presiding judge's *charge* to the trial jury on completion of testimony, arguments, and motions by all concerned. It comes after the summations by the prosecution and the defense, the latter customarily speaking last. Much thought goes, or should go, into this charge, which is intended as an exposition of the law and is delivered orally in most, although not all, cases.[105] The judge must take great care to ascertain that its contents are clear, to the point, comprehensive, and illuminating and that they pose readily discernible alternatives to the jury panelists, who may well ask for further instructions on details. But as a rule the jury may not take copies of the charge to the jury deliberation room,[106] nor may they taperecord it. No wonder that jury comprehension remains generally low. It is a highly complicated business, but it need not be. Thus, in the words of an appellate tribunal:

---

104. See the accounts in *The Philadelphia Inquirer*, August 9, 1971, p. 1, and *The Philadelphia Evening Bulletin*, December 16, 1971, p. G68. For an interesting examination of hung juries, replete with statistics, see Leo J. Flynn, "Does Justice Fail When the Jury Is Deadlocked?" 61 *Judicature* 3 (September 1977) pp. 129–34. For an account of the hung Flood jury see *Time* Magazine, February 19, 1979, p. 97.

105. An interesting study of jury-charging attitudes by fifty randomly selected federal district court judges in 1970, conducted by Jerry K. Frye of Texas Christian University, pointed to among other things, the extreme importance judges assign to *oral* instructions, its "meaningfulness" to the jurors, an average length of one and one-half hours, a strong disinclination to permit any written material to accompany the jury to the deliberation room, and considerable confidence in the average juror's listening and comprehension ability (see letter to author, plus chart, dated February 5, 1970). Two-thirds of the states (e.g., Colorado, Illinois, Michigan) have tried to make "pattern," that is, standard, model, uniform instructions by judges mandatory (see 62 *Judicature* 185 [October 1978]).

106. There are exceptions, such as Iowa State courts, where juries are permitted to take written instructions to the deliberation room. Oregon statutorily permits the judge in his discretion to deliver his instructions orally and then send an exact copy to the jury.

> The trial judge should not as a rule limit himself to stating good set terms of law culled from the codes and the reports. Jurors need not legal definitions merely. They require proper instructions as to the method of applying such definitions after reaching their conclusions on the facts.[107]

As one recent careful research project again demonstrated convincingly, it is far from impossible to develop understandable jury instructions. Rewriting instructions can improve comprehensibility dramatically.[108]

Moreover, the judge must see to it that the charge is scrupulously fair to both sides in the dispute; it is naturally of overriding importance to the accused. It should be "the safeguard of fairness and impartiality and the guarantee of judicial indifference to individuals."[109] Many a charge has, ultimately, been instrumental in causing a mistrial; many another has been found by appellate courts to be defective on points of law. In brief, the judge's charge to the jurors, which is almost always necessarily complicated, sums up the case, pinpoints the chief issues involved, and concludes with the admonition that the jury must bring in a verdict of "guilty" or "not guilty"—addressing itself to each of the charges and/or counts at issue and, if a choice is permissible under law in homicide cases, determining the degree of punishment. Any verdict of "guilty" must have taken into account the absence of *reasonable doubt*, often a very difficult open-ended problem. There are no in-between stages of a verdict, although in some instances, in several of the fifty American states, juries are empowered to mitigate their judgment of guilt in homicide cases by a recommendation of mercy, which is normally binding on the judge. It was just such a binding recommendation by the third jury in the Finch–Tregoff murder case that saved Finch from the electric chair.

Under certain limited circumstances, a judge may express a value judgment on the evidence in charging the jury, but this is valid only in isolated instances, and, indeed, has been judicially interdicted in others (e.g., in Pennsylvania)[110]. Superior Judge Leroy Dawson in the second Finch–Tregoff case startled courtroom observers by telling the deadlocked jury that the evidence showed "a willful and deliberate taking of human life." When one of the defense attorneys repeatedly attempted to stop the judge from reading his comments, he found himself twice cited for contempt. Judge Dawson cited a 1934 amendment to the California Constitution as his authority and a San Diego case in 1958 as his precedent.[111] Since his own case resulted in a hung jury, Dawson's action was not challenged further. On the other hand, judges everywhere are free to comment on a jury's verdict once it has been announced, although many jurists believe this practice, too, to be at least

---

107. *People v. Odell*, 230 N.Y. 481 (1921) at 487–88. It has been repeatedly suggested that both the testimony and the instructions in litigation be *videotaped* so as to be readily available, and "recallable" by and to deliberating juries. See David U. Strawn and G. Thomas Munsterman, "Helping Juries Handle Complex Cases," 65 *Judicature* (March–April 1982), pp. 444–48.
108. Amiram Elwork, James J. Alfini, and Bruce D. Sales, "Toward Understandable Jury Instructions," 65 *Judicature* (March–April 1982), pp. 432–43.
109. *People v. Odell*, loc. cit., at 488.
110. Philip R. Goldsmith, "Judges' Comments to Jurors Curbed," *The Philadelphia Inquirer*, April 22, 1972, p. 8.
111. *The Philadelphia Evening Bulletin*, November 6, 1960, p. 1.

unwise if not unethical; but it is not illegal unless expressly interdicted by constitutional, statutory, or judicial mandate.

Setting a Verdict Aside. In *civil* cases, but generally less commonly in *criminal* cases since only a few states permit it, a judge may *reverse* the jury's verdict. This frequently occurs in so-called *negligence* or *compensation award* cases, in which jury lawlessness, in the form of excessive verdict, is not uncommon. A much-publicized illustration of the latter is the overturning by U.S. District Court Judge Joseph Stevens of a $500,000 jury award in the alleged sex discrimination case involving onetime Metromedia anchorwoman Christine Craft. Stevens ruled that "plaintiff was not discriminated against because of her sex," that Metromedia's actions "with respect to her appearance were necessary and appropriate."[112] A federal case example of the negligence issue, one widely featured in the public press in 1959 because of an open clash between Justices Whittaker and Douglas, was *Inman v. Baltimore and Ohio Railroad.*[113] A District of Columbia jury had held the railroad negligent in stationing Inman where he could be knocked down by a drunken driver, and it awarded him $25,000. However, the judge who presided over the trial in the U.S. District Court set the verdict aside as being "irrational."[114] When the U.S. Court of Appeals upheld the district judge, Inman appealed to the U.S. Supreme Court, which, in a 5:4 opinion, affirmed the judgment below. What provoked the headlined outburst by Justice Douglas, and his insistence that the Supreme Court has a duty to enforce the guarantee of a jury trial and to prevent the lower courts from setting too strict a standard, was Justice Whittaker's concurring opinion. In it Whittaker had scoffed at the idea that the railroad had been negligent and suggested that the only way it could have prevented the accident was to have the employee encased in an army tank. This, in the full glare of an "Opinion Day" (to be described in detail in chapter 5), Douglas denounced, in person and from the bench, as "smart-alecky." Barely one year later, however, with Justices Black and Douglas dissenting vehemently, the Supreme Court itself, for the first time in twenty-four years, reversed a jury's verdict awarding damages to an injured railroad worker.[115] Judge Charles E. Wyzanski, Jr., of the federal trial court below had upheld the jury's verdict but denounced it in no uncertain terms, asserting the case was devoid of "any evidence of negligence." He had refrained from setting it aside solely because he felt bound by what until then had been Supreme Court doctrine in these cases.[116] Of course, courts may also reverse and remand an award as being "too low," although this occurs far less frequently. Thus, the U.S. Court of Appeals for the Second Circuit held a $32,000 jury-awarded pay-

---

112. *Craft v. Metromedia, Inc.,* 572 F. Supp. 868 (1983). A second trial lowered the award to $325,000, but it, too, was overturned on appeal in mid-1985 (*ibid.,* 766 F.2d 1205) by the U.S. Court of Appeals for the Eighth Circuit.

113. 361 U.S. 138.

114. An example of a state court reversal of a verdict is the action by Philadelphia Court of Common Pleas Judge Theodore L. Reimel in setting aside a $25,000 verdict by a jury for a local attorney's claim for fees due as being "excessive and perverse" (*The Philadelphia Evening Bulletin,* January 16, 1962, p. 13).

115. *New York, New Haven, and Hartford v. Hennagan,* 364 U.S. 441 (1960).

116. Ibid. As reported in 272 F. 2d 153 (1959) at 155–56.

ment to a widow for the death of her husband in an automobile accident "as grossly inadequate," basing the decision on what Judge Irving R. Kaufman noted as the unfair influence of the trial judge's charge to the jury.[117] A dramatic example of an overruling in a criminal case came in 1984 when Mobile County (Alabama) Judge Braxton Kittrell, Jr., overruled a jury that had unanimously sentenced a member of the Ku Klux Klan to life imprisonment without parole for the killing and hanging of a young black man. Judge Kittrell, rejecting the verdict as insufficient, instead sentenced the convicted Henry Francis Hay to death in the electric chair and set an execution date.[118]

Judges may also set aside a jury verdict if it is clearly based on an obviously mistaken notion of the law involved in a case. A recent instance is U.S. District Court Judge Oliver Gasch's setting aside of a $2 million libel judgment against The Washington Post for a story about Mobile Oil Corporation President William Tavoulares. Gasch ruled that the necessary evidence required in the case of a public figure under the legal precedent established in New York Times v. Sullivan[119] of proof of "knowing lies or statements made in reckless disregard of the truth" had neither been submitted nor established.[120] Yet all these practices in American courts are a far cry from Continental systems, in which the trial judge is permitted, if not expected, to comment on the weight of the evidence and the credibility of witnesses throughout the course of the trial and to allow the jury to know his or her opinion on the merits of the case.[121] On the other hand, the average judge in the United States, too, has the power in all cases to order a verdict of directed acquittal before a case goes to the jury—a motion made often by defense counsel almost as a routine matter, but rarely granted. If granted, however, it is not subject to reversal by any higher court on the federal level. Moreover, the judge may take a case out of the jury's hands if it becomes evident that only questions of law are involved and no facts are in dispute. And among the myriad of reasons why a judge may order a retrial is the finding of a clear case of basic confusion among the jurors—one that obviously affected the verdict in such a fashion that there is grave doubt in the mind of the presiding judge that the jury has fulfilled its part in seeing justice is done. Thus, in a New Jersey automobile accident case the jury had returned from its deliberations, and its foreman upon being asked by the judge, "Have you agreed upon a verdict, Mr. Foreman?" answered, "My name isn't Foreman. My name is Admerman." When the trial judge refused to recognize this interesting reply as a sufficient reason to declare a mistrial, defendant Naomi Haberli appealed to the Appellate division of the New Jersey State Superior Court, which unanimously ordered a retrial, citing Mr. Admerman's response, as well as the grossly excessive award granted by his fellow jurors, as a prima facie example of the type of "basic confusion" necessitating a new trial.[122] Not a matter of con-

---

117. Caskey v. The Village of Wayland, 362 F. 2d 1789 (1967).
118. See the account in The New York Times, February 3, 1984, p. A16.
119. 376 U.S. 254 (1964).
120. The Washington Post v. Tavoulares, 527 F. Supp. 676 (D.C.-D.C., 1983).
121. In sixteenth-century England, and until 1670, the so-called writ of atteint (the remote ancestor of today's "directed verdict") enabled a judge to refuse to accept any jury verdict he did not approve, no matter what the evidence. A new trial, with a larger jury, was then customarily held.
122. The New York Times, December 15, 1960, p. 27.

fusion was the mistrial in a rape case declared by District of Columbia Superior Judge Fred B. Ugast in 1981. When a jury of eleven was unable to reach a verdict, the Judge, upon inquiry, received the following message from jury foreman Robert W. Smoot: "Your Honor, we cannot reach a decision in this case unless two jurors are replaced. . . . Drinking problem." Two jurors had been having a veritable ball during deliberations by drinking from cups of "Seven-Up," laced with a little good Bourbon ensconced in their purses![123] But it should be understood that no trial or appellate judge will readily tamper with a jury's verdict, no matter what his or her private opinion may be.

"General" and "Special" Verdicts. On the basis of the somewhat questionable assumption that the jury fully comprehends the judge's instructions concerning the applicable substantive legal rules, it is usually required to return a general or overall verdict in favor of one party or another.. Theoretically, as already indicated, this jury verdict is based on the facts of the case, the judge himself having determined the rules of law, although it is not always possible to separate facts and law, and the U.S. Supreme Court has repeatedly dismissed challenges to statutory provisions that make juries the sole judges of the law as well as the facts in criminal trials.[124] In practice, however, the general verdict permits the jury to do what it pleases: it gives no details, simply reports its decision, and no one either really knows or may safely predict just what facts a jury found from the evidence. Judge Jerome Frank, a life-long and severe critic of the jury system as a fact-finding institution, viewed the judge's charge as little more than an elaborate ceremonial routine, and he argued that of all the possible ways that could be devised to arrive at the falsity or truth of testimony, "none could be conceived that would be more ineffective than trial by jury."[125] He and many other legal authorities have long contended that special, or fact, verdicts—employed in England for centuries, and reconfirmed with the Courts Act of 1971—in which the jury is asked to answer a specific question of fact, are a far preferable method of arriving at a verdict that is just to all concerned. In a special verdict procedure, which is now used in several of the fifty states and was authorized for federal civil suits in 1938 (but is very rarely employed), the trial judge charges the jury to report its findings—presumably even if these are simply beliefs—about certain particular issues of fact raised during the course of the trial, facts that a jury should be able to weigh and determine with a modicum of accuracy and reliability. To those facts thus "found" the judge then applies the appropriate legal rule. It has been frequently and thoughtfully suggested that a jury's ability to find appropriate facts would be enormously enhanced were it permitted to submit written interrogatories to witnesses during the course of a trial (through the presiding judge).[126] In effect, some judges have begun to experiment with such procedures in complex cases.[127] Whatever the type of jury

123. As reported by The Washington Post, May 4, 1981, p. A18.
124. See, for example, Giles v. Maryland, 372 U.S. 767 (1962).
125. Jerome Frank, Courts on Trial (Princeton, NJ: Princeton University Press, 1949), p. 20 (italics supplied). This is one of the great books on the judicial process.
126. See, e.g., Strawn and Munsterman, op. cit., p. 131, and Elwork, Alfini, and Sales, ibid.
127. See Irving R. Kaufman, "The Verdict on Juries," The New York Times Magazine, April 1, 1984, pp. 42ff.

verdict advocated, the degree of perfection one may expect from the human institutions that constitute the judicial process is necessarily a limited one.

English and Welsh judges employ a charge rather similar to that found in the tribunals of the United States, but they provide somewhat more guidance to the jury during the trial. No charge is used in the courts of France. Instead, the French presiding judge, who actively directs the proceedings in the courtroom by interrogating the accused and witnesses, submits to the jury—in the infrequent instances of its presence in a case—a list of questions which the nine panelists are required to answer with a simple "yes" or "no." Standard examples of these queries would be, "Did the accused prove his alibi?"; "Was the accused present at the scene of the crime when it was committed?"; "Was the act of homicide one of self-defense?"; and, always, "If you find the defendant guilty, were there any extenuating circumstances?" Clearly, by his interrogation the judge tries to give to the jury the most lucid picture possible as a matter of guidance. The jury, its members voting individually and in secret, answers these questions specifically and thereby reaches its verdict—if necessary by a *majority* vote, in contrast to the *unanimity* requirements of the American federal judicial system. However, should the divisions among the jurors prove to be uncomfortably close, such as 7:5 or even 6:6, the presiding judge may assume the power of determining the verdict with the aid of the two associate judges (there are always three judges at the assize-trial level). But in that event the verdict is almost certain to be one of acquittal.

In West Germany today the entire courtroom examination in criminal trials is conducted by the judges, while the prosecuting attorney and counsel for the defense sit mute and take notes. Counsel is privileged to put a question only when the judges have completed an examination calculated to bring out fully and fairly all that a witness might tell. Jurors are taken from a local list of "outstanding" citizens and impaneled for a term of one year. Judge and jury sit on the bench together and participate jointly and equally in deliberation on a case—a procedure known as a *fused* jury.

JURIES: BLESSING OR EVIL?

It is not easy to be objective about juries—and few observers are. Certainly there is but little doubt that juries throughout the Western world have declined both in significance and esteem during the past century. Often, when they are not held in utter contempt by the professional critics, they are merely tolerated as a necessary, and at times admittedly convenient, evil. In large measure, the juries have brought this opprobrium on themselves—no matter how innocent and perhaps even understandable their response to the demands of the legal process may be. But it is not easy to defend the institution in the face of so many jury-created fiascos.

Thus, we again turn to the aforementioned Finch–Tregoff case, this time the first 1960 trial, to find the jury system at its worst. According to an interview (!) granted to United Press International by one of the female members of the panel of five men and seven women that had just been declared a hung jury,

> at one point a near fight broke out. At the height of one heated debate, a male juror
> threatened to throw another [a female] out of a window and turned over the jury

table—he used to be a boxer—before she ran to the door. She was hysterical and pounded on the door for the bailiff.[128]

A different woman juror also readily and beamingly gave an interview to UPI, reporting that at least three "propositioning" notes had been passed to one of her female colleagues on the panel. An extra bailiff was then brought in to stand guard at another woman's hotel room door after those notes came to light.[129] A further illustration is the young mother from Bedford, Indiana, who confessed that as a member of a jury panel in the 1950s she had voted to convict the accused of rape— despite the fact that she believed him to be innocent. She did so against her own judgment, she readily admitted, because "I knew I had those children at home and we would never get out of there if we tried to argue it out with the others."[130] Similar "interviews" were granted by jurors in the Wallace Butts-Curtis Publishing Co. 1963 libel suit. In 1987 a juror in one of the longest trials in American history (2½ years) told the Associated Press that, although she opposed it, she went along with an award of $16 million in punitive damages against the Monsanto Company "to get it over with." She also admitted that she read newspaper accounts of the trial in direct violation of the judge's orders.[131] In 1977, T. Cullen Davis, the "victor" in his six-month, $3 million plus costs jury trial for the murder of his twelve-year-old stepdaughter, joined several jurors (and the presiding judge, the bailiff, his mistress, and friends) for a raucous victory party in Amarillo, Texas.[132] And to conclude the unfortunately almost inexhaustible instances of the kind of antics that have served to bring widespread opprobrium on the institution: In March 1961, under the guise of registering a *coup* in what it called "public service," the Hearst Corporation–owned station WBAL-TV in Baltimore induced, evidently without any difficulty, nine of twelve jurors to appear before the studio camera and reenact their deliberations that resulted in the conviction of one Melvin Davis Rees, Jr., for murder and kidnapping. This intriguing performance, which featured in great detail the thoughts and reasoning that culminated in the verdict, came on the evening *prior* to the scheduled sentencing of the convicted man! As a result, defense counsel succeeded in obtaining at least a temporary postponement of sentencing, and he raised a series of legal questions based on this jury TV debut, which the *Baltimore News Post*, also a Hearst-owned medium, termed "a reportorial breakthrough of the traditional silence of the jury room."[133] Considerations of law, ethics, morals, and taste were evidently deemed insignificant. And within hours of their acquittal of John Z. DeLorean of drug conspiracy charges in 1984, jurors were on TV—including the morning shows—providing detailed insight into their deliberations and offering sundry gratuitous advice to the government.

Evil? It is tempting to underscore the questioning of the efficacy of the institution of the jury—which Honoré Balzac once defined as "twelve men to decide who

128. *The New York Times*, March 13, 1960, p. 42.
129. Ibid. But judges may enjoin interviews (e.g., *U.S. v. Driscoll*, 276 F. Supp. 333, 1967).
130. As quoted by John F. X. Irving, "The Jury May Be Out Permanently," *National Review* 177 (September 1958).
131. *The New York Times*, October 25, 1987, p. 15.
132. *The* [Charlottesville] *Daily Progress*, November 18, 1977, p. A8.
133. See Jack Gould's article in *The New York Times*, March 25, 1961, p. 49.

has the better lawyer," Herbert Spencer called "a group of twelve people of average ignorance," and Erwin Griswold styled "the apotheosis of the amateur"—by noting that there is considerable evidence that the average jury reaches its verdict in most instances by a kind of "happy" compromise. Not being able to agree on a financial award in a civil case, for example, each panelist will write down his or her own figure; then the jury will add the total, divide it by the number of jurors, and thus attain peace of mind![134] In homicide cases a host of revelations again and again points to jury compromises. Thus, unless they are expressly forbidden to do so by statute or by the judge's charge, jurors will frequently decide a case of murder by "compromising" between first-degree murder and acquittal by settling for a second-degree conviction, even if it is not justifiable by the facts in the case. For example, the 1967 Naples, Florida, jury that convicted Dr. Carl Coppolino of the poison-murder of his first wife, Carmela, brought in a verdict of murder in the *second* degree, when, obviously, the very use of purchased poison carries with it premeditation, which calls for a *first*-degree murder conviction. Evidently, the jury had "compromised." Sometimes the flip-of-the-coin or lot method is employed in order to get the nasty business over with. Or, as was demonstrated in a Hancock County, Kentucky, case, the jury became so confused as a result of its own deliberations that it formally "retracted" an already rendered verdict![135]

Even with the best of intentions, it may well be almost impossible for the wandering mind of the ordinary juror to overcome conclusively the histrionics that so often characterize presentation by counsel. Both prosecution and defense generally conduct what is to all intents and purposes a legal sporting combat, with each side following evidence by counterevidence, examination by cross-examination, witness by counter-witness, each one sworn to tell the truth, the whole truth, and nothing but the truth. Not infrequently, this alleged search for the truth results in statements in open court that are clearly out of order. But even if the judge so holds, as he often does, and asks the jury to disregard the statement at issue, it has been uttered, of course, and it is conjectural at best whether or not it can be wiped from the jurors' minds. To arrive at the truth behind what one long-time observer of juries styled "the curtain of flimflam and obfuscation"[136] the jury may well have to decide which side, in its judgment, seemed to tell fewer lies, and in that way reach a verdict. Hence, in the words of Judge Frank, based on his many years of active experience in the legal and judicial processes:

> [T]he jury is the worst possible enemy of the "supremacy of the law." For "jury-made law" is, par excellence, capricious and arbitrary, yielding the maximum in the way of lack of uniformity, of unknowability. . . . To my mind a better instrument than the usual jury trial could scarcely be found for achieving uncertainty, capriciousness, lack of uniformity, disregard of the [rules], and unpredictability of decisions.[137]

134. In some jurisdictions (e.g., Iowa) this "averaged" verdict, known as a "quotient" verdict, if ascertained to have occurred, does become grounds for a possible reversal.
135. *The New York Times*, April 15, 1962, Sec. 4, p. E8.
136. David A. Dressler, "Trial by Combat in American Courts," 222 *Harper's Magazine* 32 (April 1960).
137. Frank, op. cit., pp. 123, 132. Mark Twain often voiced similar sentiments! For example: "The jury system puts a ban upon intelligence and honesty, and a premium upon ignorance, stupidity and perjury" (as requoted in *Time* Magazine, September 28, 1981, p. 47).

Accordingly, he and others would prefer the trial judges to hear and decide cases alone, the assumption being that judges are trained in the law, which jurors are not, and that they function in a setting that is open to considerably more scrutiny than juries. Yet the "Chicago Jury Project"[138] pointed to a significant 83 percent agreement on verdicts between judges and juries.

Blessing? A natural and main source of endorsement of the jury system is the trial lawyer, who has a vested interest in influencing it—even if this is done by persuading the generally bewildered jurors that A is really B. Few, if any, defense lawyers in a criminal case would argue against it. But the venerable institution's defense does not need to rest its case on such pragmatic grounds. Many a legal scholar, far from decrying the factors of emotion, prejudice, and sympathy that are undeniably major determinants in jury verdicts, holds that these very factors advance the cause of justice because they represent the "socially adapted intuitive law" of the various communities to which we belong. Thus, Thomas Lambert of the American Trial Lawyers Association noted in 1968 that "the glory of the jury is its beautiful lawlessness. . . . [It represents] the yeasty independence of the average man over officialdom"[139]—a view of the jury generally seconded and even expanded by Jon M. Van Dyke in a full-length work on jury selection, replete with a host of statistical trial data.[140] Charles P. Curtis and Harold J. Berman have contended repeatedly that the jury reflects "the intuitive part of us," which they view as a necessary counterbalance to the equally essential "intellectual part of us" in the judge.[141] This is particularly appropriate if one keeps in mind that, in the final analysis, the first and foremost function of a jury is to choose between conflicting testimony, testimony so frequently beclouded by histrionics and legalistics as to render an "intuitive" judgment all but inevitable—at least up to a point. Something can certainly be said for the time-honored principle of being judged by a group of one's peers. Jurors, as Holmes once put it, "introduce into their verdicts a certain amount—a very large amount. . . . of popular prejudice, and this keeps the administration of the law in accord with the wishes and feelings of the community."[142] Moreover, much of the adverse criticism would appear to depend on which side of the case one's interests lie and whether the jury sits in a civil or criminal case.

One of the most articulate and influential champions of the jury system was the distinguished John Henry Wigmore, who advanced four main arguments in favor of the principle: First, it prevents popular distrust of official justice because it gives the average member of the body politic a share in the political process—a kind of communal enactment of the democratic ideal. Second, it provides for some necessary flexibility in legal rules and regulations in that it enables an adjustment of the "general rule of law to the justice of a particular case—what de Tocqueville viewed as "a gratuitous public school, ever open"—whereas the judge is rightly

---

138. See p. 132 and n. 144, *infra.*
139. *Time* Magazine, July 26, 1968, p. 80.
140. *Jury Selection Procedures: Our Uncertain Commitment to Representative Juries* (Cambridge, MA: Ballinger Publishing, 1977).
141. See Curtis, op. cit., pp. 101–4.
142. Oliver Wendell Holmes, Jr., *Collected Legal Papers* (New York: Harcourt, Brace, and Howe, 1920), p. 237.

expected to be consistent and consequential in his rulings for all. Third, it educates the ordinary citizen in the administration of justice by cultivating the judicial habit in him and by creating in him a respect for law and order, thus making him conscious of his duty to society and his share in the governmental process. Fourth, it ameliorates the verdict because it is based on the amalgam of a host of temperaments and viewpoints.[143] In essence, this is a plea on behalf of the institution based on the recognition of the role of common sense in the judicial process. It is a plea echoed by law professors Harry Kalven, Jr., and Hans Zeisel of the University of Chicago after a monumental study of the jury system, involving the questioning of 550 judges who presided over 3,576 jury trials across the country. Their conclusion was that the freedom of a jury to inject its own sense of justice is one of the greatest strengths of the system. But it also acknowledged that "jury legislation," or the jury's conscious modification of the law to make it conform to community views of what it ought to be, was a factor in fully 50 percent of the disagreements between judge and jury of what *the law* in a given case *is*.[144]

Unquestionably, the Wigmore roster of exhortation is subject to serious exception—especially since it is based, at least in part, on a rather optimistic view of human nature and a belief in the willingness as well as the ability of the average citizen to accept and adapt to these laudatory notions of participation in the responsibilities of society and state. Some of the illustrations presented in connection with the adverse criticism of the institution would appear to raise some crucial doubts regarding Professor Wigmore's analysis. Be that as it may, despite its shortcomings the jury system has been generally regarded by the public at large as a laudable instrument in the quest for justice. "It is so justly regarded," once applauded Joseph H. Choate, "as the best and perhaps the only known means of admitting the people to a share in maintaining their wholesome interest in the administration of justice. . . ."[145] The ultimate questions remain, however: Is it? And does it? It is difficult to still the haunting doubts.[146]

FROM OFFENSE TO TRIAL: A PROCEDURAL NOTE

The practices and customs that characterize the judicial process differ widely in the various jurisdictions discussed herein. This also applies to the procedures fol-

---

143. As discussed and quoted by William Wirt Blume, "The Place of Trial in Criminal Cases," 43 *Michigan Law Review* (1944), pp. 64–65.

144. The study, Ford Foundation–financed, and known as the "Chicago Jury Project," was published under the title *The American Jury* (Boston: Little, Brown, 1966). See also Gary J. Jacobsohn, "Citizen Participation in Policy-Making: The Role of the Jury," 39 *The Journal of Politics* 1 (February 1977), pp. 73–96, particularly for the discussion on "jury nullification."

145. As quoted by Justice Bernard Botein, *Trial Judge* (New York: Simon and Schuster, 1952), p. 195. Thomas Jefferson described the jury system as "the only anchor ever yet imagined by man by which government can be held to principles of its constitution" (as quoted in *Time* Magazine, September 28, 1981, p. 44).

146. See the Symposium, "The Jury in Complex Litigation," 65 *Judicature* 8–9 (March–April 1982), which analyzes key aspects of the problem in a series of several articles. (See especially those by Peter W. Sperlich, Mark A. Nordenberg, and William V. Luneberg.) See also Justice John Marshall Harlan's thoughtful "pro" and "con" analysis in his dissenting opinion, joined by Justice Potter Stewart in *Duncan v. Louisiana*, 391 U.S. 145 (1968), at 171.

lowed in the lengthy and often difficult path that leads from the commission of the offense to its ultimate adjudication in or out of the courtroom—for the vast majority of cases are in fact settled by mutual agreement before they reach the trial stage. Indeed, on the whole it is only the so-called trouble cases—or "hard" cases, as Holmes preferred to style them—that actually traverse the tedious process through the entire courtroom sequence. The purpose of this procedural note is to illustrate, in necessarily brief and generalized fashion, the various stages that confront participants in a full-length legal proceeding. The model employed, which will distinguish between civil and criminal cases, is a typical jurisdictional unit in the United States of America. And it should be noted that the very nature of an American court case requires the presence of the following four conditions: (1) an adversary process, (2) a justiciable issue, (3) ripeness for judicial determination, and (4) an actual disposition.[147]

PROCEDURE IN CIVIL CASES

A civil case is one in which individuals or groups bring adjudicatable actions in court against other individuals or groups by whom they contend to have been wronged. *Step 1 is the commencement of the action* by the *plaintiff*, the party bringing the suit, against the *respondent* or *defendant*. If it is a matter of an *appeal* rather than the bringing of an initial suit, the party who appeals is known as the *appellant*, the other side as the *respondent* or *appellee*. The plaintiff or appellant may also be termed *petitioner*. A word of caution: although it is easy to determine who the two sides to a respective suit are at the initial stage of a new suit, once that proceeding has reached the various appellate stages, it is considerably more difficult, and the only safe way to do so is to read the first few paragraphs of the case. In order to bring the suit, a plaintiff will have to do at least three things: (1) select the correct and proper tribunal, (2) have the defendant or his or her possessions brought before it, and (3) present the charges and ask for appropriate remedies.

In order to achieve the second requirement, the plaintiff must ask the proper authorities to serve a *summons*, which is issued after the petitioner has "sworn it out." Presumably it will be obeyed. Failure to respond to the summons will normally result either in a judgment against the respondent by default or in contempt proceedings. An even more compelling order to appear is a *subpoena*, a writ that, unlike the summons, must always be served on the respondent or witness in person; it directs his or her appearance on pain of being held in contempt of court (or of whatever other judicial or quasi-judicial authority may be empowered to issue the writ). A subpoena *duces tecum*, a related writ, requires the respondent to *bring something* along, a specific document, for example. If the respondent resides outside of the court's jurisdiction, but owns property therein, the latter may be *attached* in order to commence a suit, but only if the property attached is itself the subject matter of the suit. If it is not, the respondent cannot be brought into court by attachment of business property, even if he or she resides within the jurisdiction.

Closely related to the three tasks the plaintiff performs to commence the action

---

147. See ch. 9 *infra*, in this connection. For a reference to the British system, see Doreen J. McBarnet, "Pre-Trial Procedure and the Construction of Conviction," *The Sociology of Law*, ed. by Pat Carlen (Sociological Review Monograph, no. 23, 1976).

is an attempt by the two parties to the suit to narrow the factual and legal issues involved by virtue of an exchange of one formal written statement, or a series of them, stating the claim at issue. Such statements are called *pleadings*. These follow logically as a result of the plaintiff's initiation of his or her *complaint*. *Step 2* is designed solely to formulate the issues in the case and consists of the formal pleadings, now presumably involving the legal battery for both sides. This stage of the pleadings features the formal exchange of documents between the two sides, with the respondent required to file an *answer*. Often the lawyers are able to settle matters at this stage, but since we are concerned here with a sketch of the entire procedure, we assume that instead of there being acquiescence or agreement, the future defendant will file a *motion to dismiss* the complaint, sometimes also known as a *demurrer*. If the plaintiff rejects these formal counterclaims, the stage will now have been set for the docketing of the case on the calendar of the court of proper jurisdiction. A *pretrial conference with the judge* may conceivably settle matters at this juncture and avoid an actual trial—it will very likely serve to further narrow some of the problems involved. The next formal stage is the trial itself.

The nature and character of *step 3*, the *trial*, depend largely on whether the issue between the litigants is one of law or one of fact. If the issue is solely one of *law*, the court receives the case by means of a legal *argument* presented by the attorneys for both sides. Because there are no facts to be determined, jury and witnesses are not called; the judge decides the dispute strictly on the basis of the law, as he or she sees it. But if the dispute is either "mixed" or strictly of *facts*, the case will be tried before judge and jury, depending somewhat on its nature and, as has been described earlier in the chapter, on whether or not a jury trial is waived by mutual consent when that is possible and desirable. The next four steps, *verdict*, *judgment*, *appellate review* (if any), and *enforcement*, if not self-explanatory, have already been delineated or will be discussed in subsequent chapters.

PROCEDURE IN CRIMINAL CASES

Because of the very nature of the offense, the procedure in a criminal case is *ipso facto* both more formal and more elaborate, and it involves the machinery of the state to a much greater degree. Above all, the state, as was demonstrated in chapter 1, *necessarily* is a party to the suit—at least in the sense that it is responsible for the prosecution of the offense. It is responsible because criminal proceedings pertain to actions by individuals or groups who are charged with having committed one or more antisocial acts that society, through its governmental processes, has defined as a "crime" in public law. *Step 1* in a criminal case, therefore, is very simply the *apprehension* of the prospective defendant within the territorial limitations of the governmental jurisdiction concerned—who, unless he or she voluntarily surrenders to the authorities, is literally caught and arrested, either in the act of commission, while fleeing, or as a result of an arrest warrant, which the arresting officer must obtain in advance from properly constituted authority. *Step 2*, closely related to the first, sees the arrested person—who, if indigent, is entitled to the appointment of counsel as of the arrest stage—brought before a magistrate (known until the 1960s as a "commissioner" on the federal level[148]) for the *preliminary* exami-

---

148. See p. 161, *infra*, for a brief explanation of this office.

nation, in order to determine whether he or she shall be released or *held to answer*. If the latter, the accused will be held either in *custody* or released on *bail* to await the decision of the public prosecutor or the grand jury on the question of whether or not an *information* or an *indictment* shall be filed against him or her. The preliminary examination is a crucial and highly significant stage in criminal procedure, if for no other reason than that well over half of those arrested are released here, which customarily closes the books on the matter.

Step 3 represents the formal *accusation* by grand jury indictment or by the process of "information," depending on the statutory requirements or practices in the several jurisdictions concerned. This is logically followed by the *arraignment* and pleading—although the accused may already have entered a plea at the preliminary hearing stage—which constitutes *step 4*. An arraignment consists simply of the official, formal reading of the terms of the indictment or information to the accused by the court of jurisdiction,[149] and it concludes with the question, "How do you plead?"—giving the accused the choice of *"guilty"* or *"not guilty."*[150] Here the two parties often try to reach a settlement to avoid a formal trial. Known as "plea bargaining"—a practice strongly discouraged in England—it is conducted between the prosecution and the defense, frequently with the assistance of the judge.[151] In sheer statistical terms it is employed about fifteen times more frequently than juries to "resolve" cases.

Step 5 is the *trial* itself. In a jury trial, the verdict is always the jury's to render—unless the judge directs the jury to find the defendant "not guilty." If there is no trial by jury, the judge's verdict takes its place, as happens in many, but not all, pleadings of guilty. A host of proceedings, with which we need not concern ourselves here, antedates the trial—including various motions for dismissal of the case, change of pleadings, placing of dispositions, request for changes of *venue*, plea bargaining, possible dismissal or change of charges. The trial is conducted by the judge, either with or without a jury as the case and jurisdiction may mandate, and the process terminates with the next four steps: *verdict, judgment and sentenc-*

---

149. In 1978 the Idaho Supreme Court gave effect to a new rule (43.2) governing arraignments that satisfy its requirements "either in person or by electronic audio-visual devices in the discretion of the magistrate." See Warren H. Gilmore, "Arraignment by Television: A New Way to Bring Defendants to the Courtroom," 63 *Judicature* 8 (March 1980), pp. 396ff.

150. Under some circumstances the accused may plead *nolo contendere*, or "no contest"—specifically, "I do not wish to contend"—by which he throws himself on the mercy of the court. In effect an admission of guilt without so stating formally, the *nolo contendere* penalties are potentially the same as for the plea of guilty; but the judge more often than not displays leniency in such cases—some say if for no other reason than that the plea saves time, effort, and money. Vice-President Spiro T. Agnew's plea of *nolo contendere* in federal district court in October 1973 to a charge of income tax evasion is a famous case illustration. (Concurrently he announced his resignation from the high office, to which he was succeeded by Gerald Ford.)

151. Plea bargaining—which has had official U.S. Supreme Court sanction (e.g., *Bordenkircher v. Hayes*, 98 S. Ct. 663 [1978])—played a prominent role in the Agnew case in 1973 and in many, in fact most, of the Watergate culprits' cases. Indeed, in 1978 the U.S. Department of Justice estimated that 90 percent of the country's *criminal* cases "are now resolved by the process of persuading the accused to plead guilty to a lesser crime" (*The New York Times*, January 19, 1978, p. A7). As of 1984 all states except Alaska permitted plea bargaining.

ing,[152] *appellate review,* if any, and *execution of the sentence imposed,* if any. Of course, no bare procedural sketch such as this can take into account the sundry aspects and ramifications of the manifold practices, procedures, and safeguards that surround this fascinating aspect of the judicial process; it should be regarded merely as the outline of its essential framework.

Despite the relatively drastic distinctions in judicial theory and practice between the common law lands and the statutory law lands of the free West, the justice meted out under both legal systems is similar in its ultimate degree of fairness, if not in its efficiency. Each system is characterized by obvious advantages and disadvantages that govern its "costs" and each features methods that are peculiar to the needs or predispositions of the particular governmental jurisdiction concerned. As is so preeminently true of most practices in the realm of free government, they, too, are specifically adapted to the needs of the people directly involved. They are steeped in their own culture and tradition, and it is sheer folly for outsiders to endeavor to impose their own systems, even in theory. Sir Stafford Cripps once remarked wisely that methods and institutions of government are not simply commodities of international commerce, thus echoing the statement made by Alexis de Tocqueville in his *Democracy in America* in 1831:

> The more I see of this country [the United States] the more I admit myself penetrated with this truth: that there is nothing absolute in the theroretical value of institutions, and that their efficiency depends almost always on the original circumstances and the social conditions of the people to whom they are applied.

152. In 1977 the Supreme Court of Pennsylvania ruled that henceforth all *criminal* defendants should receive a statement of *reasons* for any sentences imposed on them (*Commonwealth v. Riggins,* Pa. 507).

4

Courts at Home: I—The Lesser Tribunals

A DUAL SYSTEM OF COURTS

As a result of the federal system that prevails in the United States, the national government and fifty state governments all make and enforce law. In effect, this means that there exist, side by side, two major court systems—one could quite accurately even say fifty-one—which are wholly distinct bodies, in the sense that they are created under different basic authorities—the respective national and state constitutions. This is in marked contrast with federal India, for example, whose Constitution of 1950 provides for a single integrated judicial system, with the Supreme Court of India at the apex and subordinate (district) courts at the base. The jurisdiction of America's two systems may, and in some highly significant instances does, regularly "merge" at the bar of the final interpretative authority of the U.S. Supreme Court. However, such a "merger" can come about only if a *substantial* federal question has been validly raised in the proper state court below and, after all remedies at the state level are duly exhausted, has been successfully brought to the attention of the Supreme Court—whose authority is now *discretionary* in all but a handful of instances. It is axiomatic that the path to the highest court in the land is long, expensive, arduous, and difficult; thus it is not traveled frequently. Other than in this appellate process, and possibly in the vexatious and procedurally intricate realm of injunctive relief, the national and state courts in the United States are separate entities. Nonetheless, it should be noted that through its constitutional power to establish *"inferior courts,"*[1] Congress possesses the power to draw a rigid line between the *jurisdiction* of these federal and state courts. But it has not seen fit to do so except in certain civil rights areas, notably, some

1. U.S. Constitution, Art. III, Sec. 1, Para. 1 (italics supplied).

types of racial discrimination,[2] and in a number of fields of relatively narrow jurisdiction, such as matters involving admiralty, bankruptcy, copyright, and patent. "Judicial federalism"—the distribution of power between national and subnational judiciaries—remains a very significant, yet often overlooked, "parity" principle element of American federalism. There is no question that it raises "political, jurisdictional, and administrative stress"[3]—yet, as Chief Justice Burger contended warmly, federal and state courts must not grow too similar on pain of constituting "a possible threat to individual rights and to the quality of the state courts."[4]

THE STATE COURTS

It is in the courts of the fifty states that the great majority of the legal business of the American public begins and ends. The character, jurisdiction, quality, and complexity of these courts vary considerably from state to state in accordance with the myriad considerations of public policy, need, size, and constitutional practice that characterize the heterogeneous component parts of the nation. Every state constitution establishes a judicial branch for its invariably tripartite government or, either in whole or in part—as is true for the national level under Article III of the Constitution of the United States—authorizes the legislature to provide for a judicial system. Although the terminology and structure among the state courts differ significantly, a discernible structural pattern does exist. The base consists of a system of justices of the peace and trial courts, with the pyramid gradually winding its way upward through a more or less elaborate appellate system, culminating in a supreme court (not invariably termed "Supreme Court," however).

THE JUSTICE OF THE PEACE

With rare exception, the lowest court at the state level—and there are those who would put the noun *court* into quotation marks in this particular connection—is the *Justice of the Peace*, originally a fourteenth-century Anglo-Saxon office. The officeholder is often, and sometimes irreverently, referred to as the "J. P." (standing for "Justice for the Plaintiff," in some eyes). The J. P. is also occasionally styled *squire* and *magistrate* increasingly in many cities (e.g., New York). By no means necessarily a lawyer, this official is usually elected for a two- to six-year term in counties, townships, and towns; but sometimes he or she is appointed for a term of similar length by the executive in the cities. The office has an honorable and, indeed, ancient tradition that came to the colonies from England. It was initially designed to aid in the administration of justice in minor matters at the local level. Today the Justice of the Peace, who is usually also a notary public, still performs a modicum of court work, but many of the duties are quasi-legislative, quasi-judicial, and quasi-administrative, including, characteristically, performance of civil marriages. Most of these tasks are undertaken on a fee basis—probably a regrettable

2. For example, see certain provisions of the Civil Rights Acts of 1957, 1960, 1964, and 1968 and the Voting Rights Act of 1965, as amended in 1970, 1975, and 1982.
3. See the perceptive article by John W. Winkle, III, "Dimensions of Federalism," in 406 *The Annals* 67–76 (November 1974).
4. As quoted in *The Washington Post*, June 11, 1980, p. A12. The Chief Justice was addressing the American Law Institute.

practice in view of its close link to meting out justice. The J. P. does, however, retain at least the appearance of a court of first instance in minor civil and criminal matters. In the former, the jurisdiction normally extends only to cases involving less than $300; in the latter, it is limited almost exclusively to misdemeanors.

With notable exceptions, again usually confined to some urban areas—for example, New York City, where the magistrates have legal background, are appointed for ten-year terms of office, and receive about $86,000 annually, an unusually high figure for that office, which normally commands a far lower remuneration—the Justice of the Peace's lack of training and qualifications is exceeded only by a sure-fire penchant for convictions, which have averaged 96 percent in civil cases and 80 percent in criminal cases.[5] A study conducted in 1956 of the minor judiciary of North Carolina, found that not a single J. P. in that state then had a law degree, that 75 percent had never gone to college, and that 40 percent had never even attended high school![6] A similar study for Virginia a decade later showed that of 411 past and present members of the Association of Justices of the Peace of Virginia, a mere four were lawyers, 71 percent had never gone to college, only five of the 29 percent who did were graduated, and 18 percent were not even high school graduates.[7] In Oregon only nine of seventy J. P.s had law degrees in 1966.[8] Even in such a cosmopolitan city as Philadelphia, only six of its twenty-eight elected magistrates held a law degree in 1968. All this represents an unfortunate state of affairs, for, given suitable attributes of integrity and proper qualification, the Justice of the Peace might well still provide able and inexpensive adjudication and settlement of minor legal problems in the judicial process. But Philadelphia's then Chief Magistrate, Joseph J. Hersch, insisted in a 1961 interview, seconded in 1968 by his successor, John Patrick Walsh, that the job of a magistrate is "more social than legal"; he decried the increasing clamor for a law degree, stating:

> A law degree doesn't make a magistrate more qualified. Living with people is more essential than going to a law library to find out what it's all about. . . . If you take Purdon's law books away from them [the lawyers], they're out of business.[9]

Yet evidence of questionable judicial qualifications and aberrant on-bench behavior that have continued to surface with some consistency are not likely to stop the drive for an end to lay-judge staffing of the office. However, as noted earlier, in 1976 the U.S. Supreme Court ruled in a Kentucky case that a non-lawyer[10] jurist

5. In 1962 in Pennsylvania, of 63,040 criminal cases handled by the then 4,305 J. P.s, 51,997, or about 83 percent, resulted in convictions; another 6,375, or 10 percent, were bound over for court trial; and 4,668, or about 7 percent, were dismissed (XI *Horizons for Modern Governments* 5, May 1963, p. 4). For examples of conviction rates from 95 to 99.2 percent in Michigan, Mississippi, and Tennessee counties, see Mitchell Dawson, "The Justice of the Peace Racket," in Robert Morlan and David L. Martin, *Capitol Courthouse and City Hall*, 6th ed. (Boston: Houghton Mifflin, 1981).

6. Isham Newton, "The Minor Judiciary in North Carolina" (unpublished Ph.D. thesis, University of Pennsylvania, 1956).

7. "Justice of the Peace in Virginia: A Neglected Aspect of the Judiciary," 52 *Virginia Law Review* 151 (January 1966), describing a survey conducted by Weldon Cooper of the Institute of Government of the University of Virginia.

8. *The Christian Science Monitor*, May 9, 1967, p. 5.

9. Interview with author, December 18, 1961.

10. *North v. Russell*, 427 U.S. 328 (see ch. 2, p. 21, n. 1.)

may preside even at a criminal trial involving possible jail sentences, at least when the defendant has an opportunity, through an appeal, to obtain a second trial before a judge who *is* a lawyer. In the case at issue, the lay City Judge, C. B. Russell, had not only proved himself incompetent, but outrageously so.[11] But, following the U.S. Supreme Court's holding, a number of state supreme courts (e.g., New Hampshire, Washington, Idaho, and Florida) upheld the utilization of lay judges in sundry cases.[12] On the other hand, North Carolina enacted a statute *requiring all* judges to have a law degree.

THE MUNICIPAL COURT

Again because of varying needs, different nomenclature attends the *Municipal Court*, the next higher level of court ordinarily found in the several states. Some of the most common designations are *Traffic Court, City Court, Night Court, General District Court*, and *Police Court*. The Municipal Court, whatever it may be called, is almost always a court of original jurisdiction, and normally also the first court of record[13] in the judicial hierarchy of the state. Its jurisdiction is customarily limited to about $500 to $1,000 in civil cases and to misdemeanors when it does have criminal jurisdiction. The municipal-level courts provide the parties before them with a fast and inexpensive procedure, and they are generally staffed by judges who possess legal training[14].

THE COUNTY COURT

The next court in line is the workhorse of the average judiciary, the *County Court*. It is a court of general civil and criminal jurisdiction, as a rule covering three major types of cases and controversies: ordinary civil beyond the limit of the court of jurisdiction just below, criminal except for routine misdeameanors, plus probate and inheritance. As its name implies, the County Court's geographical jurisdiction is limited to the level of that subdivision of the state. If juries are used by a state judiciary at all—and they usually are, although there is still no *state* obligation, except in above-misdemeanor-level *criminal* cases,[15] always to provide juries under the wording and interpretation of the Bill of Rights in the *federal* Constitution— they will be found here. Although Philadelphia, for one, has a separate tribunal called the County Court (with jurisdiction over juveniles, domestic relations cases,

11. See the description of Allen Ashman and Pat Chapin, "Is the Bell Tolling for Non-Lawyer Judges?," 59 *Judicature* 9 (April 1976).

12. Thus, New Hampshire's Supreme Court, following *North*, upheld a similar arrangement for its state, which allows a *de novo* trial in the Superior Court following a lay-judge court decision below.

13. Although all courts are, presumably, required to keep records today, the expression "court of record" is still used to distinguish between courts presided over by members of the minor judiciary (magistrates or justices of the peace) and other courts of original jurisdiction presided over by judges.

14. Frequently found at the Municipal Court level is the *Court of Small Claims*. Its jurisdiction is usually limited to claims in civil disputes ranging from $150 (Texas) to $3,000 (Louisiana). Its speedy and inexpensive procedures are characterized by low court costs (averaging only $45 in 1990), no juries, often no appeals (except for a trial *de novo*), sometimes not even counsel—generally a simplified process that rarely takes more than six weeks to settle a complaint. A careful 1978 study by the National Center of Courts (see p. 175, *infra*) gave high marks to the Courts of Small Claims throughout the states.

15. See *Duncan v. Louisiana*, 391 U.S. 145 (1968), ch. 3, p. 113, and n. 40, *supra*. with respect to *criminal* cases.

certain crimes, and some civil matters), a whole coterie of allied or subsidiary courts is either present at this level or takes the place of the County Court. Among these may well be all or some of the following often self-explanatory, judicial county helpmates: *Common Pleas* (a court to hear and determine civil cases, usually where the amount in controversy is in excess of $5,000); *Oyer and Terminer* (a criminal court with jurisdiction over capital crimes and other felonies, e.g., murder, manslaughter, treason, robbery, rape, kidnapping); *Quarter Sessions* (a predominantly criminal court with jurisdiction over a few technical civil cases and over crimes not tried by Oyer and Terminer, which usually meets four times annually, and sometimes consists of the same personnel as Oyer and Terminer); *Orphans*; *Probate* (for wills, estates, and deeds); *Juvenile* (for youthful offenders); *Domestic Relations*; *Surrogate* (similar to Probate in some counties); *Chancery* (specializing in equity matters); and *Equity*.[16]

16. A highly promising "noncourt" system of case-disposition in the judicial process is Philadelphia's (and Pittsburgh's) efficient system of "compulsory arbitration" of *civil* cases—except equity cases and those involving title to real estate—involving claims of up to $20,000—$25,000 for motor vehicle actions—(exclusive of interest and costs), totals that were scheduled to go "shortly to $35,000 and then to $50,000" (May 30, 1991, letter from Mary M. Alleva, Deputy Court Administrator, Arbitration). Actually found administratively at the level of the County Court (Court of Common Pleas) in Philadelphia since its statutory adoption by the state in 1958, it consists of teams of three-member lawyer panels who hear and decide a vast number of cases that would otherwise linger on the court dockets. The lawyers are appointed by the Deputy Arbitration Commissioners from an alphabetical list of Philadelphia County-based attorney volunteers. No matter how long a hearing takes, the lawyers are each paid a fee of $200.00 for a full day's service, $100.00 for one-half. With a nominal filing fee of $42.50, the average cost per "trial" to date has been but $199.50! Not only their time and expertise but also their quarters and any necessary secretarial help are provided by these volunteer members of the bar. The atmosphere of the proceedings is judicial and judicious, but rules of evidence are given liberal construction. Any appeal taken from a panel's decision is heard by a County Court judge *de novo* with or without a jury. But such appeals have averaged only 10 percent per annum, and the successful processing of an average of 7,500 cases annually by these arbitration panels is proof positive of the system's success and common sense. (For details see the *Annual Reports* of the Commissioner of the Compulsory Arbitration Division of the County Court of Philadelphia, 1958ff.) Philadelphia, beset—as are almost all jurisdictions—by clogged dockets, is also moving lesser *criminal* offenses out of the regular court structure. Charges that carry penalties of two years or less imprisonment are handled by *special* judges who settle the cases without a jury. Any defendant dissatisfied with the result may have a formal court trial, but to date fewer than 4 percent have so requested. This has resulted in a marked decrease of untried cases. Cf. Atlanta, Baltimore, and Miami.

An intriguing development is the founding, in 1984, of "Judicate," known as "the National Private Court System." It is one of several concerns created in recent years to offer alternatives to the often costly and overcrowded legal systems. In essence "Judicate" and its prototypes are entirely private organizations that settle cases on the basis of state law, with an ironclad agreement by the parties to the suit—be it of a civil or criminal nature—that they will abide by the decision. These private "tribunals," or arbitration units, are usually headed by former judges—there were 500 in 1991—who preside in robes, hear lawyers for both sides, and question witnesses under oath. They are well paid, usually from $150.00 to 300.00 per hour. In 1988 they handled nearly 800 cases in thirty-four states; 70 percent of the caseload involved personal injury suits ("Tell It to the Rent-a-Judge," *Time* Magazine, August 29, 1988, p. 50). While state law and procedures are followed, there are usually no juries—although there may be by mutual agreement—and the public is excluded from the deliberations. Crucial is the advance agreement by all involved to abide by and accept the "judge's" decision (see the articles by Martin Tolchin in *The New York Times*, May 12, 1985, p. 38, and August 4, 1985, p. E5). See, generally, the special issue of *Judicature*, "Alternate Dispute Resolution and the Courts," Vol. 69, No. 5 (February–March 1986), pp. 251–314.

THE INTERMEDIATE COURT OF APPEALS

Beyond the County Court lies the intermediate court, or courts, of appeals, usually termed *Appellate Division, State Appellate Court, Superior Court,* or *Intermediate Court of Appeals.* The jurisdiction of this tribunal is almost wholly appellate—certain writs being the exception in some states. It receives and adjudges appeals from decisions of the County Court and the Municipal Court, and in rare cases, from others. More often than not its decisions are final, although it is, of course, possible to go up from here to the final level since it is an *intermediate* appellate court. Only about half of the states resort to such an intermediate stage, but all of the larger ones do. Some of these have an elaborate structure, indeed. New York has an intricate system of more than 150 appellate courts at this level, and the appellate structure of California enabled Caryl Whittier Chessman to file fourteen appeals in its system (which he augmented with twenty-eight appeals to the federal courts between 1948 and 1960 in an ultimately unsuccessful battle to escape San Quentin's gas chamber). Happily, in recent years several states have taken considerable strides toward the adoption of more integrated hierarchical judicial pyramids—in large measure owing to the fine example set by New Jersey under its Chief Justice, Arthur T. Vanderbilt, in the 1950s—Virginia's 1976 reorganization being a case in point.[17]

THE FINAL COURT OF APPEALS

At the apex of each state system lies its *Final Court of Appeals,* which receives and adjudicates appeals on major questions emanating from the courts below, normally from the intermediate appellate level. It will not lightly accept cases that are merely concerned with questions of fact; its main purpose is to find the law. Usually this highest state court is known as the Supreme Court, but not always. In New York, for instance—where the "Supreme Court" is a trial court at the lower rung of the state judiciary and its lowest court of record—the high tribunal is called the *Court of Appeals;* in Maine and Massachusetts it is termed the *Supreme Judicial Court.* It has the last word in the state on all constitutional questions. Its decisions are final and authoritative as to state and, by virtue of the unitary structure involved, local law. Although there are some exceptions,[18] the U.S. Supreme Court

17. See Larry C. Berkson, "The Emerging Ideal of Court Unification," 60 *Judicature* 8 March 1977), pp. 372–82, for a comprehensive, up-to-date analysis of the problem. In 1976 Virginia reorganized its judiciary with commendable economy of levels, to embrace from low to high: (1) General District Courts, one judge sitting, (2) Circuit Courts, the first court-of-record level, again just one judge sitting, and (3) the seven-member Virginia Supreme Court (chosen by the legislature). An intermediate Court of Appeals of ten members (selected in the same manner) was created in 1983 to become operative as of January 1985, and an adjunct Small Claims Court was established in certain counties in 1988.
18. *Fay v. Noia,* 372 U.S. 391 (1963), governing certain types of *habeas corpus* appeals. But cf. *Stone v. Powell.* 428 U.S. 465 (1976) and *Wainright v. Sykes,* 433 U.S. 72 (1977), rejecting at least part of the essence of the *Fay v. Noia* holding, and *Engle v. Isaac,* 456 U.S. 107 (1982), the latter insisting that objections to state trial proceedings be raised at the time of the trial. See also *Rose v. Lundy,* 455 U.S. 509 (1982), generally following the same trend of deference to the state criminal justice process in *habeas corpus* review attempts; similarly, *United States v. Frady,* 456 U.S. 152 (1982); and especially *Coleman v. Thompson,* 59 LW 4789 (1991), which all but overruled *Fay v. Noia.*

insists that "all remedies below" must have been exhausted before it will consider a request for review from a party that "lost" in the final court of appeals of a state. Nevertheless, if a federal question of a substantial nature is allegedly involved, and if that question has been properly raised below, a chance, however slim, does exist that the highest court in the land will accept the case for review. In rare instances, the Supreme Court of the United States theoretically must accept a case appealed from the highest court—but, as will be described in the next chapter, this presumed duty is not without significant loopholes.

THE FEDERAL COURTS

When we look at the other prong of the "dual system of courts" at issue, we are confronted with the federal system, which is in many ways considerably less varied and confusing than the understandably heterogeneous state system(s). Certainly the federal courts are infinitely less numerous and, indeed, the hierarchical and jurisdictional arrangements of the three major constitutional courts—demonstrated later in Chart A—are readily comprehensible and clear-cut. Nevertheless, there is more to the structure and organization of the federal system of courts than is immediately apparent. Above all, there are two major *types* of federal courts from the point of view of their creation and functions: the *constitutional* courts and the *legislative* courts. Briefly, the former are created under Article III, the judiciary article of the Constitution, whereas the latter are created under Article I, its legislative article. Consequently, the safeguards of tenure, salary, and independence that accrue to judges of the constitutional courts by virtue of the explicit and inherent safeguards of Article III are not necessarily present for the judges of the legislative courts. However, because they are created by Congress, nothing prevents that body from clothing the judges of the legislative courts by statute with the same or similar prerogatives as are constitutionally guaranteed to those of the constitutional courts. In fact, even before Congress changed the status of three erstwhile legislative courts—the U.S. Court of Claims,[19] the U.S. Customs Court, and the U.S. Court of Customs and Patent Appeals[20]—to that of constitutional courts in 1953, 1956, and 1958, respectively, it had already granted them the same "good behavior" tenure provisions enjoyed by the judges of the constitutional courts. (As described later, the Court of Claims was reestablished as an Article I—i.e., legislative—court in 1982.) A more significant difference between the two types of courts is that the legislative courts are endowed with functions that are nonjudicial, that is, legislative and administrative, as well as judicial. Moreover, although they are tied into the constitutional appellate structure for certain purposes, they are primarily created to aid in the *administration* of specified congressional statutes.

19. The constitutionality of the change was challenged, but it was upheld by the Supreme Court in a 5:2 decision in 1962 (*Glidden Co. v. Zdanok*, 370 U.S. 530). It ruled the Court of Claims to be a court properly created under Article III of the federal Constitution, and that therefore its judges may sit on all federal district and appellate courts.
20. The same verdict as that accorded to the constitutionality of the Court of Claims was applied in a challenge to the U.S. Court of Customs and Patent Appeals, and for the same reasons (*Lurk v. United States*, 370 U.S. 530).

Nonetheless, their judgments are as much *res judicata* (authoritative settled law) as are those of the constitutional courts.

As its basic power for the establishment of *legislative* courts, Congress utilizes Article I, Section 8, Clause 9, which extends to it "the power to constitute tribunals inferior to the Supreme Court." The lawmakers then expressly or implicitly join the fundamental power through the "necessary and proper" clause, the famous "implied powers" clause (I-8-18) of the Constitution,[21] with that congressional authority in the particular field in which the court is to perform its main function, for example, the taxing power (I-8-1) for the U.S. Customs Court (now a constitutional court, known as the Court of International Trade) or the power to "make rules for the government and regulation of the land and naval forces" (I-8-14) for the U.S. Court of Military Appeals. Other legislative courts have existed in the past, of which the defunct (as of 1915) *U.S. Commerce Court*, created under congressional power over interstate and foreign commerce (I-8-3), is an example. But today, if we exempt the now officially transformed and reconstituted U.S. Court of Claims, U.S. Court of Customs, and U.S. Court of Customs and Patent Appeals, there are only four bona fide legislative courts: the U.S. Court of Military Appeals, the U.S. Tax Court, the U.S. Court of Veterans Appeals, and the several Territorial Courts.

The U.S. Tax Court. Originally part and parcel of the executive branch under the Internal Revenue Service, the U.S. Tax Court was transformed into a legislative court by Congress under its taxing power (I-8-1) in 1969—heeding a longstanding recommendation of the Hoover Commission. It consists of nineteen judges—including its Chief Judge, elected by his or her colleagues for a two-year term in that post—who are appointed by the President with the advice and consent of the Senate for fifteen-year terms of office at $129,500 annually (1992), and who are still removable in the same manner as members of the independent regulatory commissions. Ten other special trial judges hear small tax cases, in which the tax due is less than $5,000. Notwithstanding its change to a legislative tribunal, the U.S. Tax Court is probably still viewable as, in effect, a quasi-administrative agency independent of the Internal Revenue Service rather than a court *qua* court. Its jurisdiction comprises the review of governmentally proposed deficiency assessments (or overpayments) of income, gift, self-employment, and prior excess profit taxes that have been challenged by the taxpayers concerned. The U.S. Commissioner of Internal Revenue is thus necessarily always the defendant party. The Tax Court, which may conduct trials anywhere in the United States—and did so in 100 cities in 1989, for example—is a busy agency, indeed, its workload having risen from 17,000 in 1979 to 52,000 as of early 1989. It is organized into subdivisions, each of which is headed by a judge. Each trial session is conducted by a single judge or by one of the five commissioners who are appointed by the Chief Judge.

---

21. See *McCulloch v. Maryland*, 4 Wheaton 315 (1819). The first federal court originated in November 1775 as a Congressional Committee on Appeals and emerged in 1780 as the autonomous Court of Appeals in Cases of Capture.

The U.S. Court of Military Appeals. This "G.I.'s Supreme Court" was created in 1950 as part of the revised Uniform Code of Military Justice, as amended subsequently (most recently in 1983); the Code had been created earlier largely because of the severe criticism heaped on the military's concepts and practice of justice before, and especially during and after, World War II. That system of justice, steeped in the court-martial tradition, had been predominantly concerned with notions of military efficiency and chain of command, and had lodged all but dictatorial powers in the persons of the various commanding officers. Other than the unlikely "court of last resort" in the person of the President of the United States, all appeals from its judgments were to higher military commanders. The new code altered this arrangement drastically and dramatically by granting accused military personnel new rights before a court-martial and by creating the civilian U.S. Court of Military Appeals (USMCA), which Chief Justice Warren dubbed the "civilian supreme court of the military." *De minimis* this meant that service personnel now had a genuine appellate tribunal to apply and interpret military law (while retaining their right of eventual appeal to the Secretary of the Army, Navy, or Air Force and, of course, the President). In effect, the door was opened for civilian observance and at least a modicum of civilian control, and as the 1950s ripened into the 1960s it became clear that service personnel had gained considerably more: the application of most of the Bill of Rights. Thus, in 1965 military personnel were assured that the Sixth Amendment's right to counsel entitled them not only to a lawyer in a military case, but to a *trained* lawyer. In April 1967 the "G.I.'s Supreme Court" ruled 2:1 that the limitations on police interrogation and confessions announced in 1966 by the Supreme Court of the United States in its historic *Miranda v. Arizona* decision[22] must also be applied in military law, because, in the words of the majority opinion written by Judge Homer Ferguson, it announced standards for the enforcement of the Fifth Amendment, which is binding on *all* federal courts—including the U.S.C.M.A.[23] And the Military Justice Act of 1968, authored by Senator Sam J. Ervin (D.-N.C.), contained sweeping safeguard provisions, including for the first time bail and insulation of military legal officers from local command pressure on court-martial decisions. The law permits defendants to demand trial by a military judge alone, instead of a jury of officers, in general courts-martial cases; and, if the defendant objects, forbids a single officer to act as prosecutor, defense counsel, judge, and jury in summary courts-martial.[24] Further liberalizations are contained in the Code's 1983 amendments.

The U.S. Court of Military Appeals is staffed by three judges who receive $137,300 (1992) annually; they must be appointed from civilian life, but may hold a reserve commission in "any armed force." They are nominated for staggered fifteen-year terms of office by the President, subject to confirmation by the Senate, and are eligible for reappointment. The President, who has the power to designate the Chief Judge, may, upon notice and hearing, remove a member of the court only for neglect of duty, malfeasance in office, or because of a mental or physical

22. 384 U.S. 436.
23. *United States v. Tempia,* 16 USCMA 629 (1976), at 635.
24. P.L. 90–632.

disability, but for no other cause. No more than two of the judges may be from the same political party. Those who had been appointed through 1984 had all had judicial and/or other public service, not necessarily excluding past military duty.[25] Indeed, the statute requires that all appointees be members of the bar of a federal court or of the highest state court. The USCMA, which determines its own rules of procedure, is authorized to review *at its discretion* decisions of courts-martial involving bad conduct discharges and prison sentences of more than one year, on being petitioned by the accused serviceperson, provided that the petition had already been passed on by a Court of Military Review appointed by the Judge Advocate General. The USCMA *must* review all courts-martial decisions, as affirmed by a Court of Military Review, in which the death penalty was decreed below, regardless of the rank of the accused, in all cases certified for its review by the Judge Advocate General after initial review by a Court of Military Review (consisting of commissioned officers or civilians, each of whom must be a member of a bar of a federal court or of the highest state court), or on "petition of the accused for good cause shown" in cases reviewed by a Court of Military Review. However, the court's powers of review extend solely to matters of law, not of fact—although that line, as we shall have occasion to note repeatedly, is sometimes a very fine one. The USCMA decides about two hundred of the 3,000 cases that now reach it yearly. Delays in rendering judgments, recently averaging three years, have led to mounting criticism of the tribunal's modus operandus.[26]

An illustration of one type of decision the Court of Military Appeals may render is the case of one Russo, a member of the Air Force, whom a duly convened court-martial had found guilty of premeditated murder and sentenced to death. On reviewing the record of the case, the staff judge advocate recommended approval of the sentence by the convening authority, but concurrently recommended that it be commuted to a dishonorable discharge from the Air Force, coupled with life imprisonment. When a Court of Military Review received the case, it indicated its belief that the suggested commutation was appropriate. However it held that it was "powerless to effect the change in penalty ... [because] Congress had not granted that power to Boards of Review." Hence, it affirmed both the findings of guilt and the originally imposed sentence. Because this judgment involved a death penalty and had been approved by a Court of Military Review below, review by the Court of Military Appeals was mandatory. In a decision again written by Judge Ferguson, the USCMA denied various other points of appeal advanced by Russo but held that both a court-martial convening authority and a Court of Military Review have the authority to lessen the severity of a death penalty. The USCMA then reversed the judgments below and returned the record of the Russo trial to the Judge Advocate General of the Air Force for action consistent with its decision.[27] More than half of all cases heard there to date have won reversals in the

---

25. For example, as of the time of his appointment in 1956 by President Eisenhower, Judge Homer Ferguson had been an attorney-at-law, a judge, a U.S. senator, and ambassador to the Philippine Islands; he had seen no military service.
26. See the scathing report of the Court's Review Committee, analyzed by Molly Moore in *The Washington Post*, February 13, 1989, p. A21.
27. *United States v. Russo*, 11 USCMA 252, 29 CMR 168 (1960).

Court of Military Appeals. One that did not was that brought by First Lt. William L. Calley, who thus unsuccessfully appealed from the twenty-year court-martial sentence meted out for his role in the slaying of "at least twenty-two" Vietnamese civilians in the 1968 My Lai massacre.[28] In 1974 that sentence was reduced by the Secretary of the Army; his conviction was overturned by a federal district court but was reinstated 8:5 by the U.S. Court of Appeals for the Fifth Circuit.[29] He then appealed to the U.S. Supreme Court which, without comment, refused to review his conviction.[30] He was freed in 1976.

Until the drastic amendments to the Military Justice Act, enacted by Congress in 1983 (discussed later), there was no direct appeal from the final judgments of the Court of Military Appeals. However, the U.S. Supreme Court, as well as the other federal constitutional courts, were able to exercise jurisdiction to review or "pick up" a case in an *habeas corpus* proceeding, such as claims of illegal detention, illegal procedure, or deprivation of fundamental constitutional rights. In 1953, the Supreme Court did indicate that it had that power in the much-discussed *Burns* case[31] that featured four separate opinions; but a majority of the Justices went on to point out that under the law federal constitutional court review would probably be limited to determinations of military court jurisdiction and considerations of "fair claims of justice." Justices Black and Douglas dissented vigorously, contending that *all* of the rights under the Fifth and Sixth Amendments of the U.S. Constitution should be held to apply to military as well as civilian trials. Regardless of the merits of the dissent, or of speculation on how the highest tribunal would "go" today, the Fifth Amendment issue has become moot in the face of the Court of Military Appeals' aforementioned 1967 confession and interrogation case,[32] in which Judge Ferguson wrote:

> The time is long since past when this court will lend an attentive ear to the argument that members of the armed forces are, by reason of their status, *ipso facto* deprived of all protections of the Bill of Rights.

The 1983 amendments governing Supreme Court review authorize the parties to petition that Court to review decisions of the USCMA through discretionary writs of *certiorari*. Given the concerns about the Supreme Court's overcrowded docket, however, the amendments were drafted in a manner that would limit the number of cases subject to direct review. Thus, cases in which the USCMA has declined to grant a petition for review are excluded, and the Supreme Court has *complete discretion* to refuse to grant petitions for writs of *certiorari*.

Without necessarily guaranteeing the application of *all* aspects of the Bill of rights in *all* circumstances to service personnel, the previously quoted Ferguson opinion, coupled with reforms readily undertaken by the armed forces themselves (led by the Air Force); the broad sweep of the Supreme Court's decisions in the

---

28. *United States v. Calley*, 22 MSCMA 534 (1973).
29. *United States v. Calley*, 519 F.2d 184 (1975).
30. *Calley v. Hoffman*, 425 U.S. 11 (1976).
31. *Burns v. Wilson*, 346 U.S. 137, at 144, 147.
32. *United States v. Tempia*, op. cit., at 635.

1960s matters affecting Amendments Four (applied and expanded again in 1982),[33] Five, Six, Seven, and Eight; the impact of the Ervin Military Justice Act of 1968 which, among others, provides protection against searches and seizures even broader than the Fifth Amendment; and the liberalizing 1983 provisions for Supreme Court review, it seems safe to say that the serviceperson's constitutional protection now comes very close to that of the American in mufti, that most, although not all (e.g., standing to sue superior officers),[34] lingering differences are being reduced or eradicated. Thus, a form of random jury selection was sanctioned by the USCMA in 1974.[35] It is noteworthy that under military law juries need not be unanimous, but a guilty verdict requires a two-thirds vote.[36] In 1980 President Carter approved changes in the Manual for Courts-Martial that largely extend to the military the same evidentiary rules that are applicable in federal criminal trials.[37] Moreover, the Supreme Court had further liberalized the rights of servicemen with a 1969 holding that gave the *civil* courts authority over "off-base, non-service-connected" offenses committed *in the United States* in peacetime.[38] On the other hand, in 1975 the Court applied brakes to the extent of ruling 6:3 that a federal District Court could *not* halt a pending court-martial proceeding against an Army captain for possession and sale of marijuana simply on the grounds that his offense was not "service connected" and therefore not under military jurisdiction. In effect, the Court thus extended to military trials the rule that federal courts will not interfere in state criminal trials *until* they have been concluded.[39] The Court also held 5:3 in 1976 that *summary* courts-martial are not "criminal prosecutions" and that hence the Sixth Amendment's guarantee of representation by counsel does not apply.[40] Yet in *bona fide* military criminal cases now not only will the defendant have the services of a lawyer free of charge but he or she will be able to *select* that lawyer, who must then be assigned "if reasonably available"—a provision going considerably beyond those governing assignment of free counsel in civilian proceedings.

The Territorial Courts. Perhaps the several Territorial Courts are in a slightly different category than the standard legislative courts, but they are established by Congress under its power to "make all needful rules and regulations respecting the territory or other property belonging to the United States. . . . " (IV-3-2). Created for, and located in, such diverse areas as Guam (1900), Puerto Rico (1900), the Vir-

---

33. *United States v. Kalscheuer*, 11 USCMA 373.
34. *Chappell v. Wallace*, 462 U.S. 296 (1983).
35. *United States v. Yager*, 7 MJ 171 (CMA 1979).
36. In a heavily publicized case involving charges of rape, attempted murder, sodomy, and abduction, Marine Corporal Lindsey Scott was acquitted, although the seven-member jury voted 4:3 to convict. The needed vote to do the latter was 5:2. Unlike civilian courts, there is no such thing as a "hung" jury in military tribunals.
37. See the informative article by Eugene R. Fidell, "Military Justice: Same Target, But Different Steps and Tactics," *The New York Times*, May 30, 1980, p. 8E. See also the book-length study by Harold F. Nufer, *American Service Members' Supreme Court: Impact of the U.S. Court of Military Appeals on Military Justice* (Washington, D.C.: University Press of America, 1982).
38. *O'Callahan v. Parker*, 395 U.S. 258.
39. *Schlesinger v. Councilman*, 420 U.S. 738.
40. *Middendorf v. Henry*, 425 U.S. 25.

gin Islands (1917), and the Northern Mariana Islands (1978),[41] these courts have jurisdiction that is, necessarily, extremely varied.[42] Generally—but specifically excluding Puerto Rico, where they have federal jurisdiction only, Puerto Rico having a set of separate local courts—it includes matters analogous to those in the jurisdiction of state and local courts as well as the federal District Courts. The judges of the Territorial Courts are appointed in the usual manner by the President and confirmed by the Senate; but their term of office, which varies from four to eight years, represents an uncommonly brief period for members of the federal judiciary. Responding to pleas, Congress in 1966 provided for lifetime ("good behavior") tenure for Puerto Rico's federal judges. In creating the various Territorial Courts, Congress has generally followed the wise policy of tailoring them to specific local needs, while retaining the *fundamental*, as distinguished from the *formal*, safeguards of the Constitution of the United States.[43]

The U.S. Court of Veterans Appeals. Established late in 1988 under Congress's power over the armed forces (Article I, Section 8, Clauses 12–14), this new tribunal is composed of a chief judge and "at least two and not more than six" associate justices, appointed by the President with the advice and consent of the Senate for fifteen-year terms at a salary of $129,500. The tribunal has exclusive jurisdiction to review decisions of the Board of Veterans Appeals, with its decisions subject to review by the U.S. Court of Appeals for the Federal Circuit. Based in the District of Columbia, the Court of Veterans Appeals gives every promise of being a busy court.

EX-LEGISLATIVE "SPECIAL" CONSTITUTIONAL COURTS

Until their conversion by Congress from their status as legislative to that of constitutional courts in the 1950s, the three most important and best known of these federal legislative courts were the Court of Claims (which was redesignated as such in 1982—see later), the Court of Customs (now the Court of International Trade), and the court of Customs and Patent Appeals (in 1982 consolidated with jurisdictional aspects of the old Court of Claims into the constitutional *U.S. Court of Appeals for the Federal Circuit*). Although they are now constitutional courts, they nevertheless still occupy a special niche in the federal court system; they may be regarded as special constitutional courts with special court duties. Despite their new station, they thus still perform, or at least may be viewed as performing, certain quasi-legislative and quasi-administrative functions. However, there is no doubt that public laws by Congress specifically changed their former status, and it must be assumed theoretically that Congress will henceforth not bestow upon these three the kind of nonjudicial powers that have always been considered inappropriate for members of the constitutional courts.

41. The Canal Zone had such a court from 1912 to 1982.
42. For statistical purposes *only*, these courts and their judges have been counted throughout this work as "U.S. District Courts."
43. See the series of *Insular Cases* (1901–5), especially *Hawaii v. Manchiki*, 190 U.S. 197 (1903) and *Rasmussen v. United States*, 197 U.S. 516 (1905), for an elaboration of the distinctions between the two terms. See also Justice Cardozo's memorable opinion for the Court in *Palko v. Connecticut*, 302 U.S. 319 (1937).

The U.S. Court of Claims. Created in 1855, after four earlier bills seeking to establish it had failed, the Court of Claims consisted of seven judges[44] who, aided by fifteen "commissioners," were given the task of adjudicating citizens' suits for damages against the government of the United States. Most, but certainly not all, of these suits represented claims arising out of public contracts. Others involved just compensation for the taking of private property for public use. Some represented suits for injuries caused by negligent or wrongful behavior of a government employee. The court was, in fact, an institutionally arranged denial of the age-old theory that the sovereign cannot be sued. Through the Court of Claims, sometimes referred to as "the keeper of the nation's conscience," the federal government did permit itself to be sued by affected persons—and thus became the only proper defendant—but only within rather narrow limits, such as the contractual disputes already mentioned. Because of the heavy volume of these complaints and the time consumed in their adjudication—it heard and its successor court hears the largest number of claims in the world—the existence of the Court of Claims, with its jurisdiction extending to territories and possessions as well as the United States proper, represented a genuine blessing to the general courts, whose dockets might otherwise be clogged considerably more than they already are. Moreover, the Court of Claims as well as the other specialty-area courts proved to be a welcome time-and-trouble-saving device for Congress itself; for there is no question that a good many of the matters now handled and adjudicated by these courts would otherwise have come to the halls of the federal legislature in the form of requests for special or local bills or of amendments to general statutes.

Essentially, the nationwide jurisdiction of the Court of Claims was limited to *original* jurisdiction in all contractual, tax, injury, and other *non-tort*[45] claims against the government of the United States. All suits against that government for money damages were and are tried here if the amount exceeds $10,000 (except in tax refund claims in which U.S. District Courts have concurrent jurisdiction and in tort claims in which the latter have exclusive jurisdiction). However, the Federal Tort Claims Act of 1946, as amended in 1959, permits claims of $2,500 or less against the government to be settled by administrative officials in instances involving damages caused by a negligent act or omission by the government or one of its agents. The Court of Claims possessed a very limited power of *concurrent appellate review* with the U.S. Circuit Courts of Appeals in certain tort actions against the federal government decided in the U.S. District Courts. Decisions of the Court of Claims are subject to Supreme Court review in appropriate instances, and some of the latter's more famous cases did in fact "come up" from the Court of Claims, among them *Humphrey's Executor (Rathbun) v. United States,*[46] which arose out of a suit against the United States to recover a sum of money allegedly due the deceased Humphrey. In 1931 William Humphrey had been reappointed a member of the Federal Trade Commission for a second seven-year term; in 1933 President Frank-

---

44. The first woman to become a judge on the Court of Claims was Charlotte Murphy, in August 1973.
45. A tort is any wrongful act, *other than a breach of contract,* for which an injured party may bring a civil action against the alleged wrongdoer.
46. 295 U.S. 602 (1935).

lin D. Roosevelt removed him. Contending that he had been illegally removed, Humphrey—and, upon his death, his executor, one Rathbun—sued to recover his salary. The Court of Claims, evidently somewhat uncertain of its grounds, certified some questions regarding the President's removal power to the Supreme Court (see Chart B, p. 180). That tribunal subsequently held unanimously that the Chief Executive had no authority to remove summarily members of independent regulatory commissions clothed with quasi-legislative, quasi-judicial, quasi-executive powers, thereby decisively restricting his power of removal. This decision stands today, reaffirmed and reinforced by a 1958 case that involved President Eisenhower's dismissal of War Claims Commissioner Wiener.[47]

Redesignated in 1982 as a *legislative* court, and restructured, now known as the *U.S. Claims Court*, the new/old tribunal has inherited all of its predecessor U.S. Court of Claims Court's *trial* jurisdiction, except for federal tort claims cases (which will continue to go to the U.S. District Courts and the regional U.S. Courts of Appeals). The new Claims Court has sixteen judges, appointed by the President with Senate advice and consent, who serve for fifteen-year terms and are paid $129,500 per annum (1992).

The U.S. Court of Customs and Patent Appeals. In 1910, utilizing the severally delegated powers to regulate commerce with foreign nations and among the states (I-8-3), to levy taxes (I-8-1), and "to promote the progress of science and useful arts" (I-8-8), Congress established the now defunct Court of Customs and Patent Appeals. Its five members, appointed in the customary manner, served "during good behavior." The functions of the court were primarily threefold: to review (1) decisions of the *Customs Court* regarding duties levied on goods imported into the United States and the classification of such goods, (2) those of the *Patent Office* regarding decisions on patents and trademarks, and (3) on a more legally restricted scale, those of the *Tariff Commission* relating to import practices.

For example, in one case on record the Tariff Commission (redesignated in 1974 as the *U.S. International Trade Commission*) on reviewing an appeal by an importer, held that the attempted importation and sale of certain synthetic sapphires and rubies described in an established U.S. patent represented not only "unfair methods of competition," but also "unfair acts in importation," both of which tended substantially to injure the industry of the patent's owner. The commission consequently recommended proceedings against the importer involved, and the latter appealed to the Court of Customs and Patent Appeals. The court held that the evidence at hand amply supported the findings below that the patent owner's industry was operated efficiently and economically within the United States, that the imported stones fell within the description of the patented articles, that the patent had been properly secured, that the importer's actions had a tendency substantially to injure the aforesaid owner within the meaning of the statute, and that where no holding of invalidity of patent was alleged, it would be regarded as valid.[48]

---

47. *Wiener v. United States,* 357 U.S. 349.
48. *Re Von Clemm,* 229 F.2d 441 (1955). For a more recent case involving the "countervailing duty," see *Zenith Radio Corp. v. United States,* 562 F.2d 1209 (1978).

A rather different instance of the work of the court concerned an action in August 1955 by President Eisenhower, who, pursuant to a recommendation of the Tariff Commission, had set certain new import duty rates on bicycles manufactured abroad. However, in so doing he had neither acted within the time limit prescribed by law nor really followed the Tariff Commission's advice—instead, his announced rates represented a *compromise* with it. The importers filed a suit in the Customs Court that held against the U.S. government. The latter appealed on the legal issue involved to the Court of Customs and Patent Appeals. The court ruled that, by following the course of action described, the President had violated the basic statute, which provides that Tariff Commission recommendations must be either accepted or rejected outright.[49] All parties concerned acquiesced in that 1960 decision. The Court of Customs and Patent Appeals, unlike the Court of Claims, possessed only *appellate* jurisdiction, and was confined to matters of law. Appeals from its decisions could go to the Supreme Court.

The already-alluded-to reorganizations of the judiciary in 1982 saw the abolition of the U.S. Court of Customs and Patent Appeals. Its functions, coupled with the trial jurisdiction (see earlier) of the old U.S. Court of Claims were consolidated into a new appellate tribunal, the twelve-member *U.S. Court of Appeals for the Federal Circuit*, the thirteenth such circuit in the federal appellate structure. This new tribunal hears appeals, including patent appeals from all federal district courts, in suits against the government for damages or refunds of federal taxes, appeals from the Court of International Trade, appeals from the Patents and Trademark Office, the Merit Systems Protection Board, and other agency review cases. In effect, the little recognized but vitally important court stands between the U.S. District Courts, the Tax Court, and various administrative bodies. Its rulings are thus binding on some 115 courts, boards, and government departments and agencies. Review of its decisions are by writ of *certiorari* to the U.S. Supreme Court, but usually the Court of Appeals for the Federal Circuit, rapidly dubbed "the business court of the United States," is the court of last resort in the significant areas alluded to..

The U.S. Customs Court. Its nomenclature changed to *U.S. Court of International Trade* in 1980, but still commonly known as the Customs Court, the busy tribunal consists of nine members, who receive $129,500 annually (1992). No more than five may be from the same political party. Growing out of the U.S. Board of General Appraisers, and with roots extending back to pre-Revolutionary days, the modern version of the court was created by Congress in 1926 under its commerce and taxing powers. Sitting in three sections or divisions of three judges each, this special court, which meets in New York headquarters and all other ports of entry in both the continental United States and the territories and insular possessions, has jurisdiction to review the rulings and appraisals on imported goods by collectors of customs. As noted, appeals from its decisions now go to the Court of Appeals for the Federal Circuit although, in rare instances, it is possible to go directly to the Supreme Court.

---

49. *United States v. Schmidt Pritchard & Co.*, 47 CCPA 152, C.A.D. 750. For a leading recent work on the U.S. Court of Customs and Patent Appeals, see Lawrence Baum, "The Court of Customs and Patent Appeals," 11 *Law and Society Review* (1977), 823–50.

An illustration of the work of the Court of International Trade—which handles roughly 3,500 cases yearly—is a case involving International Packers, Ltd., in 1959. The firm contended that it should be permitted to deduct from the appraised value of goods imported from Argentina a certain percentage of the purchase price it had to pay to the Argentine authorities on their export. The U.S. government's customs officials rejected this claim. On bringing action for adjudication in the Court of International Trade (then still officially the Customs Court), the plaintiff convinced that body that the 15 percent levy exacted by the Argentine government was a "necessary expense from the place of shipment to the place of delivery." Accordingly, the court ruled that the percentage involved was properly allowable as a deduction in computing the United States value of the merchandise under the Tariff Act.[50]

Review of tariff controversies by the Court of International Trade is not limited to the statutory provisions of the various congressional enactments. The right to sue before it applies to practically every legal controversy between an importer-taxpayer and the federal government. The fact that the Secretary of the Treasury or some other public official might have handed down an administrative ruling does not preclude an appeal to this interesting watchdog court.[51]

THE FEDERAL CONSTITUTIONAL COURTS

We now turn to the three chief *constitutional* courts, the U.S. District Courts, the U.S. (Circuit) Courts of Appeals, and the U.S. Supreme Court—but the most important of these, the Supreme Court, will be the sole subject of the next chapter. All three were created under Article III of the U.S. Constitution. In its key Section 1, that article mentions only "one supreme court," but it goes on to point to "such inferior Courts as the Congress may from time to time ordain and establish." The two lower of these three constitutional courts hence owe their origin to one of the very first acts passed by the First U.S. Congress, the Judiciary Act of 1789, of which Senator Oliver Ellsworth, who had been a delegate from Connecticut to the Constitutional Convention, and who would soon be the second Chief Justice of the United States, was a leading author. The act established and fairly well spelled out the national system of constitutional courts, which, as has been demonstrated, received no hierarchical additions until the Court of Claims was designated a constitutional court in 1953, followed by the Customs Court in 1956 and the Court of Customs and Patent Appeals in 1958. Constitutional courts and their judges are clothed with the significant and essential benefits of life (literally, "good behavior") tenure, irreducible salary, prestige, and independence. In the opinion of many an observer of the American scene, including the author of this book, there are no positions of greater desirability and prestige in the entire structure of American

---

50. *International Packers, Ltd. v. United States,* 171 F. Suppl 854.
51. Another type of special Article III constitutional court, the *Foreign Intelligence Surveillance Court,* was created in 1978 to regulate the use of electronic surveillance in foreign intelligence cases. It reviews government requests for such surveillance of suspected spies, terrorists, and, in exceptional cases, American citizens with information deemed essential to national security. In 1981, for example, the seven U.S. District Court judges—who serve part time on the tribunal—approved all of the 431 requests it received (*U.S. News & World Report,* January 1, 1982, p. 56).

government than those occupied by the members of the three leading constitutional courts.

General Jurisdiction. Omitting the jurisdiction (discussed earlier) of the several past and/or present "special" federal courts, constitutional as well as legislative, the general jurisdiction of these three top federal constitutional courts is amazingly well spelled out by Article III, Section 2, of the Constitution. In what is surely one of the most succinctly worded segments of the basic document, the first sentence of the first paragraph of that section makes clear at once that the judicial power of the United States "shall extend to all Cases, in Law and Equity, arising under this Constitution, the Laws of the United States, and Treaties made, or which shall be made under their Authority. . . . " Thus, in addition to announcing the sweeping realm of overall jurisdiction, that wording comes to grips with one of the crucial aspects of the jurisdictional process, namely, that it is limited to "Cases" (and "Controversies," by subsequent phrases in the Section). This signifies the necessity of the presence of a bona fide case or controversy involving litigants of opposing points of view who bring to the federal courts a genuine conflict of interest. In the absence of these fundamental elements, the three constitutional courts have no jurisdiction—which pinpoints the important truth that they neither can nor will accept manufactured or trumped-up cases or controversies devoid of the essential elements described, nor can or will they render *advisory* opinions per se.[52] This collective ban is as applicable to official as it is to private personages, and even extends to the influential government official who might feel the urge of convenience to run to the chambers of the Supreme Court with a fervent plea for an opinion on the legality of an issue, be it pending or dormant. Thus, as early as 1792–93, the Supreme Court declined to advise the government because it deemed the advisory function to be one more properly belonging to the Cabinet, a precedent that has not been violated.

After having disposed of that crucial aspect, the constitutional paragraph at issue goes on to outline the particular type of jurisdiction available to these courts. Generally speaking, these fall into two groups or classifications: (1) those that are based on the character or nature of the *subject matter of the case* and (2) those that are based on the character or nature of the *parties* to the suit. Under group 1 the courts may hear and dispose of cases and controversies in law and equity arising under the following:

a. The Constitution, a federal law, or a treaty.

b. Admiralty and maritime laws.

Under the necessarily larger and more complex group 2 the courts may hear and dispose of cases and controversies in law and equity in the following cases:

a. The United States is a party to the suit.

b. One of the fifty states is a party to the suit (*but*, in accordance with the provisions of the Eleventh Amendment, *not* if the suit was commenced or prosecuted *against* a state *by* either an individual—*any* individual—or a *foreign* country).

c. They are between citizens of different states.

52. For a detailed analysis of the "case and controversy" and other "maxims" of the judicial process, see ch.9, *infra*.

d. They affect ambassadors and other duly appointed bona fide representatives of an accredited *foreign* country.

e. They arise between citizens of the *same* state because of a dispute involving land grants claimed under titles of two or more states.

However, despite this very specific and extensive jurisdiction it does not necessarily follow that the federal courts will inevitably exercise it. There is no barrier in the language of the Constitution against congressional assignment of certain aspects of it (theoretically, probably even all of it) to the fifty states, either on a concurrent or even exclusive basis, for example, the requirement that the value of a controversy in civil suits between citizens of different states must exceed $50,000 (as of 1989) to qualify for original federal jurisdiction. Moreover, Congress may distribute the seven areas of federal jurisdiction among the various federal courts. It has done so and continues to do so in accordance with felt need, more often than not as a result of suggestions by the members of the judicial branch itself.

Overlapping Federal and State Jurisdiction. Whether or not Congress assigns concurrent or even exclusive jurisdiction in *federal* matters to *state* courts, it is axiomatic, of course, that in some areas the *state* courts have *exclusive* jurisdiction. It may be possible to raise a *federal issue* in a matter arising under state law or the state constitution, but the *original* jurisdiction of state courts over their own affairs is exclusive, as is that of the federal courts in their own sphere. However, there are some areas in which *both* court systems have jurisdiction[53]—as in the case of state bank embezzlement involving a federally insured bank—or in that of the theft of an automobile that subsequently crosses state lines—and where, consequently, the guilty party or parties are theoretically subject to prosecution and punishment by *both*. The U.S. Supreme Court has held repeatedly that such dual prosecution and even dual punishment violates neither the Bill-of-Rights ban of double jeopardy nor the "due process of law" clause under the Fourteenth Amendment.[54]

As indicated earlier, Congress has purposely granted *exclusive* jurisdiction over certain federal matters to the states. More often than not it has done this to reduce the federal work load in otherwise routine areas, such as the vast realm of diversity of citizenship disputes (i.e., suits between citizens of different states.)[55] It was for these cases that it enacted the 1989 requirement of a minimum value of $50,000 as the admission ticket to the federal court of jurisdiction, here the U.S. District Court. Going beyond that proviso, however, Congress has seen fit to grant *concurrent* jurisdiction in diversity of citizenship cases to the states even when the

---

53. The overall problem of jurisdiction remains a major bone of contention: for as long as a defendant can appeal an unfavorable verdict from state to federal courts, and as long as state courts can "distinguish" federal court orders, finality is often both illusory and elusive. See the perceptive book by Judge Carl McGowan of the U.S. Court of Appeals for the District of Columbia, *The Organization of Judicial Power in the United States* (Evanston: Northwestern University Press, 1969).

54. See *Bartkus v. Illinois*, 359 U.S. 121 (1959) and *Abbate v. United States*, 359 U.S. 187 (1959). But note the replete-with-the-possibility-of change 6:3 *per curiam* ruling by the Court in *Rinaldi v. United States*, 434 U.S. 22 (1977).

55. More than one-quarter of all civil federal cases now fall into that category of litigation! Indeed, they now represent the single highest category of civil cases filed in district courts. They comprise mostly insurance litigation, automobile accident cases, and other personal injury suits.

Chart A. The Jurisdiction of the Three Major Federal Constitutional Courts of the
United States (1991)

Courts Created Under Article III of the Federal Constitution[a]

1 Supreme Court of the United States, nine judges, has:
Original jurisdiction in actions or controversies:
1. Between the United States and a state.[b]
2. Between two or more states.
3. Involving *foreign* ambassadors, other *foreign* public ministers, and *foreign* consuls or
   their "domestics or domestic servants, not inconsistent with the law of nations."[b]
4. *Commenced by a state against* citizens of another state or aliens, or *against* a foreign
   country.[b] (N.B.: If these actions are *commenced by the citizen or alien against a state,*
   or by a foreign country *against* a state, the suit must *begin in state court,* according to
   the provisions of Amendment XI.)
Appellate jurisdiction from:
1. All lower federal *constitutional* courts; most, but not all, federal *legislative* courts, and
   the *territorial* courts.
2. The highest state courts having jurisdiction, when a "substantial federal question" is
   involved.

13 U.S. (Circuit) Courts of Appeals, 179 judges,[c] have:
Appellate jurisdiction *only* from:
1. U.S. District Courts.
2. U.S. Territorial Courts, the U.S. Tax Court, the U.S. Claims Court, and some
   District of Columbia Courts.
3. The U.S. Court of International Trade.
4. The U.S. Independent Regulatory Commissions.
5. The U.S. Court of Veterans Appeals.
6. Certain federal administrative agencies and departments (for review, but also for
   enforcement of certain of their actions and orders).

94 U.S. District Courts,[d] 649 judges,[e] have:
Original jurisdiction *only*[f] over:
1. All crimes against the United States.
2. All civil actions arising under the Constitution, laws, or treaties of the United States,
   wherein the matter in controversy exceeds $50,000 (unless the U.S. Supreme Court
   has jurisdiction as outlined previously).
3. Cases involving citizens of different states or citizens and aliens, provided the value
   of the controversy is in excess of $50,000.[b]
4. Admiralty, maritime, and prize cases.
5. Review and *enforcement* of orders and actions of certain federal administrative
   agencies and departments.[b]
6. All such other cases as Congress may validly prescribe by law.[g]

---

[a]For the purposes of this chart, the "special" constitutional courts (discussed on pp. 149–53) are omitted.
In 1991 they had a total of sixty-seven active and eight senior judges.

[b]*Jurisdiction not exclusive*—that is, while according to Article III of the Constitution cases are to orig-
inate here, legal arrangements may be made to have them handled by a different level court. For
example, Congress has the power to give the federal District Courts *concurrent original jurisdiction*
over cases affecting foreign ambassadors and *some* cases in which a state is a party to the suit. See
United States v. Ravara, 2 Dallas 297 (1793); *Bors v. Preston,* 111 U.S. 252 (1884); and *Ames v. Kansas,*

value meets or exceeds $50,000—provided the parties to the suit are willing to go there. As a further aid to the over-docketed federal courts, especially the work-horse District Courts, Congress in the late 1950s enacted a long overdue statute dealing with the citizenship status of corporations for purposes of legal actions. As a result, corporations are now viewed as "citizens" not only of the states in which they have been incorporated—which had been the case heretofore—but also as "citizens" of those states in which they have their principal place of business, regardless of their status of incorporation in them.

On the other hand, Congress has seen fit to vest *exclusive* original jurisdiction in the federal courts in a number of areas: suits between two or more of the fifty states (Supreme Court only), cases involving *foreign* ambassadors and other accredited *foreign* representatives, all bankruptcy proceedings, and all prosecutions for violations of *federal* criminal laws. Chart A demonstrates the overall jurisdiction of the three major federal constitutional courts.

The U.S. District Courts. By all odds the workhorses of the federal judiciary, the ninety-four District Courts, with their 649 active judges—perpetually an insufficient total—comprise the trial courts of the federal system. Established under the Judiciary Act of 1789, their jurisdiction extends to the initial trial of almost all civil and criminal cases arising in the vast realm of federal jurisdiction. It is here that the U.S. government commences, and usually ends, its prosecutions, for example, the government's victorious antitrust suit against the electrical appliance concerns for illegal price-fixing, which began and terminated in the U.S. District Court for Eastern Pennsylvania in Philadelphia in February 1961, Judge J. Cullen Ganey rendering the famous decision that saw a number of astonished top executives go to jail.[56] It is here also that most suits arising under the federal statutes begin and end (viz., one Paul Abrikossoff's action to recover certain property that had been disposed of by the Alien Property Custodian under the Trading with the Enemy Act).[57] And it is here that the trial (petit) juries sit in the federal system; they do so in roughly half of all cases commenced at that level. The District Courts have *orig-*

---

56. Case not reported in F. Supp. See Reporter's Transcript in Office of the Clerk, U.S. District Court, Eastern District of Pennsylvania. Also see Clerk Gilbert W. Ludwig's letter to author, dated June 8, 1961.

57. *Abrikossoff v. Brownell,* 145 F. Supp. 18 (1956).

---

111 U.S. 449 (1884). And in late 1964 the Supreme Court declined to review a Ninth Circuit Court decision that U.S. District Courts have jurisdiction over suits *by the United States against a state* (*California v. United States,* 379 U.S. 817).

ᶜPlus (as of 1992) 71 "senior" (retired appeals judges, voluntarily serving part or even full time. *Not* counted are the 264 bankruptcy judges who are distributed over the 94 districts, and are appointed by the regional courts.

ᵈIncludes the district courts for Guam, Puerto Rico, the Virgin Islands, and the Northern Mariana Islands, all of which have local as well as federal jurisdiction.

ᵉPlus about 259 "senior" (retired) district judges as of 1992 voluntarily serving part or even full time.

ᶠA case can be made for the contention that it also has a measure of *appellate* jurisdiction, involving certain actions tried before especially designated U.S. magistrates.

ᵍAs Congress did, for example, when in 1984 it restructured the bankrupt courts by assigning to the U.S. District Courts jurisdiction over Title 11 of the U.S. Code.

inal jurisdiction only. However, when necessary, they do have the obligation to *enforce* as well as review actions and orders of certain federal administration agencies and departments; certain actions tried before U.S. magistrates, formerly known as commissioners (see later), may be reviewed by them; and certain other classes of cases may be *removed* to them from the state courts under certain specific statutory authorization. Hence, in the vast majority of instances, the decisions of the District Courts are, in effect, final. And there is a veritable flood of business: they now decide upwards of 600,000 cases annually. In 1989–90, a total of 992,267 proceedings were *commenced* in the District Courts. The average civil caseload has grown by at least 4 percent every year since World War II, doubling every 15–20 years.[58] No wonder delays are common here, as well as elsewhere in the understaffed, overly litigious American judicial system.[59] At the level of the *federal* courts the time interval between the point when a case was "at issue" and the trial itself ranged from 4.1 months to 39.1 months in 1959; from 3.9 to 48.7 months in 1965–66; from 1.0 months to 52.0 months in 1982–83; and from 1.0 to 66.0 months in 1989–90. In the *state* courts, it varied from 1.0 months to 52.9 months in 1959; from 4.3 to 69.5 months in 1965–66; and then from 0.6 months to 59.1 months in 1982–83.[60] A poignant and pertinent illustration: a ten-year-old girl, Nancy Verona, was hit by a car while riding her bike. When her case at last came to trial, she was a young mother, aged nineteen, who took her baby to the court with her![61]

The Speedy Trial Act of 1974, enacted by Congress to be effective as of July 1, 1975, set up a schedule to be implemented over a four-year period on the federal level (with several states adopting similar measures). It provided for time limits, ultimately reaching 100 days (as of July 1, 1979), within which *criminal* charges must either be brought to trial or dismissed. Indeed, as of November 1980, 96 percent of District Court criminal cases reached trial within those 100 days. Not astonishingly, this legislation found itself quickly in a number of procedural as well as interpretative difficulties. It came under heavy constitutional challenge, chiefly on separation of powers grounds, and was held unconstitutional by U.S. District Court

---

58. To be precise: 217,879 civil, 48,904 criminal, and 725,484 bankruptcy cases, representing an overall increase of about 50 percent in ten years (*Annual Reports* of the U.S. District Courts). (The case backlog doubled between 1960 and 1975 and again since. See T. B. Marvell, "Caseload Growth—Past and Future Trends," 71 *Judicature* 3 [October–November 1987], pp. 151–61.

59. In 1976 a total of 5,320 civil rights suits were brought against employers—a 1500 percent increase since 1970. (*The New York Times*, May 22, 1977, Section 4, p. E7). *Civil* suits filed between 1960 and 1980 tripled and quadrupled by 1990!

60. See the symposium, "Lagging Justice," 328 *The Annals of the American Academy of Political and Social Science* (March 1960); the series by Howard James in *The Christian Science Monitor*, "Crisis in the Courts," April–July 1967, and James's book, *Crisis in the Courts*, rev. ed. (New York: David McKay Co., 1971); the statistics cited by Victor G. Rosenblum in *The 50 States and Their Local Governments*, ed. by James W. Fesler (New York: Alfred A. Knopf, 1967), pp. 434–35; and the *Annual Reports* of the Administrative Office of the U.S. Courts, 1972ff. See also the special issues of *Judicature* 65–66 (August 1981 and June–July 1982), "Court Delay: Diagnosing the Problem, Testing New Treatments;" "U.S. Courts Being Swamped . . . " *The New York Times*, July 9, 1984, p. A1; and "Rehnquist Cites Costs in Delays to a Swift Trial," *The Daily Progress*, April 11, 1987, p. A1.

61. Cited by Louis Banks, "The Crisis in the Courts," 64 *Fortune* Magazine 86 (December 1961) at 88.

Judge Joseph Young in *United States v. Howard*, 440 F. Supp. 1106 (1977). His decision was promptly appealed by the government. No final disposition having been rendered as of fall 1979, Congress postponed the law until July 1, 1980. The courts subsequently managed to skirt the constitutional issue,[62] and the statute has proved to be generally successful, although hardly inevitably so.[63]

Each of the fifty states of the Union, the District of Columbia, Puerto Rico, Guam, the Canal Zone, the Northern Mariana Islands, and the Virgin Islands contains at least one federal district with a District Court and a District Court judge, who receives $129,500 (1992) annually. There is no cutting across state lines, but in many instances the large number of cases to be adjudicated compels a subdivision of labor within a particular district. Almost all districts today (1992) have two or more judges, although there are still a few districts with only one, such as Guam and the Mariana Islands. The Southern District of New York (New York County, i.e., Manhattan; Bronx County; and the adjacent suburban counties to the north),[64] with its high proportion of complex commercial litigation, had the 1992 maximum—twenty-eight. Almost half of all litigation occurs in the twelve District Courts that are located in the larger metropolitan areas. The Chief Justice of the United States (the Chief Justice of the Supreme Court) has the authority to transfer district judges temporarily from their home circuit to a more congested one, but only with their consent. These judges are then known as "visiting" or "designated" judges. It was as Visiting Judge for the Eastern District of Arkansas that U.S. District Judge Ronald N. Davies, whose home district was North Dakota, issued the now famous injunction[65] against Governor Orval E. Faubus and other state officials of Arkansas in September 1957, after they had actively interfered with an earlier court order upholding the Little Rock School Board's desegregation plan.[66] Judge Davies had been temporarily transferred to help deal with a mounting backlog of cases. To cite one other procedural example: in order to remedy a staggering backlog of civil jury cases in the U.S. District Court for the Southern District of New York, Chief Justice Warren, acting on the urging of Chief Judge Sidney Sugarman of that court in 1968 to help clear the accumulation, assigned ten district judges from other parts of the country (one each from Oregon, California, Iowa, Kansas, Utah, Tennessee, New Mexico, and the Eastern District of New York, and two from Connecticut). The team did just that within two months. In 1978, however, the Justice Department's Office for Improvement in the Administration of Justice proposed new limits in such assignments, ultimately embraced generally, confining the latter to instances covering a regular judge's absence from his or her home circuit because of "illness, disability, or official business, or [if] a vacancy exists," but not merely because of a heavy work load.

---

62. See Henry J. Abraham, *Freedom and the Court: Civil Rights and Liberties in the United States*, 5th ed. (New York: Oxford University Press, 1988), p. 99.

63. In 1990 the Vermont Supreme Court unanimously upheld a six-month delay in *civil* jury trials in the state, holding that the constitutional guarantees of speedy trials do not mean "instant" ones (see *The New York Times*, June 5, 1990, p. A24).

64. Columbia, Dutchess, Greene, Orange, Putnam, Rockland, Sullivan, Ulster, and Westchester.

65. *United States v. Faubus*, 156 F. Supp. 220 (1957).

66. *Aaron v. Cooper*, 143 F. Supp. 855 (1956).

No matter how many judges may be permanently or temporarily assigned to a federal district, it is customary for a lone District Court judge, sitting with a jury—unless that institution has been validly waived—to preside over a trial in the roughly 400 localities where they now are held in the United States. However, in some instances of particular importance, Congress has statutorily provided for adjudication by *three-judge District Courts*. They customarily consist of two district judges and one circuit judge, the Judicial Code providing that at least one judge must be from the circuit, the next higher echelon in the judicial system. As a matter of practice, the Chief Judge of the Circuit Court involved, rarely, if ever, assigns more than that absolute minimum. Suits required to be heard by these three-judge District Courts—from which lies direct appeal to the Supreme Court of the United States as a matter of right in appropriate cases—are usually those seeking to restrain by an *injunction*, on grounds of unconstitutionality, the enforcement, operation, or execution of both federal and state statutes and orders of state administrative agencies dealing with apportionment or reapportionment of legislative districts and, similarly, in instances in which such a court is required by specific act of Congress, for example, the Civil Rights Act of 1964 and the Voting Rights Act of 1965, as amended, and the Federal Election Campaign Act of 1974.

Considerable sentiment exists for the discontinuation of the use of these three-judge tribunals—more than tripling in the number of cases handled by them during the past decade—for they have unquestionably added to the judicial workload, in general, and to Supreme Court review, in particular. Chief Justice Burger has been a leading and insistent spokesman for their abolition,[67] and, though not abolishing the three-judge tribunals, Congress, in 1976, and again dramatically in 1989, restricted the type of cases in which they may henceforth be impaneled,[68] resulting in an enormous drop in their caseload.

The busy judges of the district courts are provided with a number of assistants to carry on their tasks, all of whom are appointed by the judges themselves (some were mentioned in chapter 3). Among them are the U.S. magistrates, law clerks, bailiffs, court reporters, stenographers, clerks, probation officers, and, as of 1971, professional administrators to relieve the chief judges of management duties at the appellate level as well as here at the trial level. These positions are more or less self-explanatory, except for that of the important and influential parajudicial *U.S. Magistrate*, who not only is in charge of some of the preliminary steps involved in the pretrial process but has been granted considerably enhanced powers. Thus, he or she may issue arrest warrants; hear evidence to determine whether or not to hold an accused person for grand jury action and, if so, set the bail; and assume jurisdiction in certain minor federal offenses when the defendant waives the right to confront a federal judge and jury. Moreover, a magistrate is active in pretrial and discovery proceedings, considers preliminary petitions, and appoints legal counsel

---

67. See the "Freund Report," published by the Federal Judicial Center, January 1973; *The New York Times*, August 15, 1972, p. 1; and *U.S. News and World Report*, August 21, 1972, p. 41, for illustrative commentary. (See also Winkel, op. cit.)
68. See p. 188, *infra* for specifics.

for indigent defendants under the Criminal Justice Act of 1964.[69] As a result of the Federal Magistrates Act of 1979, full-time magistrates can now try any civil case, with the consent of all parties, as well as all misdemeanors, again such consent being granted, and the cases may be heard with or without a jury. As of 1979, too, appeals from a magistrate's judgments may, in a civil case, be taken directly to the U.S. Court of Appeals. In the instance of magistrate-conducted *criminal* misdemeanor trials, defendants must explicitly waive their right to a trial by a U.S. District Court judge, however. And although the Supreme Court ruled unanimously in 1989 that magistrates do not have the legal authority to preside over jury selection in felony cases without the defendant's consent, it held 5:4 two years later that they *may* sometimes substitute for *federal* judges in presiding over jury selection even in federal criminal trials.[70] The 1979 statute details requirements for merit appointments: candidates are appointed by District Court judges for eight- and four-year terms of office, and they must have been members of the bar for at least five years prior to their selection. Often they are former law clerks or other close associates of the district judges who appoint them (e.g., assistant U.S. Attorneys). In 1990 there were 476 authorized positions for magistrates plus a staff of 613. Salaries are geared to workload—up to $119,140 annually (1992)—but gone are the days when magistrates (then called commissioners) were paid out of court fees.[71] In 1989–90 the magistrates handled 425,211 items of judicial business.[72] Their 1979 statute-strengthened powers and duties[73] were specifically upheld by the U.S. Supreme Court, largely because a *judge* retains authority to accept, reject, or modify any rulings by a magistrate.[74]

The two most significant officers at the district level are the *U.S. Marshal* and the *U.S. Attorney*. Appointed for each of the districts by the President with the advice and consent of the Senate—with the senators of the President's political party the prime source of recommendation—the U.S. Attorney functions under the authority of the Attorney General (rather than that of the district judge). The "A.G." also appoints a number of Assistant U.S. Attorneys, often in conjunction with the patronage wishes of influential members of his political party. The U.S. Marshal,[75] appointed in the same manner as the U.S. Attorney, makes arrests; guards and transports prisoners; determines where a prisoner is to serve his or her

---

69. In 1976 the Supreme Court specifically, and unanimously, upheld the power of U.S. magistrates to review preliminary law suits involving Social Security benefits and have them prepare proposed decisions and findings for U.S. District Court judges (*Mathews v. Weber*, 423 U.S. 261).

70. *Gomez v. United States*, 490 U.S. 858, and *Peretz v. United States*, 59 LW 4830, respectively.

71. For an excellent article on recent developments in this little-known office, see Steven Pruro, Roger L. Goldman, and Alice Padawer-Singer's authoritative article in 64 *Judicature* 10 (May 1981); Carroll Seron's "Magistrates and the Work of Federal Courts: A New Division of Labor," 69 *Judicature* 6 (April–May 1986); and Christopher E. Smith's "Who are the U.S. Magistrates?" 71 *Judicature* 3 (October–November 1987), pp. 143–50.

72. *Annual Report*, Administrative Office of the United States Courts, 1990, pp. 275–86.

73. P.L. 96-82, 93 Stat. 643.

74. *United States v. Raddox*, 447 U.S. 667 (1980).

75. The origin of the office traces back to medieval England, where the Old French word *mareshal* (groom) came to mean a sort of royal sheriff in charge of procuring witnesses for the monarch.

sentence; disburses federal judicial funds; serves court orders, writs, and processes,[76] guards and transports all federal court documents, from jury notices to Supreme Court orders; ascertains the security of witnesses; generally maintains the decorum of the courtroom of the District Court of the United States; and, when called upon, aids in riot control. In 1991 there were 94 such marshals and 2,000 deputy and chief deputy marshals.[77]

The U.S. (Circuit) Courts of Appeals. Initially established in 1891 as a group of nine, and standing immediately above the U.S. District Courts in the federal constitutional court hierarchy, are the thirteen U.S. (Circuit) Courts of Appeals, twelve of these on geographic lines. The thirteenth (described briefly earlier)[78] the 1982-created U.S. Court of Appeals for the Federal Circuit, does not have a specific regional/geographic base, but "counts" as a full-fledged circuit court of appeals. They are all essentially what their name implies: appellate courts only. They do, however, have a statutory obligation to enforce, when necessary, as well as review actions of a host of federal executive agencies that are clothed with quasi-judicial functions. Among these, to cite but a few, are certain rulings of the National Labor Relations Board, wage orders of the Administration of Wage and Hour Division of the Department of Labor, and orders under antitrust or unfair practice laws of the Interstate Commerce Commission, the Federal Communications Commission, the Civil Aeronautics Board, and the Board of Governors of the Federal Reserve System. But even if one were to classify aspects of the review and enforcement of the activities of these quasi-judicial units of the federal government as original jurisdiction—and they are that only by stretching the concept considerably—the vast majority of the work of the U.S. Courts of Appeals is clearly appellate. It is, in the words of an astute commentator, a "mini Supreme Court in the vast majority of cases,"[79] for, in effect, it is at once the first and last stop for appeals from below in all instances but those that go on up to the U.S. Supreme Court and those few that are permitted to bypass it from below en route to the Supreme Court. Other than the appeals from the highest state courts of record, which go directly to the Supreme Court without touching the other federal courts, the Circuit Courts of Appeals may be validly bypassed only if (1) direct appeal lies from a decision by a three-judge District Court, as explained before, (2) there is a direct appeal statutorily authorized to the Supreme Court from a limited number of ordinary

76. This is a task that frequently takes considerable ingenuity. For example, to serve a desegregation injunction on the evasive and defiant Alabama Governor George Wallace in 1963, one deputy marshal stowed away in the men's room aboard the governor's plane!

77. See Annual Report of the U.S. District Courts and telephone interview with William Dempsey, Congressional and Public Affairs Office, U.S. Marshal's Service, October 15, 1991. Appointees must have attained a qualifying grade on the Treasury Enforcement Examination and have at least five years of investigative experience. For an excellent recent treatment see Frederick S. Calhoun, The Lawmen: United States Marshals and Their Deputies, 1789–1989 (Washington, D.C.: Smithsonian Institution Press, 1989).

78. See p. 155, supra.

79. J. Woodford Howard, Jr., Courts of Appeals in the Federal Judicial System (Princeton, NJ: Princeton University Press, 1981), p. 58.

District Court cases, such as a case in which a federal statute has been held unconstitutional by a District Court and the United States is a party to the suit, and (3) it is shown that a case is of "such imperative public importance as to justify the deviation from normal appellate process and require immediate settlement [in the Supreme Court]," as was true in such momentous controversies as those represented by the 1952 *Steel Seizure* and 1974 *Nixon Tapes* Cases.[80]

But in all other instances, both civil and criminal, the Circuit Court of Appeals is the natural appellate tribunal for the approximately 41,000 cases—an increase of 2000 percent between 1942 and 1992—that now (1992) come up to it annually from the U.S. District Courts in the fifty states, the District of Columbia, and the territories, and from the many independent regulatory commissions, agencies, and cabinet departments that are endowed with quasi-judicial powers and functions. In effect, it *finally* decides approximately 85 percent of all federal cases. For example, the Court of Appeals for the District of Columbia, sometimes referred to as the second most important federal tribunal, held, on reviewing the denial of one Shachtman's passport application by the Department of State, that the latter had violated the due process of law clause of the Fifth Amendment in the circumstances at issue.[81] The Department of State subsequently complied with the court's mandate. Illustrations of cases arising from a decision of a District Court rather than that of an administrative agency or department are the (unsuccessful) appeal to the U.S. Court of Appeals for the Second Circuit by Alger Hiss seeking reversal of his conviction on perjury charges in connection with the theft of U.S. government documents and the (equally unsuccessful) appeal by President Nixon to the Court of Appeals for the District of Columbia from Judge John J. Sirica's order to turn nine of the Watergate tapes over to him for scrutiny.[82]

Although officially stripped of the term *circuit* in 1948, the courts on this important level in the federal judicial process are still generally referred to as Circuit Courts. There are eleven such *numbered* circuits in the United States plus an unnumbered twelfth one, known as the *Court of Appeals for the District of Columbia*,[83] and the thirteenth, the *Court of Appeals for the Federal Circuit*, a 1982-created consolidation of parts of the jurisdiction of the old Court of Claims and the Court of Customs and Patent Appeals:

---

80. *Youngstown Sheet and Tube Co. v. Sawyer*, 343 U.S. 579 and *United States v. Nixon*, 417 U.S. 683, respectively.

81. *Shachtman v. Dulles*, 225 F. 2d 938 (1955).

82. *United States v. Hiss*, 185 F. 2d 822 (1950) and *Nixon v. Sirica*, 487 F. 2d 700 (1973), respectively.

83. In 1933 the U.S. Supreme Court ruled that both the U.S. District Court for the District of Columbia and the U.S. Court of Appeals for the District of Columbia are at the same time "constitutional" and "legislative" courts (*O'Donoghue v. United States*, 289 U.S. 516). In 1930 it had held that "it is recognized that the courts of the District of Columbia are not created under the judiciary article of the Constitution but are legislative courts. . . . " (*Federal Radio Commission v. General Electric Company*, 281 U.S. 464, at 468). But, of course, *O'Donoghue* governs today. However, the Court ruled unanimously in 1977 that these federal courts have no jurisdictional role in purely local criminal cases—that the judges of the home-ruled District of Columbia court structure have the competence to decide *all*, even constitutional problem, cases (*Swain v. Pressley*, 430 U.S. 372).

First Circuit:	Maine, Massachusetts, New Hampshire, Rhode Island, Puerto Rico
Second Circuit:[84]	Connecticut, New York, Vermont
Third Circuit:	Delaware, New Jersey, Pennsylvania, Virgin Islands
Fourth Circuit:	Maryland, North Carolina, South Carolina, Virginia, West Virginia
Fifth Circuit:	Louisiana, Mississippi, Texas
Sixth Circuit:	Kentucky, Michigan, Ohio, Tennessee
Seventh Circuit:	Illinois, Indiana, Wisconsin
Eighth Circuit:	Arkansas, Iowa, Minnesota, Missouri, Nebraska North Dakota, South Dakota
Ninth Circuit:	Alaska, Arizona, California, Hawaii, Idaho, Montana, Nevada, Oregon, Washington, Guam, Northern Mariana Islands
Tenth Circuit:	Colorado, Kansas, New Mexico, Oklahoma, Utah, Wyoming
Eleventh Circuit:	Alabama, Florida, Georgia

Each of these circuits is theoretically headed by one of the nine justices of the U.S. Supreme Court. By tradition they are said to be "riding circuit"—the junior Justices usually, but not necessarily, being assigned the "extra" circuits.[85] Indeed, this is what the Justices used to do, literally—and a frightful physical burden it was![86]—at the beginning of America's nationhood, but the practice fell into disuse approximately three-quarters of a century later with the enactment of the Judiciary Acts of 1869 and 1891. Today, lack of time prevents them from more than nominal participation, although they continue to be faithfully and formally "assigned" at the beginning of each term. And, of course, they do retain the power to act on certain pleas that arise from court actions, particularly dispositive orders, in "their" circuits. A typical illustration is Justice White's refusal to set aside an Oklahoma District Court decision that had nullified the state's May 1964 primary and had ordered a new primary for that September on a "one-man, one-vote" basis. White, as the Justice in administrative charge of the Tenth Circuit, of which Oklahoma is a part, simply wrote "stay denied," and "that," in Justice Holmes's language,

---

84. Styled by the then President-elect of the American Bar Association, Lawrence E. Walsh, as "for practical purposes, the court of last resort for the most important commercial and financial problems of one of the great financial centers of the world" (*The New York Times*, April 27, 1975, sec. 4, p. 5.)
85. In 1977–78 they were instead assigned to the then two most senior members of the Court, Chief Justice Burger and ranking Associate Justice Brennan.
86. Justice Iredell commented that he felt like a "travelling postboy" in the 1790s, as he rode over 4,000 miles to cover the Southern Circuit (quoted in John P. Frank's *The Marble Palace* [New York: Alfred A. Knopf, 1958], p. 10.) In 1838 the nine Supreme Court Justices reported having traveled an average of 2,975 miles, with Justice McKinley's "logging" fully 10,000! (See Felix Frankfurter and James M. Landis, *The Business of the Supreme Court* [New York: Macmillan, 1928], pp. 49–50.

"was that!" Supreme Court Justices are also empowered to preside over U.S. District Court proceedings but seldom do so (a rare exception being Justice Rehnquist's trial of *Heislup v. Town of Colonial Branch* on June 18–19, 1984).[87]

The thirteen Circuit Courts of Appeals comprise a statutorily authorized total of 179 (1992) judges—salaried at $137,300 (1992) annually—who, except for the judges of the District of Columbia, must be residents of the assigned circuit during the time they serve and even thereafter, because, though they may have retired, they are still subject to assignments by the Chief Justice of the United States. Each of the Circuit Courts has a Chief Judge, who is customarily the judge with the longest service and who may serve for a total of seven years. (No one is eligible for the post if over the age of sixty-four at the time his or her seniority-based turn comes.) Upon reaching the voluntary retirement age of seventy, the incumbent Chief Judge retains powers as a full-fledged member of the court—assuming the judge neither chooses to retire nor has accumulated sufficient time to do so on full salary—but ceases to be its head. This arrangement also applies in the District Courts that have two or more judges but *not* in the Supreme Court.

Each court consists of between four and twenty-eight judges, depending on the amount of work in the circuit.[88] Usually three judges sit to decide cases; a quorum is two. In rare instances the entire membership of circuits sits *en banc*. Proceedings before the Courts of Appeals are conducted on the basis of the record established below—that is, before the U.S. District Courts or one of the administrative agencies. The most important cases are selected for rare oral argument—for example, the constitutionality of the Federal Election Campaign Act of 1974[89]—while the lesser ones, which are the majority, are decided on the basis of submitted documents (except in the Second Circuit, which has a history of hearing oral argument in *all* cases). At least in theory, *new* evidence may not be presented at the bar of this appellate tribunal, just as it may not be introduced in the appellate cases reaching the highest ranking court in America's judicial hierarchy, the Supreme Court of the United States. The Courts of Appeals' decisions are subject to review on appeal to the U.S. Supreme Court. More often than not the tendency is to affirm the intermediate appellate tribunal, but by no means inevitably. Thus, in the 1983–84 term, by May 1984 the Supreme Court had issued full opinions in fifteen of the Ninth Circuit's decisions, and in all fifteen had totally or substantially reversed that Court's judgments. It might be noted that sixteen of the then twenty-three active Ninth Circuit Court judges were appointed by President Carter.[90]

---

87. 84–340R. Justice Rehnquist served at the invitation of U.S. District Court Judge D. Dortch Warriner of the Eastern District of Virginia, trying the case in Richmond.
88. In 1991 the Ninth had twenty-eight, the Fifth had seventeen, and the Eleventh had twelve. ("Senior" status judges, of whom the Ninth had eight, are not counted here.)
89. *Buckley v. Valeo*, 519 F.2d 821 (1975).
90. *The Washington Post*, May 23, 1984, p. A19. See also Gerard F. Uelmen, "The Influence of the Solicitor General upon Supreme Court Disposition of Federal Circuit Court Decisions: A Closer Look at the Ninth Circuit Record," 69 *Judicature* 6 (April–May, 1986), pp. 361–66.

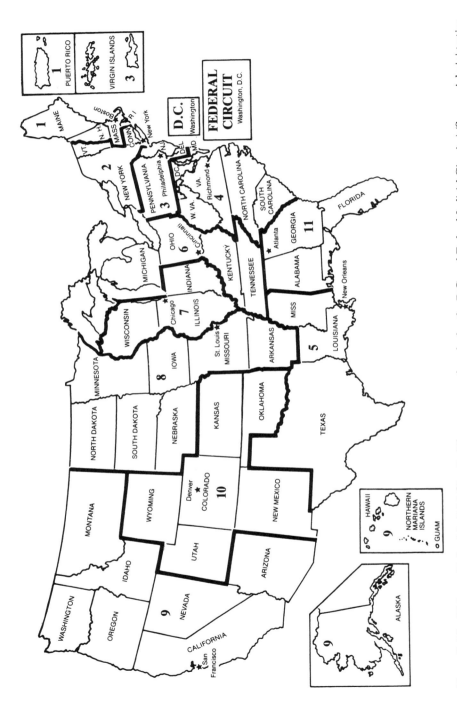

Figure 2. The Thirteen Federal Judicial Circuits (Eleven are numbered, plus the D.C. and Federal Judicial Circuits.) (Source: Administrative Office of the United States Courts, September 1991.)

ADMINISTERING THE FEDERAL JUDICIARY

Before turning to a discussion of the Supreme Court, something should be said about the administration of the federal judicial system. While considerable thought may well have been given for many years to the establishment of a centralized administrative structure for these courts, it was actually not until shortly prior to the second quarter of this century that the judicial and legislative branches, particularly the former, recognized the urgency of the problem to the extent of doing something about it—other than to declaim and exhort on what had become an increasingly deplorable state of administrative anarchy. Fortunately, Congress yielded to mounting pressure by bar, bench, and interested laypersons, and the establishment of the Judicial Conference of the United States and the Administrative Office of the U.S. Courts in 1922 and 1939, respectively, effected considerable

The Judicial Conference of the United States. The 1922 statute requires "the Chief Justice . . . to submit to Congress an annual report of the proceedings of the Judicial Conference and its recommendation for legislation." This is done faithfully and to considerable advantage by the "Chief," who is head of that body. In addition to him, it consists (1992) of the chief judge of each of the thirteen federal judicial circuits (see Figure 2), twelve district court judges, one from each of these circuits except the thirteenth (the U.S. Court of Appeals for the Federal Circuit)—chosen for a term of three years by the judges of the Circuit at its annual judicial Conference, and two bankruptcy judges. The Judicial Conference meets at least twice a year at the Supreme Court in absolute secrecy for the legislatively established purpose of making a "comprehensive survey of the conditions of business in the courts of the United States and [of preparing] plans for assignment of judges to or from circuits or districts where necessary." It is also required to submit suggestions to the various courts "in the interest of uniformity and expedition of business." This vital body of twenty-eight prestigious and influential experts has made an excellent job of keeping abreast of the needs of an efficient judiciary and has done its utmost—in conjunction with the Administrative Office of the U.S. Courts, for which it establishes policy—to realize these needs. In that capacity, to cite an example of its administrative and personnel role, it sent out the following admonition to all federal judges: "No justice or judge of the United States shall serve in the capacity of officer or director or employee of any corporation organized for profit."[91] Repeatedly, it has called on all federal trial courts to adopt rules limiting what lawyers may say publicly about criminal cases.

Although not all of the Judicial Conference's policy recommendations have either been adopted, or adopted speedily, by Congress—this applies especially to those involving the creation of new judgeships—the legislative branch has displayed considerable regard for the wisdom of the Judicial Conference. Thus, in 1958 Congress passed a Conference-recommended law authorizing the Judicial Conference to set up committees of judges, lawyers, and law professors to study the rules of procedure in the federal courts. On receiving such committees' rec-

91. As quoted in its *Annual Report* for 1978.

ommendations, the Judicial Conference passes judgment on them and then sends them on to the Supreme Court for its action. Adopted changes become effective in ninety days unless they are specifically disapproved by Congress during that time. Congress also acquiesced in the Conference's request for federally appropriated funds for the defense of the indigents in federal courts, a move that resulted in the Criminal Justice Act of 1964, and in the late 1970s and 1980s it yielded to repeated calls for a marked increase in judicial salaries as well as in the number of federal judges.

The Administrative Office of the U.S. Courts. This judicial housekeeping agency (and veritable gold mine of statistics) is the executive arm of the Judicial Conference. It is headed by the director and the deputy director, both of whom are appointed by the Chief Justice of the Supreme Court. The director possesses no administrative jurisdiction vis-à-vis the Supreme Court, but the director and his or her subordinates are crucially involved in the administrative business of the subordinate federal courts. (Indeed, an increasing number of the fifty states have begun to establish similar bodies—e.g., California, Iowa, New York, and Pennsylvania.) Among these tasks of the now more than 500-members agency are the compilation of the suggested budgets, determination of personnel needs, examination of the dockets, auditing of accounts, procurement and allocation of supplies, preparation of all vital statistics in connection with the business of the courts (its Annual Report has become essential for all those interested in the judicial process), and all such other duties as may be assigned to the director and his staff by either the Supreme Court or the Judicial Conference—both of which are headed by the Chief Justice of the United States. The Administrative Office of the U.S. Court has become an essential arm of the judicial system; it has been widely and justly acclaimed; it has, in effect, become indispensable to the orderly and successful operation of the courts. Judge John J. Parker, who characterized it at the time of its creation in 1939 as "probably the greatest piece of legislation affecting the judiciary since the Judiciary Act of 1789,"[92] was quite correct in his analysis. Nonetheless, constant efforts to bring about further improvement in the operation and function of the courts, high as well as low, are essential. The establishment in 1967 of the Federal Judicial Center as the research and training agency of the federal judicial system, with the Chief Justice of the United States as chairman of the board and the director of the Administrative Office of the U.S. Courts one of its members, is a highly commendable step in the right direction.[93] So is the creation of State/Federal Judicial Councils in almost all of the states (to alleviate friction between the two jurisdictions and to resolve overlapping between the two court systems) largely due to the efforts of Chief Justice Burger; his call for a National Institute of Justice (to devise proposals to ameliorate various aspects of the judicial process); the establishment of the Institute for Court Management in Denver in 1970; and the 1972 creation of the National Center for State Courts in historic Williamsburg, Virginia (to assist those courts in research and development to meet

92. As quoted by James Willard Hurst, The Growth of American Law: The Law Makers (Boston: Little, Brown, 1950), pp. 114, 454.
93. For a brief sketch of the Center's functions, see n. 146, p. 95, ch. 2, supra.

cascading burdens of litigation and adjudication).[94] There remains much room, of course, for additional improvement, especially in the realm of judicial education in which, however, aided by the establishment of some of these bodies—plus the American Academy of Judicial Education, the Institute of Judicial Administration in New York, and the National College of the State Judiciary—major studies are being undertaken to maintain and improve professional competence through, as the American Bar Association put it, "continuing professorial education."[95]

94. See the interview with Chief Justice Warren E. Burger, "New Ways to Speed Up Justice," *U.S. News and World Report*, August 21, 1972, pp. 38–46; "Burger Renews Pleas for Agency," *The New York Times*, December 7, 1972, p. 31; and his comprehensive, forthright annual "State of the Judiciary" messages to the profession and to the country, 1972ff. See also the imaginative new Judicial Fellows program.
95. See *60 Judicature* 7 (February 1977), pp. 334–42. As of 1975 at least three states—Minnesota, Iowa, and Wisconsin—made "refresher courses" for sitting judges compulsory. Early in 1978 Chief Justice Burger, in a series of much publicized lectures and speeches well received publicly, reportedly charged that up to "50 percent" of the lawyers who practiced in trial courts were inadequate.

5

Courts at Home: II—The Supreme Court

AT THE ZENITH: THE U.S. SUPREME COURT

The most dazzling jewel in the judicial crown of the United States is the revered and often controversial U.S. Supreme Court. It is the sole court mentioned specifically in Article III or in any other part of the Constitution, all other federal courts having been created by statute. The Supreme Court, the national symbol of justice, stands at the very pinnacle of the judiciary: there is no higher court, and all others bow before it—or, at least, are expected to do so. It is, in Alpheus Thomas Mason's words—so prophetic for the Watergate crisis of 1974—"the American counterpart of the British Crown, but unlike a queen on the throne, the Court has real power. It can bring Congress, President, state governors and legislators to heel."[1] At times having had as few as five, and at other times as many as ten, Justices in the first eighty years of its venerable history, the Court has stood at nine ever since the first term of President Grant in 1869. Before that date, and as dictated by various policy considerations, its membership, which is fixed by Congress, comprised five in 1789, six in 1790, seven in 1807, nine in 1837, ten in 1863, and eight in 1866.

The Supreme Court consists of the Chief Justice and eight Associate Justices, the former being currently (1992) rewarded with an annual salary of $166,200, the latter with $159,500 each,[2] usually, but not always, subject to annual incre-

---

1. "Judicial Activism: Old and New," 55 *Virginia Law Review* 411 (1969).
2. An illustration of petty congressional pique vis-à-vis the Supreme Court, motivated chiefly by its momentous and trail-blazing civil rights and civil liberties decisions of the 1950s and 1960s, was the refusal of Congress in 1964 and again in 1965 to give the Chief Justice and his associates on the Court the same $7,500 pay increase then granted all lower federal court judges. Instead, the members of the highest tribunal had to settle for a $4,500 raise.

ments.[3] Yet the nonsalary compensations, frequently called "psychic income" by college professors, are undoubtedly considerable. (The retirement prerogatives were discussed in chapter 2.)

ORIGINAL JURISDICTION

The U.S. Supreme Court has both *original* and *appellate* jurisdiction, but it exercises the former only in rare instances. Moreover, the Eleventh Amendment to the Constitution, ratified in 1798, has seriously abridged that phase of its work by removing from its, and the lower federal courts', jurisdiction all those cases in which one of its own citizens or one of another state or of a foreign country, or even a sovereign foreign country itself, wishes to sue one of the states of the United States. In effect, the Eleventh Amendment enacted the necessity of obtaining a *state's permission to sue it* in all litigation involving these categories.

That Amendment was adopted as a direct result of a Supreme Court decision in 1793 in the case of *Chisholm v. Georgia*.[4] There the Court, in a broad decision, but in accordance with the terminology of Article III of the Constitution, held 4:1[5] that Chisholm, a citizen of one state (South Carolina), could sue another state (Georgia) in the federal courts—an outrageous and shocking pronouncement in the eyes of citizens with confirmed states-rights views. It was especially galling because the matter involved debts owed to a then-deceased British creditor, one Robert Farquhar, a merchant who had resided in Charleston, South Carolina, for whom Chisholm acted as an executor. (But it ought to be noted that the debts were for supplies sold in 1777 to Georgia in full accordance with the wishes and at the direction of Georgia's Executive Council.) The Supreme Court's judgment, which had been handed down without benefit of argument by Georgia, triggered instantaneous and profound opposition. For example, the lower house of the legislature of the State of Georgia passed a bill to punish by hanging "without benefit of clergy" any person endeavoring to aid in the enforcement of the decision! Merely two days had passed after the announcement in *Chisholm v. Georgia* when the future Eleventh Amendment was introduced into both houses of Congress.

Thereafter, the *original* jurisdiction docket of the Supreme Court became a very minor factor in its work. Not counting *memorandum orders* (to be explained later), at the outset of its 1991–92 term the Court had *rendered decisions* under the original jurisdiction clause of the Constitution—Article III, Section 2, Paragraph 2, as amended—in only 165 cases since its first term in 1789.[6] The cases that now still

---

3. Under the Federal Salary Act of 1975, which provided for these incremental arrangements, the percentage is left to Presidential discretion—or, as President Carter ordered for 1978–79, they may be omitted entirely. The increments ordinarily ranged from 4.3 to 8.7 percent. None at all were authorized for federal judges for 1988. But Congress provided a hefty 25 percent increase as of January 1991.

4. 2 Dallas 419. Actually, *Chisholm* involved the review of a case that had reached the Court from the Circuit Court below, entitled *Farquhar v. Georgia (Farquhar's Executor v. Georgia)* (Case File, Records of U.S. Circuit Court, District of Georgia, Case A, Box 1).

5. William Paterson had been commissioned an Associate Justice in 1793, but he did not participate in the case.

6. For a detailed analysis, including a list of 123 of these cases as of June 1959, see "The Original Jurisdiction of the United States Supreme Court," 11 *Stanford Law Review* (July 1959), pp. 665–719.

presumably commence there under it do so as a *matter of right* under its provisions. Theoretically, they comprise the following four categories of cases or controversies: (1) those between the United States and one of the fifty states,[7] (2) those between two or more states; (3) those involving *foreign* ambassadors, other *foreign* public ministers, and *foreign* consuls, or their "domestics or domestic servants not inconsistent with the law of nations"; and (4) those *commenced by a state* against citizens of another state or aliens or *against* a foreign country. (But note that if these actions are *commenced by the citizens*[8] or *alien or even the foreign country*[9] against a state, that litigation *must begin in state court*, in accordance with the provisions of the Eleventh Amendment.)

However, the Supreme Court does not exercise *exclusive* original jurisdiction even in the four categories cited, with the sole exception of category (2), that is, cases or controversies involving two or more of the several states. There it, and it alone, exercises original jurisdiction. But Congress, with the hearty approval of the Court, has extended *concurrent original* jurisdiction to the federal District Courts in litigation affecting category (3) and in *some*, but not all, cases in categories (1) and (4) in which a state is party to the suit at issue. Hence, most of the cases the Supreme Court has heard on its original jurisdiction docket have indeed involved two or more states. For example, the nine successive actions the state of Virginia filed against West Virginia in the lengthy and trying history of their debt controversy were all heard at the bar of the Supreme Court.[10] More recent controversies have involved Michigan and Ohio in a possession dispute over a 200-square-mile tract in the Maumee Bay area of mineral-rich Lake Erie,[11] California and Arizona in their persistent water rights squabbles,[12] a river boundary dispute between Louisiana and Texas,[13] Delaware's unsuccessful attempt to have the Court declare unconstitutional the electoral college vote count in presidential elections,[14] the evidently eternal Virginia–Maryland "war of the oyster beds,"[15] a Mississippi river bed area dispute between Mississippi and Arkansas,[16] and another river border dispute between Ohio and Kentucky.[17] All of these cases must, and do, commence in the Supreme Court. Yet if a determination of *facts* is required, the Court here often utilizes the device of referring these disputes to a special *master*—frequently an ex-jurist—for a hearing and report to it, as it did in the Virginia–Maryland oyster dis-

7. E.g., *United States v. Maine*, 420 U.S. 515 (1975), involving the always live question of whether the states or the federal government have jurisdiction over oil deposits outside the three-mile limit. The federal government emerged victorious, 8:0, the White opinion being largely based on a *stare decisis* interpretation, bottomed on the 1953 Submerged Lands and Outer Continental Shelf Acts, as construed in, for example, *United States v. California II*, 381 U.S. 139 (1965).
8. See *Hans v. Louisiana*, 134 U.S. 1 (1890).
9. See *Monaco v. Mississippi*, 292 U.S. 313 (1934).
10. E.g., *Virginia v. West Virginia*, 246 U.S. 565 (1918).
11. *Michigan v. Ohio*, 386 U.S. 1029 (1967).
12. *Arizona v. California*, 370 U.S. 906 (1961); ibid., 373 U.S. 546 (1963); ibid., rehearing denied, 375 U.S. 892 (1963). But see its "return" in 1983: 460 U.S. 605.
13. *Texas v. Louisiana*, 410 U.S. 702 (1973).
14. *Delaware et al., v. New York et al.*, 385 U.S. 895 (1966).
15. E.g., *Virginia v. Maryland*, 355 U.S. 946 (1958).
16. *Mississippi v. Arkansas*, 415 U.S. 302 (1974), involving the so-called Luna Bar.
17. *Ohio v. Kentucky*, 444 U.S. 335 (1980); rehearing denied, 445 U.S. 939.

pute, the Western water litigation cases, the 1966 suit by Ohio against Kentucky in a dispute over their boundary, and in the federal–state jurisdictional squabble over offshore oil deposits.[18]

APPELLATE JURISDICTION

The primary task of the Court is *appellate*. In that capacity it serves as the final arbiter in the construction of the Constitution of the United States and it thus provides a uniform interpretation of the law, although its very power to do so also enables it to change its mind from case to case. However, at least to a considerable degree, it attempts to adhere to precedent, the aforementioned doctrine known as *stare decisis*, that is, let the decision stand, giving to precedents the authority of established law. (We shall examine this philosophy of law and the extent of its success in chapter 8.)

Appellate cases come to the Supreme Court from the subordinate federal courts and the state courts of last resort (which are usually, but not always, the state supreme courts). Actually, there are five different sources of the appellate cases that reach the Court: (1) the state court of last resort having jurisdiction in a particular action, provided that a federal question has been raised validly, and further provided that all remedies have been duly exhausted below, (2) the thirteen U.S. Circuit Courts of Appeals, (3) the U.S. District Courts, (4) one of the special constitutional legislative courts, and (5) the territorial courts.

WRITS OF REVIEW

Cases or controversies normally reach the Supreme Court for purposes of review under its appellate jurisdiction in one of three principal ways, as each member of the Court considers every application for review: (1) on a writ of appeal, as a matter of right (usually simply called appeal), a writ severely limited in 1988[19]; (2) on a *writ of certiorari*, as a matter of Court discretion (usually simply called *certiorari* or *cert*); and (3) by *certification*. The old *writ of* error, a common law process roughly akin to today's writ of appeal, was statutorily discontinued in the federal courts in 1928. It brought the entire record of a proceeding in a lower court before the Supreme Court for its consideration of "errors of law," allegedly committed at a low level. We may also quickly dispose of *certification*. Rarely employed, it presents the Court with even fewer cases than those on its original jurisdiction docket. It covers

18. The four masters involved in these four decisions were, respectively, retired U.S. Supreme Court Associate Justice Stanley F. Reed, retired U.S. District Court Judge Simon H. Rifkind, retired U.S. Court of Appeals Judge Percy Foreman, and retired U.S. Court of Appeals Judge Albert B. Maris. Masters' reports are normally accepted by the Court, but not always: For example, in 1974 the Court rejected a master's proposal in connection with a long-standing dispute between New York and Vermont over water pollution in Lake Champlain. (*Vermont v. New York*, 415 U.S. 270). And, on occasion, a disappointed litigant may seek Court reconsideration of an accepted master's recommendation, as Maine and eleven other states did in 1975 opposing Master Maris's ruling against the states and in favor of the federal government as to jurisdiction over offshore Atlantic Coast oil deposits outside the three-mile limit (*United States v. Maine*, 420 U.S. 515). The Court, basing its decision on both Judge Maris's recommendation and *stare decisis*, stuck to its holding that it was indeed the federal government that owned the rights to the deposits in question.

19. P.L. 100-352, June 27, 1988, "An Act to improve the administration of justice . . . and for other purposes."

"any question of law in any civil or criminal case in which instructions are desired" by the lower court, usually a Court of Appeals or the Court of Claims. (Arguably, a fourth way for cases to reach the Court is by "extraordinary writ," such as *habeas corpus* or *quo warranto*.)

Appeal. In the instance of a writ of appeal, which, as noted, has been drastically curtailed, the aggrieved party—known as the *appellant*; the answering party is the *appellee* or *respondent*—has an absolute, statutorily granted right to carry a case to the U.S. Supreme Court, which in theory must review it. It was used frequently until, bowing to the pleas of the case-beleaguered judiciary, Congress took its 1988 curtailing action. In any event, since 1928 the high tribunal has had the very considerable discretionary power to reject such an appeal on the ground that the federal question, otherwise validly raised, is "insubstantial."[20] Moreover, the federal question must have been validly raised early in the state court—when the matter begins as a state issue. Even then the Supreme Court might not take the case if the state court's judgment can be sustained on an independent ground of state law. This highly significant multiple discretionary element in the area of the Court's so-called compulsory appellate jurisdiction caused it to dismiss over 90 percent of the appeals and petitions presented to it in the 1986–87 term, for example. Of these, at least half were rejected "for want of a substantial federal question" or a "properly presented" one,[21] the balance on other jurisdictional grounds. An average of 50 to 60 percent of the writs of appeal are dismissed or the judgment below affirmed without printing the record or oral argument, and Justice Douglas contended in an important statistical article that, as a rule, the Court actually grants no more than 15 percent.[22]

Hence, the appeal was thus always used but sparingly, generally in only about 9 percent of all cases or controversies *presented* to the Court, but Douglas claimed that this 9 percent constituted 90 percent of all "meritorious" cases.[23] As a result of the 1988 changes, the writ of appeal is now confined to those situations in which a U.S. Three-Judge District Court (which includes at least one judge from the U.S. Court of Appeals) has granted or denied an interlocutory or permanent injunction in any proceeding required by an act of Congress to be heard by such a tribunal. An example would be the 1964 decision in *Schiro v. Bynum*,[24] in which the Supreme Court unanimously and summarily affirmed a Three-Judge District Court decision striking down a Louisiana law requiring racial segregation of sports events and entertainment open to the general public. The constitutional issue thus adjudicated here was the meaning of the equal protection of the laws clause of the Fourteenth Amendment. Many racial and gender discrimination cases have

---

20. See *Kohrig v. Illinois*, 479 U.S. 1073 (1987), in which the Court rejected Elizabeth J. Kohrig's appeal challenging Illinois's mandatory seatbelt law as lacking a substantial federal question.
21. E.g., *Albanese v. United States*, 350 U.S. 845 (1955), *certiorari* denied (the Court's refusal to interfere with a Connecticut law that allows a person injured by a drunk to sue the person who sold the drink), and *Doe v. Delaware*, 450 U.S. 382, (1981) *per curiam*, respectively.
22. William O. Douglas, "The Supreme Court and Its Case Load," 45 *Cornell Law Quarterly* 401 (Spring 1960) at 410.
23. *Ibid.*, at 409. In 1987 the appeal route was successfully utilized in some 220 of the 4,000 cases acted upon, comprising 5.1 percent of the docket.
24. 375 U.S. 395.

reached the Supreme Court by this route and may be expected to continue to do so.[25]

Certiorari. In all other cases involving a "federal question of substance"—which now means in almost all instances—the disappointed litigant in a suit has *no right* to appeal to the Supreme Court the adverse decision he sustained; *but,* he or she does have the *privilege* of petitioning the highest bench in the land to grant a writ of *certiorari*—a Latin term meaning "made more certain," or "better informed." Generally, each such petition,[26] a copy of which goes to every Justice with a record of the proceedings below, comprises the two sides' arguments both for and against its grant—the party bringing the action known as the *plaintiff* or *petitioner,* the other as the *respondent.* Ninety percent of the cases decided by the Supreme Court reach it by that method, and most of these come to it from the Circuit Courts of Appeal. Neither in *certiorari* nor in *appeal* proceedings is a formal printed record necessary until such time as the writ of *certiorari* is granted or the appeal noted. However, forty copies of the petition must be filed within thirty to ninety days, depending on the type of case,[27] after final judgment and denial of rehearing in the lower courts, and they must be accompanied by a $200 fee.

The grant of *certiorari* signifies the willingness of the Supreme Court to review a case, based on a written petition initiated by the plaintiff together with a reply from the other side, which often urges a denial of *certiorari*. A grant of the petition—"petes for cert.," Justice Holmes used to call them—directs the lower court to send up the record in the case for review so that the decision "may be made more certain." Needless to say, the Court is quite chary of granting its writs of *certiorari* and, unless it detects an issue of substantial significance or controversy in the case or happens to be especially interested in it, chances are that the application for the writ will be rejected with a terse "*certiorari* denied," as is evident from the published listing of a large number of petitions thus disposed of. The Court's own Rule 19 states that *certiorari* will be granted only "when there are special and important reasons therefor. . . . [in order to settle] important questions of federal law, which [have] not been settled by this Court." Among these, according to the language of Rule 19 of the Court's Revised Rules of 1967, are the following: (1) when two federal Circuit Courts of Appeals or two Three-Judge Federal District Courts have rendered conflicting decisions (e.g., in one case, two diametrically opposed judgments involving the constitutionality of the so-called Blue Laws were handed down by two Three-Judge Federal District Courts, sitting in Boston and Philadelphia, striking down and upholding such Massachusetts and Pennsylvania laws, respectively,[28] and, in another case, equally opposing judgments, this time on

25. E.g., *Brown v. Board of Education of Topeka*, 347 U.S. 483 (1954) and *Swann v. Charlotte-Mecklen-burg Board of Education*, 402 U.S. 1 (1971).
26. The petition must set forth the basis for the Court's jurisdiction, frame the questions presented for review, state the facts material to a consideration of those questions, and, in the words of Chief Justice Vinson, "explain why it is vital that the questions involved be decided finally by the Supreme Court" (from his talk to a group of University of Pennsylvania students, April 16, 1952).
27. The Court's *Rules* require a thirty-day deadline in *federal criminal* cases, ninety days in *federal civil,* cases, and ninety days also in *any state* case (letter from Clerk's Office, October 9, 1976).
28. *Crown Kosher Super Market v. Gallagher*, 176 F. Supp. 466 (1959), and *Two Guys from Harrison Allentown v. McGinley*, 179 F. Supp. 944 (1959).

the constitutionality of the Public Accommodations Title of the Civil Rights Act of 1964, were rendered by two Three-Judge courts in the same circuit—the Fifth—in Atlanta and Birmingham, respectively, upholding and striking down that title of the Act)[29]; (2) when a state court or a federal appellate court has passed on an important question of federal law on which the Supreme Court has never passed[30]; (3) when these lower courts have rendered a decision that conflicts with applicable precedent established by the Supreme Court[31]; or (4) when a federal court has so far departed from the accepted canons of judicial proceedings as to call for exercise of the Supreme Court's power of supervision.[32] In any case, as Justice Frankfurter viewed the Court's power to control its docket, "[it] carries with it the responsibility of granting review only in cases that demand adjudication of the basis of importance to the operation of our federal system; importance of the outcome merely to the parties is not enough."[33] In an address to a group of Illinois lawyers he illustrated what the Chief Justice, who plays an important role in certiorari grants, might say:

> This is a very interesting and important question . . ., but we can't do any better than Judge Julian Mack [late judge of the U. S. Court of Appeal] did with it below. He really knows more about this field of law than the rest of us. I suggest we deny this petition for certiorari.[34]

This posture is symptomatic of what Justice Frankfurter used to term the need for "alert deference" to lower court opinions in general. It echoes Chief Justice Vinson's contention that the Supreme Court "is not, and never has been, primarily concerned with the corrections of errors in lower court decisions. . . . [Its] function is, therefore, to resolve conflict of opinions on federal questions of wide import under the Constitution, laws and treaties of the United States, and to exercise supervisory power over the lower courts."[35]

Still, a case of substance is not necessarily a "big" or "major" case. For example, the Supreme Court once reached down to the Police Court of Louisville, Kentucky, to set aside, as a violation of the due process of law clause of the Fourteenth Amendment to the Constitution, two $10 fines for loitering and disorderly conduct.[36] This case symbolizes the willingness of the highest court in the land to look

---

29. Heart of Atlanta Motel v. United States, 231 F. Supp. 393 (1964), and McClung v. Katzenbach, 233 F. Supp. 815 (1964). Another, more recent illustration was the issue of "selective" prosecution of individuals failing to register for the draft, with the Ninth Circuit approving and the Sixth Circuit disapproving: United States v. Wayte, 710 F.2d 1385 (CA 9) and United States v. Schmucker, 721 F. 2d 1046 (CA 6), respectively (the U.S. Supreme Court ultimately ruled 7:2 in favor of the Ninth Circuit in 1985 in Wayte v. United States, 53 LW 4319).

·30. Furman v. Georgia, 408 U.S. 238 (1972).

31. E.g., Biddle v. Perovich, 274 U.S. 480 (1927), and United States v. O'Brien plus O'Brien v. United States, 391 U.S. 367 (1969).

32. E.g., United States v. District Court (United States v. Haley), 371 U.S. 18 (1962).

33. Quoting from Wilkerson v. McCarthy, 336 N.J. 53 (1949).

34. As quoted by Anthony Lewis, "How the Supreme Court Reaches Decisions," The New York Times Magazine, December 1, 1957, pp. 51–54.

35. Address to the Annual Meeting of the American Bar Association, St. Louis, Mo., September 7, 1949. See also Justice Harlan's similar sentiments in Cohen v. California, 403 U.S. 15 (1971).

36. Thompson v. City of Louisville et al. 362 U.S. 199 (1960).

at the smallest matters if it is necessary to do so to ensure justice. Here, in a criminal proceeding, one Sam Thompson, a man who had been convicted of disorderly public conduct for "shuffling" in a cafe, successfully took his claim of lack of evidence to the Supreme Court on *certiorari* because, under Kentucky law, the fines involved were too small to be reviewed by any state appellate court—under Kentucky law $20.00 was the minimum per offense.[37] Speaking for the unanimous Court, Justice Black noted: "Our examination of the record presented in the petition for *certiorari* convinced us that *although the fines here are small, the due process questions presented are substantial and we* therefore granted *certiorari* to review the police court's judgment."[38] And, in the oral argument before the Court, the case was given *twice* the customary time allotted.

Since the Court has complete discretionary power over grants of *certiorari*—a power bestowed on it by the necessary and desirable "Judges Bill" of 1925,[39] which was largely the creation of Chief Justice Taft and Justice Van Devanter—it denies between 85 and 90 percent of all *certiorari* applications, and does not usually explain its reason for the denial.[40] Prior to the 1925 statute the Court's appellate jurisdiction was obligatory to the extent of some 80 percent of its business. Gone now are the days when the Court, its docket jammed with mandatory appeals, was expected to devote an all-too-large portion of its valuable time and energy merely to correcting errors of lower courts that primarily affected the rights of parties to a particular case or controversy. Today, it must concentrate on those cases whose resolution will have immediate importance far beyond the particular facts and parties involved. On the other hand, the Court has never forgotten the oft-quoted admonition of Chief Justice Marshall in *Cohens v. Virginia*, back in 1821:

> It is most true that this Court will not take jurisdiction if it should not: but it is equally true that it must take jurisdiction if it should. The judiciary cannot, as the legislature may, avoid a measure because it approaches the confines of the Constitution. We cannot pass it by because it is doubtful. With whatever doubts, with whatever difficulties, a case may be attended, we must decide it if it be brought before us. We have

37. Actually, it was the Dr. Wynant Dean family for whom he worked who urged Thompson to appeal his case, for they felt that the police had been harassing him; they hired Louis Lusky, a distinguished New York lawyer with an abiding interest in civil liberties, to take the case.

38. Ibid., at 203 (italics supplied). See also the charming 1976 case of the "Nevada One Inch Pupfish" (*Cappaert v. United States*, 426 U.S. 128) and the 1978 case of the three-inch "Tennessee Snail Darter" (*Tennessee Valley Authority v. Hill*, 437 U.S. 153).

39. 43 Stat. 936.

40. An examination of a forty-year period (1945–85) indicates that it does so in less than 1 percent of all such denials. However, on occasion one or more disappointed judges will write an *opinion*, or a note, on the Court's refusal to grant *certiorari* in a certain case—for example, Justice Douglas's lengthy one from the Court's refusal to hear a test of the constitutionality of New York's criminal syndicalism law in 1968 (*Epton v. New York*, 390 U.S. 29). But the more common approach is simply to record a dissent from the Court's negative action on the request to grant the writ—as Chief Justice Burger and Justice Douglas did, for example, in *Buckley v. American Federation of T.V. and Radio Artists*, 419 U.S. 1093 (1974), and as Justices Brennan and Marshall did in *Franklin v. Lynaugh*, 487 U.S. 64 (1988). See also the bitter dissenting opinion by Justice Rehnquist, joined by Chief Justice Burger and Justice White, from the Court's refusal to grant *certiorari* in the potentially highly significant affirmative action/reverse discrimination case of *Bushey v. New York State Civil Service Commission*, 469 U.S. 1117 (1985).

no more right to decline the exercise of jurisdiction which is given than to usurp that which is not given. The one or the other would be treason to the Constitution.[41]

Indeed, a glance at the subject matter represented on the Court's 1990–91 docket points to a veritable *smörgasbord*, ranging the alphabetical gamut from abortion to zoning discrimination. However, there exists a distinct tendency on the Court's part to favor reviews sought by the federal government as a petitioning party. This is true both in terms of fully discussed cases and in the decisions of the Chief Justice (and the Clerk of Court) to "special list" cases for possible review in the first place.

To grant *certiorari*, at least four of the Justices must vote to do so. That decision is reached and formalized at the Court's weekly Conference, in which those petitions deemed worthy of consideration by any one Justice have been put on the Conference discussion list, each Justice, without direct consultation with any other, having reached his or her own conclusions as to whether the application should be considered at all. The Justice may have reached that decision either by reading a particular petition personally, by having shared that task with his or her law clerks, or by having asked them for a summary or "bench" memorandum. A novel Burger Court development, authored by Justice Powell, has been the so-called *cert.* pool, an arrangement presently (1992) subscribed to by eight[42] of the nine Justices, under which their respective law clerks—a total of twenty-seven— work together in analyzing petitions for *certiorari*. A working rule devised by the Court itself, this Rule of Four also applies to noting probable jurisdiction on writs of appeal, an interesting development in view of the important distinction that theoretically governs the two writs. Of course, the Court can change its mind on a grant for review; there is nothing to prevent it, on thinking the matter over, from ultimately dismissing a writ as having been "improvidently granted."[43] According to a statute of 1863, however, *six* Justices constitute a quorum to hand down a decision.[44] This means that a plurality of four Justices can *decide* a case. In the event of a tie vote, the decision of the lower court stands as the final word in the controversy at issue.[45] But a single Justice may—unless, or until, overruled by action of peers on the bench—grant a stay of execution or a writ of *habeas corpus*. A pertinent illustration of this significant prerogative is the grant of a request for a stay of execution, although denying a request for a writ of *habeas corpus*, by Justice Douglas, in the sensational case of the convicted atom spies, Ethel and Julius Rosenberg, in June 1953. While vacating the stay of execution just twenty-four hours after it had been granted, Chief Justice Vinson took note inferentially of the intemperate reaction in the public press, and especially in Congress (where bills of

41. 6 Wheaton 264, at 404.
42. Scalia, White, Blackmun, Kennedy, Rehnquist, O'Connor, Souter and Thomas. (Stevens has his own clerks screen cases; so did Brennan and Marshall.)
43. E.g., *Cichos v. Indiana*, 385 U.S. 76 (1966), a state double jeopardy case which it had originally accepted for review; the "smut" case of *Carlos v. New York*, 396 U.S. 119 (1969); one aspect of *Nixon v. United States*, 418 U.S. 683 (1974); and *Florida v. Casal and Garcia*, 462 U.S. 637 (1983).
44. Early in 1970, when Justice Harlan abruptly removed himself from an important case involving oil shale mining rights, the niceties of judicial ethics dictated the cancellation of a Supreme Court hearing in midargument—for Harlan's departure left but five Justices on the bench (The *New York Times*, January 22, 1970, p. 22).
45. E.g., Maryland's highest court's 1971 finding that the Swedish film *I Am Curious (Yellow)* was obscene (*Grove Press, Inc. v. Maryland State Board of Censors*, 401 U.S. 480).

impeachment were at once introduced in the House of Representatives), by writing that "Mr. Justice Douglas had power to issue the stay. No one has disputed this, and we think the proposition is indisputable."[46]

Considerable disagreement exists, not only among the many observers of the Court, but among the Justices themselves, as to the true meaning of a denial of an application for a writ of *certiorari*. Justice Jackson viewed "sincere worthiness" as a tacit agreement by a quorum of the Justices that the decision below is good enough to stand. "The fatal sentence," he wrote, "that in real life writes finis to many causes cannot in legal theory be a complete blank."[47] Justice Frankfurter, however, always insisted that no significance attaches to the denial of *certiorari*, that it "in no wise" implies Court approval of the decision below. All it means, he would point out, is that, for reasons seldom if ever disclosed, six or more Justices evidently do not think that a case ought to be adjudicated on its merits. On one occasion he spelled out his reasoning:

> [it] seemed . . . to at least six members [of the Court] . . . that the issue was either not ripe enough or too moribund for adjudication; that the question had better wait for the perspective of time or that time would bury the question or, for one reason or another, it was desirable to wait and see; or that the constitutional issue was entangled with nonconstitutional issues that raised doubt whether the constitutional issue could be effectively isolated; or for various other reasons not related to the merits.[48]

No matter which of these two contrasting views may be "correct," the effect in the eyes of the disappointed petitioner is necessarily the same: at least for the present, he or she has lost.[49] (See Chart B, *infra*, pp. 180–81, for a summary of this section.)

WORKLOAD

All cases to be disposed of are placed on one of the Court's three dockets: the *original*, the *appellate*, and the *miscellaneous*. In the 1989–90 term the Court had 5,746 cases on these dockets and *disposed* of 4,987 with finality. But of those many cases the Court disposed of, it decided only 205 *on the merits*, with *full written opinions* handed down in 143 (129 of these signed) cases, the remainder being disposed of either *per curiam* or by *memorandum orders* (e.g., "affirmed," "reversed," "dismissed," or "vacated").[50] Yet it must be recognized that the Court does *act on*

46. *Rosenberg v. United States*, 346 U.S. 273 (1953), at 285. Each Supreme Court Justice is responsible for considering appeals for stays in any matters that come up in his or her circuit. However, if someone seeking a stay is turned down by the Justice presiding over the circuit, the petitioner can further appeal to any or all of the other members of the Court for relief. When Douglas was savagely attacked for granting the Rosenbergs' stay, Senator William Langer (R.-N.D.) offered him solace: "Douglas, they have thrown several buckets of shit over you. But by God, none of it stuck. And I am proud" (*Go East, Young Man. The Early Years: The Autobiography of William O. Douglas* [New York: Random House, 1974], p. 469).
47. Concurring opinion in *Brown v. Allen*, 344 U.S. 443 (1953), at 543.
48. Dissenting opinion in *Darr v. Burford*, 339 U.S. 200 (1950), at 227. See, similarly, Justice Brennan's statement in "State Court Decisions and the Supreme Court," 31 *Pennsylvania Bar Association Quarterly* (1960), pp. 399–400.
49. See pp. 179–187, *infra*.
50. Such "summary" decisions *cum* dispositions are not infrequently targets of strong intra-Court adverse criticism (e.g., see a sixteen-page memorandum by Justices Brennan and Marshall, described in detail in *The New York Times*, November 9, 1976, p. C24).

Chart B. U.S. Supreme Court Review

Cases Normally Reach the U.S. Supreme Court for Purposes of Review (as distinct from original jurisdiction) in One of Two Principal Ways:

1. On APPEAL, i.e., as a matter of right.
2. On a writ of *CERTIORARI*, as a matter of Court discretion.

(A third way, by CERTIFICATION, will be omitted for present purposes. It is rarely used, presenting the court with even fewer cases than those on its original docket. It covers "any question of law in any civil or criminal case as to which instructions are desired" by the lower court, usually a Court of Appeals.[a] The old writ of ERROR, a common law process strongly akin to (1) above, was statutorily discontinued in the federal courts in 1928. It brought the entire record of a case proceeding in a lower court before the Supreme Court for its consideration for alleged "errors of law" committed below.)

N.B.: Title 28 of the U.S. Code, formulated as a result of congressional legislation, governs the types of review available to an appellant. (See ch. 81, Secs. 1252, 1254, and 1257.)

I. *Cases reaching the U.S. Supreme Court on APPEAL* (i.e., the Court reviews because it *must*).

    A.1. When a *special three-judge District Court* (which must include at least one circuit judge) has granted or denied an interlocutory or permanent injunction in any proceeding required to be heard by such a court. These three-judge courts now sit only in suits brought to restrain, on grounds of unconstitutionality, *enforcement, operation, or execution of federal or state statutes* dealing with apportionment or reapportionment of legislative districts; in actions challenging the constitutionality of any statewide legislative body; and in instances in which such a court is *required* by specific acts of Congress, such as the Civil Rights Act of 1964 and the Voting Rights Act of 1965, both as amended, and the Presidential Election Campaign Act of 1974[b] (§ 1253).

II. *Cases reaching the U.S. Supreme Court on a writ of CERTIORARI* (i.e., because a minimum of four Supreme Court Justices had agreed to a review). Writs of *certiorari* are granted or denied at the *discretion* of the Court—subject always to the latent power of the Court.

    A. From the state court of last resort having statutory jurisdiction in any particular case (usually, but not always, the *"highest court of a state,"* which normally, but not always, is the state supreme court).

      1. In cases where the validity of a treaty or statute of the United States is drawn in question or where the validity of a statute of any State is drawn in question on the ground of its being repugnant to the Constitution, treaties, or laws of the United States, or where any title, right, privilege, or immunity is specially set up or claimed under the Constitution or the treaties or statutes of, or any commission held or authority exercised under, the United States (§ 1257).

    B. From the U.S. (circuit) courts of appeals and, in all pertinent cases, from other lower courts of the United States, such as legislative courts (§ 1254).

      1. By writ of certiorari granted upon petition of any party to any civil or criminal case, before or after rendition of judgment or decree.

Chart B. U.S. Supreme Court Review (*continued*)

___

2. By certification at any time by a court of appeals of any question of law in any civil or criminal case as to which instructions are desired, and upon such certification the Supreme Court may give binding instructions or require the entire record to be sent up for decision of the entire matter in controversy (§ 1254).

___

[a]One of the very infrequent illustrations of its use is that by the Fifth U.S. Circuit Court of Appeals in 1963, which certified the question of whether or not its criminal contempt citation of Governor Ross R. Barnett and Lieutenant Governor Paul B. Johnson, Jr., of Mississippi necessitated a trial by jury. The intermediate appellate tribunal was evenly divided (4:4) when it turned to the Supreme Court in this ticklish case, which had arisen out of the admission of a black man, James H. Meredith, to the University of Mississippi at Oxford (*United States* v. *Barnett*, 375 U.S. 805). The highest tribunal ruled 5:4 against Barnett and Johnson (ibid., 376 U.S. 681) in 1964. But one year later the Circuit Court cleared the two because of "changed circumstances and conditions" (ibid., 346 F. 2d 99).

[b]Until Congress, heeding repeated entreaties by Chief Justice Burger and other students of the judicial process, limited these courts' jurisdiction in 1972 and, even more dramatically in 1976 and 1988, their authority embraced a host of other areas, for example, orders of the Interstate Commerce Commission.

___

every case of which it disposes, whatever the nature of that disposition. The large number of cases docketed and disposed of, representing a major increase in the work load over previous years, has come chiefly in the so-called *miscellaneous* cases, which are largely handwritten or typewritten papers filed by indigent persons, often prison inmates, and, unlike the formal petitions for *certiorari* on the appellate docket, need not follow a particular form or even contain material normally considered essential in petitions. Indigents obtain authority to file from the federal *in forma pauperis* statute,[51] which gives to a citizen of the United States the right to enter proceedings in any federal court, provided he or she executes an oath. Of course, this does not guarantee a Supreme Court review, although of the cases the Court heard in its 1990–91 term, for example, more than half came to it *in forma pauperis!* Naturally, it did summarily vacate or reverse a fair number of other lower court decisions challenged by indigent persons, most of these cases being "frivolous" or without a substantial federal claim. And early in 1991 the Court endeavored to draw a line: In a 6:3 *per curiam* decision, it ruled that it had had it with *in forma pauperis* petitioners like Michael Sindram, who, in the past three years, had filed forty-two separate petitions and motions, twenty-four in the 1990–91 term alone! Henceforth it would simply reject "repetitious and frivolous" requests.[52] The purpose of the interesting *in forma pauperis* statute clearly was to protect indigent persons—a large proportion of whom, according to a bitter remark by Justice Jackson, represent "our convict population." And Justice Douglas, certainly a sympathetic friend of the underdog, once commented that the claims made in these pauper cases "are often fantastic, surpassing credulity . . . [and] are

___

51. 28 USC 1915 (a). See also Supreme Court Rule 53.5.
52. *In re Sindram*, 59LW 3458. Soon thereafter, the Court, in an opinion by Justice White, confirmed the extensive power of federal judges to levy fines against those who abuse the court system (*Chambers* v. *NASCO*, 59 LW 4595).

for the most part frivolous."[53] Nevertheless, many vital criminal cases have reached the Court by this path—indeed, they have increased more than fortyfold since 1930 and today represent well over half of all case filings. Among them was the momentous *Gideon v. Wainwright*[54] in 1963, which resulted in the overruling of the *Betts v. Brady*[55] precedent that had stood for two decades. Clarence Earl Gideon had petitioned the Supreme Court for a writ of *habeas corpus*—the principal device available to those who attack state judgments—in a hand-penciled letter from his Florida prison cell.[56]

Of the total number of 5,746 cases filed during the 1989–90 term, 757 were not disposed of and thus went over to the 1990–91 docket. That residue is a low average number of cases carried forward, the record—since the Clerk of the Supreme Court began to keep these statistics in 1930—was the 1203 cases not disposed of by the 1973–74 term of the Court. Although there is some disagreement among the Justices themselves on the point, notably on the part of Douglas, who insisted time and again that the Court is "underworked—not overworked,"[57] most observers of the work of the Court believe firmly that it is overburdened with cases. In large measure, this is due to the flood of petitions that reach it; but to some degree it may also be because the Court has persisted in taking cases that are at best trivial, sometimes dealing simply with issues that did not present any truly imperative constitutional questions. This, of course, is a matter of judgment. Yet it would seem that at least in tax cases or in railroad and maritime injury-negligence cases, particularly the latter, which usually involve a question of fact as to who was at fault in the accident, the Court has at times unnecessarily overextended itself in granting petitions for review. That a good many of the Justices feel quite strongly about the matter is indicated by a veritable stream of comments by Justice Frankfurter, who, in case after case in this field, would pen a comment to the effect that "the case . . . is so trivial that the Court should dismiss its grant of review as improvident." And in one dispute, answering in the affirmative the question whether or not a jury should hear the case of a wrench falling on a seaman's "left great toe," Justice Harlan, speaking for a minority of four Justices, delivered a three-page dissent that began:

> At the opening of a term which finds the court's docket crowded with more important and difficult litigation than in many years, it is not without irony that we should be witnessing among the first matters to be heard a routine negligence . . . case involving only issues of facts. I continue to believe that such cases, distressing and important as they are for unsuccessful plaintiffs, do not belong in this Court.[58]

53. Address to the Cornell University School of Law, April 15, 1960.
54. 372 U.S. 335.
55. 316 U.S. 455 (1942).
56. See the superb book on the *Gideon* case by Anthony Lewis, *Gideon's Trumpet* (New York: Random House, 1964), which, in addition to its basic story, is highly instructive in the judicial process.
57. E.g., again in an interview on December 7, 1972 (*The Daily Progress*, Charlottesville, Va., p. 2). His colleague Brennan formally seconded Douglas in an interesting article in 59 *American Bar Association Journal* 835 (August 1973), "Justice Brennan Calls National Court of Appeals Proposal 'Fundamentally Unnecessary and Ill Advised.'" Douglas reiterated this view in 1975: "I found it a comfortable burden carried even in the months of my hospitalization." (*The New York Times*, June 27, 1975, p. C17).
58. *Michalic v. Cleveland Tankers, Inc.*, 364 U.S. 325 (1960) at 332–33.

Justice Frankfurter went even further here, contending the Court should not even have agreed to consider such an issue in the first place; and he once again voiced his long-standing lament against consideration of minor negligence cases. Chief Justice Rehnquist, a Frankfurter admirer, embarked on a major course of case reduction as of 1986–87.

Among several suggestions advanced in the mid-1970s by the blue-ribbon Study Group on the Case Load of the Supreme Court, usually referred to as the Freund Committee (after Prof. Paul A. Freund of Harvard University Law School), was one to abandon the appellate jurisdiction of the Court and leave a writ of *certiorari* as the only means of obtaining review by the Supreme Court. In other words, direct appeals to the highest judicial body, whether from a one-judge court under the antitrust Expediting Act or from a three-judge court convened to consider the constitutionality of a state or federal statute, would be abolished other than through *certiorari*. Congress began to talk about the proposal in 1979 and by 1988 wrote many of these suggestions into law. (See text and Chart B, *supra*, pp. 181–89.) But it did not act on the Freund Committee's widely discussed, Chief Justice Burger–backed proposal to create a new appellate court, known as the National Court of Appeals, nor a Senate Judiciary's proposal for an "Intercircuit Panel," as a "buffer" between the U.S. Court of Appeals and the U.S. Supreme Court.

An intriguing, and possibly highly significant, decision by the Court during its 1960–61 term gave Justice Frankfurter additional reasons for expounding on the theme of unwise, nonjurisdictional, unnecessary case work. Over his lone fifty-eight-page dissenting opinion, the eight-man majority held that policemen and other local officials who violated a citizen's constitutional rights under the Civil Rights Act of 1871 could be sued for damage in *federal* courts *even if these officials acted without state authority*. Frankfurter in his dissent not only charged the majority with violating federal–state relationships, relying heavily on the legislative history of the act as he saw it to prove his point, but he also decried what he viewed as rank court interference. Envisaging a veritable flood of petitions, he insisted that the broad construction adopted here by the Supreme Court made the federal Constitution

> a law to regulate the quotidian business of every traffic policeman, every registrar of elections, every city inspector or investigator, every clerk in every municipal license bureau in this country.[59]

59. *Monroe v. Pape*, 365 U.S. 167 (1961). Frankfurter would have been repulsed in the face of 1978 and 1980 decisions by the Court which, going well beyond the 1961 holding, in effect stripped away the long immunity enjoyed by local (and, by implication, by federal) governments, ruling that such governments were subject to lawsuits for violations of civil rights and that having acted in "good faith" was not an acceptable defense (*Monell v. New York Department of Social Services*, 436 U.S. 658 and *Owen v. City of Independence, Missouri*, 445 U.S. 622, respectively). *Ergo*, a "person" in such litigation now extends to municipalities and other governmental entities; it is no longer limited to their officials. He would have been even more repulsed had he lived to note the Court's astonishing 6:3 decision in *Maine v. Thiboutot*, 448 U.S. 1 (1980), holding that not only can state and local officials be sued for damages for violations of civil rights, as established previously, but that the Civil Rights Act of 1871 *also* created a right to sue those officials for alleged denial of *any* federal benefit provided through them (e.g., food stamps, educational benefits, and other welfare programs enacted by the federal government). (See p. 263, *infra*, for related explications of suits against governments and their officials.)

Whatever the number of cases docketed, it ought to be fairly obvious that the lawyer who grandiosely and proudly informs both the client and the public press that "we'll fight this case all the way to the Supreme Court," really means that *if* the funds are present he or she will *attempt* to do so—unless a pauper's oath is involved, the standard case will consume a solid outlay of upward of $10,000—and *if* the Court will grant review he or she will *endeavor* to convince it of the righteousness of the client's case. An average case takes from two to five years to reach the highest bench. The preparation and printing of the record and the writing of briefs alone normally consume five months. Seldom does the Court actually *hear oral arguments* on more than 125 to 150 of the cases it disposes of annually; the balance is dismissed on procedural or some other jurisdictional ground. Of those actually heard, formal *written opinions* by the Court are usually handed down in 75 to 85 percent of the cases, the others being decided *per curiam*—an anonymous opinion expressing the summary judgment of the Court as a whole and not the opinion of a single Justice with whom the others concur. In other words, a *per curiam* is an *unsigned*, more often than not brief, opinion for the Court, applying *res judicata* (settled law), its authorship unknown to the outside world, although, in Professor Schubert's opinion, "it seems probable that most . . . are written by the Chief Justice or for him by one of his . . . law clerks."[60] For example, it was employed in the initial disposition of the controversial 1972 *Capital Punishment Cases*.[61] Usually *per curiam* opinions are written for a unanimous Court, but there are exceptions. For instance, in 1966 Justice Clark wrote a formal dissenting opinion to the Court's *per curiam* in *Riggan v. Virginia*[62] in which he was specifically joined by his colleagues Black, Harlan, and Stewart. There, the now readily identifiable majority of five (Warren, Douglas, Brennan, White, and Fortas) reversed *without briefs or arguments* a lower court decision upholding the validity of a search warrant issued by a Virginia tribunal. Considerable criticism about the increasing resort to *per curiam* decisions has ensued. However, it may very well be that this simply constitutes an attempt by the Court to resolve the conflict between rendering fully reasoned opinions and affording the finality of Supreme Court adjudication to as large a number of litigants as possible. Or it may simply represent a stopgap expedient, such as the Court's *per curiam* decision in a group of obscenity cases in 1967,[63] an area that has defied a firm, universally applicable rule of law—notwithstanding continuing attempts to determine one.[64]

Reconsideration. A petitioner whose request for review has been *denied* by the Court for one or more of the reasons discussed earlier is not, of course, barred from trying again. Accordingly, some sanguine souls are rather persistent in these efforts—although they rarely, if ever, succeed unless their new petition serves to convince four Justices of the merits of the renewed appeal. Thus, in a two-sentence

60. Glendon Schubert, *Judicial Policy-making: The Political Role of the Courts* (Glenview, IL: Scott, Foresman, 1965), p. 73. The statement concerning the role of the law clerks is subject to considerable doubt, however (see pp. 239–44 *infra*).
61. *Furman v. Georgia*, 408 U.S. 238.
62. 384 U.S. 152.
63. *Redrup v. New York, Austin v. Kentucky, and Gent v. Arkansas*, 386 U.S. 767 (decided together).
64. See, for example, the Court's efforts in a series of 5:4 decisions handed down in 1973 (*Miller v. California* 413 U.S. 15 and *Paris Adult Theatre v. Slaton*, 413 U.S. 49).

statement included on the forty-second page of a forty-five page list of orders in nearly one thousand cases filed at the start of the Court's 1976–77 term, it refused to reconsider[65] its July 2, 1976, decision[66] upholding the death penalty for murder, thus lifting the stay that had been blocking the states from implementing that decision. Among well-known illustrations of such unsuccessful attempts are the cases of Morton Sobell, convicted of complicity in the atomic espionage case of Ethel and Julius Rosenberg, and the doomed Caryl Chessman. Sobell filed eight formal petitions for review of his conviction between 1953 and 1958; all were denied by the Court without comment.[67] Chessman filed fully sixteen petitions for review with the Court between his conviction in 1948 for seventeen crimes (including kidnapping, attempted rape, sex perversion, robbery, and car theft) and his execution in 1960, prompting even Justice Douglas to comment: "The conclusion is inevitable that Chessman is playing a game with the courts, stalling for time. . . . This is not a case of a helpless man who was given no opportunity to participate in the settlement of the record."[68] Chessman's battle ended in failure only after he had filed a total of forty-two appeals[69] with various federal and state courts! The struggle covered twelve years, caused extensive debates on the merits of capital punishment, and made Chessman's name a household word throughout the world.[70] A rare occurrence in this realm of the judicial process is a Court-*solicited* or -encouraged reconsideration, such as that specifically requested by the 1961–62 bench when, in granting review to prison inmate Gideon,[71] it requested argument on the specific *quaere*[72] whether or not it should now reconsider its 1942 ruling in

65. *Gregg v. Georgia*, 428 U.S. 1301 (1976).
66. *Gregg v. Georgia*, 428 U.S. 153 (1976).
67. He came close with his ninth attempt, in 1968, when he gained the vote of three of the necessary four Justices (Douglas, Harlan, and Brennan). He was released after his tenth appeal one year later.
68. *Chessman v. Teets*, 354 U.S. 156 (1957), at 170.
69. But it would not be long before Chessman's record became the rule rather than the exception in capital punishment cases. Ergo, emphasizing the need to limit repeated, seemingly endless, challenges and appeals in these and other criminal convicts, the Court, speaking through Justice O'Connor, ruled in 1982 that there would simply have to be some limits to that game (*United States v. Frady*, 456 U.S. 152, *Rose v. Lundy*, 455 U.S. 509, and *Engle v. Issac*, 456 U.S. 107). And in 1991, in a Georgia death penalty case, the Court (6:3) set a standard for lower federal courts under which a prisoner's second or subsequent *habeas corpus* petition must be dismissed except in unusual circumstances, to be governed by the judicial doctrine known as "abuse of the writ" (*McCleskey v. Zant*, 59 LW 4288).
70. Chessman's record years on death row were exceeded in 1966 by the thirteen years spent by both Edgar Labat and Clifton Alton Poret, two blacks who had been convicted of raping a young white woman in 1950. However, not only were they released from death row, but they were ordered freed from jail by the Fifth U.S. Circuit Court of Appeals because they had been convicted by juries from which blacks were *systematically* excluded. Their death row record was exceeded in turn by Edgar H. Smith, freed in 1971 after having served more than fourteen years for the murder of a fifteen-year-old girl. (A few years later he was back in jail for a new felony.) Willie Jasper Darden, executed in 1988, had also been on death row for over fourteen years, as had Pierre Dale Selby, executed in 1987.
71. *Gideon v. Cochran*, 370 U.S. 908 (1962). (See n. 56, *supra*.)
72. "Should this Court's holding in *Betts v. Brady*, 316 U.S., be overruled?" In *Betts* the Court had held 6:3 that indigent state criminal defendants are automatically entitled to state-furnished counsel *only in capital criminal cases*—unless certain "special circumstances" attend the case (and, in the Court's judgment, they did not in *Betts*).

Betts v. Brady.[73] An embarrassing illustration is the Court's request to the parties in an already-decided case "to address an additional question," namely, the possible modification of the Fourth Amendment's "exclusionary rule" to permit a "good faith" exception—only to conclude, "with apologies to all," that because "the issue we framed for the parties was not presented to the Illinois courts [we] ... do not address it [here and now]."[74] It would, in fact, be tackled one year later.[75]

Rehearing. On the other hand, it is also possible for a *defeated* litigant to petition the Supreme Court for a *rehearing* within twenty-five days after the announcement of an unfavorable decision, in the dim hope that the Court, in the person of one or more of the Justices, may undergo a change of mind on rehearing the case. This is especially true when the original decision was a very close one and featured a sharply divided Court. But under the Court's rules, such a rehearing may not be granted unless a member of the *majority* in the original decision votes for one, and the Court in effect granted only six rehearings between 1950 and 1975, to cite an otherwise especially active quarter-century.

A notable illustration of one of the infrequent successes gained by a petitioner on rehearing—one of but three such victories in the twenty-five year period indicated—was the group of "military justice" cases, involving Mesdames Clarice Covert and Dorothy Smith-Krueger, both civilians, who killed their unfaithful Master Sergeant and Colonel spouses with ax and knife, respectively, while with them at overseas bases. The cases had been argued together at the bar of the Supreme Court initially in 1956, the constitutional issue being the validity of the section of the U.S. Uniform Military Code of Justice that authorized the military trial of civilians accompanying the armed forces abroad.[76] The Court had upheld the disputed section in a 5:3 decision, delivered by Justice Clark, whereas the three dissenters—Warren, Black, and Douglas—had protested they were being rushed at term's end, and Justice Frankfurter had refused to participate other than to file a "reservation" because of "lack of adequate time to consider" the issues involved and "their complexity." Clearly, this was the type of decision in which counsel for defendants might well see a distinct hope for a rehearing. A motion for one was duly filed; it was accepted by a 5:3 vote, the three original dissenters and Justice Frankfurter being joined in approving the petition for rehearing moved by Justice Harlan, a member of the original majority.[77] Matters certainly seemed to look up for the widows.

The case was duly reargued early in 1957, and during the waning days of that term the Court handed down its decision, reversing itself by declaring the section in question unconstitutional by a 6:2 vote.[78] Only Justices Clark and Burton remained of the former majority; Justices Minton and Reed having retired from

73. 316 U.S. 455 (1942). When the *Gideon* decision came down in 1963, *Betts v. Brady* stood unanimously overruled—in a triumphant opinion for the Court by Justice Black, one of the three dissenters in *Betts* (*Gideon v. Wainwright*, 372 U.S. 335).

74. *Illinois v. Gates*, 462 U.S. 213 (1983), at 217.

75. *United States v. Leon* and *Massachusetts v. Sheppard*, 468 U.S. 897, and 981 (1984), respectively.

76. *Kinsella v. Krueger*, 351 U.S. 470 and *Reid v. Covert*, 351 U.S. 487 (June 11, 1956).

77. *Reid v. Covert and Kinsella v. Krueger*, 352 U.S. 901 (November 5, 1956). On petition for rehearing.

78. *Reid v. Covert and Kinsella v. Krueger*, 354 U.S. 1 (June 10, 1957). On rehearing.

the Court, Justice Harlan having changed his mind, and a new member, Justice Brennan, joining the majority. The ninth member, Justice Whittaker, just appointed to replace Justice Reed, did not participate in the decision. It should be reemphasized, however, that a grant of a petition for rehearing is the exception to the rule. The latter finds support in the prominent example of a petition for a rehearing of the so-called Hyde Amendment case, *Harris v. McRae*, brought in 1980 by 286 organizations and 70 law professors. The Court refused, thus staying with its original 5:4 ruling that had upheld a four-year-old ban on the use of Medicaid funds for abortions (with certain exceptions).[79] An indication of a possible chance for a rehearing, but certainly no assurance, is, of course, an officially announced change of mind from the bench, such as Justice Douglas's announcement, in the *New York Prayer Case*,[80] that he *now* believed that the *New Jersey Bus Case* of 1947, in which he had provided the crucial fifth vote,[81] had been wrongly decided. Yet the latter has never been overruled.

Reargument. A related, but distinct, practice is an order for *reargument*, in which the Court, for reasons best known to itself, orders a case back on the docket for reargument rather than hand down a decision. At the end of what became known as the "libertarian 1956–57 term," it did this in ten cases that had already been briefed and argued before it. The famed *Segregation Cases*[82] are a pertinent earlier example. Initially argued in December 1952, they were ordered reargued in December 1953 and were decided in May 1954. Another illustration is the aforementioned controversial water-dispute case between Arizona and California, which the Supreme Court ordered reargued in 1962, as an original jurisdiction case, despite the fact that the Court had spent a week hearing arguments in that complex litigation during the preceding January. A crucial reason for this order was Chief Justice Warren's voluntary disqualification—he had been governor of California—coupled with Justice Frankfurter's illness and Justice Whittaker's retirement; Whittaker's successor, Justice White, had not heard the initial arguments. A decision was ultimately handed down, in June of 1963. The Chief Justice did not participate, but both Justice Goldberg, who had replaced the then-retired Justice Frankfurter, and Justice White took part and sided with the 7:1 Black majority opinion.[83] A later petition for a rehearing by the "loser," California, was denied.[84] And in the spring of 1985 Justice Powell requested reargument in five of the 57 cases he had missed because of a protracted illness, all five of which had ended in 4:4 ties.

---

79. 448 U.S. 297. A successful plea for a rehearing in 1980 came in a complex antitrust case (*McLain v. Real Estate Board of New Orleans, Inc.*, 444 U.S. 232).

80. *Engel v. Vitale*, 370 U.S. 421 (1962), at 443.

81. *Everson v. Board of Education of Ewing Township*, 330 U.S. 1.

82. *Brown v. Board of Education of Topeka*, 347 U.S. 483 (1954), and *Bolling v. Sharpe*, 347 U.S. 497 (1954).

83. *Arizona v. California*, 373 U.S. 546.

84. 375 U.S. 892 (1963). But the issue continued to percolate: cf. *Arizona v. California*, 460 U.S. 605 (1983). *United States v. Brewster*, 404 U.S. 1055 (1972), which dealt with the range and extent of senatorial immunity, represents another pertinent illustration of a reargument order, as does a counsel case, *Kirby v. Illinois*, 406 U.S. 683 (1973), and two cases dealing with rights of aliens, *Weinberger v. Diaz*, 426 U.S. 77 and *Hampton v. Mow Sun Wong*, 426 U.S. 88, both 1976 actions.

THE U.S. SUPREME COURT AT WORK

How does this most impressive and most dignified of all governmental bodies in the United States *generally* conduct its tasks? Since 1873 it has customarily sat for thirty-six weeks annually, from the first or second Monday in October until the end of June.[85] Now and then, as in the 1971 *Pentagon Papers Case*[86] and in the dramatic Nixon tapes ruling of 1974,[87] the Court may briefly extend its term because of the felt necessity to render a decision prior to adjournment. And on rare occasions, such as in the case involving the Little Rock, Arkansas, school desegregation crisis in August–September 1957[88] and in that of the seven German saboteurs in 1942,[89] a Special Session may be convened, although there have been only four such sessions in this century. Yet it must be stated at once that the business of judging, at least at the level of the federal government, is a year-round occupation, regardless of the formal calendar.

All of the Court's sessions are now held in its own magnificent Greek-style, Corinthian-order, white marble structure, at 1 First Street, S.E., near Capitol Hill in Washington, D.C. The Court's present home[90] (its construction began in 1932 and was completed in 1935) is patterned after the Temple of Diana at Ephesus, the noble words "Equal Justice Under Law" carved above the two great 6½ ton

---

85. Its longest session to date (1990–91) ended on July 7, 1978.
86. *The New York Times Co. v. United States* and *United States v. The Washington Post Co.*, 403 U.S. 713.
87. *United States v. Nixon*, 417 U.S. 683.
88. *Cooper v. Aaron*, 358 U.S. 1.
89. *Ex parte Quirin*, 317 U.S. 1.
90. The first term of the Supreme Court was the February term 1790. Jay and his colleagues failed initially of a quorum because of mired roads (other than the Chief Justice, only Justices James Wilson of Pennsylvania and William Cushing of Massachusetts were in attendance of the original six appointees). It began on February 1 of that year and was held in the Royal Exchange Building—designed as an open air market for butchers, with meeting facilities on the second floor—in New York City, which was then the seat of the federal government. That term lasted ten days, devoted to the admission of attorneys who wished to practice before it. The second term lasted two days. In July 1790, Congress moved the young nation's capital to Philadelphia, where in February 1791, the Court began to sit in the (now restored) State House, later known as Independence Hall, on Fifth and Chestnut streets. It met there for one term and then moved to nearby Old City Hall until August 1800, where it had to share space with the Mayor's Court. It switched to the County Court House for one term, but in February 1801 joined the government in its move to Washington, D.C., to the office of the Clerk of the Senate (on the main floor of the East Wing of the then still unfinished Capitol Building). It remained there until its own beautiful chamber in that edifice, created by famed American architect Benjamin Henry Latrobe, was readied in 1810, although it had to meet in rented houses and private homes because of the destruction wrought in the War of 1812 when the British had used Supreme Court documents to set fire to the Capital. (Fully restored to its 1860 splendor in 1975, it is now open to the public, designated as the "Old Supreme Court Chamber.") In 1860, the court moved directly above to what is today known as the "Old Senate Chamber," where it functioned until 1935, more or less restricted to a total of four rooms, when the Cass Gilbert–designed present beautiful structure was ready for its occupancy across the plaza. Congress had appropriated $9,740,000 for the latter's construction; $93,532.02 was returned unexpended! The magnificent edifice stands as one of *the* greatest construction bargains in history. Unfortunately, neither Gilbert, its architect (who died in 1934) nor Chief Justice Taft, its "midwife" (who died in 1930) lived to see its completion.

bronze doors of the majestic entrance. The resplendent 82-by-91-foot courtroom itself, which is ringed on three sides by the Justices' chambers, has a 44-foot dome, supported by twenty-four Ionic columns of light Siena old convent marble from the Liguria region of Italy, and ivory vein marble walls from Alicante, Spain. The carvings on the walls depict both real and symbolic judicial figures (on one wall those of the pre-Christian era, on the other those of the Christian). Here convenes the Supreme Court of the United States, its nine Justices clad in black judicial vestments—which Judge Jerome Frank always wanted to banish.[91] (The building still houses its own seamstress to sew those judicial robes as well as a woodworking shop to repair the chairs.) They are seated behind the raised half-hexagon bench of marble and Honduran mahogany in high-backed black leather, swivel rocking chairs of various sizes,[92] which stand against a background of full purplish red draperies. At the appointed hour, the drapes part and from behind them appears the Chief Justice, followed by the eight Associate Justices, seriatim in order of seniority. They, as well as all those assembled in the courtroom, remain standing until the Marshal has completed his time-honored introduction: "Oyez, Oyez, Oyez! All persons having business before the Honorable, the Supreme Court of the United States, are admonished to draw near and give their attention, for the Court is now sitting. God save the United States and this Honorable Court" (a remark that has been the butt of a number of tasteless jokes).[93] The Justices' seats are arranged according to length of continuous service on the bench: the Chief Justice sits in the center, flanked by the Senior Associate Justice on his immediate right, the second-ranking on his immediate left, then alternating in that manner in declining order of seniority (see Figure 3).

ORAL ARGUMENT

In this impressive setting, guarded by its special thirty-three-member police detail on round-the-clock security, and attended by four court attendants[94] (since 1963 mercifully no longer in knickers, long black stockings, and double-breasted jackets), the Court listens to oral arguments—in the cases it has agreed to hear—normally for the first three, but sometimes four, days in two weeks out of each month. (Until 1955 it used to sit for oral argument five days each week.) Its Justices spend the other two weeks behind closed doors considering cases and writing opinions. Accompanied by a $100 fee, forty copies of the printed briefs to be presented in the case at bar—one set to each Justice—have to be filed with the Clerk of the Court well in advance (to be exact, within forty-five days after the case is placed

91. See his amusing "The Cult of the Robe" in his classic Courts on Trial: Myth and Reality in American Justice (Princeton, NJ: Princeton University Press, 1949), ch. 18.

92. In late 1974 Chief Justice Burger let it be known that he was desirous of uniformity in the chairs, but some of his colleagues demurred successfully.

93. At the Court's first session of each new term in October, the Chief Justice will announce, as William H. Rehnquist did on that occasion in 1986: "I have the honor to announce that the October 1986, term of the Supreme Court of the United States has convened" (October 6, 1986).

94. For the first time in its 182-year history the Court, in September 1972, appointed a female page— fourteen-year-old Deborah Gelin of Rockville, Md. At the beginning of the October term 1975, the Court discontinued the practice of utilizing teenage "pages," which originated in 1865, and replaced them with mature "court attendants," usually night students at area colleges and universities.

on the docket by the party bringing suit) and the answering brief has to be filed thirty days after this.[95] The briefs, which are filed in accordance with prescribed format and nowadays are preferably no longer than twenty-five pages,[96] generally state the facts, issues, questions to be presented, decisions of lower courts, and all relevant legal arguments, together with the statutes and citations of cases to which they apply—contemporarily also laced with social science data as part and parcel of a so-called Brandeis Brief, that is, one that stresses such data explicitly and usually extensively; it was first used by Louis D. Brandeis when he argued for Oregon in the 1908 maximum hour law case of *Muller v. Oregon*, 208 U.S. 412. (As already explained, those bona fide paupers whose cases are treated on the special miscellaneous docket may file handwritten or typewritten briefs.)

Oral argument, now heard on designated days from 10:00 A.M. to 12:00 P.M. and from 1:00 P.M. until 3:00 P.M.,[97] is at once the most significant, the most human, and the most fascinating aspect of the *public* portion of the Court's work. (All oral argument began to be taperecorded in 1955; all tapes are being preserved but become publicly available only three years after the ultimate decision date.) Of the 300 seats available, 112 are allotted to the Justices' families, members of the bar, and

THE SUPREME COURT OF THE UNITED STATES

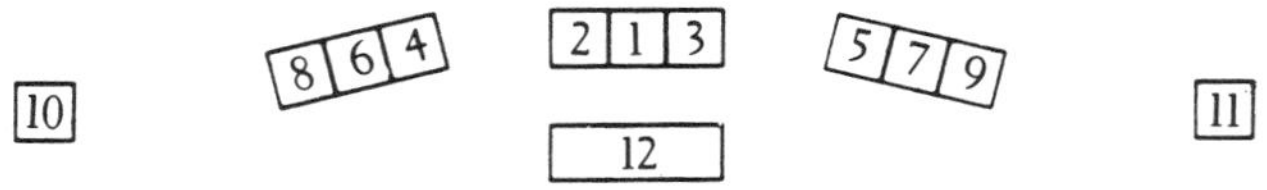

1. Chief Justice Burger

2. Justice Brennan	3. Justice White
4. Justice Marshall	5. Justice Blackmun
6. Justice Powell	7. Justice Rehnquist
8. Justice Stevens	9. Justice O'Connor
10. Clerk of the Court	11. Marshal of the Court

12. Counsel

Silence is Requested

Figure 3. The Supreme Court of the United States, 1991–1992

95. All printed documents filed in the Court must be on 6½- by 9¼-inch paper, with type no smaller than 11-point, "adequately leaded," and the paper must be "opaque and unglazed."

96. In 1974 the Court *rejected* a 107-page brief by L. S. Huffman, the prosecuting attorney of Allen County, Ohio, as not being brief enough under its rules. In rejecting it, the Justices cited a rule that all briefs be "concise and free from burdensome, irrelevant, immaterial and scandalous matter." Mr. Huffman, who had lost below in a case involving his attempts to close down a movie theater for allegedly showing an obscene film, had also attached an appendix comprising more than 4,500 small photos of sexual acitvity from the film! In 1976, visibly irritated, Chief Justice Burger veritably roasted Sylvester Petro, a Winston-Salem, N.C., lawyer who had filed a 216-page brief (*The* [Charlottesville, Va.] *Daily Progress*, November 10, 1976, p. A3).

97. From 1873 until 1961 the Court met from 12:00 P.M. until 4:30 P.M., and from 1898 until 1970 it allowed but half an hour for lunch. Then Chief Justice Burger ordered the more humane break of one hour, now in force.

the media (nineteen positions complete with writing desks) with the remaining 188 being available to the general public, generally on a "first come, first served" basis.[98] Usually there are two public queues for those seats—one a three-minute-stay line, the other a "stay as long as you wish" one, the latter normally needing advance arrangements with the Marshal's office.

There is at least a chance that skillful oral arguments, in supplementing the printed brief by oral emphasis,[99] may sway members on the spot, although this is far less likely in the great than in the small cases. Still, first impressions count—and Justice Douglas, for one, insisted that "oral arguments win or lose the case."[100] Chief Justice Warren, on the other hand, regarded oral argument as "not highly persuasive."[101] But Justice Souter acknowledged that his mind was changed by oral argument in 5 to 10 percent of the cases he heard during his first term on the Court (1990–91).[102] And Justice Holmes seldom found it significant, often taking catnaps during it. The pressure on the arguing lawyers, who must speak from the floor level, naturally is enormous; they must indeed be quick of tongue and feet! They are frequently questioned sharply by the Justices, who often have a bench memorandum prepared before the argument, and their questions may conceivably forecast the ultimate decision of the Court, although in few, if any, instances is it possible, let alone safe, to give an accurate prognosis. Some Justices (e.g., Douglas, Brennan, Blackmun, and Powell) customarily ask very few questions; others (Frankfurter, the most impassioned advocate of oral argument, who would not read the briefs antecedent to it, Stevens, and Scalia) have a habit of asking a great many. John P. Frank reported that in one particular case he witnessed—perhaps a somewhat extreme illustration—the Justices interrupted counsel 84 times during 120 minutes of oral argument, with 93 questions and interpolations, chargeable to Justice Frankfurter alone![103] Woe to the counsel who is ill-prepared or uncertain— and the Justices frown on reading from the prepared text. In fact, the Court's Rule 44 states that it looks "with disfavor" on such a practice. But the Justices may also well prove to be helpful to counsel. Thus, during one oral argument heard in the 1960–61 term, Justice Frankfurter sharply questioned an obviously flustered lawyer several times, only to see Justice Douglas intervene each time with a helpful answer. "I thought *you* were arguing this case," shot Frankfurter to grateful coun-

---

98. By adding chairs in spare spaces, 500 people (including 14 additional media positions in the alcoves behind the regular 19) may be admitted on days of maximum public interest—such as oral argument in the 1974 *Nixon tapes case*—but that is rarely done (*United States v. Nixon*, 417 U.S. 683).

99. See John M. Harlan, "What Role Does Oral Argument Play in the Conduct of an Appeal?" 41 *Cornell Law Quarterly* 6 (1955) and Stephen M. Shapiro, "Oral Argument in the Supreme Court: The Felt Necessities of the Time," *Supreme Historical Society Yearbook, 1985*, pp. 22–34.

100. *The Philadelphia Inquirer*, April 9, 1963, "Oral argument," as Frankfurter once put it, "has a force beyond what the written word conveys" (as quoted by Kenneth Turan, "Let Them Entertain You," *The Washington Post*, "Potomac." February 2, 1975, p. 11).

101. "Seminar with Mr. Chief Justice Warren," University of Virginia Legal Forum, April 25, 1973, p. 9.

102. Remarks to a group of the author's graduate students, the Supreme Court, Washington, D.C., March 25, 1991.

103. *The Marble Palace* (New York: Alfred A. Knopf, 1958), pp. 104–5.

sel, who responded, "I am, but I can use all the help I can get."[104] It should be clear that the Court, as Frankfurter once put it, does not see itself as "a dozing audience for the reading of soliloquies, but as a questioning body, utilizing oral argument as a means for exposing the difficulties of a case with a view to meeting them."[105]

Unlike the old days, especially during Chief Justice John Marshall's reign, when argument often seemed interminable, and when a Daniel Webster would sometimes address the Court with mounting eloquence for days, present-day lawyers are severely limited in the time granted to them for argument. Normally, the limit is one-half hour for each side; sometimes an hour is allotted. One of the rare suspensions of the time limit rule took place in the case of *United Steel Workers of America v. United States*,[106] involving the legality of the injunctive provisions of the Taft-Hartley Act. In the average term only about 250 hours of argument are allotted to the attorneys for their oral presentations.[107] They use a lectern to which two lights are attached; five minutes before time is up a white light flashes; when the second light, appropriately a red one, flashes, the lawyer must stop instantly, unless he or she is granted permission by the Chief Justice to continue. According to one of Chief Justice Hughes's law clerks, the "Chief" was so strict on the score of time that he once stopped a leader of the New York Bar in the middle of the word "if"; on another occasion, on being asked by the same attorney how much time remained, Hughes replied icily, "Fourteen seconds, Mr. Counsel."[108]

To argue cases at the bar of the Supreme Court a lawyer must be admitted to practice before it. This is now a relatively routine matter,[109] one that requires two

104. As reported by Anthony Lewis in "The Justices' Supreme Job," *The New York Times Magazine*, June 11, 1961 (italics supplied). For an engaging recent analysis, see Mary Scallcup, "Questions from the Bench," *Manhattan Lawyer*, May 24–30, 1988, n.p. She divided the 1988 Court into three categories: "Fundamentalists" (Rehnquist, White, Marshall, O'Connor, and Kennedy); "Mental Gymnasts," (Stevens and Scalia); and "Observers" (Brennan and Blackmun).

105. From "Memorial for Stanley M. Silverberg," *Of Law and Men*, ed. by Philip Elman (New York: Harcourt, Brace, 1956), pp. 320–21 (which does not mean that there has never been dozing on the high bench!). Almost all the Justices agree on the desirability and the significance of oral argument, but there are exceptions—for example, Justice Minton, who was always restive and bored during oral argument. Of course, the Court does not *have* to hear oral argument in order to render a formal decision in a case. Thus, in 1978, without hearing oral argument, and basing their judgment entirely on the legal papers submitted—a procedure they use infrequently—the Justices held 7:2 that reducing the benefits of welfare recipients who move from the United States to Puerto Rico is not a violation of their constitutional right to travel (*Califano v. Torres*, 435 U.S. 1). Also in the 1981 holding in *California v. Prysock*, 453 U.S. 355, in which it ruled 6:3, without hearing formal argument, that the *Miranda* warnings do not require "talismanic incantation" from the police.

106. 361 U.S. 49 (1959). Six hours were provided in that case. Another was *Arizona v. California*, sixteen hours (!) in 1962; a third was *Brown v. Board of Education II* in 1955, for which fourteen hours were allotted (370 U.S. 906 and 349 U.S. 294, respectively).

107. In the 1977–78 term, for example, 225 hours.

108. Edwin McElwain, "The Business of the Supreme Court as Conducted by Chief Justice Hughes," 63 *Harvard Law Review* 6 (1949).

109. But see Chief Justice Burger's objections to one Daniel S. Zevin in 1984, forcing a formal vote on his admission, which Burger lost 6:3. (See *The New York Times*, May 1, 1984, p. A10.) "His application," explained Burger, "appears to me a clear attempt to use membership in this Court's bar to 'launder' his past conduct to offset the negative impact of the very lenient disciplinary reprimand imposed by the Georgia Supreme Court."

sponsors, three years of good standing before the highest court of a state, and payment of a $100 fee. Gone are the days, in vogue until 1970, when the Chief Justice would formally welcome and chat with each lawyer newly admitted to practice before the Court.[110] Approximately 200,000 attorneys have been admitted to date (1991), averaging 5,000 annually. The $100 "admission fee" is used by the Supreme Court to cover travel and printing expenses of Court-assigned lawyers who represent indigent parties that come before it. Admission may, however, be revoked, as occurred, for example, in the case of attorney Wilmer D. Rekeweg of Paulding, Ohio, in June 1967. Because of certain professional aberrations resulting in his disbarment from the practice of law in all courts of Ohio by order of the Supreme Court of Ohio, the Supreme Court of the United States, after a "show cause" procedure, suspended and then disbarred him in a special Order, which read: "it is ordered that the said Wilmer D. Rekeweg be, and he is hereby disbarred, and that his name be stricken from the roll of attorneys admitted to practice before the bar of this court."[111] A similar fate befell G. Gordon Liddy, one of the convicted Watergate burglars, who was disbarred in 1973,[112] and former White House Counsel John W. Dean III, in 1975.[113] In July 1976 the Court, 7:0, accepted ex-President Nixon's resignation from the Court's bar. (He had been disbarred in New York.) Former Nixon Administration official Attorney General John N. Mitchell and former White House Assistant John D. Ehrlichman were disbarred by the Court in 1977.[114] So was another former Nixon Attorney General Richard G. Kleindienst, by a vote of 7:0, in 1982.[115] And so, in 1989, were former Representative Mario Biaggi (D.-N.Y.), who had been convicted of racketeering, and former U.S. District Court Judge Walter L. Nixon, who had been impeached and convicted by Congress for lying to a grand jury.

The Solicitor General. The *Solicitor General* is the third-ranking official in the U.S. Department of Justice, following the Attorney General and the Deputy Attorney General. Because of its special relationship to the Supreme Court, the post of Solicitor General has always enjoyed a high reputation in legal circles, has been eagerly sought by members of the legal profession, and has not infrequently been filled by legal scholars (e.g., President Kennedy's 1961 appointment of Professor Archibald Cox of Harvard University Law School, President Johnson's of Cox's Dean, Erwin N. Griswold,[116] in 1967, succeeding Thurgood Marshall, President Nixon's of Yale Law School Professor Robert H. Bork in 1973, President Reagan's

---

110. In the 1975–76 term, for example, the Court admitted *sage und schreibe* 5,691 persons to practice before it (*Washington Counsel,* September–October 1976, p. 49). The first member of the Supreme Court bar was Elias Boudinot of New Jersey, who was admitted on February 5, 1790. The first black was Dr. John S. Rock, admitted on February 1, 1865; the first woman was Belva A. Lockwood on March 3, 1879.

111. "Actions in United States Supreme Court," June 5, 1967 (as reported in *The New York Times,* June 6, 1967) (Order 1346 Misc.).

112. *In the Matter of the Disbarment of George Gordon Liddy,* 414 U.S. 1037.

113. *In the Matter of Disbarment of John W. Dean III,* 421 U.S. 985.

114. *In re Mitchell* and *in re Ehrlichman,* 434 U.S. 917.

115. *In the Matter of Disbarment of Richard G. Kleindienst,* 459 U.S. 811 (1982).

116. Griswold was before the bench a total of 114 times, more than any other modern Solicitor General.

of Brigham Young Law School Dean Rex Lee in 1981, and Harvard's Charles Fried in 1985).

The Solicitor General is in charge of all of the government's litigation in the Supreme Court, which constitutes in excess of 50 percent of the Court's total workload. That official plus deputies and assistants argue all of the government's cases before it. The Solicitor General's office supervises all government briefs filed in the Court, and the Solicitor General must personally approve or disapprove any case before the government takes it to the Court. Moreover, the Solicitor General has supervisory authority over other government appeals. Only if he or she gives approval may the government appeal from an adverse decision in a trial court, but, of course, it must be remembered that both the federal and state governments are checked by the Fifth (and Fourteenth) Amendment safeguards against double jeopardy. Sometimes, to the chagrin of certain members of both the executive and legislative branches, the Solicitor General's office exercises its commendable tradition of alertness toward any unfairness in government cases. When he or she detects such unfairness, the Solicitor General will usually file a "Confession of Error" in the Supreme Court, in which he or she asks that it set aside a victory won by the government in the lower court. Although this practice is of the very essence of justice—which, after all, should be the aim of all litigation—it may well be doubted that a large number of private counsel would be similarly willing to forgo a victory. All too frequently litigation is viewed as a courtroom battle between two opposing teams of high-powered trial lawyers bent on "victory" rather than on the triumph of justice.

BEHIND CLOSED DOORS

During the Court's term, each Friday and, at Chief Justice Burger's behest, since 1974 also at 3:00 P.M. on Wednesdays, is *Conference Day*.[117] On that day (there are about thirty each term of Court) the Justices, summoned by a buzzer five minutes before the hour, meet in a strictly closed session, usually from 9:30 or 10:00 A.M. until 5:30 or 6:00 P.M. (with a ten-minute mid-morning refreshment break and less than one hour for lunch) in the beautiful, oak-paneled conference chamber on the first (main) floor, under the chairmanship of the Chief Justice, whose offices are adjacent to it.[118] The role of the "Chief" is that of *primus inter pares*, although some have tended to be more *primus* than *pares*, and vice versa (as we shall presently see). Here the Justices discuss the cases they have heard, as well as all pending motions and applications for *certiorari*. Prior to each weekly conference the Chief Justice circulates two lists of cases that establish the basis for conference discus-

---

117. Until changed by Chief Justice Warren, Saturday was Conference Day, and it used to go on until seven or eight at night (as quoted by Jim Mann, *Los Angeles Times*, May 10, 1983, p. D1). Chief Justice John Marshall insisted that the Justices stay at the same boarding house, where they discussed cases over leisurely meals and, under Marshall's genial leadership, achieved the unanimity which "the Chief" accurately believed would result in greater prestige and authority for the fledgling tribunal.

118. The conference room is a large ceremonial anteroom between the two offices occupied by the Chief Justice.

sions. On the first, the "Discuss List," are those few cases deemed worthy of conference time. The other, much longer one, the "Dead List," contains those deemed unworthy—which are usually simply denied. Upward of three-quarters of the *certiorari* petitions are thus dismissed without even having merited conference discussion. Among those Justice Brennan, for one, thus considered frivolous in 1973 were the following propounded questions: "Are Negroes in fact Indians and therefore entitled to Indians' exemption from federal income taxes?" "Are the federal income tax laws unconstitutional insofar as they do not provide a deduction for the depletion of the human body?" "Is the Sixteenth Amendment unconstitutional as a violation of the Fourteenth Amendment?" and "Does a ban on drivers' turning right on a red light constitute an unreasonable burden on interstate commerce?"[119] Each Justice is expected to be ready to indicate his or her tentative stand, which he normally will have noted on the copy of the agenda, having been previously advised which cases would be up for discussion—generally those just heard by the Court on the three or, rarely, four "argument days" during that week or those recently heard in the course of conferences meeting during the two recess weeks in which no oral arguments are presented. The conference "list" may run from 25 to 150 items; 75 is about normal. The importance of this traditional conference, or for that matter any conference of appellate judges at which law cases and controversies are reviewed, was stated ably by Justice Jesse W. Carter of the California Supreme Court:

> [The conference] is not a prayer meeting where everyone is expected to nod "amen"; it is more like a battleground where opposing philosophies meet in hand-to-hand combat.[120]

Or, as Justice Powell observed almost two decades later:

> [The conference] affords the principal opportunity for discussion, debate, and group deliberation. Justices may speak as frequently and as long as they wish . . . and not infrequently a conference has altered my original tentative view.[121]

But there are dissenters to that positive evaluation, e.g., Justice Antonin Scalia, who commented in 1988: "To call our discussion of a case a conference is really something of a misnomer. It's much more of a statement of the views of each of the nine Justices, after which the totals are added and the case is assigned. I don't like that. Maybe it's just because I'm new. [He had joined the Court in 1986.] Maybe it's because I'm an academic. Maybe it's just because I am right."[122]

The Justices are seated around a large rectangular mahogany conference table, each of the nine highbacked chairs bearing a nameplate; about twenty-five carts loaded with needed data stand nearby. In accordance with a tradition established by Chief Justice Fuller in 1888—some credit its authorship to then Associate Justice Edward D. White (1894–1910)—all shake hands with one another on entering the room. The Chief Justice sits at the south end and the Senior Associate

119. 59 *Journal of the American Bar Association* 846 (August 1973).
120. As quoted in *The New York Times*, March 16, 1959, p. 31.
121. As quoted by Richard L. Williams, *Smithsonian*, February 1977, p. 89.
122. As quoted in *The New York Times*, February 22, 1988, p. A16.

Justice at the north end. Three of the other Justices sit on one side, four on the other, but not necessarily in the usual order of seniority.[123] Looking down on this scene is the sole portrait in the room, that of Chief Justice John Marshall. The incumbent Chief Justice, whose personality and administrative talent loom large in these meetings, customarily gives his own view first in the case up for discussion, and he is followed by the other Justices in order of seniority. Each Justice, refreshed by coffee from a silver urn, must be prepared to recite and do so persuasively, if he or she feels strongly about an issue involved. Upon completion of this phase of their deliberations, the nine members of the Court take a tentative ballot on the case, for some time now voting in the same order as in the discussion phase.[124] Each Justice has a hinged, lockable docket book, in which all votes are duly recorded.

The Role of the Chief Justice. Although he is theoretically merely *primus inter pares*—and he does have but one vote among nine—the "Chief" has a potential influence that may well outweigh that of any ordinary presiding officer. Justice Hughes suggested some reasons for this:

> Popular interest naturally centers in the Chief Justice as the titular head of the Court. He is its executive officer; he presides at its sessions and its conferences, and announces its orders. By virtue of the distinctive function of the Court he is the most important judicial officer in the world; he is the Chief Justice of the United States.[125]

Several of his functions lend themselves ideally to the exercise of that influence: one is the chairmanship of the Court's own conference, including his highly important role in the sifting of writs of *certiorari*, the other his assignment of opinions (to be more fully described later in this section). When the "Chief" opens discussion of a case by giving his own views first, he has an excellent opportunity to state the case as he sees it, to indicate the questions to be decided, and to give his opinions on the issue or issues involved. This "speak first" rule is a far from inconsiderable power, for there is a chance that his initial analysis of a problem will have at least some influence on that of others in the room. It is, of course, by no means inevitable that the person who selects the issues to be discussed will dominate or determine the ultimate results—to which the lasting and profound differences in reading the

123. In a letter to me, dated September 28, 1970, Justice Brennan described the Court's seating arrangement at that time as follows: "The Chief Justice sits on one end and Justice Black on the other end of the table. On the Chief's right sit Justice Marshall, myself, and Justice Douglas in that order. On his left sit Justice Stewart, Justice White, Justice Blackmun, and Justice Harlan in that order." In an article in *The New York Times* (February 6, 1975, p. M31) Warren Weaver professed to have knowledge of a quite different contemporary seating arrangement, based strictly on "clockwise by seniority," with Douglas beginning the order on Burger's left. But in a letter to me, dated August 4, 1975, Barrett McGurn, the Court's information officer, declared Weaver to be wrong and, having checked with the Clerk of the Court, provided a diagram, which is very close to the data on the seating of the Justices supplied by Justice Brennan.

124. For a good many years it was customary to have the most junior justice in seniority vote first. Some disagreement exists as to just when that practice was dropped. But Justice O'Connor told me that "now the Chief Justice speaks and votes first, and the junior justice speaks and votes last" (interview, the Supreme Court, March 21, 1988). And a letter from Chief Justice Rehnquist not only confirmed that assertion but makes clear that that was and is the practice in his Court [May 19, 1989]).

125. As quoted in *The New York Times*, June 24, 1969, p. 25.

meaning of the Constitution among Justices on a host of issues bear witness. Still, there is a good chance that such will indeed be the case. An interesting example, gleaned from the Harold H. Burton papers, among others, is Chief Justice Warren's role in speaking first in the Court's Conferences on the *1954 and 1955 Segregation Cases.*[126]

Other tasks, implied or actual, confront a Chief Justice and play a role in history's regard of him as an effective or ineffective leader. Among these is the ability to keep peace among the several Justices, who are often deeply divided along intellectual and personal lines. Justices Jackson and Black, for example, became increasingly hostile during the waning days of Chief Justice Stone's tenure (partly due to Jackson's long assignment in Nürnberg), resulting, or so it is believed, in President Truman's compromise "peacemaker appointment" of Fred Vinson as Stone's successor on the latter's death in 1946. Vinson, a person of far less judicial and intellectual stature than Stone, had a reputation as a conciliator and, apparently, succeeded at least in keeping the feud between the two Justices *en famille.* Justice McReynolds, a confirmed anti-Semite, refused even to speak to his newly appointed colleague, Justice Brandeis, from 1916 to 1919. Chief Justice White was unable to alter the situation, but the amiable and popular Chief Justice Taft apparently succeeded in mitigating it somewhat. Still, McReynolds caused Taft constant difficulties, too. For instance, he refused to sit for the Court's annual photograph in 1924 because he would have found himself seated next to Brandeis in seniority—and no photo was taken. And two years earlier he had declined to accompany the Court to a Philadelphia ceremony, writing to Taft: "As you know, I am not always to be found when there is a Hebrew aboard. Therefore, my 'inability to attend' must not surprise you."[127] In 1939 he refused to attend Felix Frankfurter's robing ceremony; he would not sign the Court's routine retirement resolution when Brandeis left; and he habitually turned his back on Justice Cardozo. Other McReynolds quirks were almost constant carping at practically every opinion authored by Stone, whom he disliked for philosophical reasons, and his overt hostility toward Justice John H. Clarke. McReynolds, who, as Wilson's Attorney General, had played a role in Clarke's appointment to the bench, felt "betrayed" because Clarke failed to vote on the Court as McReynolds thought he should and would.[128] Although he was by no means able to stop entirely the public barbs exchanged on the bench on occasion between, for example, Justices Frankfurter and Whittaker on the one hand, and Justices Black and Douglas on the other, Chief Justice Warren apparently smoothed over many a ruffled feeling, despite his personal involvement in an outburst or two, as some of the illustrations to follow will indicate. Yet it is vital to be aware of a basic fact of life on the Court: *no* Chief

126. *Brown v. Board of Education of Topeka,* 347 U.S. 483 (1954); ibid., 349 U.S. 294 (1955); and *Bolling v. Sharpe,* 347 U.S. 497 (1954). See the account by S. Sidney Ulmer in *Courts as . . . Small Groups* (New York: General Learning Press, 1971), pp. 23–26; the Warren obituary, *The New York Times,* July 11, 1974, p. A35; and Richard Kluger's *Simple Justice* (New York: Alfred A. Knopf, 1975).

127. As quoted by Alpheus T. Mason in his *William Howard Taft: Chief Justice* (New York: Simon and Schuster, 1965), pp. 216–17.

128. Any of the following types of applicants to a clerkship were disqualified with McReynolds: those who were "smokers," 'drinkers," Jews, married, or engaged!

Justice can command the beliefs of his associates, and the Court has never lacked for strong personalities and strong convictions, nor will it henceforth.

Another significant facet of the Chief's work is to keep an eye on the clock during the conference, with a view of getting its tasks accomplished. Although there has been disagreement on the extent of the Court's burden, there is little doubt that the pressure of case work is enormous. Unless a firm hand rules the conference, time will flee, especially as the Justices are, quite naturally, given to extensive speaking—Justice Oliver Wendell Holmes, Jr., interestingly enough, was a notable exception. No Chief Justice since Marshall controlled his flock so firmly as did Hughes, whom most students and observers of the Court, as well as those who served with him on the high tribunal, have generally regarded as the most effective—even if on occasion somewhat arbitrary—organizer, leader, and disciplinarian since Marshall's taut judicial regime.[129]

For example, Hughes would accord an average of three and one-half minutes of conference time, and no more, to a petition for *certiorari*, having himself gone through and thoroughly analyzed all of them *before* the conference and being fully prepared to make recommendations on each to his colleagues. And he would often force the end of a discussion that he viewed as unprofitable or dilatory by intoning: "Brethren, the only way to settle this is vote. So let us do just that—now." Justice Stone, whose philosophy of his role as Chief was drastically different, declined to put any time on either *certiorari* discussions or a particular series of cases. Stone simply refused to engage in what he viewed as "high pressure tactics." Thus, whereas Hughes finished a conference docket in four hours, Stone would require four days for a similar docket. This did not make Stone a less qualified jurist, but it probably made him a far less effective Chief than Hughes—or Taft, another assertive, resourceful, and popular Chief Justice, whose caliber, however, was certainly considerably below that of Stone as a *jurist*. (Taft was infinitely happier as Chief Justice than as President; he regarded the former office as possessing both more power and more prestige than the latter.) Some observers, although distinctly a minority, believe that the virtues of Hughes as Chief Justice were overstated and those of Stone underrated. One of these, John P. Frank, a law clerk for Justice Black, complained that Hughes's tactics of "business efficiency" meant that "discussion in conference was perforce a statement of conclusions more than an exchange of mutually stimulating ideas . . ." and he charged the Chief Justice with "intellectual flexibility for the sake of the appearance of unanimity."[130] Be that as it may, Chief Justice Hughes was immensely popular as a leader of his bench, and he was the only member of the Court to whom Justice McReynolds would defer. We have Justice Frankfurter's word that "if he made others feel his moral superiority, they merely felt a fact . . . all who served with him recognized [his] extraor-

129. This does not mean that even Hughes was able to control the idiosyncrasies of the cantankerous Justice McReynolds, who, upon being informed by a messenger from the Chief Justice that it was time to convene for a Court session, sent the messenger packing with the reply that he did "not work for" the Chief Justice. As reported by James F. Simon, *In His Own Image: The Supreme Court in Richard Nixon's America* (New York: David McKay, 1973), p. 55.
130. John P. Frank, "Harlan Fiske Stone: An Estimate," 9 *Stanford Law Review* 692n (1957).

dinary qualities. . . . To see him preside was like [seeing] Toscanini leading an orchestra."[131] Justice Black attested to his own "more than impersonal and detached admiration [for Hughes's] extraordinary intellectual gifts."[132] And Justice Roberts wrote that "Men whose views were as sharply opposed as those of Van Devanter and Brandeis, or those of Sutherland and Cardozo, were at one in their admiration and affectionate regard for their presiding officer."[133] There is little, if any, doubt that Charles Evans Hughes was the epitome of a great Chief Justice. And history may arguably place Earl Warren into a similar bracket—perhaps even higher, next to John Marshall. For to both Warren and Marshall the Court was more than "a mystically passive weigher of 'the law,' but also a participant, along with other agencies of the government, in the practical process of realizing the objectives set out in the Constitution's preamble."[134]

ASSIGNING AND WRITING OPINIONS

As Eugene V. Rostow wrote when he was dean of the Yale School of Law, "Judges must write down their reasons for a decision because they are partners with us, the citizenry, in an agreed procedure for reaching responsible decisions."[135] The practice of writing the Opinion of the Court[136] goes back to the days of Chief Justice John Marshall. Prior to his adoption of this time-saving procedure, the Justices usually delivered their opinions *seriatim*[137] in about one-quarter to one-third of the cases, a practice still prevalent among the Law Lords of the British House of Lords, and one that Jefferson, as President, wanted to institutionalize in the face of Marshall's powerful objections. Marshall realistically believed that the Court's power and prestige would be enhanced if it were to speak with a single voice.[138] Today, full opinions are written for the Court (some of these *per curiam*, as we have seen) in all cases heard by it on the merits, other than those decided by memorandum order. However, if there is a tie vote, no opinion is written, and the Court does not announce on which side of the tie the Justices stood. In the event of such a vote, the decision of the highest court below, from which the case came to the Supreme Court, is sustained; for example, the Court's 4:4 vote in the case of *Bailey v.*

131. *Of Law and Men*, op. cit., pp. 133, 148.
132. Black to Hughes, June 3, 1941, Hughes Papers.
133. New York County Lawyers' Association, December 12, 1948.
134. Alpheus Thomas Mason, "Judicial Activism: Old and New," 55 *Virginia Law Review* 424 (1969). Fred Graham placed Warren just below Marshall and above Taney in an interesting evaluative article, "180 Years of Chief Justices: Some Nonentities, Some Giants," *The New York Times*, June 24, 1969, p. 25.
135. *The Sovereign Prerogative: The Supreme Court and the Quest for Law* (New Haven: Yale University Press, 1962), p. 89.
136. John P. Frank, a careful observer and student of the Court, once divided the writing styles of the Justices into four categories: "legal lumpy," "legal massive," "rock-bottom contemporary," and "legal lucid." *The Marble Palace*, op. cit., pp. 295 ff.
137. A well-known illustration is the group of *seriatim* opinions by Associate Justices Chase, Paterson, and Iredell in the 1796 case of *Hylton v. United States*, 3 Dallas 171.
138. The judges of Italy's Constitutional Court, the highest tribunal in the land (see ch. 7 *infra*, pp. 297ff.) are statutorily *forbidden* to file individual opinions and, in general, to make their votes known.

Richardson[139] affirmed the 2:1 upholding of the loyalty dismissal of Dorothy Bailey by the federal government in the Court of Appeals for the District of Columbia. In this instance the even division of the Court came about as a result of Justice Tom Clark's failure to participate in the case; because he had been the U.S. Attorney General at the time of Miss Bailey's travail and dismissal, he deemed it unethical to be involved in the disposition of her appeal. Another illustration is the Court's failure, because of Justice John Paul Steven's refusal to agree with either side, to resolve an important jury instruction controversy.[140]

Abstentions. The members of today's Supreme Court, unlike most members of Congress, are extremely cautious about even the faintest taint of conflict of interest, be it of a social, economic, personal, or political nature.[141] Among the Justices, "When in doubt, do not sit" is a firmly established custom, called "recusing," partially reinforced by two federal statutes and a canon of the American Bar Association.[142] This was not always so, particularly not in the early days of the Court— witness Marshall's refusal to disqualify himself in *Marbury v. Madison*,[143] in which he was personally and directly involved.

Assignments Generally. The work load of preparing opinions of the Court is usually very well distributed. If the Court is unanimous, or if the Chief Justice is in the majority, he may, and often does, write the opinion of the Court himself. In the latter instance, provided he speaks for at least four other Justices, it would be known as the *majority opinion.*

But, of course, nothing prevents the Chief from asking another member of the Court to write the opinion either when it is unanimous or when he is on the side of the majority. The only exception to this practice is the long-standing tradition of permitting every newcomer to the Court to select the first opinion he will write. Long gone are the days of Chief Justice Marshall who, especially during his early

139. 341 U.S. 918 (1951). Three other illustrations are the Court's 4:4 split (Justice Lewis F. Powell, a prominent Richmond educational leader, abstaining) in the 1973 Richmond school consolidation cases (*School Board of Richmond v. Bradley* and *Bradley v. State Board of Education of the Commonwealth of Virginia*, 411 U.S. 913); a freedom of expression case affirming *per curiam* 4:4 a lower court's declaration of unconstitutionality (*Common Cause v. Schmitt*, 455 U.S. 129 [1982]; and a 3:3 split in a visa denial case (*Reagan v. Abourezk*, 484 U.S. [1987], Justices Blackmun and Scalia not voting and Justice Powell's vacancy still unfilled).

140. *Connecticut v. Johnson*, 460 U.S. 73 (1983).

141. As a fledgling member of the Court in 1972, Justice Rehnquist, notwithstanding the highly critical reaction of large segments of the legal and academic communities, refused to disqualify himself in at least three 5:4 decisions that had been within his jurisdiction as an official in the Justice Department prior to his appointment to the Supreme Court—but he did *not* participate in *United States v. Nixon*.

142. For their exact verbiage, see Title 29, Sec. 454, U.S.C.A., Title 28, Sec. 455, U.S.C.A., and the Fourth Canon of the American Bar Association's Canons of Judicial Ethics. The frequent abstentions of the then still recently appointed Justice Thurgood Marshall in his first term on the Court (1967–68), largely because he had been Solicitor General of the United States as well as a prominent civil rights attorney, caused considerable consternation. By the end of the first five months of the term he had abstained in thirty-one of the forty-four formally decided cases. For a warm plea against excessive recusing, see Erwin N. Griswold and Ernest Gellhorn, "200 Cases in Which Justices Recused Themselves," *The Washington Post*, October 18, 1988, p. A25.

143. 1 Cranch 137 (1803).

years on the bench, would himself write practically every opinion, no doubt at least partly because his fellow Justices were rather lethargic (some would say brow-beaten).[144] In fact, during his first four full years (1801–5) he personally authored all but two of the opinions of the Court![145] Chief Justice Warren, on the other hand, in assigning 80 percent of all the Court's opinions during his sixteen-year tenure, self-assigned but 10 percent, and Chief Justice Burger during his first fifteen terms (1969–84) self-assigned a similar percentage in assigning 84.8 percent of all cases.[146]

When the Chief Justice is on the minority side of a decision, however, the Senior Associate Justice on the side of the majority either writes the opinion of the Court himself or herself or assigns it to one of the other members among the major-ity. All assignments are made by sending a formal note to the prospective author a few days after the conference. Professor Spaeth's significant study of Chief Justice Burger's assignment practices documents a remarkable record of distributive equality—better than that of any of his five immediate predecessors (Warren, Vin-son, Stone, Hughes, and Taft). The 1990–91 term serves as an illustration of an equitable distribution of the workload[147] of preparing the 113 written opinions of the Court: Chief Justice Rehnquist and Justice O'Connor wrote 15 each; Justices Blackmun, White, and Justice Stevens 14; Justice Kennedy 13; Justice Marshall 12; Justice Scalia 11; and Justice Souter 7. (He did not join the Court until February 1988.) Five opinions were *per curiam.* Of the 64 written *concurring* opinions filed, Justice Scalia led his colleagues with 15; next was Justice White with 13; Justice Brennan 11; O'Connor 8; Justice Stevens 6; Chief Justice Rehnquist 2; Justices Blackmun and Kennedy 4 each; and Justice Marshall 1. Justice Stevens led the Court in its written dissenting opinions with 17; he was followed by Justice Bren-nan's and Justice Marshall's 13 each; Chief Justice Rehnquist wrote 7; Justices White and Scalia 11; Justice Blackmun 10; Justice O'Connor 12; and Justice Ken-nedy 3. (There were additional dissents without written opinions.)

144. According to a wistful 1822 letter from Justice William Johnson to Thomas Jefferson, the former soon perceived the real reason his Chief, John Marshall, "delivered all the opinions. . . . Cushing was incompetent, Chase could not be got to think or write—Patterson [sic] was a slow man and willingly declined the trouble, and the other two judges [Marshall and Bushrod Washington] are commonly estimated as one judge. . . . ("Letter of December 10, 1822, quoted in Donald G. Mor-gan, *Justice William Johnson: The First Dissenter.* Columbia: University of South Carolina Press, 1954, pp. 181–82). During their twenty-nine years together on the Supreme Court Washington disagreed with Marshall only thrice!

145. In all, he wrote 519 of his Court's 1,106 opinions, dissenting only nine times in his thirty-four and one-half years on the high bench; and he wrote 36 of the 62 decisions involving constitutional questions (see Robert J. Steamer, *The Supreme Court in Crisis: A History of Conflict* [Amherst: University of Massachusetts Press, 1971], p. 35).

146. Harold J. Spaeth, "Distributive Justice: Majority Opinion Assignments in the Burger Court," 67 *Judicature* 6 (December–January 1984), p. 301, and *ibid.,* Table 1, and accompanying text.

147. During his thirty-six-and-one-half-year tenure—which ended on November 15, 1975—Justice Douglas wrote 1,628 majority, concurring, dissenting, and other opinions. In 1972–73 he authored a record 53(!) His written dissents rank him as by far the most prolific dissenter to date (1992). Holmes, although known as the "great dissenter," wrote only 74, ranking him rather modestly in that category. Brennan, second at his retirement in 1990, had penned 409. However, Holmes wrote more opinions on behalf of the entire Court (885) than anyone else. Douglas had penned the most opinions *qua* opinions as of the end of the 1991–92 term; Brennan's 1,258 were in second place.

Although until circa 1930 the Court tended to be unanimous in approximately 80 to 85 percent of its decisions, as a rule unanimous opinions have since then been rendered in a minority of full opinion cases, averaging 25 to 35 percent through the years, only barely 20 percent in 1967–77—although 1982–83 and 1983–84 witnessed a welcome climb to 39 and 44 percent, respectively; in 1987–88 and in 1990–91 it was 35 percent.[148] A partial explanation for that fifty-odd-year drop in the number of unanimous decisions is the plethora of complex and novel cases that the Court has had to deal with contemporarily. In the 1981–82 term thirty-three cases—nearly one-fifth of the all full opinions issued—were decided by a one-vote margin, twice as many as in the previous term of the Court. That figure changed little in 1982–83, 1983–84, and 1984–85, with 19, 21, and 18 percent, respectively. It jumped to 25 percent in 1985–86 but dropped under the post-Brennan Rehnquist Court to 19 percent in 1990–91. Memorandum orders, which, quite naturally, enjoy a far higher degree of unanimity, were up to 82.1 percent.[149] Most opinions are rendered as *majority* opinions, but an unfortunately increasing number do not command a majority and are thus delivered as *plurality* opinions. In the latter, the Court, although ruling on the issue(s) at hand, commands only a plurality of the Justices in favor of that particular ruling; that is, there may be a 4:3:2 decision— seven favoring the side of the "winner" but for dissimilar reasons. Until 1953 only forty-seven plurality decisions had been rendered in the Court's history; but the Warren Court handed down forty in the ensuing fifteen years, and the Burger Court presented the annals with eighty-eight between 1969 and 1981.[150] Subsequent terms have borne witness to some but relatively little improvement.

Dissenting Opinions. As these statistics demonstrate, dissenting and concurring opinions as well as simple dissents and concurrences are now quite common.[151] Yet only when the formal opinion method of registering disagreement with the decision and/or the opinion of the majority is employed does the practice become meaningful for the governmental process. A simple *dissent*, without explanation, such as "Mr. Justice Butler dissents" in *Palko v. Connecticut*,[152] represents a vote on the other side; but it says little to the expert and layperson alike, save that a Justice, for reasons known only to himself, or herself, chose to dissent. It is entirely

---

148. A total of 647 orally argued Warren Court cases were decided without dissent, as were 860 Burger Court cases. These totals are based on case citation rather than docket number and they comprise 36.1 percent of the Warren Court's 1793 cases and 35.8 percent of the Burger Court's 2,403 cases (72 *Judicature* 5 [February–March 1989], p. 276).

149. Several good sources for these statistics exist; among others are the *Annual Report of the Director of Administrative office of the U.S. Courts* and the law reviews, especially the November issue of the *Harvard Law Review.*

150. *The Washington Post,* June 25, 1981, p. A13.

151. Apparently there exists a tradition, albeit not an unbroken one, that precludes any qualifying opinion in a decision involving a new Justice's first opinion for the Court. See Wallace Mendelson's "Neo-Behavioralism—A Rebuttal," 57 *American Political Science Review* 952 (December 1963), n. 7. Thus Justice Antonin Scalia's first opinion for the Court came in a 9:0 holding in a tax case (*O'Connor v. United States,* 479 U.S. 27 1986). Justice David H. Souter's "maiden" opinion was for a 9:0 Court in 1991 in a capital punishment jury problem case. (*Ford v. Georgia,* 59 LW 4111).

152. 302 U.S. 319 (1937).

possible, of course, for honest, competent jurists to arrive at sharply divided opinions in a case; hence, *dissenting opinions*, both short and long, are quite common. In fact, the first *reported* decision of the Supreme Court was rendered by a divided Court, Justices William Cushing and Thomas Johnson dissenting from the Court majority's grant of an injunction to Georgia.[153] Thomas Jefferson believed early that dissents rendered the Court a more open, a more democratic institution—and that belief represented a major reason why he wanted the Court always to render *seriatim* opinions (a practice opposed, and discarded, by John Marshall when he became Chief Justice). As one of the best-known dissenters, Justice Holmes, said, "General propositions do not decide particular cases." One of the classic statements on the subject was made by the then ex–Associate Justice and future Chief Justice Charles Evans Hughes:

> A dissent in a court of last resort is an appeal to the brooding spirit of the law, to the intelligence of a future day, when a later decision may possibly correct the error into which the dissenting judge believes the court to have been betrayed.[154]

This from the pen of a jurist who rarely wrote dissenting opinions himself, who rarely dissented, and who exerted a greater dominance over the Court than any other Chief Justice save Marshall. Hughes often expressed the view that there is no reason to expect more unanimity on difficult problems of law than in the "higher reaches" of physics, theology, or philosophy. Justice Carter, the colorful state of California jurist mentioned earlier, was fond of observing: "I welcome dissents, for they test the soundness of my own opinions. . . . The dissenting opinion is . . . a forecast of things to come. The writers of dissents are usually men who look forward—not back, nor to the immediate present, but to the future."[155] Or, as Roscoe Pound once remarked, " . . . dissenting opinions may be the symptom of life in the law of time."[156] To Thomas Reed Powell they were "most valuable equilibrators in the undulating course of the law."[157] And in his very last public statement on the last day of his sixteen-year tenure as Chief Justice of the United States, Earl Warren, responding to President Nixon, said:

> We do not always agree [on the bench]. I hope the Court will never agree on all things. I am sure that its virility will have been sapped because it is composed of nine independent men who have no one to be responsible to except their own conscience.[158]

153. *Georgia v. Braisford*, 2 Dallas 402 (1792). What scholars regard as the first "real" dissenting opinion on the Court, however, came from the "Father of Dissent," the Jefferson-appointed William Johnson, in 1805, in *Huidekoper's Lessee v. Douglas*, 3 Cranch 1. Johnson wrote most of the dissenting opinions during Marshall's Supreme Court Chief Justiceship. The latter was not amused.
154. C. Evans Hughes, *The Supreme Court of the United States* (New York: Columbia University Press, 1928), p. 68.
155. As quoted in *The New York Times*, March 16, 1959, p. 31.
156. "Preface," in *Justice Musmanno Dissents* (Indianpolis: Bobbs-Merrill, 1956).
157. "The Logic and Rhetoric of Constitutional Law," 15 *Journal of Philosophy, Psychology, and Scientific Method* 654 (1918).
158. As quoted in *The New York Times*, June 24, 1969, p. 1.

On the other hand, his colleague Potter Stewart labeled dissents "subversive literature."[159]

Many among the most memorable opinions of the Court initially on the dissenting side have eventually become majority opinions—especially some by famed spokesmen of erstwhile minority viewpoints, such as Justices William Johnson, Harlan, Sr., Holmes—although he categorized dissents in his first as "useless" and "undesirable,"[160]—Brandeis, Stone, Black, and Brennan. One obvious example is the lone Harlan dissenting opinion in 1896, his eloquent remonstrance against the "separate but equal" doctrine in Plessy v. Ferguson,[161] which became the unanimous opinion of the Court in 1954 in Brown v. Board of Education of Topeka.[162] Another is the lone dissenting opinion of Stone in 1940 in the Gobitis case.[163] Stone argued forcefully, but unsuccessfully, against the compulsory flag salute required by the Minersville, Pennsylvania, school district even from those who found it to be religiously objectionable. Scarcely three years later this became the opinion of the Court when a majority of six—over a memorable dissent by Justice Frankfurter—held a similar West Virginia Board of Education requirement to be an unconstitutional attachment of freedom of religion in the Barnette case.[164] Justice Cardozo, also a frequent dissenter, viewed the dissenting opinion as an entirely proper place for recording "the best inspiration of the time," for instruction in moral values still battling for general acceptance in the political process.[165] "It's grand to fight," once remarked Justice Black. "The Supreme Court does disagree. I hope it always will. It does have men who express their differences. I hope it always will have. Because I subscribe to the theory that there is no progress when differences are stifled."[166] It was Black who was given the honor of writing the opinion for the unanimous Court in the 1963 Gideon case, which extended to indigents the right to be furnished counsel in non-capital as well as capital criminal cases, a decision that overruled the Betts case of 1942 in which Black had vigorously dissented (joined by his brothers Douglas and Murphy).[167]

There is little doubt that a dissenting opinion is preeminently the result of a profoundly held conviction; consequently, it may well be regarded as strengthening rather than weakening the authority of a particular case. However, as Learned Hand contended, it may also weaken the Court's authority. Moreover, it may also serve to muddy the waters, to force extremist positions, and to confuse the public. For example, there are those students of the Dred Scott case—and not necessarily only the apologists for Chief Justice Taney—who contend that Taney's extremist

159. William J. Brennan, Jr., "In Defense of Dissents," Hastings College of Law Lecture, November 18, 1985, p. 3.

160. Northern Securities Co. v. United States, 193 U.S. 197 (1904), at 400.

161. 163 U.S. 537. Harlan's memorable words: "Our Constitution is color-blind, and neither knows nor tolerates classes among citizens" (at 559).

162. 347 U.S. 483.

163. Minersville School District v. Gobitis, 310 U.S. 586.

164. West Virginia State Board of Education v. Barnette, 319 U.S. 624 (1943).

165. Benjamin M. Cardozo, Selected Writings, ed. by Margaret E. Hall (New York: Fallon Publishers, 1947), p. 274.

166. Quoted in The New York Times, June 5, 1961, p. 10

167. See nn. 56, 72, 73, 74, supra.

position for the majority was a reaction to the extremist position taken by the politically ambitious Justice McLean in his dissenting opinion.[168] (It should be noted
here that dissent is *much* less common in the fifty state courts, in which the average rate of dissent at the highest appellate level is but one case in ten.)[169] *De minimis*, as Harlan Fiske Stone observed at the outset of his Chief Justiceship that
dissent "is some assurance to counsel and to the public that decision has not been
perfunctory, which is one of the most important objects of decision-writing."[170] Dissent is indeed essential to an effective judiciary in democratic society.[171] In Justice
Brennan's 1985 words: "Through dynamic interaction among members of the
present Court and through dialogue across time with the future Court we ensure
the continuing contemporary relevance and hence vitality of our fundamental
charter.[172]

Concurring Opinions. At times the reasoning of the Justice assigned to write
the opinion of the Court may not be palatable to all of the members of the majority
side. In that event, one or more *concurring opinions* may be written, an increasingly common practice during the past few decades. Broadly speaking, it usually
signifies the concurrence of its author in the *decision*, but not in the *reasoning* of
the Court. One illustration would be the two separate concurring opinions of
Justices Black and Douglas in the 8:0 decision of the Supreme Court in *Rochin v.
California*.[173] While agreeing with the Court that the State of California had
engaged in grossly brutal, and hence obviously illegal, conduct in its apprehension
and conviction of Rochin, a narcotics peddler, the two Justices strongly disagreed
with the *ground* on which the Court based its reversal of Rochin's conviction: violation of the due process of law clause of the Fourteenth Amendment of the U.S.
Constitution. In the firmly held judgment of Black and Douglas, California had
actually violated individual liberty safeguards specifically enumerated in the Bill of
Rights—in fact thus contending, as they had done ever since their appointment to
the Court in 1937 and 1939, respectively, that the specific provisions are per se

---

168. In his essay on "politically minded" Justices, Alexander M. Bickel calls McLean the "most noto-
riously so." See his *Politics and the Warren Court* (New York: Harper & Row, 1965), p. 135.
Indeed, McLean was a presidential candidate of sorts five times: in 1832 as an Anti-Mason, in 1836
as an Independent, in 1848 as *both* a Whig and a Free-Soiler; in 1852 he refused the Native American party's nomination; and in 1856 came his most serious candidacy, as a Republican. No doctrinaire he! See Francis P. Weisenburger, *The Life of John McLean: A Politician on the United
States Supreme Court* (Columbus: Ohio State University Press, 1937).
169. See the interesting article by Robert J. Sickles, "The illusion of Judicial Consensus," 59 *The American Political Science Review* 100 (March 1965). See also Steven A. Peterson and Kenneth N.
Vines, "Acceptance of Dissent by American Legal Elites" (Paper prepared for delivery at the
Southern Political Science Association's annual meetings in Atlanta, Georgia, November 4–6,
1976).
170. "Dissenting Opinions Are Not Without Value," 26 *Journal of the American Judicature Society* 78
(1942).
171. See Justice Frankfurter's opinion in *Ferguson v. Moore–McCormack Lines*, 352 U.S. 528 (1957)
and, generally, Steven A. Peterson, "Dissent in American Courts," 43 *The Journal of Politics* 412
(May 1981).
172. "In Defense of Dissents," op. cit., n. 159, p. 14.
173. 342 U.S. 165 (1952).

applicable to the states (by means of the Fourteenth Amendment) as well as to the federal government.[174]

Another example of the use of the concurring opinion is that by Justice Frankfurter, a frequent "concurrer," in *Cooper v. Aaron (The Little Rock Case)*,[175] which was decided in the Special Session in the summer of 1958. There, not only in order to show its continuous unanimity in cases basically following *Brown v. Board of Education*,[176] but also to make clear that those Justices (Harlan, Brennan, and Whittaker) who had not participated in *Brown* were at one with the remaining six members of that historic opinion, the Supreme Court issued its opinion in the unique format of a joint authorship, with the names of each of its nine unanimous members specifically listed *seriatim* at the head of the "Opinion of the Court." However, Justice Frankfurter was obviously deeply grieved and disturbed by the clear flouting of the law and crass defiance of the federal judiciary by the officials of the State of Arkansas, led by Governor Orval E. Faubus—so much so that, notwithstanding the unusual joint authorship described, he was moved to write a separate concurring opinion, which was issued and published some weeks thereafter (an action that infuriated Chief Justice Warren, who had understood that there would be *no* separate opinion of any kind). In it, Frankfurter gave what, in effect, was a profound and moving lecture to the country in general, and the South in particular, on the meaning of "the supreme Law of the Land" and the federal system. Written with scholarship and feeling, this independent statement nevertheless probably somewhat diminished the effect of the joint opinion of the Court. There are many legal scholars who are convinced that, whereas *dissenting* opinions are both eminently justifiable and necessary, *concurring* opinions are neither—that they are frequently nothing more than ego manifestations and/or "quibbling," which would more profitably be confined to footnotes in the body of the majority opinion. Chief Justice Warren, for one, strongly opposed resort to concurring opinions.[177] Yet there is no doubt that the concurring opinion is a significant tool in the judicial process.

Techniques of Assignment. The preceding discussion raises the interesting problem of the selection of the opinion writers by the Chief Justice, or by the Senior Associate Justice when the duty of designation devolves on him. Giving due attention to the need of distributing the work load relatively evenly (and, as explained earlier, permitting a Court newcomer to select his own first opinion to write), the average Chief Justice's assignments—approximately 80 to 85 percent of the cases—may well be said to follow a fairly common pattern. It is a pattern, based on the considerable influence that governs the actions of the Chief in making his selections, that will take account of all of the following considerations. First, the so-called great, big, or important constitutional cases—although these are neces-

---

174. See my *Freedom and the Court: Civil Rights and Liberties in the United States,* 4th ed. (New York: Oxford University Press, 1982), ch. 3.
175. 358 U.S. 1 (1958).
176. 347 U.S. 483 (1954).
177. "Seminar with Mr. Chief Justice Warren," op. cit., p. 5.

sarily somewhat subjective concepts[178]—should be authored by the Chief himself; for example, Chief Justice Warren speaking for the unanimous Court in *Brown v. Board of Education,*[179]—of which, as he was quoted after his retirement, he had written "every blessed word."[180]

> I assigned myself to write the decision, for it seemed to me that something so important ought to issue over the name of the Chief Justice of the United States. In drafting it, I sought to use low-key, unemotional language and to keep it short enough so that it could be published in full in every newspaper in the country. I kept the text secret (it was locked in my safe) until I read from the bench.[181]

In Chief Justice Hughes's majority opinion for the narrowly divided Court (5:4) in the immensely significant case of *West Coast Hotel Co. v. Parrish,*[182] upholding the state of Washington minimum wage law for women—sometimes, perhaps flippantly but probably not altogether unjustly, called "the-switch-in-time-that-saved-nine" case—the Court departed from its erstwhile stubborn adherence to the narrow construction of the concept of "freedom of contract" under the Fifth and Fourteenth Amendments to the Constitution by overruling the specific precedent of *Adkins v. Children's Hospital*[183] (in which it had struck down [5:3] a similar, though federal, law for the District of Columbia). That departure clearly indicated a change of position by the Chief Justice *and* Justice Roberts. The latter's switch was especially significant because prior thereto he had normally represented the "swing vote" between the so-called pro– and anti–New Deal factions on the Court. His new stance heralded more or less clear sailing, at least on constitutional grounds, for the legislative programs enacted by the then still high-riding New Deal Roosevelt Administration.

178. In his impressively researched, ably analytical study (see n. 146, p. 201, *supra*), Harold J. Spaeth deals with the vexatious concept of "important" cases and their assignments during the first twelve Burger Court years (1969–80). Surprisingly, of the 170 cases styled as important that the Chief Justice assigned, Burger self-assigned only 43 (a total of 25.3 percent). Justice Brennan, on the other hand, when assignment devolved on him as Senior Associate Justice, self-assigned 12 of his 31, that is, 38.7 percent (op. cit., pp. 303–04).

179. 347 U.S. 483 (1954).

180. As quoted by James F. Simon, *In His Own Image: The Supreme Court in Richard Nixon's America* (New York: David McKay, 1973), p. 55.

181. *The New York Times,* July 11, 1974, p. A35. He had elaborated in his University of Virginia "Seminar," op. cit. n. 101, *supra:*

> I decided that the opinion in *Brown* would be short and that it would be written in simple, easy to understand English. I wanted the full text of the opinion to be short enough to be carried in every newspaper in the country in total and I wanted every citizen to be able to read and understand our decision since it would affect their lives. Frankfurter wrote his opinions for the legal experts. He thought that if they could understand them, they could explain them to others and that was all that was necessary. I didn't agree with that philosophy. I wrote my opinions for the common man to read. I don't deserve any credit for the *Brown* decision. Some say I united the Court in that decision. But I didn't. [Yet see p. 213, *infra*, for a rather different interpretation.] The real individuals who deserve credit for the *Brown* decision are the men from the South who were on the Court, that is Black from Alabama, Reed from Kentucky, and Clark from Texas. These men are responsible for the full Court or unanimous Court. These men couldn't go back home to their states for ten years after the decision in the case. A decision with three dissents from the Court's Southern members would not have been as persuasive as was the unanimous decision.

182. 300 U.S. 379 (1937).

183. 262 U.S. 525 (1923).

In 1974 it was Chief Justice Burger who assigned himself the writing of the momentous opinion for his unanimous Court in *United States v. Nixon*[184] (consisting also of Justices Douglas, Brennan, Stewart, White, Marshall, Blackmun, and Powell). Obviously, he had and/or managed the necessary votes—as is not always the case, of course, as the 1978 decision in the long-anticipated *Bakke* ruling proved only too well to the chagrin of a good many students of the judicial process. In *Bakke*, instead of a unified and unifying holding written by the Chief, a badly split six-opinion, 154-page divider came down, authored by Justice Powell, who mustered a bare 5:4 margin in the two prongs of this potentially significant "reverse discrimination/affirmative action" controversy.[185] Five years later, it was once again Chief Justice Burger who spoke for his 7:2 (or 6:3, depending on one's analysis of Justice Powell's concurring opinion) Court, when the high tribunal declared unconstitutional the then fifty-year-old practice of the one-house or two-house "legislative veto," imbedded in 212 statutes (62 of these active) over executive action. A decision of momentous significance, it was a "natural" for the Chief Justice's authorship—as was his 7:2 majority opinion in the crucial 1986 *Bowsher v. Synar* holding that pulled a key tooth from the "Gramm-Rudman-Hollins" statute.[186]

Second, no matter what the importance of a case, the selection of a Justice to write the opinion must take into account the possible importance of the decision as a precedent. Justices may well differ in their views on whether the decision should be lodged on a broad or a narrow construction of the issue and on the ground on which the decision is to be based. For instance, the movie *Lady Chatterley's Lover* had been banned by the New York State Board of Regents on grounds of a statutory provision that forbade showing of films that present "acts of sexual immorality, perversion or lewdness" as being "desirable, acceptable, or proper patterns of behavior," and the Court agreed unanimously that the movie did not fall under that ban. But a majority of only five Justices (Warren, Black, Douglas, Brennan, and Stewart) would join in Stewart's opinion for the Court holding that particular provision of the New York licensing statute to be an unconstitutional violation of the Fourteenth and First Amendments. There were five *concurring* opinions, of which the principal opinion by Harlan (joined by Frankfurter and Whittaker), while agreeing that the New York statute could not be validly applied in this case, argued that the Court should have reversed New York on *statutory construction* grounds without reaching the *constitutional issues*. Frankfurter also penned an individual concurrence, and Clark noted that he concurred "in the result." Black and Douglas, although members of the majority of five, joined one another in the two remaining concurring opinions, in which they contended that this statute, like all other prior censorship of movies, should be thrown out as being "unconstitutional on its face" as a prior restraint on freedom of speech

---

184. 417 U.S. 683. Justice Rehnquist, a one-time Assistant Attorney General in the Nixon Administration, recused himself in the case.
185. *Regents of the University of California v. Bakke*, 429 U.S. 953.
186. *Immigration and Naturalization Service v. Chadha*, 462 U.S. 919 (1983) and 478 U.S. 914, respectively.

and press.[187] Obviously, here the Chief Justice's assignment had to take into account which prospective authorship would be sufficiently acceptable, or least offensive, to five Justices—in this case, evidently Stewart's.

Third, although some observers would disagree, there is considerable evidence that the Chief is conscious of an element of public relations in designating his opinion writer. This is particularly true in cases that are undoubtedly going to be unpopular to a sizable segment of the population. In other words, he is not unmindful of the importance of attempting to make a decision acceptable to the public, or, when necessary, of coating the bitter pill that must be swallowed. A fascinating illustration of this point was brought to light by Professor Alpheus T. Mason in his fine biography, *Harlan Fiske Stone: Pillar of the Law*.[188] In 1944 the Court conference on the Texas "White Primary" case, *Smith v. Allwright*,[189] had clearly evidenced that all of the Justices save Roberts were agreed that this constitutionally challenged Texas statute was unconstitutional as a violation of the Fifteenth Amendment. The South was bound to react with great vehemence. Chief Justice Stone assigned the opinion to Justice Frankfurter, an eloquent stylist and a profoundly serious and scholarly jurist, not given to pamphleteering. One day after the conference, having discussed his strong misgivings with some of his colleagues, Justice Jackson—a good friend of the principals involved—wrote a highly unusual, and, indeed, probably quite unprecedented, letter to the Chief Justice, candidly and fervently suggesting that the nature and the importance of the issue in the case were so far-reaching and made of such emotional matter that the Frankfurter selection was bound to "grate on Southern sensibilities." He explained:

> Mr. Justice Frankfurter unites in a rare degree factors which unhappily excite prejudice. In the first place, he is a Jew. In the second place, he is from New England, the seat of the abolition movement. In the third place, he has not been thought of as a person particularly sympathetic with the Democratic party in the past.[190]

Jackson went on to point out that he realized a consideration of every one of the listed factors was utterly distasteful and he mentioned them only with the greatest reluctance and "frank fear of being misunderstood." He had, of course, discussed the matter with Frankfurter and had advised him of his intention to write to the Chief Justice. Evidently persuaded by Jackson's argument, Stone, with Frankfurter's knowledge and agreement, substituted Justice Stanley Reed, who was (a) an old-line Kentuckian, (b) a Protestant, (c) native-born, in contrast to Justice Frankfurter, who was born in Vienna, and (d) a Democrat of long standing. This did not render the wounds of the South less severe, but at least they were administered, in a manner of speaking, by a one-time kinsman.

In the same general vein, the Chief Justice will normally make it a practice to

---

187. *Kingsley International Pictures Corporation v. Regents*, 360 U.S. 684 (1959)—which featured a total of six opinions.

188. Alpheus T. Mason, *Harlan Fiske Stone: Pillar of the Law* (New York: The Viking Press, 1956), pp. 614–15.

189. 321 U.S. 649 (1944).

190. Mason, loc. cit., p. 615. Justice Frankfurter was not exactly pleased about the publicity given this event—in fact, the revelation infuriated him.

assign so-called liberal opinions of the Court to "conservative" Justices and so-called conservative opinions to "liberal" Justices—again in the hope of making them more palatable. Thus, Chief Justice Stone assigned to one of the Court's leading liberals, Justice Black, the majority opinion in what has been widely labeled as the "most racist" decision in this century's history of the tribunal, *Korematsu v. United States*.[191] There the Court upheld 6:3 the forcible exclusion of 112,000 persons of Japanese ancestry, including 77,000 native-born American citizens, and their removal from their West Coast homes to inland war relocation centers. Although not one of these evacuees had been specifically accused of disloyalty, the Black opinion upheld the exclusion order as a validly authorized emergency measure necessitated by the facts of life of wartime, as an "exercise of power of the government to take steps necessary to prevent espionage and sabotage in an area threatened by Japanese attack." When the Court, in a 7:1 opinion in 1957, severely limited the application of the Smith Act in the prosecution of Communist party leaders and members, Chief Justice Warren assigned the case to a member usually found on the conservative side, Justice Harlan.[192] When the Court, in the emotion-charged field of religion, in 1963 decided 8:1 that no state or locality may either require or sanction the recitation of the Lord's Prayer or the reading of verses from the Holy Bible in the public schools, the Chief Justice assigned that delicate case to Justice Clark, a Presbyterian who was active in the affairs of his church. (He was joined, in separate concurring opinions, by the Court's only Catholic, Justice Brennan, and its only Jew, Justice Goldberg.)[193] In 1976 Chief Justice Burger assigned to his only black colleague, Justice Marshall, the writing of the opinion in a case charging employer discrimination against whites. Speaking for a unanimous Court, Marshall held that the provisions of the Civil Rights Act of 1964, barring such discrimination, are "not limited to discrimination against members of any particular race."[194] And in two 1989 prisoners' rights cases Chief Justice Rehnquist assigned the normally liberal Justice Blackmun opinions in which the latter expanded the power of prison wardens to control what prisoners may read and whom they may see.[195] Such strategy or tactic is not always employed, but it is resorted to with sufficient regularity to make a distinct pattern, mild and unpredictable though it may be.

Fourth, when the conference has indicated a split decision, no matter how many Justices may be in the latent minority, the Chief Justice will endeavor to assign the opinion to a Justice whose views come closest to the would-be dissenters, without, however, being one of them. The theory here is that the Justice would, in this case—and probably in others—be a "center Justice," whose "middle" approach would be acceptable, more or less, to both majority and minority.[196] For

191. 323 U.S. 214 (1944).
192. *Yates v. United States*, 354 U.S. 298.
193. *Abington School District v. Schempp* and *Murray v. Curlett*, 374 U.S. 203.
194. *McDonald v. Santa Fé Transportation Co.*, 427 U.S. 273.
195. *Thornburgh v. Abbott* and *Kentucky v. Thompson*. 109 S.Ct. 1874 and 109 S.Ct. 1904, respectively.
196. For an able and extensive discussion of this and related points, see the interesting paper by David J. Danelski, "The Influence of the Chief Justice in the Decisional Process of the Supreme Court," presented at the 1960 American Political Science Association Meeting, New York City, September 9, 1960.

example, in *United States v. Butler*[197] a majority of six declared the Agricultural Adjustment Act of 1933 unconstitutional, as an illegal use by Congress of its powers over taxation and commerce at the expense of the principle of "dual federalism." This was one of thirteen New Deal laws or provisions thereof that the Court would invalidate on constitutional grounds in little more than one year's time during 1935–36. Reasoning that an opinion by one of the four "ultra-conservative" justices—Butler, McReynolds, Van Devanter, and Sutherland—would only serve to increase the fury of both the executive and legislative branches, Chief Justice Hughes assigned Justice Roberts to speak for the Court. The latter wrote an opinion that adopted the broad Hamilton–Story interpretation of the "general welfare" clause of the Constitution (I-8-1) but struck down the particular tax at issue as substantially an illegal regulation of local affairs. There is evidence that the Chief Justice went along with the majority only because Roberts wrote the opinion— and there was enough in that opinion to permit the minority of three, and their allies on both ends of Pennsylvania Avenue, to nourish hopes for a better day. It came scarcely a year later.

The critical role of the Chief Justice in assigning opinions is thus axiomatic. Much depends on his skill, diplomacy, tact, and sheer powers of persuasion. On retiring, Chief Justice Warren was frankly proud of the record of "his" Court on that score: "During all the years I was there I never had any of the Justices urge me to give them opinions to write, nor did I ever have anyone object to any opinion that I assigned to him or anyone else."[198] "My biggest consideration," he elaborated shortly prior to his death, "was always who could best express the wishes of the majority; who could write it best; and who could best unite the rest." He rejected any notions of "expertise" on the part of individual Justices, but he did

> sometimes assign an opinion to a Justice because he had an interest in a particular area and evinced a desire to write the opinion. . . . I often did that with Justice Black who, I knew, wanted to write the majority opinions in cases which adopted ideas he had expressed in dissent years earlier. He had been on the Court many years, and it was something I could do for him.[199]

The Chief Justice's assignment to Black of the Court's unanimous opinion in *Gideon v. Wainwright* is prominent confirmation of that point.[200] No other Chief, in the opinion of Justice Frankfurter, a longtime member of the bench who served under four Chief Justices and knew three others, "equalled Chief Justice Hughes in the skill and wisdom and disinterestedness with which he made his assignments." He closed his observations with this wise admonition:

> The grounds for the assignment may not always be obvious to the outsider. Indeed, they are not always so to the members of the Court; the reasons normally

197. 297 U.S. 1 (1936).
198. Comment to Anthony Lewis, "A Talk with Warren on Crime, the Court, the Country," *The New York Times Magazine*, October 19, 1969, p. 130.
199. "Seminar with Chief Justice Warren," op. cit., pp. 1–2.
200. 372 U.S. 335 (1963). *Gideon* overruled *Betts v. Brady*, 316 U.S. 455 (1952), in which Justice Black had written the dissenting opinion. (See p. 185, *supra*.)

remain within the breast of the chief justice. But these involve, if the duty is wisely discharged, perhaps the most delicate judgment demanded of the chief justice.[201]

Yet no matter how hard he may try, or how skillful he may be, a Chief Justice cannot compel unanimity. As we have already seen, separate opinions are the rule rather than the exception. It is thus not at all uncommon to find five, six, seven, eight, and occasionally even nine opinions in a single case. The *Dred Scott Case*, the *License Cases*, the 1971 *Pentagon Papers Case*, the 1972 *Capital Punishment Cases*, and the 1990 *Abortion Cases*, each featured nine such opinions.[202] The *Steel Seizure Case*[203] had seven; the *Connecticut Birth Control Case*,[204] *Baker v. Carr*,[205] the 1973 *Abortion Cases*,[206] the *Nixon Recordings and Materials Case* of 1977,[207] and the 1978 *Bakke "Reverse Discrimination" Case*[208] each six; and *Dennis*,[209] the *Bible Reading Cases*,[210] *Ginzburg v. United States*,[211] and the 1982 *Free Public Education for Children of Illegal Aliens Case*[212] each had five opinions. The practice of writing separate opinions may be valuable and intriguing, yet it hardly lends itself to certainty in the judicial process. However, certainty is not inevitably an end in itself; indeed, certainty and unanimity in the law are generally possessed only under a dictatorial system of government—to which, in fact, they are indispensable.

Drafting and Circulating Opinions: The Key Stage. After the assignment of opinions—which does not take place at the Conference itself, but formally, in writing, a few days to two weeks thereafter—the laborious task of drafting commences. The power of persuasion by the author, presumably actively supported by the Chief Justice, whenever feasible, looms large in this phase of the judicial decision-making process. An opinion, as Justice Holmes once commented, not only must be informative and persuasive, it must show that the "judge can dance the sword dance; that is he can justify an obvious result without stepping on either blade of

---

201. *Of Law and Men*, op. cit., pp. 137, 142. Frankfurter regarded Marshall, Taney, and Hughes as the greatest Chief Justices.

202. *Dred Scott Case*, 19 Howard 393 (1857): Taney (Opinion of the Court); Wayne, Nelson, Grier, Daniel, Campbell, and Catron (Concurring Opinions), and McLean and Curtis (Dissenting Opinions). *License Cases:* 7 Howard 283 (1849). *Pentagon Papers Case: The New York Times v. United States* and *United Stated v. The Washington Post*, 403 U.S. 713. The 1990 *Abortion Cases: Hodgson v. Minnesota I and II*, 58 LW 4957 and *Ohio v. Akron Center for Reproduction*, 58 LW 4979. *Capital Punishment Cases: Furman v. Georgia*, 408 U.S. 238.

203. *Youngstown Sheet and Tube Co. v. Sawyer*, 343 U.S. 579 (1952).

204. *Griswold v. Connecticut*, 381 U.S. 479 (1965).

205. 369 U.S. 186 (1962).

206. *Roe v. Wade*, 410 U.S. 113, and *Doe v. Bolton*, 410 U.S. 179. In his memoir of his father, *My Father: A Remembrance* (New York: Random House, 1975), Hugo Black, Jr., touches on those decisions' controversial impact: "When Justice Harry Blackmun wrote the 'abortion' opinion, poor Daddy in his grave contemplating infinity, was crucified about the decision—he actually received over 1,000 letters of protest" (p. 148).

207. *Nixon v. Administrator of General Services*, 433 U.S. 425.

208. *Regents of the University of California v. Bakke*, 438 U.S. 265.

209. *Dennis v. United States*, 341 U.S. 494 (1951).

210. *Abington School District v. Schempp* and *Murray v. Curlett*, 374 U.S. 203 (1963).

211. 383 U.S. 463 (1966).

212. *Plyler v. Doe*, 457 U.S. 202 (1982).

opposing fallacies."[213] Again, we know but little of what takes place during these backstage activities, but from those sources that are available—papers, biographies, former law clerks, various memoirs, the research of persistent political scientists, and, as of the early 1980s, led by Justice Blackmun's arguably questionable public candor, a string of television, newspaper, and magazine interviews as well as public speeches by the Justices themselves—we do acquire an outline of this terminal phase of the preparation of a Supreme Court opinion, collective as an end product but with the distinct imprint of the minds and labor of nine individuals. As opinions are drafted, and on whatever side of the tentative decision they may be, printed "proof" copies are circulated by their authors among the members of the Court. Unlike most of his colleagues, Justice Stevens writes all his first drafts in longhand on yellow legal pads. He then dictates them for the clerks to flesh out and to analyze and evaluate them with him.[214] These copies—indeed all of the Court's publications—are composed by a special unit of printers who labor in secrecy (to the extent of locking themselves in during working hours) and utilize the basement of the Court building for their work rather than the Government Printing Office. A private Supreme Court library, with a staff of fourteen and all conceivable facilities, is at the disposal of the Justices and their law clerks at all times.

Depending on comments by his or her colleagues, an author of an opinion may draw additional drafts in an attempt to gain adherence or a concurrence rather than a dissent; or he or she may use any one of the other devices that may soften disagreement where disagreement exists, or make more forceful an opinion where unanimity seems attainable. Justice Brennan reported that once he circulated ten printed drafts before one was accepted as the Opinion of the Court,[215] and Justice Powell acknowledged having rewritten one opinion at least ten times also.[216] This labor of persuasion is undertaken irrespective of how the several Justices may have voted in conference, the theory being that there is always hope for their views to win out in future years. The process of opinion writing is frequently a difficult and laborious task, sometimes running into months, occasionally even years—although the normal length of the labor ranges from thirty-five to fifty-eight days. The opinion for *Brown v. Board of Education* was in various stages of writing from 1952 to 1954, probably largely owing to Chief Justice Warren's herculean efforts to obtain not only a unanimous Court, but also a single opinion, undoubtedly a delicate and

213. Alpheus T. Mason, reviewing *The Holmes-Einstein Letters* (New York: St. Martin's Press, 1965), in *The New York Times Book Review*, November 22, 1964, p. 60. See, for example, some of the important work concerning the innards of the Conference by lawyer–political scientists David J. Danelski of Cornell University, S. Sidney Ulmer of the University of Kentucky, and Walter F. Murphy of Princeton University. See also the excellent article by J. Woodford Howard, Jr., "On the Fluidity of Judicial Choice," 52 *American Political Science Review* 43 (March 1968) which, relying heavily on Murphy papers, provides fascinating and important insights. Ditto David M. O'Brien's *Storm Center: The Supreme Court in American Politics*, 2d ed. (New York: W. W. Norton, 1991).

214. See Stuart Taylor, Jr., "The Last Moderate," *The American Lawyer*, June 1990, p. 51.

215. "Inside View of the High Court," *The New York Times Magazine*, October 6, 1963, p. 11.

216. J. Harvie Wilkinson, III, *Serving Justice: A Supreme Court Clerk's View* (New York: Charterhouse, 1974), p. 93.

difficult matter on the subject at issue—the declaration of unconstitutionality of compulsory-racial segregation in the public schools.[217] Although still very much a case of conjecture, apparently the last holdout on the Court was Justice Reed.[218] It is certain that this decision was the collective product of inordinately painstaking labor.

We do know of many specific cases of persuasion—"bargaining" would not at all be an inappropriate term here—thanks to the papers left by the Justices. In one instance, Justice Butler, who had voted in conference to reverse the decision of the lower court, evidently succumbed to the persuasive powers of his colleague Stone. Sending a copy of his "surrender" to Chief Justice Taft, who ever tried to turn a dissenting opinion into silent acquiescence, he wrote to case-author Stone as follows:

> I voted to reverse. While this sustains your conclusion to affirm, I still think reversal would be better. But I shall in silence acquiesce. Dissents seldom aid in the right development or statement of the law. They often do harm. For myself I say: "lead us not into temptation."[219]

It is quite clear that all of the Justices, at one time or another, are thus willingly constrained by group and institutional concerns. About another and later Stone opinion, Chief Justice Hughes wrote to him: "I choke a little at swallowing your analysis, still I do not think it would serve any useful purpose to expose my views."[220] Although, as Chief Justice, Stone exercised far less persuasive pressure than Hughes, he did work for unanimity whenever possible. At times, this would involve—as it does quite frequently—a switch from a decisional ground initially agreed on to another. For example, in one of the cases brought during Stone's tenure, *Edwards v. California*,[221] he successfully persuaded Justice Byrnes to change his conference vote. Now delivering the opinion of the Court, Byrnes' switch resulted in adopting a *ground* for the decision on which five members of the Court could agree—the interstate commerce, rather than the "privileges and immuni-

---

217. As he reported some years later:

> Ordinarily, the Justices at our Friday conferences stated their positions, offered debate and then voted. But in Brown we were all conscious of the case, so I held off a vote from conference to conference while we discussed it. If you'll remember, Brown was argued in the fall of 1953, and I did not call for a vote until the middle of the following February, when I was certain we would be unanimous. We took one vote, and that was it.

(*The New York Times*, July 11, 1974, p. A35). For a view that strongly *disapproves* of this obviously so deliberately planned and achieved unanimity, see Charles S. Hyneman, *The Supreme Court on Trial* (New York: Atherton Press, 1963), pp. 211–14.

218. According to Yale Law Professor Fred Rodell, three Justices (evidently Reed and Jackson plus either Burton, Clark, or Minton) came close to dissenting, and the bare minimum of four had voted to grant *certiorari* in the case. See his "It Is the Earl Warren Court," *The New York Times Magazine*, March 13, 1966, p. 93. In a letter to Reed, Frankfurter noted there probably would have been four dissenters (Reed one of them) had the case been decided just one term earlier (letter displayed in Retrospective Memorial Exhibit in honor of Justice Felix Frankfurter's Ninety-fifth Birthday, October 21, 1977).

219. As quoted by David J. Danelski in "The Influence of the Chief Justice in the Decisional Process of the Supreme Court," pp. 19–20. See n. 196, *supra*.

220. Danelski, loc cit., at p. 21. The case was *Stanford v. Commissioner*, 308 U.S. 39 (1939).

221. 314 U.S. 160 (1941).

ties" clause of the Constitution. Four Justices concurred in the decision, thus rendering it unanimous, but indicated their preference for the latter ground. An extreme example of the drive for agreement was provided in a difficult double jeopardy case in 1959, when Justice Brennan wrote the opinion of the Court *and a separate opinion* in which he expressed views he had evidently been unable to persuade his colleagues to accept, stating that " . . . it cannot be suggested that in cases where the author is the mere instrument of the Court he must forego expression of his own convictions."[222] It is essential to recognize that Justices may shift positions between the Conference and their final vote—a "testament," as Professor Howard put it, "to the limitations of conference and the effectiveness of the argumentation system."[223]

Much of what has been said of the backstage give-and-take is documented by an excellent study by Professor Alexander M. Bickel of Yale University Law School (one of Justice Frankfurter's law clerks) entitled *The Unpublished Opinions of Mr. Justice Brandeis.*[224] Based on the private papers of Louis Dembitz Brandeis as they relate to his career as Justice of the Supreme Court of the United States from 1916 to 1939, the book is rich in illustrations of the persuasive processes that accompany the drafting of opinions for ultimate delivery. One or two examples will suffice: a photograph of a note from Holmes to Brandeis indicates that Holmes had revised his opinion in *Bullock v. Florida*[225] by adopting the result Brandeis had urged on him. Having been persuaded by Brandeis's point of view, Holmes did so willingly enough; but his note showed much concern lest his changed opinion cause dissatisfaction among the former majority and perhaps result in a reassignment of the case to someone else. That did not happen, however.[226]

In another instance, it was Brandeis's turn to give in. He had felt quite strongly about the construction of a statute at issue in a 1924 railroad case opinion, which had been assigned to Justice McReynolds.[227] In discussing the case some years later with then Professor of Law Felix Frankfurter, Brandeis said that he had told the Chief Justice (Taft) that "he couldn't stand for" McReynolds's opinion, that it contained too much that would "bother us in the future." Justice Van Devanter, continued Brandeis,

worked with McReynolds and made changes, and the Chief asked me whether that will remove my sting. The corrections weren't adequate, and finally the Chief took

222. *Abbate v. United States,* 359 U.S. 187 (1959), at 196, fn. 1. Other similar illustrations cited by Brennan are the actions of Justice Jackson in *Wheeling Steel Corporationv. Glander,* 337 U.S. 562 (1949) at 576; those of Justice Cardozo in *Helvering v. Davis,* 301 U.S. 619 (1937) at 639–41; and Justice Blackmun's in *Logan v. Zimmerman Brush Co.,* 455 U.S. 438–42 (1982). There, Blackmun, writing the majority opinion, turned around and also penned a separate plurality "addendum" to his own opinion. The lawyers in the case noted that they were still trying to figure out just what it meant. See also Justice Stevens's intriguingly diverse actions in *South Carolina v. Regan,* 52 LW 4232 (1984), at 4241, in which he registered a dissent along with a partial concurrence.
223. Howard, loc cit., p. 47 (Justice Brennan told me that post-Conference "lineup" switches are far more common than is generally believed).
224. (Cambridge: Harvard University Press, 1957.) Subtitled, *The Supreme Court at Work.*
225. 254 U.S. 513 (1921).
226. Bickel, loc cit., insert between pp. 118–19, last photographic plate.
227. *Railroad Commission of California v. Southern Pacific Railway Co.,* 264 U.S. 331.

over the opinion and put out what is now the Court's opinion and I suppressed my dissent, because, after all, it's merely a question of statutory construction and the worst things were removed by the Chief.[228]

On the other hand, the persuasion *cum* bargaining may well be blunt and direct, as evidenced by a memorandum sent by the usually gentle Justice Stone to the not-so-gentle Justice Frankfurter: "If you wish to write [the opinion] placing the case on the ground which I think tenable and desirable, I shall cheerfully join you. If not, I will add a few observations for myself."[229]

Toward the End Product. By far the most important fact revealed by this glimpse into the Supreme Court's inner sanctum is that many, if not all, of the Court's opinions, though ostensibly the work of one person are really the product of many minds, in the sense that the Justice who writes the opinion often has to add to, delete, or modify the original draft in order to be able to retain the support of his colleagues, many of whom are far from agreeing with him or with each other. If this involves changes of mind, even reversals, so be it—such behavior is very human. In fact, one close student of the Court's 1940 decade was tempted to avow that hardly any decision during that period "was free from significant alteration of vote and language before announcement to the public."[230] Moreover, studies based on the Justices' papers make abundantly clear that Justices of *all* ideological persuasions ponder, bargain, and argue in the course of reaching their decisions—even at the risk of compromising their ideologies.[231] Those who see facile niches and categories for the Justices may need to do a bit more applied research. It is essential to recognize that each member of the Court participates in every stage of the consideration of a case. Once we grasp this, we can readily understand why a considerable number of the Court's decisions are vague or contain several apparently contradictory statements. Because the views reflected in a given opinion are rarely identical, it may well turn out to be either ambiguous or maintain several varying postures, in order that each Justice who supports it will be able to reconcile it with his or her own particular position. A pertinent example is the laborious forging of Chief Justice Stone's majority opinion in *In Re Yamashita*,[232] in which the Court upheld the conviction by a U.S. military commission of the Japanese general who was accused of violating the laws of war in failing to prevent his troops from committing atrocities against American and Philippine citizens. The decision is quite unclear on the question of whether the due process clause of the Fifth Amendment is binding on such a military commission. On the whole, the opinion tends to give the impression that the answer to this question is in the negative, but some slight support can be found for the contrary view. According to Professor Mason, Stone's biographer, the latter's original draft contained the assertion that Yamashita's trial would have to adhere to the requirement of this clause. However, to meet at least in part the objections of Justices Black and Reed, who apparently were of the opinion that these commissions were not bound by the provisions of the due process

228. As quoted and described by Bickel, loc cit., pp. 209–10.
229. Quoted by Mason in *Harlan Fiske Stone*, op. cit., p. 501 (Stone's letter was dated January 20, 1941).
230. *Howard*, op. cit., p. 44.
231. See, for example, ibid., pp. 55–56.
232. 327 U.S. 1 (1946).

clause, Stone deleted the assertion and substituted some nebulous additions that Black and Reed could more or less reconcile with their own views on this matter.[233] The end product, though it did not entirely satisfy either its readers or the bench as a whole, at least had the virtue—if that it be—of receiving the support of the majority of the Court.

Secrecy of Deliberations. Even though these various data undoubtedly are intriguing and are important to an understanding of the Court's *modus operandus,* the absolute secrecy that attends the backstage work and deliberations of the Supreme Court—the "Purple Curtain," as Professor Fowler Harper once called it—is essential. Until 1910 it was customary for two page boys to be present, but since that time (the Justices suspected a leak by one or more of the pages in a decision) no one but the nine Justices has been present in the conference; no record of the discussions is kept. When clerks bring messages, the Justice who is junior in seniority, no matter what his or her chronological age, goes to the door to get them. There simply are no leaks. This is not to say, however, that no leaks have ever occurred. The most serious of these on record came in connection with the *Dred Scott* decision.[234] In that case not only did the pro-slavery Justice John Catron evidently tell President-elect James Buchanan the "line-up" of the Justices in the pending decision one month prior to its announcement, but segments of the Northern press published the dissenting opinion of Justice Curtis. The incoming President, troubled and weak, used the Catron information in his inaugural address on March 4, 1857, and told the country that the Court would soon settle the much disputed territorial question. Two days later Chief Justice Taney delivered the 7:2 opinion of the Court, which, as history would prove all too soon, did anything but settle the problem. Indeed, it acted as a catalyst in bringing on the Civil War.

However, that instance was a rare and crass exception.[235] Complete secrecy does, and must, exist. The Court can neither open its backstage deliberations to the public nor hold news conferences. To do either would fatally affect its position as well as its effectiveness. For a description of what goes on behind the doors, we depend almost entirely on the kind of papers and biographies of the Justices dis-

---

233. Mason, op. cit., pp. 667–69.

234. *Dred Scott v. Sandford,* 19 Howard 393 (1857). See Stanley I. Kutler, *The Dred Scott Decision: Law or Politics* (Boston: Houghton Mifflin, 1967); Vincent C. Hopkins, S. J., *Dred Scott Case* (New York: Atheneum, 1967); and D. E. Fehrenbacher, *The Dred Scott Case* (New York: Oxford University Press, 1978) for book-length analyses.

235. Justice Jackson's biographer, Eugene C. Gerhart, buttressed by other Court observers and biographers, professes to be satisfied of proof of about six to eight decisional leaks, commencing with *Luther v. Borden* 7 Howard 1 (1849) and ending with *United States v. South-East Underwriters Assn.,* 22 U.S. 533 (1944). See *America's Advocate: Robert H. Jackson* (Indianapolis: Bobbs-Merrill, 1958), pp. 258–69. He points to Drew Pearson and his friendship with Justices Black and Douglas as the culprits. Two years prior to Gerhart's assertions, Alpheus Thomas Mason had already related in his *Harlan Fiske Stone: Pillar of the Law* that Pearson obtained advance leaks from the Conference room through Douglas in at least two cases, citing *United States v. Hope Natural Gas Co.,* 320 U.S. 59 (1944) as well as the *South-Eastern Underwriters* case (Mason, op. cit., p. 625). See also the allegations surrounding the Court's denial of *certiorari* in 1977 in the "Watergate Three" conviction case; two alleged "print shop" leaks in 1979; and evidence that Justice Fortas provided information to President Johnson in the mid-1960s in certain pending wiretap cases (see *The New York Times,* January 23, 1990, p. A19).

cussed earlier, duly analyzed by scholars, and, on occasion, on revelations, usually appearing after the death of the Justice involved, by their former law clerks. Yet even these revelations are more often than not confined to matters of procedure. This is emphatically as it should be. We know enough of the operation and functions of the highest court in the land to enable us to appreciate, study, and, we hope, understand them in the context of the Court's significant role in the process of free government. To repeat, the secrecy of the Court's proceedings behind that "Purple Curtain" is a necessary by-product of its work. In a widely read article endeavoring to explain Justice Roberts's famous so-called switch-in-time to the side of the "liberals" on the Court in 1937, Justice Frankfurter viewed the Court's reticence in these terms:

> Disclosure of Court happenings not made public by the Court itself, in its opinions and orders, presents a ticklish problem. The *secrecy that envelops the Court's work is not due to love of secrecy or want of responsible regard for the claims of a democratic society to know how it is governed.* That the Supreme Court should not be amenable to the forces of publicity to which the Executive and the Congress are subjected is essential to the effective functioning of the Court. But the passage of time may enervate the reasons for this restriction, particularly if disclosure rests not on tittle-tattle or self-serving declarations. . . . [236]

OPINION DAY(S)

The final stage in the Supreme Court's decision-making process occurs on *Opinion Day.* On that important occasion, now commonly tied into the public oral argument hearing days of each month during the term,[237] the Court announces, or "hands down," the decisions it has reached. Other than those disposed of *per curiam* or decided by memorandum order,[238] the now made-public cases—all of which are filed with the Clerk of the Court—cover the full reasoning of the Court and set forth all viewpoints expressed by the Justices. Commencing with the junior

---

236. "Mr. Justice Roberts" 104 *University of Pennsylvania Law Review* 313 (1955) (italics supplied). For further insights "behind the scenes," see Walter F. Murphy, *Elements of Judicial Strategy* (Chicago: University of Chicago Press, 1964), especially ch. 3, "Marshalling the Court," and O'Brien, *Storm Center,* op. cit., p. 223, n. 213.

237. Until April 11, 1965, when Chief Justice Warren announced that he and the Court saw no reason why decisions should be announced only on Mondays, that day of the week was in fact "reserved" for that purpose. And in the 1970–71 term of "his" Court, Chief Justice Burger commenced a pointed—although but marginally, successful—effort to avoid Mondays, chiefly to vitiate the high overtime payments to printers in the Court's printshop incurred by first-day-of-the-week pressures. By the 1980s Tuesdays and Wednesdays had become the main, although not exclusive, Opinion Days.

238. A device increasingly, and controversially, resorted to, for example, the Court's 1976 summary 6:3 affirmation of a 2:1 three-judge District Court action that had rejected a challenge to a Virginia law prohibiting even private, adult consensual sodomy (*Doe v. CommonwealthAttorney for City of Richmond,* 425 U.S. 901). See the interesting article by John P. McKenzie, "4-Word High Court Rulings Questioned," *The Washington Post,* April 18, 1976, p. 2, highly critical of "the judgment is affirmed" syndrome. For another simple summary affirmance without oral argument of a very significant voting rights issue, see *Mississippi Republican Executive Committee v. Brooks,* 469 U.S. 1002 (1984).

Justices, and proceeding in ascending order of seniority, the various opinions may be either read verbatim or paraphrased or summarized, the customary and Chief Justice–preferred method, by their authors as the spirit and the occasion may dictate; sometimes the decision is simply announced by the author or by the Chief Justice. Justice Whittaker used to read from his text, whereas Justice Frankfurter never looked at his, but would expound from memory. Thus, techniques vary widely.[239] The reading of the opinions may run from a few minutes to more than an hour[240]—although the Chief Justice would almost certainly try to discourage the latter. Nonetheless, Earl Warren spent more than an hour in reading the entire 61-page opinion he had penned in *Miranda v. Arizona*.[241] And although the process has indeed been increasingly speeded up of late, normally resulting merely in a summary by the author of the majority opinion, a visitor to the Supreme Court on an Opinion Day ought to be prepared for the possibility, albeit no longer the probability, of up to two hours' reading duration—as was true of the *Bakke* case opinions in late June of 1978. It was similarly true of Justice Stewart's protracted stinging dissenting opinion in the 1980 *Fullilove* case, an opinion he read aloud in full,[242] and of the majority and dissenting opinions by Justices Brennan and Stevens, respectively, in the emotion-charged "flag burning" case of 1989, in which the Court 5:4 declared unconstitutional forty-eight state laws that proscribed flag desecration, followed one year later by that of the federal statute by the same vote and lineup.[243] Despite a bad cold, Justice O'Connor insisted on reading her full solo dissenting opinion in *Pacific Mutual Life v. Haslip* in 1991, in which the 7:1 Court rejected appeals from business groups to impose strict constitutional constraints on the award of punitive damages.[244] The interesting practice of announcing opinions orally is not generally followed in the lower courts, in which a case is "announced" simply by filing its disposition with the clerk. Prior to the Chief Justiceship of Charles Evans Hughes, the Court's announcements were even lengthier, for the Justices generally persisted in reading opinions word for word, not infrequently in an unrelieved monotone. Hughes, however, sensing a golden opportunity—in the words of Edwin McElwain, who was one of his law clerks—to make "a public demonstration of the dignity and responsibility of the Court to the bar and to the

239. See Donald D. Gregory and Stephen L. Wasby, "How to Get an Idea from Here to There: The Court and Communication Overload," 3 *Public Affairs Bulletin* 5 (November–December 1970), passim.
240. One of Justice Holmes's many virtues was brevity, which one of his most ardent on-the-bench admirers, Justice Robert H. Jackson, attributed to Holmes's lifelong practice of writing his opinions in longhand while *standing* at a desk of draftsman's height. When fatigue set in, Holmes would write finis to the opinion. See Eugene C. Gerhart, *Robert H. Jackson: Lawyer's Judge* (Albany: Q Corporation, 1961), pp. 109–10. The average length of Holmes's opinions was 3.54 pages—by far the briefest among the Justices who served with him; the longest, 12.24 pages per opinion, were written by Justice Horace Gray.
241. 384 U.S. 436 (1966).
242. *Regents of the University of California v. Bakke*, 438 U.S. 265 and *Fullilove v. Klutznick*, 448 U.S. 448, respectively. The 1901 *Insular Cases* took six hours to deliver.
243. *Texas v. Johnson*, 57 LW 3679 (1989) and *United States v. Eichman*, 58 LW 4744 (1990).
244. 59 LW 4157.

thousands of visitors who came to the new Supreme Court Building during his regime,"[245] not only encouraged paraphrasing and summarizing of opinions, but also impressed on his colleagues of the bench the need to deliver them forcefully and convincingly. The Chief Justice himself was such an impressive figure—with his magnificent head, white beard, and sonorous voice—that visitors to an Opinion Day, hearing him deliver one of his opinions with dramatic impact, often likened him to a latter-day Moses, a concept not entirely displeasing to Hughes, not so much for himself, but for Court and Law.

Even after the Justices have assembled for the announcement of their opinions, should any one of their number have some last-minute qualms regarding one about to be handed down, all he or she has to do is to ask the Chief Justice to "let it go over"—such is the concern with each Justice's sensibilities. It cannot be emphasized too strongly that *each and every Justice* passes on all aspects of a case, at *each* of its stages; the Court most emphatically does not function by committee, panel, or section. The now published opinions presumably confine themselves to the issue involved in the various cases, but the voicing of profoundly held beliefs, and at times even a swipe at a colleague, is quite common. Thus, cleavages among the Justices of an intellectual, policy, and, at times, even personal nature become apparent in the written opinions—no matter how skilled an arbiter the Chief Justice may be. Fortunately, less frequent are *ad hoc* outbursts from the bench on Opinion Day; these are not found in the written record, but they do occur. Perhaps the most famous one is Justice McReynolds's explosion in 1935, while reading his dissent in the *Gold Clause Cases*,[246] when he veritably screamed from the bench: "This is Nero at his worst. The Constitution is gone!"

Judicial Tempers. To give some brief, contemporary illustrations of this aspect of Opinion Day: In November 1960, Justice Douglas, having just heard Justice Whittaker read the 6:3 opinion for the Court in a tax case,[247] commented acidly from the bench that the issue decided this day was "narrow and technical"; that he would not have filed a dissent had not the "majority's error been so egregious"; and he closed with the observation: "But six make the law, and sometimes very bad law." Earlier that year, Justice Frankfurter had characterized as a "judicial somersault" an opinion for the Court by Justice Stewart in a criminal law case.[248] On Opinion Monday, March 30, 1959, Justice Frankfurter, while reading the majority opinion upholding the successive federal and state trials of one Bartkus for the same criminal act, against the charge of double jeopardy, made a passing reference to "the so-called Bill of Rights." When Justice Black's turn came to read his dissent in the case, he declared passionately: "This case concerns the Bill of Rights, not the 'so-called Bill of Rights'!"[249] Eight years later, the normally gentle Black, dissenting from a new interpretation of the constitutionality of eavesdrop-

---

245. "The Business of the Supreme Court as Conducted by Chief Justice Hughes," 63 *Harvard Law Review* 20 (1949).
246. *Norman v. Baltimore & Ohio Railroad Co.* 294 U.S. 240.
247. *Meyers et al. v. United States*, 364 U.S. 410 (1960).
248. *Elkins and Clark v. United States*, 364 U.S. 206 (1960).
249. As reported by Anthony Lewis, "Justice Black at 75: Still the Dissenter," *The New York Times Magazine*, February 26, 1961, p. 74.

ping in the *Katz* case, accused his brothers of being "language-stretching judges" whose aim was to "rewrite" the Constitution, who lacked "scholarship, common sense and candor," who had engaged in "clever word juggling."[250] On an Opinion Monday in April 1971, the usually affable Justice Brennan began his dissent from the Court's 5:4 decision ruling that some foreign-born U.S. Citizens could lose their citizenship merely on certain residential grounds by bitterly observing: "Since the Court this term has already downgraded citizens receiving public welfare, and citizens having the misfortune to be illegitimate, I suppose today's decision downgrading citizens born outside the United States should have been expected."[251]

During the waning days of the 1960–61 term, the public and the Court were treated to two serious *ad hoc* outbursts from the bench on two Opinion Days, involving Chief Justice Warren and, again, Justice Frankfurter. In the first instance, a sharp dissent by the latter provoked an oral rebuttal by the former, which was even more unusual because the Chief Justice, on the side of the 5:4 majority, had written no opinion in the case. But in stating his dissent, Justice Frankfurter took nearly fifteen minutes to sharpen the written language and heighten his criticism of the majority opinion in the criminal case at issue. Evidently hurt and annoyed by Frankfurter's tone of voice and the contents of his summation, the Chief Justice told the courtroom that "since so much has been said here that was not in any written opinion," he wanted to add a word as to why he joined the majority.[252]

An even more serious manifestation of judicial temper-flaring occurred several Opinion Days later, again featuring the same two Justices. The Court, once again by a 5:4 vote, as is so frequently the case in criminal cases involving Bill-of-Rights interpretations, had reversed the murder conviction of one Willie Lee Stewart. In a ringing dissent, Justice Frankfurter, going far beyond anything he had written, accused the majority of "plucking out" of the lengthy trial record an isolated episode, and suggested that judges find in the record "what the mind is looking for." He went on to categorize the majority opinion as an "indefensible example of finicky appellate review of criminal cases" and warned against "turning a criminal appeal into a quest for error." When he had finished, Chief Justice Warren leaned forward, his face deeply flushed, and with evident emotion stated that the dissent just heard was not a proper statement of an opinion, but rather a

> lecture . . . a closing argument by a prosecutor to a jury. It is properly made, perhaps, in the conference room [of the Court], but not in the court room. . . . The purpose of reporting an opinion [here] is to inform the public and is not for the purpose of degrading this Court.

Warren then turned to Frankfurter, who was seated to his immediate left, and whispered an invitation to respond. Frankfurter said: "The Chief Justice urges me to comment on what he said, but of course I won't. I have another case."[253] Yet at

---

250. Comment from the bench in *Katz v. United States*, 389 U.S. 347, on December 18, 1967.
251. *Rogers v. Bellei*, 401 U.S. 815.
252. As reported in *The New York Times*, March 21, 1961, p. 18.
253. As reported in *The Philadelphia Evening Bulletin*, April 25, 1961, p. 3, and in *The New York Times*, April 25, 1961, p. 27. (The case is *Stewart v. United States*, 366 U.S. 1.)

the end of the session the two adversaries were engaged in friendly and cordial conversation! Even Supreme Court Justices are human. . . . [254]

254. Since the preceding exchanges took place, there have been other memorable judicial outbursts—among them an unusually sharp attack by Justice Douglas on his brother Black in *Arizona v. California*, 373 U.S. 546 (1963); an acid exchange between Black and Justice Harlan in the congressional redistricting case of *Wesberry V. Sanders*, 376 U.S. 1 (1964); Harlan's scathing attack on the entire Court in the key reapportionment cases of 1964, headed by *Reynolds v. Sims*, 377 U.S. 533; Justice White's sarcastic references to his colleague Goldberg's reasoning in the now famous case of *Escobedo v. Illinois*, 378 U.S. 478 (1964); Justice Black's blistering attack on what he regarded as the "loosest construction of the Constitution in this court's history" by its two leading alleged and avowed "strict constructionists," Chief Justice Burger and Justice Blackmun, in the "gratis divorce proceedings case" of *Boddie v. Connecticut*, 401 U.S. 371 (1971); Justice Stewart's angry charge in a 1974 repossession case (*Mitchell v. W. T. Grant Co.*, 416 U.S. 600) that "recent changes in the Court's composition—instead of principles of law—caused a break with precedent less than two years old!"; and Justice Blackmun's biting comment that Justice Stewart's 5:4 majority opinion for the Court in the late 1976 complicated tax case of *United States v. Foster Lumber Co.*, 429 U.S. 32, was "a wooden and unimaginative reading of the tax law," and his characterization of another Stewart Opinion in a 1981 custody case as "virtually incredible" (*Lassiter v. Department of Social Services*, 452 U.S. 18). In a much-quoted outburst Justice Rehnquist accused his colleagues of continuing "to evade some responsibility for this mockery of our criminal justice system [the Court's reluctance to uphold death sentences]," charging the "Court and the lower Federal courts" of having "converted the constitutional limits upon imposition of the death penalty by the States and the Federal Government into arcane niceties which parallel the equity court practices described in Charles Dickens's 'Bleak House'" (*The New York Times*, April 28, 1981, p. D23). Rehnquist returned to the fray in the 1983 reversal of a drug suspect's "airport profile" conviction, commenting sarcastically that the Court's plurality opinion "betrays a mindset more useful to those who officiate at shuffleboard games, primarily concerned with which particular square the disk has landed on, than to those who are seeking to administer a system of justice whose twin purposes are the conviction of the guilty and the vindication of the innocent" (*Royer v. Florida*, 460 U.S. 491, at 520). Earlier, Justice Brennan had accused Rehnquist and his allies of "judicial activism," "sheer demagoguery," and "unvarnished hostility to constitutional claims" (*The Washington Post*, April 22, 1982, p. A11). Justice O'Connor—much sniped at by some of her brethren—returned fire on one occasion by finding Justice Brennan's views on at least one instance to "carry more rhetorical force than substance" and referring to a Blackmun opinion as simply an "absurdity" (*The Washington Times*, November 18, 1982, p. A10). And, beginning in 1982, Justice Stevens commenced a continuing barrage of public criticism of his colleagues for what he considered a "pro-prosecution" tilt, a charge in which he was joined by Justices Marshall and Blackmun (e.g., *The [Charlottesville, Va.] Daily Progress*, August 7, 1982, p. A3; *The Washington Post*, April 24, 1984, p. A4; *The New York Times*, Aug. 5, 1984, p. 1; and *The Washington Post*, Sept. 24, 1984, p. A1 and Oct. 26, 1985, p. A8). Bruising rhetoric was rampant in the municipal religious display case of *Allegheny County v. Greater Pittsburgh ACLU*, 492 U.S. 573 (1989), in which Justice Kennedy damned his colleague Blackmun for his "latent hostility to religion" and his "callous indifference." Blackmun found this "offensive and absurd," and they charged each other with "Orwellian newspeak." The acute fractiousness of the national abortion controversy engendered by the Court's 5:4 decision in *Webster v. Reproductive Health Services*, 492 U.S. 490 (1989), is reflected by the heated charges and countercharges voiced by several Justices in that case, which upheld sundry restrictive Missouri measures on abortion and raised the spectre of overturning *Roe v. Wade*, 410 U.S. 113 (1973). Thus, Justice Scalia excoriated Justice O'Connor (although both were on the prevailing side of the case) for her reluctance to meet the latter issue in her concurring opinion. He characterized her opinion as one that "could not be taken seriously," that was "irrational" and "preserved a chaos that is evident to anyone who can read and count." Justice Blackmun, the author of *Roe*, found Chief Justice Rehnquist's opinion for the plurality that sustained Missouri's restrictive legislation "unadulterated nonsense," "deceptive," "feigned," "disingenuous," "contrived . . . in the hope of precipitating a constitutional crisis," and deserving of charges of "cowardice and illegitimacy." He professed fear "for the integrity of, and public esteem for, this Court"

Ratio Decidendi *and* Obiter Dictum. It is important to distinguish—although this is sometimes far more easily said than done—between the *ratio decidendi* of an opinion and the frequently present *obiter dictum* or *obiter dicta*. *Ratio decidendi* refers to the essence, the vitals, the necessary legal or constitutional core of the decision; *obiter dictum* is a more or less extraneous point, presumably unnecessary to the decision, made by the author of an opinion. In other words, the former constitutes the legal rule to be followed and adhered to; the latter is an expression of a belief, viewpoint, or sentiment, which, at least in theory, has no binding effect. It is not surprising, however, that, on occasion, an *obiter dictum* lives long after the *ratio decidendi* has been forgotten! Moreover, as U.S. District Court Judge P. M. Hall of California once put the matter, "I am not unmindful of the fact that in the last analysis the Judges of the Supreme Court are the final arbiters as to what is or is not *dicta* in a previous opinion."[255] Justice Brennan once observed that *obiter dicta* reflected "the gas on the stomach felt by the Justice at the time he was writing the decision."[256] But it is the *ratio decidendi* that makes the decided case one of record and renders the matter at issue *res judicata*, that is, a matter on which a competent court of law has passed judgment.

One of the most famous expounders of the *obiter dictum* was Chief Justice John Marshall, who delighted in employing that technique as a medium for the constitutional education of the public. His celebrated opinions in *Marbury v. Madison*,[257] *McCulloch v. Maryland*,[258] and *Gibbons v. Ogden*,[259] for example, are full of *dicta* that history has so merged with the *ratio decidendi* in these cases that the two concepts are almost indistinguishable. Nor has that approach become extinct in our own day, to which illustrations on two levels of the judiciary bear witness: In the case of *Shachtman v. Dulles*,[260] three judges of the U.S. Circuit Court of Appeals for the District of Columbia held unanimously that the grounds for the Secretary of State's denial of a passport to the petitioner constituted an arbitrary, and hence unconstitutional, denial of due process of law under the Fifth Amendment. That was the *ratio decidendi* of the case, but the author of the opinion of the tribunal, Circuit Judge Fahy, in an interesting *obiter dictum*, based the privilege of a passport on the "natural right" to travel, "to go from place to place as the means of transportation permit." At the level of the Supreme Court, *Watkins v. United States*[261] dealt with the refusal of a former labor organizer, John T. Watkins, to answer certain questions put to him by a subcommittee of the House Committee on Un-American Activities, which was investigating "Communist activities in the Chicago area." In a 6:1 decision, speaking through Chief Justice Warren, the

(see *Manhattan Lawyer*, August 8–14, 1989, p. 11). Yet outbursts such as Blackmun's and his colleagues' will hardly serve to enhance that image.

255. *Odikubo v. Bonesteel*, 60 F. Supp. 916 (1945) at 930, fn. 28. As Lord Lloyd of Hamstead once observed in his *Introduction to Jurisprudence*, 3d ed., discussing the use of *dicta:* "A battery of howitzers off the target is more impressive than a pop gun on it" (New York: Praeger Publishers, 1972, p. 711).

256. Remark made to me, December 18, 1969, in the Justice's chambers.

257. 1 Cranch 137 (1803).

258. 4 Wheaton 316 (1819).

259. 9 Wheaton 1 (1824).

260. 225 F. 2d 938 (1955).

261. 354 U.S. 178 (1957).

Court set aside Watkins's conviction for contempt of Congress in the District Court below because neither Congress nor the Committee had ever satisfactorily apprised him whether or not the questions he had refused to answer were "pertinent to the subject under inquiry." This failure on the part of the legislature was thus held to render the conviction void on the ground of vagueness under the due process of law clause of the Fifth Amendment. Here we have the *ratio decidendi* of the *Watkins* case. But, resorting to the device of the *obiter dictum*, Chief Justice Warren also discussed matters, however related, which had not really been specifically raised by the petitioner Watkins in his allegations. In the face of charges of "overstatement" and "lily-gilding," Warren's long and fervent *dictum* clearly represented a lecture to Congress—and, he hoped, to the public at large—on the rights of individuals and Congress's abuse of its power to investigate. In it was this admonition: "We have no doubt that there is no congressional power to expose for the sake of exposure."[262] Another important example is the Court's footnote *dictum* in *United States v. Barnett*,[263] which indicated that anyone convicted of criminal contempt by a judge could not be given a sentence more severe than might be imposed for a "petty offense."

After the announcement and reading of an opinion the case is presumably finished, insofar as the members of the Court are concerned, and no further public comment thereon will normally emanate from the Justices. On rare occasion, however, the public reception of a decision may move a Justice to comment further. This occurred, for example, as a result of the *New York Prayer Case*,[264] when Justice Clark seized upon the occasion of a public speech to take note of the decision's critical reception by "explaining" his vote as a member of the majority. Referring to the Court's 8:1 judgment that New York's state-composed twenty-two-word nondenominational prayer for use in the state's public schools constituted a violation of the principle of separation of church and state as imbedded in the First and Fourteenth Amendments, he stated simply: "No to me means no. That is all the court decided, not that there should be no recognition of a supreme being."

COMPLIANCE

When officially announced as decided, the case becomes binding on all lower federal courts and on all state courts when and where applicable. It is now *the* controlling opinion, *res judicata*—the law of the land—as enunciated and/or interpreted by its highest tribunal. It is then duly recorded and published—printed by a computer for the first time in October 1981—by the federal government in an invaluable series of volumes known as the *United States Reports*, which, duly compiled and edited by the Supreme Court's Reporter of Decisions, constitute the sole *official* record of the actions of the Court. Several unofficial publications are also available.[265] (The *Reports* and their forerunners are on file back to 1790.) However,

262. Ibid., at 200.
263. 376 U.S. 681 (1964), at 695, n. 12.
264. *Engel v. Vitale*, 370 U.S. 421 (1962).
265. For example, the *Supreme Court Reporter*, the *Lawyers' Edition of the Opinions of the United States Supreme Court*, and *United States Law Week*.

although compliance with the Court's decisions may be expected to be a foregone conclusion insofar as the lower *federal* courts are concerned (Chapter 8 will discuss some of the problems of compliance, and of enforcement by *nonjudicial* governmental bodies generally), it is not always necessarily simple and automatic.

By Federal Courts. For example, in September 1960, Judge Ashton Williams of the U.S. District Court for South Carolina disqualified himself from a desegregation suit on the ground that *he* considered the Supreme Court's decision and subsequent order in *Brown v. Board of Education*[266] to be unconstitutional. He announced that another judge would have to hear the case, brought by four Charleston blacks, which involved compulsory segregation of the Charleston municipal golf course. Contending that the Supreme Court's decision barring separate facilities for whites and blacks in such public recreational facilities was based "on no constitutional grounds," he nonetheless stepped aside rather than disobey, and declared: "Since as a Federal judge I have to follow that decision I will disqualify myself because I have taken an oath to sustain the Constitution."[267]

Another U.S. District Court jurist, the then eighty-seven-year-old Judge William H. Atwell of Texas, went considerably further in 1956; he simply *refused* to carry out the desegregation ruling of the Court, and resorted to every conceivable judicial roadblock to prevent it. Although his ruling had been reversed by the Fifth U.S. Circuit Court of Appeals,[268] after his initial rejection of the plaintiffs' petition,[269] he again refused to set a date of desegregation of the Dallas school district because such a step would cause "civil wrongs." In order to make quite clear where he stood on the issue, Atwell announced:

> I believe that it will be seen that the [Supreme] Court based its decision on no law but rather on what the Court regarded as more authoritative, more psychological knowledge.... It will be recalled that in 1952, Mr. Justice Frankfurter said it [the Supreme Court] was not competent to take judicial notice of "claims of social scientists."[270]

The Court of Appeals, naturally, again reversed the second Atwell decision in short order.[271] But far from acquiescing, Judge Atwell now embarked on a course of action in the opposite extreme by ordering all Dallas schools integrated in the middle of the academic year.[272] This decision was also reversed by the higher court.[273] Three or four years later, Atwell retired permanently—he had been recalled for temporary duty—and another federal District Court judge ultimately ordered a "mild" form of desegregation. This was broadened and amended by the Fifth Circuit Court of Appeals in accordance with the Supreme Court's 1954 and 1955 mandates,[274] with desegregation scheduled to begin on a one-grade-a-year

266. 347 U.S. 483 (1954) and 349 U.S. 294 (1955).
267. As reported in *The New York Times*, September 8, 1960, p. 27.
268. *Brown v. Rippy*, 233 F. 2d 796 (1956).
269. *Bell v. Rippy*, 133 F. Supp. 811 (1955).
270. *Bell v. Rippy*, 146 F. Supp. 485 (1956) at 486.
271. *Borders v. Rippy*, 247 F. 2d 268 (1957).
272. 2 *Race Relations Law Reporter* 985 (1957).
273. *Rippy v. Borders*, 250 F. 2d 690 (1957).
274. *Brown v. Board of Education*, 347 U.S. 483 (1954), and ibid., 349 U.S. 294 (1955).

basis in September of 1961[275]—which indeed it did, without incident. It should be pointed out, however, that the nature of the implementation order, as handed down by the Court in the second *Brown* case,[276] was tailor-made for dilatory tactics by federal District Court judges. It vested in them inherent authority to use their discretion in ordering desegregation by suggesting that they take notice of the peculiarities of the local situation. In effect, they were guided solely by the Court's mandate that the judges require a "prompt and reasonable start toward full compliance" and that they take such action as may be necessary to bring about the end of racial segregation in the public schools "with all deliberate speed."[277] This open-ended order has naturally also resulted in contentious, far-reaching, "judicial activist" desegregation orders, increasingly utilized by a plethora of U.S. District Court Judges as of the mid-1960s, and even accelerating in the 1970s. Examples are Judge W. A. Garrity, Jr.'s orders in connection with the Boston school desegregation controversy of 1974–75, including a federal takeover of the school system and some of the extensive compliance orders by, for instance, U.S. District Court Judge Frank M. Johnson of the Middle District of Alabama, *inter alia* requiring such specific mandates as college degrees for the athletic coaches and dieticians of state institutions and *x* number of feet of urinal space for each male inmate of a state prison or mental institution.[278]

But lest the impression arise that all defiance and deviation from the law as stated by the Court are confined to the segregation–integration controversy, we have another, and quite different example, this one involving an eminent jurist, Chief Judge John J. Parker of the Fourth U.S. Circuit Court of Appeals. In 1940 the Supreme Court had held 8:1 in the first of the *Flag Salute* cases[279] that Pennsylvania could validly require children of Jehovah's Witnesses attending public schools to salute the flag, despite claims of violation of their constitutionally guaranteed freedom of religion. Only Justice Stone had dissented. But no Supreme Court reversal still having taken place two years later, Judge Parker held an *identical* West Virginia statute unconstitutional.[280] He went to some length to point

---

275. *Boston v. Rippy*, 275 F. 2d 850 (1960).
276. Loc. cit., 349 U.S. 294 (1955).
277. Ibid., at 296. The term "all deliberate speed" was suggested by Justice Frankfurter, who lifted it from Justice Holmes's opinion in *Virginia v. West Virginia*, 222 U.S. 17 (1911), at 30—a case dealing with a monetary controversy between the two states. After more than fourteen years of "deliberate speed" compliance, the Court unanimously abandoned that doctrine in October 1969, ordering desegregation "at once" by and for all school systems so as henceforth to "operate now and hereafter only unitary schools" (*Alexander v. Holmes County Board of Education of Mississippi*, 396 U.S. 19. Rehearing denied, 396 U.S. 976 [1969]).
278. *Morgan v. Hennigan*, 379 F. Supp. 410 (Mass., 1974), schools; Alabama: *Wyatt v. Stickney*, 344 F. Supp. 373 (1972), Bryce Hospital; *Pugh v. Locke*, 406 F. Supp. 318 (1976), prisons, E.g., *Pugh* required "in working order one toilet per 15 inmates, one urinal or one foot of urinal trough per 15 inmates, one shower per 20 inmates, and one lavatory per 10 inmates," at 334. "Each inmate who requires a special diet for reasons of health or religion shall be provided a diet to meet his or her individual need," at 334. "Visitors shall not be subjected to any unreasonable searches," at 334. "Qualified staff sufficient to maintain institutional order and to administer programs shall be employed," at 335.
279. *Minersville School District v. Gobitis*, 310 U.S. 586 (1940).
280. *Barnette v. West Virginia*, 47 F. Supp. 251 (1942) at 253.

out that this really was not defiance, because three members of the 1940 majority had publicly confessed error on the occasion of a different case involving another constitutional claim by Jehovah's Witnesses,[281] and two others[282] had retired from the bench in the two-year interim, thus leaving the supporters of the compulsory flag salute in a minority of three.[283] His analysis and implied prediction proved to be correct, because the Court did specifically overrule itself, 6:3, when that very same West Virginia case[284] reached it, but, of course, Judge Parker could neither safely predict that event, nor did it lessen the fact of his deviation.[285]

A grotesque illustration of defiance on the lower federal court level, is the astonishing case of the then eighty-six-year-old U.S. District Court Judge T. Whitfield Davidson of Dallas. In 1962, fully four years after he had been ordered to do so by the Supreme Court of the United States, Judge Davidson refused resolutely to impose a $506.11 penalty on a Texas farmer who had wilfully and illegally exceeded his planting allotment of wheat under federal regulations by forty-three acres. The venerable judge simply insisted on his own conclusions that the statute involved was unconstitutional—despite several Supreme Court holdings to the precise contrary[286]—and he further ruled that the highest court had no jurisdiction in the case at bar! When the federal authorities ultimately appealed Judge Davidson's obstructions to the Supreme Court, the latter made clear, in a curt and unsigned opinion, that it did indeed have jurisdiction and that it wanted its orders carried out forthwith "without delay."[287] They were! Had they not been, the Court could have issued a writ of *mandamus* to him, as it did in 1969 to U.S. District Judge John F. Dooling, Jr., of Brooklyn, who not only had ignored a trial jury's guilty verdict *and* dismissed the grand jury's indictment against four members of the "Mafia," but had ignored a writ by the U.S. Court of Appeals for the Second Circuit.[288]

And, as a last example of a lower federal jurist's fling of the gauntlet of outright refusal to abide by a Supreme Court ruling, we have the contemporary action by U.S. District Court Judge W. Brevard Hand of the Southern District of Alabama, who in 1983 declared unconstitutional the highest tribunal's 1962 ban on state-mandated prayers in public schools.[289] Hand's sixty-six-page ruling[290] was bottomed on the proposition that the Supreme Court had misread history by incorporating

---

281. *Jones v. Opelika*, 316 U.S. 584 (1942) at 623–24. The three were Justices Black, Douglas, and Murphy.
282. Chief Justice Hughes and Justice Byrnes.
283. Justices Roberts, Reed, and Frankfurter. The six constituting the new majority were the new Chief Justice (Stone), the three "confessors-of-error" (Black, Douglas, and Murphy), and the two new-comers to the bench, Justices Jackson and Rutledge.
284. *West Virginia State Board of Education v. Barnette*, 319 U.S. 624 (1943).
285. For an enlightening article on compliance generally, see Walter Murphy, "Lower Court Checks on Supreme Court Power," 53 *American PoliticalScience Review* (December 1959), pp. 1017–31.
286. The leading, and unanimous, decision was *Wickard v. Filburn* 317 U.S. 111 (1942), which upheld the constitutionality of the Agricultural Adjustment Act of 1938.
287. *UnitedStates v. District Court (United States v. Haley)*, 371 U.S. 18.
288. *Perzico v. United States*, 395 U.S. 911 (1969).
289. *Engel v. Vitale*, 370 U.S. 421.
290. *Jaffree v. Board of School Commissioners of Mobile County*, 554 F. Supp. 1104 (USDC S. Ala.).

the First Amendment and misinterpreted the separation of church and state clause when it handed down its historic decision. Hand's order was stayed by Justice Powell, pending action on appeal by the U.S. Court of Appeals for the Eleventh Circuit. The latter subsequently reversed Judge Hand unanimously.[291]

However, these illustrations of deviations by lower court *federal* judges are exceptions to the general rule of compliance with the orders emanating from the highest tribunal. There may be disagreement with such an order, but one must, and may, expect that it be followed. The following comments by U.S. District Court Judge Charles E. Wyzanski, Jr., of Boston are in the best tradition of compliance, no matter how extensive the substantive disagreement. At issue was one of those time-consuming negligence cases, involving a trial jury's grant of $30,000 in damages to an injured New Haven Railroad worker, one Mrs. Henagan. The New Haven, on receiving the jury's verdict in Judge Wyzanski's court, asked him to set it aside. He replied that he would if he could, but that he was not free to do so because the Supreme Court had consistently held in favor of railroad employees in similar cases and that the Court's precedent commanded his obedience. But he went on to indicate his feelings in no uncertain terms:

> I cannot read the record as a whole in a way to find any evidence of negligence [by the New Haven]. But I know that my method of reading the record is different from that of a majority of the Supreme Court of the United States as exhibited in past cases, and I hope *I am a lawful judge*, and I recognize the limits of my authority whether appellate judges do or not.[292]

Ironically, as matters developed, the Supreme Court, for the first time in a quarter of a century of rulings in Federal Employers' Liability Act cases, a short time thereafter reversed a jury verdict by a 6:2 majority because it found insufficient negligence on the part of the railroad—and the case was Mrs. Henagan's![293]

It should also be noted that the Court, by special order, may bypass proceedings in the lower federal courts, although this is not commonly done, as Congressman Adam Clayton Powell (D.-N.Y.) found out in 1967 when he unsuccessfully sought a Supreme Court order to bypass the U.S. Court of Appeals, where his appeal from an adverse decision from a U.S. District Court on his exclusion from the U.S. House of Representatives then lodged. However, an example of a successful plea is a 1964 antitrust action under the Clayton Act commenced by the federal government against the El Paso Natural Gas Co. There, Justice Douglas directed that

---

291. Ibid., 705 F. 2d 1526 (CA 11) (1983).
292. *New York, New Haven, & Hartford v. Henagan*, as reported in 272 F. 2d 153 (1959), at 155–56 (italics supplied). For a similar stance see the statement of U.S. Court of Appeals for the Fifth Circuit in *Griffin v. Breckenridge*, 410 F. 2d 817 (1969), a case it wanted to overrule but did not, because "[s]ince we may not adopt what the Supreme Court has expressly rejected, we obediently abide the mandate in [*Collins v. Hardyman*, 341 U.S. 651, 1951, at 826–27]." Another apposite example is U.S. District Court Judge Adrian G. Duplantier's publicly voiced agreement with Justice White's *dissenting* opinion in *Roe v. Wade* as he struck down Louisiana's 1991 antiabortion law because he considered himself bound by Justice Blackmun's majority opinion in that controversial case (*Sojourner v. Roemer*, 772 F. Supp. 930 [1991]).
293. *New York, New Haven, & Hartford, v. Henagan*, 364 U.S. 441 (1960).

El Paso divest itself of a firm it had acquired "without delay"—and without "further proceedings in the lower courts,"—an order from which only Justice Harlan dissented.[294]

By State Courts. When it comes to compliance with Supreme Court decisions by *state* courts, an entirely different element enters. In effect, the Supreme Court has no power to make a *final determination* of any case in which it reviews *state* court judgments. All it can do in these instances is to *decide the federal issue* and *remand* it to the state court below for final judgment "not inconsistent with this opinion."[295] Because the state courts possess the power to raise new issues, issues based on "independent and adequate state grounds,"[296] after they receive the case back from above, they are provided with an opportunity to evade the substantive effects of the reversal by the Supreme Court in a number of ways.[297] And once a new issue is raised, the ultimate disposition of the case may, of course, go either way. A notorious illustration is the case of Virgil Hawkins, a then forty-two-year-old Florida black, who was denied admission to the University of Florida Law School in 1949. After lengthy legal stratagems, delays, and assorted maneuvers on all levels of the judiciary over a period of nine years, *de minimis* involving a dozen court cases, Hawkins was finally ordered admitted by the U.S. Supreme Court after the Florida Supreme Court continued to stall—yet he was in fact never allowed to go to the university, and he gave up.[298] He finally earned his law degree at the New England School of Law in 1965, when he was fifty-eight years of age, and he was at last admitted to the Florida Bar—without having to take the bar examination—in 1976, at age 70! He opened a law office in his hometown of Leesburg, but soon found himself in a lot of financial difficulties; was charged with incompetence and malfeasance; and was arrested for embezzling $15,000. In 1985, aged seventy-nine, he resigned from the bar. But he had succeeded in integrating Florida's legal structure. Seven months after his death at eighty in 1986, the Florida Bar—after a unanimous vote of the state's Supreme Court—reinstated Hawkins posthumously.

That this whole matter of spotty and often unpredictable state court compliance is not an illusory conclusion is well demonstrated by, for instance, certain sta-

---

294. *United States v. El Paso Natural Gas Co.*, 376 U.S. 251.
295. E.g., see the grisly history of the case of *Williams v. Georgia*, 349 U.S. 375 (1955) and 350 U.S. 950 (1956).
296. See *Murdock v. City of Memphis*, 87 U.S. 590 (1874). However, to be "independent" that state ground must not depend for its support on, or be intertwined with, the federal question.
297. E.g., the New York State Court of Appeals' "reviving" of that state's eavesdropping law in 1967 (*People v. Kaiser*, 286 N.Y. 52 & 801), notwithstanding the U.S. Supreme Court's mandate of unconstitutionality pronounced six months earlier in *Berger v. New York*, 388 U.S. 41.
298. Among the seven Supreme Court Hawkins cases were: *Florida ex rel Hawkins v. Board of Control*, 347 U.S. 971 (1954); ibid., 350 U.S. 413 (1956); and ibid., 355 U.S. 839 (1957). See the account of the Hawkins dilemma in Walter F. Murphy and C. Herman Pritchett, *Courts, Judges, and Politics* (New York: Random House, 1961), pp. 606–18. For more recent ones, see Daryl Paulson and Paul Hawkes, "Desegregating the University of Florida Law School: Virgil Hawkins v. The Florida Board of Control," 12 *Florida State University Law Review* 1 (Spring 1984), and Barbara Stewart, "The Law and Virgil Hawkins," *Florida Magazine of The Orlando Sentinel*, March 8, 1987, pp. 14–17.

tistics gathered and published by the *Harvard Law Review* some years ago.[299] For example, from 1941 to 1951, the Supreme Court remanded 175 cases to the various state courts for further proceedings "not inconsistent with this judgment." In 46 of these (almost 27 percent of the total), further litigation ensued, with 22 of the parties who won in the Supreme Court now *losing* in the state courts as a result of the final judgment below. In the decade immediately preceding, the Court had reviewed 187 state court cases and remanded them. In 34 of these (somewhat above 18 percent), new issues were raised below, and in a mere 9 of these the ultimate state court decision favored the party who had "won" in the Supreme Court of the United States. Especially certain state supreme courts, who are very much the creatures of the political system in which they operate, may invoke "judicial federalism" by relying on state constitutions as independent sources of constitutional authority.[300]

Whatever the difference in the degree of compliance with the decisions of the highest court in the land,[301] it is fair to conclude that their nationwide impact is often uneven. The many diverse local conditions that characterize the federal system are all but tailor-made for considerable latitude in compliance. This fact of constitutional life clearly accounts for the spotty, often utter lack of compliance in the 1954 and 1955 decisions concerning desegregation, yet, conversely, also for the amazingly speedy acceptance and compliance, however varied, with the reapportionment-redistricting decision of the 1960s, following the historic Supreme Court ruling in *Baker v. Carr.*[302] On the other hand, some public school districts, egged on by local and state authorities, openly defied, and others circumvented by "interpretations" that seemed to ignore, the language of the Supreme Court's ruling in the *Prayer and Bible Reading Cases* of 1962 and 1963.[303] Indeed, nearly 13 percent of the nation's public schools—and 50 percent of those in the South—were continuing their defiance as the 1960s turned into the 1970s,[304] although, happily, the nationwide figure had dropped to 10 percent by early 1975.[305] But there are more than a few examples of continuing efforts of defiance, such as Alabama's during

299. See the two *Notes*, "Final Disposition of State Court Decisions Reversed and Remanded by the Supreme Court, October Term 1931 to October Term 1940," 55 *Harvard Law Review* 1357 (1942), and "Evasion of Supreme Court Mandates in Cases Remanded to State Courts since 1941," 67 *Harvard Law Review* 1251 (1954).

300. See the illuminating article by Mary Cornelia Porter and G. Alan Tarr, "The New Judicial Federalism and the Ohio Supreme Court: Anatomy of a Failure," 45 *Ohio State Law Journal* 1 (1984).

301. For a study that found no significant degree of difference in the compliance rate of federal and state courts, see Edward N. Beiser, "A Comparative Analysis of State and Federal Judicial Behavior: The Reapportionment Cases," 62 *American Political Science Review* 788 (September 1968).

302. 369 U.S. 186 (1962). Barely six years later all but a handful of states had either complied voluntarily or done so as a result of U.S. District Court orders. What had once been an average deviation of close to 11 percent in population representation had sunk to less than 1 percent—an amazing manifestation of compliance.

303. See, for example, "The Supreme Court and the Bible Belt: Tennessee Reaction to the 'Schempp' Decision," by Robert H. Birkby, 10 *Midwest Journal of Political Science* 3 (August 1966). Also see Henry J. Abraham and Robert R. Benedetti, "The State Attorney General: A Friend of the Court?" 117 *University of Pennsylvania Law Review* 6 (April 1969).

304. *The New York Times*, March 26, 1969, p. 1.

305. *The New York Times*, February 5, 1975, p. 24.

1981–83.[306] And until the Court issued its contentious but specific and plainly understood rules in its historic criminal justice decision in *Miranda v. Arizona*,[307] different state courts—even so sophisticated a court as the Supreme Court of New Jersey—interpreted the decision in *Miranda's* antecedent, *Escobedo v. Illinois*,[308] in a host of diverse, frequently clearly defiant, ways. If properly supported by responsible public and private sources of power and influence, the Court will of course ultimately generally have its way, more or less—unless it is reversed by legislative action or constitutional amendment, or if it overrules or modifies its own decisions (of which much more will be said in chapters 7 and 8). But it must be accorded appropriate executive support—as indeed it was in Little Rock, Arkansas, Oxford, Mississippi, and Tuscaloosa, Alabama—for, as will be emphasized and reemphasized in these pages, the Court's only effective power is the power to persuade: purse and sword, as Hamilton noted so presciently in *Federalist No. 78*, are in other hands.

OUTSIDE INFLUENCES ON COURT PERSONNEL

Much has been written and pronounced on various outside sources that allegedly prey on and lobby the Court and endeavor to influence its decision-making process. A good deal of this commentary has been exaggerated; much has been spurious; some has been made with nothing less than evil intent and ill will; and some has been sheer nonsense. Of course, the Justices are subject to "influence." Any governmental body with the power to make significant discretionary choices, which the Court assuredly possesses, may be expected to be a target of interest groups and interest seekers. But it is an entirely different type of "influence" from that normally associated with lobbying. Let it be stated at once and unequivocally, that the sort of lobbying and the button-holing and back-slapping approaches used to influence (1) legislators and (2) executives and administrators, not only would not work with the members of the federal judiciary in general, and the Justices of the Supreme Court in particular, but would meet with withering disdain. As the British would say, "this simply is not done!" Moreover, the so welcome and necessary independence of the federal judiciary, and the almost Olympian position of awe, if not necessarily always majoritarian regard and esteem, the Justices rightfully enjoy in the popular mind would militate against any of the myriad approaches, ingenuous or ingenious, to which the average official or unofficial lobbyist resorts in Washington and the various other seats of federal and state power in the United States of America. If, however, we mean by "influence" a well-reasoned and ably written brief, be it by one of the litigants or a brief *amicus curiae* (see pp. 236–39, *infra*); a persuasive oral argument on behalf of an issue at bar; a timely, thoughtful, and convincing book, monograph, speech, or, notably, a law review article on the general or specific issue; a strategically timed use of a bona fide test case—*that* type of influence, as well as the intriguing concept of the "cli-

306. See p. 227, *supra*.
307. 384 U.S. 436 (1966).
308. 378 U.S. 478 (1964).

mate of public opinion" (to be discussed in chapter 7), falls into a different category. In the final analysis, here the Justices remain the complete masters of their own house.

In elaborating somewhat on the several sources of outside influence that may bear on the Court, we may omit the more obvious and self-explanatory, such as the well-written brief, the persuasive oral argument, and most literature. Some others do deserve separate treatment, including the alleged "gray eminences" behind the Justices, the law clerks.

LEGAL PERIODICALS

Articles that appear in law reviews and other legal periodicals undoubtedly have exerted a formative influence on the law for some time. This is only natural, because the best legal thinking finds expression in these periodicals (only the top law students "work on" law reviews while in law school). The jurists are part of the legal process and are quite naturally generally familiar with the thinking that presents itself in the pages of the reviews; indeed, they must be familiar with it if they wish to keep their fingers on the pulse of the profession and, as Justice Holmes put it so cogently, "the felt necessities of the times." In a pioneering article based on work leading to his doctorate, Chester A. Newland presented the results of a close study of the use made by the Supreme Court of legal periodicals during the period between 1924 and 1956.[309] In most cases the law review and other articles cited by the Justices constituted minor references in the opinions concerned, although a few seemed to be close to the *ratio decidendi*. An avowed and indeed acknowledged illustration of the latter is Justice Brandeis's significant opinion in the landmark case of *Erie v. Tompkins* of 1938,[310] which overruled the almost-century-old precedent on the judicial application of common law laid down in *Swift v. Tyson* by Justice Story in 1842.[311] Brandeis, who is generally regarded as the principal originator of the use of law review articles, made a point of crediting "the research of a competent scholar"—Charles Warren's article, "New Light on the History of the Federal Judiciary Act of 1789," 37 *Harvard Law Review* 49 (1923).[312] In any event, there were numerous references in each term after 1937, with an average of twenty-five opinions (or about one-fifth of the number handed down by the Court in a typical term) citing a total of between forty and seventy periodicals. Not surprisingly, the Justices varied in the frequency of use they made of these references, depending, more or less, on their scholarly bent and interest. Of the Justices appointed after 1937 and before 1957 who cited legal periodicals in at least twenty opinions during that period, Justice Rutledge, with a per-term average of 7.4 opinions, headed the list; next came Justice Frankfurter with 5.5; third was Justice Jackson with 4.1; low man was Justice Burton with 2.0. For whatever sig-

---

309. "Legal Periodicals and the United States Supreme Court," 3 *Midwest Journal of Political Science* 58–74 (February 1959).
310. 304 U.S. 64.
311. 16 Peters 1 (1842). As a result of *Erie*, the Judicial Code now provides that "the laws of the several states . . . shall be regarded as rules of decision in trials at common law in the courts of the United States." Equity, admiralty, and criminal cases are *excluded* from the clause's operation, however.
312. 304 U.S. 64, at 72–73.

nificance it may have, the statistics also indicate that the four most frequently cited journals during the thirty-two-year period covered by Professor Newland's study, and the number of times they were referred to, were *The Harvard Law Review* (399), *Yale Law Journal* (194), *The Columbia Law Review* (176), and *The Michigan Law Review* (165).

There is little doubt that reliance on the legal periodicals by both bar and courts has increased further. Thus, a study published a generation after Newland's demonstrated, *inter alia*,[313] that the U.S. Supreme Court used thirty-six law review references in *Miranda v. Arizona*, (1966), forty-five in *Furman v. Georgia*, (1972), and fifteen in *Stone v. Powell* (1976).[314] Although difficult to determine objectively, this particular genre of the written word exerts a formative influence, and it does, of course, represent an outside influence. Yet it may well be asked how much "outside" this particular type of influence is. Moreover, commentators as well as students of the legal process hardly agree on its extent. To cite one of the more extreme points of view on the matter, in a speech in the House of Representatives, Congressman Wright Patman (D.-Tex.) viewed any reliance on legal periodicals as all but evil and sinister, and contended that it was subversive of traditional judicial processes:

> In adopting and relying upon such pseudo-legalistic papers disseminated by the lobbyist-authors thereof the result is that the theories advanced by these pretended authorities were presented and received by the Court in an ex parte fashion.[315]

Replying to Patman in his article, Professor Newland charged the veteran congressman with "some measure of naïveté," and pointed out that if law reviews and other legal journals were not to limit their interests solely to the past, they were bound to be vehicles for the expression of views on current policy issues.[316] He concluded his observations by putting the problem into its proper focus:

> Critics may properly object that some views expressed in legal periodicals and adopted by the courts are contrary to policies which they deem desirable. But no greater unanimity of opinion usually exists among law faculties and reviews than exists on the Supreme Court. Legal periodicals appear to be "political" in somewhat the same way that the Courts are.[317]

SOCIAL SCIENCE DATA

Related to the judicial use of legal periodicals, but in a rather different category, is the resort by members of the Court to *social science data*, either on the basis of independent research and utilization by the Justices themselves or, more frequently, because of their presentation in briefs by the litigants. The literature on the phenomenon has increased markedly, and a pioneering 1978 "Report on the Uses of Social Science in Judicial Decision Making" by Professor Victor G. Rosen-

---

313. Steven R. Schlesinger, *The Facts, Evidence, and Law* (Lanham, MD: University Press of America, 1983), pp. 37–42.

314. *Congressional Record, 85th Cong. 1st sess.*, Vol. 103, Part 12, p. 16160.

315. Newland, op. cit., pp. 73–74.

316. Ibid., p. 74.

317. Ibid.

blum of Northwestern University and colleagues throws considerable, if perhaps inconclusive, light on the matter. What follows relies heavily on that interesting study.[318]

"Social science data" (or "materials") are usually bracketed under the disciplines of political science, economics, sociology, psychology, history, anthropology, and a few others. Utilizing that classificiation, the Rosenblum research examined the use of such data as a tool of decisional aid by members of the Supreme Court during the 1954, 1959, 1964, 1969, and 1974 terms—1954, of course, including the *Brown v. Board* desegregation decision, which made frank use of social science data, and 1969 representing the end of the Warren and the beginning of the Burger eras. During that twenty-year period, the sitting Justices numbered twenty-one—ranging in order of seniority from Black through Rehnquist—and wrote about 800 majority and concurring and 470 dissenting opinions in a total of 601 cases. In roughly one-third of their opinions the Justices resorted to identifiable social science materials, although these were not necessarily crucial to the *ratio decidendi*. The cases featuring the usage were almost evenly divided between civil and criminal suits and similarly divided between those coming to the Court on appeal or *certiorari*. In descending order of frequency, the social science disciplines represented (with their appearance frequency noted in parentheses) were political science (43 percent), economics (20.1 percent), sociology (18.8 percent), psychology (9.4 percent), history (4.0 percent), anthropology (1.3 percent), and others (3.4 percent). By far the heaviest concentration of utilization by the Justices occurred in four fields of litigation: legislative apportionment, criminal procedure, racial discrimination, and election and voting laws. Almost 60 percent of the total were brought on "equal protection of the laws" grounds, with those coming up under "due process of law" a clear but distant second (13 percent).

Among some of the both interesting and significant findings of the Rosenblum study were the following: A larger percentage of use and reliance on social science materials occurred on the *winning* side of the cases involved. Unexpectedly, perhaps, there was *no* correlation between the use of social science data and so-called liberal and conservative Justices. The four most frequent *absolute* users were, in descending order, Harlan, Douglas, White, and Stewart; the most frequent *relative* ones were, in the same order, White, Goldberg, Marshall, and Frankfurter. Three of the twenty-one Justices *never* employed social science data, namely, Burton, Minton, and Whittaker—but they were among the least productive opinion authors and, arguably, the least effective members of that Court. Some Justices utilized the materials *solely* in majority opinions, never in dissent: Frankfurter, Warren, Goldberg, Burger, and Powell; others resorted to them chiefly in dissenting opinions: Black, Douglas, and Stewart. Certain members of the Court proved themselves to be demonstrably comfortable with the use of social science findings; for example, Warren, Marshall, Brennan, and White, whereas others, for example, Black and Clark, in particular, were extremely wary of them. Whatever conclu-

---

318. Unpublished manuscript, April 1978 (used by permission of the author).

sions one may draw from it, the phenomenon is one to be reckoned with in the judicial process and bids fair to find continued utilization.[319]

TEST CASES

Because the American federal judicial system is based on the concept of litigation by virtue of an actual case or controversy brought before the courts by parties directly concerned, who must have standing to sue either as individuals or as personally and directly involved members of a class (see chapter 9), the solution of an issue in the judicial process depends on the decision handed down by the tribunal having jurisdiction. Consequently, neither the U.S. Supreme Court nor any of the lower constitutional courts can decide an issue unless it is before that court. Hence the employment of "test cases" becomes a fortiori crucial, and both the timing and the presentation of the case are of the utmost importance. As long as the plaintiff or petitioner is a bona fide litigant it does not matter whether or not he or she pays for the almost always considerable expenses involved; nor does it matter to the outcome whether he or she personally is vitally interested in the decision. Provided that any individual is directly involved and is willing to go to court, it is of no legal significance that, in effect, he or she may thus well act as a front or a foil. Some states do have laws against "barratry," a form of induced litigation, but it is extremely difficult to prove that barratry has been practiced unless a litigant so acknowledges. This is particularly unlikely in those "class action" cases (see chapter 9) epitomized by the segregation–integration controversy.

The first really important case in that realm came before the Supreme Court through the auspices of a Missouri black, Lloyd Gaines, to whom that state had statutorily denied admission to its public law school,[320] but who mysteriously disappeared just a few days prior to his significant 7:2 victory in the Court. (Gaines was never heard from again.) Ever since that time, test cases have been brought with increasing frequency by blacks who have been discriminated against, with the active encouragement, backing, and financing of the interest groups such as the National Association for the Advancement of Colored People (NAACP). It is neither surprising nor subject to doubt that that organization, dedicated to the aim inherent in its title, has acted, and will assuredly continue to act, very much like a strategy board of a field command, with due regard to the manifold tactical and strategic problems that beset such a command. In that sense, it resorts to the device of the test case to get its day in court, as do a host of other organizations for their own purposes. The American Civil Liberties Union (ACLU) is a similarly apposite and highly visible example of the practice.

Another illustration of the use of test cases is the concerted drive by the Jehovah's Witnesses to obtain a maximum of religious freedom, as the Witnesses conceive of it, through the device of testing in the courts what they consider to be

319. See the critical analysis of the phenomenon by David M. O'Brien, "The Seduction of the Judiciary: Social Science and the Courts," 64 *Judicature* (June–July 1980), and its defense by Peter W. Sperlich, "Social Science Evidence and the Courts," ibid. 63 (December–January 1980). See also Louis Fisher, "Social Influences on Constitutional Law," *Journal of Political Science* (Spring 1987).
320. *Missouri ex rel Gaines v. Canada*, 305 U.S. 337 (1938).

restrictions and attacks on their members. During the second quarter of this century, individual members of that sect, actively supported by the parent body, brought more than fifty bona fide test cases to the Supreme Court. Of these they won all but five! Nor is this practice confined to so-called minority groups. Almost every segment of the body politic has resorted to the device of the test case to gain—or lose—a point. The question arises, just how much pressure or influence-peddling on the Court *is* involved here? Those who suspect a burglar under every judicial bed quite naturally view test cases as an all but subversive scheme. Yet test case or regular case, a case is a case, provided it meets the jurisdictional requirements of the Court. And the line between a "plotted" or "instigated" case and a "real" or "natural" one is so thin that it almost defies detection except in the most obvious instances. Moreover, the Court is the master of its own calendar and will not accept frivolous litigation, much less hand down a decision on it. Finally, if an issue of constitutional magnitude is duly and properly brought before the Court— all legal remedies below having been exhausted, and all the requirements of the judicial process having been met—and the Court has agreed to review it, does it *really matter* whether the issue was instigated or just happened in the natural course of events?

THE BRIEF *AMICUS CURIAE*

Closely related, indeed often essential, to the technique of test cases encouraged and supported by interest groups is the resort to the brief *amicus curiae.* It is a partisan brief filed by an outside individual, corporation, governmental unit, or group who is not a litigant in the suit but is vitally interested in a decision favorable to the side it espouses. Long gone is the original concept of the *amicus curiae*— namely, that it "acts for no one, but simply seeks to give information to the Court."[321] The device of the brief *amicus curiae*, that is, "friend of the court," which may well be a misnomer in some situations, "friend of the *cause*" being far more accurate,[322] enables the interested party filing these briefs to enter the case, however tangentially, either by way of a written statement, or by participating in oral argument, or both. But there are obstacles as well as limitations to the filing of an *amicus curiae.* Thus, if all parties consent to the filing of such a brief, the Supreme Court's rules still require its own acquiescence thereto. However, mutual consent by the litigants is by no means always readily forthcoming. In that event, any party may petition the Court itself for permission to file an *amicus curiae*, a request that may or may not be granted, depending entirely on the judgment of the Justices.[323] Moreover, in cases in which the U.S. government is a party to a suit, which is true of approximately one-half or even more of the total number of all cases before the Supreme Court, consent for leave to file briefs *amici curiae* must, at least in theory, be given by the Solicitor General before the Court will admit them. In general, that high government official has been quite willing to do so, but

321. *Campbell v. Swasey*, 12 Ind. 70 (1859) at 72.
322. See the persuasive article, "'Friend of the Court' More Properly Means 'Friend of the Cause,'" by Fred Barbash, *The Washington Post*, December 27, 1980, p. A4.
323. Thus, in *Lemon v. Kurtzman*, 397 U.S. 1042 (1969), probable jurisdiction having been noted, the Court *granted* one motion to file an *amicus curiae* and *denied* another.

on some occasions the Court has also granted organizational requests for briefs *amici curiae* over his refusal to consent. The same general approach is true of cases involving *state* government or its subsidiaries, as was demonstrated by the Supreme Court's acceptance of briefs *amici curiae* in the 1965 case testing Connecticut's birth control statute over that state's objections.[324] By and large, the Supreme Court has been quite accessible to a wide array of requests for the admission of briefs *amici curiae*, especially by organized interests.

Who files these briefs? Theoretically any interested party may do so; in practice, however, most briefs *amici curiae* come from active civic organizations and other pressure groups and, not surprisingly, from the federal government itself through the Solicitor General. According to an authoritative study of applicants for leave to file during relatively recent times,[325] most requests have been filed by the following organizations: the ACLU (a tireless and effective battler for civil rights and liberties)[326]; the NAACP (persistent and broadly successful spokesperson for blacks); the American Jewish Congress and the American Jewish Committee (in roughly the same category as the ACLU, but with emphasis on cases concerning matters involving its own particular interests); the chief interest group for the vast labor movement, the AFL-CIO; and, of course, a host of business interests, such as the Chamber of Commerce and the National Association of Manufacturers (NAM). Also very active have been the American Bar Association, sundry consumer groups (often led by Ralph Nader and Common Cause), various veterans' pressure groups, led by the American Legion, and, quite often of late in matters involving reapportionment–redistricting, sexual discrimination, and segregation–integration (but not only those), the U.S. government.[327] Participation is not confined to the "merit" stage of the judicial process: roughly one-third of the briefs *amici curiae* actions are directed to petitions for writs of *certiorari* and/or jurisdictional statements on writs of appeal.[328]

To cite a specific example of the successful use of an *amicus curiae* by the last,

---

324. *Griswold v. Connecticut*, 381 U.S. 479. See the illuminating article in *Time* Magazine, February 26, 1965, pp. 50–51.

325. Clement E. Vose, "Litigation as a Form of Pressure Group Activity," 319 *Annals of the American Academy of Political and Social Science* (September 1958), pp. 20–31.

326. Between 15 and 20 percent of the cases the Court agreed to review in the last generation.

327. In one fairly typical stretch of six terms of Court (1962–68), the U.S. government participated as *amicus curiae* in 121 cases (about 15 percent of the total number of cases heard by the Court). Roughly half of these 121 dealt with race and apportionment matters. See Samuel Krislov, *The Role of the Attorney General as Amicus Curia* (Washington, D.C.: American Enterprise Institute for Public Policy Research, July 1968), pp. 71–103. In the 1970s, discrimination other than on the basis of race replaced apportionment as the government's second major concern. A more recent study by Karen O'Connor demonstrates the continuing, and indeed mounting, *amicus curiae* role of the federal government in Supreme Court litigation. Thus, in the decade from 1970 through 1979 covered by her research, the Office of the Solicitor General of the United States participated as *amicus curiae* in 285 cases, comprising a total of 17 percent of all cases. (But the government also took part as the direct party in an *additional* 713 cases, comprising an additional 42 percent of all cases. See 66 *Judicature* 6 [December–January 1983], pp. 257–64.)

328. See Gregory A. Caldeira and John R. Wright, "Amici Curiae before the Supreme Court: Who Participates, When, and How Much?" 52 *Journal of Politics* 3 (August 1990), pp. 782–806.

the government filed such a brief in a 1960 case, *Boynton v. Virginia*,[329] through the auspices of Solicitor General J. Lee Rankin. Here a bus terminal restaurant in Richmond, Virginia, segregated passengers according to color, regardless of their destination. The plaintiff rested his brief on the equal protection of the laws clause of the Fourteenth Amendment, under which so many cases in the area of racial segregation had been won—and would continue to be won—by black petitioners. However, the Solicitor General's brief *amicus curiae* used an entirely different approach, contending that since the restaurant involved was an "integral part" of a bus line's interstate passenger service, the Interstate Commerce Act of 1887—a federal statute—forbade such segregation. More or less ignoring the litigants' arguments and briefs, the Supreme Court fastened on the contents of Mr. Rankin's *amicus curiae* and decided 7:2 in the plaintiff's favor. Justice Whittaker, however, in a dissenting opinion in which he was joined by Justice Clark, chided the Court majority for deciding the case on the commerce clause which had been raised *solely* by the government as *amicus curiae*.

Unless the evidence is as clear-cut as it was in the preceding instance, it is very difficult to determine how far, if at all, the Court's decision and opinion make use of briefs *amici curiae*. What some commentators in this field report as the gospel's truth is not infrequently laced with conjecture and sheer guesswork, and some of it with prejudiced motivation. On the other hand, it would be fair to state that the flood of briefs *amici curiae* filed by the NAACP in the area of its own special interest had evinced persuasive influence in the outcome of the many cases handed down by the Court in the fifteen years between the end of World War II and 1960, for example, in which cases the cause espoused by the NAACP gained fifty victories. A specific illustration of one of these is the momentous decision by the Court in *Shelley v. Kraemer*, the most important of the *Restrictive Covenant* cases.[330] That case held the record until 1963 for the number of main briefs and briefs *amici curiae* filed and accepted: nineteen by the NAACP and others favorably disposed to its point of view, five by opposing groups, chiefly real-estate interests, and one by Solicitor General Philip B. Perlman on behalf of the U.S. Department of Justice, siding with the black plaintiff.[331] Speaking for the unanimous six-man Court—Justices Reed, Jackson, and Rutledge having disqualified themselves from participation—Chief Justice Vinson ruled that although racially restrictive *private* covenants did not in themselves violate the Fourteenth Amendment of the Constitution, *court enforcement* of such contracts would constitute state action and thereby violate the equal protection of the laws clause of that Amendment— a signal victory for the cause of the NAACP.

Other illustrations of the use of briefs *amici curiae* on *both* sides are *Gideon v. Wainwright*, the influential 1963 decision that extended the right of indigents to be assigned counsel for *non*capital as well as capital criminal cases; *DeFunis v. Odegaard* which, in 1974, raised the delicate question of "reverse discrimination"

---

329. 364 U.S. 454.
330. 334 U.S. 1 (1948) plus *Hurd v. Hodge*, 334 U.S. 24 (1948) and *Barrows v. Jackson*, 346 U.S. 249 (1953).
331. Clement E. Vose, *Caucasians Only: The Supreme Court, the NAACP, and the Restrictive Covenent Cases* (Berkeley and Los Angeles: University of California Press, 1959), Ch. 8.

in university admissions; and *Regents of the University of California v. Bakke*, which again raised that issue insistently in 1977–78 after the Court had "mooted" it in *DeFunis*.[332] In *Gideon*, twenty-four such briefs were filed on behalf of Clarence Earl Gideon, two on behalf of Florida Prison Warden Wainwright, thus toppling the erstwhile record submittals. In *DeFunis*, eight briefs were filed for law student Marco DeFunis and nineteen for University of Washington President Charles Odegaard, another record. It was surpassed, however, in *Bakke* with the filing of 120 briefs, 83 on the side of the University of California, 32 for Alan Bakke, and 5 that were "neutral." But that record, too, was shattered in 1984, in *Sony Corporation of America v. Universal City Studios*, when 140 briefs *amici curiae* entered the fascinating fray involving the right of American citizens regularly to copy television programs at home on videotape recorders, such as those manufactured by Betamax.[333] The contentious abortion issue case of *Webster v. Reproductive Health Services*, which gave promise of reopening the seminal *Roe v. Wade* decision of 1973, saw 80 briefs *amici curiae* filed.[334]

Surely, briefs *amici curiae* may, and sometimes do, influence members of the Court. To acknowledge that entirely plausible, and in many cases quite conceivably salutary, phenomenon is one thing; to lower it to the level of a sinister or subversive cops-and-robbers plot is quite another. In this realm of alleged outside influence, as well as in those discussed earlier, the fact remains that, when all is said and done, the Justices have the final word on whether or how far, if at all, they permit themselves to be influenced within the accepted framework of the judicial process.

THE LAW CLERKS

In a somewhat different category among the "pressures" on the Court are its law clerks. Depending on the point of view advanced, these able and intelligent young aides to the Justices, almost all recent law-school graduates in their mid-twenties, are in the category either of a private secretary aide-de-camp to their Justices or of a gray eminence, a sort of judicial Rasputin—indeed, the veritable power behind the throne. Thus, in an angry 1958 speech on the Senate floor, U.S. Senator John Stennis (D.-Miss.), a vigorous critic of the Court's attitude on segregation and subversion cases, took pains to call for an investigation of the activities of the clerks, the establishment of statutory minimum qualifications for them, and their confirmation by the Senate just like the Justices themselves—all this because of what the Senator termed "their ever-increasing importance and influence." The law clerks, he said, might be occupying roles in government far more important than those occupied by undersecretaries and assistant secretaries of the executive branch, and that

> [to] the extent that they participate in shaping the work of the court, they are deciding vital questions of national effect. Within the Judicial branch, these are equivalent to policy-level decisions in the executive branch.[335]

332. 372 U.S. 335; 416 U.S. 312; and 429 U.S. 109, respectively. (One of the briefs *amici curiae* for Alan Bakke was filed by Marco DeFunis.)
333. 464 U.S. 417.
334. 492 U.S. 490 (1989).
335. As reported in *The New York Times*, May 7, 1958, p. 27.

Yet we have the word of ex-law clerk after ex-law clerk that their influence on the Justices to whom they were assigned was nil insofar as the actual judicial decision-making process was concerned. John P. Frank, once clerk to Justice Black, wrote that, in his years at the court, "my Justice made approximately one thousand decisions, and I had precisely no influence on any of them."[336] Frank related that a Douglas clerk, having substantially taken it upon himself to reorganize a draft opinion by his Justice, was told by the latter: "I can see you've done a lot of work, but you are off base here. If and when you get appointed to the Supreme Court, you can write opinions as you choose."[337] "Sometimes," commented another Black clerk, "a clerk can get a word or comma accepted, but the substance and decision are never anything but Black's alone."[338] Dean Acheson, one of several of Justice Brandeis's law clerks who later rose to national prominence, reported that his Justice would sometimes let him work on a draft opinion, largely for the sake of criticism, but:

> When I finished my work on a draft which had been assigned to me or got as far as I could, I gave it to him. [As is evident from the Brandeis files] he tore it to pieces, sometimes using a little, sometimes none [of it].[339]

Justice Byron R. White, who clerked for Chief Justice Vinson (1946–53), recalled later: "I don't think anything I ever did or said influenced my Justice. I felt I was doing him a service by making sure that relevant considerations were placed before him. . . . "[340] "Judging is not delegated!" snapped Justice Brennan once in response to a reporter's taunt.[341] And of all the law clerks who have written or otherwise reported on their experiences behind the "Purple Curtain," only one, William H. Rehnquist[342]—who was appointed to the Supreme Court by President Nixon late in 1971 from his former position of U.S. Assistant Attorney General, and whom President Reagan would appoint to Chief Justice in 1986—suggested the possibility of some "unconscious slanting of material by clerks."[343] But even he, who had served as Justice Jackson's clerk in the 1952–53 term, readily admitted that the notion of the law clerk "exerting an important influence on the cases actually decided by the Court, may be discarded at once . . . I certainly learned of none."[344] He would reiterate that conviction repeatedly during his ensuing career on the Court, as both Associate and Chief Justice. During his often heated confirmation hearings, a memorandum came to light in which Rehnquist had argued to Jackson

336. *The Marble Palace*, op. cit., p. 119. See his "The Supreme Court: The Muckrakers Return," *Journal of the American Bar Association* (February 1980), pp. 160ff.
337. " . . . The Muckrakers Return," loc. cit., p. 164.
338. Daniel J. Meador, "Justice Black and His Law Clerks," 15 *Alabama Law Review* 57 (1962) at 59–60.
339. As quoted by Bickel, *The Unpublished Opinions* . . . , op. cit., p. 92.
340. As quoted by Williams, op. cit., n. 113, pp. 90–91.
341. *Time Magazine*, June 5, 1964, p. 67.
342. Rehnquist was the second of three contemporary Supreme Court Justices to have served as law clerks themselves; the other two were White and John Paul Stevens (the latter for Wiley Rutledge in 1947–48).
343. "Who Writes Decisions of the Supreme Court?" *U.S. News and World Report*, December 13, 1957, p. 275.
344. Ibid.

that the "separate but equal" doctrine in education should not be overturned because it "was right and should be reaffirmed."[345] Yet Jackson subsequently joined the unanimous Court in declaring that doctrine unconstitutional in 1954.[346]

These law clerks, almost without exception, have gone on to notable careers.[347] Just who are they, and how are they selected? As indicated, they are recent law-school graduates of the highest caliber, and all were men until the first two women, Lucille Loman and Margaret Corcoran, were appointed by Justices Douglas and Black, respectively, in 1944 and 1966. In 1948 Justice Frankfurter appointed the first black Supreme Court clerk, William T. Coleman (who would later serve as Secretary of Transportation under President Ford). Each is chosen by an individual Justice to work for him or her for a year, sometimes for two.[348] The practice[349] was initiated in the Supreme Court in 1882 by Justice Horace Gray, who had begun using the clerks during his tenure on the Massachusetts bench. Gray, whose opinions were consistently longer than those of his colleagues, hired recent top Harvard Law School graduates for one year, and he paid his clerks out of his own pocket until 1886, when Congress appropriated $1,600 annually for a "stenographic clerk" for each Justice.[350] That figure had risen to $37,294 by 1991–92. Today (mid-1992) there are thirty-four clerks (including ten women). Each Associate Justice except Justice Stevens uses four. The latter and Chief Justice Rehnquist select only three. Since 1972 the Chief also has been entitled to an "Administrative Assistant to the Chief Justice," a post created by Congress to help in planning, leadership, and administrative responsibilities for the federal judiciary.[351]

Some Justices do their own selecting of clerks, either by personal interview or by considering written data, almost always the former; others rely chiefly on experts' recommendations (e.g, Justice Frankfurter, whose clerks were chosen for him by Professors Sachs and Freund at the Harvard Law School), as indeed "F. F." used to select all of Justice Brandeis's clerks, and as Justice Brennan had mem-

345. *The New York Times*, December 7, 1971, p. C20.

346. *Brown v. Board of Education of Topeka*, 347 U.S. 483 (1954) and *Bolling v. Sharpe*, 347 U.S. 497 (1954). See also Kluger's account, op. cit. (n. 126 *surpa*).

347. E.g., Dean Acheson (U.S. Secretary of State), Francis Biddle (U.S. Attorney General), Irving Olds (President of U.S. Steel Corp.), David Riesman (famed professor of sociology), Elliot Richardson (Attorney General, Secretary of Defense, Undersecretary of State, Secretary of Health, Education and Welfare, and Secretary of Commerce), and the aforementioned Associate Justices White, Rehnquist, and Stevens.

348. But Justice Joseph McKenna (1898–1925) kept his first clerk for twelve years and had only two other clerks during his remaining twelve years on the Court. And there was one law clerk who served with four Justices, beginning with Justice J. Rufus Peckham (1896–1909) in 1905 and ending with Justice George Sutherland (1922–38) in 1924, for a record total of nineteen years (see Wilkinson, op. cit., pp. 48–49).

349. At the state level the practice has generally been customary only since circa 1950, and it has become extensive only since 1970 (see John B. Oakley and Robert S. Thompson, *Law Clerks and the Judicial Process*. Berkeley: University of California Press, 1981).

350. Until 1973, when each of the Justices was at last assigned two secretaries, they had to content themselves with just one, plus the use of the stenographic pool.

351. In 1985 the active federal constitutional judges employed 1,507 law clerks; and additional 281 served senior judges and 243 bankruptcy judges. Each of these 2,000-plus clerks, whose ages ranged from twenty-five to thirty, was paid between $26,000 and $31,000 annually (see *The Wall Street Journal*, July 28, 1986, p. 14). Clerks are routinely paid at federal pay scale grade 12, step 1.

bers of that faculty do during his early tenure on the Court. From Harvard, Professor of Law Felix Frankfurter sent a number of his own outstanding students, sometimes referred to as "Felix's Happy Hot Dogs," to the Court as clerks (and to government service with the New Deal). In short, the clerks are really the purely personal patronage of the Justices, who are free to base their selections on whatever criteria they desire. John P. Frank avowed that his Justice, Hugo Black tried "to get Southern boys—and tennis players where possible."[352] Justice Stewart preferred Yale Law School graduates, Justice Murphy those from Michigan, Justice Butler Minnesotans, Justice Minton Indianans, Chief Justice Vinson those who had their degrees from Northwestern University, Chief Justice Warren Californians, Justice Clark graduates of lesser-known law schools, and Justice Powell Virginians. Justice Harlan II ordinarily chose one applicant from Harvard and one from a New York City law school, and Justice Douglas usually turned to a West Coast law school for his choice. Alone among his colleagues to do so, Justice Stevens selected a *state* supreme court clerk as one of his two clerks for 1984–85. Justice Marshall, who in his latter years on the Court gave his clerks more responsibilities than any of his colleagues were inclined to do, had his sitting clerks select future clerks. Justice Brennan relied on his law school contacts to send him the kind of clerks he would be comfortable with. In the 1965–66 term of the Court, to cite one Court's pattern, nineteen law clerks were chosen by the nine members of the court, Chief Justice Warren selecting three, Justice Douglas one, and all the others two; there was also one assigned jointly to retired Justices Reed and Burton, who were still "on call" for lower federal court spot tasks, as assigned by the Chief Justice. The young lawyers came from ten different law schools: six from Harvard University, three each from Yale University and the University of Pennsylvania, two each from the University of Virginia and Stanford University, and one each from Columbia University, the University of Texas, and the University of North Carolina. The 1984–85 "lineup" (excluding Chief Justice Burger's four), reflecting the increased number of clerks allotted as well as greater diversity, provided the following data, in descending order of frequency: Harvard, five; Chicago and Columbia, four; Yale, three; Stanford, two; and one each from George Washington, U.C.L.A., Maine, Virginia, Illinois, Howard, Pennsylvania, Georgetown, New York University, Michigan, Tulane, and Boston University. In recent years the clerks have tended to reflect the liberal political philosophy of the elite law schools whence they come. Thus, of the thirty-three clerks who served in the 1985–86 Court only six (18 percent) had voted for Ronald Reagan in 1984.[353]

Exactly what work a Justice assigns or delegates to his clerk depends on the former's inclination—or, as Justice Jackson once stated, "on the Justice's temperament and experience." In any event, they are a hardworking lot: usually a seven-day, ninety-hour week. Apparently, most but not all of the Justices use their clerks to wade through the manifold petitions for *certiorari* that are filed annually (Justices Frankfurter and Brennan[354] are on record as being notable exceptions to the prac-

---

352. *The Marble Palace*, op. cit., pp. 115–16.
353. As reported by Terry Eastland, "While Justice Sleeps," *National Review*, April 21, 1989, p. 26
354. See 59 *American Bar Association Journal* 836 (August 1973) for Justice Brennan's assertions on the issue. But in the 1980s Brennan began to use his clerks for a good bit of "cert. work."

tice). Typically, a law clerk may read such a petition and the opposing party's response and then type or pen a brief memorandum to his or her Justice stating the issues involved and setting forth arguments for and against a grant of the desired writ. Suffice it to note that the Justice concerned will, of course, make up his or her own mind; yet the *certiorari* work by the clerks may well become crucial in the Court's endeavor to handle the ever-mounting case load.[355] In the manifestation of unusual public self-criticism *cum* confessional, Justice Stevens observed that he had "found it necessary to delegate a great deal of responsibility in the review of petitions [of *certiorari*]" to his law clerks. "They examine them all and select a small minority that they believe I should read myself. As a result, I do not even look at the papers in over 80 percent of the cases that are filed."[356] No wonder, then, that *The Brethren* would attribute such a degree of importance to the law clerks![357]

Some of the Justices may go somewhat further in employing their clerks, asking for a so-called bench memorandum on a particular case now and then. Such a memorandum may note whether the case is properly before the Court, state what federal issues are presented and how these were decided by the courts below, summarize the positions of the parties pro and con on the grant of the writ, propound certain approaches and points of precedent, and thereby suggest questions to be asked of counsel by the Justices during oral argument. The most intensive task performed by the law clerks is probably that of the necessary drudgery of research once an opinion has been assigned to a particular Justice. Then commences the time-consuming chore of investigating, of sorting and checking precedents, citations, historical data, congressional records—the host of materials so vital to the decision-making process. Beyond that, the chief role of the law clerk is to serve as a foil, friend, critic, and sounding board. In the final analysis, however, as one former clerk wrote:

> In the course of my year, we never changed the Justice's mind on the result of any case. Our influence was close to nil. There was the fullest discussion, but he made the decisions. . . . The judge will listen if you say that some statement in his draft opinion is too broad or that a case is cited incorrectly. But if you tell him that such-and-such a constitutional amendment doesn't mean what he believes, you might as well stay in bed.[358]

The clerks are important tools for the Justices in the judicial process,[359] perhaps indispensable ones, yet they are hardly classifiable as veritable powers behind the throne. The picture painted in *The Brethren*—a highly controversial book, based to a very considerable extent on the assertions of 170 anonymous law clerks—is

355. For an interesting analysis, which contends that the Court could not function without the clerks' *certiorari* role, see Arthur S. Miller, "High Court Secrets," *The New York Times*, November 17, 1971, p. M45.

356. Address to the American Judicature Society, San Francisco, August 8, 1982.

357. Bob Woodward and Scott Armstrong, *The Brethren: Inside the Supreme Court* (New York: Simon and Schuster, 1979), passim.

358. As quoted anonymously in *The New York Times*, October 14, 1957, p. 29.

359. See Michael Slaughter, "Judicial Clerkships in Perspective," 59 *Judicature* 5 (December 1975), pp. 248–52.

misleading.[360] In the words of Justice Powell's first clerk: "The idea that law clerks represent some independent force of resistance within the Court or that they somehow thwart or undermine a Justice's personal will, is a piece of mythology that ought to be rejected."[361] Essentially, they are law *clerks:* able, intelligent, and undoubtedly often, if not always, of considerable procedural aid to their Justices. But they are not members of the Court in any sense of the term. And, as has been contended repeatedly in connection with the entire matter of influence on it, the Supreme Court of the United States is, in fine, master of its own house—which does not, however, mean that it is not aware of the existence of other houses both in and out of the governmental compound.

As we conclude this extensive consideration of the Supreme Court of the United States at work, it is both easy and natural to assent to a perceptive statement made by *The New York Times* reporter and columnist Anthony Lewis as he left his seven-year coverage of the Court for a new assignment in London in 1965: "The wonderful thing about the Supreme Court is that it does its work. It decides, as it has to decide. There has never been a Rules Committee to save the Justices on tough problems. . . . [T]he Supreme Court . . . is the last stronghold of personal responsibility for decision."[362]

360. *The Brethren,* op. cit.
361. Wilkinson, op. cit., p. 61. Justice Frankfurter's then law clerk, Philip Elman, tried unsuccessfully to dissuade the Justice from penning his famous dissenting opinion in *West Virginia State Board of Education* v. *Barnette,* 319 U.S. 624 (1943) at 646. (See pp. 226–27, *supra.*) Frankfurter told his clerk with some acerbity: "This is my opinion, not yours" (as reported by Israel Shenker, *The New York Times,* October 23, 1977, p. 34).
362. *The New York Times Magazine,* January 17, 1965, pp. 56–58.

6

Courts Abroad

Wherever appropriate, reference has been made to the practices and theories of jurists and judicial systems of sundry lands, since the comparative element is one of the essential characteristics of this work. Newly emergent states of the world adapt their needs to the legal and social patterns of older ones. The United States has both profited from and contributed to other systems. Basically English in origin and design, features of its judicial system and process nevertheless both resemble, and differ drastically from, its progenitor as well as that of others. The legal systems of England, Wales, and France, are most useful in an analysis in this connection. In the following pages a relatively brief view of the courts of these countries will be presented.

THE COURTS OF ENGLAND AND WALES

It is incorrect to think of the courts of Great Britain or of the United Kingdom as a unified judicial system. For actually *three different systems* exist in the United Kingdom of Great Britain and Northern Ireland: one for England and Wales, one for Scotland, and one for Northern Ireland. Only at the ultimate appellate level of the House of Lords is it possible to speak with accuracy of a unified system for the United Kingdom; because that body in its judicial role represents the final court of appeals, in those very few cases that manage to reach it, from the judgments of the highest courts of Scotland and Northern Ireland as well as from those of England and Wales. The following description is of the judicial system of England and

Wales—for convenience hereafter referred to as England—unless specified otherwise[1] (see Figure 4, p. 251, *infra*.)

In the United States the *same* tribunals ordinarily have *both* civil and criminal jurisdiction, with some minor exceptions for certain low-level state courts, such as the Court of Small Claims in Pennsylvania. But in the England of today justice is meted out in two separated judicial hierarchies, one for civil cases and one for criminal cases, although the sitting judges are often the same individuals. (There are fewer than 500 full-time judges in England, but they are augmented by more than 25,000 lay magistrates or justices of the peace.) The separation between civil and criminal court jurisdiction is based on the Supreme Court of Judicature (Consolidation) Act of 1925, as amended, the progeny of a series of Judicature Acts which commenced in 1873. That statute brought order into what had been a truly bewildering array of distinct tribunals—for example, some seven or eight leading courts had original jurisdiction in civil cases! However, unlike France, neither England nor the United States has a bona fide system of administrative courts, although some of the English administrative courts such as Railway Rate Tribunals existed long before World War II, and others have begun to make their appearance since the war; also, some of the special and/or legislative tribunals in the United States are at least quasi-administrative.[2]

THE CRIMINAL COURTS' HIERARCHY

It is perhaps somewhat unorthodox to discuss the criminal courts' hierarchy before that of the civil courts, but the English structure lends itself peculiarly well to such a procedure, in part because of a considerable amount of interchange of judges between the two hierarchies, despite the rigid structural segregation inherent in the system. Jurisdiction over criminal offenses has been exercised as a separate entity for some 700 years.

The Justice of the Peace or Magistrate and the Stipendiary Magistrate. At the base of the criminal courts hierarchy in England is the unpaid, volunteer lay magistrate, the *Justice of the Peace* or *Magistrate*, who must live within fifteen miles of the judicial area of jurisdiction. It is an office established by law in 1326 or 1327 during the reign of Edward II. The approximately 26,000 J.P.s or Magistrates are at work today (1991) in some 500 magistrate courts in most of the larger cities, but also in a few smaller ones. In the larger cities there is instead the *Stipendiary Magistrate*—London alone, where he or she is called Metropolitan Magistrate, has roughly thirty-five of these officials—who, unlike the Justice of the Peace or Magistrate, must be a full-time professional lawyer, usually a barrister, and is salaried at £50,500 (1992), again unlike the unpaid lay J.P.s or Magistrates. With the exception of the Duchy of Lancaster, where they are designated by its own Chancellor,

---

1. These courts are presided over by judges who often, but certainly no longer always, wear wigs—either shoulder-length ("full-bottomed") or short—and robes of office, with the color of their robes depending on the law they administer. Common law judges as well as those who administer to the criminal law wear scarlet robes; the others wear black. The atmosphere in an English courtroom remains much more formal than in an American one, but English judges have become rather tolerant of the manner in which people dress in court.

2. See chapter 4, *supra*, for details.

the Magistrates at this lowest level of the criminal hierarchy are appointed on behalf of the Crown by the Lord Chancellor after careful screening and recommendation by local advisory committees in each county.[3] This politically designated officer, who was discussed earlier,[4] is not only the highest judicial officer in the whole British system, he is also a member of the Cabinet, its foremost legal adviser, and a member as well as *ex officio* presiding officer of the House of Lords. (The Lord Chief Justice is the highest judicial officer for England alone.)

Sitting *en banc* in twos or threes (more often the latter) without a jury—the Stipendiary Magistrate sits alone—the Justice of the Peace or Magistrate, in his or her role (10,000, or 40 percent were women in 1983)[5] as a tribunal of first instance, is exclusively a court of summary jurisdiction for criminal offenses. Indeed, more than nine out of ten criminal cases begin and end there. But he or she may also double as a committing judicial officer by holding an accused for action by a higher court in the event of "indictable" offenses. These would normally require grand jury action at the federal level in the United States; but in England, since the statutory abolition of the grand jury in 1933, the process of "information" has replaced it. Except for minor matters, trials at this lowest level of original jurisdiction are conducted by one, two, or three justices of the peace, but by only one Stipendiary Magistrate—a vital distinction between the two similar types of officials. The latter's chief function is to try relatively minor criminal offenses, although they have an important jurisdiction in certain domestic relations—matrimonial, bastardy, and poll tax (since 1989) cases, and some administrative functions, such as licensing— and, as indicated, to determine whether or not evidence is sufficient to commit the alleged offender for trial before a jury in a higher court. Barristers and solicitors have equal rights of access in these tribunals.

Many of the offenses handled by the J.P. or Magistrate or the Stipendiary Magistrate concern traffic violations with limited fines.[6] Generally speaking, his or her jurisdiction is now (1991) restricted to cases involving a maximum fine of £1,000 or a six-months jail sentence, or both, although there are exceptions, such as customs cases. In many instances the accused is permitted the option of a trial before the Justice of the Peace or Magistrate or the Stipendiary Magistrate or before a higher judge (and jury, when appropriate). Experience has demonstrated that the accused will often choose the lower-level tribunal because of considerations of expeditiousness, but he or she may have the right to a trial and wish to exercise it.

Still apropos the first level of the judiciary, when two or more Justices of the Peace or Magistrates or one Stipendiary Magistrate are sitting, a *Court of Petty Sessions* is said to exist. As will be explained subsequently, appeals from this level are possible either to the Crown Court or to a three-judge Divisional Court of the Queen's Bench Division of the High Court of Justice, depending on the nature of

3. For an excellent discussion of the magistrate level of the English judiciary, see E. C. Friesen and I. R. Scott, *English Criminal Justice* (Birmingham: Institute of Judicial Administration, University of Birmingham, 1977).
4. See chapter 2, *supra*.
5. *The Economist* (August 13, 1983, p. 51) claims 48 percent to be a more accurate figure.
6. A late 1980s study found three-quarters of nontraffic sentences in the Magistrate-level courts to be in the form of fines.

the appeal and provided that the defendant did not plead guilty, although in London he or she is free to appeal even in the latter event if the sentence is more than one month in prison or a fine of more than £3. Appeals in matrimonial cases go to the Divisional Court of the Family Division of the High Court of Justice.

The Crown Court. Immediately above the J.P. level is the *Crown Court,* established by the Courts Act of 1971; it replaced the fourteenth-century *Court of Quarter Sessions* and the twelfth-century *Assize Courts.* Clothed with appellate as well as original jurisdiction, averaging 60,000 cases annually, it is the first court in which an accused, given the proper circumstances, is entitled to a trial by jury. The Crown Court is statutorily enabled to sit anywhere in England and Wales—it sat in ninety-seven centers in 1988—and is staffed by High Court judges, the newly created Circuit judges, and Recorders. They sit with Justices of the Peace or Magistrates in case of appeals and committals of sentence, but no more than nine members of the Court may sit *en banc* in any given case. In some boroughs the Court consists merely of the paid *Recorder,* usually selected from barristers of at least five years' experience. A Recorder serves only occasionally as such, however, and continues in practice as a barrister. Ordinarily, the Court's session is presided over by a professional Circuit judge or, on limited occasions, by a High Court of Justice (a civil court) in London. It was Lord Parker, the Lord Chief Justice of England who, in his capacity as a judge of its Queen's Bench Division, presided over the important Blake spy trial that took place in the spring of 1961 in England's capital. (The Lord Chief Justice, who is England's highest judicial officer, is the head of the Queen's Bench Division.)

Because of the nature of the offenses tried before them—all trials on indictment, including all major felonies such as homicide, robbery, larceny, and rape—the assizes still always sit with a jury. Much traditional pageantry and fanfare attend their sessions, the proper judicial manner being very much in evidence. The Crown Court for Metropolitan London is the Central Criminal Court, widely known as the "Old Bailey" because of the name of the building where it meets for its twelve sessions annually, one each month.[7]

Appeals from judgments of the Crown Court are possible to the next higher level court, the Court of Appeal Criminal Division, on both points of law and fact. On the former, any convicted defendant may appeal; and he or she may do so on a point of fact with leave of the Crown Court judge or that of the Court of Appeal itself. The latter permission is mandatory for an appeal against the sentence.

The Court of Appeal. Appeals from the two lower levels in the hierarchy, to which only the defendant is entitled—the Prosecution may not appeal from a verdict of acquittal, although the Attorney General may refer a point of law—were formerly taken directly to the *Court of Criminal Appeal,* created in 1907. Recently, however, the separate Court of *Criminal Appeal* was abolished, and its functions taken over by a *Criminal Division* of the *Court of Appeal,* an arrangement of chiefly administrative importance. Appeals come to the Criminal Division in the same way they used to go to the Court of Criminal Appeal, assuming the necessary

---

7. *Bailley* was the tenth-century English word for "enclosure," and the Old Bailey stands on the site of an enclosure, originally part of Newgate Prison, where public executions took place until 1868.

jurisdiction is present and leave to file has been obtained. It is the most important tribunal of appellate jurisdiction in the criminal hierarchy of England. Sitting without a jury, it hears 6,000 to 7,000 appeals annually based on the transcripts of the evidence taken at the trial. The Court of Appeal is composed of the legally qualified and salaried judges of the Queen's Bench Division of the High Court of Justice and often there may be one or two members of the Lords Justices who form the Court of Appeal. Usually there are three members, the customary quorum, but in civil cases sometimes only two.

Because of the stipulated assumption that any appeal constitutes a "retrial," the Court of Appeal has the power to revise (i.e., alter or vary) the original sentence in three situations: (1) if it is not legally justified, (2) if it was based on improper evidence, and (3) if the length or severity of the sentence points to an error in "some matter of principle" by the trial court. The Court of Appeal may even substitute conviction on another offense for the initial one if it appears that the defendant should have been convicted for it rather than for the one for which he or she was convicted below. But it has no power to order a trial *de novo* unless there has been a mistrial in the lower court.

The House of Lords. In rare instances, the accused—never the Prosecution— has one last and very much restricted path of appeal, from the Court of Appeal to the *House of Lords* (an institution to be more fully described in connection with the civil hierarchy). Yet such an appeal is possible only when a point of law of "general public importance" is involved, and leave to file for appeal to that august body must be given by the Court of Appeal or the Divisional Court of the Queen's Bench Division of the High Court of Justice, or by the House of Lords itself if the appeal is refused by the aforementioned tribunals. Moreover, since the House of Lords often confines its rulings on the specific, sometimes narrow, point of law involved, broad legal pronouncements are uncommon.[8]

Until a statutory change was effected in 1960, permission to appeal to the House of Lords was even more circumscribed than the present procedure. Leave to appeal could be granted only by the Attorney General, the senior law officer of the Crown, and then only if the point of law involved was deemed of "*exceptional* public importance." Thus, in the famous Guenther Padola loss-of-memory murder case of 1959, the Attorney General, Sir Reginald Manningham-Buller, refused to grant such permission. All other channels of appeal had previously been exhausted, and the Old Bailey jury had decided in the trial court that the alleged amnesia was faked. The accused consequently paid the ultimate penalty.

THE CIVIL COURTS' HIERARCHY

Although some of the terminology will be similar and some of the judicial personnel are in fact, the same, the existing hierarchical distinctions between the crimi-

---

8. See Richard M. Jackson, *The Machinery of Justice in England,* 8th ed., revised by J. R. Spencer (Cambridge: Cambridge University Press, 1989). This is an excellent book, and one of the very few relatively up-to-date ones available on the British judiciary. It presents a superb explanation and analysis of its subject matter.

nal and civil courts are highly pertinent to a proper understanding of the judicial process in England. Again, we commence at the lowest level of the courts.[9]

The County Court. The court of first instance in civil matters is the *County Court*, so called by virtue of the adoption of the ancient name of the local courts of the county in early Anglo-Norman times, despite the fact that the jurisdiction of these tribunals today does not necessarily coincide with county boundaries. Indeed, it has nothing to do with them. The districts they serve are arranged so that a County Court is within ready reach everywhere; they are subject to geographic alteration by the Lord Chancellor. The more than 500 county courts are grouped into over fifty circuits, with at least one judge for each such circuit, who holds court in each district at least once a month but daily in busy circuits. The judges, called "circuit judges" since the Courts Act of 1971, are appointed by the Crown on the advice of the Lord Chancellor—again with the exception of those in the Duchy of Lancaster, as in the case of the Justices of the Peace. To qualify, they must be barristers in good standing with at least seven years of experience. They retire at seventy-two or, exceptionally, at seventy-five.

The County Court's "circuit judges," who earn £61,000 (1992), are prone to live in their districts. They hold court daily in London and once or twice a month in appropriate towns, referred to as their circuit, depending on the work load docketed. Each County Court is assigned a *Registrar* (now known as "District Judge,") a senior practicing barrister or solicitor appointed by and subject to removal by the Lord Chancellor, who is not only in charge of the court's office staff but who may also act as a lesser judge. By leave of his or her county court judge, and in the absence of objections by any of the parties, the Registrar deals mainly with matters not involving more than £75 but may exercise wider jurisdiction with the consent of the litigants.

The jurisdiction of the County Court is now statutorily unlimited as a result of its dramatic restructuring by the Courts and Legal Services Act of 1990 (effective as of 1991), and the number of cases commenced at this level is vast. In 1982, for instance, a total of 2,301,364 proceedings were entered in the county courts.[10] Broadly speaking, the large majority of cases fall into the area of actions based on contract and tort claims up to a maximum of £1,000, with a handful of exceptions (e.g., libel and slander). Yet many of these cases do not exceed £150 in value. Other areas of County Court jurisdiction include equity matters up to £5,000, real-estate actions for the recovery of land in which the net annual value of the land's rating is not above the County Court limit, and a limited range of admiralty and bankruptcy matters. And a highly significant field of its jurisdiction arises under so-called social or collectivist statutes, a by-product of today's welfare state. Since 1934, an appeal from the County Court must be taken directly to the Court of Appeal, thus bypassing the next higher court level.

The High Court of Justice. Immediately above the County Court in the hierarchy of the civil courts stands the *High Court of Justice*, an ancient institution deriving from the Norman *curia regis*, which was the monarch's personal instrument for dispensing justice. It has chiefly original but also some divisionally

---

9. Below the County Courts there are, in addition to the Magistrates Courts and the Juvenile Courts, also the Small Claims Courts. In the latter nobody is permitted to employ a lawyer.
10. Bray, op. cit., ch. 2, p. 97, n. 137.

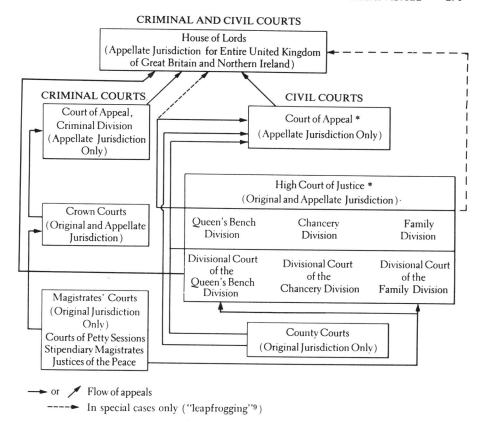

CRIMINAL AND CIVIL COURTS

House of Lords
(Appellate Jurisdiction for Entire United Kingdom
of Great Britain and Northern Ireland)

CRIMINAL COURTS

Court of Appeal,
Criminal Division
(Appellate Jurisdiction
Only)

Crown Courts
(Original and Appellate
Jurisdiction)

Magistrates' Courts
(Original Jurisdiction
Only)
Courts of Petty Sessions
Stipendiary Magistrates
Justices of the Peace

CIVIL COURTS

Court of Appeal *
(Appellate Jurisdiction Only)

High Court of Justice *
(Original and Appellate Jurisdiction)·

Queen's Bench
Division

Chancery
Division

Family
Division

Divisional Court
of the
Queen's Bench
Division

Divisional Court
of the
Chancery Division

Divisional Court
of the
Family Division

County Courts
(Original Jurisdiction Only)

→ or ✦ Flow of appeals

----► In special cases only ("leapfrogging"9)

* The Court of Appeal and the High Court of Justice form the *Supreme Court of Judicature* (known simply as "The Supreme Court") which, in effect, however, is neither "supreme" nor a "court". (See p. 265, *infra.*)

Figure 4. The criminal and civil courts of England and Wales (1992)

restricted appellate jurisdiction. This famous tribunal, established in 1837, is now (1992) staffed by eighty (seventy-seven plus three senior pending judges) distinguished *puisne* judges,[11] salaried at £84,250 (1992), who have had a minimum of ten years of experience as barristers—many have had twenty or twenty-five years. The three divisions of the "High Court," as it is commonly called, thus comprise the forty-nine–member *Queen's Bench Division*, including its presiding officer, the Lord Chief Justice of England who ranks immediately after the Lord Chancellor

11. The first woman to be appointed to the High Court of Justice was County Court Judge Elizabeth Lane, Q.C., who reached her country's No. 3 tribunal in August 1965. A minor crisis arose over what to call the first woman judge. Would it be "Mr. Justice" or "Your Lordship"? Not at all, decreed the Lord Chancellor, Lord Gardiner: Instead, upon her confirmation by Queen Elizabeth it was announced that "henceforth and hereafter" Dame Elizabeth Lane would be addressed as "The Honorable Mrs. Justice Lane," and inside the courtroom she would be addressed as "My Lady" or "Your Ladyship" (*The Christian Science Monitor*, September 19, 1965, p. 11).

in the judicial hierarchy; the thirteen-member *Chancery Division*, plus its non-sitting presiding officer, the Lord Chancellor (its effective head is known as "Vice-President"); and the President and sixteen judges of the *Family Division* (formerly known as the *Probate, Divorce, and Admiralty Division*).

Of the three, the Queen's Division is by far the largest and busiest, partly because its judges must participate also in the work of the criminal courts as a matter of exercising original jurisdiction—as was explained earlier—and partly because, with three or five of its judges sitting as the *Divisional Court* of the Queen's Bench Division, it hears certain appeals in criminal cases from the courts of summary jurisdiction, that is, the Justice of the Peace or Magistrate and Stipendiary Magistrate Court and the Crown Court. Coupled with its jurisdiction over the general field of the common law, its work range thus extends to (1) ordinary civil actions (normally those claims with more than £5,000 at stake), (2) its appellate and supervisory jurisdiction *en banc* in its mantle of Divisional Court of the Queen's Bench Division, (3) appellate functions exercised by a single judge, and (4) its limited original criminal jurisdiction. Its annual case load usually encompasses between 1,500 and 2,000 full trials.

As the presiding officer of the Queen's Bench Division, the Lord Chief Justice enjoys a considerable degree of authority and prestige. In his capacity he is the directing figure of the criminal courts of England, although, unlike the Lord Chancellor, he has no direct say in government. The L.C.J.'s stature depends on a good deal on his individual personality; yet what he says on any given occasion may influence not only the other judges but also the lawyers, the magistrates, and even the police. The Lord Chief Justice is regarded with much awe, confidence, and respect.

The Chancery Division has exclusive jurisdiction in some cases and concurrent jurisdiction with the Queen's Bench Division in others. In the extensive former category—averaging 700 trials yearly—are equity matters of bankruptcy, companies, tax, finance, execution of trusts, wardships, patent cases, foreclosures of mortgages, and so on. Appeals from county courts in bankruptcy matters lie to a *Divisional Court of the Chancery Division*.

The Family Division has jurisdiction in the areas implied by its name: giving valid title to the estate of deceased persons; matrimonial decrees as to divorce (the new growth area for English lawyers), nullity, restitution of conjugal rights, judicial separation, presumption of death, and dissolution of marriage; and declaration of legitimacy. Its *Divisional Court* hears appeals from the Magistrates' Courts level in matrimonial cases. The Family Division, which deals with the astounding number of 2 to 3 million cases annually, also used to have jurisdiction over various matters affecting ships under maritime law, but since the administration of Justice Act of 1970 there is an Admiralty Court as part of the Queen's Bench Division to take Admiralty business.[12]

12. In popular lingo, the Family Division used to be referred to as "Wrecks" Division, because it was said to deal with "wills, wives, and wrecks." Lord Goddard, who was Lord Chief Justice for twelve years, amended this jest by quipping that the Division deals with "wrecks of wills . . . marriages . . . and ships" (Lord Goddard, "Organization and Jurisdiction of the Courts of England," 44 *Journal of the American Judicature Society* 62 [August 1960]; see his entire article for a fine description, pp. 60–65).

In addition to its specialized jurisdiction, just explained, the High Court of Justice has overall jurisdiction in all cases that are eligible for hearings in the County Court as well as those that lie outside that tribunal's jurisdiction. But, if it is asked to take cases under its original jurisdiction when these can be handled by the County Court, for example, routine controversies with a value of less than £1,000, even the successful plaintiff may have to pay court costs. Together with the Court of Appeal, the High Court of Justice forms the *Supreme Court of Judicature*, which usually sits in London. It is a body that is actually neither supreme nor a court, but serves as a type of cover-all for the Common Law and Chancery branches of the civil courts system.

The Court of Appeal. Appeals from any of the Divisions of the High Court of Justice go to the *Court of Appeal*,[13] which consists of the Master of the Rolls (England's third highest judicial officer), who is the presiding judge in the Court of Appeal, plus seventeen Lord Justices of Appeal, the regular sitting members—usually in groups of three—who must have had fifteen years of experience as barristers or been High Court judges. The Court of Appeal's appellate jurisdiction extends to points of law arising out of civil cases from the County Court or the High Court of Justice. There may now also be appeals on fact from High Court decisions, but they rarely succeed. The Court of Appeals' annual case load is circa 1,500 cases. As a general rule, in contrast to practices prevalent in the United States judicial system, there is no unqualified right of appeal in England. It would be entirely accurate to note that there the trend is to limit rather than to extend appellate review.

Appeals on points of law coming from the County Court reach the Court of Appeal as a matter of right if the amount of the claim involved exceeds £20, or when the remedy is an injunction. In other appeals the judge below must give permission. In the cases coming from the High Court, appeal is automatic on points of law but not on points of fact. If the Court of Appeal grants an appeal, retrial of the case will normally take place below; however, it may also reconsider the evidence itself, but without taking new testimony from witnesses.

The House of Lords. From the Court of Appeal, if the matter of law involved is deemed to be of sufficient importance, there remains the final path of appeal to the *House of Lords* (an expensive one—£1,000 for printing costs alone is an average expenditure, the cost of reaching the Lords commonly running to £20,000) provided that the appeal has been certified by the Court of Appeal[14] or granted by the House of Lords itself, a historic right dating back to the practices of the Nor-

13. The Administration of Justice Act of 1969 provides for appeals in some cases directly from the High Court to the House of Lords, thus "leapfrogging" the Court of Appeal. Thus, under its Part II, appeals from the High Court in certain civil proceedings may be brought directly to the House of Lords ("leapfrog" over the Court of Appeal) on the certificate of the High Court and leave of the House of Lords. For an insightful study of the English appellate process, see Robert J. Martineau, *Appellate Justice in England and the United States: A Comparative Analysis* (New York: William S. Hein, 1990).

14. A famous illustration of a refusal by the Court of Appeal so to certify an appeal was the case of Dr. Robert A. Soblen in 1962. The sixty-one-year-old psychiatrist had fled the United States while under a life sentence for wartime espionage for the Soviet Union and asked Britain to grant him asylum. The British Home Office refused, and Soblen commenced a lengthy, ultimately unsuccessful, series of legal maneuvers to escape deportation. He later committed suicide rather than be sent back to the States.

man institution of the *magnum concilium*, the Great Council. The Lords do not, of course, sit in a mass body for that purpose: there were 1,185 members in December of 1988 (although the average daily attendance was but 290).[15] Instead, the legal section of the House of Lords comprises a small, highly skilled, distinguished group of judicial experts, the nine *Law Lords*, known as the *Lords of Appeal in Ordinary*, plus the Lord Chancellor, the presiding officer of the House of Lords. These ten officials, who thus constitute the final court of appeal, are augmented by any other peer who has held, or now holds, high judicial office under the Crown.

This small group of appellate[16] experts, who sit in *bancs* of five, was created originally by the Appellate Jurisdiction Act of 1876 to supplement the judicial strength of the House of Lords. It remains the sole kingdomwide judicial body, and as such always has some members from Scotland (usually two) and, on occasion, one from Northern Ireland. These few dignitaries, who have backgrounds of at least fifteen years as barristers in England or Northern Ireland or as practicing advocates in Scotland, or of two years in high judicial office, are all professional, paid judges with life peerages. They constitute the highest judicial authority of the United Kingdom of Great Britain and Northern Ireland. But in contrast to the Supreme Court of the United States, and the other U.S. federal and state courts, neither the House of Lords nor any other English or Welsh court, no matter how high, possesses the power of judicial review as that exists in the United States, namely, that ultimate power of *striking down* legislative and executive actions as being unconstitutional (which will be fully described in the following chapter). But courts in the United Kingdom do, of course, possess authority to review decisions of the Government and subordinate legislation to determine whether that is in conformity with the enabling statute or existing law, or is "reasonable." And, as noted earlier, the European Court of Justice, the Court of the European Communities, does have power to find that legislation by any of the member states is not in conformity with Directives or other binding requirements of the European Commission, of which the United Kingdom is a member.

The Judicial Committee of the Privy Council. One other appellate tribunal, sitting somewhat astride the regular court system just described, exists in the British Isles. It is the *Judicial Committee of the Privy Council*, which constitutes the final court of appeal for cases from the ecclesiastical courts of the Church of England, colonies, protectorates, trust territories, the Isle of Man, and the Channel Islands. It is also available as the ultimate appellate body for all those members of the Commonwealth that might wish to avail themselves of its services. But in recent years, with few exceptions, such as Jamaica on the death penalty, Commonwealth members have normally preferred to adjudicate their problems in their own judicial structure. The Judicial Committee of the Privy Council constituted the final court

---

15. *The International Yearbook and Statesmen's Who's Who* (East Grinstead, West Sussex, England: Thomas Skinner Directories, 1988).

16. The House of Lords has *original* jurisdiction in civil cases of claims to peerages and decisions as to disputed elections. (In criminal matters it has both original and appellate jurisdiction, but it is very rarely exercised.) All in all, the Law Lords handle about sixty cases annually. See Louis Blom-Cooper and Gavin Drewry, *Final Appeal: A Study of the House of Lords in its Judicial Capacity* (New York: Oxford University Press, 1972), and Alan Paterson, *The Law Lords* (Toronto: University of Toronto Press, 1982).

of appeal from Canada on constitutional matters until 1949, when the right to appeal to it was abolished there by statute.

Only privy councilors are eligible for membership on the Judicial Committee. In practice, most of the work has been done by the Law Lords of the House of Lords, but other high judicial officers from the United Kingdom, as well as from the Commonwealth and other jurisdictions that the Judicial Committee serves, have participated in its functions.

THE COURTS OF FRANCE

If imitation may be regarded as indication of approval, the popularity and acceptance of the French judicial system among the older as well as the newer states of the world represent such approval in the highest degree. The French administration of justice, far more than the Anglo-American, has become a model abroad. To a large extent this is attributable to its base: those legendary civil, criminal, penal, commercial, and procedural codes, drafted under the often personal direction of Napoleon Bonaparte at the end of the eighteenth century, and especially at the beginning of the nineteenth, culminating in the famous, and still very much alive, *Code Napoleon*. With full justice the French codes have been called "well-balanced pieces of jurisprudential art, utterly systematic and conveniently accessible."[17] Here French logic was truly at its best.

Yet the judicial structure that applies the codes—which, of course, have been periodically amended—is far from a simple and readily comprehensible one. A maze of tribunals stud the countryside, just as in Napoleon's time, despite a number of revisions in the hierarchy of one of the two major court systems under the de Gaulle Republic in 1959, 1963, 1965, and 1967, and under Charles de Gaulle's successors, Georges Pompidou, in 1972, Valéry Giscard d'Estaing, in 1974 and 1979, and François Mitterand, in 1981–82. The French authorities have gone so far as to take due public cognizance of the problem in an official governmental release, which noted that "judicial organization in France is exceptionally complex," but they went on to point out that "it is the product of successive contributions from centuries of our history, and in it, tradition continues to play a very important role."[18] This acknowledgment may not be of much comfort to the student of the system, but it does serve as an explanation. The government bulletin might have added that one of the reasons for the complexity and profusion of the French courts is the generally admirable notion that justice should be provided quickly, efficiently, inexpensively, and conveniently.

TWO MAJOR DIVISIONS

The courts of France are characterized by two quite separate and distinct hierarchies: first, the *ordinary* or *regular* courts; second, the *administrative courts*. (A sub-

17. Robert G. Neumann, *European and Comparative Government*, 4th ed. (New York: McGraw-Hill Book, 1968), p. 330. On the other hand, a good many women have considered them still hostile toward egalitarianism.
18. As quoted in *European Political Systems*, 3d ed., ed. Taylor Cole (New York: Alfred A. Knopf, 1959), p. 234.

structure of commercial and certain other special courts need not concern us at this juncture; they may be viewed as falling generally under the ordinary courts, although appeal from some of them lies to the Conseil d'État.) In case of doubt as to proper jurisdiction, the eight-member Tribunal des Conflits (Tribunal of Conflicts), created especially for that umpire role and headed by the Minister of Justice, who votes only in case of a tie, determines unappealably to which of the two major court systems a case goes.

Again, the chief reason for this division of responsibility between the two judicial hierarchies is an historic one. Fearful that the ordinary courts might interfere with the administrative or executive branch of the government, the legislative bodies of France, dating all the way back to the days of the Revolution, wrote into laws and constitutions specific provisions that expressly forbade judicial bodies to intervene. For example, the Law of December 22, 1789, provided: "Judicial power should not trouble local administrative agencies in the exercise of their functions." And that of August 16–24, 1790, spelled the matter out more clearly:

> The judicial functions are and will remain forever separate from the administrative functions. The judges will not be allowed, under penalty of forfeiture, to disturb in any manner whatsoever, the activities of the administrative corps, nor to summon before them the administrators, concerning their functions.[19]

This was all very well in theory, but it soon became clear that someone or something would be needed to check certain administrative excesses of power beyond the mediating and advisory services rendered by the Conseil d'État on matters in dispute between the citizen and the government. Hence the eventual adoption of the system of administrative courts—comprising the Conseil plus developing subordinate administrative tribunals—designed to check administrative abuses and at the same time retain the cherished principle of separation of powers insofar as the judicial and executive–administrative functions are concerned. The separated hierarchies have flourished, and they survive essentially unchanged in design and principle, although not in certain organizational structure and nomenclature.

THE ORDINARY OR REGULAR COURTS' HIERARCHY

On March 1, 1959, the de Gaulle government effected the first group of several contemporary judicial reforms—based upon the ordinance of December 22, 1958—chiefly designed to give the courts a corps of more specialized judges and to distribute these more equitably geographically in a rearranged system of ordinary courts, geared closely to modern demands and realistic population distribution. The effect of these changes, as augmented in 1963, 1965, and 1967, most recently and extensively in 1972, and again in 1981, is reflected in the following description.

The Court of Instance (TRIBUNAL D'INSTANCE). The first de Gaulle Reorganization Bill abolished the time-honored but outdated lowest of the ordinary courts, the local Juge de Paix—again, our friend the Justice of the Peace—and replaced

---

19. Stephan Riesengeld, "The French System of Administrative Justice: A Model for American Law," 18 Boston University Law Review 48 (1938). See also Margherita Rendel's excellent work, The Administrative Function of the French Conseil d'État (London: Weidenfeld and Nicolson, 1970).

that popular institution with a new local court of first instance in all minor civil cases, the *Tribunal d'Instance*. Theretofore *juges de paix*, armed with law diplomas, unlike most of their English and American counterparts, had brought justice, more or less, to the 3,040 cantons of France by way of a completely informal, inexpensive, and often inconsequential procedure in the usual type of petty, chiefly civil, infractions, which obliged them to "ride circuit." Since 1959, however, the new *tribunaux d'instance*, numbering 455, have existed in the capitals of the various *arrondissements*, the administrative geographical levels above the canton. Each of these courts may have several judges, who are required to live in the area of jurisdiction of the tribunal, but decisions are rendered by a single judge. The *tribunaux d'instance* and their judges have been given considerably more effective adjudicatory power than that possessed by the old *juges de paix*. Indeed, they are fully intended to become the most important basic unit in the revised judicial system.

The Court of Major Instance (TRIBUNAL DE GRANDE INSTANCE). The old civil Court of First Instance (*Tribunal de Première Instance*), one of which was located in every *arrondissement*, gave way to the newly created *Tribunal de Grande Instance*. The erstwhile criminal section of this level, the Correctional Court (*Tribunal Correctionnel*), has been retained but was moved to the criminal side of the judicial structure (see Figure 5). In place of the original 359 courts, the new 181

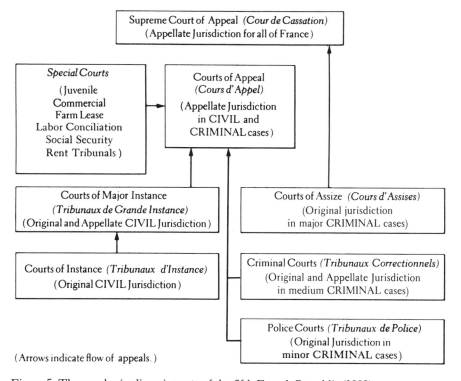

Figure 5. The regular (ordinary) courts of the fifth French Republic (1992)

tribunaux de grande instance have unlimited civil jurisdiction throughout the *région* and the *département*, the highest administrative subdivisions in France, not merely in a single *arrondissement*. According to the number of inhabitants and the "degree of economic activity,"[20] the larger *départements* are entitled to two or more of the tribunals. Each case is tried by several judges sitting *en banc*, usually three, but always an uneven number, with the decision reached by majority vote. Appeals from the *tribunaux de grande instance* lie to the Courts of Appeals.

The reforms established *Police Courts (Tribunaux de Police)* as the basic tribunal for minor offenses (e.g., parking violations) on the *criminal* side of the organizational ledger. Numbering 455 like the *tribunaux d'instance*, its judge (or judges) may well be the same individual as that at the basic civil level. The Police Court's jurisdiction is limited to offenses not exceeding penalties of sixty days in prison and/or small fines.

At the next higher level of the criminal hierarchy of the ordinary courts are the aforementioned Correctional or Criminal Courts *(Tribunaux Correctionnels)*. Like their counterparts on the civil side, the *tribunaux de grande instance*, there are 181 units, composed of three or more judges. Their jurisdiction extends to more serious offenses, covering penalties of up to five years' imprisonment and fines upward of F.F. 200.

The Assize Court (COUR D'ASSISES). The original tribunal for most criminal cases above the *tribunaux correctionnels* is the *Assize Court (Cour d'Assises)*. Its *original* jurisdiction thus extends to all major criminal cases, such as homicide, its penalty power ranging from fines to life imprisonment. A lot-chosen jury of nine "*de simples citoyens*" (plain citizens), who represent "*la souveraineté populaire*" (popular sovereignty), plus three judges sit in cases of original jurisdiction. (A verdict of guilty requires a majority of eight votes.) There are ninety-five assizes, one in each *département*, each being usually staffed with three judges from the twenty-seven units of the courts of appeal above. However, depending on the work load and the availability of personnel, two of the three judges may be drafted from a local lower tribunal, but the presiding judge is invariably a member of the *Cour d'Appel*.

The Court of Appeal (COUR D'APPEL). The 1959 and subsequent reforms did not make any substantial changes in the structure of the *Court of Appeal (Cour d'Appel)*, the appellate tribunal for civil cases from below, and none at all in the number of the twenty-seven judicial districts *(Chambres)*, each of which includes several *départements*, in which one of these tribunals operates. However, the jurisdiction of the *Cour d'Appel* was naturally extended not only to take appeals on all matters of fact from both the civil and criminal courts below but also to include the special courts alluded to earlier, and other newly created ones, particularly in the field of social and economic legislation. Thus, in addition to civil appeals from the *tribunaux de grande instance*, appeals to a *Cour d'Appel* may come from such as any one of the following (in addition to the considerable number of appeals that reach it from the *tribunaux de grande instance* in the regular hierarchy below): The aforementioned *Tribunal Correctionnel* and *Tribunal de Police*; the *Labor Conciliation Board (Conseil de Prud'hommes)*, composed of an equal number of employers and

---

20. *Ambassade de France*, French Affairs Bulletin No. 84 (May, 1959), p. 32.

employees who, chosen by their own groups for six years (one-half retiring every three years), hear disputes arising out of industrial contracts and arbitrate these; the *Commercial Court (Tribunal de Commerce)*, consisting of business persons elected by their local peers for two-year terms to act in certain statutorily designated commercial cases; the *Juvenile Court (Tribunal pour Enfants)*, one judge sitting for three years, chosen from a *tribunal de grande instance*; the *Farm Lease Court, (Tribunal des Baux Ruraux)* found at the seat of each *tribunal d'instance*; the *Social Security Court*, which consists of one judge from the *tribunal d'instance* plus two representatives of "interested parties," and the similarly composed *Rent Tribunal (Tribunal des Loyers)*. All of these special courts have several court units throughout the country. Each of the twenty-seven courts of appeal, with from three to five judges sitting—seven in the Parisian tribunal—hears a case before it entirely *de novo*; their decisions on points of *fact* are final. On points of *law* further appeal lies to the *Cour de Cassation*.

In 1963, Parliament created a complicated and controversial special tribunal to combat "subversive activity," the *Permanent Court of State Security (Cour de Sûreté de l'État)*, largely as a direct result of terrorist activity by both civil and military elements involved in the government's attempts to settle the difficult problem of Algeria. The tribunal, which consisted of civilian judges and senior military officers and sat without a jury, the sole appeal from its decisions being to the *Cour de Cassation*, was abolished in June 1981 as one of the Mitterand Administration's first acts.

The Supreme Court of Appeal (Cour de Cassation). At the pinnacle of the regular courts of France stands its Supreme Court of Appeal *(Cour de Cassation)*. Although it was largely unaffected by the Judicial Reorganization Acts of 1959, 1963, 1965, 1967, and 1981, reforms did reach it. Appropriately sitting in Paris—as ever, the heart and pulse of *la patrie*—it consists of eighty-four judges, or, more precisely, seventy-seven counselors *(conseillers)*, the Chief Justice *(Premier Président)*, and six presidents of sections; twenty-seven *conseillers-référendaires;* one *procureur général;* one *premier avocat général;* and nineteen *avocats généraux*. Its jurisdiction, which is interpretatively final in both civil and criminal cases on points of *law*, extends throughout the French Republic. The high tribunal enjoys great prestige and respect.

The *Cour de Cassation* is divided into six sections *(chambres)* of up to fifteen "*environ*" judges (and supportive personnel), each headed by a *président*, a favorite French title, with the entire tribunal presided over by the First President, or Chief Justice. Five judges constitute a quorum to hear a case. Five sections deal with civil matters (two of these with personal and family status and property). The three civil other *chambres* handle commercial and social matters, respectively. The sixth section deals with criminal appeals. Like the House of Lords, but unlike the Supreme Court of the United States, the *Cour de Cassation* has no original jurisdiction; all cases that come to it through the hierarchy of the ordinary courts do so by way of appeal from the assizes (a majority of the cases) and the courts of appeal below.

Casser, the French for "to break," or "to smash," indicates the actual role of this respected and dignified tribunal. That role is distinctly limited, for the *Cour de*

Cassation rules only on the legal appropriateness of the decision rendered—that is, it merely passes judgment on *the point of law involved in the decision,* emphatically not on the substance of the case. It neither "decides" nor "retries" a case. It simply possesses the power to quash *(casser)* the legal point of a case, and *then to remand it below for retrial* by a court of the same category and rank as the one from which it came, but not to the same court. In the event of a second appeal in a case that it had sent back down initially, the Court will give an authoritative interpretation which *must* be followed by the lower tribunal. In sum, the *Cour de Cassation's* legal holdings are binding on all lower courts.

In no sense does the *Cour de Cassation,* "an offspring of the revolutionary legislators' profound distrust of the judges,"[21] have the power of judicial review. In 1974 President Giscard d'Estaing's government did promise to consider its adoption in a future reform of the judiciary, and so did President Mitterand's as of 1981; but it had not materialized by mid-1992. Indeed, as the Court itself did rule, in a case involving the newspaper *Le National,* a law that had been "deliberately promulgated according to constitutional forms" is beyond attacks on grounds of unconstitutionality under the French system of separation of powers.[22] The absence of *bona fide* judicial review[23] is a deficiency of power the French courts have shared with their friends across the Channel. However, a system of what might be called quasi-judicial review, lodged in an extra-judicial body lying outside the judicial hierarchy, the *Constitutional Council (Conseil Constitutionnel)*—to be described in the following chapter—was adopted by the Constitution of the Fifth Republic as a successor to its rather anemic relative of the Fourth Republic, the *Constitutional Committee (Comité Constitutionnel).* But as will be readily perceived, the French system of quasi-judicial review is a far cry from the *bona fide* power and authority vested in the U.S. judiciary—although it may have been undergoing a modicum of strengthening since 1974.

ADMINISTRATIVE TRIBUNALS GENERALLY

We now turn to what is unquestionably the more novel second judicial hierarchy in France, the popular and entirely separate *administrative courts,* which are more or less foreign to the Anglo-Saxon world. Despite some significant post–World War II modifications, especially in England and Wales, beginning with the Rules of the Supreme Court of 1977 that radically amended its Order 53 and were incorporated into the Supreme Court Act of 1981 (discussed later), the United Kingdom and the United States still hold, by and large, to the ancient Anglo-Saxon principle that "the King can do no wrong"—which, in effect, signifies that the sovereign, the state, cannot be sued without its expressed consent. This concept of governmental immunity, dating from the reign of Henry II (1154–89), has its legal roots in the prerogatives of the King of England, who was the "Fountainhead of Justice

21. Mauro Cappelletti, *Judicial Review in the Contemporary World* (Indianapolis: Bobbs-Merrill, 1971), p. 13.
22. See 7 *Political Studies* 51–53 and 60–61 (February 1959).
23. Except insofar as the *Conseil d'État* (see pp. 266ff., *infra*) reviews decrees under Arts. 38 and 39 of the Constitution. For recent developments see William Safran, *The French Polity,* 3d ed. (New York Longmans Books, 1991).

and Equity" under the law of the feudal state. During the sixteenth century, the personal immunity of the monarch was enlarged to include that of the state—hence the King (State) can do no wrong. Accordingly, in the Anglo-Saxon world of our day the acts of government officials are viewed as the acts of ordinary citizens and are judged by exactly the same rules of law and before the same courts. After all, it is one of the underlying principles of the philosophy of democratic government that any citizen is presumably capable of participating in it (a notion dear to the heart of President Andrew Jackson, and well popularized by him, who used it to justify, and some erroneously contend, to invent, the "spoils system"). Thus, as one of Britain's great students of government, A. V. Dicey, often put it, every government official, from the Prime Minister on down to the lowliest clerk, is "under the same responsibility for every act done without legal justification as any other citizen."[24]

Until fairly recently (see earlier discussion) this has meant that a British or American citizen who believes himself or herself to have been aggrieved or injured by a government official in either of the two lands and wants to take action would have to sue that official—who, in turn, would have to justify his or her actions at the bar of the regular courts. Thus, if citizen John Smith believes that he has been wronged or maltreated by Sheriff James Doe in the latter's capacity as an officer of the law, he may bring suit. But such a suit must be brought against Sheriff James Doe, in a regular court of jurisdiction, not against Doe's state of Virginia, whose laws he was presumably enforcing (or not against the United States, if the arresting officer had been a federal official), and the suit will normally read Smith v. Doe. Moreover, to collect damages, which would presumably come out of Doe's pocket, citizen Smith must demonstrate successfully that Sheriff Doe has exceeded his discretionary authority under the law, an extremely difficult task in most instances. However, as alluded to earlier, the adoption in England and Wales of new rules, capped by the Supreme Court Act of 1981, render feasible the application of what the British term "judicial review" in order to seek redress through prerogative writs, such as mandamus, certiorari, or prohibition. Not judicial review in the same sense as it is understood in the United States, the English and Welsh practice facilitates application for redress for alleged grievances against government directly to a court of law.[25]

Whatever the underlying philosophical justifications for personal liability of governmental officials, its practical implications are often unsatisfactory, to say the least, and may well be fraught with danger both to the individuals involved and the system they serve and under which they live. Among these implications and the lessons of experience are the possibility that an official may perform his or her duties timidly or haphazardly or not perform them in accordance with his or her most considered judgment but according to expediency; the difficulty, already alluded to, of collecting from an individual government servant; and the question why, in performing a governmental duty, a civil servant should be personally

24. For example, see his Introduction to the Study of the Law of the Constitution, 10th ed. (New York: Macmillan, 1961).
25. See especially H. W. R. Wade, Administrative Law, 5th ed. (Oxford: Oxford University Press, 1982), particularly pp. 572–76.

responsible in the first place. Moreover, there are the inevitable delays in getting a case docketed in the courts; the slowly grinding judicial process, especially in as large and litigation-happy a country as the United States; and the inconvenience and expense of bringing a case to court. All these represent factors that may well, and often do, outweight any monetary recompense that might eventually accrue to the plaintiff.

In recognition of these very real problems, England and the United States have gradually begun to provide tribunals in which the state may be sued directly. No abandonment of the old philosophy of a single, unified judiciary has taken place, nor is it likely to take place in the near future. However, both countries have shown considerable interest in the institution of the Scandinavian *ombudsman*,[26] a sort of "people's watchdog" over administrative abuses, who commands a good deal of influence and esteem, though little direct power, and who disposes of some thousand cases annually with dispatch and expertise. Indeed, with the enactment of the Parliamentary Commissioner Act of 1967, Britain adopted a limited, rather restricted, and watered down version of it.

Moreover, both Britain and the United States have taken some tangible steps in the direction of rendering matters a bit more palatable to government employees and citizens alike. Thus, Britain adopted the Crown Proceedings Act of 1947, which, under certain circumstances, makes the government responsible for the actions of its servants. Purposely provided with many loopholes and exceptions, the act nevertheless now enables ordinary citizens to sue the government in the same manner and before the same tribunals "as if the Crown were a fellow-citizen." Hence, the injured or aggrieved party sues the state as a matter of right.[27] Furthermore, the act makes government departments responsible for common law as well as statutory duties. However, it should be noted that the act confines itself, more or less, to the *non-law-enforcing* agencies of government, thus leaving unchanged the path of claims that might arise under the law-enforcing units, such as police, military services, foreign affairs. Nevertheless, this unquestionably valuable statute does represent a wholesome and welcome change.[28]

What this statute did for Britain, the Federal Tort Claims Act of 1946 had done, broadly speaking, for the United States one year earlier, insofar as the federal government is concerned. Under it, a citizen who feels he or she has been injured or aggrieved by an employee of the federal government, or the government itself, may bring suit in any civil action other than a breach of contract (which is not a tort) against the United States for negligence or wrongful acts, no maximum monetary ceiling existing on the claim. The Act requires lawsuits against governmental

26. See the compendium on the *ombudsman*, edited by D. C. Rowat, *The Ombudsman: Citizen's Defender*, 2d ed. (London: Allen & Unwin, 1968), containing chapters on Britain and the United States; the chapter on the United States is my "The Need for Ombudsmen in the United States." See also my "Denmark's *Folketingets Ombudsmand*: A People's Watchdog," 20 *Public Administration Review* 152 (Summer 1960), and the compendium, edited by Roy V. Peel, "The Ombudsman or Citizen's Defender: A Modern Institution," 377 *The Annals* (May 1968), pp. iii–240.

27. Thus, if a citizen is run over by a Post Office van, he can sue the Post Office instead of proceeding against the Attorney General by Petition of Right.

28. For a brief evaluation of the Act, see Harry Street, *Government Liability: A Comparative Study* (Cambridge: Cambridge University Press, 1953).

agencies to be decided by a judge, not a jury, and does not allow punitive damages. The statute, as amended in 1966, also renders possible making claims of less than $25,000—and above that with the approval of the Attorney General—directly to the head of any federal agency alleged to be responsible for a loss caused by "negligent or wrongful act of omission of an employee," but the agency is *not required* to sanction such claims. Appeals under the provisions of the Tort Claims Act may be taken to the U.S. Court of Appeals for the Federal Circuit and, under certain conditions, to the regular constitutional court hierarchy.[29]

The Court of Claims, established in 1855, redesigned and reconstituted as the U.S. Claims Court in 1982 (as was demonstrated in some detail in chapter 4), is itself a vehicle for citizens to sue the federal government for damages and as such represents a modification of the "sovereign-can-do-no-wrong" principle. But its limited jurisdiction is confined to contractual, tax, and other non-tort claims against the government of the United States. The Tort Claims Act contains, as its British counterpart, many deliberate exceptions and ambiguities. For example, it *excludes*

> any claim based upon an act or omission of an employee of the Government exercising due care, in the exercise of a statute or regulation, whether or not such statute or regulation be valid, or based upon the exercise or performance or the failure to exercise or perform a discretionary function or duty on the part of a federal agency or an employee of the Government, whether or not the discretion involved be abused. . . . [30]

but it is hoped that it personifies a salutary trend in adjudication. In effect, the act, together with the U.S. Claims Court and the U.S. Tax Court (see pp. 144ff., *supra*), represents one of three forms of "consent in advance" under which a citizen may now bring suit against the federal government.[31]

Mention should be made of the remarkable series of Burger Court cases stripping government officials of their immunity from damage suits for violating rights established under the federal Constitution or federal law. In *Butz v. Economou*, 438 U.S. 478 (1978), the Court permitted suits against *federal* officials who were or should have been aware that they were violating constitutional rights except when it is demonstrated that absolute immunity is essential for conducting the public

29. Thus, early in 1988, in a series of rulings, the U.S. Supreme Court let die the last appeal by civilians suing the federal government for deaths, cancers, and other illnesses that were allegedly caused by open-air atomic bomb tests in Nevada from 1951 to 1962 (see the detailed account in *The New York Times*, January 12, 1988). On the other hand, the Court, also in 1988, eased the way to sue the United States for safety policy violations if, and only if, officials violated "specific mandatory directives contained in statutes, regulations, etc." (*Berkowitz v. United States*, 56 LW 4549).

30. It should not be forgotten, of course, that in both countries exist numerous *quasi-judicial* agencies and/or tribunals that, among other duties, *adjudicate administratively* claims on the government. These are, for example, the "independent" regulatory commissions and agencies in the United States, and the ministerially appointed "special administrative tribunals" in the United Kingdom, established to deal with cases arising out of the application of social policy, for example, the Licensing Authority for Public Service Vehicles. An important development in connection with these British tribunals was the creation of the Council on Tribunals, established under the Tribunals and Inquiries Act of 1958, following the Franks Committee Report; it is charged with general supervision over all British administrative tribunals. For a perceptive explanation and analysis, see H. W. R. Wade, "The Council on Tribunals," *Public Law* 351 (1960).

business. In *Monell v. New York City Dept. of Social Services*, 436 U.S. 658 (1978), *local* governments were made subject to damage suits for civil rights violations. In *Owen v. City of Independence, Missouri*, 445 U.S. 622 (1980), the Court made it clear that a *municipality* may not assert the good faith of its officials as a defense. If a constitutional violation occurs, a city may be held accountable for damages for the actual loss in court. An even more liberal decision was *Maine v. Thiboutot*, 448 U.S. 1 (1980), in which the Court ruled that private citizens, under the Civil Rights Act of 1871, are entitled to sue their own states whenever state policy allegedly violates any federal law. By reducing the barrier to suing government officials, the Court has made it easier for private citizens to assert equal protection and due process claims. Indeed, the 1871 statute—known as Section 1983, Title 42, of the United States Code, Annotated—which had been passed by a Reconstruction Congress to protect former slaves from maltreatment by local officials, is clearly becoming an ever more powerful pool for challenging a widening array of official actions that have nothing to do with race.[32] The law permits suits by anyone whose *federal* constitutional or legal rights may have been violated by a public official or agency acting by authority of state law; a state or local official; a local governmental body; a county; or a school board.

That there are limits to the Court's largesse, however, was demonstrated by several contemporary rulings, including two in 1981 (both 6:3). In the first, the Court held that local governments are immune from "punitive damages" that go beyond *compensating* the victim for injuries caused by violations of constitutional rights (*Newport v. Fact Concerts*, 453 U.S. 247). In the second, the Court determined that individuals could not sue for damages against alleged unconstitutional behavior by state and local officials if the laws involved in the claim themselves provide adequate remedies for the alleged violations—here the federal water pollution laws (*Middlesex County v. National Sea Clammers*, 453 U.S. 1). In 1988, ruling 7:1, the Court, giving local governments broad protection from civil rights suits, limited liability to violations resulting from *officially* sanctioned policies.[33] And in 1989 the Court specifically declined to open *states* to the same liability it had applied to *local* government in the *Monell* case. On the other hand, in 1984 the Court, dividing 5:4, had ruled that state and local (and, by implication, federal) judges may be subjected to limited civil rights for damages to pay the legal fees of criminal suspects whose rights they had allegedly violated (*Pulliam v. Allen and Nicholson*, 466 U.S. 522). In 1985, in a seven-opinion case, it held that federal cabinet officers have but "qualified" immunity: that they cannot act in willful disregard of the law.[34] In 1989 it held 9:0 that cities can be sued for damages if the failure to give police officers or other employees adequate training results in the violation

---

31. For an approach designed to simplify as well as facilitate suits against government, see Peter H. Schuck, *Suing Government: Citizen Remedies for Official Wrongs* (New Haven: Yale University Press, 1983).
32. See the excellent column by Linda Greenhouse, "1871 Law Now Used for Many Causes," *The New York Times*, August 26, 1988, p. B6.
33. *City of St. Louis v. Praprotnik*, 485 U.S. 112.
34. *Mitchell v. Forsyth*, 472 U.S. 511. But compare the states' absolute immunity against antitrust suit for their official action (*Columbia v. Omni Outdooor Advertising*, 59 LW 5429 [1991]).

of someone's constitutional rights.[35] And two years later it ruled 8:0 that state officials can be forced to pay monetary damages out of their own pockets if their official actions violate people's rights.[36]

THE FRENCH ADMINISTRATIVE COURTS

The hierarchy of courts that administers the *droit administratif* in France is very much part and parcel of the governmental system, however separated it is from the ordinary courts. To the French—and to many careful observers in the Anglo-Saxon world as well—theirs is the only logical system of supervising the administrative branch of the government, not only because of its rapid, convenient, and efficient adjudicatory process, but also because of the expertise inherent in the judicial personnel that staff its administrative courts. This is even more remarkable because the French administrative courts are actually more closely linked to the executive than to the judicial branch. Evolving gradually since revolutionary days, the predominantly "judge-made" *droit administratif* has a long and honorable history, beginning with the creation of the first *Council of State (Conseil d'État)* under Napoleon Bonaparte in the year VIII (1799).

The structure of the French administrative court system is infinitely less complicated than the regular court system. It consists of but two levels: first, the *Regional Councils* or *Administrative Tribunals (Tribunaux Administratifs)*, since they are arranged no longer in *départements*, as of yore, but in twenty-three national regions plus Paris; second, the famous multipurpose and powerful *Council of State (Conseil d'État)* at the apex. (There are also a number of special collateral administrative tribunals, sometimes known as "inferior councils," such as the *Council of Public Instruction [Conseil d'Instruction Publique]* and the *Draft Review Board [Conseil Militaire de Revision]*, which may be omitted for present purposes.)

The Regional Councils (TRIBUNAUX ADMINISTRATIFS). It is to the *Tribunal Administratif* of the appropriate region that a French citizen with a complaint against the administrative branch of *La République* or local authorities turns initially. In almost all instances involving the *droit administratif*, the *Tribunal Administratif* acts as the administrative court of first instance. It has power either to annul an illegal decision or action or to cause payment of damages. It is staffed by able, experienced civil servants of whom a majority have been recruited either directly from the *École Nationale d'Administration* (discussed later), or from the administrative branch itself—provided they have law degrees—or are merit appointees who have passed competitive examinations; a few have come from political or semipolitical posts.[37] The caliber of the four to six members of each *tribunal administratif*—one *président*, of course, and three to five *conseillers*—is almost always outstanding even at this first instance level.

The administrative court system of France is both simple and inexpensive: all

---

35. *City of Canton v. Harris*, 57 LW 4270.
36. *Hafer v. Melo*, 60 LW 4001.
37. Margherita Rendel, "The Political Impact of the French *Conseil d'Etat*." Paper presented at the meeting of the International Political Science Association, Montreal, Canada, Aug. 21, 1973, p. 3.

a plaintiff at the bar of his *Tribunal Administratif* has to do is to execute and file the official complaint form, which costs practically nothing. Normally, the tribunal will conduct the investigation of the complaint by way of written statements to both sides of the complaint. Sometimes an oral hearing is held, at which the litigants may either present arguments personally or through legal counsel. When the tribunal is ready to render a decision it will do so publicly; usually that settles the matter. Far more often than not, the complaining *citoyen* wins his or her suit, and can then look forward to normally speedy compensation from the public treasury for any damages. So prevalent have these citizen victories been that considerable criticism has ensued among both legal scholars and practitioners who believe that the administrative court system has caused the French government to be "too tough on itself," that there exists what might be viewed as a distinct bias *against* it.

The Council of State (LE CONSEIL D'ÉTAT). With its appellate jurisdiction from the *tribunaux administratifs*[38]—approximately 20 to 25 percent of the lower tribunals' decisions are appealed[39]—as well as original jurisdiction in certain stipulated "important" and/or "delicate" cases, the *Conseil d'État*, housed in the Palais-Royal, justly enjoys enormous prestige. Actually, it is far more than a merely administrative tribunal; only one of its seven sections—a most renowned one, the *Litigation Section (Section du Contentieux)*—deals with the *droit administratif*. The other six are concerned with drafting of legislation for the cabinet, giving advisory opinions on legislative and executive matters, supervising rules of public administration, and performing sundry other significant functions in the governmental process. In the words of one of the foremost students of the *Conseil d'État*, it is its policy "to ensure a reasonable and proper administrative method, and to try to achieve consistency and completeness, so that administrative agencies are not driven to stretching or twisting the law in order to carry out their policies."[40] Plainly, it will insist on what it regards as proper procedures.

Roughly one-half of the Council's membership of 271, headed titularly by the Minister of Justice but effectively by its vice-president, works in the administrative court section, and its personnel, supported by twenty-two high-ranking *fonctionnaires*, is uniquely trained and qualified. The members of that Litigation Section are recruited in two ways, as are those of the other branches of the council: the "second class auditors" *(auditeurs de 2e classe)*—those who enter the council at the bottom of the ladder—are drawn from graduates of the three-year course at the justly celebrated *École Nationale d'Administration*, which provides expert personnel destined for the highest levels of the corps of civil servants in France. Admission to the *École* is by stiff competitive examination, most of the applicants having had some training in the law or in political science. The school graduates only about fifty to sixty students annually, a figure that represents at most 5 percent of

38. As a result of law, enacted on December 31, 1987, and initiated on January 1, 1989, five special *cours administratifs* were created as an intermediate appellate tribunal between the Regional Councils and the Council of State. They are located in Paris, Bordeaux, Lyon, Nancy, and Nantes.
39. *Les Cahiers Français*, Nos. 156–157, September–December 1972, "La Justice," Notice 1 (Paris: La Documentation Française, 1972).
40. Margherita Rendel, *The Administrative Function of the French* Conseil d'État, op. cit., p. 248.

the initial applicants. A small proportion of the personnel of the higher echelons of the council come from the upper levels of the ministries, the ranks of the prefects, or the legal profession, but most are promoted from lower echelons. France is justly proud of her distinguished corps of *conseillers* in the Council of State; it is truly an elite civil service body and richly merits its great prestige and acclaim.

Nine subsections, numbered chronologically, constitute the section of the council which handles the *droit administratif*. Each of these subsections consists of a *président* and a number of *conseillers*. Although all the subsections operate independently in readying cases for decision, they may hear cases either singly or in pairs. Important cases are considered by the full "judicial section," consisting of the President of the section, the two Deputy Presidents, the *conseillers* (who are also members of the Administrative Section), and the *rapporteurs*. The highest organ of the *Conseil d'État* is its Litigation Assembly, for which are reserved cases of "extreme importance." It is composed of the Vice-President of the *Conseil*, the Presidents of the sections, the Deputy Presidents of the Litigation Section, the Presidents of the subsections that originally dealt with the case, and the *rapporteur*. Decisions by all of these organs are of equal weight, and they are final and binding.

Review Procedure. As already illustrated briefly, the procedure for obtaining review in the French administrative court hierarchy is as simple as it is inexpensive. In large measure, it is inexpensive because the French state assumes responsibility for investigating both the facts and the law involved in a plaintiff's petition. Moreover, because under the French inquisitorial procedure the judiciary plays an active role throughout the administration of justice, the role of the petitioner is reduced to a summary statement as to the alleged facts and the relief prayed. He or she may request either of two types of review actions: (1) proceedings for the annulment of an *ultra vires*—beyond powers—administrative act *(recours pour excès de pouvoir)* or (2) proceedings to order some type of affirmative administrative action, such as payment of monetary damages *(recours de pleine jurisdiction)*. Most petitions for review fall into the first category. Having received the petition, the administrative tribunal takes over; petitioner need not even retain legal counsel in the first type of case unless he or she chooses to do so. In any event, the petitioner need not worry: his or her interests will be amply guarded by the mills of the *droit administratif*. Moreover, the Council of State, *on its own cognizance*, has added a third ground for review going beyond the concept inherent in *ultra vires* (i.e., an official action beyond the scope of legal authority) namely, the famous French administrative law concept of *détournement de pouvoir*, best translated as rank *abuse* of power. In its eyes, *abuse* of power is a concept different from that of an illegal *application* of power, which is governed by the first review category under *ultra vires*.[41] Its deliberations are secret.

Once the Council of State has granted the availability of review, it must define the extent or scope of its reviewing power on the merits. This is especially true in the first category cases, under which the legality of an administrative action may be challenged on three grounds, all of which fall under the *ultra vires* con-

---

41. Roughly comparable to the Anglo-Saxon distinction between "*misfeasance*" and "*malfeasance*."

cept: (1) lack of jurisdiction, (2) failure to observe procedures defined by law, and (3) error of law. To these three the special category of abuse of power is then added.

Even President de Gaulle had to bow to a Council ruling in 1962 under the *excès de pouvoir* category: He had set up a special military tribunal to try terrorists who aided European extremists in Algeria. But when the lawyer for one of the leaders of the terrorist secret army charged de Gaulle with "an illegal administrative act" in setting up the tribunal, and took the matter to the Council of State, the latter agreed and ruled it illegal indeed. (One year later Parliament created the now abolished Court of State Security, described earlier.) On the other hand, later that year the Council found itself impotent in the face of its defiance by de Gaulle in connection with his call for a national referendum on direct election of the *Président* (see p. 292, *infra*). It did, however, win a qualified victory over him in May 1968 when, following its declaration of unconstitutionality of de Gaulle's proposed national referendum on his leadership during a series of sustained student uprisings, the *Président*, sensing a hostile political climate, yielded. (Yet he won an unprecedented victory in the national *elections* he then called instead of the abortive referendum.) The *Conseil d'État's* role of constitutional watchdog, manifested in these illustrations, prompted one expert, Professor Mauro Cappelletti, to assert that it has come near to assuming the power to invalidate statutes per se—since it seems now ready to review "all *executive* acts, decrees, and ordinances, even those legislative in nature . . . in adversary, party-initiated proceedings for conformity with applicable statutes, the provisions of the Constitution, and the general principles of law."[42] But it still lacks actual power to declare a law unconstitutional.

Evaluation. It is hardly surprising that the Council of State is literally swamped with petitions for action and review! The same applies to the lower rung of the administrative court system. The French people look up to it as a reliable and virile guardian of individual rights against administrative encroachment. Moreover, they have great faith in the ability of these high-class civil servants to dispose of the thousands upon thousands of cases that reach them every year, as well they might. Small wonder that Anglo-Saxon states have given considerable thought to the adoption of a similar system. The Task Force of the Second Hoover Commission in the United States, for one, urgently suggested some form of administrative court system for our federal government.

Not only does the French system provide for fuller review of administrative action than the average Anglo-Saxon one, but the cost of litigation is smaller, accessibility to the courts is greater, review is more easily available, scope of review is larger, state liability for damages is less circumscribed, and settlement is far more prompt and efficient. The French state, whatever the wisdom of its philosophy of government here may be, simply considers itself totally liable for service-connected faults of public officers and state agencies. That liability has even been extended to cover most cases in which the damage is caused by personal fault of public officials, for the administrative courts have held that such faults are often inseparably connected with the administrative service of which the official is an agent. In such cases, the state indemnifies the damages to the injured citizen.

42. *Judicial Review in the Contemporary World*, op cit., p. 18. Margherita Rendel (see fnn. 19, 37, 40, and 43 of this chapter) concurs readily.

Yet the French state accepts liability not only for fault under the *droit administratif* but, as outlined earlier, also for risk. In other words, if proper administrative action results in an unequal burden on, or a social injustice to, a citizen, the state bears the cost of equalizing the burden—without the need to introduce a private bill in the legislature. In effect, the *droit administratif* is developing in the direction of absolute liability to ensure equitable sharing among all citizens of the burden of government action. This may well be far from an unmixed blessing, but the French administrative court system, with the *Conseild'État* standing at its apex, has operated so successfully and has proved to be such a bulwark against arbitrary actions by the centralized state, that it richly merits the careful attention that has increasingly been extended to it by students and practitioners of government alike. And the political implications of its jurisdictional growth in constitutional matters—perhaps "its most important development in the last quarter of [the] century"[43]—will undoubtedly enhance that attention.

43. Margherita Rendel, "The Political Impact of the French *Conseil d'État*," op. cit. p. 12.

7

Judicial Review: I—The Supreme Power

DEFINING JUDICIAL REVIEW

Certainly the most controversial and at the same time the most fascinating role of the courts of the United States in general, and of the Supreme Court in particular, is the exercise of the power of *judicial review*. It is commonly viewed with almost equal amounts of reverence and suspicion. Edward S. Corwin regarded it as "American democracy's way of hedging its bet."[1] Although about seventy countries—chiefly in Western Europe, Latin America, Africa, Australasia and the Far East—had adopted some form of judicial review by late 1991, in its full majesty and range it is a power that the *ordinary* courts (i.e, those that are part of the formal judicial hierarchy) of only a handful of lands possess effectively. Chief among these are Australia, Brazil, Canada, India, Pakistan, and Japan, of whom all except Japan have federal systems of government, with Australia and Canada[2] being closest to

1. Review of Benjamin F. Wright's article, "Growth of American Constitutional Law," 56 *Harvard Law Review* 487 (1942).
2. In 1982, in connection with its adoption of a "Charter of Rights and Freedom," Canada embraced an intriguing "legislative override." Under this process, if either the federal or a provincial government believes that the Canadian Supreme Court has erroneously struck down one of their statutes as being violative of a Charter right, it is authorized to *reenact* the offending legislation with the proviso that it should take effect "notwithstanding" the Charter. Thus, on December 8, 1988, the Quebec government, in what was only the third time the provision was invoked, overrode a 5:0 Supreme Court decision, thereby voting to continue to require that only the French language be used on outdoor commercial signs in the province.

270

the American model.[3] Experience has demonstrated that countries which have exhibited stable or moderately stable traditions of judicial review are generally characterized by (1) regime stability, (2) a competitive political party system, (3) significant horizontal power distribution, (4) a strong tradition of judicial independence, and (5) a high degree of political freedom.[4]

Briefly stated, judicial review in the United States comprises the power of any court to *hold unconstitutional and hence unenforceable any law, any official action based on a law, or any other action by a public official that it deems*— upon careful, normally painstaking, reflection and in line with the canons of the taught tradition of the law as well as judicial self-restraint—*to be in conflict with the basic law, in the United States its Constitution.* In other words, by invoking the power of judicial review, which, of course, may "approve" as well as "veto", a court applies the *superior* of two laws, which at the level of the federal judiciary of the United States signifies the Constitution instead of the legislative statute or some action by a public official allegedly or actually based on it.

In the United States, the chief subject in this treatment of judicial review, this highly significant instrument of power, "the principled process of enunciating and applying certain enduring values of our society"[5] is possessed theoretically by every court of record, no matter how high or low on the judicial ladder. Although admit-

---

3. For an informative summary discussion, see K. C. Wheare, *Federal Government,* 4th ed. (New York: Oxford University Press, 1964, reprinted in 1980), ch. 4, "The Constitution, the Courts, and the Law." Judicial review in Switzerland is confined to cantonal legislation, but serious consideration has been given to its introduction at the *federal* level. India's Supreme Court had been flexing its muscles increasingly in the 1950s and 1960s. For example, it struck down 10:1 Prime Minister Indira Gandhi's Bank Nationalization Act, ruling that the July 1969 takeover of the fourteen biggest banks was "hostile discrimination" because other Indian banks and foreign banks were excluded (*The New York Times,* February 11, 1970, p. 1). By 1975 it had held more than one hundred federal and state laws unconstitutional. But late in that year came Mrs. Gandhi's "emergency" usurpation of all effective governmental power, and the Indian judiciary, especially its Supreme Court, lay low. However, on Mrs. Gandhi's defeat in early 1977, the Court reasserted itself markedly. See Robert L. Hardgrave, Jr., *India: Government and Politics in a Developing Nation,* 3d ed. (New York: Harcourt Brace Jovanovich, 1980). Yet it did not take very long on her return to power in 1980 to note an indubitable return to the *status quo ante* (see, among others, Ved Metha, *A Family Affair: India Under Three Prime Ministers* [New York: Oxford University Press, 1982] and Aroun Thourie, *Mrs. Gandhi's Second Reign* [New Delhi: Vikas Publishing House, 1983]). Buttressed by the enactment in 1982 of the Canadian Charter of Rights and Freedom, Canada's Supreme Court evinced rapid cognizance of its implied powers to flex its interpretative muscle, frequently citing America's initial embrace of judicial review under the leadership of John Marshall (see, for example, Michael T. Kaufman, "Canada's Judiciary Starts Using New Powers," *The New York Times,* May 6, 1984, p. 14). See also Christopher S. Wren, "Canada Supreme Court Rules Solely English Laws Invalid," ibid., June 14, 1985, p. A3; see 2, *supra.* Sweden adopted a somewhat limited form of judicial review, with a legislative override, relative to any act of the executive or Parliament (the *riksdag*) in 1974 (but had not employed it significantly as of mid-1991). The applicable provision (Article 14 of Chapter 11) of Sweden's Constitution (as amended in 1981) concludes as follows: "However, if the provision [at issue] has been decided by the *riksdag* or by the Government, the provision may be set aside only if the inaccuracy is obvious and apparent."

4. See the perceptive paper by Donald P. Kommers, "Cross-National Comparisons of Constitutional Courts: Toward a Theory of Judicial Review," presented at the Annual Meeting of the American Political Science Association, Los Angeles, Calif., September 11, 1970.

5. Alexander M. Bickel, *The Least Dangerous Branch* (Indianapolis: Bobbs-Merrill, 1962), p. 58.

tedly it happens rarely, it is not at all impossible for a judge in a low-level court of one of the fifty states to declare a federal law unconstitutional; such a decision would quite naturally at once be appealed to higher judicial echelons for review. Conscious of the nature and purpose of federalism and, especially, the need to permit legislative bodies to act in accordance with their judgment, no matter how unwise that may be at times, courts are understandably loath to invoke the judicial veto. Yet their power to do so, and particularly that of the Supreme Court of the United States, serves as an omnipresent and potentially omnipotent check on the legislative and executive branches of government. Thus, although that highest tribunal has to date (fall 1992) declared but 141 or 142 provisions of *federal* laws unconstitutional in whole or in part,[6] out of a total of almost 95,000 public and private laws enacted, some 1200 *state* laws and provisions of *state* constitutions[7] have run wholly or partly afoul of that judicial checkmate since 1789—about 850 of these after 1870. An example of the latter action is the Court's unanimous ruling in *Torcaso v. Watkins*:[8] there it struck down a provision of the Maryland Constitution on the ground that to compel officeholders to declare belief in God constituted a "religious test for public office" that invaded the individual's right to religious freedom. In many ways, the Court's power over state actions is of more significance to the federal system than the much more publicized, and more well-known, power over federal actions. It ought to be added that approximately 110 *federal* executive branch ordinances have also been invalidated since the turn of the century.

Tables 8 and 9 illustrate in some detail the power of judicial review over *legislative enactments* as exercised by the Supreme Court at the *federal level only*. But it is interesting to note that more statutes of the State of Louisiana have been declared unconstitutional than those of any other state, Louisiana being the only one of the fifty to employ *civil* (Roman or statutory) *law* as its judicial system (see Chapter 1, *supra*). Regarding the sparse number of federal statutes held unconstitutional by the post-"anti New Deal" Supreme Court in recent times, the sixty-nine provisions of congressional enactments that as of this writing (fall 1992) have fallen since 1937—actually since 1943—all but ten did so because they infringed on certain personal rights and liberties safeguarded under the Constitution. Those sixty-eight instances were as follows:

1. *Tot v. United States* (1943).[9] A statutory presumption that a known criminal in possession of firearms or ammunition must have carried them in violation of the Federal Firearms Act of 1938, Section 2(f), was invalidated 8:0 as a violation of the due process of law clause of the Fifth Amendment.

---

6. It was not until 1965 that the Supreme Court invalidated an *act of Congress* on First Amendment expression grounds (*Lamont v. Postmaster General*, 38k U.S. 301) and not until 1971 one (actually just a segment thereof) in a First Amendment religion case (*Tilton v. Richardson*, 403 U.S. 672).

7. In an unpublished monograph, "Judicial Review of State Laws and the National Policy-Making Role of the Supreme Court in Protecting Fundamental Rights," David G. Barnum suggests the appropriate figure to be 848 between 1809 and 1974 (undated manuscript, p. 11). That would appear to be on the low side, however.

8. 367 U.S. 488 (1961).

9. 319 U.S. 463.

Table 8. U.S. Supreme Court Declarations of Unconstitutionality of Federal Statutes (in Whole or in Part), I (arranged chronologically in accordance with tenure of Chief Justices)[a]

Time Span	Chief Justice	Number of Declarations of Unconstitutionality	Commentary
1798–1801	Jay	0	
	J. Rutledge	0	Weak, placid Court
	Ellsworth	0	
1801–1835	Marshall	1	1803: *Marbury v. Madison*
1836–1864	Taney	1	1857: *Dred Scott v. Sandford*
1864–1873	Chase	10	1870: *Legal Tender cases*
1874–1888	Waite	9	1883: *Civil Rights cases*[b]
1888–1910	Fuller	14 (15)	1895: *Income Tax cases*
1910–1921	White	12	1918: *Child Labor case*
1921–1930	Taft	12	1923: *Minimum Wage case*
1930–1936	Hughes	14	Of these, 13 came in 1934–36!
1936–1941	Hughes	0	The New Deal Court emerges following the "switch-in-time that saved nine" in 1937
1941–1946	Stone	2	New Libertarian emphasis
1946–1953	Vinson	1	Abstemious Court
1953–1969	Warren	25	High watermark of Libertarianism
1969–1986	Burger	34	Chiefly First, Fifth, and Fourteenth Amendment concerns
1986–present[a]	Rehnquist	6	Moderate move to the right
		141 (142)	

[a] As of fall 1992.
[b] Consolidated five different cases in *one* opinion (here counted as one).

2. *United States v. Lovett* (1946).[10] Section 304 of the Urgent Defense Appropriation Act of 1943, which barred the salaries of certain specifically named federal employees, was struck down 8:0 as violative of the constitutional prohibition against a Bill of Attainder.

3. *United States v. Cardiff* (1952).[11] Section 704 of the Food, Drug, and Cosmetic Act, which deals with factory inspection, fell 8:1 as unconstitutionally vague under the due process clause of the Fifth Amendment.

4. *Bolling v. Sharpe* (1954).[12] The federal companion case to the *Public School Segregation Cases*, involving an 1862 federal statute that, insofar as pertinent here,

10. 328 U.S. 303.
11. 344 U.S. 174.
12. 347 U.S. 497. (The states cases' citation is *Brown v. Board of Education of Topeka, Kansas, et al.*, 347 U.S. 483.)

Table 9. U.S. Supreme Court Declarations of Unconstitutionality of Federal Statutes (in Whole or in Part), II[a]

Under Chief Justice	Recorded Declaration Number	Citation of Case and Year Decided	Vote
Marshall	1	*Marbury v. Madison,* 1 Cranch 137 (1803)	4:0
Taney	2	*Dred Scott v. Sandford,* 19 Howard 393 (1857)	
Chase	3	*Gordon v. United States,* 2 Wallace 561 (1865)	
Chase	4	*Ex parte Garland,* 4 Wallace 33 (1867)	5:4
Chase	5	*Reichart v. Felps,* 6 Wallace 160 (1868)	8:0
Chase	6	*The Alicia,* 7 Wallace 571 (1869)	8:0
Chase	7/8/9[b]	*Hepburn v. Griswold,* 8 Wallace 603 (1870)	4:3
Chase	10	*United States v. DeWitt,* 9 Wallace 41 (1870)	9:0
Chase	11	*The Justices v. Murray,* 9 Wallace 274 (1870)	9:0
Chase	12	*United States v. Klein,* 13 Wallace 128 (1872)	7:2
Waite	13	*United States v. Reese,* 92 U.S. 214 (1876)	7:2
Waite	14	*United States v. Fox,* 95 U.S. 670 (1878)	9:0
Waite	15/16[c]	*Trade Mark cases,* 100 U.S. 82 (1879)	9:0
Waite	17	*United States v. Harris,* 106 U.S. 629 (1883)	8:1
Waite	18	*Civil Rights cases,*[d] 109 U.S. 3 (1883)	8:1
Waite	19	*Boyd v. United States,* 116 U.S. 616 (1886)	7:2
Waite	20	*Baldwin v. Franks,* 120 U.S. 678 (1887)	7:1
None[e]	21	*Callan v. Wilson,* 127 U.S. 540 (1888)	8:0
Fuller	22	*Monongahela Nav. Co. v. U.S.,* 148 U.S. 312 (1893)	8:0
Fuller	23	*Pollock v. Farmers' L. & T. Co.,* 157 U.S. 429 (1895)	6:2
Fuller	23A[f]	*Pollock v. Farmers' L. & T. Co.,* 158 U.S. 601 (1895)	5:4
Fuller	24	*Wong Wing v. United States,* 163 U.S. 228 (1896)	8:0
Fuller	25	*Kirby v. United States,* 174 U.S. 47 (1899)	6:2

Under Chief Justice	Recorded Declaration Number	Citation of Case and Year Decided	Vote
Fuller	26	Jones v. Meehan, 175 U.S. 1 (1899)	9:0
Fuller	27	Fairbank v. United States, 181 U.S. 283 (1901)	5:4
Fuller	28	James v. Bowman, 190 U.S. 127 (1903)	6:2
Fuller	29	Matter of Heff, 197 U.S. 488 (1905)	8:1
Fuller	30	Rassmussen v. United States, 197 U.S. 516 (1905)	9:0
Fuller	31	Hodges v. United States, 203 U.S. 1 (1906)	7:2
Fuller	32	Employers' Liability cases, 207 U.S. 463 (1908)	5:4
Fuller	33	Adair v. United States, 208 U.S. 161 (1908)	6:2
Fuller	34	Keller v. United States, 213 U.S. 138 (1909)	6:3
Fuller	35	United States v. Evans, 213 U.S. 297 (1909)	9:0
White	36	Muskrat v. United States, 219 U.S. 346 (1911)	9:0
White	37	Coyle v. Oklahoma, 221 U.S. 559 (1911)	7:2
White	38	Choate v. Trapp, 224 U.S. 665 (1912)	9:0
White	39	United States v. Hvoslef, 237 U.S. 1 (1915)	8:0
White	40	Thames & Mersey Mar. Ins. Co. v. United States, 237 U.S. 19 (1915)	8:0
White	41	Hammer v. Dagenhart, 247 U.S. 251 (1918)	5:4
White	42	Knickerbocker Ice Co. v. Stewart, 253 U.S. 149 (1920)	5:4
White	43	Eisner v. Macomber, 252 U.S. 189 (1920)	5:4
White	44	Evans v. Gore, 253 U.S. 245 (1920)	7:2
White	45	United States v. Cohen Grocery Co., 255 U.S. 81 (1921)	6:2
White	46	Weeds, Inc. v. United States, 255 U.S. 109 (1921)	6:2
White	47	Newberry v. United States, 256 U.S. 232 (1921)	5:4
Taft	48	United States v. Moreland, 258 U.S. 433 (1922)	5:3

Table 9. (Continued)

Under Chief Justice	Recorded Declaration Number	Citation of Case and Year Decided	Vote
Taft	49	Child Labor Tax case, 259 U.S. 20 (1922)	8:1
Taft	50	Hill v. Wallace, 259 U.S. 44 (1922)	9:0
Taft	51	Keller v. Potomac Electric Co., 261 U.S. 525 (1923)	9:0
Taft	52	Adkins v. Children's Hospital, 261 U.S. 525 (1923)	5:3
Taft	53	Washington v. Dawson, 264 U.S. 219 (1924)	7:2
Taft	54	Miles v. Graham, 268 U.S. 501 (1925)	8:1
Taft	55	Trusler v. Crooks, 269 U.S. 475 (1926)	9:0
Taft	56	Myers v. United States, 272 U.S. 52 (1926)	6:3
Taft	57	Nichols v. Coolidge, 274 U.S. 531 (1927)	9:0
Taft	58	Untermyer v. Anderson, 276 U.S. 440 (1928)	6:3
Taft	59	National Life Insurance Co. v. United States, 277 U.S. 508 (1928)	6:3
Hughes	60	Heiner v. Donnan, 285 U.S. 312 (1932)	6:2
Hughes	61	Booth v. United States, 291 U.S. 339 (1934)	9:0
Hughes	62	Lynch v. United States, 292 U.S. 571 (1934)	9:0
Hughes	63	Panama Refining Co. v. Ryan et al., 293 U.S. 388 (1935)	8:1
Hughes	64	Perry v. United States, 294 U.S. 330 (1935)	5:4
Hughes	65	Railroad Retirement Bd. v. Alton R. R., 295 U.S. 330 (1935)	5:4
Hughes	66	Schechter Poultry Corp. v. United States, 295 U.S. 495 (1935)	9:0
Hughes	67	Louisville Joint Stock Land Bank v. Radford, 295 U.S. 555 (1935)	9:0
Hughes	68	United States v. Constantine, 296 U.S. 287 (1935)	6:3
Hughes	69	Hopkins Federal Savings and Loan Association v. Cleary, 296 U.S. 315 (1935)	9:0
Hughes	70	United States v. Butler, 297 U.S. 1 (1936)	6:3
Hughes	71	Rickert Rice Mills v. Fontenot, 297 U.S. 110 (1936)	9:0

Under Chief Justice	Recorded Declaration Number	Citation of Case and Year Decided	Vote
	72	*Carter v. Carter Coal Co.,* 298 U.S. 238 (1936)	5:4
Hughes	73	*Ashton v. Cameron County Water Improvement District,* 298 U.S. 513 (1936)	5:4
Stone	74	*Tot v. United States,* 319 U.S. 436 (1943)	8:0
None[g]	75	*United States v. Lovett,* 328 U.S. 303 (1946)	8:0
Vinson	76	*United States v. Cardiff,* 344 U.S. 174 (1952)	8:0
Warren	77	*Bolling v. Sharpe,* 347 U.S. 497 (1954)	9:0
Warren	78	*United States ex rel Toth v. Quarles,* 350 U.S. 11 (1955)	6:3
Warren	79	*Reid v. Covert and Kinsella v. Krueger,*[h] 354 U.S. 1 (1957)	6:2
Warren	80	*Trop v. Dulles,* 356 U.S. 86 (1958)	5:4
Warren	81	*Kinsella v. United States ex rel Singleton,*[h] 361 U.S. 234 (1960)	7:2
Warren	82	*Grisham v. Hagan,* 361 U.S. 278[h] (1960) plus *McElroy v. United States,* 361 U.S. 281 (1960)[i]	6:2
Warren Warren	83	*Kennedy v. Mendoza-Martinez* plus *Rusk v. Cort*[l] 372 U.S. 144 (1963)	5:4
Warren	84		
Warren	85	*Schneider v. Rusk,* 377 U.S. 163 (1964)	5:3
Warren	86	*Aptheker v. Secretary of State,* 378 U.S. 500 (1964)	6:3
Warren	87	*Lamont v. Postmaster-General* plus *Fixa v. Heilberg,*[l] 381 U.S. 301 (1965)	8:0
Warren	88	*United States v. Brown* 381 U.S. 437 (1965)	5:4
Warren	89	*United States v. Romano,* 382 U.S. 136 (1965)	9:0
Warren	90	*Afroyim v. Rusk,*[k] 387 U.S. 253 (1967)	5:4
Warren	91	*United States v. Robel,* 389 U.S. 258 (1967)	6:2
Warren	92	*Marchetti v. United States,* 390 U.S. 39 (1968)	7:1
Warren	93	*Grosso v. United States,* 390 U.S. 62 (1968)	7:1

Table 9. (Continued)

Under Chief Justice	Recorded Declaration Number	Citation of Case and Year Decided	Vote
Warren	94	Haynes v. United States, 390 U.S. 85 (1968)	7:1
Warren	95	United States v. Jackson, 390 U.S. 569 (1968)	6:2
Warren	96	Washington v. Legrant (Shapiro v. Thompson) 394 U.S. 618 (1969)	6:3
Warren	97–101[l]	Leary v. United States, 395 U.S. 6 (1969)	9:0
Burger	102	Turner v. Untied States, 396 U.S. 398 (1970)	6:2
Burger	103	Schacht v. United States, 398 U.S. 58 (1970)	5:4
Burger	104	Oregon v. Mitchell, 400 U.S. 112 (1970)	5:4
Burger	105/106[m]	Blount v. Rizzi and United States v. The Book Bin, 400 U.S. 410 (1971)	9:0
Burger	107	Tilton v. Richardson, 403 U.S. 672 (1971)	9:0
Burger	108	Chief of Capitol Police v. Jeanette Rankin Brigade, 409 U.S. 972 (1972)	9:0
Burger	109[l]	Richardson v. Davis and Richardson v. Griffin, 409 U.S. 1069 (1972)	6:3
Burger	110	United States Department of Agriculture v. Murry, 413 U.S. 508 (1973)	5:4
Burger	111	United States Department of Agriculture v. Moreno, 413 U.S. 528 (1973)	7:2
Burger	112/113[n]	Frontiero v. Richardson, 411 U.S. 677 (1973)	8:1
Burger	114	Jiminez v. Weinberger, 417 U.S. 628 (1974)	8:1
Burger	115	Weinberger v. Wiesenfeld, 420 U.S. 636 (1975)	8:0
Burger	116/117[o]	Buckley v. Valeo, 421 U.S. 1 (1976)	8:0/6:2
Burger	118/119[p]	National League of Cities v. Usery, 426 U.S. 833 (1976)	5:4
Burger	120	Califano v. Goldfarb, 430 U.S. 199 (1977)	5:4
Burger	121	Califano v. Silbowitz, 430 U.S. 924 (1977)	9:0
Burger	122	Railroad Retirement Board v. Kalina, 431 U.S. 909 (1977)	9:0

Under Chief Justice	Recorded Declaration Number	Citation of Case and Year Decided	Vote
Burger	123	*Marshall v. Barlow's, Inc.* 436 U.S. 307 (1978)	5:3
Burger	124	*Califano v. Westcott,* 443 U.S. 76 (1979)	9:0
Burger	125/126^q	*United States v. Will,* 449 U.S. 200 (1981)	8:0
Burger	127	*Common Cause v. Schmitt,* 455 U.S. 129 (1982)	4:4^r
Burger	128	*Railway Labor Executive Association v. Gibbons,* 455 U.S. 457 (1982)	9:0
Burger	129	*Northern Pipeline Construction Co. v. Marathon Pipeline Co.,* 458 U.S. 50 (1982)	6:3
Burger	130	*United States v. Grace,* 461 U.S. 171 (1983)	8:1
Burger	131^s	*Immigration and Naturalization Service v. Chadha,* 462 U.S. 919 (1983)	7:2
Burger	132	*Bolger v. Youngs Drugs,* 463 U.S. 60 (1983)	8:0
Burger	133	*FCC v. League of Women Voters of California,* 468 U.S. 364 (1984)	5:4
Burger	134	*Regan v. Time, Inc.,* 468 U.S. 641 (1984)	8:1
Burger	135	*F.E.C. v. National Conservative Pol. Action Comm.* 470 U.S. 480 (1985)	7:2
Burger	136	*Bowsher v. Synar,* 478 U.S. 714 (1986)	7:2
Rehnquist	137^k	*F.E.C. v. Massachusetts Citizens for Life,* 479 U.S. 238 (1986)	5:4
Rehnquist	138^k	*Boos v. Barry,* 485 U.S. 312 (1988)	5:3
Rehnquist	139	*Sable Communications v. F.C.C.,* 492 U.S. 115 (1989)	9:0
Rehnquist	140^i	*United States v. Eichman and United States v. Haggerty,* 496 U.S. 310 (1990)	7:2
Rehnquist	141	*Metropolitan Washington Airport Authority v. Citizens for the Abatement of Aircraft Noise,* 59 LW 4660 (1991)	6:3
Rehnquist	142	*New York v. United States,* 60 LW 4603 (1992)	6:3

^{a} As of fall 1992.
^{b} Same case but parts of three statutes.
^{c} Same case but two different statutes.
^{d} Consolidated five cases, in *one* opinion.

Table 9. *(Continued)*

---

e Chief Justice Waite died before the case was heard and was not replaced by Chief Justice Fuller until after it had been decided.
f Rehearing of the earlier case.
g Chief Justice Stone had died before the case was heard and Chief Justice Vinson did not take his place on the bench until after it had been decided. (Counted under Stone.)
h See pp. 280–81, *infra*, for elaboration.
i Two separate cases but the same statute and the same citation.
j The two cases were reported under the same citation, but there were two declarations of unconstitutionality involving segments of two separate statutes. (See p. 281, *infra*.)
k Although the holding refers specifically only to one aspect of the statute, its breadth may be interpreted as reaching several more.
l One citation but involving four provisions of one statute and one of another.
m Two separate cases invalidating two different statutes, but same citation.
n One citation but involving two different statutes.
o Two different provisions of the same statute, but differing votes: 8:0 on constitutionality, 6:2 on expenditure limits.
p Two different amendments to the same statute.
q Same case and same issue, but two different statutes.
r Affirmed by an equally divided Court (4:4), Justice O'Connor not sitting, *per curiam*, but with full opinion affirming the declaration of unconstitutionality by two lower federal courts of record.
s Case could be read (6:3) as declaring unconstitutional 212 statutes with similar provisions, 62 of these still active. But here *Chadha* is viewed as just a *single* declaration of unconstitutionality.

provided for separate schools for white and black children, was unanimously held unconstitutional as a violation of the due process of law clause of the Fifth Amendment.

5. *United States ex rel Toth v. Quarles* (1955).[13] The Court held unconstitutional 6:3, Article 3A of the Uniform Code of Military Justice when applied to a *former* member of the U.S. Air Force as violative of the guarantees of the civilian judicial process inherent in Article III of the Constitution.

6–8. *Reid v. Covert* and *Kinsella v. Krueger* (1957), later coupled with *Kinsella v. United States ex rel Singleton and Grisham v. Hagan* and *McElroy v. United States* (1960).[14] These cases concerned a series of related decisions in which the Court, over a three-year period, dealt with several aspects of Article 2(11) of the Uniform Code of Military Justice, and, by votes ranging from a high of 7:2 to a low of 5:4, found some of these unconstitutional as applied to various civilians accompanying the armed forces. The pertinent sections of the Code in these multiple cases fell as violative of the individuals' rights under Article III and Amendments V and VI of the Constitution, including the right to a trial by jury, indictment by grand jury, and public trial in a civilian court before an impartial jury of one's peers.

9. *Trop v. Dulles* (1958).[15] Here the narrowly divided Court struck down Section 401(G) of the Nationality Act of 1940, holding that Congress had exceeded its mil-

13. 350 U.S. 11.
14. 354 U.S. 1; 361 U.S. 234; 361 U.S. 278 and 361 U.S. 281, respectively.
15. 356 U.S. 86.

itary and expatriation powers in making desertion in time of war punishable by expatriation. The Court ruled 5:4 that to expatriate for such a reason constituted "cruel and unusual punishment," forbidden by Amendment VIII.

10 and 11. *Kennedy v. Mendoza-Martinez* and *Rusk v. Cort* (1963).[16] Although these two cases were decided together (and under the same citation), the Court's 5:4 decision in effect held two sections of different congressional statutes unconstitutional as violative of procedural safeguards found in Amendments V and VI. Thus affected were Section 349(a)(10) of the Immigration and Nationality Act of 1952 and Section 401(j) of the Nationality Act of 1940, which had provided for automatic expatriation of U.S. citizens who, in order to evade military service, either fled the country or refused to return upon draft-board notification.

12. *Schneider v. Rusk* (1964).[17] In another citizenship decision the Supreme Court here invalidated 5:3 Section 352(a)(1) of the 1940 Immigration and Nationality Act, chiefly on due process of law grounds under the Fifth Amendment. Section 352 had deprived *naturalized* American citizens of their citizenship if they returned to the territory of their birth and then resided there for more than three years.

13. *Aptheker v. Secretary of State* (1964).[18] Here a 6:3 majority of the Court declared unconstitutional on its face Section 6 of Title I of the Subversive Activities Control Act of 1950, which proscribed the application for or the use of a U.S. passport by any member of an organization required to register under the Act's provisions. The Court held that Section 6 "too broadly and indiscriminately restricts the right of travel and thereby abridges the liberty guaranteed by the Fifth Amendment."

14. *Lamont v. Postmaster-General* and *Fixa v. Heilberg* (1965).[19] In its *first* decision voiding an Act of *Congress* on the ground that it violated the freedom of speech guarantee of the First Amendment, the Court unanimously declared unconstitutional a section of the Postal Services and Federal Employees Salary Act of 1962, which provided that all mail matter originating abroad, except first class mail, that the Secretary of the Treasury held to be "communist political propaganda," was to be detained and that the addressee was to be notified that it could be delivered only if the addressee sent a card stating that desire.

15. *United States v. Brown* (1965).[20] The Court, in one of its rare applications of the Bill of Attainder prohibition, held 5:4 that Section 504 of the Labor–Management Reporting and Disclosures (Landrum–Griffin) Act of 1959, making it a crime for a member of the Communist party to serve as an officer or employee of a labor union, was in fact such an unconstitutional piece of legislation.

16. *United States v. Romano* (1965).[21] Unanimously, the Court reversed a conviction under a section of the Internal Revenue Code providing that the presence of a defendant at the site of an illegal still was sufficient to authorize a conviction

16. 372 U.S. 144.
17. 377 U.S. 163.
18. 378 U.S. 500.
19. 381 U.S. 301.
20. 381 U.S. 437.
21. 382 U.S. 136.

for possession and control of that still, unless the defendant satisfactorily explained his or her presence to the jury. It held such a statutory presumption of guilt to be an unconstitutional violation of substantive due process of law under the Fifth Amendment.

17. *Afroyim v. Rusk* (1967).[22] Here, in an enormously significant decision, the Court ruled 5:4 that Congress, under Section 1 of Amendment Fourteen, lacks the constitutional authority to pass any laws that strip American citizens of their nationality *without their express consent*. Specifically, it declared unconstitutional that section of the already tattered Nationality Act of 1940 which deprived U.S. citizens of their nationality if they voted in a foreign election—and thereby overruled a 1958 decision that had held 5:4 to the contrary.[23]

18. *United States v. Robel* (1967).[24] On that term's last Opinion Day, the Court struck down 6:2 as an unconstitutional infringement of the freedom of association guarantees of the First Amendment a section of the much-battered Subversive Activities Control Act of 1950 that made it a crime for Communist party members to work in defense plants.

19–21. *Marchetti v. United States* and *Grosso v. United States* and *Haynes v. United States* (1968).[25] Here, in three separate 7:1 decisions delivered simultaneously, the Court declared unconstitutional as a violation of the Fifth Amendment's privilege against compulsory self-incrimination two separate sections of the Gambling Tax Act of 1951 in the first two cases named and one of the Firearms Act's of 1934 in the third.

22. *United States v. Jackson* (1968).[26] A section of the "Lindberg Anti-Kidnapping Law" (12–1A of the Title 18 of the Criminal Code), dealing with pleas and sentencing, fell as violative of the self-incrimination and jury guarantees of Amendments V and VI, respectively.

23. *Washington v. Legrant* (1969).[27] The Court declared unconstitutional, as a violation of the Fifth Amendment's due process of law, a District of Columbia statutory provision that denied welfare assistance to those residents of the District who had not resided there for at least one year prior to their application for assistance.

24–28. *Leary v. United States* (1969).[28] Unanimously, the Court here struck down five provisions of two federal laws dealing with marijuana controls as violative of the Fifth Amendment's strictures against compulsory self-incrimination. One law required payment of a tax for transportation of marijuana; the other established that anyone with marijuana in his or her possession upon entrance into the United States could be presumed to have imported it knowingly.

22. 387 U.S. 253.
23. *Perez v. Brownell*, 356 U.S. 44.
24. 389 U.S. 258.
25. 390 U.S. 39; 390 U.S. 62; and 390 U.S. 85, respectively. (Two separate laws were involved, the two cases first cited coming under the first.)
26. 390 U.S. 569.
27. 394 U.S. 618 (This is usually cited under *Shapiro v. Thompson*, the state welfare case with which it was consolidated.)
28. 395 U.S. 6.

29. *Turner v. United States* (1970).[29] Similarly to the *Leary* decisions, the Court subsequently held unconstitutional 6:2 a provision of the Narcotics Import and Export Act that created a presumption that possessors of cocaine knew of its illegal importation into the United States.

30. *Schacht v. United States* (1970).[30] Down unanimously, on grounds of crass violation of First Amendment freedom of expression, went a quaint federal law that made it a crime for an actor to wear U.S. military apparel in a theatrical production if the portrayal reflected "discredit" on the armed forces—it was perfectly acceptable to wear it if it was a "favorable" portrayal!

31. *Oregon v. Mitchell* (1970).[31] While the Court *upheld* 5:4 a newly enacted federal law that provided for the lowering of the voting age to eighteen in *national* elections, it ruled unconstitutional (Justice Black, the author of both opinions, switching to the other side) a collateral provision of the law that would also have lowered the voting age similarly for *state and local* elections as violative of Article I, Sec. 2 of the U.S. Constitution governing state electoral authority.

32 and 33. *Blount v. Rizzi* and *United States v. The Book Bin* (1971).[32] Two so-called "mail block" laws were unanimously held to constitute unconstitutional invasions of First Amendment guarantees of freedom of expression, because they authorized the Post Office Department to cut off postal service to mail order houses that deal in pornography, without providing prompt judicial review of the issues of "pornography."

34. *Tilton v. Richardson* (1971).[33] A provision of the Federal Higher Educational Assistance Act of 1963 here fell unanimously afoul of First Amendment strictures against the violation of the principle of separation of church and state, by permitting church-affiliated schools to use buildings erected with federal construction funds for religious purposes after a twenty-year hiatus.

35. *Chief of Capitol Police v. Jeannette Rankin Brigade* (1972).[34] This saw another unanimous declaration of unconstitutionality of a federal statute, one enacted in 1882, on First and Fifth Amendment invasion grounds. The law, adjudged an impermissibly vague restriction of free speech and assembly, had banned "all unauthorized demonstrations" on the grounds of the U.S. Capitol.

36. *Richardson v. Davis* and *Richardson v. Griffin* (1972).[35] Here the Court struck down 6:3, as an unconstitutional infringement of due process of law guarantees under the Fifth Amendment, Section 203(a) of the Social Security Act of 1935, as amended, which provided that "illegitimate children get benefit payments only to the extent payments to widows and other children of wage earners do not exhaust 'maximum family' benefits."

37 and 38. *United States Department of Agriculture v. Murry* and *United States*

29. 396 U.S. 398.
30. 398 U.S. 258.
31. 400 U.S. 112.
32. 400 U.S. 410.
33. 403 U.S. 672.
34. 409 U.S. 972.
35. 409 U.S. 1069.

Department of Agriculture v. Moreno (1973).[36] By votes of 5:4 and 7:2, respectively, the Court here backed challenges to the constitutionality of Sections 5(b) and 3(e) of the Food Stamp Act of 1964, as amended, as violations of due process of law under the Fifth Amendment. In the former instance, the program denied eligibility to certain household residents on "over-age" grounds, in the latter to "unrelated" persons; the Court's majorities regarded both provisions as at war with the legislation's stated purpose.

39 and 40. *Frontiero v. Richardson* (1973).[37] With only Justice Rehnquist in dissent, the Court struck down as violative of the due process of law clause of the Fifth Amendment sections of 37 and 10 U.S.C. that provided for greater statutory dependency benefits to servicemen than to servicewomen.

41. *Jiminez v. Weinberger* (1974).[38] Again with only Justice Rehnquist dissenting, the Court declared unconstitutional, also on due process grounds, a provision of the Social Security Act of 1935, as amended—42 U.S.C. 416(h)(3)(B)—which denied benefits to illegitimate children of a disabled mother just because they were born after the disability began.

42. *Weinberger v. Wiesenfeld* (1975).[39] Unanimously (8:0) the Court, once again on due process grounds, struck down another provision of the Social Security Act, Section 402(g), which authorized survivors' benefits for the widows of deceased workers with children but denied them to widowers in the same position.

43 and 44. *Buckley v. Valeo* (1976).[40] By vote of 6:2 and 8:0 the Court threw out two separate provisions of the Federal Election Campaign Act of 1974, the former on First Amendment (freedom of expression) grounds, the latter as a violation of the separation of powers because of the manner in which the FEC commissioners were to be appointed.

45 and 46. *National League of Cities v. Usery* (1976).[41] By identical 5:4 votes the Court declared unconstitutional as an impermissible extension of the congressional power over interstate commerce two amendments to the Fair Labor Standards Act, added in 1966 and 1974, that mandated the application of the act's minimum wage provisions to state and municipal employees. The majority held the amendments to be coercive.

47. *Califano v. Goldfarb* (1977).[42] Another 5:4 decision declared unconstitutional as a violation of due process of law of the Fifth Amendment an OASDI requirement that rendered it more difficult for widowers than for widows to collect Social Security survivor's benefits. (42 U.S.C., Section 402[f][1][D].)

48. *Califano v. Silbowitz* (1977).[43] In a summary *per curiam* decision the Court, without recorded dissent, struck down, again on due process grounds, yet another

36. 413 U.S. 508 and 413 U.S. 528, respectively. (This involved two separate decisions governing two distinct sections of the statute.)

37. 411 U.S. 677. (The provisions of the two separate statutes were disposed of in the same case.)

38. 417 U.S. 628.

39. 420 U.S. 636.

40. 421 U.S. 1.

41. 426 U.S. 833. Nine years later, with Justice Blackmun switching his *Usery* vote, the Court overruled that opinion 5:4 in *Garcia v. San Antonio Metropolitan Transit Authority,* 469 U.S. 528 (1985).

42. 430 U.S. 199.

43. 430 U.S. 934.

OASDI provision, 42 U.S.C., Section 402(c)(1)(C), that required men but not women seeking Social Security benefits through their spouse's earned benefits to prove that they received at least one-half of their support from said spouse.

49. *Railroad Retirement Board v. Kalina* (1977).[44] In still another deprivation of due process holding, the Court declared unconstitutional 45 U.S.C., Section 231(a)(c)(3)(ii), which permitted the wife of a retired railroad employee to qualify for her spouse's annuity without a showing of actual dependency, while requiring the husband of a retired female railroad employee to demonstrate actual dependency in order to qualify for such benefits.

50. *Marshall v. Barlow's, Inc.* (1978).[45] A fractured 5:3 Court here held unconstitutional the statutory authorization for warrantless inspections pursuant to Section 8(a) of the Occupational Health and Safety Act (OSHA) of 1970, deeming it violative of the Fourth Amendment's unreasonable searches and seizure strictures.

51. *Califano v. Westcott* (1979).[46] One more Social Security case saw a provision of 42 U.S.C. Section 407 fall 9:0 (5:4) on violation of due process *cum* equal protection grounds. It had provided for welfare payments to families with an unemployed father but *not* in cases in which a mother became unemployed. The Court was unanimous on the provision's unconstitutionality, but it split 5:4 on statutory construction grounds.

52 and 53. *United States v. Will* (1981).[47] Two statutes (enacted in 1977 and 1982, respectively) that rescinded judicial pay increases *after* they had already gone into effect were declared unconstitutional 8:0 as a violation of Article III, Section 1. (Public Laws 94–440, 90 Stat. 1439 and 96–86, 93 Stat. 565).

54. *Common Cause v. Schmitt* (1982).[48] A U.S. Court of Appeals decision that the Presidential Election Campaign Fund Act's prohibition against expenditure over $1,000 by unauthorized political committees to further a presidential candidate's election violates the First Amendment (and that federal district courts lack jurisdiction to hear private citizens' suits to enforce the act) was affirmed by an equally divided 4:4 Court.

55. *Railway Labor Executives' Association v. Gibbons* (1982).[49] Unanimously, the Court held unconstitutional Section 701 of the Staggers Rail Act of 1980, which had reenacted an earlier lower-federal-court-voided segment (Sects. 106 and 110) of the Rock Island Railway Transition and Employee Assistance Act (RITA) that had been deemed an uncompensated taking of private property for a public purpose in violation of the Just Compensation Clause of the Fifth Amendment. The Supreme Court ruled 9:0 that the Staggers Act's provisions as reenacted are repugnant to Article I, Section 8, Clause 4 of the Constitution, which empowers Congress to enact "uniform Laws on the subject of Bankruptcies throughout the United States."

44. 431 U.S. 909.
45. 436 U.S. 307.
46. 443 U.S. 76.
47. 449 U.S. 200.
48. 455 U.S. 129.
49. 455 U.S. 457. But in 1991 the Court refused to hear a challenge to that law's section that makes it a crime to hold a demonstration on the marble plaza in front of the Supreme Court building (*Pearson v. United States*, 60 LW 3257).

56. *Northern Pipeline Construction Co. v. Marathon Pipeline Co.* (1982).[50] Struck down 6:3 Section 241(a) of the Bankruptcy Act of 1978 for giving excessive power to bankruptcy judges who lacked the constitutional protections of Article III judges (such as "good behavior" tenure and guarantees against salary reductions while in office).

57. *United States v. Grace* (1983).[51] A section of federal law, barring the distribution of leaflets or picketing on the public sidewalk surrounding the Supreme Court of the United States in Washington, D. C., was declared unconstitutional 8:1 as a *prima facie* violation of the First Amendment's freedom of speech, press, and assembly guarantees.

58. *Immigration and Naturalization Service v. Chadha* (1983).[52] The "one house" legislative veto provisions, contained in Section 224(c)(2) of the federal immigration and naturalization statute, were declared unconstitutional 7:2 as "severable" encroachment on executive power and as *ultra vires* congressional authority under Article I, Section 7. (In effect, the Court's sweeping holding declared unconstitutional 6:3 one- and/or two-house legislative vetos in fully 212 statutes enacted by Congress since 1932, with sixty-two of these still active in 1983.)[53]

59. *Bolger v. Youngs Drugs* (1983).[54] Section 3001(e)(2) of Title 39 U.S.C., which prohibited the mailing of unsolicited advertisements for contraceptive devices, was declared unconstitutional 8:0 as a violation of First Amendment guarantees of freedom of expression.

60. *FCC v. League of Women Voters of California* (1984).[55] In a 5:4 decision, the Court declared unconstitutional the provision of 47 U.S.C. 399, which had barred editorials on public radio and TV stations that receive funding from the Corporation for Public Broadcasting, as an impermissible violation of the First Amendment's freedom of expression.

61. *Regan v. Time, Inc.* (1984).[56] A complex and multiopinioned 8:1 ruling struck down as a First Amendment violation 18 U.S.C. Section 504's mandated *exception* to 18 U.S.C. 474's ban on use of photographic reproductions of U.S. currency "for philatelic, numismatic, educational, historical, or newsworthy purposes," as discriminating on basis of *content* of the photograph and message it conveys "and thus cannot survive First Amendment challenge as reasonable time, place, and manner regulation."

62. *F.E.C. v. National Conservative Political Action Committee* (1985).[57] By a 7:2 vote the Court struck down as an unconstitutional infringement on First Amendment rights of free speech and association 9012 (f) of 26 U.S.C. 9011, which limited the amount of money political action committees (PACs) could spend on behalf of presidential nominees.

50. 458 U.S. 50.
51. 461 U.S. 171.
52. 462 U.S. 919.
53. *Chadha* is here counted as just a *single* declaration of unconstitutionality, however.
54. 463 U.S. 60.
55. 468 U.S. 364.
56. 468 U.S. 641.
57. *F.E.C. v. National Conservative Political Action Committee,* 470 U.S. 480 (1985).

63. *Bowsher v. Synar* (1986).[58] In a dramatic four-opinion 7:2 holding, the Court struck down as a violation of the separation of powers a key provision (Sec. 251) of the "Gramm–Rudman–Hollins" Balanced Budget and Emergency Deficit Control Act of 1985, which had vested in the Comptroller General of the United States certain actions deemed "executive" by the Court's majority.

64. *FEC v. Massachusetts Citizens for Life* (1986).[59] By a 5:4 margin, the Court declared unconstitutional as a violation of the First Amendment the regulation in the federal election campaign statute (Sec. 316) that prohibited *independent* political expenditures by nonprofit advocacy groups.

65. *Boos v. Barry* (1988).[60] In a splintered multiopinion 5:3 decision, the Court declared unconstitutional as a violation of the First Amendment a section of the District of Columbia's Code (§22–1115, enacted in 1938) that had made it a crime to display signs within 500 feet of any foreign embassy or any other building used by foreign officials in Washington, D.C., if the signs would bring the foreign government involved into "public odium" or "disrepute."

66. *Sable Communications v. FCC* (1989).[61] In a unanimous opinion, the Court ruled that the portion of the 1988 federal ban on commercial telephone messages (§223 (b) of the Federal Communications Act of 1934) that are merely "indecent" but not "obscene" violates the First Amendment right of adults to access of such messages. (But §223 (a) as to obscene was upheld 6:3.)

67. *United States v. Eichman* (1990).[62] In an emotion-charged 5:4 holding, the Court—in one of Justice Brennan's last opinions—declared unconstitutional the Federal Flag Protection Act of 1989 that had proscribed the knowing mutilation, defacing, defiling, burning, maintaining on the floor or ground, or trampling of "any flag of the United States." (One year earlier, employing similar reasoning, the Court had struck down 5:4 a portion of the Texas Criminal Code, forbidding the same type of conduct, in *Texas v. Johnson*.[63])

68. *Metropolitan Washington Airports Authority v. Citizens for the Abatement of Aircraft Noise* (1991).[64] Voting 6:3, the majority, led by Justice Stevens, struck down as a violation of the separation of powers a part of the legislation establishing an authority to operate Dulles International and National Airports, reasoning that Congress had impermissably created a review board consisting of nine members of Congress with a veto power over majority decisions by the executive authority.

69. *New York v. United States* (1992).[65] By a 6:3 vote the Court struck down §5 (d)(2)(c) of the 1985 Low-Level Radioactive Waste Policy Act, which had been designed to force states to find disposal sites for low-level radioactive waste.

58. 478 U.S. 714.
59. 479 U.S. 238.
60. 485 U.S. 312.
61. 492 U.S. 115.
62. 496 U.S. 310.
63. 491 U.S. 397.
64. 59 LW 4660.
65. 60 LW 4603.

After the famous decision in *Marbury v. Madison* in 1803 in which Chief Justice Marshall enunciated the doctrine of judicial review—although it was not really the first instance of its application (see this chapter, pp. 303–05) no other federal legislation and only thirty-six state statutes were declared unconstitutional by his Court during the remaining thirty-two years of his long tenure of thirty-four years.[66] Nevertheless, the Marshall Court wielded immense power and, guided by the dominant figure of the great Chief Justice, probably did more than either of the other two branches of the national government to make the young United States a strong, vigorous, powerful nation, and its Constitution a living, effective, elastic basic law. Not until Chief Justice Taney's painful decision in *Dred Scott v. Sandford* (19 Howard 393) in 1857 was another federal statute struck down by the Court; and the greatest crisis evoked by that power of the Supreme Court did not arrive until, dominated by the doctrinaire conservatives among the so-called Nine Old Men, the Court in 1934–36 declared unconstitutional no fewer than thirteen New Deal laws.

JUDICIAL REVIEW ABROAD

As already indicated, the practice of judicial review in its ultimate and awesome U.S. application of striking down, of utterly negating, legislative and/or executive action, is not likely to be found in nonfederal states. Hence the other two major subject lands of this study either do not (as in the case of Britain, except in the sense of the aforedescribed "application for judicial review" under the Supreme Court Act of 1981) or did not, until the adoption of the Constitution of 1958 (in the case of France), clothe their courts with the *bona fide* power of judicial review as it is known in America, Australia, and Canada, for example. And in the instance of the French Fifth Republic, it is "judicial review" only to a limited degree, if indeed it is classifiable as "judicial review" at all (although the *Conseil d'État* is able to review the constitutionality of *réglements d'administration publique*). But as noted earlier, the Giscard d'Estaing government, which came into office in May 1974, pledged moves toward *bona fide* judicial review. Although it had not achieved that when it gave way to the Mitterand administration in 1981, it did see enacted into law a provision expanding the role of the Constitutional Council (discussed later), and President Mitterand has promised to move in the spirit of his predecessor.

BRITAIN

In Britain, Parliament is supreme in the sense that any law that has been enacted by it and has received the routine approval of the Crown becomes the law of the land and is *ipso facto* beyond overturning by the British courts. By virtue of the ancient English writ of *quo warranto*[67] the courts do, of course, possess the authority to interpret legislation (which also continually crops up in ordinary litigation), and particularly administrative action based on it, for all government officials are

---

66. The Circuit Court of Appeals for the District of Columbia did strike down by a vote of 2:1 a congressional statute in *U.S. v. Benjamin More* only six months after *Marbury v. Madison*.
67. It requires a person to show by what authority he or she exercises a "public office, franchise, or liberty."

potentially accountable to the courts for their actions. The construction, the interpretation, and the meaning of the words of an act of Parliament are a matter of law for the courts. *But the courts may not strike down the law itself.* In the immortal words of Walter Bagehot, the famous British economist and journalist, "there is nothing the British Parliament cannot do except transform a man into a woman and a woman into a man." Although he expressed this fact of governmental life more than a century ago, it is still fundamentally true today (albeit not in medical contemplation!).

The people of Britain, although no longer as homogeneous as of yore, are deeply steeped in the common experience of centuries, tradition, custom, and a firm if hardly uncritical faith in Westminster and Whitehall, and they continue to be generally resolved to entrust their treasured freedoms to the good judgment of their representatives assembled in Parliament. These representatives are duly checked—"controlled" is a more appropriate term—by the powerful executive arm, the political parties, the continuing dedication to the "cricket" factor, and public opinion itself. The British courts are broadly revered and esteemed as necessary concomitants of the democratic process, but emphatically not to the degree of being ultimate guardians of the Constitution as are the American courts. On the other hand, as recent muscle flexing by the Law Lords has indicated,[68] the British judiciary will endeavor to guard the Constitution in its own way by taking on Cabinet ministers. Even if that should turn out to be merely symbolic in the long run, it nonetheless points to the presence of a guardianship that could be regarded as both tentative and revisionist.[69]

FRANCE

The French, too, insisting that a law is the expression of the sovereign will, had not endowed their courts with authority to declare laws unconstitutional, even in a limited manner, until the proclamation of the Constitution of the Fifth Republic in 1958. However, prior to it they did devise a rather interesting safeguard in order to ascertain that suggested legislation of dubious constitutionality did not become law per se short of an amendment to the Constitution. That safeguard was established by the framers of the Constitution of the Fourth Republic in the form of a special thirteen-member committee known as the *Constitutional Committee (Comité Constitutionnel)*.

Chaired by the President of the Republic, the Constitutional Committee consisted, in addition to the President of the National Assembly and the President of the Council of the Republic, of three members selected by the latter and seven by the former branch of the legislature. In each instance these ten were chosen from personnel outside the membership of the respective chambers, usually professors of law in general concord with the several political parties represented in Parlia-

---

68. For two examples, see *Laker Airways v. Department of Trade* (1977) Q.B. 643 and *Padfield v. Minister of Agriculture, Fisheries, and Food* (1968) A.C. 977.
69. For a fairly recent insightful appraisal, see ch. 7, "Judicial Decision-Making," in Dan Budge and David McKay, et al., *The New British Political System: Government and Society in the 1980s* (London: Longman Group, 1983).

ment. Whenever it was requested to do so—and only then!—by the President of the Council of the Republic and an absolute majority of its members, the committee was empowered to examine a law prior to its final promulgation to determine whether or not it was of such a nature as to require its recasting as a *constitutional amendment* rather than simply pass as a *law*. If the committee concurred that a law did in fact imply an amendment to the Constitution, it was sent back to the National Assembly for appropriate action. Not surprisingly, the Constitutional Committee was hardly a very busy institution; it was called on in merely a few cases, and only one of these gave it an opportunity to perform a significant role. Whatever its performance, the institution was a far cry from bona fide judicial review.

The Constitutional Council. However, France moved closer to the latter, without actually attaining it, with the adoption of a provision in the de Gaulle Constitution of 1958 calling for a *Constitutional Council (Conseil Constitutionnel).* Not a court at all, it actually lies outside the judicial system of the government; neither individual citizens nor groups (except as noted on p. 312, *infra*) nor courts of law can appeal to it. The council is theoretically composed of all ex-Presidents of France surviving and not holding any other elective public office, regardless of which Republic they may have headed, plus nine other distinguished personages, of whom the President of the Republic, the President of the Senate, and the President of the National Assembly each select three. *M. le président* of the council is chosen from among its membership by the incumbent President of the Republic, who enjoys a seven-year term of office, without limits as to renewability. The members may hold no public office of any kind, other than already held civil service appointments, for it was the intention of the authors of the institution that its membership be wholly independent, exercising no outside remunerative public activity whatsoever.

The nine appointive members of the Constitutional Council—usually lawyers who have been active in politics (five of the original nine had been active Gaullists)—serve for one nonrenewable, staggered nine-year term of office, whereas all ex-Presidents of France serve for life. In theory, the latter may not resign, but one, the venerable Vincent Auriol, first President of the Fourth Republic, announced on July 2, 1960, that, in protest of three allegedly unconstitutional actions taken by President de Gaulle, he would no longer participate in the Council's work. The disputed actions were, first, a measure to increase vastly state aid to denominational schools, second, de Gaulle's refusal, in March 1960, to convene Parliament in special session despite a request by a majority of the deputies, duly backed by a constitutional provision, and, third, the short-cut procedure employed to revise the Constitution on the structure of the French Community. The then seventy-five-year-old popular Socialist, who had done much to bring de Gaulle to power in the dark days of May 1958, concluded his letter of resignation to Council President Léon Noel as follows:

> This lack of deference for the national sovereignty and our fundamental charter orients the constitutional regime of 1958 toward a system of personal and arbitrary power in opposition to the essential rules and principles of democracy. . . . [T]hus, not

wanting to remain powerless and mute before attacks on the national sovereignty, I regret to inform you that I will no longer sit with the Constitutional Council.[70]

On the other hand, when ex-President Giscard d'Estaing stood for an elective legislative post in 1984, while trying to retain his seat on the *Counseil Constitutionnel*, the latter ruled him ineligible for continued membership thereon.[71]

The Council has the preventive power to declare unconstitutional all *organic laws* (Article 46 of the Constitution) and *standing orders* (rules of procedure) of the houses of Parliament; both these categories *must* be submitted to the council prior to their promulgation. It is also empowered to strike down or hold up, pending rectification, those *ordinary laws, treaties,* and *protocols* that *may* be voluntarily referred to it before final enactment or ratification by the President of the Republic, the Premier, or the Presidents of the two houses of Parliament (Articles 54–55). Thus, Senate President Alain Poher, who had unsuccessfully opposed President Georges Pompidou in the 1969 elections, referred an antifreedom of association bill to it in 1971. It was a measure that had been bitterly criticized by liberals and leftists and passed over the Senate's objections. In a milestone decision, the Council declared it unconstitutional, marking the first time that the body, dominated by the ruling Gaullist party, had effectively opposed the government on a fundamental point of law.[72] It was also the first time that the *Conseil* based a decision on the *Preamble* of the Constitution of 1946, rather than on an article in the body of that document. Four years later, it refused to consider the delicate question whether the text of a treaty was compromised by a law dealing with voluntary abortions.[73]

Normally, the Council is expected to hand down a decision within one month, but if the government categorizes a referred measure as "urgent," it must rule on the matter within eight days. Among the other main functions of the Council are supervision of the "regularity" of the elections of the President of the Republic, the members of Parliament—the Constitutional Council, not Parliament, establishes the credentials of the deputies[74] and senators—and of all popular referenda; it may decide disputes between the government (the Ministry) and Parliament regarding the "delimitation of executive and legislative competence";[75] and it *must* be consulted by the President of the Republic when he is contemplating the assumption of emergency powers under Article 16 of the Constitution, as de Gaulle did in April 1961, with regard to both the existence of the emergency and the measures he proposes to take under it.

---

70. As reported by Robert C. Doty in *The New York Times* (International Edition), July 2, 1960.
71. *Décision du 7 Novembre 1984.*
72. *Decision du Juillet July 16, 1971* (see the articles in the International Edition of the *Herald Tribune,* July 19, 1971, and *The New York Times,* July 18, 1971, p. 13).
73. *Décision du 15 Janvier 1975.* (See explanatory letter from *Conseil* staff member Nicole de Montricher February 6, 1988.)
74. Thus, after the November 1962 elections to the National Assembly, the Council invalidated the results in four assembly districts.
75. By the end of 1969, the Council had decided sixty-six such disputes. See Roy Pierce, *French Politics and Political Institutions,* 2d ed. (New York: Harper & Row, 1973), pp. 94–95. In only seven of the disputes did the Council side with Parliament.

The Council (which meets *in camera*) does not initiate action in constitutional cases, but it is autonomous regarding the other delimited areas of its power just outlined. A quorum for a valid decision is seven members, yet an absolute majority is required to certify Presidential disability, another of its responsibilities. A single opinion is delivered in behalf of the entire body (there are no concurring or dissenting opinions), but all decisions of the Council must be written. There is no oral argument, although representatives from the political branches may be asked to be present by the *rapporteur* of a particular case. Its decisions, which are based on written documents and briefs, there being no oral argument at all, are final and binding and are not appealable to "any jurisdiction whatsoever." Yet the Council has no power to enforce its decisions, other than the power to persuade.

Given its limited range of power and authority,[76] it would be highly misleading to characterize the functions of the Constitutional Council as full judicial review per se. For there are three cardinal weaknesses: First, the inability of private individuals to challenge the constitutionality of a law, because only the high public officers named previously and, since 1974, sixty deputies or senators, acting in a group petition—which has resulted in a tenfold increase of laws brought before the *Conseil*—possess that right as an adjunct of their official station, although both in 1990 and in 1991 President Mitterand signaled his hope that, as soon as feasible, it would become possible for *individuals* to take a case directly to the "C.C." (no action had been taken as of early 1992). Second, a challenge to the constitutionality of a law even by those authorized to do so is possible solely as to the *substance* of the law and not as to its procedural application (one of the most frequent causes of court review in the United States, for example). Third, the extremely short period of time permitted to the Council for its deliberation on a validly challenged measure makes all but a mockery of the concept of an appeal—especially since its power is exercisable only *prior to* promulgation. On the other hand, its record to date (1992) indicates a definite inclination to assert itself not only in the constitutional evaluation of the writing of parliamentary rules, but also in other areas of its presumed competence. However, in the still more or less apposite opinion is one of the most astute commentators on the French scene, *le Conseil Constitutionnel* is best thought of as an adjunct to the President of the Republic in his or her endeavors to ensure respect for the 1958 Constitution.[77] This appraisal was assuredly vindicated when President de Gaulle in October 1962 called for a national referendum on direct election of the President—despite the Council's objections, and those by the *conseil d'état*, to such a referendum call on the obvious ground that the Constitution of 1958 did not provide for such direct action and that, indeed, the President's call represented a patent violation of the letter and the spirit

---

76. Between 1958 and 1975, the Council rendered 484 decisions, including 35 certifications of results of elections and referenda. During that same period it examined the constitutionality of organic laws just twenty times, that of ordinary laws eleven times, and that of treaties just once (Louis Favoreu and Loic Philip, "La jurisprudence du Conseil constitionnel," 91 *Revue du droit et de la science politique*, January–February 1975, pp. 165–200). See the latter journal's subsequent annual volumes for current statistics. Between 1981 and January 1987 the *Conseil* handed down 82 decisions under Article 61 *(control de constitutiionnalité)* (see Nicole de Montricher, loc. cit.).

77. William Pickles, *The French Constitution*, October 4, 1958 (London: Stevens, 1960), p. 33.

of the basic document. But when, predictably, de Gaulle refused to be stopped, held the referendum, won it (albeit by a narrow margin), and then saw his action and the attendant results challenged at the bar of the Council, the latter promptly declared itself "incompetent" to rule on the "subject matter approved" by and in the referendum.

The French Constitutional Council is no Supreme Court of the United States, despite the efforts implicit in the Giscard d'Estaing reforms of 1974 that, in theory, indeed may represent "un gramme de démocratie."[78] Arguably more than that: for in a 1971 decision, dubbed as the "Marbury v. Madison of France," the Conseil interpreted the French Constitution as effectively incorporating the 1789 Declaration of the Rights of Man, and subsequent decisions incorporated additional rights declared in prior French laws and constitutions.[79] Indeed, in 1977 the Giscard government did push through further legislation to expand the watchdog role of the Council, which has used it a number of times, including on a budget. Although there is still a long way to go, even under a Socialist administration, such as Mitterand's, there is no doubt that the past two decades have witnessed what one of its leading interpreters regards as a "profound transformation" leading to a "heretofore unimaginable statue of genuine prestige."[80] The legitimacy of the Conseil's work as the guardian of constitutional values is now widely accepted,[81] a fact of French government and politics enshrined by the representatives of four of the five major political parties in a joint declaration in the National Assembly in March 1987. In that historic setting they formally acknowledged the supremacy of the French Constitution, as interpreted by the "neuf sages" (nine wise men). Yet the Conseil itself made clear that it "does not possess the same general power of political judgment that the Parlement does."[82] And with an obvious glance at the United States judiciary, it asserted that it is not authorized "to substitute its own views for those of the legislature"; that it would hew to a general rule of not intervening except in the case of "une erreur manifeste"—something akin to James Bradley Thayer's famed exhortation to the United States Supreme Court, namely, to exercise its ultimate power of judicial review only in the presence of a "clear mistake."[83]

SOME OTHER SPECIAL CONSTITUTIONAL TRIBUNALS

Several countries—perhaps recognizing traditional distinctions between natural and positive law—have created judicial bodies that approach or even feature some of the manifestations of the power of judicial review, yet they are usually found outside or astride the ordinary court structure. Among the more visible of these

78. See Maurice Duverger, "Un gramme de démocratie," Le Monde, October 11, 1974.
79. See F. L. Morton, "Judicial Review in France: A Comparative Analysis," Occasional Papers Series Research Study 3.3., Faculty of Social Science, University of Calgary, December 9, 1987, p. 2.
80. Louis Favoreu, "Le droit constitutionnel jurisprudentiel en 1981–1982," Revue du Droit Public et de la Science Politique en France et a L'Étranger, February 1983, pp. 337–39.
81. See Alec Stone, "In the Shadow of the Constitutional Council: The Juridicization of the Legislative Process in France," West European Politics, July 1988.
82. Morton, op. cit., n. 79.
83. "The Origin and Scope of the American Doctrine of Constitutional Laws," Harvard Law Review (1893).

bodies are the constitutional courts of West Germany, Italy, and Austria, all of which practice at least some measure of judicial review. There are others, but a brief treatment of these three will suffice to illustrate the point. The three states, each in a post–World War II development, empowered their special constitutional courts to guard against infringement of their constitutions by simple legislation and other governmental action, such as any action that would violate the constitutional guarantee, present in almost identical form in all three lands, that "all persons shall be equal before the law." There has been fairly general acceptance of their purpose and functions.[84]

By far the most active and most successful among the three is West Germany's *Federal Constitutional Court (Bundesverfassungsgericht)*, created in 1951—responding to U.S. advocacy of an independent judiciary and the power of judicial review—under the Basic Law of 1949, as amended, most recently under the unification treaty of 1991, and seated in Karlsruhe. (The framers of the Weimar Republic had rejected judicial review both because of an inherent and endemic bias against it but also because of what they regarded as the "stultifying actions" of the U.S. Supreme Court!)[85] It consists of sixteen judges of at least forty years of age; all have considerable past judicial, legal, professional, or other high public experience and are elegible for judicial office as well as for election to the *Bundestag* (though they cannot be members of it). They are elected half by the lower house *(Bundestag)* by a special committee of twelve electors set up by it on the basis of proportional representation in the *Bundestag*—hence dominated by the major parties—with eight of the twelve votes necessary for selection, and half by the upper house *(Bundesrat)* of Parliament by a two-thirds majority. The *Bundesrat* is representative of the partisan and regional interests of the *Länder* (states). The selections by the two houses are made from a list provided by the Ministry of Justice. It comprises *all* federal judges eligible for elevation to the *Bundesverfassungsgericht* as well as any other legally trained candidates who are nominated by the federal government, by the *Länder*, and by the political parties. Only six of those selected—three from each of its two eight-member chambers,[86] *must* come from the ranks of professionally trained, sitting federal judges; the others may, but need not, be drawn from such judgeships. All judges serve for nonrenewable twelve-year terms of office; they must retire at age sixty-eight.

In response to disputes or cases brought by agencies, institutions, and individuals empowered to invoke its jurisdiction, the Federal Constitutional Court possesses the extensive power to decide all disputes involving the meaning and interpretation of the Basic Law *(Grundgesetz)*; it decides the constitutional validity of any federal or state *(Land)* statute, whether or not a case involving it has already

84. See the informative article by Taylor Cole, "The Constitutional Courts: A Comparison," in 53 *American Political Science Review* (December 1959), pp. 963–84. See also Mauro Cappelletti, *Judicial Review in the Contemporary World* (Indianapolis: Bobbs-Merrill, 1971), ch. 3, "The Modern Systems of Judicial Review: The Organs of Control," pp. 45–68.
85. The High State Court *(Staatsgerichtshof)* did, however, have express authority to settle constitutional conflicts between levels and branches of government. See Peter Merkl, ed., *Forty Years of West German Politics* (New York: New York University Press, 1989).
86. Each house of Parliament elects one-half of each of the two chambers (senates).

come before one of the regular courts; and it adjudicates disputes between organs of government at the national level. Out of these powers arise the Court's two most significant functions: jurisdiction over disputes between the Federal Republic and the *Länder* regarding the latter's administration of the former's statutes,[87] and guardianship over the fundamental rights and privileges of citizens as determined by the Basic Law both on substantive and procedural grounds, like judicial review in the United States and unlike its restricted, if conceivably ultimately widening, practice in France.

As indicated, the *Bundesverfassungsgericht*[88] is composed of two chambers or senates of eight judges each. Initially, one handled all cases dealing with civil and constitutional rights and the other handled all other cases. But to even out the caseload *both* senates now decide individual rights or constitutional complaints. The first senate thus has jurisdiction over complaints involving the interpretation of Articles 1–17 (speech, religion, equal protection, right to trade, etc.), whereas the second senate decides complaints involving procedural due process rights (Articles 101, 103, and 104).[89] Votes in both senates are recorded in each published case, (but when there are no *written* dissenting opinions the judges remain anonymous. Only such *written* opinions bear the names of their authors. The author of the majority opinion is *never* identified—such opinions being viewed as institutional. Dissenting opinions are still rare occurrences; a strong bias against them holds sway on the Court. The *Bundesverfassungsgericht* has been a busy and assertive court—now exceeding 3,500 cases annually (approaching the work load of the U.S. Supreme Court)—and to the surprise of many a skeptic it has acted with considerable courage and vigor. For example, it braved the wrath and power of Chancellor Konrad Adenauer when, in a momentous decision early in 1961, it declared unconstitutional, as a violation of principles of federalism guaranteed in Article 30 of the Basic Law, his executive action setting up a federally controlled second television network that was to be financed largely through commercials,[90] a plan that had been expressly rejected by Parliament earlier. The decision was particularly remarkable because it resulted from a suit filed some months earlier by four *Länder* dominated by the Chancellor's opposition, the Social Democrats.

Two other significant decisions served to declare unconstitutional both the Communist party in 1956 and the socialist *Reich* party (a neo-Nazi organization) in 1952 as being militantly resistant to the constitutional and democratic order of the state.[91] And as another illustration of the Court's virility and assertiveness, it

---

87. See the excellent study on the Court's federalism jurisprudence by Philip M. Blair, *Federalism and Judicial Review in West Germany* (Oxford: Clarendon Press, 1981).
88. There are several modes of access to the *Bundesverfassungsgericht*, the three most important ones being (1) *Richterklage*—request by an inferior court to have the BVG render a judgment on a constitutional question in a pending case; (2) *Parteienklage*—appeal by a constitutional organ (federal or state); (3) *Bürgerklage* or *Verfassungsbeschwerde*—in cases concerning questions of violation of basic rights of individuals involving any statute, judicial decision, or administrative act or in the case of local governments, "the right of self-government." (No cases had been filed under category 1 as of late 1991.)
89. This division of jurisdiction was announced in 14/BVerfGE (1971).
90. 12 BVerfGE 60 (1961).
91. BVerf GE 85 (1956) and 2 BVerf GE 1 (1952).

did not hesitate to strike down an executive decree based on what the Court viewed as unconstitutional delegation of legislative power by the *Bundestag* to the Executive.[92] The reasoning employed here was quite similar to that used by the U.S. Supreme Court in 1935, in the "Hot Oil" cases,[93] when it declared unconstitutional, as an illegal delegation of legislative power to the Chief Executive, an important section of the National Industrial Recovery Act, which was soon to fall in its entirety. A further example of the Court's versatile jurisdictional determination came in 1966 when it declared unconstitutional the federal statutes under which the three major political parties had been subsidized from public funds to the tune of DM 38 million (about $14 million) annually. The Court held that such funds could be authorized only for legitimate election campaign expenses, not for general propaganda, and would have to be made available to splinter parties as well. "In a free society," said the tribunal, "the process of forming public opinion should be free of the state, and should move from the people themselves to the state institutions rather than from the state down to the people."[94] And the BVG made worldwide headlines early in 1975 when it struck down 6:2, as unconstitutional, a federal law permitting abortions on request during the first three months of pregnancy, holding the 1974 statute to violate Article I of the Constitution's "human dignity clause" that comprehends a guarantee that "everyone shall have the right to life." In the words of the unidentified majority opinion's author, "[T]he bitter experience of the Nazi period in Germany provides historical grounds for determining that protection of human life should receive absolute priority."[95]

It is fair to say that the *Bundesverfassungsgericht* has assumed an importance hardly predictable, and that it has thus become a significant and prestigious element in the constitutional *modus operandi* of the new German federalism. Between 1951 and 1980 it declared 107 statutes unconstitutional, partly or entirely. In the judgment of one seasoned observer, "the Court clearly has become the most important source of judicial influence in German politics and the most active and powerful tribunal in Western Europe."[96] On the other hand, there are those who would conclude, with Professor Fritz Nova, that the BVG "has checked its exercise of power with a strong sense of self-restraint" and the latter phenomenon, coupled with limited creativity, has "characterized its performance."[97] As another expert on the BVG concludes, while the tribunal's impact has indeed been "sub-

---

92. 1 BVerf GE 14 (1951).
93. *Panama Refining Co. v. Ryan*, 293 U.S. 388 (1935).
94. 20 BVerf GE 56–59, 119, 134 (1966).
95. 39 BVerf GE 1–95 (1975). See the incisive analysis by Donald P. Kommers, "Abortion and Constitution: United States and West Germany," 25 *The American Journal of Comparative Law* 2 (Spring 1977). On the other hand, the *Canadian* Supreme Court struck down a federal law *restricting* the practice in 1988 (5:2), employing reasoning very similar to Justice Blackmun's majority opinion in *Roe v. Wade* in 1973.
96. Lewis J. Edinger, *Politics in Germany: Attitudes and Processes*, 2d ed. (Boston: Little, Brown, 1976), p. 323.
97. "Political Innovation of the West German Federal Constitutional Court: The State of Discussion on Judicial Review," 70 *The American Political Science Review* 1 (March 1976), p. 124.

stantial," it would be wise at this time to avoid "an inflated conception of the Court's significance in the German system."[98]

Still another modern special Constitutional tribunal is Italy's *Constitutional Court (Corte Costituzionale)*, established under the Italian Constitution of 1948—although it did not begin to function until January 1, 1956. This fifteen-member body is staffed with distinguished, mature personages who come from three groups: (1) members of the bar with at least twenty years of experience as practicing lawyers; (2) upper-level, broadly experienced judges; and (3) full professors of law with considerable seniority. In all categories political allegiance plays a role. (Once more we note the high esteem in which the professor is still held in Europe.) The members of the Court are appointed for staggered nine-year terms: five are chosen by the President of the Republic of Italy with the Premier's countersignature (a mere *pro forma* requirement, for the selection is exclusively the President's jealously guarded prerogative); five by a three-fifths vote of Parliament in joint session, reflecting political adherence and power; and five by the "ordinary and administrative judiciary," that is, three by the *Corte di Cassazione* (Court of Cassation), one by the *Consiglio di Stato* (Council of State), and one by the *Corte dei Conti* (Court of Accounts). The *Corte Costituzionale*, whose votes are by secret ballot—there are no concurring or dissenting opinions—is the final interpreter of the Constitution. As such it has the power to declare both national and regional laws unconstitutional—as it did in the case of a 1934 law that denied Sunday rest to shepherds and, a decade later, in that of a government ban on foreign cable TV[99]—and it serves as arbiter in disputes between organs of government at the national level. In that role it also acts as legitimator: for example, it validated the controversial Divorce Act of 1971, a law enacted only after a long and bitter Parliamentary struggle, that for the first time in Italy's history enables married people to dissolve their wedlock.[100] Access of individuals to it, although utilized increasingly, is considerably less readily available than in West Germany. That fact, plus a general tendency to tread more cautiously, at first rendered the *Corte Costituzionale* less of a peacemaker in matters of constitutional checks than its counterpart north of the Alps. The *Corte's* average annual caseload has been quite heavy. Thus, in 1989 a total of 883 *new* cases were brought to the Court, 869 in 1990. The Court decided 1043 in 1989 and 960 in 1990. It carried over 420 in 1989 and 329 in 1990. And it has sporadically asserted itself, particularly so when dealing with the now familiar

98. Donald P. Kommers, *Judicial Politics in West Germany: A Study of the Federal Constitutional Court* (Beverly Hills: Sage Publications, 1976), p. 301. See also C. C. Schweitzer, Taylor Cole, Donald P. Kommers et al. (eds.), *Politics and Government in the Federal Republic of Germany* (London: Berg Publishers, 1983; New York: St. Martins, 1984).

99. Decisions of July 22, 1962 and 1974, respectively. A few months prior to the former decision, the Corte Costituzionale upheld the constitutionality of Articles 559 and 560 of Italy's penal code, which had provided for sterner punishment for adulterous wives than for unfaithful husbands. That judgment, however, was overruled on contemporary egalitarian grounds in 1968, the Court holding that the different responsibilites and punishments established thereunder for men and women were violative of Act III of the Italian Constitution's "equal protection clause" (Gurisprudenza Corte Costituzionale No. 126 [1968], overruling Guir. Cost. No. 64 [1961], resp.)

100. Giur. Cost. No. 169 (1971).

illegal delegation of legislative power to the executive branch, and in the realms of family relations, women's rights, and criminal procedure. It likes to employ an interpretive technique, leading to the so-called *sentenze additive* that sees the Court "adding" a rule to a statutory provision, especially in welfare legislation. This technique prompted two knowledgeable commentators to conclude, arguably somewhat expansively, that the Court has not only "insisted upon its prerogatives and successfully defended its position," but that it has "become a bulwark for freedom in Italian society."[101] On the other hand, although the Court's decisions are generally obeyed, they have occasionally also been deliberately ignored by officials; one such instance in 1957 caused the resignation of Enrico De Nicola, the Court's first President, when a cabinet minister resolutely refused to adhere to a decision of the Court.[102] Thus, antagonism between the judicial and other branches has indeed flared sporadically, but not frequently or significantly. The Court has been generally cautious and deferential. By and large, it is fair to conclude, with Professor Giovanni Bognetti, one of its closest students, who contends that it is primarily a rather discreet presence in Italian political life"—that, all things being equal, the Italian Constitutional Court prefers "exhortations to orders."[103] Yet the influential *Consigliere de Stato*, Professor Guglielmo Negri—quite possibly a candidate for membership on the Court himself—is convinced that the *Corte Costitutzionale* has become an increasingly significant defender of the Constitution and its inherent rights and liberties. Another distinguished student of Italy's judicial system, Professor Roberto Toniatti of the University of Trento, dissents from that sanguine analysis. If he once did view the *Corte* in that role in the later 1960s and the 1970s, he now no longer regards it as the "protector" of human rights. Indeed, he perceives a significant tendency to invoke judicial restraint via the political branches of the government.[104]

Austria, too, has its Constitutional Court, the *Verfassungsgerichtshof*. This fourteen-member tribunal (there are always six substitute members available) was reinstituted in 1945, based on the Austrian Constitution of 1920, as amended in 1925

101. Guglielmo Negri and Joseph La Palombara, "Principles of Italian Constitutional Law and the Structure of Central Government," in Guglielmo Negri, *Three Essays on Comparative Politics* (Milan: D. A. Ciuffre, 1964), pp. 33–37 and p. 8, respectively.
102. See Norman Kogan, *The Government of Italy* (New York: Thomas Y. Crowell, 1965), p. 120.
103. "The Political Role of the Italian Constitutional Court," 49 *Notre Dame Lawyer* 5 (June 1974), pp. 982–98.
104. Interview with Professor Negri at the Palazzo del Quirinale, Rome, Italy, July 2, 1987, and with Professor Toniatti via mail in October and November 1991. A partly concurring and partly dissenting view as to the Court's power is voiced by one of the Court's recently most prolific commentators, Dr. Maria Rosaria Ferrarese, who is dismayed by the tribunal's arcane procedures and what she views as its passive tendencies, but who now also professes to detect activist signs along the lines of Professor Negri's judgement (see her "Civil Justice and the Judicial Role in Italy," 13 *The Justice System Journal* 2 [1988–89]). Her optimism may well be centered in courts other than the *Corte Costituzionale*, however. Her and Professor Toniatti's critical views are broadly echoed by Professor Carlo Guarnieri of the University of Bologna, who characterizes it as having but "limited autonomy." See his "Check, Without Balance: Judicial Power and Politics in Italy," 5 *Italian Journal* 344 (1991) pp. 8–13.

and 1929. Of its members, the Chief Justice, his or her substitute, six justices, and three substitute justices are appointed by the President of the Republic of Austria from nominees of the federal government. The other six justices and three substitutes are chosen by the President on the recommendations of the lower house (National Council) and the upper house (Federal Council) of Parliament. All must be trained in the law. They serve for life—unlike the German and Italian justices—up to the compulsory retirement age of seventy. As the only Austrian court with the power to declare legislation unconstitutional, the tribunal reviews laws and decides jurisdictional disputes between the courts and administrative authorities; the legality of executive orders, international law and treaties, and election contests. It also rules in impeachment proceedings. Until 1975 individuals had less ready access to the *Verfassungsgerichtshof* than their German neighbors had to their constitutional court but more than Italians to theirs. As a result of a constitutional amendment adopted in that year, however, individuals are entitled to file complaints *(Beschwerde)* not merely because they believe their constitutionally guaranteed rights have been violated by an act of the *administration*—as they had been able to do since at least 1920—but now also if they believe one of their rights has been violated by a *law* (an act of the legislature). Thus, there has been a *rapprochement* to the German conception of judicial review. The Austrian *Verfassungsgerichtshof*, too, now asserts itself; it has not been loath to examine challenged legislation, even legislation that, like the subject of an increasing number of cases handled by the Italian *Corte Costituzionale*, extends to the socioeconomic and egalitarian realm: for example, it held unconstitutional a section of the Income Tax Law that differentiated between the sexes for tax purposes (decision of March 29, 1958). In the view of at least one astute Austrian lawyer–political scientist observer, the *Verfassungsgerichtshof*, which customarily disposes of about 500 cases annually, is now a type of "upper house" of the Austrian political system.[105] Still, its power is restricted, and its decisions may now be overturned by Austria's Parliament—as the latter did, for example, when it voted permissible a restriction on pensions to $100,000 annually that the *Verfassungsgerichtshof* had ruled impermissible in 1987.[106]

Yet of all the issues that have confronted these three constitutional courts of Europe, by far the greatest number has concerned the interpretation and application of respective constitutional provisions in the vexatious areas of delegation of legislative authority, federalism, and equality before the law. With varying emphasis, they are very much in the constitutional weather eye of the U.S. judiciary as well—contemporarily especially the latter.

105. Manfried Welan, *"Der Verfassungsgerichtshof—eine Nebenregierung?"* in Heinz Fischer, *Das Politische System Österreichs* (Vienna: Europaverlag, 1977), p. 313. The most insightful work on the Austrian Constitution is Ludwig K. Adamovich (longtime Chief Justice of the VG) and Bernd-Christian Funk, *Österreichisches Verfassungsrecht*, 3d ed. (New York: Springer Verlag, 1985).

106. The power to overturn the high tribunal's decision stems from a recent constitutional amendment. Enacting amendments necessitates a two-thirds majority of both houses of Austria's Parliament. (see letter from mag. jur. Helgar G. Schneider, Graz-Andritz, Austria, September 5, 1991).

A HISTORICAL NOTE

The notion that courts, or some other body, should exercise judicial review as the guardian of the theoretical primacy of a basic law or constitution[107] stems primarily from the early European rejection of the idea of the inviolability of an enacted law. One of the first statements clamoring for a type of judicial review in that connection was made in England—oddly enough in view of its subsequent rejection of the concept. It arose out of the famous *Dr. Bonham's Case* in 1610. The King, pursuant to an Act of Parliament, had granted to members of the London College of Physicians the exclusive right to issue licenses to practice medicine in that city. Dr. Bonham was charged with practicing medicine illegally, for he was not a member of that College, the latter having refused to license him. The College then fined him, confiscating half of the fine for itself. When the case came before Sir Edward Coke, the Lord Chief Justice, he declared the charter void as a violation of the common law. Holding the latter to be supreme, Sir Edward simply stated that the courts could declare acts of Parliament null and void; therefore, he held in the now famous dictum "[W]hen an act of Parliament is against common right and reason, or repugnant, or impossible to be performed, the common law will controul it and adjudge such act to be void."[108] Parliament then simply reenacted the statute! If Sir Edward's view of judicial review was ever seriously adopted at all anywhere in England, it found itself soon superseded when the Glorious Revolution of 1688 clearly established the supremacy of Parliament. In fact, already in 1653 Lord Coke's peers had held in *Captain Streater's Case*[109] that "we must submit to the legislative power else things would run around."[110]

Nevertheless, the concept of judicial review—a product of our common Western history and the "logical result of centuries of European thought and colonial experience"[111]—subsequently found its way across the Atlantic Ocean to the British Colonies, there to be nurtured by several colonial courts. In eight or nine separate early judgments these courts refused to enforce legislative enactments that they deemed to be against "the laws of nature" (shades of Locke and future events) or "the laws of natural equity," in a sense against the latent, unwritten Constitution.

---

107. An intriguing development on that front, albeit a still somewhat unreliable one, in terms of its genuine role and meaning, is the establishment in 1964 of Yugoslavia's eleven-member Constitutional Court, elected by the Federal Assembly for a once renewable eight-year term of office. See Winston M. Fisk and Alvin Z. Rubinstein, "Yugoslavia's Constitutional Court," 15 *East Europe* 7 (July 1966). It has evinced some muscle-flexing by taking on a number of local fiefdoms, but it does not seem to be destined for a genuine counterfoil to medium- and upper-level governmental authority.
108. 8 Co. 188a.
109. 5 How St. Trs. 365.
110. However, there are those who argue—a bit tortuously—that, in effect, by their common law power of *interpreting* legislation, the courts of England *do* practice judicial review. See, for example, A. Wilson, in "the Doctrine and Practice of Judicial Review of Legislation," 4 *Me Judice* 20 (January 1962).
111. Mauro Cappelletti, *Judicial Review in the Contemporary World*, op. cit., p. 25.

JUDICIAL REVIEW AT HOME

Yet if the principle of judicial review was imbedded in the minds of the American Founding Fathers, they assuredly failed to spell it out literally, although the records of the Constitutional Convention in Philadelphia in 1787 prove conclusively that the idea of judicial review was widely recognized and accepted; that the matter was very much on the minds of the delegates, who after all distrusted unrestrained popular government; and that it was widely debated. In any event, the massed evidence is quite persuasive that a vast majority of the delegates, Anti-Federalists as well as Federalists, favored it, although for quite different reasons. Between twenty-five and thirty-two of the forty delegates—including three-fourths of the Convention's leaders—are generally considered to have called for it. Distinguished constitutional authorities, such as Professors Beard, Corwin, Berger, and Mason, fully agree on that interpretation of the wishes of the delegates[112] who, with less than a handful of dissenters, in effect concurred in the pronouncement by Gouverneur Morris of Pennsylvania that the courts should decline to give the weight of law to "a direct violation of the Constitution." Morris admitted that such control over the legislature might have "its inconveniences," but that it was nonetheless necessary because even the "most virtuous citizens will often as members of a legislative body concur in measures which afterward in their private capacity they will be ashamed of."[113]

So prominent a framer as Alexander Hamilton declared in his famous *Federalist Paper* No. 78 that judicial review was definitely meant to be incorporated into the prerogatives of the judiciary; that "the courts were designed to be an intermediate body between the people and the legislature, in order among other things, to keep the latter within the limits assigned to their authority. The interpretation of the laws is the proper and peculiar province of the courts." *Federalist* No. 78 should be

112. See Charles Beard, "The Supreme Court—Usurper or Grantee?" 27 *Political Science Quarterly* 1 (1912); Max Farrand, *The Framing of the Constitution of the United States* (New Haven, CT: Yale University Press, 1913); Edward C. Corwin, *The Doctrine of Judicial Review; Its Legal and Historical Basis and Other Essays* (Princeton, NJ: Princeton University Press, 1914); John Schmidhauser, *The Supreme Court as Final Arbiter in Federal-State Relations, 1789–1957* (Chapel Hill: University of North Carolina Press, 1958), especially chs. 1 and 11; Raoul Berger, *Government by Judiciary: The Transformation of the Fourteenth Amendment* (Cambridge: Harvard University Press, 1977); and Alpheus T. Mason, *The States' Rights Debate: Antifederalism and the Constitution*, 2d ed. (New York: Oxford University Press, 1972). See also Beard's classic, *The Supreme Court and the Constitution*, rev. ed., with an introduction by Alan F. Westin (Englewood Cliffs, NJ: Prentice-Hall, 1962). Benjamin F. Wright, however, puts the number of "pro"-delegates at the much lower level of seven to seventeen. One reason for the difference in numbers may well be that the larger figure may include those delegates who embraced the idea of a "Council of Revision," which would have consisted of the President and "a convenient number of the National Judiciary" empowered to examine every act of Congress and by its dissent to constitute a veto. The Founding Fathers thrice rejected the Council, however. They also rejected the "Congressional Negative," which would have empowered Congress to disallow *state* laws deemed to contravene the Constitution.

113. As quoted by Alpheus T. Mason and Richard H. Leach, *In Quest of Freedom* (Englewood Cliffs, NJ: Prentice-Hall, 1959), p. 124. Morris was the individual who wrote out the final draft of the *circa* 10,000-word Constitution in longhand.

read in conjunction with Nos. 79, 80, 81, and 83 to derive fuller benefit of Hamilton's view of judicial power, of which a crucial ingredient was his conviction, as he put it in No. 80, that "no man ought certainly to be a judge in his own cause, or in any cause in respect to which he has the least interest or bias." The "Father of the Constitution" himself, James Madison, wrote:

> Judiciary is truly the only defensive armor of the Federal Government, or rather for the Constitution and laws of the United States. Strip it of that armor and the door is wide open for nullification, anarchy and convulsion.[114]

And in his famed Philadelphia lectures of 1790–91, James Wilson, probably the most influential Founding Father after James Madison, and by then an Associate Justice of the U.S. Supreme Court, observed that the Constitution was supreme law, that it was for the judges to declare and apply it, that what was subordinate must give way, and that because one branch of the government infringed the Constitution was no reason that another should abet such infringement.[115] Despite this solid evidence it is still a matter of some academic dispute whether or not the framers intended the power of judicial review to be given to the courts. But there are sundry additional grounds for the conclusion that such doubts as still remain ought to be laid to rest—that the debate over the legitimacy of judicial review has been settled by history.

FURTHER HISTORICAL ROOTS

The Constitution itself, while admittedly not providing *expressly* for the power of judicial review in so many words, assuredly alludes to it by implication. The supremacy clause of Article VI (Section 2) relating to the duty of state judges, may very well be viewed as implying judicial review by federal tribunals over *state actions*. Moreover, that same provision of the Constitution requires acts of Congress to be made "in pursuance thereof," which would seem to call for someone to act as arbiter. It may be well to quote the entire supremacy clause:

> This Constitution, and the laws of the United States which shall be made in pursuance thereof, and all treaties made or which shall be made under the authority of the United States, shall be the supreme law of the land; and the judges in every state shall be bound thereby, anything in the Constitution or laws of any state to the contrary notwithstanding.

Another clearly relevant provision of the basic document is to be found in Article III, Section 2, which states:

> The judicial power shall extend to all cases, in law and equity, arising under this Constitution, the laws of the United States and treaties made or which shall be made, under the authority. . . .

If nothing else, this section strongly articulates the authority of the judiciary over cases in a vast area of constitutional interpretation and thus implies its finite power as to the legality of those cases.

---

114. As quoted by Charles Warren in *The Supreme Court in United States History* (Boston: Little, Brown, 1937), 1, p. 740.
115. Ibid., 1, p. 460.

Moreover, as has already been briefly indicated, it is noteworthy that in the colonial period the British Privy Council had *established* judicial review over acts passed by the colonial legislatures—and indeed exercised it 469 times in the seventeenth and eighteenth centuries.[116] At least eight states' ratifying conventions expressly discussed and accepted the power to pronounce legislative acts null and void.[117] Furthermore, between 1789 and 1803 the courts in ten of the states had *exercised* that power by declaring state laws to be in conflict with state constitutions, and prior to 1789 eight instances[118] of state court judicial review deciding against their state legislature had taken place. And Section 25 of the Judiciary Act 1789, the law under which the First Congress created the national judiciary, con-ferred on the federal government specific authority to *reverse* provisions of state laws and state constitutions that conflicted with the "Constitution, treaty, statute, or commission of the United States."[119] Still, because neither the Constitution for any level of government nor the Judiciary Act of 1789 for the national level *spe-cifically* provided for judicial review, it remained for the Supreme Court of the United States to do so. This it did in 1803, in *Marbury v. Madison*[120]—though, as Thomas Reed Powell noted in his *Vagaries and Varieties in Constitutional Inter-pretation*, no one "had any premonition that the point of judicial review would be relevant to the disposition of the controversy."[121]

SPELLING IT OUT: MARBURY V. MADISON

With the possible exception of *McCulloch v. Maryland*[122]—of which James Brad-ley Thayer and Felix Frankfurter thought "that the conception of the nation which Marshall derived from the Constitution and set forth [in it] is his greatest single judicial performance"[123]—and, perhaps, *Gibbons v. Ogden*[124] (but for differ-ent reasons), no more seminal case at early American constitutional law exists than the hallowed and revered *Marbury v. Madison*, which has been called "the rib of the Constitution."[125] All three were written by that great national constitutionalist, Chief Justice John Marshall, who had himself been a delegate to the Ratifying Convention of Virginia and a one-term congressman from that state. The back-

116. Robert K. Carr, *The Supreme Court and Judicial Review* (New York: Farrar & Rinehart, 1942), p. 43.
117. Virginia, Rhode Island, New York, Connecticut, Massachusetts, New Jersey, North Carolina, and South Carolina. For examples of its application in several cases, see Charles Grove Haines, *The American Doctrine of Judicial Supremacy*, 2d ed., rev. and enl. (Berkeley: University of California Press, 1959).
118. E. G., *Holmes v. Walton* (New Jersey, 1780) and *Trevett v. Wheeden* (Rhode Island, 1786).
119. Act of September 24, 1789, c.20, 25, I Statutes at Large 73, 87.
120. 1 Cranch 137.
121. (New York: Columbia University Press, 1956), p. 11.
122. 4 Wheaton 315 (1819).
123. "John Marshall and the Judicial Function," in *Government Under Law* (Cambridge: Harvard Uni-versity Press, 1956), p. 8. For an incisive study and analysis of Thayer's influential "reasonable doubt" test, see Sanford B. Gabin, *Judicial Review and the Reasonable Doubt Test* (Port Wash-ington, NY: Kennikat Press, 1980).
124. 9 Wheaton 1 (1824).
125. Glendon A. Schubert, *Constitutional Politics* (New York: Holt, Rinehart and Winston, 1960), p. 178.

ground of the *Marbury* decision is so colorful, and the decision itself so important, that no treatment of the judicial process would be complete without at least a brief analysis of the case, one that is still frequently cited by courts not only in the United States but also in other countries, for example, Italy, Japan, and India.

Prompt enactment of the Judiciary Act of 1789 enabled the national judiciary to begin to function at once in the fledging United States, but questions of the existence of the power of judicial review and any possible challenge of it did not arise immediately. However, the issue was simmering. For example, in *Hayburn's case* Associate Justices Blair and Wilson, riding circuit in Pennsylvania in 1792, had refused to carry out a congressional statute that they deemed contrary to the Constitution, contending that they could not perform certain duties imposed on them by the law because they were not "judicial in nature."[126] Together with District Judge Peters they were to pass on disputed pension claims of invalid war veterans, with *their* determination subject to review by the Secretary of War and Congress. If nothing else, this judicial refusal to carry out a legislative act called attention to the constitutional problem. Three years later, in *Van Horne's Lessee v. Dorrance*[127] Justice William Paterson—who had been a delegate to the Constitutional Convention from New Jersey—held for the Court: "Whatever may be the case in other countries, yet in this *there can be no doubt that every act of the Legislature repugnant to the Constitution, is absolutely void.*"[128] A similar judgment was expressed by Justice Samuel Chase on another occasion soon thereafter.[129]

Moreover, the Supreme Court had struck down at least two relatively minor *state* enactments,[130] although, in fact, the second of these decisions was of considerable importance because it held state laws subject to treaties by ruling that the Anglo-American Peace Treaty overrode a Virginia law on the delicate and potentially explosive issue of debts owed to British subjects by Americans.[131] Furthermore, depending on the historical source, the Supreme Court even held an insignificant *federal* pension claim law unconstitutional in the case of *United States v. Yale Todd*, which was decided in 1794 but not officially reported until it became a footnote almost sixty years later in *United States v. Ferreira*.[132] Nevertheless, this was evidently the first instance of the declaration of unconstitutionality of a federal statute. Finally, two years after *Yale Todd*, the Court—with three of its six justices not participating—expressly *upheld* a congressional statute imposing a duty on carriages as not being a "direct tax" and therefore not unconstitutional.[133] (Exactly ninety-nine years later the Supreme Court in effect overruled this decision in the *Second Income Tax Case*,[134] thus precipitating the Sixteenth Amendment.) Yet

126. 2 Dallas 409 (1792). See also the unreported *Chandler v. Secretary of War* (dec. 2/14/1794).
127. 2 Dallas 304 (1795).
128. Ibid., at 308 (italics supplied).
129. *Cooper v. Telfair*, 2 Dallas 14 (1800) at 19.
130. *Clerke v. Harwood*, 3 Dallas 342 (1797) and *Ware v. Hylton*, 3 Dallas 199 (1796).
131. *Ware v. Hylton*, loc. cit.
132. 13 Howard 40 (1851)
133. *Hylton v. United States*, 3 Dallas 171 (1796).
134. *Pollock v. Farmers Loan & Trust Co.*, 158 U.S. 601 (1895).

regardless of these aforegone instances of incipient concern with judicial review, it was not until 1803 and *Marbury v. Madison* that matters actually came to a climax.

The Factual Setting. The second President of the United States, John Adams, had been defeated in his bid for re-election in 1800 by his political arch-rival, Thomas Jefferson. Laboring desperately to salvage something for his prostate Federalist party, Adams was determined to pack the federal judiciary with as many judgeships as humanly and statutorily possible. With the aid of a more than obliging lame-duck Federalist Congress, which passed both the Circuit Court Act[135] and the District of Columbia Organic Law Act early in 1801, Adams, before leaving office on March 3, 1801,[136] was able to nominate, have approved by the Senate, and commission the following fifty-nine persons into office: sixteen new circuit judges (under the Circuit Court Act), forty-two new Justices of the Peace (under the District of Columbia Act), and one Chief Justice of the U.S. Supreme Court, his own Secretary of State, the forty-five-year-old staunch Federalist John Marshall (who in 1789 had refused Washington's offer of an Associate Justiceship). These nominees have often been called "Adams' Midnight Judges" because the President devoted his waning hours in office to signing their commissions of appointment.

It fell to the outgoing premier of the cabinet—Marshall, whose appointment Adams came to regard as the single most important act of his administration (just as President Hoover would ultimately regard his of Cardozo more than 125 years later)—to affix to them the Great Seal of the United States and then to deliver the new judgeship commissions to the various appointees. But Marshall, at once fatigued and exhilarated on Inauguration Eve, failed to deliver seventeen of the forty-two Justices of the Peace commissions, although, aided by his brother James, he worked until late into the evening and indeed had taken care of all the important new circuit judgeships plus most of the other appointments. However, he would begin his first full day as Chief Justice in the morning, a post to which he had been appointed almost two months earlier upon the resignation of the elderly and feeble Oliver Ellsworth in favor of a diplomatic position,[137] and upon John Jay's summary refusal to accept Adams' proffered second appointment as Chief Justice—duly confirmed by the Senate—because, as Jay felt, the Court, at the head of a judicial "system so defective," lacked "energy, weight, and dignity."[138] As head of the Court, Marshall would have the somewhat less than delightful duty of administering the oath of the Presidency to his avowed political enemy (and distant cousin) Thomas Jefferson, who would later frequently refer to Marshall as "that

---

135. The Act, which was repealed in March 1802 at Jefferson's insistence, also provided that the next vacancy on the Supreme Court should *not* be filled, thus reducing the Court's membership from six to five and thereby rendering impossible any automatic vacancy-filling appointment by the incoming Jefferson, a "Democratic-Republican" rather than a Federalist. Barely one year later the new President succeeded in having Congress reestablish the membership at six.

136. Since the enactment of the Twentieth Amendment to the Constitution in 1933, the outgoing President leaves office at noon on January 20.

137. See Albert J. Beveridge, *The Life of John Marshall* (Boston: Houghton Mifflin, 1919).

138. See Frank Monaghan's biography, *John Jay: Defender of Liberty* (New York: Bobbs-Merrill, 1935). See p. 338 *infra,* for additional data on the matter.

gloomy malignity." He left the undelivered commissions to the incoming Secretary of State, James Madison.[139] The stage was thus set for a towering battle of three veritable titans of the early days of Constitution and Nation.

Preliminaries. Angry because of the sustained packing of the judiciary with Federalist appointees, Jefferson on taking office was delighted to find the seventeen undelivered Justice of the Peace commissions on the desk of the Secretary of State (Madison arrived somewhat later). The new President, subsequently seconded enthusiastically by his new Secretary of State, determined not to deliver them, declaring that the "nominations crowded in by Mr. Adams after he knew he was not appointing for himself I treat as mere nullities."[140] And, according to one account, the commissions at issue were "disposed of with the other waste paper and rubbish of the office."[141] Neither subsequent pleas nor threats by such disappointed office-seekers as William Marbury were to sway them. Marbury, a forty-one-year-old Washingtonian, and three other staunch Federalists—Denis Ramsay, William Harper, and Robert Townshend Hooe—subsequently sought aid of counsel and hired Charles Lee, Attorney General under George Washington and John Adams.

Lee turned to the law and to the courts. He found what he believed to be the applicable law in a provision of the Judiciary Act of 1789: Section 13 of that important statute extended to the Supreme Court of the United States the power to issue a *writ of mandamus* (Latin for "we command"), an old Anglo-Saxon writ used as early as the twelfth-century reign of Henry II, commanding a public official to perform his official, ministerial, nondiscretionary duty. Invoking that provision, Lee petitioned the Court for appropriate action, and, at the next term of the Court in 1803 (Congress's angry Jeffersonian majority having canceled the Court's 1802 term), *Marbury v. Madison* reached the original docket of the highest court of the land. It could readily have dismissed the petition for want of jurisdiction under the 1789 statute in this type of case, but, as will become apparent, this would hardly have suited the purposes of the Chief Justice. For presiding over the Supreme Court now, of course, was Jefferson's mortal political enemy and Adams's loyal supporter, John Marshall, who had transmitted an order to Madison, who promptly ignored it, to show cause why the requested writ of mandamus should not be issued against him. Surely Marshall's decision would be in favor of Marbury, especially in view of the seemingly clear language of Section 13!

Marshall, C. J., for the Court. But both the Federalists and the Jeffersonian Republicans had underestimated the boldness and judiciousness, the craftsmanship and shrewd political acumen, the farsightedness and statesmanship, and above

139. For a penetrating analysis of the more technical aspects of *Marbury v. Madison*, see Justice Harold H. Burton's article, "The Cornerstone of Constitutional Law: The Extraordinary Case of *Marbury v. Madison*," 36 *American Bar Association Journal* 805 (October 1950). See also the more historical piece by John A. Garraty, "The Case of the Missing Commissions," in his *Quarrels that Have Shaped the Constitution*, rev. ed. (New York: Harper & Row, 1987), and analysis by George L. Haskins, "Law versus Politics in the Early Years of the Marshall Court," 130 *University of Pennsylvania Law Review* (November 1981), pp. 1–27.
140. Warren, op. cit., 1, p. 201.
141. Charles S. Hyneman, *The Supreme Court on Trial* (New York: Atherton Press, 1963), p. 75.

all, the powerful dedication to the Constitution—*as he saw it and wanted to see it*—of the fourth Chief Justice of the U.S. Supreme Court. And it was John Marshall who spoke for the unanimous Court in a twenty-seven-page opinion, despite the fact that he had a direct personal interest in the case at bar—which today would almost certainly result in self-disqualification (recusing) from the case. Whatever one may think of his failure to abstain, it is not difficult to agree with Professor Corwin that "his compact presentation of the case marches to its conclusion with all the precision of a demonstration of Euclid."[142] The Chief Justice was confronted with a dilemma: if he were to grant the writ in the face of almost certain disobedience by Madison, the Court would be powerless, and if he were to refuse to grant it, Jefferson would triumph.

Marshall's heart, of course, was on the side of Marbury's cause—which happened to be that of his fellow Federalists—and he did not hesitate to chide Jefferson and Madison from the bench, to castigate them for their "rascality." Moreover, he distinctly concurred with the plaintiff's contention that (1) he had a legal right to the commission and (2) the laws of the land afforded him a remedy. These 9,000 words of *obiter dicta* consumed twenty of the twenty-seven pages. But as to the remedy, Marshall, an experienced political savant, here confronted with an utterly political situation, announced unmistakably that a writ of mandamus, issued by the Supreme Court under Section 13 of the Judiciary Act, was definitely *not* such a remedy, for it was *unconstitutional!*

It was unconstitutional, explained Marshall for himself and his unanimous Associate Justices, Paterson, Chase, and Washington (Cushing and Moore not sitting in the case), because by *incorporating it into the Judiciary Act of 1789, Congress had added to the original jurisdiction of the Supreme Court by law,* an action which Article III, the judicial article of the Constitution, does not sanction. And, continued Marshall in an unprecedented, pithy, 1,500-word display of judicial self-abnegation combined with judicial assumption of power (for there is no doubt that judicial review, "the ultimate conservative response to the 'evils of democracy,' "[143] was a goal of the democracy-distrusting Federalists) in Section 13 Congress had given the Court a power it could not legally receive. (That section of the act had actually figured in earlier Supreme Court decisions, yet no one had chosen to raise the present constitutional issue.) *"An act repugnant to the Constitution is void,"* explained Marshall, thus echoing Hamilton's *Federalist* No. 78, and, in so stating the matter, he enunciated clearly the doctrine of judicial review.[144] He elaborated:

> It is emphatically the province and duty of the judicial department to say what the law is. Those who apply the rule to particular cases, must of necessity expound and

---

142. A lecture at Princeton University, September 25, 1950.

143. Wallace Mendelson, *Capitalism, Democracy, and the Supreme Court* (New York: Appleton-Century-Crofts, 1960), p. 20.

144. For a different view, though wholly "pro" judicial review, see Charles L. Black, Jr., *The People and the Court: Judicial Review in a Democracy* (New York: Macmillan, 1960), pp. 25ff. Black contends that judicial review had already been firmly established by then, and he calls a "myth" the usual belief that it was Marshall who gave it authoritative expression.

interpret that rule. . . . A law repugnant to the Constitution is void; . . . courts as well as other departments are bound by that instrument.[145]

Significance and Summary. In brief, John Marshall—thus ingeniously having managed to have his cake and eat it too, in what Senator Albert J. Beveridge of Indiana, his earliest and most voluminous biographer, perhaps somewhat extravagantly described as "a coup as bold in design and as daring as that by which the Constitution had been framed"[146]—clearly, cogently, and quite emphatically enunciated and interpreted three principles of the utmost significance to the young nation: (1) that the courts have the power of judicial review, (2) that the Constitution of the United States is the supreme law of the land, (3) that the *original* jurisdiction of the Supreme Court cannot be changed by simple law of Congress, since that particular jurisdiction is specifically limited by the language of the Constitution, although, plainly, the *appellate* jurisdiction may indeed be changed by simple legislation because the letter of the Constitution so permits.

This, of course, has been done since, with the most pertinent example being the intriguing post–Civil War case of *ex parte McCardle*.[147] Here the Supreme Court had under consideration an appeal, already argued before it in an 1868 *habeas corpus* proceeding, which was specifically authorized under a statute of 1867 that provided for a direct appeal to the Supreme Court in such cases—having unanimously rejected the government's motion to dismiss it for want of jurisdiction—in which the constitutionality of one of the Reconstruction Acts was at issue. Fearful that the Court might declare the act involved unconstitutional, and thus conceivably strike a mortal blow against the entire Reconstruction program, Congress, over President Andrew Johnson's courageous but fruitless veto that March, quickly amended the 1867 statute defining the appellate jurisdiction of the Supreme Court in these instances. Congress did this, in a rider to a customs and revenue appeals bill, by withdrawing from that jurisdiction direct appeals to the Supreme Court from the circuit courts in certain classes of *habeas corpus* proceedings, including the present one.[148] Incidentally, the majority of the Court who, led by Chief Justice Salmon P. Chase, had simply postponed action pending the legislative and executive moves, was far from displeased about the congressional victory, although

---

145. *Marbury v. Madison*, 1 Cranch 137 (1803).
146. Op. cit., vol. 1, p. 223, and vol. III, p. 142.
147. 7 Wallace 506 (1869). Colonel William H. McCardle, editor of the *Vicksburg [Miss.] Times* in the Fourth Reconstruction District, whose paper had been vociferously critical of Reconstruction policies and forces under the command of General Edward O. C. Ord, had been charged with numerous offenses, court-martialed, and sentenced to be shot.
148. In a letter to his son, Battle, shortly before he died (he was released by the military in due course and never tried in civil court for his alleged crimes and lived to a ripe old age), McCardle wrote that the Supreme Court had actually agreed to decide the case in his favor before Congress acted, the vote being 5:3 to hold his arrest unconstitutional. (He did not say how he became privy to those data.) It is a fact, however, that Chief Justice Chase, in a post–McCardle letter to U.S. District Court Judge Hill (who had initially denied bail to McCardle) confided that, had the case been tried on the merits, "the Court would doubtless have held that his imprisonment for trial before a military commission was illegal" (see Charles Fairman, 6 *History of the Supreme Court of the United States: Reconstruction and Reunion 1864–88*, Part 1 [New York: Macmillan, 1971], at p. 494).

Associate Justices Field and Grier issued a bitter public dissent against what they viewed as an evasion of constitutional responsibility and deliberate procrastination. But the Court was unanimous in upholding the action of Congress—and the Reconstruction Acts were never tested by it.

Whether or not one accepts Leonard Baker's enthusiastic encomium, namely, that Marshall's opinion in *Marbury v. Madison* "was one of civilization's finest hours, one of mankind's greatest achievements,"[149] the importance of Marshall's decision in *Marbury v. Madison* to American constitutional development can hardly be overestimated.[150] There is no question that judicial review is crucial to the governmental process in the United States under its federal character, its separation of powers principle: the whole nature of its constitutionalism. Yet it cannot be gainsaid that Marshall strained the judicial process in making *Marbury v. Madison* his vehicle for the announcement of the doctrine of the judicial veto. We have already noted that he should probably have disqualified himself from sitting in the case because of his direct and personal involvement with both its fundamental issue and its *dramatis personae*—after all, the case in effect arose out of his own negligence or apathy—and that, in any event, he did not really have to accept the case for review. He could readily have dismissed it for lack of original jurisdiction in this case. Moreover, based on available precedent, he could easily have interpreted Section 13 and its empowering provision—indeed, he probably should have—in such a manner as to raise no substantial questions regarding *substantive* statutory additions to the Court's original jurisdiction. For a good case could be made for the contention, based on the intent of its framers in the First Congress (which included future Chief Justice Oliver Ellsworth), that Section 13 signified nothing more than that the Court had the *procedural* power to grant writs of mandamus in all instances when such a remedy would be appropriate in the disposition of cases duly and properly brought before it, either on its original or its appellate docket. Specifically, the section stated that the Supreme Court could issue the writ to "persons holding office under the authority of the United States," and the justices *had* issued that writ in earlier cases without questioning Section 13 for a moment.[151] By no means was Section 13 thus necessarily intended to enlarge the original jurisdiction of the Court; but Marshall now claimed that the Court could not issue a writ of mandamus *except* in cases that came to it on appeal from a lower court. Yet he could quite simply have ruled that Congress did not seek to enlarge the Supreme Court's original jurisdiction under Section 13, but merely authorized the use of writs of mandamus when the Court exercised jurisdiction assigned by the Constitution.

However, none of the preceding suggested alternate courses of action would have suited Marshall's purposes, one of which also was to avoid the potential embarrassment that would have resulted from the almost certain defiance by President Jefferson. Having said and recognized that—and noting David P. Currie's

---

149. *John Marshall: A Life in Law* (New York: Macmillan, 1974), p. 409.
150. Marbury and his fellow litigants disappeared into the obscurity from which they had come at the conclusion of the case, although Marbury did become president of a Georgetown bank in 1814. He died in the same year as Marshall, 1835.
151. See, for example, Beveridge's *Marshall*, op. cit., 3, p. 130, no. 1 and 2, and 1 Cranch, generally.

charge that Marshall "stooped to deceptive reasoning, flouted precedent, and dodged the real issues"—[152]we should nonetheless avowedly acknowledge the genius of that powerful figure in American history and of the great service he performed in expounding the doctrine of judicial review when he did—a doctrine for which he fought hard in the Virginia Ratification Convention.[153] Far from being a usurpation, it has powerful claims to authenticity, based on more than a century of history, a strong line of precedents, and convincing contemporary literature. That debate on the justification and wisdom of the doctrine ensued almost at once, and that it has never really ceased, merely serves to add stature to its progenitor.[154] In the words of Charles P. Curtis, John Marshall "snatched from the majority and offered to our courts, the function of rendering our political decencies and aspirations into immanent law. What we owe to Marshall is the opportunity he gave us of combining a reign of conscience with a republic."[155]

152. *The Constitution in the Supreme Court: The First Hundred Years* (Chicago: University of Chicago Press, 1985), p. 74.
153. There are some latter-day dissenters from that generally accepted point of view. Thus, Robert Lowry Clinton argues in his *Marbury v. Madison and Judicial Review* (Lawrence: University of Kansas Press, 1989) that Marshall's decision in *Marbury v. Madison* was anything but a radical departure from legal tradition; that the accepted view of that case is a historical and represents a misunderstanding by both legal scholars and historians. And the feisty Leonard W. Levy declares in his *Original Intent and the Framers' Constitution* (Chicago: University of Chicago Press, 1988) that the Court in *Marbury v. Madison* held unconstitutional "an act of undoubted validity," concluding that "to the extent that judicial review rests on *Marbury* it rests on rubbish [sic], notwithstanding the imperishable lines of Marshall's opinion on the supremacy of fundamental law and the indisputable need to respect constitutional limitations" (at 87–88).
154. For a thoughtfully advocative contention that John Marshall, far from being a "usurper" or a "judicial activist," merely "followed [the] basic design [of the Founding Fathers] to create a system in which the parts could no longer emasculate the whole," see Wallace Mendelson, "Was Chief Justice Marshall an Activist?" in S. C. Halpern and C. M. Lamb (eds.), *Supreme Court Activism and Restraint* (Lexington, MA: Lexington Books, 1982), pp. 57–76.
155. "Review and Majority Rule," in *Supreme Court and Supreme Law*, ed., by Edmond Cahn (New York: Simon and Schuster, 1971), p. 198, Professor Cahn's own essay in his collection, "An American Constitution," is a fascinating analysis of both the wisdom *and* the justification of judicial review.

8

Judicial Review: II—Controversy and Limitations

JUDICIAL REVIEW IN A DEMOCRATIC STATE: SAINT OR SINNER?

That no other federal law, or section thereof, was declared unconstitutional by the Supreme Court between *Marbury v. Madison*[1] in 1803 and the *Dred Scott* case,[2] a full fifty-four years later, did not lessen the debate on the doctrine of judicial review. That it has remained fresh, indeed, and has lost none of its controversial characteristics, is testified to vividly and contemporarily by—to employ an obvious illustration—the widespread public, often emotion-charged, debate surrounding the unanimous decision for the Court by Chief Justice Warren in the 1954 *Segregation cases*,[3] in a sense the grandchildren of the Taney Court's decision in *Dred Scott*. The charge against the Warren Court: in holding compulsory segregation on account of race in the public schools to be a violation of the "equal protection of the laws" clause of the Fourteenth Amendment to the U.S. Constitution in the state cases, and the due "process of law" clause of the Fifth in the federal case, the Court had not *judged*, not *interpreted*, not *reviewed*, but *legislated*. Two decades later, to use an even more contemporary illustration, the same indictment would be levied against the Burger Court's historic and contentious *Abortion cases*[4] by what came to be known as the "pro-life" forces (with the "pro-choice" forces on the other side). The indictment of judicial legislation is directly related, of course,

---

1. 1 Cranch 137.
2. *Dred Scott v. Sandford,* 19 Howard 393 (1857).
3. *Brown v. Board of Education,* 347 U.S. 483 (1954) and *Bolling v. Sharpe,* 347 U.S. 497 (1954). *Brown* was a Kansas case; *Bolling* came from the District of Columbia.
4. *Roe v. Wade* and *Doe v. Bolton,* 410 U.S. 113 and 410 U.S. 179 (1973), respectively.

to the power and doctrine of judicial review, once characterized as "the people's institutionalized means of self-control."[5]

INVOKING AUTHORITY

Unfortunately, all too few professional observers of the judicial process and quite naturally even fewer laypersons, however informed they may be, are resolutely consistent in their attitude toward either judicial review or the institution that exercises the power. To abide by Paul A. Freund's exhortation that "criticism . . . be informed by perspective and informed by philosophy"[6] is difficult. More often than not "it all depends whose ox is being gored," to employ Al Smith's pungent phrase. Yet it is entirely feasible to determine both articulate and reasonable "con" and "pro" positions regarding the doctrine without embracing the postures of the more passionate partisans of the controversy. Although a great deal of literature on the subject is available, we may well permit two of America's most honored and most literate governmental personages to speak for the two sides. It is fair to say that, had they not lived and functioned considerably more than a century apart, they would have respected and admired one another and would have made a worthy set of opponents in any public debate on the issue: Thomas Jefferson *con*, and Benjamin Cardozo *pro* judicial review. With due allowance for certain deviations, their points of view, even their verbiage, are today very much representative of the two divergent attitudes on the question.

Con. Although, as a strong believer in the necessity of an independent judiciary, Thomas Jefferson was in fact among the first to suggest judicial review as a means of harmonizing the federal system, and although evidence contained in at least two

5. Charles L. Black, Jr., *The People and the Court: Judicial Review in a Democracy* (New York: Macmillan, 1960), p. 20. For some other vital contemporary works on judicial review, with varying points of view, cf. Alexander M. Bickel, *The Least Dangerous Branch* (Indianpolis: Bobbs-Merrill, 1962) and his *The Supreme Court and the Idea of Progress* (New York: Harper & Row, 1970); Herbert Wechsler, *Principles, Politics and Fundamental Law* (Cambridge: Harvard University Press, 1961); Charles S. Hyneman, *The Supreme Court on Trial* (New York: Atherton Press, 1963); Howard E. Dean, *Judicial Review and Democracy* (New York: Random House, 1966); Arthur A. North, S. J., *The Supreme Court: Judicial Process and Judicial Politics* (New York: Appleton-Century-Crofts, 1966); Louis Lusky. *By What Right? A Commentary on the Supreme Court's Power to Revise the Constitution* (Charlottesville, VA: Michie, 1975); Raoul Berger, *Government by Judiciary: The Transformation of the Fourteenth Amendment* (Cambridge: Harvard University Press, 1977); Jesse H. Choper, *Judicial Review and the National Political Process* (Chicago: University of Chicago Press, 1980); John Hart Ely, *Democracy and Distrust: A Theory of Judicial Review* (Cambridge: Harvard University Press, 1980); Sanford B. Gabin, *Judicial Review and the Reasonable Doubt Test* (New York: Kennikat Press, 1981); Arthur S. Miller, *Toward Increased Judicial Activism: The Political Role of the Supreme Court* (Westport, CT: Greenwood Press, 1982); Michael J. Perry, *The Constitution, the Courts, and Human Rights: An Inquiry into the Legitimacy of Policy-Making by the Judiciary* (New Haven, CT: Yale University Press, 1982); Christopher Wolfe, *The Rise of Modern Judicial Review* (New York: Basic Books, 1986); John Agresto, *The Supreme Court and Constitutional Democracy* (Ithaca: Cornell University Press, 1984); Sotirios A. Barber, *On What the Constitution Means* (Baltimore: Johns Hopkins University Press, 1984); Bernard H. Siegan, *The Supreme Court's Constitution: An Inquiry into Judicial Review and Its Impact on Society* (New Brunswick, NJ: Transaction Books, 1987); and Paul R. Dimond, *The Supreme Court and Judicial Review: The Role of Provisional Review in a Democracy* (Ann Arbor: University of Michigan Press, 1989).

6. *The Supreme Court of the United States* (Cleveland and New York: World Publishing, 1961), p. 77.

letters written from Paris to James Madison is persuasive that Jefferson had favored some type or degree of direct judicial control at the time of the framing of the Constitution in Philadelphia and even almost two years later,[7] the great Virginian certainly never accepted the notion of judicial review as it was subsequently expounded by his political opponent, John Marshall. Some observers[8] trace the genesis of his hostility to the enforcement of the hated Alien and Sedition Acts of 1798: prior to this he was demonstrably not opposed to judicial review, at least not in theory. In any event, Jefferson's opposition to overriding judicial power was based on two major concepts: first, that the doctrine of judicial review—and certainly as applied by Marshall, for he saw no one else do it—violates that of the constitutionally mandated theory of the separation of powers, and second, that it represents a patent denial of the veritable popular will, the majority will, as expressed by the sovereign people through their duly elected representatives "in Congress assembled" (and in any other properly constituted legislative body). That the second assertion did not, however, blind him to the potential excesses of these representatives, is indicated clearly in one of his letters to Madison, to whom he voiced the fear that "the tyranny of the legislatures is the most formidable dread at present and will be for many years."[9]

Nonetheless, Jefferson vehemently rejected the contention that the Founding Fathers had intended to give to one of the three branches the sole right to prescribe rules for the government of the others "and to that one, too, which is unelected by and independent of the nation." He insisted that each of the three branches, being independent, "has an equal right to decide for itself the meaning of the Constitution in the cases submitted to its action; where it is to act ultimately without appeal; [and that] the court is neither more learned nor more objective than the political branches of the government."[10] He did grant its salutary role in protecting constitutional rights.[11] Yet, in fine, to Jefferson the doctrine of judicial review, with its inherent possibilities of leading to judicial *supremacy*, was both elitist and *antidemocratic*—although, of course, on close examination one sees that *all* agencies of government have their "undemocratic" aspects. Moreover, it is entirely possible to categorize the sage of Monticello's stance on judicial review not so much as opposition *qua* opposition, but opposition based on its presence as a tool in the hands of John Marshall.

Jefferson's position on the nonexclusiveness of the power to interpret the Constitution has been echoed frequently since, but by none better than Justice John B. Gibson of the Supreme Court of Pennsylvania, a contemporary of Jefferson and essentially an advocate of legislative supremacy, who was probably the most able

7. December 20, 1787, and March 15, 1789.
8. E.g., Wallace Mendelson "Jefferson on Judicial Review: Consistency through Change," 29 *University of Chicago Law Review* (Winter 1962), pp. 327–37.
9. Letter of March 15, 1789.
10. From his letter to Judge Spencer Roane of the Virginia Supreme Court, September 6, 1819. See also his letter to Abigail Adams, September 11, 1804, when he wrote: "You seem to think it devolves on the judges to decide on the validity of the Sedition Law. But nothing in the Constitution gives them a right to decide for the executive, more than the executive to decide for them." As quoted by Saul K. Padover, *A Jefferson Profile* (New York: John Day, 1956), p. 154.
11. Letter to William Jarvis, September 28, 1820.

adversary of judicial review in his day. From that bench in 1825, in his now famous dissenting opinion in *Eakin v. Raub*,[12] in which his colleagues upheld the power of Pennsylvania's state courts to declare state statutes unconstitutional, Gibson, insisting that "[t]he oath to support the Constitution is not peculiar to the judges, but is taken indiscriminately by every officer of the government. . .," lucidly and forcefully challenged Marshall's argument in *Marbury v. Madison* along the lines of the Jeffersonian response. One of his key points was the classic concept of popular democracy: that it is a "postulate in the theory of our government . . . that the people are wise, virtuous, and competent to manage their own affairs."[13] Yet Gibson had apparently modified his viewpoint twenty years later. When an attorney, pleading his case before the Pennsylvania Supreme Court, cited the Gibson dissent in *Eakin v. Raub*, that Justice replied from the bench that he had changed his opinion for two reasons: one, that the Pennsylvania Constitutional Convention of 1838, by remaining silent on judicial review, had "sanctioned the pretensions of the court to deal freely with the act of the legislature," and two, "from experience of the necessity of the case."[14] This does not necessarily connote a change of mind, but it assuredly does indicate at least that Justice Gibson, true to his philosophy of the representative legislative function, had accepted the latter's "surrender" to the doctrine. It ought to be noted here that Gibson never intended his opposition to judicial review to extend to the *federal* judiciary's power to declare *state* laws unconstitutional. For *that* power he perceived as clearly stipulated by the obligations of Article VI of the U.S. Constitution, the supremacy clause. Nonetheless, when Gibson, supported by John C. Calhoun, was under consideration for the U.S. Supreme Court vacancy caused by Justice Bushrod Washington's death in 1829, his well-known *Eakin* rationale truncated his candidacy.

Pro. Although he greatly admired Jefferson as a human being, a democratic leader, and a political philosopher, Benjamin N. Cardozo, who served for eighteen years on the New York State Court of Appeals as well as an Associate Justice of the U.S. Supreme Court for the regrettably brief period from 1932 to 1938, disagreed strongly with Jefferson's approach to, and rejection of, judicial review. Cardozo anchored his belief in that doctrine on the firm conviction that although it must be employed cautiously and sparingly, as he himself did, it serves nonetheless as a necessary and proper check on possible excesses by both the federal and state legislatures. But it would be utterly wrong to label him a "judicial activist." More than a decade prior to his universally hailed appointment to the Supreme Court, where he filled the seat vacated by Justice Oliver Wendell Holmes, Jr., Cardozo had advanced his key contention that it is the *restraining influence of its presence* rather than the frequency of its application that renders judicial review so vital to the governmental process in the United States of America. His characteristically beautiful style and language must be quoted directly:

> By conscious or subconscious influence, the presence of this restraining power aloof in the background, but none the less always in reserve, *tends to stabilize and rational-*

---

12. 12 S. & R. (Pa. S. Ct.) 330.
13. Ibid., at 355.
14. See *Norris v. Clymer*, 2 Pa. St. 277 (1845) at 281, as reported by Robert F. Cushman, *Cases in Constitutional Law*, 6th ed. (Englewood Cliffs, NJ: Prentice-Hall, 1984), p. 12.

ize the legislative judgment, to infuse it with the glow of principle, to hold the standard aloft and visible for those who must run the race and keep the faith. . . . The restraining power of the judiciary does not manifest its chief worth in the few cases in which the legislature has gone beyond the lines that mark the limits of discretion. Rather shall we find *its chief worth in making vocal and audible the ideals that might otherwise be silenced, in giving them continuity of life and expression, in guiding and directing choice within the limits where choice ranges.* This function should preserve to the courts the power that now belongs to them; if only the power is exercised with insight into social values, and with suppleness of adaption to changing social needs.[15]

The great jurist whom Cardozo had succeeded was familiar with this passage, fully concurred in its sentiment and credo, and had practiced it throughout his three decades on the highest bench of the land. However, although Holmes was willing to grant that the United States would not "come to an end if we lost our power to declare an Act of Congress void," he firmly insisted that "the Union would be imperiled if we could not make that declaration as to the laws of the several states."[16] U.S. Circuit Court Judge Learned Hand, the distinguished contemporary of Holmes and Cardozo, frequently echoed this Holmesian creed. But Hand went considerably further than Holmes when, writing several years after his retirement from the bench, he endeavored to devise a test that would provide another modification of the doctrine. Although agreeing that the Supreme Court must have the power and authority to review *grants* of power to and by Congress, he believed that it should not possess these sanctions regarding "a review of how the power has been *exercised.*"[17] It is difficult to see how such an amendment of the doctrine of judicial review would not wound it seriously, if not fatally.

The Jefferson and Cardozo viewpoints—and their attempted modifications— have manifold ardent and articulate adherents.[18] Yet there is no longer any doubt that judicial review is a permanent fixture in the American structure and operation of government, notwithstanding the repeated frontal and guerilla attacks from both public and private sources.[19] It is, after all, an essential adjunct of our consti-

---

15. Benjamin N. Cardozo, *The Nature of the Judicial Process* (New Haven, CT: Yale University Press, 1921), pp. 93–94 (italics supplied).
16. Oliver Wendell Holmes, Jr., "Law and the Court," in *Collected Legal Papers* (New York: Harcourt, Brace, 1920), p. 295.
17. Learned Hand, *The Bill of Rights* (Cambridge: Harvard University Press, 1958), pps. 66, 93–94 (italics supplied).
18. For a conveniently "tabularized" list of arguments in favor and against judicial review, see Alan F. Westin's "Introduction" to the paperback edition of Charles A. Beard's classic, *The Supreme Court and the Constitution* (Englewood Cliffs, NJ: Prentice-Hall, 1962), pp. 6–7.
19. For summary analysis of attempted legislative checks on the power, see Sheldon D. Elliott, "Court-Curbing Proposals in Congress," 33 *Notre Dame Lawyer* (August 1958), pp. 597–605. Five excellent books dealing with the problem are Walter F. Murphy, *Congress and the Court* (Chicago: University of Chicago Press, 1962); C. Herman Pritchett, *Congress versus the Supreme Court* (Minneapolis: University of Minnesota Press, 1961); Raoul Berger, *Congress v. The Supreme Court* (Cambridge: Harvard University Press, 1969); Adam C. Breckenridge, *Congress against the Court* (Lincoln: University of Nebraska Press, 1971); and John R. Schmidhauser and Larry L. Berg, *The Supreme Court and Congress: Conflict and Interaction, 1945–1968* (New York: Free Press, 1972). See also the important study in the late 1960s, undertaken by Stuart S. Nagel, which demonstrates that between 1802 and 1959 there were seven periods of high-frequency and an equal number of low-frequency Court-curbing legislation. He found a total of 165 bills introduced in Congress during those 157 years that

tutional firmament, a normal fact of American governmental life—ringingly recon-firmed contemporarily in such seminal decisions as *United States v. Nixon* in 1974, *Immigration and Naturalization Service v. Chadha* in 1983, and *United States v. Eichman* in 1990.[20]

DRAWING THE LINE—OR ATTEMPTING TO DO SO

Directly and intimately entwined in the controversy over the doctrine of judicial review is the thus perpetually voiced charge that the Supreme Court of the United States—and in varying lesser degrees the lower components of the judiciary, is guilty of *judicial legislating*; in other words, that many of its decisions are tanta-mount to legislating rather than judging. More often than not, this indictment of the judiciary admits, and indeed grants, that the Court must have the power to *interpret* legislation and, if "absolutely necessary," hold unconstitutional a law that is *clearly* contrary to the Constitution, although no yardstick is provided on the connotation of the modifier "clearly." But this school of thought insists that a line must be drawn between the exercise of judicial *judgment* and the imposition of judicial *will*. Judicial will is accordingly equated with legislating, presumably reserved to Congress and the legislatures of the fifty states. Like all fine lines, the one between "interpreting" or "judging" and "legislating" is highly tenuous. How is it to be drawn? by whom? where? under what circumstances? Clearly there is no simple or single response to these questions, so crucial to line-drawing in general, and the line at issue in particular. Justice Robert H. Jackson's memorable exhor-tation *cum caveat*, one year prior to his death in 1954, that "We are not final because we are infallible; but we are infallible only because we are final,"[21] is indeed apposite.

JUDICIAL LEGISLATING

The polar extremes in the endless controversy over the absence or presence of the concept of judicial legislating become readily apparent in the following two quotes, taken from active and honorable participants on both sides of the aisle, institution-ally as well as philosophically. Early in 1930, rising on the floor of the U.S. Senate, of which he was one of the finest and most purposeful members for many years, George W. Norris of Nebraska, the "gentle-knight of progressive ideals," shouted:

> We have a legislative body, called the House of Representatives, of over 400 men.
> We have another legislative body, called the Senate, of less than 100 men. We have,

---

were designed to curb the power of the Court: 49 were aimed at changing or eliminating the power of judicial review, 49 at changing its personnel, 45 at limiting its jurisdiction, and 22 representing mis-cellaneous "curbing" proposals. See "Court Curbing Periods in American History," in his *The Legal Process from a Behavioral Perspective* (Homewood, IL: Dorsey Press, 1969), pp. 285–93. In the first five months of 1981 alone, 23 Court-curbing proposals were introduced in the House and 4 in the Senate. For a trenchant recent study of Court curbing, see Gary L. McDowell, *Curbing the Courts: The Constitution and the Limits of Judicial Power* (Baton Rouge: Louisiana State University Press, 1988).

20. 417 U.S. 683, 462 U.S. 919, and 496 U.S. 310, respectively.

21. *Brown v. Allen*, 344 U.S. 443 (1953), at 540, concurring opinion.

in reality, another legislative body, called the Supreme Court, of nine men; and they are more powerful than all the others put together.[22]

The diametrically opposite point of view is represented in a passage from an address to the New York State Bar Association in 1893 by Justice David Brewer of the U.S. Supreme Court:

> They [courts and judges] make no law, they establish no policy, they never enter into the domain of popular action. They do not govern. Their functions in relation to the state are limited to seeing that popular action does not trespass upon right and justice as it exists in written constitutions and natural law.[23]

Both expressions are equally extreme in their thesis, of course; they represent gross oversimplifications, notwithstanding the sincerity and conviction of the two speakers involved. Indeed, most of the Justices of the highest tribunal do not claim to have a pat answer to the vexatious question presented by the controversy over *the line*. But they have often come to grips with the crux of the matter in recognizing the human element that is so inevitably involved in the judicial process. In the realistic words of Justice John H. Clarke:

> I have never known any judges, no difference how austere of manner, who discharged their judicial duties in an atmosphere of pure, unadulterated reason. Alas! we are all "the common growth of Mother Earth,"—even those of us who wear the long robe.[24]

The blunt-spoken Justice McReynolds insisted that a judge should not be "an amorphous dummy, unspotted by human emotions"—and he was more than a little spotted! "Judges are men, not disembodied spirits," once remarked Justice Frankfurter; "as men they respond to human situations. They do not reside in a vacuum." "Our judges are not monks or scientists," wrote Chief Justice Warren, "but participants in the living stream of our national life, steering the law between the dangers of rigidity on the one hand and formlessness on the other."[25] He thus echoed the realistic appraisal made by Thomas Reed Powell four decades earlier, who had commented:

> Judges have preferences for social policies as you and I. They form their judgments after the varying fashions in which you and I form ours. They have hands, organs, dimensions, senses, affections, passions. They are warmed by the same winter and summer and by the same ideas as a layman is.[26]

As Chief Justice Rehnquist observed simply in 1988, "Judges are shaped in what's going on in the world around them."[27]

In any event, the Justices are agreed that they endeavor to judge the cases and controversies that reach the Court in accordance with the perceived commands

22. *Congressional Record*, 71 Cong. 2d Sess., Vol. 72, Part 4, p. 3566 (February 13, 1930).
23. Address to the New York State Bar Association, *Proceedings* (1893).
24. Hoyt L. Warner, *The Life of Mr. Justice Clarke* (Cleveland: Western Reserve University Press, 1959), p. 69.
25. "The Law and the Future," 52 *Fortune* 106 (November 1955).
26. "The Logic and Rhetoric of Constitutional Law," 15 *Journal of Philosophy, Psychology, and Scientific Method* 656 (1918).
27. As quoted in *The Washington Post*, May 25, 1988, p. A15.

of the Constitution and the laws of the land. There is no doubt that the nine Justices—in fact the judges on all levels of the judicial process—necessarily "legislate" in interpreting constitutional phraseology. The question is how much and how far they are justified in such judicial legislating. The often quoted jurist, however apocryphal the story may be, who responded to the question of whether judges make law replied, "Of course we do; made some myself last Monday," is undoubtedly close to the truth. One of the wisest among those who graced the bench of the Supreme Court, the revered Justice Holmes, who has been so well described as the official judicial philospher for the modern age,[28] also recognized "without hesitation" that judges *do and must legislate*"; but he added that they "can do so only interstitially; they are confined from molar to molecular motions."[29] In a valedictory interview, Chief Justice Warren readily acknowledged that the Court, in effect, does make law:

> It doesn't make it consciously, it doesn't do it by intending to usurp the role of Congress but because of the very nature of our job. When two litigants come into court, one says the act of Congress means this, the other says the act of Congress means the opposite of that, and we say the act of Congress means something—either one of the two or something in between. We are making law, aren't we?[30]

Chief Justice Marshall, however, who was fully aware of the problem at issue, nevertheless insisted that "judicial power, as contradistinguished from the power of the law, has no existence. Courts are the mere instruments of the law, and can will nothing."[31] Yet this statesman, who is generally recognized as the most influential, competent, and successful of all the Chief Justices to date and is ranked among the two or three most powerful and influential jurists ever to sit on the Supreme Court, was hardly loath to interpret broadly the Constitution and legislation passed under its authority—and in accordance with what Justice Holmes later referred to as "the felt necessities of the time." After all, had not that same Marshall written, in the great *McCulloch v. Maryland* decision, that our laws were made under a Constitution that was "intended to endure for ages to come, and consequently, to be adapted to the various *crises* of human affairs"?[32] Probably no Justice has done more of this "adapting," and more incisively, than did Chief Justice Marshall, who often reminded his fellow citizens that "we must never forget that it is a *Constitution* we are expounding!"[33] Did he *interpret* or did he *legislate?* Undoubtedly both.

More on the Line and on the Goring of Oxen. Marshall's long-term successor, Chief Justice Roger B. Taney, stared into the heart of the problem when, in rendering the majority opinion in the *Dred Scott* case, he held that the Constitution

> speaks not only in the same words, but with the same meaning and intent with which it spoke when it came from the hands of its framers, and was voted on and adopted

28. Fred V. Cahill, Jr., *Judicial Legislation* (New York: Ronald Press, 1952), p. 32.
29. *Southern Pacific Co. v. Jensen*, 244 U.S. 205 (1916), at 221 (italics supplied).
30. Sacramento, California, June 26, 1969, as quoted in *The New York Times*, June 27, 1969, p. 17.
31. *Osborn v. United States Bank*, 9 Wheaton 739 (1824) at 865.
32. Wheaton 315 (1819) at 413 (italics in original).
33. Justice Frankfurter considered this Marshall statement to be "the single most important utterance in the literature of constitutional law—most important because most comprehensive and comprehending" ("John Marshall and the Judicial Function," 69 *Harvard Law Review* 217 [1955] at 219).

by the people of the United States. Any other rule of construction would abrogate the judicial character of this court, and make it the mere reflex of the popular opinion or passion of the day.[34]

But the *Dred Scott* decision has been denounced more often as sheer "legislation" than any other decision of the Court, with the possible exception of the 1954 *Segregation cases*.[35] When he was informed of the decision in *Dred Scott*, Senator Hale of New Hampshire introduced a resolution to *abolish* the Supreme Court. Yet again depending on the point of view, those people who hailed the 1857 *Dred Scott* judgment as "statesmanlike interpretation" would have violently denounced the 1954 *Segregation cases* as "blatant legislation," whereas the champions of the latter decisions would have roundly denounced the former. Indeed, some of the torrent of abuse poured on the Court by the latter day *Segregation cases* critics is almost identical in verbiage to that employed by the enemies of their Southern ancestors, the Radical Republicans of the North, in attacking *Dred Scott*. Could it be that the popular judgment does, in fact, depend on whose ox is being gored?

Justice Owen J. Roberts, always searching for, if not inevitably contributing to, a modicum of consistency on the bench, attempted to draw the line once and for all in 1936—"the slot machine theory," commented Roscoe Pound acidly—when he spoke for a majority of six in the significant case of *United States v. Butler*, in which the Court struck down the New Deal's Agricultural Adjustment Act of 1933:

> When an act of Congress is appropriately challenged in the Courts as not conforming to the constitutional mandate the judicial branch of the Government has only one duty—*to lay the article of the Constutition which is invoked beside the statute which is challenged and to decide whether the latter squares with the former.*[36]

"Bravo," applauded the *opponents* of the New Deal, "great judicial statesmanship, proper and precise interpretation of the Constitution!" "An unwarranted, outrageous assumption of legislative authority," countered the *proponents* of the New Deal, "arrogant disregard of constitutional limitations of judicial power." And President Roosevelt, scarcely one year after *Butler*, moved unsuccessfully to pack the Court by statutory provision, setting off one of the most interesting, most heated, and most sustained controversies in the entire history of Court and nation.[37]

It was in the *Butler* case that the issue was perhaps most nearly joined by Justice Harlan Fiske Stone, not too many years later to be the Chief Justice, when he dissented from the opinion of the majority and admonished the members on that side of the decision that

> [w]hile unconstitutional exercise of power by the executive and legislative branches is subject to judicial restraint, *the only check on our own exercise of power is our own*

---

34. *Dred Scott v. Sandford*, 19 Howard 393 (1857).
35. *Brown v. Board of Education*, 347 U.S. 483 (1954) and *Bolling v. Sharpe*, 347 U.S. 497 (1954). The 1973 *Abortion Cases* decision in *Roe v. Wade*, 410 U.S. 113, represent another obvious illustration of charges and countercharges.
36. 297 U.S. 1 (1936) at 62 (italics supplied).
37. For two engagingly written accounts, see Joseph Alsop and Turner Catledge, *The 168 Days* (New York: Doubleday, Doran, 1938) and Leonard Baker, *Back to Back: The Duel between F.D.R. and the Supreme Court* (New York: Macmillan, 1967).

sense of self-restraint. . . . Courts are not the only agency of government that must be assumed to have capacity to govern. . . . For the removal of unwise laws from the statute books appeal lies not to the courts but to the ballot and to the processes of democratic government.[38]

This would seem to be as close to the facts of judicial life as is attainable. In a sense, and although he would very likely have disapproved of the comparison, the Stone comment was almost an echo of a famous statement made twenty years earlier by Charles Evans Hughes while he was the Republican presidential nominee. He had just become an ex-Associate Justice of the U.S. Supreme Court, was an ex-Governor of New York, a future member of the Permanent Court of Arbitration and Judge of the Permanent Court of International Justice, a future Secretary of State in the Administrations of Presidents Harding and Coolidge, and ultimately would ascend the Court for a second tenure, this time as Chief Justice. While stumping during the campaign, a campaign which almost won him the presidency, he publicly repeated a pronouncement he had made in 1907 while he was still governor: *"We are under Constitution, but the Constitution is what the judges say it is.* . . ."[39] That assertion represents both too drastic and too simplified an analysis of the complex position of the judiciary and the Court, and it is subject to considerable substantive modification. Surely, in the final analysis, the Constitution is or becomes what the people of the nation want it to be or to become—a fact of political life that is very much on the mind of judges—and it must be considered, as Holmes said, "in the light of our whole experience and not merely in that of what was said a hundred years ago." In the words of his long-time friend and colleague, Brandeis:

> Our Constitution is not a straight jacket. It is a living organism. As such it is capable of growth—of expansion and adaptation to new conditions. Growth implies changes, political, economic, and social. Growth which is significant manifests itself rather in intellectual and moral conceptions than in material things.[40]

Moreover, for the sake of argument, the Constitution may well be what the judges say it is, but this by no means makes certain appropriate compliance, as has been repeatedly demonstrated. With these essential qualifications in mind, however, the Hughes campaign statement, coupled with the Stone dissent in the *Butler*

38. *United States v. Butler,* 297 U.S. 1 (1936) at 78, 88. (italics supplied). In an intriguing, if hardly non-controversial, analysis, Professor Bradley C. Canon identifies six specific elements or dimensions that give general structure to the concept of "judicial activism": (1) *majoritarianism*—the degree to which policies adopted through democratic processes are judicially negated. (2) *interpretive stability*—the degree to which earlier court decisions, doctrines, or interpretations are altered. (3) *Interpretive fidelity*—the degree to which constitutional provisions are interpreted contrary to the clear intentions of their drafters or the clear implications of the language used. (4) *substance/democratic process distinction*—the degree to which judicial decisions make substantive policy rather than affect the preservation of democratic political processes. (5) *specificity of policy*—the degree to which a judicial decision establishes policy itself as opposed to leaving discretion to other agencies or individuals. (6) *availability of an alternate policymaker*—the degree to which a judicial decision supersedes serious consideration of the same problem by other governmental agencies. "Defining the Dimensions of Judicial Activism," 66 *Judicature* 6 (December–January 1983), pp. 237–47.
39. Charles Evans Hughes, *Addresses,* 2d ed. (New York: Putnam, 1916), p. 185 (italics supplied).
40. An unpublished passage in *United States v. Moreland,* 258 U.S. 433 (1922), as quoted by Alexander Bickel in his *The Supreme Court and the Idea of Progress* (New York: Harper & Row, 1970), p. 20.

case, could serve largely as the definitive view of the Court's attitude. It has frequently been echoed by other articulate members of the highest bench, such as that philosophical devotee of British legislative supremacy and majority rule, Justice Frankfurter, who, in dissenting in the controversial expatriation case of *Trop v. Dulles,* lectured that

> All power is, in Madison's phrase, "of an encroaching nature." . . . Judicial power is not immune against this human weakness. It must also be on guard against encroaching beyond its proper bounds, and not the less so since *the only restraint upon it is self-restraint.* . . .[41]

Vast differences about this aspect of the vexatious line exist now, and have always existed, among the Justices themselves, but most, in fact probably all, would candidly subscribe to the essence of the suggested Stone–Hughes formula, however at variance their interpretation and application of it may be. One thing is above all clear, in the realistic words of Justice Cardozo, not only one of the most proficient and most beloved Justices ever to sit on the Supreme Court but also one of its finest and most haunting stylists: *"The great tides and currents which engulf the rest of men, do not turn aside in their course, and pass the judges idly by."*[42]

Justice George Sutherland, one of the six-man majority in the *Butler* case, justified judicial activism—which he and his jurisprudential soulmates, Justices Van Devanter, McReynolds, and Butler applied chiefly in the economic *laisser faire* camp—as natural judicial involvement. As one Sutherland student analyzed his posture, the oath of office taken by each Justice required him to decide cases in terms of his own best judgment. As he put it: "Self-restraint, therefore, had no place among judicial duties. To surrender one's deliberate judgment, indeed, except as it might be modified by the persuasion of those holding different views, would constitute a violation of his oath of office."[43] To quote Sutherland directly from his dissenting opinion in the 1937 "switch-in-time-that-saved-nine" *West Coast Hotel* case:

> Self-restraint belongs in the domain of will and not of judgment. The check upon the judge is that imposed by his oath of office, by the Constitution, and by his own conscientious and informed convictions. . . .[44]

It is delicious irony that his jurisprudential and philosophical opposite, Justice William O. Douglas, could just as easily have written these words and applied them to *his* posture in the realm of civil rights and liberties! In any event, as Justice Frankfurter put the matter cogently, the Court cannot, in the long run, escape judging; it must adjudicate; it must decide. Not one to judge lightly or hastily— Professor Wallace Mendelson has aptly called him a "humilitarian" among jurists with respect to the judicial process[45]—Frankfurter, while deeply dedicated to the

41. 356 U.S. 86 (1958) at 113 (italics supplied).
42. Benjamin N. Cardozo, *The Nature of the Judicial Process,* op. cit., p. 168 (italics supplied).
43. Carl Brent Swisher, *The Growth of Constitutional Power in the United States,* 2d ed. (Chicago: University of Chicago Press, 1963), p. 221.
44. *West Coast Hotel Co. v. Parrish,* 300 U.S. 379, at 402.
45. "Mr. Justice Frankfurter—Law and Choice," 10 *Vanderbilt Law Review* 333 (February 1957).

concept of judicial self-restraint, nevertheless clearly faced the problem in his concurring opinion in the often-cited *Sweezy* case:

> To be sure, this [opinion] is a conclusion based on a judicial judgment in balancing two contending principles—the right of a citizen to political privacy, as protected by the Fourteenth Amendment, and the right of the State to self-protection. And striking the balance implies the exercise of judgment. This is the inescapable judicial task in giving substantive content, legally enforced, to the Due Process Clause, and it is a task ultimately committed to this Court. It must not be an exercise of whim or will. *It must be an overriding judgment founded on something much deeper and more justifiable than personal preference. As far as it lies within human limitations, it must be impersonal judgment. It must rest on fundamental presuppositions rooted in history to which widespread acceptance may fairly be attributed.* Such a judgment must be arrived at in a spirit of humility when it counters the judgment of the State's highest court. *But, in the end, judgment cannot be escaped—the judgment of this Court.*[46]

That this awesome and even agonizing duty of finding and drawing the line between judicial will and judicial judgment in rendering a necessary decision conscientiously is not confined to the highest level of the federal judiciary may be illustrated by a decision of the Supreme Court of Michigan. In a consortium case replete with human factors, a closely divided (4:3) Court not only reversed a lower court decision but negated precedent of long standing. Speaking for the majority, Justice Talbot Smith recognized that the decision represented a drastic departure from the past and would surely be viewed as judicial legislating. Yet having braved the expected storm, he admitted that the decision to permit the wife of a man seriously injured in an automobile accident to sue for loss of consortium (i.e., marital comfort, affection, and companionship) marked a stride away from the "outworn legal views" derived from old English and Roman law that a wife is merely a "vassal, chattel, and household drudge." He concluded:

> Were we to rule upon precedent alone, we would have no trouble with this case. We would simply tell this woman to be gone, and take her shattered husband with her. . . . Legally today, the wife stands on a par with her husband. . . . *The obstacles to the wife's [court] action were judge-invented and they are herewith judge-destroyed.*[47]

The anticipated critical storm of charges of crass judicial legislating broke over the heads of author and Court at once. Yet, perhaps Justice Smith had simply been unusually frank in writing his opinion as he did, rather than disguising it in judicial semantics. Perhaps he had not been unaware of the famous expression of judicial philosophy by Chancellor Kent of New York a century and a half earlier:

> I saw where justice lay, and the moral issue decided the court [Kent] half the time; and I then sat down to search the authorities. . . . I might once in a while be embar-

---

46. *Sweezy v. New Hampshire, by Wyman, Attorney-General,* 354 U.S. 234 (1957) at 266–67 (italics supplied).
47. *Montgomery v. Stephan,* 359 Mich. 33 (1960). Eight years later the New York Court of Appeals handed down an almost identical decision, and also by a 4:3 vote (*Millington v. Southern Elevator Co.,* 293 N.Y.S. 2d 305).

rassed by a technical rule, but I almost always found principles suited to my views of the case. . . .[48]

In summary, depending, of course, on the facts and posture of each individual case, both verbiage and line are very much matters of degree. But, as Justice Frankfurter took pains to admonish, to say that courts make law just as legislatures do is "to deny essential features in the history of our democracy. It denies that legislation and adjudication have had different lines of growth, serve vitally different purposes, function under different conditions, and bear different responsibilities."[49]

JUDGES LIMITED: THE TAUGHT TRADITION OF THE LAW

Moreover, it must be clearly understood that judges are not free agents in rendering their decisions, regardless of the impression given by some. Again in Frankfurter's words: "We do not sit like a kadi under a tree dispensing justice according to considerations of individual expediency."[50] A deplorable tendency exists in the mind of the public to oversimplify the process of judicial decision making, the area of government obviously least understood by the average citizen. Although it may perhaps overstate the case somewhat, there is much merit in the contention of the just-cited Justice Talbot Smith, that we are rigidly bound within walls that are unseen by the layperson. These walls are built of the heritage of the law, the spirit of the Anglo-Saxon law, the impact of the cases as they come down through the years—in brief, *the taught tradition of the law*. No one has expressed the heart of the matter better than Justice Cardozo:

> A jurist is not to innovate at pleasure. He is not a knight-errant, roaming at will in pursuit of his own ideal of beauty or of goodness. He is to draw his inspiration from consecrated principles. He is not to yield to spasmodic sentiment, to vague and unregulated benevolence. He is to exercise a discretion informed by tradition, methodized by analogy, disciplined by system, and subordinated to the primordial necessity of order in the social life.[51]

Among the vital aspects of his taught tradition of judicial self-restraint[52] are an abiding sense of judicial integrity, a close and necessary regard for the rules of pro-

---

48. William Kent, ed., *The Memoirs and Letters of James Kent* (Boston: Little, Brown, 1898), pp. 158–59.
49. "Reflections on Reading Statutes," 2 *The Record* 213 (June 1947).
50. *Terminiello v. Chicago*, 337 U.S. 1 (1949) at 11, dissenting opinion.
51. Benjamin N. Cardozo, *The Nature of the Judicial Process*, op. cit., p. 141.
52. Professor Philip B. Kurland makes six basic assumptions for the doctrine of judicial self-restraint:

> One is history and the obligation that constitutionalism imposes to adhere to the essential meaning put in the document by its framers. A second is the intrinsically undemocratic nature of the Supreme Court. A third is a corollary to the second, an abiding respect for the judgments of those branches of the government that are elected representatives of their constituents. A fourth is the recognition that judicial error at this level is more difficult of correction than other forms of judicial action. A fifth is respect for the judgments of earlier courts. But [sixth], the essential feature of judicial restraint that has gained most attention and aroused the greatest doubts probably because few men are themselves big enough to abide by its command—is the notion of rejection of personal preference [*Mr. Justice Frankfurter and the Supreme Court* (Chicago: University of Chicago Press, 1971), p. 5].

cedure, considerations of equal treatment before the law, the deference shown to legislative enactments, judicial recognition of the realities of the cultural, ideological, and institutional setting the judges share with their fellow citizens, not excluding the political realities, and *stare decisis,* the adherence to precedent.

STARE DECISIS

The desirability and, indeed, the need for certainty in planning our affairs, in both their internal (professional) and external aspects, render reliance on precedent an attractive and useful doctrine. "Imitation of the past," observed Justice Holmes, "until we have a clear reason for change, no more needs justification than appetite. It is a form of the inevitable to be accepted until we have a clear vision of what different things we want."[53] Yet, be it noted at once that *stare decisis* is a principle of policy and not a mechanical formula of adherence to the latest decision, "however recent and questionable, when such adherence involves collision with a prior doctrine more embracing in its scope, intrinsically sounder, and verified by experience."[54] "*Stare decisis,*" in the words of Justice Brandeis,

> is usually the wise policy, because in most matters it is more important that the applicable rule of law be settled than it be settled right. . . . This is commonly true even where the error is a matter of serious concern, *provided correction can be had by legislation.* But in cases involving the Federal Constitution, where correction through legislative action is practically impossible, this Court has often overruled its earlier decisions. The Court bows to the lessons of experience and the force of better reasoning, recognizes that the process of trial and error, so fruitful in the physical sciences, is appropriate also in the judicial function.[55]

Thus, quoting the first sentence of the preceding statement some fourteen years later, Justice Douglas went on to observe that "throughout the history of the Court *stare decisis* has had only a limited application in the field of constitutional law. And it is a wise policy which largely restricts it to those areas of the law *where correction can be had by legislation.* Otherwise the Court loses the flexibility necessary if it is to serve the need of succeeding generations."[56] Douglas's jurisprudential opposite, Chief Justice Rehnquist, echoed both his and Justice Brandeis's sentiments in authoring the majority opinion for his 6:3 Court in overturning two recent 5:4 precedents in *Payne v. Tennessee* in 1991. He added that *stare decisis* is not "an inexorable command; rather, it is a principle of policy and not a mechanical formula of adherence to the latest decision." And, he contended significantly, "considerations in favor of *stare decisis* are at their acme in involving *property and contract* rights, where reliance interests are involved; the opposite is true in cases such as the present one involving procedural and evidentiary rules."[57]

The doctrine of *stare decisis* requires a careful weighing in each doubtful case "of the advantages of adherence to precedent and the necessity for judicially

---

53. "Holdsworth's English Law," in *Collected Legal Papers* (Boston: A. Harcourt, 1920), p. 290.
54. Justice Frankfurter, for the Court, in *Helvering v. Hallock,* 309 U.S. 106 (1940) at 110.
55. *Burnet v. Coronado Oil & Gas Co.,* 285 U.S. 293 (1932) at 406 (italics supplied).
56. *New York v. United States,* 322 U.S. 572 (1946) at 590–91 (italics supplied).
57. 59 LW 4814, at 4819. The two precedents *Payne* overruled were *Booth v. Maryland,* 482 U.S. 496 (1987), and *South Carolina v. Gathers,* 490 U.S. 804 (1989).

planned social and economic progress."[58] The law, as Dean Pound has stated, must be stable and yet it cannot stand still. Or, as Viscount Kilmuir, then the Lord High Chancellor of Britain, told a distinguished audience of legal scholars in 1960: "Critics are apt to allege that we treat existing law with such reverence that every antique is replaced unaltered. I believe in an occasional spring cleaning."[59] Just such a "spring cleaning" occurred in an intriguing 9:0 decision by the Court in 1975, when it ruled that liability in a maritime collision must be *apportioned* among the ships involved according to their *proportionate* ("relative") degree of responsibility, thus abolishing the then-120-year-old rule that damages be divided "equally."[60]

Reliance on precedent presents difficult problems to the judge, especially since the question to be resolved comes, normally speaking, to a *choice* of precedents. "Sometimes," commented Justice Jackson wistfully in his last book, "one is tempted to quote his former self, not only to pay his respects to the author, but to demonstrate the consistency of his views, if not their correctness."[61] Precedents abound and not all precedents are of equal rank; a good many judges generally seem to accord considerably more sanctity to very old and hallowed "precedents," such as most of Chief Justice John Marshall's decisions, than to those of relatively recent vintage. Progress, in any event, does not stand still, and a precedent may have to be overruled or reversed in time. "Our assurance that our children will live, as we have, under a constitutional democracy," commented the then U.S. Solicitor General Stanley F. Reed, "rests upon the power of the form of government to adjust itself. . . . The Position of the Supreme Court on *stare decisis* makes that adjustment possible."[62] Between 1810 (when it rejected a two-year-old precedent) and 1991, the Supreme Court of the United States *overruled* its own previous determinations 260 times. During Earl Warren's sixteen-year Chief Justiceship, it did so sixty-three times; during the seventeen years of Warren E. Burger, sixty-one precedents fell; and so far (mid-1992) sixteen did so under the Chief Justiceship of William H. Rehnquist. Obviously, overruling of precedents is not confined to any particular jurisprudential philosophy.[63] Many additional cases are *distinguished* from precedent, which is somehow viewed as a less disrespectful device. "From age to age," commented Justice Douglas in an able treatment of the issue,

> the problem of constitutional adjudication is the same. It is to keep the power of government unrestrained by the social or economic theories that one set of judges may

---

58. Robert A. Sprecher, "The Development of the Doctrine of *Stare Decisis* and the Extent to Which It Should Be Applied," 31 *American Bar Association Journal* 501–9 (1945).
59. Speech on the occasion of the dedication ceremony of the University of Chicago Law Center, April 30, 1960.
60. *United States v. Reliable Transfer Co.,* 421 U.S. 397, overruling *Schooner Catherine v. Dickinson,* 17 Howard 170 (1854).
61. Robert H. Jackson, *The Supreme Court in the American System of Government* (Cambridge: Harvard University Press, 1955), p. 11.
62. "Stare Decisis," 35 *Pennsylvania Bar Association Journal Quarterly* 150 (1938).
63. See Linda Greenhouse, "A Longtime Precedent for Disregarding Precedent," *The New York Times,* July 21, 1991, p. 4E. For somewhat different yet basically similar statistics, see Christopher P. Banks, "The Supreme Court and Precedent: An Analysis of Natural Courts and Reversal Trends," 75 *Judicature* 5 (February–March 1992), Table 1, p. 263.

entertain. *It is to keep one age unfettered by the fears or limited vision of another.* . . . A judge looking at a constitutional decision may have compulsions to revere past history and accept what was once written. But he remembers above all else that it is the Constitution which he swore to support and defend, not the gloss which his predecessors may have put on it.[64]

Or, as Justice Potter Stewart admitted after twelve years on the Court, in an important 1970 labor case, quoting Justice Frankfurter: "Wisdom too often never comes, and so one ought not to reject it merely because it comes late."[65] Precedents, as Justice Talbot Smith said, being "judge-invented," may thus be "judge-destroyed." The judge must speak and through him society speaks. His function, as one leading student of constitutional law put it so lucidly, is "necessarily something more than to be a grammarian . . . [but] it is decidely less than to be a zealot."[66] Lord Coke's practice to the contrary, few, if any, judges today would create a maxim out of whole cloth and then recite, "as the old maxim saith. . . ." (Yet it was the same Lord Coke who lauded *stare decisis* as "the known certaintie of the law which is the saftie of all."[67]) "The rule of *stare decisis*," in New York Court of Appeals' Chief Judge Stanley H. Fuld's words, "was intended not to effect a petrifying rigidity, but to assure the justice that flows from certainty and stability. If, instead, adherence to precedent offers not justice but unfairness, not certainty but doubt and confusion, it loses its right to survive and no principle constrains us to follow it."[68] In Justice Antonin Scalia's words: "I would think it a violation of my oath to adhere to what I consider a plainly unjustified intrusion upon the democratic process [here considerations of state policy in criminal justice] in order that the Court might save face."[69]

To sum up, the judge is assuredly not a free agent. Indeed, the second Justice John Marshall Harlan underscored that fact of judicial life poignantly, when he wrote a concurring memo in a coerced confession case:

> [D]espite my strong inclination to join in the dissent of my Brother White, I can find no acceptable avenue of escape from *Miranda v. Arizona* [384 U.S. 436, 1966] in judging this case. . . . Therefore, and purely out of respect for *stare decisis*, I reluctantly feel compelled to acquiesce in today's decision of the Court, at the same time observing that the constitutional condemnation of this perfectly sensible, proper, and indeed commendable police work, highlights the unsoundness of *Miranda*.[70]

But Stewart joined White's dissent, responding to Harlan's action with the statement "It seems to me that those who dissented [*in Miranda*] remain free not only

---

64. William O. Douglas, *Stare Decisis* (New York: The Association of the Bar of the City of New York, 1949), p. 31, and ibid., 49 *Columbia Law Review* 735–36 (1949).
65. *Boys Market v. Retail Clerks' Union*, 398 U.S. 235 (1970) at 255.
66. Paul A. Freund, *The Christian Science Monitor*, March 27, 1956, p. 16.
67. Robert von Moschzisker, "Stare Decisis," 37 *Harvard Law Review* 409 (1924) at 429.
68. *Time* Magazine, May 10, 1971, p. 43.
69. *South Carolina v. Gathers*, 490 U.S. 805 (1989), dissenting opinion, at 823–25. See also his subsequent concurring opinion in *Payne v. Tennessee* two years later (op. cit., n. 57).
70. *Orozco v. Texas*, 394 U.S. 324 (1969) at 327–28.

to express our continuing disagreement with that decision, but also to oppose any broadening of its impact."[71]

No matter what it may be termed or how it may be styled, of necessity the judge "makes" the law—to some degree, at least. The delicate question will ever be how to aid its development without violating the confines of the constitutional structure. Let Justice Cardozo state the case:

> [but] no doubt the limits for the judges are narrower. He legislates only between gaps. He fills the open spaces of the law. How far he may go without traveling beyond the walls of the interstices cannot be staked out for him upon a chart. He must learn it for himself as he gains the sense of fitness and proportion that comes with years of the practice of an art. . . . None the less, within the confines of those open spaces and those of precedent and traditions, choice moves with a freedom which stamps its actions as creative. The law which is the resulting product is not found, but made. The process, being legislative, demands the legislator's wisdom.[72]

Surely, to echo a comment once made by Max Lerner, "judicial decisions are not babies brought by constitutional storks." They are the carefully considered, more or less practical, judgments by the human beings who, sensitive to their calling, wield judicial authority—as judges, not as legislators.[73]

OTHER LIMITATIONS ON JUDICIAL POWER AND EFFECTIVENESS

Yet there remain several other qualifying considerations—checks may be a better term—on judicial authority, even at the highest level of the federal courts. First, the Supreme Court's rulings may be effectively reversed by other participants in the processes of government; second, they are almost inevitably responsive to overall policy formulations, sooner or later; third, for enforcement they must look to the executive branch of the government; and fourth, as demonstrated in chapter 5, compliance with them is not necessarily automatic.

REVERSING THE COURT

In a variety of ways, although not without some toil and trouble, the Supreme Court of the United States may be reversed by direct or indirect action of other institutions in the political process. Although its decisions unquestionably constitute the supreme law of the land—as they must if government under law is to have

---

71. Ibid., at 331. Justice Tom C. Clark retrospectively contended that he had developed what a biographer called a "no subsequent dissent" rule. Not entirely convincing on the record, the rule professed a policy of dissenting from a precedent *only* during the term in which it was established. Thereafter, it would be the law of the land, and Clark would consider himself bound by it—unless he could later marshal a majority of his colleagues in establishing a new precedent in the older one's place. See Dennis D. Dorin, "Tom C. Clark: The Justice as Administrator," 61 *Judicature* 6 (December–January 1978).

72. *The Nature of the Judicial Process*, op. cit., pp. 113–15.

73. See the perceptive historical analysis by Robert J. Harris, "Judicial Review: Vagaries and Varieties," 38 *The Journal of Politics* 173 (August 1976).

any meaning in American society—and are thus final and binding, even that high body may have the last say "only for a time." Congressional activity to countermand Supreme Court decisions constitutes living proof of that fact.

Thus, as of January 1992, Congress had enacted 123 statutes in response to one or more Supreme Court decisions,[74] thereby reversing the Court either totally or in substantial measure, as it did in passing the Federal Employers' Liability Act of April 22, 1908, designed to replace that of 1906 which the Court had declared unconstitutional 5:4 as an illegal invasion of instrastate commerce in the *First Employers' Liability cases* earlier in 1908. Since Congress seemed to have corrected the alleged constitutional deficiency of the earlier statute, the Court found no difficulty in unanimously upholding it when the test came in the *Second Employers' Liability cases*[75] in 1912. Two better-known recent illustrations are Congress's 1978 overturning by statutory amendment of Title VII of the Civil Rights Act of 1964 of a 1976 Court ruling that had upheld private employers in their refusal to provide "disability benefits" for pregnant workers[76]; and its speedy 1982 legislative overturning of a 1981 Court holding that had upheld a federal statute declaring retirement pension pay to regular and reserve army commissioned officers "off limits" in divorce settlements[77]; ditto its 1987 law negating a 1986 Court holding that sanctioned 5:4 the Defense Department's ban on wearing religious headgear[78]; its "Civil Rights Restoration Act of 1988" over President Reagan's veto, that overturned the effect of the Court's 6:3 ruling in *Grove City v. Bell* in 1984[79]; and its Civil Rights Act of 1991, which overturned or significantly modified a series of 1989–90 adverse affirmative action decisions.

In other instances the circumstances or situation of the controversy had either changed or become moot, thus rendering insignificant or totally unimportant the erstwhile decision handed down by the Court—as, for example, the withdrawal of improperly delegated legislative power by action of the legislature or the revocation or amendment of a challenged administrative or executive order, both actions coming prior to the full effect of the Court's decisions.[80] In some instances the

---

74. See Richard A. Paschal, "The Continuing Colloquy: Congress and the Finality of the Supreme Court," VIII *The Journal of Law & Politics* 1 (1991), p. 203 and Appendix B. During the five-year period of 1985–90 the number of bills *introduced* to overturn or modify Supreme Court decisions totalled eighty-two, addressing fifty-six separate Supreme Court decisions. (Ibid., p. 200 and Appendix A.)

75. 223 U.S. 1 and 207 U.S. 463, respectively. Another instance was the Court's declaration of unconstitutionality of a federal municipal bankruptcy act in 1936 (*Ashton v. Cameron County Water Improvement District*, 298 U.S. 513), which Congress "corrected" with the enactment of a slightly revised law that was upheld by the Court two years later (*United States v. Bekins*, 304 U.S. 27).

76, *General Electric Co. v. Gilbert*, 429 U.S. 125. For two tables concentrating on congressional reversal action, see Robert A. Dahl's updated 1957 article in Thomas P. Jahnige and Sheldon Goldman, eds., "The Supreme Court's Role in National Policy Making," in *The Federal Judicial System: Readings in Process and Behavior* (New York: Holt, Rinehart and Winston, 1968), pp. 358–63.

77. *McCarty v. McCarty*, 453 U.S. 210.

78. *Goldman v. Weinberger*, 475 U.S. 503.

79. 465 U.S. 555.

80. E.g., *Lewis Publishing Co. v. Wyman*, 228 U.S. 610 (1913).

Court simply *distinguished* cases from often very similar earlier decisions, as it did when it upheld the second New Deal Agricultural Act of 1938 in *Mulford v. Smith* in 1939 even though it had struck down the first A.A.A. in *U.S. v. Butler*[81] three years earlier. True, the statutes were not exactly alike, and the personnel of the Court had changed, but the essential features, impact, and purpose of the statutes were unchanged. In other cases, the Court itself questioned, reversed, modified, or even negated its earlier judgments—by no means solely because of changes in its personnel—as it did so prominently in the four *Covert-Krueger* cases between 1955 and 1960.[82] And in six to nine (depending on one's point of view) instances, Amendments to the Constitution were passed in order to reverse the Court: the *Eleventh* (1798), reversing the 1793 decision in *Chisholm v. Georgia,*[83] by amending the original jurisdiction of the Supreme Court to hear certain suits against the several states; the *Thirteenth, Fourteenth,* and *Fifteenth* (the Civil War Amendments, adopted in 1865, 1868, and 1870, respectively), reversing various Supreme Court decisions, including the *Dred Scott case,*[84] dealing with suffrage, slavery, and civil rights; the *Sixteenth* (1913), the Income Tax Amendment, giving Congress power to tax incomes from whatever source derived, thereby effectively reversing the 1895 decisions in *Pollock v. Farmers' Loan and Trust Co.,*[85] which had held various income tax *statutes,* designed to accomplish the same end, unconstitutional as a violation of Article 1, Section 9, Clause 4; and the *Twenty-Sixth,* overturning the Court's 1970 ruling in *Oregon v. Mitchell*[86] by granting the franchise to eighteen-year-olds in *state* elections (the Court having upheld the statute insofar as it dealt with *federal* elections). Some would include the *Seventeenth* (direct election of U.S. Senators), the *Nineteenth* (women's suffrage, 1920), and the *Twenty-Fourth* (abolition of the poll tax in federal elections). The adoption of a constitutional amendment is the most authoritative and most certain method of reversing the Court, but it is also usually the most difficult politically to attain and almost always the most time-consuming.[87]

Going beyond the 140 or 141 provisions struck down by it, the Court *overruled* 156 of its decisions between 1937 and 1992, beginning with the immediate post-"switch-in-time-that-saved-nine" era. Prior to this, the Court had overruled itself at least 104 times. (These two figures cover not only overrulings of provisions previously held unconstitutional, but also those made on other than constitutional grounds.) Unless it seems to be absolutely necessary, however, the Court is disin-

---

81. 307 U.S. 38 and 297 U.S. 1, respectively.
82. 'Kinsella v. Krueger, 357 U.S. 470 and *Reid v. Covert* 351 U.S. 487 (June 11, 1956); 352 U.S. 901 (November 5, 1956); 354 U.S. 1 (June 10, 1957); and *Kinsella v. Singleton* 361 U.S. 234 and *Grisham v. Hagan,* 361 U.S. 278 (January 18, 1960).
83. 2 Dallas 419.
84. *Dred Scott v. Sandford,* 19 Howard 393 (1857).
85. 158 U.S. 601 and 157 U.S. 429.
86. 400 U.S. 112.
87. By spring 1985 some 10,000 amendments had been proposed in Congress, but only 33 were passed by *both* houses and sent to the states for ratification procedures. See Gary L. McDowell, "On Meddling with the Constitution," 5 *Journal of Contemporary Studies* 4 (Fall 1982), pp. 8–9.

clined to resort to the strong concept of *overruling*. Thus, in only 16 instances among the aforementioned 156 did the Court in subsequent decisions *specifically* and *literally* acknowledge an overruling, as it did, for example, in upholding the entire federal Fair Labor Standards Act of 1938 in the case of *United States v. Darby* in 1941. There, among others, addressing itself to the child labor provisions of that statute, it *specifically* overruled its 1918 decision in *Hammer v. Dagenhart*,[88] in which it had declared the federal Keating–Owen Child Labor Law of 1916 unconstitutional. An interesting example of the Court's overruling one of its own precedents of long standing came in 1976 when by an 8:0 vote, it unanimously overturned an 1871 (!) decision[89]—*Low v. Austin*, 13 Wall. 29—declaring it "wrongly decided" and thereby opened the way for state and local governments to place taxes on imported goods still in their original package but stored in warehouses, a type of taxation heretofore forbidden by the holding in the *Low v. Austin* case. Overruling differs from reversing in definition: technically speaking, a case may be *reversed* only on rehearing; thus, the original decision and the reversing decision are applicable to the *identical case*. An example of that procedure is the Court's decision in *Jones v. Opelika*, 316 U.S. 584, on June 8, 1942, upholding 5:4 an Opelika, Alabama, statute which required payment of the usual license tax or fee even by those groups (here the Jehovah Witnesses) that claimed exemption on grounds of freedom of religion—a decision that the Court *vacated* 5:4 on rehearing less than eleven months later, in *Jones v. Opelika*, 319 U.S. 103, on May 3, 1943, and then *reversed* on the same day in *Murdock v. Pennsylvania*, 319 U.S. 105.

The various statistics just cited do not take into account the many instances in which the Court overrules precedents *sub silentio*—that is, when it overrules an earlier decision without saying so but the effect is clearly the same as an expressed overruling—as it did on several occasions in the last quarter of the past century and the first quarter of this century in the realm of commerce and taxation. Nor do these figures account for those instances in which Congress, disagreeing with the Supreme Court's reading of a statute, simply rewrites or repeals it. For example, between 1944 and 1984 alone, Congress took sixty-three actions in economic matters that collectively overturned eighty-nine Supreme Court rulings.

Thus, although most of the Supreme Court's decisions on questions of constitutionality last, quite a few are ultimately modified or neutralized by the Court itself or by valid action of other branches of the government, led by Congress. America's system of judicial review, as Professor Freund has noted cogently, indeed produces frustrations, but it has a saving grace of resiliency.

POLICY FORMULATIONS AND CONSIDERATIONS

In any case, the policy views of the Court, the members of which, after all, in Professor Robert G. McCloskey's words, are "children of their times," never remain for long out of line with the policy views of the lawmaking majority—with the probable, but not inevitable, exception of decisions involving the Bill of Rights,

88. 312 U.S. 100 and 247 U.S. 251, respectively.
89. *Michelin Tire Co. v. Wages*, 423 U.S. 276.

particularly those made between 1940–49 and 1954–57 when the Court on a good number of occasions stood as a veritable bastion against the popular majority viewpoint. On major public policy issues, both the Chief Executive and Congress may be expected to succeed, speaking generally and *in the long run*— "... and the run must not be too long either!," as Professor Edward S. Corwin once observed[90]— although in the short run they may well have to bow. If the Court is to thrive, as Professor Wallace Mendelson has said so well, it "must respect the social forces that determine elections and other major political settlements. No court can long withstand the morals of its era."[91] The Court, however, cannot be a mere register of public opinion; it must be the latter's sporadic molder and leader. Yet, in the final analysis, as Francis Biddle well noted, its Justices "must not get away too far from life and should continually touch earth for renewed vitality."[92] An intriguing suggestion to formalize the issue was dramatically, albeit unsuccessfully, propounded by President Theodore Roosevelt in a speech in Columbus, Ohio, in 1912 when he called for a popular right of petition to bring before the voters "at some subsequent election" whether or not the judicial "interpretation of the Constitution" in a particular case, about which the public feels strongly, "is to be sustained ... or reversed," that is, recalled.[93]

Judicial alignment with the other two major branches on overriding policy matters may not always follow axiomatically, but it comes very close to reality. Some observers of the scene have even contended that far from representing a dependable means of preventing "legislative tyranny," judicial review of national policy seems to have but marginal value.[94] Whatever the actual merits of this contentious judgment may be, the Court is well aware of the limitations on its powers. Justice Frankfurter, the "conscience of the Court" during most of his lengthy tenure, thus addressed himself to the question of reversing the Supreme Court in his now well-known separate concurring opinion in the unanimously decided Little Rock School case, *Cooper v. Aaron,*[95] in which he quoted at length from his concurring opinion in the *United Mine Workers* case of 1947:

> Even this court has the last say only for a time. Being composed of fallible men, it may err. But revision of its errors must be by orderly process of law. The court may

90. *Court over Constitution* (Princeton, NJ: Princeton University Press, 1938), p. 127.
91. *Justices Black and Frankfurter: Conflict in the Court*, 2d ed. (Chicago: University of Chicago Press, 1966), pp. 75–76. On this point see also the intriguing, although somewhat interpretatively misleading, article by Robert A. Dahl, "Decision-Making in a Democracy: The Supreme Court as a National Policy-Maker," 6 *Journal of Public Law* 279 (1957), updated a decade later (see n. 76, *supra*). For a telling response to Dahl, pointing out convincingly that the Court's policy-making influence is considerably more extensive than Dahl's rather narrowly based thesis would have us believe, see Jonathan D. Casper, "The Supreme Court and National Policy Making," 70 *The American Political Science Review* 1 (March 1976), pp. 50–63.
92. *Justice Holmes, Natural Law, and the Supreme Court* (New York: Macmillan, 1961), p. 73.
93. See Stephen Stagner, "The Recall of Judicial Decisions and the Due Process Debate," 24 *The American Journal of Legal History* 3 (July 1980), pp. 257–58.
94. E.g., S. Sidney Ulmer, "Judicial Review as Political Behavior: A Temporary Check on Congress," 4 *Administrative Science Quarterly* 426 (March 1960).
95. 358 U.S. 1 (1958).

be asked to reconsider its decisions, and this has been done successfully again and again throughout our history. Or, what this court has deemed its duty to decide may be changed by legislation; as it often has been, and, on occasion, by constitutional amendment.[96]

He might have added that one of the major catalysts in revision and reconsideration is the inevitably changing personnel composition of the Court—yet any recognition of that crucial element in judicial decision-making must carefully guard against a pat and oversimplified catch-all analysis of its significance. In any event, reversal of judicial action is possible, and it has frequently been effectuated. Decisions running counter to the broad consensus simply do not last *in the long run*. The toast offered in 1801 at a dinner honoring the Justices, "To the Judiciary of the United States—independent of party, independent of power, independent of popularity!"[97] merits skeptical analysis. Still, time and again the Court has come through nobly when the constitutional chips have been down, as it did in July 1974, when it was confronted with the expansive claims of Executive Privilege advanced by President Nixon during the Watergate controversy. Its unanimous 8:0 ruling[98] against these claims constituted a—probably *the*—major catalyst in his subsequent resignation from office on August 9 of that fateful year.

COMPLIANCE AND ENFORCEMENT

But there is more to be said. Aspects of chapter 5 demonstrated at some length that the judgments of the Supreme Court of the United States are not necessarily accepted as automatically binding by those who ought to be bound. A decision may be simply ignored, as was proved by, for example, the continuation of the practice of "released time"[99] in numerous public secondary schools in situations and settings identical to that struck down as an unconstitutional violation of the principle of separation of state and church in *McCollum v. Board of Education*.[100] In 1966, four years after the decisions in the *Prayer and Bible Reading cases*,[101] some 60 percent of the states reported continued violations of the Court's mandates.[102] Or a decision may be circumvented, and even opposed by force, to which the his-

96. *United States v. United Mine Workers*, 330 U.S. 258. An embattled U.S. District Court Judge, James B. McMillan, sitting in key desegregation cases in the Western District of North Carolina, put it similarly:

> In the long run . . . a majority of the people will have their way. . . . If the Constitution is amended or the higher courts rule so as to allow continued segregation in the local public schools, this court will have to be governed by such amendment or decisions. In the meanwhile the duty of this and other courts is to seek to follow the Constitution in the light of the existing rulings of the Supreme Court, and under the belief that the constitutional rights of people should not be swept away by temporary local or national public opinion or political manipulation (*Swann v. Charlotte-Mecklenburg Board of Education*, 318 F. Supp. 786).

97. As quoted in *Connecticut Courant*, February 9 and 16, 1801.

98. *United States v. Nixon*, 417 U.S. 683.

99. For an explanation and an analysis of "released time" see my *Freedom and the Court: Civil Rights and Liberties in the United States*, 4th ed. (New York: Oxford University Press, 1982), ch. 6.

100. 333 U.S. 203 (1948).

101. *Engel v. Vitale*, 370 U. S. 421 (1962) and *Abington School District v. Schempp* and *Murray v. Curlett*, 374 U.S. 203 (1963).

102. See Ellis Katz, "Patterns of Compliance with the *Schempp* Decision," 14 *Journal of Public Law* 2 (1966); and Henry J. Abraham and Robert R. Benedetti, "The State Attorney-General: A Friend of the Court?" 117 *University of Pennsylvania Law Review* 795 (April 1969).

tory of the 1954 and 1955 *Segregation cases* and their progeny bear ample witness. And there is the already described host of calculated, interminable delays in compliance.[103]

Moreover, with the very few exceptions of its original jurisdiction docket cases, the Court formulates *general* policy. It is the lower federal and state courts, as the case may be, that *apply* it, presumably "not inconsistent with this opinion," as the Supreme Court's mandate normally reads. In so applying the opinion, the lower courts may, and often do, materially modify the Supreme Court's determination. These modifications, moreover, are not at all astonishing in view of the not infrequent habit of Supreme Court Justices to mix dogma with dicta. On the other hand, some of the so-called modifications or interpretations clearly have been little short of outright defiance—especially by state courts.[104] Indeed, as an astute observer of judicial power noted confidently, "a material gap exists between what the Court orders to be done and what the people will do."[105]

There is also the obvious fact that, lacking any source of physical power of its own, the Supreme Court depends on the political branches of the government for the enforcement of its mandates, in particular on the Chief Executive, who has the vital obligation to ascertain obedience to all Court orders. If the Court fails to obtain that cooperation in those instances in which it is vital for compliance, it necessarily stands helplessly on the sidelines. The most famous case in point is the comment, perhaps apocryphal, by President Andrew Jackson who, according to Chief Justice Marshall's biographer, exploded, "John Marshall has made his decision:—*now let him enforce it!*"[106] The outburst reputedly occurred as a result of Marshall's decision in *Worcester v. Georgia*,[107] in which his Court upheld the rights of the Cherokees in a dispute with Georgia, and in which he strongly implied in his opinion that it was the President's duty to honor and back the Cherokee Nation's rights under federal law. Aprocryphal or not, the Jackson comment illustrates the Court's dependence and its quandary when the necessary executive support is not forthcoming. Its effectiveness in the absence of the executive sword is as limited as its operations in general would be without the necessary appropriations from the legislative purse, and the legislative assent to its jurisdictional and procedural needs. In essence, as Justice Jackson starkly stated this fact of judicial life, "[the Court] can perform but one function—that of deciding litigations—and can proceed in no manner except by the judicial process.[108] Thus, he echoed an

---

103. See ch. 5, pp. 224–31, *supra*.
104. On this general point see the informative article by Walter Murphy. "Lower Court Checks upon Supreme Court Power," 53 *American Political Science Review* (December 1959), pp. 1017–31.
105. Choper, *Judicial Review and the National Political Process*, op. cit., p. 150, n. 5.
106. Albert J. Beveridge, *The Life of John Marshall*, vol. 4 (Boston: Houghton Mifflin, 1919), p. 551 (italics supplied).
107. 6 Peters 515 (1832). Worcester, a citizen of Vermont, was a missionary preaching the gospel, who had entered the territory of the Cherokee Nation under President Jackson's authorization, but without the permission that the state of Georgia required by statute. The Court declared the statute unconstitutional; yet, ironically, Jackson now sided with Georgia! It may well be that he did so because he did not wish to drive Georgia into the South Carolina-led tariff nullification camp.
108. *The Supreme Court in the American System of Government* (Cambridge: Harvard University Press, 1955), p. 12.

oft-quoted remark by Justice Samuel Miller that "in the division of the powers of government between the three great departments, executive, legislative, and judicial, the judicial is the weakest for purposes of self-protection and for the enforcement of the power which it exercises."[109] But not only do we often expect too much from the Court, we let it, or wish it would, settle *policy* matters that ought to be settled by one of the other two branches, notably the legislative, but which for a variety of reasons, chiefly political, are not.[110] Glaring illustrations of such policy matters are reapportionment/redistricting, segregation/desegregation—"let the Court decide!" urged Senators Paul Douglas (D.-Ill.) and Kenneth Keating (R.-N.Y.) during the acrimonious debates on controversial provisions of the Civil Rights Act of 1964[111]—and aspects of criminal justice. And there is a host of others in which the proverbial buck has been passed eagerly to the judicial branch.

MACHTKAMPF: THE SUPREME COURT IN THE POLITICAL POWER STRUGGLE

Whatever the implications of the preceding paragaphs, the Supreme Court has indeed been a participant in what may be viewed as a continuous struggle by the three "separated branches" of the federal government to attain a position of dominance, if not ultimate control, in the American political system. Because it lacks the potent weapons of the other two branches, especially weapons that would aid its self-protection and its enforcement of the powers it exercises, the Court has neccessarily been less prominent in this *Machtkampf* (struggle for power), but its own important tool of judicial review has provided it with a genuine measure of authority. And, as just pointed out, it has often been propelled into action precisely because the other organs of government have failed to fulfill their own responsibilities.

Victory in the *Machtkampf* of the three branches has been in the form of supremacy, which has alternated from branch to branch; although sometimes the struggle has been featured by a quasi-alliance of two branches against the third over a period of time. A pertinent example is the frustrated and frustrating protracted effort of the closely allied New Deal legislature and New Deal executive commencing in 1933, which, on many major issues, had to wait for victory over the Supreme Court until four years later, when the "switch-in-time-that-saved-nine" took place.

In general, however, the *tone* of dominance has been set by the person and personality of the elected Chief Executive, who, after all, is the sole individual in the American federal governmental process to have a nationwide constituency, and who, within limits, is in the position of interpreting his power narrowly or broadly. In other words, whenever the President has been of the category commonly called "active" or "strong" (e.g., Washington, Jackson, Polk, Lincoln, Wilson, the two Roosevelts, Lyndon Johnson, and Reagan in his first six years) the

---

109. *In re Neagle*, 135 U.S. 1 (1890), at 63.
110. On that point see the address by Justice Harlan at dedication ceremonies of the American Bar Center at Chicago, Illinois, August 13, 1963.
111. 110 *Congressional Record* 13434 (1964).

executive branch, *in the long run*, has been able to acquire supremacy. Where he has been "passive" or "weak," perhaps did not manifest sufficient concern for, understanding of, or even interest in the political process, or simply lacked sufficient support in Congress or by the people (e.g., John Quincy Adams, Pierce, Buchanan, Andrew Johnson, Grant, McKinley, Harding, Coolidge, Hoover, Eisenhower, Ford, and Carter), supremacy was acquired by Congress or, on occasion, by the Supreme Court. In several instances no clear-cut supremacy can be pinpointed. This is true, for example, of the presidencies of Madison and Monroe, Hayes, Cleveland, Taft, Truman, and Eisenhower, Kennedy, and the last two years of Reagan's. It should also be noted that during some presidencies, or at least parts thereof, the executive has tended to dominate in foreign affairs and Congress in internal matters (e.g., Truman, Eisenhower, Kennedy, and Bush). The abortive presidency of Richard M. Nixon falls into a special category: Expansive assertions and practices of presidential power enabled him to engage in sundry policy innovations in foreign affairs at the expense of domestic tranquility and achievements. His perceptions of executive power and privilege escalated until the "Watergate syndrome" engulfed him and his administration, ultimately resulting in his resignation from office on August 9, 1974—the first President to resign in the history of the Republic. The precipitous "full, free, and absolute" pardon, granted but one month later by the Nixon-selected successor, Gerald Ford, for all offenses "committed or that may have been committed" by the resignee in the course of his entire presidency, exacerbated prevalent national frustrations and anger and raised fundamental questions for the principle of equal justice under law as well as for the future of the separation of powers and checks and balances.

At the risk of some oversimplification and generalization—which inevitably attend categorization and classification—Table 10 is designed to indicate periods of American history in which existed fairly discernible tendencies toward supremacy by one branch or two allied branches against a third. Some periods are necessarily listed in more than one category: for example, the first four years of the New Deal era, when presidential supremacy was unquestioned—or, rather, when Congress surrendered to President Roosevelt, but during which time the Supreme Court proved to be a major roadblock to the New Deal program.

There is no doubt that the Supreme Court of the United States has sporadically *challenged* the authority of both President and Congress. But in spite of the four or five indicated periods of tendencies toward judicial supremacy, the Court has never really actively *bid* for the role of dominant governmental agency of the land, although a good case could be made for there having been such a bid during the era of Chief Justice Marshall. During that period, as well as during the heyday of the Hughes anti-New Deal Court, we may speak of periodic "government by judiciary" or "judicial supremacy," yet even then there was never any genuine likelihood that the Court would *in the final analysis* effectively *dominate* the executive and/or the legislative branches. When all is said and done, the Supreme Court of the United States does not possess the political power, the arsenal of potent weapons of government, the tools of the publicity media, or the strategic position in the government or in the body politic generally enjoyed by the other two branches.

A Historical Note. If we take a closer look at the Supreme Court's role in the

Table 10. Periods of Discernible Tendencies Toward Supremacy of Branches of the Government

Years	President(s)	Chief Justice(s)	Commentary
A. *Tendencies Toward Legislative Supremacy*			
1809–29	Madison Monroe J. Q. Adams	Marshall	Supremacy facilitated and advanced by powerful Court
1837–45	Van Buren W. H. Harrison Tyler	Taney	Aided by strong Court and passive Presidents
1849–61	Taylor Fillmore Pierce Buchanan	Taney	Nadir of presidency *Dred Scott* case
1865–85	Johnson Grant Hayes Garfield Arthur	S. P. Chase Waite	Partially effective opposition by Johnson and Hayes
1919–21	Wilson	White	Defeat of League President ill
1921–33	Harding Coolidge Hoover	Taft Hughes	Co-operative Court Weak, passive Presidents
1974–77	Ford	Burger	"Healing" President
1977–81	Carter	Burger	Tentative, cautious President
1987–89	Reagan	Rehnquist	Lame Duck Presidency
B. *Tendencies Toward Executive Supremacy*			
1789–97	Washington	Jay Rutledge Ellsworth	Cooperative Congress and Court Ineffective, docile Court
1801–9	Jefferson	Marshall	Some doubt about Executive Supremacy, but generally present. Strong Court
1829–37	Jackson	Marshall Taney	President in high form Last years of Marshall Court
1845–49	Polk	Taney	Underrated President
1861–65	Lincoln	Taney S. P. Chase	High-water mark of Presidency Civil War
1901–9	T. Roosevelt	Fuller	Popular President Assertive Court

Years	President(s)	Chief Justice(s)	Commentary
1913–19	Wilson	White	President lost control to Republican congressional majority in 1919, however
1933–45	F. D. Roosevelt	Hughes	Revolution on Court, 1937 "Packing"
1945–47	Truman	Stone Vinson	Powerful President Truman "honeymoon"
1963–69	L. B. Johnson	Warren	Powerful President
1969–74	Nixon	Burger	Vast claims to presidential power—truncated by Watergate
1981–87	Reagan	Burger Rehnquist	Very popular President

C. *Tendencies Toward Judicial Supremacy*

Years	President(s)	Chief Justice(s)	Commentary
1801–29	Jefferson Madison Monroe J. Q. Adams	Marshall	The great Chief Justice at power's peak
1857	Pierce Buchanan	Taney	The *Dred Scott* fiasco
1889–1901	B. Harrison Cleveland McKinley	Fuller	Judiciary's embrace of *laissez-faire*
1935–37	F. D. Roosevelt	Hughes	Thirteen New Deal Laws declared unconstitutional
1954–57	Eisenhower	Warren	Civil libertarian activism

D. *Supremacy Tendencies Not Readily Discernible*

Years	President(s)	Chief Justice(s)	Commentary
1797–1801	John Adams	Ellsworth	President and Congress shared power
1885–89	Cleveland	Waite Fuller	Probably President, but . . .
1910–13	Taft	White	Uncertainty (Taft wants to be on Court.)
1947–53	Truman	Vinson	Divided foreign and domestic tendencies but strong, assertive President
1959–61	Eisenhower	Warren	Gradual assertion of power by President after initial and sporadic passivity. Strong, activist Court Democratic congressional majority

Table 10 (*Continued*)

Years	President(s)	Chief Justice(s)	Commentary
1961–63	Kennedy	Warren	Divided foreign and domestic tendencies Strong, activist Court Popular young Presiident
1968–69	Johnson	Warren	Vietnam War becomes Johnson's political Waterloo
1989–	Bush	Rehnquist	Democratic Congress, Assertive Court, initially popular President, plagued by programmatic indecisiveness domestically

Machtkampf on the American political scene we see that the high tribunal began on a very inauspicious note. Its dozen or so pre-Marshall years, during which three Chief Justices came and went—the second of whom, John Rutledge, was not confirmed by the Senate—were characterized by a lack of popular esteem and understanding, little work, and dissatisfied personnel. The first Chief Justice, John Jay, so thoroughly disliked his job and so loathed circuit-riding—he handled some four hundred cases on circuit himself—that he not only spent one year during his tenure in England on a diplomatic mission, but twice ran for governor of New York, succeeding on the second try, whereupon he happily resigned the Chief Justiceship. When President Adams offered to reappoint him as Chief Justice in 1800, he refused categorically. Nonetheless, Adams appointed him on December 19, 1800; the Senate confirmed him: Adams and Marshall signed his commission; but Jay declined on January 2, 1801, citing his health (which was good). And, as already pointed out, the third Chief Justice, Oliver Ellsworth, eagerly left his office for a diplomatic post in France, where he then resigned, allegedly because of ill health. The Court did, however, soon make clear that it intended to act as an arbiter in disputes between the states and the federal government; and it became quickly apparent that its judicial sympathies lay with the latter, for which Jay had set the tone rather successfully.

The Marshall era, of course, brought about a drastic metamorphosis in the Supreme Court's prestige. The Chief Justice completely dominated the Court[112]— with dissents confined almost solely to Justice William Johnson who is justly regarded as "the father" of both dissenting and concurring opinions. It is quite clear that Marshall, more than any other man in the history of the judiciary, determined the character of America's federal constitutional system. From its lowly, if not dis-

112. See ch. 5, *supra*, esp. n. 144.

credited, level John Marshall raised the U.S. Supreme Court to a position of equality with the executive and the legislature—perhaps even one of dominance during
the heyday of his Chief Justiceship. He called his constitutional interpretations as
he saw them, always adhering to his previously discussed, oft-expressed doctrine
that " . . . it is a *Constitution* we are expounding . . . intended to endure for ages to
come and, consequently, to be adapted to the various crises of human affairs."[113]
Yet, as we know, he hastened to insist that "[j]udicial power, as contradistinguished from the power of law, has no existence. Courts are the mere instruments
of the law, and can will nothing."[114] Thus, "willing nothing," Marshall handed
down, among many others, four of the most momentous decisions in the history
of, and the future for, Court, Constitution, and country, without which it is at best
doubtful that the nation would have grown and prospered as it has: (1) *Marbury v.
Madison*[115] (judicial review, supremacy of the U.S. Constitution), (2) *McCulloch v.
Maryland*[116] (implied powers of Congress, reaffirmation of the supremacy of the
U.S. Constitution, federal immunity from involuntary state taxation, federal government held to have its powers directly from the people rather than from the
states), (3) *Gibbons v. Ogden*[117] (plenary federal authority over interstate and foreign commerce), and (4) *Dartmouth College v. Woodward*[118] (inviolability of contracts). Truly, the Court led and, leading, gave the federal government the means
to develop and work.

Whereas the Marshall Court had by its decisions placed the emphasis on the
national commercial-creditor-propertied classes, its successor, the also powerful
Taney Court, pursued a different emphasis. The sanctity of property remained a
primary consideration of the tribunal, but it devolved on a different segment of
society and, incidentally, of the country. A Southerner from Maryland, the Jack-
son-appointed Roger B. Taney, a Democrat and a Catholic—the first of his religious persuasion to be on the bench—by his decisions favored states' rights and
agrarian property, that is, land and slaves. From a totally different milieu than the
powerful constitutional nationalist who preceded him, Taney, and with him a
majority of his Court, demonstrated a faithful attachment to the economic interests of the South and the rapidly developing frontier of the West. But disaster
loomed on the horizon: after pursuing the aforementioned policies determinedly,
and with little, if any, interference from the other two branches for twenty years,
Taney, then in his eightieth year, lonely and frustrated, met his and the Court's
judicial Waterloo in 1857 with his monumentally aberrant opinion in *Dred Scott
v. Sandford*[119]—the thrust of which was leaked in advance by Justice John Catron
to President Buchanan,[120] the sole known major breach of secrecy on record,
although a handful of alleged others have been reported.[121]

113. *Osborn v. United States Bank*, 9 Wheaton 739 (1824) at 865.
114. *McCulloch v. Maryland*, 4 Wheaton 315 (1819).
115. 1 Cranch 137 (1803).
116. Op. cit., n. 114.
117. 9 Wheaton 1 (1824).
118. 4 Wheaton 518 (1819).
119. 19 Howard 393.
120. Justice Robert O. Grier had also *scienter* to the leak; indeed, it was he who encouraged Catron to
    spill the proverbial beans.
121. See Ch. 5, *supra*, n. 235, for illustrations.

This decision called "the worst constitutional decision of the 19th century" by Judge Robert H. Bork and "more than a crime . . . a blunder"[122] by Professor Alexander M. Bickel by Taney's Southern-dominated Court, with but two Justices dissenting, John McLean[123] and Benjamin Curtis (Curtis's opinion having been circulated in advance in the Northern press), featured nine separate opinions, including the leading one by Taney, who ironically had freed his own slaves thirty years earlier. The ruling stipulated among other things that no Negro could be a citizen, that the Negro was "a person of an inferior order," that he was a slave and thus his master's permanent property no matter whether the latter took him to slave or free parts of the country, that the Missouri Compromise was unconstitutional, and that no individual of African descent was "a portion of this American people." *Dred Scott* permanently beclouded Taney's reputation—notwithstanding his towering contributions to constitutional development—dragged the Supreme Court of the United States into its lowest depths, and hastened the dawn of the Civil War and with it the Emancipation Proclamation and the Civil War Amendments (XIII, XIV, and XV). In the words of a Washington newspaperman, "If epithets and denunciations could sink a judicial body, the Supreme Court of the United States would never be heard of again."[124]

With *Dred Scott*, which has been widely viewed as the most disastrous opinion ever issued by the high bench,[125] the Court invited a violent congressional reaction. Whereas that took a while to materialize, the influence of the Court declined at once. The country as a whole was hardly willing to consider, let alone accept, Justice James M. Wayne's anxious explanation *cum* plea in his concurring opionion that

> there had become such a difference of opinion that the peace and harmony of the country required the settlement of the slavery issues by judicial decision. . . . In our action we have only discharged our duty as a distinct and efficient department of the Government, as the framers of the Constitution meant the judiciary to be. . . .[126]

Far from alleviating the incipient sectional strife, the Court had aggravated it. During and after the Civil War, with Taney reduced to bitterness and unhappiness, Congress demonstrated its utter contempt of the Supreme Court by *thrice* changing its size in six years: up from nine to ten in 1863, down from ten to seven in 1866, up again from seven to nine in 1869. Quite obviously, all this was done for policy purposes. And, as seen earlier in these pages, when in 1868–69 the post-Taney Court indicated a possible declaration of unconstitutionality of some of the military Reconstruction Acts, an angry Congress, acting under its powers derived from the Constitution to limit the Court's appellate jurisdiction, simply deprived it of the

122. Bickel, *The Least Dangerous Branch*, op cit., p. 45. (The phrase is Talleyrand's.)
123. For a discussion of McLean's political motivations and aspirations see n. 168, ch. 5, *supra*. See also Bickel's commentary in his *Politics and the Warren Court* (New York: Harper & Row, 1965), p. 135.
124. As quoted by Hyneman, op. cit., p. 31.
125. Robert G. McCloskey, *The American Supreme Court* (Chicago: University of Chicago Press, 1961), p. 94.
126. *Dred Scott v. Sandford*, loc. cit., at 454–55.

power to decide the case.[127] This was the beginning of the Chief Justiceships of the politically ambitious Salmon P. Chase (1864–74)[128] and of Morrison R. Waite (1874–88), both Northern Republicans, during whose tenure the Court, predictably, was chiefly concerned, in addition to safeguarding property, with maintaining the status quo: state authority over individuals and federal authority over interstate commerce—the two great post-Civil War problems. The former included the Waite Court's nullification of the attempted use of the due process of law clause of the Fourteenth Amendment by the federal government as a national arm to protect civil rights in the states in the historic *Civil Rights Cases*,[129] something the Chase Court had already done in connection with the Amendment's "privileges or immunities" clause when citizens of Louisiana attempted to invoke it.[130] Indeed, the Chase Court, in a burst of judicial activism, did declare nine acts of Congress unconstitutional; but, as explained earlier, in the final analysis it bowed before the power of the Radical Republicans in Congress, and it was effectively "packed" by President Grant in 1871, thus nullifying within fifteen months its briefly successful attempt to battle for what it had regarded as stable currency in the *Legal Tender cases*.[131] One important contribution of the Waite Court to be noted, notwithstanding its generally proprietarian bent, was the highly significant development of the "affectation with the public interest" doctrine, announced by the Chief Justice himself in his opinion for a majority of seven in the leading *Granger* case of *Munn v. Illinois*.[132] There, while still clinging to the notion of due process laid down in *The Slaughterhousecases*,[133] Waite held that, under certain circumstances, the state police power could be employed to regulate private property in the public interest.

With the long Chief Justiceship of the Cleveland-appointed Melville W. Fuller of Illinois, however, the Court all but bid for policy leadership. It did this, above all, by striking out on a path designed to reassure the sanctity of property, as the majority of the Court saw it. This majority was now composed of a group of highly conservative, property-conscious Justices, who, when given the opportunity, began to strike down as unconstitutional a fair number of federal and state laws in the conomic and social sphere. *Laissez faire* seemed secure, indeed! Until roughly this time, state laws, for example, had been held unconstitutional largely because they were viewed as conflicting either with the interstate commerce or the obligation-of-contract clauses of the Constitution. Of 128 state laws invalidated by the federal courts *before* 1888, 50 involved the former clause, 50 the latter, and only one the taking of property "without due process of law." The Fuller Court, on the other hand, ultimately struck down a large number of state laws on that last ground, hold-

---

127. *Ex parte McCardle*, 7 Wallace 506 (1869).
128. Prior to his assumption of the Chief Justiceship, Chase had been a candidate at the Republican presidential conventions of 1856 and 1860. In 1868, while on the highest bench, he unsuccessfully sought the presidential nomination on *both* tickets!
129. 109 U.S. 3(1883).
130. *The Slaughterhouse Cases*, 16 Wallace 36 (1873).
131. 12 Wallace 457 (1871) and *Hepburn v. Griswold*, 8 Wallace 603 (1870).
132. 94 U.S. 113 (1877).
133. 16 Wallace 36 (1873). See my *Freedom and the Court: Civil Rights and Liberties in the United States*, 4th ed. (New York: Oxford University Press, 1982), pp. 41–49.

ing that the several legislative "experimentations" at issue deprived "persons" of liberty and property without *substantive* due process of law. Substantive due process had truly come of age! The Supreme Court had become the arbiter "between the voters on the one hand and the property owners on the other."[134] And the concept of "persons" now also included *corporations*, thanks to a unanimous Court ruling in the *Santa Clara* case,[135] a decision invalidating assessments on portions of railroad property. It was featured by a casual *announcement*, without benefit of argument, by Chief Justice Waite, who did not even write the opinion: "The Court does not wish to hear argument on the question whether the provision in the Fourteenth Amendment ot the Constitution, which forbids a State to deny to any person within its jurisdiction the equal protection of the laws, applies to these Corporations. We are all of the opinion that it does."[136] This was a rather cavalier manner of disposing of a highly significant constitutional issue—one that was neither before the Court nor had been argued in the case at bar.

The states, however, and, considerably later, the federal government insistently wished to pioneer in the realm of economic and social legislation, as they deemed that to be the desire of the majority of the voters. Yet in most areas (viz., maximum hours, minimum wages, working conditions, regulation of woman and child labor, compulsory arbitration, employer liability, and many others), the legislatures ran into the judicial vetoes not only of the Fuller Court, but also those of his successors, the White and Taft Courts and, until 1937, the Hughes Court—despite the established Waite "affectation with the public interest" doctrine. Throughout this period the Supreme Court demonstrated again and again a remarkable regard for the protection of *property* under its interpretations of the "liberty and property" phrases of the "due process of law" clauses of the Fifth and Fourteenth Amendments to the U.S. Constitution. But, oddly enough, the Court found these clauses no barrier against legislative invasions of the *cultural and political* realms, often referred to as "civil rights" or "civil liberties."

From the turn of the century on, when the great Oliver Wendell Holmes, Jr., was appointed by President Theodore Roosevelt to what was to be his thirty-year tenure on the Court, dissenting voices to the majority's policies were increasingly heard. As of 1916 Holmes was joined in dissents, although frequently for different reasons, by his colleague Louis D. Brandeis; and with the advent of Justices Harlan F. Stone in 1925 and Benjamin N. Cardozo in 1932, the dissenting voices in this area had settled to just one short of a majority. The previously described switch by Chief Justice Hughes, and, to a lesser extent, by Justice Owen D. Roberts, ultimately brought on what the eminent American constitutionalist Edward S. Corwin aptly called "a Constitutional Revolution." Having lost the battle of packing the Court in February 1937, President F. D. Roosevelt won the war when fate, in the form of deaths and resignations, weeded out the remaining four ultra-conservative Justices on the bench between 1937 and 1941—Associate Justices Willis Van Devanter, George Sutherland, James C. McReynolds, and Pierce Butler—

---

134. Arthur J. Hadley, "The Constitutional Position of Property in America," 64 *The Independent* 837 (1904).
135. *Santa Clara County v. Southern Pacific Railroad Co.*, 118 U.S. 394 (1886).
136. Ibid., at 396.

ultimately allowing him to fill nine vacancies on the court[137] (second only to Washington's ten).[138]

By no means did all of these Roosevelt appointees see the law at all times as he had hoped they would; but certainly the New Deal now had clear sailing, and there was no doubt that the new Justices rejected outright the "thou-shalt-not-pass" doctrines of their predecessors relative to legislative experimentation in the economic-proprietarian sphere. As Justice Black was to comment later: "Whether the legislature takes for its textbook Adam Smith, Herbert Spencer, Lord Keynes, or some other is no concern of ours."[139] Judicial self-restraint on legislative policymaking in these areas of public life became the avowed policy of the Court—just as the "Old Court" had practiced a similar restraint on legislative policies in the cultural and political realms (e.g., the "separate but equal" concept and abridgement on speech, press, and assembly). Yet, interestingly enough, the "New Court" immediately commenced to complete the cycle of policy reversal by throwing up judicial vetoes in the face of a good many legislative encroachments, as the Court saw them, on civil rights and liberties. Thus, the nature and character of the Court's labors began to change dramatically. Of the 160 decisions in which it had written opinions in the 1935–36 term, a mere two had dealt with civil rights and liberties. That ratio began to climb steadily so that a decade later twenty times as many opinions fell into that category, and fifteen years later fully fifty-four cases dealt with that vital area of public life—a fact of judicial life that has not only continued to the present, but has accelerated, with well over half of the Court's written opinions now regularly concerning the libertarian sector (87 of 160, 84 of 150, 91 of 152, and 59 of 116, respectively, in the Court's 1976, 1981, 1986, and 1991 terms, for example).

When Justices Murphy and Wiley Rutledge joined Chief Justice Stone and Justices Black and Douglas in the early 1940s, these "libertarian activists" were generally in firm control—certainly until the death of the Chief Justice in April 1946. They briefly relinquished that control during the last four years of the Vinson Court upon the deaths of Justices Murphy and Rutledge in 1949 and their replacement by Justices Clark and Minton, when the Court tended, broadly speaking, to side with government rather than the individual in the general field of national security, that so difficult and emotion-charged Cold War problem. But they more or less regained it during the first four years of the Warren Court, from 1953 to 1957, Chief Justice Warren having replaced Chief Justice Vinson on Vinson's death. However, with the Court led by the consistently "nonactivist" Justice Frankfurter, the 1957–58 term saw a return to readily discernible judicial self-restraint even in that area of public and constitutional policy—some would contend largely as a result of the veritable barrage of congressional and public criticism against the Court following its spate of "pro–civil liberty" decisions in 1956–57. Yet with the retirement of Justices Whittaker and Frankfurter in 1962, and their replacement by Justices Byron White and Arthur Goldberg, the latter in turn

137. Black, Reed, Frankfurter, Douglas, Murphy, Stone (promotion to Chief Justice), Byrnes, Jackson, and Rutledge.
138. See text, p. 73 and n. 112, ch. 2, "Staffing the Courts,", *supra.*
139. *Ferguson v. Skrupa*, 372 U.S. 726 (1963), at 732.

yielding to Abe Fortas in 1965, plus the Thurgood Marshall replacement of Justice Clark, the libertarian image of the Warren Court was restored. It continued and indeed mounted until the Chief Justice's resignation in 1969. His replacement by Warren Earl Burger was characterized by a somewhat moderating tenor and by some retrenchment in the criminal justice sector, but there was no general return to pre–Warren Court doctrine. Indeed, it evinced an overriding concern for civil rights and liberties, with particular emphasis upon potent egalitarian strivings on the frontiers of race, gender, and age—all of which witnessed major advances.

When the great issues of executive power that had arisen in the Watergate affair reached the Burger Court in July 1974, it took on President Nixon in *United States, Petitioner, v. Richard M. Nixon, President of the United States.*[140] In an 8:0 decision, the unanimous Court, including three of the Nixon appointees (the fourth, Justice Rehnquist, having disqualified himself), ruled, in effect, that no man was above the law, that the President was duty-bound to comply with a valid judicial order to turn over evidence desired in a criminal trial, and that there was no "absolute, unqualified presidential privilege of immunity from judicial process under all circumstances." Here, fifteen days prior to Nixon's resignation, Chief Justice Burger, resorting to John Marshall's immortal words, told the President, the nation, and the world: "We therefore reaffirm that it is 'emphatically the province and the duty' of this Court 'to say what the law is.' "

When Associate Justice William H. Rehnquist succeeded the retired Chief Justice Warren E. Burger in the center chair in 1986, Judge Antonin Scalia filled the Burger vacancy, and Judge Anthony M. Kennedy replaced Justice Lewis F. Powell, Jr., in 1987, a "rightward" turn in the Court's juriprudential majority was widely assumed. It materialized moderately, being initially largely, although not exclusively, confined to the criminal justice sector and to the contentious realms of abortion and affirmative action. Relative to abortion, the now Rehnquist Court enabled the states to exercise considerably more regulatory leeway[141] than at any time since pre–*Roe v. Wade*[142] days. In that of affirmative action, it handed down a quintet[143] of critical decisions in 1989 that limited the heretofore expansively liberal application of the doctrine, drawing rapid attempts by Congress to overturn or amend these holdings, resulting in the late 1991 enactment of the Civil Rights Act of 1991. When the aged leading liberal Justices William J. Brennan, Jr., and Thurgood Marshall stepped down in 1990 and 1991, respectively, and were replaced by two centrist federal appellate judges, David H. Souter and Clarence Thomas, the Court's turn to the right seemed to be clearly at hand, in particular on the criminal justice front,[144] amid considerable popular approbation. To what extent the Rehnquist Court would in fact consummate a major jurisprudential

---

140. 417 U.S. 683.
141. See *Webster v. Reproductive Health Services*, 492 U.S. 490 (1989).
142. 410 U.S. 113 (1973).
143. *Wards Cove Packing Co. v. Atonia*, 490 U.S. 642; *Martin v. Wilks*, 490 U.S. 755; *Lorance v. A.T.&T. Technologies*, 490 U.S. 900; *Jett v. Dallas Independent School District*, 491 U.S. 701; *Patterson v. McLean Credit Union*, 491 U.S. 164.
144. E.g., *Florida v. Bostick*, 59 LW 4708; *California v. Acevedo*, 59 LW 4559; *Florida v. Jimeno*, 59 LW 4471; and *Payne v. Tennessee*, 59 LW 4814.

metamorphosis remains to be seen. To predict the behavior of Justices of the Supreme Court is at best chancy and at worst foolhardy.

If we reflect on these several considerations in this analysis of the *Machtkampf*, the work of the Supreme Court and the force and implications of its decisions come into closer focus. At times the Court has clearly led the a country (e.g., the Marshall era); at other times it has more or less held the line (e.g., the Chase–Waite era—with important qualifications); at times it has deliberately stimulated social and economic progress (e.g., the post-1937 Court); at others it has deliberately delayed it (e.g., the Fuller Court). At times it has looked to a majority sentiment, as it were, by following the election returns (e.g., the *Insular* decisions at the turn of the last century)[145]; at others it has defied majority sentiment (e.g., some of the 1956–57 term civil liberties decisions).[146] At times its decisions have been seemingly motivated by sectional or class considerations (e.g., *Dred Scott*,[147] proclaiming corporations as "persons,"[148] and the 1954 *Segregation cases*[149]); at others they have been truly national in spirit and effect (e.g., the four major John Marshall decisions, cited earlier).[150] In a very real sense, the Court through the years has thus been the conscience of the country. In a measure, it has represented the Rousseauist *volonté générale* of the land, in a qualitative rather than a quantitative sense. It has done this through its decisions, speaking through its Justices, who—far more often than not of a high caliber—have interpreted the Constitution as they saw it, in line with the taught tradition of the law.

Of course, the Supreme Court of the United States is engaged in the political process, but, in Justice Frankfurter's admonitory prose, it is "the Nation's ultimate judicial tribunal, not a super-legal aid bureau."[151] His jurisprudential heir, Justice John Marshall Harlan, seconded and extended this point by observing that the "Constitution is not a panacea for every blot upon the public welfare, nor should this Court, ordained as a judicial body, be thought of as a general haven for reform movements."[152] Of course, the Justices—who, in the words of E. V. Rostow, are "inevitably teachers in a vital national seminar"[153]—consult their own policy preferences. But they do so in an institutional setting that forces responsibility on them. Judges, as Paul A. Freund put it, should not be influenced by the weather of the day, but they are necessarily influenced by the climate of the age.[154] And in Chief Justice Rehnquist's pithy observation, they are "shaped by what's going on in the world around them."[155] They must meet and maintain high standards of integrity, intelligence, logic, reflectiveness, and consistency. They must ever demonstrate a

145. *Downes v. Bidwell*, 182 U.S. 244 (1901) and *De Lima v. Bidwell*, 182 U.S. 1 (1901).

146. E.g, *Watkins v. United States*, 354 U.S. 178; *Jencks v. United States*, 353 U.S. 657; *Yates v. United States*, 354 U.S. 298.

147. *Dred Scott v. Sandford*, loc. cit.

148. *Santa Clara County v. Southern Pacific Railroad Co.*, loc. cit.

149. *Brown v. Board of Education*, 347 U.S. 483 and *Bolling v. Sharpe*, 347 U.S. 497.

150. See p. 000 *supra*.

151. *Uveges v. Pennsylvania*, 335 U.S. 437 (1948) at 450.

152. *Reynolds v. Sims*, 377 U.S. 533 (1964), dissenting opinion, at 624.

143. "The Democratic Character of Judicial Review," 66 *Harvard Law Review* 195 (1952).

154. As quoted in *The Washington Post*, May 25, 1988, p. A15.

155. *Ibid.*

sense of history complete with the realities and vagaries of public affairs, a task that Judge J. C. Hutcheson, Jr., of Texas once called "the hunch of intuition about the inner life of American democracy."[156] They have the exciting, yet delicate task of heeding the "felt necessities of the time"—to employ once again Justice Holmes's inspired phrase[157] while holding aloft the banner of constitutional fundamentals. It was Daniel Webster, not a present-day observer or participant of the governmental process, who put his finger on what should be obvious. Speaking in the House of Representatives in support of a judiciary bill, he intoned that "the maintenance of the judicial power is essential and indispensable to the very being of this government. The Constitution without it would be no constitution; the government no government."[158]

156. As quoted by Rostow in his *The Sovereign Prerogative: The Supreme Court and the Quest for Law* (New Haven, CT: Yale University Press, 1962), p. 110.
157. Oliver Wendell Holmes, Jr., *The Common Law* (Boston: Little, Brown, 1881), p. 1.
158. As quoted by Chief Justice Earl Warren, "Webster and the Court," *Dartmouth College Alumni Magazine*, May 19, 1969, p. 34.

9

Coda:
A Realistic
Bulwark

If the foregoing analysis of the role of the Supreme Court of the United States in the political process has proved anything at all, it ought to be that there is a recognition of the overriding need for judicial self-restraint. Its acceptance plays an omnipresent and omnipotent part in the attitude of the nine members of the highest court in the United States. No matter how the judicial record of these nine individuals may appear on a chart or graph; no matter how predictable or unpredictable their position on certain issues may be—a factor that on balance is probably far more of a blessing than a curse—they are fully aware of their role in, and responsibility to, the democratic body politic they serve with such dedication. They serve as a collective institution of government; but it is an institution that is characterized by individual absorption in the tasks at hand, an absorption that calls for direct personal evaluation and decision making. As has been demonstrated throughout these pages, *each member of the Supreme Court* normally participates in every stage of the consideration of a case—from the review stage through the evaluation of briefs, through oral argument, through discussion and vote in Conference, to the writing of or participation in the ultimate opinion of the Court. At every stage of the life of a case the Justices are fully aware of their responsibilities as members of the governmental process, and thus practice much procedural as well as substantive judicial self-restraint, both in the type of cases they will hear and in the kind of decisions they will render. This emphasis on what Alexander Bickel wisely termed "passive virtues"[1] is a simple, and yet immensely complicated, fact of judicial life—whatever the opinion of expert as well as lay outsiders

---

1. *The Least Dangerous Branch: The Supreme Court at the Bar of Politics* (Indianapolis: Bobbs-Merrill, 1962), title of ch. 4.

on judicial legislating may be. But there is little doubt that the Justices believe with Johann Wolfgang von Goethe that "self-limitation is the first mark of the master."[2]

Throughout the almost two centuries of its existence, the Court has developed a host of unwritten laws, practices, precedents, and attitudes which we may well view as a code of behavior for the highest judicial body in the United States, a series of significant *maxims of judicial self-restraint*. In analyzing the most commonly accepted of these, the reader should be aware that any such enumeration will necessarily involve some generalization and that maxims, like rules, are sometimes broken quite deliberately.[3]

THE SIXTEEN GREAT MAXIMS OF JUDICIAL SELF-RESTRAINT

There is nothing sacred about either the number of these maxims or the order in which they will appear. They are presented roughly in the order in which they would normally confront the Justices as an issue reaches the Supreme Court in the form of a case of controversy, presumably when it has become "ripe" for adjudication.

One: Before the Court will even glance at a particular issue or dispute officially, a definite "case" or "controversy" at law or in equity between bona fide adversaries under the Constitution must exist, involving the protection or enforcement of valuable legal rights, or the punishment, prevention, or redress of wrongs directly concerning the party or parties bringing the justiciable suit. A "case" may be either civil or criminal; a "controversy" is always a civil action or suit. Justice Jackson viewed this maxim as "perhaps the most significant and least comprehended limitation upon the judicial power."[4] The judicial system of the United States is constructed on specific cases with specific facts. Thus, when a group of federal employees endeavored to join one George P. Poole in a suit testing the validity of that portion of the Hatch Act of 1939 which forbids members of the executive civil service to take an active part in "political management or in political campaigns," the Supreme Court disqualified them as appellants because they, unlike Poole, had not violated the provision in question.[5] Refusing to take jurisdiction, the Court thereby reiterated its oft-expressed stand against "every form of pronouncement on abstract, contingent, or hypothetical issues."[6] Except for Poole's claims, no case or controversy directly involving the interest of the appellants was involved here in the face of the Supreme Court's first maxim, regardless of what lower tribunals might have held. Probably the most famous illustration of the "case or controversy" problems is the Court's 1911 decision in *Muskrat v. United States*.[7] At issue

2. From the sonnet "Was Wir Bringen," 1802 ("In der Beschränkung zeigt sich erst der Meister").

3. See the perceptive treatment of the overall issue by Gary L. McDowell in his *Curbing the Court* (Baton Rouge: Louisiana State University Press, 1988), especially ch. 6, "The Forms and Limits of Judicial Power."

4. Robert H. Jackson, *The Supreme Court in the American System of Government* (Cambridge: Harvard University Press, 1955), p. 11.

5. *United Public Workers of America v. Mitchell*, 330 U.S. 75 (1947). The *Poole* case issue is also apposite to the "standing" maxim, item "Two," *infra*.

6. Jackson, loc. cit., p. 12.

7. 219 U.S. 346.

was an act of Congress that had authorized Muskrat and others to bring suit in the U.S. Court of Claims, with an appeal to the Supreme Court to *determine the validity of certain acts of Congress* that altered the terms of some prior allotments of Cherokee Indian lands. Speaking for a unanimous Court, Justice Day rejected the appeal as not meeting the "case or controversy," requirement. "If such actions as are here attempted, to determine the validity of legislation are sustained," lectured Day, "the result will be that this court, instead of keeping within the limits of judicial power and deciding cases or controversies arising between opposing parties, as the Constitution intended it should, will be required to give opinions in the nature of advice concerning legislative action, *a function never conferred upon it by the Constitution. . . .*"[8]

Two: Closely related to the need for the presence of a case or controversy is the logical demand that the *party or parties bringing suit must have "standing."* The gist of the question of standing, as the Court elucidated it in *Baker v. Carr,* "is whether the party seeking relief has alleged such a personal stake in the outcome of the controversy as to assure that concrete adverseness which sharpens the presentation of issues upon which the court so largely depends for illumination of difficult constitutional questions."[9] There are two major aspects to the difficult and intricate concept of standing.[10] The *first,* to raise a constitutional issue with proper standing, is that it must be shown that the one who seeks to challenge the statute or action is personally and substantially injured by it, or is in substantial danger of such injury. A relaxation of that rule, at least in the sensitive free speech area, was introduced with the Court's landmark 1965 ruling in *Dombrowski v. Pfister,* where it held 5:2 that federal district judges should have the power to enjoin the enforcement of unconstitutional laws (i.e., laws presumed unconstitutional "on their face"), if these laws, as per Justice Brennan's majority opinion, pose a "chilling effect" on freedom of expression by mere "fact of prosecution, unaffected by the prospects of its success or failure. . . .[Thus, courts may] avoid making vindication of freedom of expression await the outcome of protracted litigation."[11] But the relaxation was short-lived. District judges, prodded by aggressive attorneys for litigants, followed the Supreme Court's *Dombrowski* ruling with such gusto that state laws on obscenity, abortion, subversion, homosexuality, vagrancy, and so on,

---

8. Ibid., at 362 (italics supplied). President Nixon's counsel unsuccessfully argued the absence of a "case" or "controversy" in *United States v. Nixon,* 417 U.S. 683 (1974).

9. 369 U.S. 186 (1962), at 204.

10. "Standing," noted Chief Justice Warren on one often reported occasion, quoting the noted constitutional law expert Paul Freund, "has been called 'one of the most amorphous [concepts] in the entire domain of public law.' Some of the complexities peculiar to standing problems result because standing 'serves on occasion, as a shorthand expression for all the various elements of justiciability.' In addition, there are at work in the standing doctrine the many subtle pressures which tend to cause policy considerations to blend into constitutional limitations" (*Flast v. Cohen,* 392 U.S. 83 [1968] at 92). For other pithy references to the incredible difficulties surrounding the issue and concept of "standing," see the excellent article, and its important notes, especially 1 and 3, by Karen Orren, "Standing to Sue: Interest Group Conflict in the Federal Courts," 70 *The American Political Science Review* (September 1976), pp. 723–41; the similarly perceptive essay by Tinsley E. Yarbrough, "Litigant Access Doctrine and the Burger Court," 31 *Vanderbilt Law Review* (January 1978), pp. 33–70; and the major work by McDowell, op. cit., p. 369, n. 3..

11. 380 U.S. 479, at 487.

began to fall like tenpins; in 1971 the Burger Court called a halt, in a significant decision which instructed the lower federal courts to estop state prosecutions *only* when state officials were "cynically harassing" defendants, causing "irreparable injury."[12] In other words, six years after *Dombrowski* the Court substituted a test of "irreparable injury" for "chilling effect."

The *second* aspect of standing is that a petitioner, endeavoring to speak for a group or "class" of similarly affected and/or interested parties, must not only have a personal and substantial interest infringed by the statute or action but must also "bring himself, by proper averment and showing, within the class as to whom the act thus attacked is unconstitutional."[13] It will not do merely to demonstrate an

12. *Younger v. Harris*, 401 U.S. 37 (1971). The Court applied its *Younger* ruling to six cases before it on the same day as the parent case (February 23, 1971). The opinions in *Younger* and the six were written by Justice Black, with but Justice Douglas in dissent.

13. *Southern Railroad Co. v. King*. 217 U.S. 524 (1910) at 534. The reference to "class" in the quotation points to the vexatious legal phenomenon called a "class action" that is, a suit filed by the person allegedly wronged on behalf of himself or herself and perhaps hundreds or thousands of unnamed others *who can be classified with him or her as similarly wronged*. Thus, class actions, when successful, provide a way for the claims of many individuals to be settled at one time, eliminating repetitious litigation and establishing an economical route to obtaining redress, since the legal fees can be taken from the total damages awarded. Celebrated illustrations of successful class action suits are the school desegregation cases of 1954 and the "one-person, one-vote" cases of 1964. In the decade that followed more and more class action suits were brought (they doubled between 1970 and 1975) and finally the Burger Court began to draw a line. The first such limiting decision was rendered late in 1973, in a 6:3 vote against the plaintiff in a pollution case. Although certain kinds of class actions, such as those involving antitrust and the large number of civil rights suits, will still not be affected by the Court's herein pronounced limitation since they have no statutory minimum requirement (e.g., *U.S. Steel Corporation v. Dickerson*, 421 U.S. 948 [1975], involving charges of discrimination brought by three black employees on behalf of *all* blacks working in the company's plant), the new policy brought the following changes: When, for example, parties from different states are henceforth involved (i.e., in diversity of citizenship cases [see ch. 4, *supra*] which, since an increase in 1989 from $10,000 to $50,000, provide that), *every* plaintiff must now meet the $50,000 minimum damage allegation requirement *separately!* No longer will a "collective" total of $50,000 thus bring proper class action standing (*Zahn v. International Paper Co.*, 414 U.S. 291 [1974]. A further narrowing of class action availability came with a unanimous ruling handed down in May 1974, that hereafter a person bringing such a suit must notify *all* members of the class potentially benefitting *and* bear the costs of such notice, even if that should be prohibitively high (*Eisen v. Carlisle and Jacqueline*, 416 U.S. 1979), which the court in 1978 unanimously expanded to extend to the *compiling* of the names and address of the affected class in *Oppenheimer Fund v. Sander*, (437 U.S. 340). Consequently, the Court thus quickly declined to review a ruling below that had held a group of *Carte Blanche* credit card holders could *not* bring a class action suit on behalf of all 800,000 such owners in order to challenge financing provisions imposed by the issuing company (*Katz v. Carte Blanche Corporation*,419 U.S. 885 [1974]). And a lower federal court accordingly ruled that one S. L. Cartt's suit, challenging Standard Oil of California's claims for its F-310 gasoline, could not proceed until she notified *each* of the 700,000 Standard credit card holders in the state. (That would have cost her $42,000, and as she was unable to raise that amount, her class action suit failed.) While the early 1980s saw a number of split decisions that seemed to strengthen procedural opportunities to file class action suits (e.g. *Deposit Guarantee National Bank v. Roper*, 445 U.S. 326 (1980); *U.S. Parole Commission v. Geraghty*, 445 U.S. 388 [1980]; *Merrill Lynch v. Curran*, 456 U.S. 353 [1982]; and *Board of Education v. Pico*, 457 U.S. 853 [1982]) that same period also witnessed the contrary (e.g., *Middlesex Country Sewer Authority v. Sea Clammers*, 453 U.S. 1 [1981] and *Los Angeles v. Lyons*, 46 U.S. 95 [1983]. The last word has hardly been spoken here; but one should not expect a comprehensive return to the easy-access days of the 1950s–1970s.

interest shared with all other citizens "generally." Thus, the Supreme Court ruled 6:3 in late 1970 that the Commonwealth of Massachusetts lacked *standing* to litigate the question of the constitutionality of the Vietnam War by attempting to challenge it in behalf of its individual citizens.[14] A lower appellate court did accept the war-legality question as a justiciable controversy a year later, and then upheld its legality, but the Supreme Court, predictably, denied *certiorari*.[15] Among the federal judiciary's prudential limitations, thus, is found the rule that "normally" it will not grant standing when the harm alleged "is a 'generalized grievance' shared in substantial measure by all or a large class of citizens,"[16] the strong implication being that *legislative* redress ought to be sought instead. Nor, as the Court lectured in a 5:4 opinion written by Justice Rehnquist in 1982, will it condone the use of the federal courts by citizen groups who seem to endeavor to employ them as if they were "constituted as ombudsmen of the general welfare" or as "college debating societies" or as podiums for those who "would roam the country in search of governmental wrong doing."[17]

One of the most famous illustrations of a *lack of standing* on record is the case of Dr. Wilder Tileston, a Connecticut physician who wanted to challenge the constitutionality of that state's statutory prohibition[18]—enforced but three times between the time of its birth in 1879 and its death at the bar of the U.S. Supreme Court in 1965[19]—of the "use of drugs or instruments to prevent conception, and the giving of assistance or counsel in their use." Having lost his appeal in the Connecticut Supreme Court of Errors below, he endeavored to get federal Supreme Court review. Because of their importance to the concept of standing, the pertinent sections of that court's *per curiam* decision should be quoted:

> Appellant [Dr. Tileston] alleged that the statute, if applicable to him, would prevent his giving professional advice concerning the use of contraceptives to three patients whose condition of health was such that their lives would be endangered by childbearing, and that appellees [Abraham S. Ullman and other law enforcement officers of the state], intend to prosecute any offense against the statute and "claim or may claim" that the proposed professional advice would constitute such an offense. The complaint set out in detail the danger to the lives of appellant's patients in the event that they should bear children, but *contained no allegation asserting any claim under*

14. *Massachusetts v. Laird*, 400 886, Justices Douglas, Harlan, and Stewart dissenting.
15. *Orlando v. Laird*, 404 U.S. 869 (1971), Justices Douglas and Brennan dissenting. (The Circuit Court's citation was 443 F. 2d 1039.) Another attempt in 1972 also failed (*DaCosta v. Laird*, 405 U.S. 979, *certiorari denied*, with Justice Douglas dissenting from the denial).
16. Thus, see the heavily criticized decision in *Warth v. Seldin*, 422 U.S. 490 (1975) at 498–99, quoting *Baker v. Carr*, op. cit., n. 9, *supra*, holding 5:4, through Justice Powell's majority opinion, that city taxpayers of Rochester, New York, residents of a zoned suburb, a builders' association looking for work in the suburb, and a citizen housing group lacked standing to sue to challenge the suburban zoning restriction at issue just as much as central city low- and moderate-income dwellers did. See also the Court's 5:3 opinion in *Allen v. Wright*, authored by Justice O'Connor, holding that a lower federal court had improperly permitted a group of black parents to challenge the manner in which the IRS grants tax exemption to private schools. (468 U.S. 737 [1984]).
17. *Valley Forge Christian College v. Americans United for the Separation of Church and State*, 454 U.S. 464, at 473, 487.
18. *Tileston v. Ullman*, 318 U.S. 44 (1943).
19. *Griswold v. Connecticut*, 381 U.S. 479.

the Fourteenth Amendment of infringement of appellant's liberty or his property rights. The relief prayed was a declaratory judgment [to be explained in the next maxim] as to whether the statutes are applicable to appellant and if so whether they constitute a valid exercise of constitutional power "within the meaning and intent of Amendment XIV of the Constitution of the United States prohibiting a state from depriving any person of *life* without due process of law." . . .

We are of the opinion that the proceedings in the state courts *present no constitutional question which appellant has standing to assert. The sole constitutional attack upon the statutes under the Fourteenth Amendment is confined to their deprivation of life—obviously not appellant's but his patients'.* There is no allegation or proof that *appellant's life is in danger. His patients are not parties to this proceeding* and there is no basis on which we can say that he has standing to secure an adjudication of his *patient's constitutional right to life, which they do not assert in their own behalf. . . . No question is raised in the record with respect to the deprivation of appellant's liberty or property in contravention of the Fourteenth Amendment. . . . Since the appeal must be dismissed on the grounds that appellant has no standing to litigate the constitutional question which the record presents,* it is unnecessary to consider whether the record shows the existence of a genuine case or controversy essential to the exercise of jurisdiction of this Court. . . . Dismissed.[20]

In short, Dr. Tileston had no standing to sue: his patients might well have had such, but *they* did not bring suit; *he* might have had such, but he brought suit on non-justiciable grounds. The Court was not about to get into the delicate matter of birth control if it could avoid doing so (it would ultimately become involved protractedly—and amidst withering criticism—two decades later).

Not to be outdone, opponents of the Connecticut statute tried again in 1961, and this time with patients *and* a physician as plaintiffs. The Supreme Court was hard pressed to reject the appeal for adjudication of the issue and thus continue to refuse to get enmeshed in the sticky problem. But it managed: Led, not surprisingly, by Justice Frankfurter, and narrowly dividing 5:4, the majority held the controversy *not* to be "fit for adjudication", that no one had in fact been injured, such as being jailed or fined, and that consequently, "this Court cannot be umpire to debates concerning harmless, empty shadows."[21] Frankfurter pointed out that the law in question had rarely been the subject of a prosecution, that perhaps it had died of disuse and would therefore not ever be enforced. Yet the statute's opponents were not mollified: more determined than ever to test its constitutionality, they continued to try to obtain standing to challenge it. They opened a birth-control clinic in New Haven, frankly advertising its existence—and, to their utter delight, the state decided to prosecute them. Best of all, Mrs. Estelle T. Griswold, the executive director of the Planned Parenthood League of Connecticut, and Dr. C. Lee Buxton, a licensed physician, who served as medical director for the league's New Haven Center, found themselves convicted and fined $100 each. Now they had standing at last! Losing in the courts below, they appealed to the Supreme Court on the ground that the Connecticut statute, as applied to them, violated the Fourteenth Amendment. In 1965 the Court granted their appeal, pointing out that persons prosecuted under a relevant statute must surely have standing to challenge

20. *Tileston v. Ullman*, loc. cit., at 46 (italics supplied).
21. *Poe v. Ullman and Buxton v. Ullman*, 367 U.S. 497 (1961).

it. And by a vote of 7:2 in an expansive, heavily attacked opinion by Justice Douglas—plus three concurring and two dissenting ones—it declared the law to be an unconstitutional infringement not only of Amendment XIV, but also of Amendments I, III, IV, V, and IX by way of "penumbras formed by emanations" therefrom.[22] Whatever the merits of the Connecticut case may be, standing is assuredly essential to an orderly and efficacious judicial process.[23]

22. *Griswold v. Connecticut*, 381 U.S. 479 (1965) at 484.

23. Another fascinating and contentious aspect of this problem is the precedent established by the Supreme Court ruling in *Frothingham v. Mellon*, 262 U.S. 447 (1923), which determined that an "ordinary taxpayer" is generally precluded from contesting the constitutionality of *federal* expenditures, such as expenditures to sectarian schools and other institutions, on the ground that he or she does not possess "sufficient interest" to bring suit. In *Frothingham* (often identified as *Massachusetts v. Mellon*, the two were argued, considered, and disposed of together). Justice Sutherland held for the unanimous Court that a taxpayer's interest in the moneys of the Treasury (here regarding the Federal Maternity Act) "is shared with millions of others; is comparatively minute and indeterminable; the effect upon future taxation . . . is so remote . . . that no basis is afforded for an appeal to the preventive power of the Court." As a consequence, a *federal* taxpayer (but not necessarily a *state* taxpayer in his or her capacity as a state citizen, for many states do allow such "taxpayer suits"), whose rights guaranteed by, for example, the First Amendment, are actually deemed violated, may be without a judicial remedy. This dilemma became particularly acute with the passage of the Federal Elementary and Secondary Aid of Education Act of 1965, given its attendant overtones of the separation of church and state controversy. Consequently, legislation to provide for judicial review of the constitutionality of grants and loans under seven specific federal statutes, including the aid-to-education measure just mentioned, plus any other statute administered by the Department of Health, Education, and Welfare, was introduced. Although it had early rough going—it passed the Senate on four occasions, only to die in the House in each instance—two bills formally authorizing the Court to review the constitutionality of legislation dealing with such aid as that prescribed in the 1965 statute, became law in 1965 and 1967. And in a dramatic development the Court in October 1967 decided to hear arguments of seven taxpayers (*Flast v. Gardner*, 389 U.S. 895) who contended that they had a right as *federal* citizens to challenge the constitutionality of federal aid to parochial schools, notwithstanding the *Frothingham* precedent. In June 1968 the Court agreed, 8:1, in *Flast v. Cohen*, 392 U.S. 83, provided that the taxpayer can establish a two-part "nexus": (1) that he or she establish a "logical link between that [taxpayer] status and the type of legislative enactment attacked [which legislation must be based on the congressional exercise of its taxing and spending power under I-8:1]; and (2)) that he or she can show that the challenged enactment exceeds specific constitutional limitations imposed upon the exercise of the congressional taxing and spending power . . ." (at 102–3). Abuse of legislative power *must* be demonstrated. Thus, in two celebrated late 1974 cases, the Court ruled *against* two taxpayer suits based on *Flast*, denying standing in both instances. The first (*United States v. Richardson*, 418 U.S. 166) sought to have declared unconstitutional congressional legislation authorizing the nondisclosure of Central Intelligence Agency receipts and expenditures under the CIA Act of 1949, the suit alleging that the arrangement violated the requirement for regular accounting of public fund expenditures under 1-9-7 of the Constitution. The second (*Schlesinger v. Reservists Committee to Stop the War*, 418 U.S. 208) challenged the reserve status of members of Congress, alleging violation of the "incompatability" clause of the Constitution (I-6-2). In both instances the prevailing Court majorities, 5:4 and 6:3, respectively, saw either a failure of a sufficient *Flast* "nexus" especially its part 1, or regarded the taxpayer claims as being of the nonjusticiable "general citizen" or "voter grievance" type or both. It is a fair question to ask whether the Court distinguished or in effect contrasted *Flast*. But a 1978 suit filed by six federal taxpayers *qua* federal taxpayers succeeded in obtaining Supreme Court review: It involved New York City's use of Title I of the Federal Elementary and Secondary Aid to Education Act of 1965 program federal funds on parochial school premises to teach remedial classes. Accepting the taxpayer suit, and deciding it on the merits, the Court, in a 5:4 opinion by Justice Brennan, ruled seven years later that the expenditures involved violated the constitutionally mandated separation of church and state (*Aguilar v. Felton*, 473 U.S. 402 [1985]).

Three. The Court does not render advisory opinions, that is, judicial rulings on the constitutionality of governmental action in the absence of a case or controversy requiring such a ruling for its disposition—nor do the lower federal constitutional courts. In effect, this was settled as early as 1793, when President Washington addressed the members of the Supreme Court, asking them to define for him the authority given him by the Constitution to decide certain questions involved in the U.S. policy of neutrality with respect to a war such as the one then in progress in Europe. Chief Justice Jay responded for the Court that it would not and could not tender legal advice—that its role was confined to the decision of cases that arose in the course of bona fide litigation. *Legislative* courts, however, may give advisory opinions, and, when authorized by their constitutions, so do some of the courts of the fifty states, such as Colorado, Massachusetts, and South Dakota.

All courts, on the other hand, are empowered to render *declaratory judgments*, a device that enables courts generally to enter a final judgment between litigants *in an actual controversy*, defining their respective rights under a statute, contract, will, or other document, *without* attaching to the otherwise binding judgment any consequential or coercive relief. The crucial distinction between a declaratory judgment and an advisory opinion is the presence of an actual controversy in the case of a declaratory judgment, whereas an advisory opinion would deal with an abstract, hypothetical question insofar as the judicial process is concerned. Today, three-quarters of the states[24] and the federal government under the Federal Declaratory Judgment Act of 1934, permit declaratory judgments. In the words of the federal statute, such a judgment—which is reviewable above—answers the following question in an actual controversy: "whether or not further relief is or could be prayed." As then Associate Justice Rehnquist put it on one occasion: "A declaratory judgment is simply a statement of rights, not a binding order."[25] It was for just such a declaratory judgment that Dr. Tileston had pleaded initially, and unsuccessfully, because he then lacked standing.

The Supreme Court itself has admitted the obvious: that the line between advisory opinions and declaratory judgments is a thin one—the controversial abortion decision of 1973 is a pertinent example[26]—and that "it would be difficult, if it would be possible, to fashion a precise test for determining in every case whether there is such a controversy [as is demanded by a declaratory judgment]."[27] But it insisted in the *Ashwander* case[28] that the Federal Declaratory Judgment Act "does not

24. A famed declaratory judgment was the 7:0 fifty-nine pages ruling by the New Jersey Supreme Court, authorizing the father of Karen Ann Quinlan, Joseph T. Quinlan, to have her life terminated medically by arranging for the disconnection of the life-sustaining machinery that had kept the comatose Karen Ann alive for over a year as of 1976. The state of New Jersey appealed its highest court's verdict to the U.S. Supreme Court, but the latter denied review. (*Garger v. New Jersey*, 429 U.S. 922, [1976]) (*In the Matter of Karen Ann Quinlan*, decided March 31, 1976). This action was taken shortly after the judicial decision, but the stricken girl "lived" comatose for almost ten more years, death came, as a friend, in June 1985.
25. *Steffel v. Thompson*, 415 U.S. 452 (1974) at 482
26. *Roe v. Wade* and *Doe v. Bolton*, 410 U.S. 113 and 410 U.S. 179, respectively. See also McDowell, op. cit., p. 369, n. 3.
27. *Maryland Casualty Co. v. Pacific Coal and Oil Co.*, 312 U.S. 270 (1941) at 273.
28. *Ashwander v. Tennessee Valley Authority*, 297 U.S. 288 (1936) at 325.

attempt to change the essential requisites for the exercise of judicial power"; and, on another occasion, it stated that it cannot be invoked to "obtain an advisory decree upon a hypothetical state of facts."[29]

Four. Not only must the complainant in federal court expressly declare that he or she is invoking the Constitution of the United States—"the ultimate touchstone of constitutionality," in Justice Frankfurter's phrase—*but a specific live rather than dead constitutional issue citing the particular provision on which he or she relies in that document must be raised by him or her; the Court will not entertain generalities.* Indeed, it has held specifically that an attack on a statute as "violative of the Constitution of the United States" is insufficient on its face.[30] Nor will a simple contention that a statute is "in violation of the Fifth or Seventh Amendments to the Constitution" do.[31] Specific, careful, closely reasoned documentation is essential. Moreover, the issue must be raised *seasonably*; that is *timely* assertion of the constitutional issue must be made before a tribunal having proper jurisdiction, and it must be reasserted at every opportunity in the course of the litigation. The Court is not concerned with dead or moot and thus inappropriate problems, as, for example, one caused by the death of the defendant in an appeal in a criminal action.[32]

Five. The Court looks askance on any attempt to have the judicial decision-cake and eat it too. Thus, *it will not pass on the constitutionality of a statute or of an official action at the instance of one who has availed himself or herself of its benefits, but then decides to challenge its legality anyway.* An illustration is the case of a St. Louis, Missouri, casting company, in the role of owner of property within a special sewer district who connected his premises with a freshly constructed sewer and availed himself of its benefits. But then he challenged the validity of the statute that permitted a tax levy against him as a recipient of the services as being an unconstitutional infringement of his property rights under the Fourteenth Amendment.[33] The Supreme Court held unanimously that by accepting and availing himself of the benefits of the construction and zoning involved, the owner was "estopped from maintaining a suit" on the grounds and under the circumstances here involved.

Six. All remedies in the pertinent lower federal and/or state courts must have been exhausted, and prescribed lower court procedure duly followed before making application to the U.S. Supreme Court for review. As Judge Augustus N. Hand of the U.S. Court of Appeals for the Second Circuit Court once observed, the rule of exhaustion is the only rule which is consistent with orderly government." Thus,

29. *Electric Bond & Share Co. v. Securities & Exchange Commission*, 303 U.S. 419 (1938) at 443.
30. *Herndon v. Georgia*, 295 U.S. 441 (1935).
31. *Chapin v. Frye*, 179 U.S. 127 (1900).
32. *List v. Pennsylvania*, 131 U.S. 396 (1888). See also *DeFunis v. Odegaard*, 416 U.S. 312 (1974) for a controversially "mooted" case (that had nothing to do with death). See also the Court's mooting in *National Organization of Women v. Idaho*, 459 U.S. 809 (1982) and in *Carmen v. Idaho*, 459 U.S. 809 (1982) of two interesting questions involving the proposed Equal Rights Amendment: (1) whether or not states could change a "yes" vote to a "no" vote and (2) whether or not Congress had acted constitutionally when it extended the ERA ratification date by simple majority vote rather than by a two-thirds vote. The Court held both questions moot because even the majority-vote extension of three years had expired on June 30, 1982.
33. *St. Louis v. Prendergast Co.*, 260 U.S. 459 (1923).

the highest court of the land will not review a judgment of a state court unless on the face of the record it affirmatively appears that a *federal question constituting an appropriate ground* for such review was presented in, and expressly or necessarily decided by, such a state court. For example, in 1963 the Court ruled 6:3 that a New York state judgment had not been taken to the highest New York court empowered to consider it, as statutorily required for Supreme Court review. Hence it dismissed a writ it had granted earlier to hear the case as having been "improvidentially granted."[34] A decade later, the Court sternly and unanimously rejected a challenge by a group of legal rights organizations to a new system of New York State court registration and supervision being applied to charitable corporations practicing law in that state by the Appellate Division of the New York State Supreme Court. The U.S. Supreme Court held that the groups had to apply to the Appellate Division for an exception to the registration requirements and be refused *before* they could bring a constitutional challenge to the supervision system.[35] No matter how vital, inviting, timely, or attractive the issue involved may be, the Supreme Court will not accept a case unless the remedies below have been exhausted; nor does it matter that a lower tribunal might not be "friendly" to the substance of a suit, as has occurred frequently in connection with state court adjudication of such contentious problems as desegregation, criminal justice, and Bible-reading in the public schools.[36] Orderly procedure is of the very essence of the judicial process; judicial and administrative chaos is the alternative. Thus, although the principle has come under recent attack by the Court,[37] it will not normally review judgments of state courts that rest on *"adequate and independent"* state grounds.

   Seven. Assuming it has been properly raised, *the federal question at issue must be substantial rather than trivial; it must be the pivotal point of the case; and it must be part of the plaintiff's case rather than a part of his adversary's defense.* Whatever the subjective overtones of the term "substantial" may be, it is normally not an overwhelming job to distinguish between a "substantial" and a "trivial" federal question. For example, the controversies surrounding the extent of the federal government's authority in connection with the Tennessee Valley Authority projects, raised in sundry respects in the famous case of *Ashwander v. T.V.A.,*[38] and the attempts by the State of California to close its borders to a destitute non-citizen traveling in interstate commerce as well as those by Connecticut and others to deny welfare benefits to persons recently migrated from other states,[39] are pertinent instances of substantial federal questions. On the other hand, the endeavors of some Greek-letter fraternities on various campuses in New York to have the Supreme Court review sundry nondiscrimination requirements by the Trustees of

---

34. *Gotthilf v. Sills,* 375 U.S. 79. See also *United States v. Raines,* 362 U.S. 17 (1960) at 21.
35. *Young Lords Party v. Supreme Court of New York,* 414 U.S. 1088 (1973).
36. E.g., *Michel v. Louisiana,* 350 U.S. 91 (1955) and *Wallace v. Jaffree,* 472 U.S. 38 (1984). See also *Fay v. Noia,* 372 U.S. 319 (1963) for both sides of the exhaustion controversy.
37. *Michigan v. Long,* 463 U.S. 1032 (1983), per Justice O'Connor.
38. *Ashwander v. Tennessee Valley Authority,* 297 U.S. 288 (1936).
39. *Edwards v. California,* 314 U.S. 160 (1941) and *Shapiro v. Thompson,* 394 U.S. 618 (1969), respectively.

the State University of New York; those of the University of Colorado setting deadlines on removing restrictive racial and/or religious clauses from fraternity "constitutions" on pain of revocation of campus privileges, and a student's legal challenge to an F he received in a Chemistry course were summarily—and quite predictably—turned aside as not involving such a substantial question.[40]

Eight. Although it would be an oversimplification, if not entirely incorrect, to state that the Supreme Court reviews only questions of law, it is nonetheless generally true that *questions of fact, as distinct from questions of law, are not normally accepted as proper bases for review.* This is especially true of the area of judicial review of administrative construction of statutes, when a *purely* factual question has no chance of a hearing, for Congress has statutorily provided for the finality of administrative finding of fact.

However, it is axiomatic that the problem of which questions are of "law," which are of "fact," and which are "mixtures" is a difficult one. Any attempt to draw a rigid line poses a genuine problem because of the very nature of the two concepts, as was demonstrated again in a station house "show-up" identification case in late 1972, in which the Court, dividing 5:3, held that the dispute between the litigants was not so much over "the elemental facts" as over the "constitutional significance to be attached to them."[41] In the words of an expert on the subject, "matters of law grow downward into roots of fact, and matters of fact reach upward, without a break, into matters of law."[42] In any event, the Court will not permit administrative procedures, which most frequently are at issue in this particular dichotomy, to fall below what it is prone to regard as a "constitutional minimum," a concept that is clearly a matter of law subject to judicial review.

Nine. While, as already indicated, Britain's highest tribunal, the House of Lords, considered itself *bound* by its own prior decisions until it publicly and expressly modified that doctrine in 1966,[43] *the Supreme Court of the United States has never held itself absolutely bound by its precedents.* It has often adhered to many of these, of course, and will presumably continue to do so, but it has not permitted itself to become enslaved by past decisions. Nor could it do so: the law does not stand still; Justice Holmes's aforementioned "felt necessities of the time" are ever-compelling facts of governmental life. We must not expect from the Court, in Chief Justice Hughe's trenchant warning, "the icy stratosphere of certainty." And in Justice Cardozo's immortal truth: "Somewhere between worship

40. *Webb v. State University of New York,* 348 U.S. 867 (1954); The *New York Times,* June 18, 1965, p. 1, and ibid., September 3, 1966, p. 10; and *Mercurio v. Board of Regents of the University of Nebraska,* 463 U.S. 1214 (1983), respectively.

41. *Neil v. Biggers,* 409 U.S. 188. The majority comprised the Chief Justice and Associate Justices Powell (the author of the opinion), White, Blackmun, and Rehnquist; in dissent were Douglas, Brennan, and Stewart. (Marshall did not participate.)

42. John Dickinson, *Administrative Justice and the Supremacy of Law* (Cambridge: Harvard University Press, 1927), p. 55.

43. See the Lord Chancellor's (Lord Gardiner's) announcement, in *House of Lords Official Reports,* vol. 276, no. 43, col. 677, July 26, 1966. *Parliamentary Debate (Hansard Weekly)* and 1 W.L.R. 1234 (1966). For an interesting, pertinent, recent House of Lords decision, see *Broome v. Cassell & Co.* [1972] 2 W.L.R. 645, in particular Lord Diplock, at 721.

of the past and exaltation of the present, the path of safety will be found."[44] But a decision of the Supreme Court is utterly binding *in federal matters* on all courts below, state as well as federal, regardless of sporadic foot-dragging and aberrations.[45]

Ten. The Court has been inclined to defer to certain legislative or executive actions by classifying an issue otherwise quite properly before it as a political question, hence refusing to come to grips with it. Depending on one's point of view— after all, is not every constitutional question or decision "political" to some extent?—this intriguing practice or formula is either a mere *device* for transferring the responsibility for a question or decision to another branch of the government, or it is in fact *required* by the constitutionally explicit or implicit realities and necessities of the presence of the separation of powers principle. What really *is* a "political question"? Giving short shrift to this inquiry, Justice Holmes, coming to the core of an issue briskly and pithily as always, once characterized it as "little more than a play on words."[46] He would have no part of the concept as a judicial mechanism, though nevertheless fully recognizing, of course, the realities of the political facts of life. Jefferson, on the contrary, regarded all questions involving the constitutionality of acts of Congress that might come before the Court as "political questions."

Professor Edward S. Corwin essayed the following, perhaps not entirely helpful, definition of the vexatious verbiage in his last monumental annotation of the Constitution:

> a political question relates to the possession of political power, of sovereignty, of government, the determination of which is vested in Congress and the President, and whose decisions are binding on the courts.[47]

In a different vein, Professor J. W. Peltason, one of the students of the revered Princeton scholar, preferred to view political questions as "those which judges choose not to decide, and a question becomes political by the judges' refusal to decide it."[48] Professor Charles C. Post regarded the term as an "open sesame word" that "instantly relieved [the Court] of all control over the problem."[49] And Judge Learned Hand labeled it, insofar as its scope is undefined, as a "stench in the nostrils of strict constructionists."[50] A good many of the Supreme Court's decisions, though not necessarily invalidating Corwin's analysis, would seem to support Peltason's more realistic evaluation. However, judges can, and do, change their minds, depending on the posture and setting of an issue; what may be rejected or avoided

---

44. Benjamin N. Cardozo, *The Nature of the Judicial Process* (New Haven, Ct: Yale University Press, 1921), p. 160.
45. See pp. 224–31 and 332–34, *supra.*
46. *Nixon v. Herndon,* 273 U.S. 536 (1927) at 540.
47. Edward S. Corwin, *The Consitution of the United States,* revised and annotated (Washington, DC: U.S. Government Printing Office, 1953), p. 547.
48. Jack W. Peltason, *Federal Courts in the Political Process* (Garden City, NY: Doubleday, 1955), p. 10.
49. *The Supreme Court and Political Questions* (Baltimore: The Johns Hopkins University Press, 1936), p. 11.
50. *The Bill of Rights* (Cambridge: Harvard University Press, 1958), p. 15, n. 3.

as a political question today may quite conceivably be accepted for review on its merit at a later date, of which the legislative reapportionment–redistricting decisions are pertinent illustrations.

For years—to be precise, until its precedent-shattering decision in what must be regarded as one of the two or at most three most significant Supreme Court decisions of the twentieth century, namely *Baker v. Carr* in 1962[51]—the Court simply would not get involved in the question of the constitutionality or even the justiciability of the way in which legislatures and constitutions either did or did not apportion or district state and/or congressional districts, no matter how obvious, how outrageous, and even how illegal the apportionment or districting or lack of it might have been! The Court, in the words of the main advocate of this determined and consistent stand, Justice Frankfurter (to whom Fred Rodell liked to refer as "the Court's Emily Post"), was not going to get itself involved in such a "patently political question," in such a "political thicket," which in his view was, after all, an area of the "exclusive authority" of legislatures.[52]

Thus, the constitutionality of the well-known county unit system of Georgia, a prime example of antiurban, pro-rural legislative gerrymandering, had been before the Court on several occasions. Under that system, each of the various counties received a minimum of two and a maximum of six electoral votes for the eight most populous counties, including Fulton County (Atlanta), with each county's electoral vote going to the candidate receiving the highest popular vote therein. The net effect had been that the one million inhabitants of Fulton County, of whom a considerable proportion of registered votes were black, received but one-third more votes than the handful of residents in numerous small rural counties. In other words a vote in the small counties of Georgia had from 11 to 120 times as much weight as one in Fulton! Yet attempts to have the Supreme Court come to grips with the matter had come to naught as relatively recently as 1950, 1951, 1958, and 1959. The Court stood by its pronouncement in the first of these cases, *South v. Peters*,[53] that "a state's geographical distribution of electoral strength among its political subdivision" is a political question. Thereby the Court continued to cling to the general philosophy and tactics it had enunciated in *Colegrove v. Green* in 1946,[54] a case concerning congressional districts in Illinois. Here appellants had contended that the Illinois law apportioning them was unconstitutional because the various districts were characterized by rank inequalities. For example, one in Chicago had 914,053 inhabitants, whereas one in southern Illinois comprised a mere 112,116. But in its decision the Supreme Court, with only seven Justices participating, and these split three ways, nevertheless held, through Justice Frankfurter and Associate Justices Reed and Burton, that it could not intervene in such a political question, which it regarded as being up to the legislature to determine and alleviate. If the Court did intervene, wrote Frankfurter, it would be entering into a "political thicket," and that, anyway, it is "hostile to a democratic system to

51. 369 U.S. 186.
52. See his opinion for the Court in *Colegrove v. Green*, 328 U.S. 549 (1946) and his dissenting opinion in *Baker v. Carr*, 369 U.S. 186 (1962), both discussed later.
53. 339 U.S. 276 (1950).
54. 328 U.S. 549.

involve the judiciary in the politics of the people."⁵⁵ Justice Black, speaking also for Justices Douglas and Murphy, dissented vigorously, contending that the state of Illinois's failure to redistrict was tantamount to "willful legislative discrimination" and constituted a denial of the equal protection of the laws presumably guaranteed by the Fourteenth Amendment ot the Constitution of the United States.

But the days of the "political question" doctrine in this sector of public law were clearly numbered when the Court, after twice having noted probable jurisdiction in its 1960–61 term, agreed to hear argument in a 1961 Tennessee case involving that state's outright refusal to reapportion the General Assembly among its ninety-five counties, seats that had been arbitrarily and capriciously apportioned by a 1901 statute—and never touched since, despite an almost fivefold growth of eligible voters and major shifts of population from rural to urban areas generally. The case was Baker v. Carr. Knowing its significance, the Supreme Court ordered three and a half hours of oral argument,⁵⁶ with U.S. Solicitor General Archibald Cox arguing as amicus curiae on the side of the plaintiff on behalf of the U.S. government. The mere willingness to accept Baker v. Carr for review served notice of the possibility, if not the probability, of a dramatic "political question" shift. And it was dramatic, indeed. There were six opinions, covering a total of 165 pages, with Justice Frankfurter's agitated and angry dissenting opinion for Justice Harlan and himself consuming 65 pages alone! Still what Justice Brennan actually decided in his opinion for the Court can be described quickly: (1) that the federal courts do have jurisdiction in apportionment–districting cases, (2) that the Baker complaint did present a justiciable controversy, and (3) that Baker and his co-appellants had standing to bring the suit. Notwithstanding Frankfurter's deeply felt warnings, in what was to prove his last opinion prior to his retirement for reasons of health later that year (1962), that the judiciary was damaging itself by getting into such "a political thicket," that it was immersing itself dangerously and wrongly in a "mathematical quagmire," the Court majority of six (Justice Whittaker had not participated in the case), without addressing itself to the specific merits of Baker's contentions, (a) regarded them as eminently justiciable in the courts (i.e., capable of adjudication) and (b) remanded the case to the lower federal court from which it came for purposes of such adjudication. (Ultimately, Tennessee was ordered to redistrict. It complied, albeit haltingly.) In short, rejecting the Frankfurter admonition that "in a democratic society like ours, relief [for political mischief] must come through an aroused popular conscience that sears the conscience of the people's representatives,"⁵⁷ the highest court in the land in effect reformulated the "political question" concept and doctrine. No longer would it apply to the matter at issue. In Brennan's words, the political question doctrine relates properly to "the relationship between

55. Ibid., at 554. The decisive fourth vote in the case was provided by Justice Rutledge who, in effect, agreed with the three dissenters that the issue per se was justiciable, but nonetheless chose to concur in the Frankfurther opinion for the Court in view of "the shortness of time remaining" before the next election and the difficulties of an election at large in a state with so many congressional districts. Justice Jackson did not sit; he was at the Nuremberg war crimes trials. Chief Justice Stone had just died, and his successor, Fred M. Vinson, had not yet been sworn in.
56. Baker v. Carr, 368 U.S. 804 (1961).
57. Ibid., 369 U.S. 186 (1962) at 270.

the judiciary and the coordinate branches of the Federal Government, and not the federal judiciary's relationship to the states . . ."[58] Over Frankfurter's specific disagreement on the point, Brennan thus confined "political questions," by way of the *Baker v. Carr* decision, to "a function of the separation of powers."[59]

As a logical result of the decision, the Supreme Court subsequently struck down as unconstitutional the infamous, although by then somewhat revised, Georgia County Unit System for state legislative apportionment in *Gray v. Sanders* in 1963,[60] plus state legislative malapportionment of congressional districts in 1964 in *Wesberry v. Sanders*.[61] Later in 1964, in the most far-reaching and most contentious of all of the myriad of post-*Baker v. Carr*–related decisions, the Court required that *both* houses of state legislatures be apportioned on the basis of *population*, a decision handed down in a six-case "package" known by its lead case, *Reynolds v. Sims*.[62] In 1968 the principle was extended to local government,[63] and in 1969 the Court made clear, 6:3, that states would have to justify *any* numerical deviation between districts on pain of findings of unconstitutionality.[64] Decisions in 1970 held the "one-person one-vote" rule to apply to all elective bodies exercising "*general* governmental authority"[65]—even school boards (although not all of them)[66]—but *not* to those that, like the New York City Board of Estimate, do not possess that kind of power,[67] nor, in 1973, accordingly, to elected *judges*.[68] Ultimately, deviations were sanctioned for certain political boundaries at the state level,[69] but not even as much as 0.7(!) percent for congressional districts,[70] and there are distinct limits on how much even a state may deviate.[71] Not at all surprisingly, the Court indicated in 1986 that it might adjudicate "egregious" examples of the age-old political shenanigans practice of the gerry-mander—although it refused to do so then.[72]

It should be clear, however, that the important contraction brought about by

58. Ibid., at 210.
59. Ibid., at 217.
60. 372 U.S. 368. (Its famed "one-person, one-vote" statement is at 381.)
61. 376 U.S. 1.
62. 377 U.S. 533.
63. *Avery v. Midland County*, 390 U.S. 474.
64. *Wells v. Rockefeller*, 394 U.S. 542.
65. E.g., *Hadley v. Junior College District of Metropolitan Kansas City*, 397 U.S. 50.
66. *Rosenthal v. Board of Education of Central High School*, 420 U.S. 985 (1975), where a *central* school board of eight appointees was selected: two each from four districts of elected town school board memberships. On the other hand, the Court applied the "one-person, one-vote" principle anew by refusing to review its embrace below in the 1975 case of *Regional High School District # 5 v. Baker*, 423 U.S. 995.
67. *Bergerman v. Lindsay*, 398 U.S. 955.
68. *Wells v. Edwards*, 409 U.S. 1095 (1973). Yet in 1991 the Court ruled 6:3 in *Chisom v. Roemer*, 59 LW 4696, that the Voting Rights Act of 1982 embraced judicial elections within its coverage, thus signaling a distinguishing, if not even an outright overruling, of *Wells v. Edwards*.
69. *City of Virginia Beach v. Howell*, 410 U.S. 315 (1973); *Gaffney v. Cummings*, 412 U.S. 735 (1973); and *White v. Regester*, 412 U.S. 755 (1973).
70. *Karcher v. Daggett*, 462 U.S. 725 (1983).
71. See, e.g., the Court's unanimous "no" in 1975 to a North Dakota attempt to institute multimember senatorial districts and to deviate up to 20 percent (*Chapman v. Meier*, 420 U.S. 1).
72. *Davis v. Bandemer*, 478 U.S. 109.

Baker v. Carr has by no means removed the concept of "political question" doctrine as such. A case like the well-known 1849 *Luther v. Borden*[73] would today assuredly continue to be treated, in line with the new Brennan formula announced in *Baker v. Carr*, as a political question. *Luther v. Borden* arose out of the Rhode Island Dorr Rebellion, early in America's history. Very briefly, the facts of the case were such that the Supreme Court found itself confronted with the crucial decision as to *which one* of two governments battling for legal supremacy in Rhode Island in 1842 was *the* legal one. The Court concluded that this was clearly a "political question": For the President of the United States, John Tyler, in reserving the right to exercise the power, conferred on the Chief Executive by Congress in 1795, to send federal troops to aid states in suppressing insurrection, had, by mobilizing the militia (though short of calling it out) in response to the Charter government's plea, indicated that he regarded the original (the "Charter") government as the lawful one of the two, and that this judgment was binding on the judiciary.

If one accepts the concept of the political question at all, the *Luther* example is obviously a much more clear-cut one than those involving legislative apportionment. Yet what a political question *is* remains difficult to determine. Generalization of the doctrine is still virtually impossible. Moreover, as Justice Brennan pointed out in *Baker v. Carr*, "the mere fact that [a] suit seeks protection of a political right does not mean it presents a political question. Such an objection is little more than a play upon words."[74] As his colleague Clark put the matter in his concurring opinion, "national respect for the courts is more enhanced through the forthright enforcement of [basic national rights such as fair legislative apportionment] than by rendering them nugatory through the interposition of subterfuges."[75] And, as Professor Louis Henkin asked suggestively: "Would not the part of the courts in our system, the institution of judicial review, and their public and intellectual acceptance, fare better if we broke open that package, assign its components elsewhere, and threw the package away?"[76] Undaunted, Justice Powell, reflecting upon *Baker v. Carr*, in which he did not participate, endeavored to condense the "P.Q." inquiry to three questions in his concurring opinion in *Goldwater v. Carter*, in 1979, sixteen years after *Baker*: (1) Does the issue involve resolution of questions committed by the text of the Constitution to a coordinate branch of the government? (2) Would resolution of the question demand that a court move beyond areas of judicial expertise? (3) Do prudential considerations counsel against judicial intervention?[77] Yet, arguably, despite Justice Powell's careful formulation, however attractive it may be in theory, "political question" maxim is a treadmill; perhaps to a fatal degree its supporting logic is circular.

Eleven. In the event of a validly challenged statute, the presumption of its constitutionality is always in its favor—although the Court's contemporary "double standard" policy, with its diverse tiers or levels of review, headed by "strict" or

73. 7 Howard 1.
74. Opinion for the Court, 369 U.S. 186, at 209.
75. Ibid., at 261–62. See also the Court's forthright disposition of potentially delicate political issues in *Powell v. McCormack*, 395 U.S. 486 (1969).
76. "Is There a 'Political Question' Doctrine?" 85 *Yale Law Journal* 597 (1976), p. 625.
77. 444 U.S. 999.

"suspect" scrutiny, may be regarded as a converse approach, certainly in civil rights cases.[78] As early as 1827, Justice Bushrod Washington wrote:

> It is but a decent respect to the wisdom, integrity, and patriotism of the legislative body, by which any law is passed, to presume in favor of its validity, until its violation of the Constitution is proved beyond a reasonable doubt.[79]

Hence, as the history of the Court shows, if a legislative enactment can be construed to be in reasonable harmony with the Constitution, a majority of the Court will almost always do so. Obviously, the views of the Justices have differed somewhat, often drastically, on the meaning of the word "reasonable." Thus, although there is today practically no judicial interference with legislation dealing with economic and social matters, the Court remains seriously divided on what constitutes "reasonable" legislative restrictions in certain areas of civil rights and liberties, such as the national security sector in the face of the specific guarantees under the First Amendment. For example, generally speaking, a hard core of five members of the 1966–67 Warren bench—the Chief Justice himself and Justices Black, Douglas, Brennan, and Fortas—would brook little, if any, legislative encroachments in this sector, whereas a hard core of three—Justices Clark, Harlan, and White—would exercise more or less judicial self-restraint, with Justice Stewart more unpredictable here, given his pronounced concern both for freedom of expression and judicial abstemiousness.

In any event, the Court will not normally formulate a rule of constitutional law broader than is required by the precise facts to which it is to be applied. "The cardinal principle of statutory construction," wrote Chief Justice Hughes in a famous case,

> is to save and not to destroy. We have repeatedly held that as between two possible interpretations of a statute, by one of which it would be unconstitutional and the other valid, our plain duty is to adopt that which will save the act. Even to avoid a serious doubt the rule is the same.[80]

On the other hand, Justice Stone, normally a firm adherent to the philosophy of presumption of constitutionality, implied an important exception to the general rule in his footnote in the otherwise rather unimportant *Carolene Products* case,[81] which footnote became one of the most famous of all time. It was there that he stated that perhaps there might be occasion for departing from the normal presumption of constitutionality for legislation in cases *where the legislative action in question involved a restriction or curtailment of the ordinary political processes which could generally be expected to be employed to bring about the negation of undesirable legislation, or where it appeared to be within "a specific prohibition of the Constitution, such as those of the first ten amendments, which are deemed*

---

78. See Henry J. Abraham, *Freedom and the Court: Civil Rights and Liberties in the United States,* 5th ed. (New York: Oxford University Press, 1988), ch. 2, "The Double Standard."
79. *Ogden v. Saunders,* 12 Wheaton 213 (1827).
80. *N.L.R.B. v. Jones & Laughlin Steel Corporation,* 301 U.S. 1 (1937).
81. *United States v. Carolene Products Co.,* 304 U.S. 144 (1938) at 152–53, n. 4.

equally specific when held to be embraced within the Fourteenth.[82] And as of the late 1960s, the Burger Court adopted a posture of judicial "suspicion" under which it began to regard legislative activity in certain categories as "suspect," notably in those of race, national origin, and alienage. In those areas, legislatures (and executives) would henceforth have to prove the existence of a "compelling state interest" rather than, as heretofore, a mere "rational relationship" in order to see their actions survive "close" judicial scrutiny.

Twelve. In the exercise of what some commentators have been fond of styling "judicial parsimony," *if a case or controversy can be decided on any other than constitutional grounds—such as by statutory construction, which constitutes the greatest single area of the Court's work, or if it can rest on an independent state ground—the Court will be eager to do so.* For normally it will not decide questions of a constitutional nature unless absolutely necessary to the decision of the case, and even then it will draw such a decision as narrowly as possible, being ever loath to formulate a rule of constitutional law broader than is clearly required by the precise facts to which it is to be applied. Nor will it anticipate a question of constitutional law in advance of the necessity of deciding it. As Justice White put it in an "obscenity" case, the proper approach is "not to invalidate . . . but to construe . . . narrowly."[83] Justice Frankfurter succinctly underscored the point of anticipation in an edifying exchange with Thurman Arnold, who was acting as counsel for Dr. J. P. Peters, petitioner in the loyalty-security case of *Peters v. Hobby.*[84] Mr. Arnold pleaded with the Court that he would not like to win the case on the narrow procedural, statutory ground to which a majority of the members of the bench was evidently inclining. Responded Justice Frankfurter: "The question is not whether you want to win the case on that ground or not. This Court reaches constitutional issues last, not first." He might well have quoted Justice Brandeis's famous assertion that the "most important thing we do is not doing." And "not doing" is what Justice Rehnquist did in 1977 by putting off a potentially significant decision on parental commitment of unwilling children to Pennsylvania mental institutions, ruling: "The fact that it would be convenient for the parties and the public to have promptly decided whether this legislation assailed is valid cannot justify a departure from these settled rules of status and class."[85]

The loyalty-security field affords a host of pertinent illustrations of the Court's preference for a resort to its potent weapon of statuory construction rather than to constitutional grounds. This delicate and emotion-laden area of public policy is tailor-made for such an approach, which preserves the statute while sometimes smoothing certain ragged edges. Thus, the Court effects a gain, however moderate it may be, for individual civil rights, while retaining the generally popular and politically desirable law. To cite some instances: it is precisely what the Court did in narrowing executive authority to dismiss government employees under the Sum-

82. Ibid., (italics supplied). On the issue of what has been regarded as a judicial "double standard," see my *Freedom and the Court,* op. cit., p. 385, n. 77.
83. *United States v. Thirty-Seven (37) Photographs,* 402 U.S. 363 (1971) at 375, plurality opinion.
84. 349 U.S. 311 (1955). The exchange is reported in 23 *U.S. Law Week* 265–66 (1955).
85. *Kremens v. Bartley,* 431 U.S. 119 (1977), quoting Justice Brandeis's opinion in *Ashwander v. Tennessee Valley Authority,* 297 U.S. 288 (1936).

mary Suspension Act of 1950 by ruling that the act did not authorize dismissal of employees holding "non-sensitive" positions,[86] in limiting the power of the Secretary of State to withhold a passport from a citizen "for any substantive reason he may choose," holding that the Immigration and Nationality Act of 1952 did not authorize such sweeping discretionary powers,[87] 60 and in finding that, while the Magnuson Seaman's Act of 1950 had given the executive branch the authority to act to prevent sabotage, it had emphatically not provided it with the authority to inquire into seamen's beliefs and associations before granting them seamen's licenses.[88] In each of these instances, congressional reaction was to the effect that "we did *so* intend to authorize what you say we did not," but in the absence of the passage of any clarifying or amplifying amendments the two statutes stood as judicially construed. After all, statutory construction is an act of judgment and, as Justice Holmes once observed succinctly, applies to cases "in which there is a fair contest between two readings." On the other hand, there are also instances when there is really *no* contest, as the Court held unanimously in no uncertain terms when, in 1975, it rejected the President's "impounding" of $9 billion in water pollution funds because the legislation establishing the program had clearly *not* given him that authority.[89] In Justice Cardozo's words, "avoidance of a difficulty will not be pressed to the point of disingenuous evasion. When the intention of Congress is revealed . . . [the] problem must be faced and answered."[90]

Thirteen. The Court will not ordinarily impute illegal motives to the lawmakers. "So long as Congress acts in pursuance of its constitutional power," explained Justice Harlan in a much-debated decision upholding certain aspects of the investigative authority of the House Committee on Un-American Activities,[91] "the judiciary lacks authority to intervene *on the basis of the motives* which spurred the exercise of that power." This sentiment was echoed by Justice Black in one of his last opinions, in which he wrote that no precedent existed for holding a law violative of "equal protection solely because of the motivations of the men who voted for it."[92] And as early as 1810 Chief Justice Marshall had written that it "may well be doubted how far the validity of a law depends upon the motives of its framers."[93] Indeed, the Court is not supposed to consider *motives* at all; but, as Max Radin once wrote, that concept is indeed a "transparent and absurd fiction"[94]—to which the decision in the *Child Labor Tax case*[95] of 1922, for example, bears eloquent witness.

However, to compound the problem, the Supreme Court is expected to, and very frequently does, take legislative *intent* or *purpose* into account; yet, it is no

---

86. *Cole v. Young,* 351 U.S. 536 (1956).
87. *Kent and Briehl v. Dulles,* 357 U.S. 116 (1958).
88. *Schneider v. Smith,* 390 U.S. 17 (1968). For an excellent more recent illustration, see *T.W.A. v. Hardison,* 432 U.S. 63 (1977).
89. *Train v. City of New York,* 420 U.S. 35.
90. *Moore Ice Cream Co. v. Rose,* 289 U.S. 373 (1932), at 379.
91. *Barenblatt v. United States,* 360 U.S. 109 (1959) (italics supplied).
92. *Palmer v. Thompson,* 403 U.S. 217 (1971), majority opinion, at 224.
93. *Fletcher v. Peck,* 6 Cranch 87, at 130.
94. "Statutory Interpretation," 43 *Harvard Law Review* 863d (April 1930).
95. *Baily v. Drexel Furniture Co.,* 259 U.S. 20.

easy task to separate motives and intent, and Justice Frankfurter, for one, consistently refused to do so. The Court, however, has to essay judgments: thus, it answered in the negative, although by a margin of but one vote (5:4), the question of whether or not anything in the current patent laws demonstrated a congressional intent to deny patents to *inventions that happen to be living organisms*, thereby in effect telling the scientific community that it may patent new forms of life.[96] Justice Holmes wrote, "I only want to know what the words mean." Still: "A ... word is not a crystal, transparent and unchanged, it is the skin of a living thought and may vary greatly in color and content according to the circumstances and time in which it is used."[97] And he found *policy* in words.[98] Or, as Justice Cardozo wrote so appropriately, "a great principle of constitutional law is not susceptible of comprehensive statement in an adjective."[99] The *Steel Seizure case*[100] of 1952, in which seven separate opinions were written, provided a basis for an opinion for the Court only because a sufficient number of Justices was able to agree on the single point that Congress, in enacting the Taft–Hartley Act, had deliberately *intended* not to provide for presidential authority to seize struck plants. Here the intent of Congress proved to be the basis for the Court's judgment that the Chief Executive had usurped legislative power, with the Justices, as is their custom, equating intent with legislative history.

This approach is sometimes styled "psychoanalyzing Congress" by some of the less reverent observers of the governmental scene, who have considerable—and perhaps well-grounded—doubt of the infallibility of the Holmesian contention, frequently quoted by Justice Frankfurter, that "a page of history is worth a volume of logic."[101] Yet whatever their merits otherwise, for this purpose at least the *Congressional Record* and the reports of the various committees of Congress are a constant and evidently fertile source of reference for the members of the Supreme Court. Thus, in unanimously upholding the Voting Rights Act of 1965, the Court repeatedly referred to congressional intent to eradicate the "substantial voting discrimination" in *specific* sections of the country because it "knew" about these and wanted to remove them. Again and again Chief Justice Warren used the term "Congress knew," thus underscoring its intent or purpose.[102] Conversely, we have the example of utter disregard by a five-member Court majority, led by Justice Brennan, in its contentious 1979 *Weber* racial quotas-in-employment case, wherein it contravened not only the express language of Title VII of the Civil Rights Act of 1964, but also its demonstrable congressional intent![103] Commenting

96. *Diamond v. Chakrabarty*, 447 U.S. 303 (1980). See also *Diamond v. Diehr*, 450 U.S. 175 (1981).
97. *Town v. Eisner*, 245 U.S. 418 (1917) at 424.
98. See Felix Frankfurter, "Some Reflections on the Readings of Statutes," Sixth Annual Benjamin N. Cardozo Lecture before the Association of the Bar of the City of New York, March 8, 1947 (reprinted in 47 *Columbia Law Review* [1947], 527–46).
99. *Carter v. Carter Coal Co.*, 298 U.S. 238 (1936) at 327.
100. *Youngstown Sheet and Tube Co. v. Sawyer*, 343 U.S. 579.
101. *New York Trust Co. v. Eisner*, 256 U.S. 345 (1921) at 349.
102. *South Carolina v. Katzenbach* 383 U.S. 301 (1966), opinion for the Court.
103. *United Steel Workers v. Weber*, 443 U.S. 193. Justice Brennan justified his reasoning by contending that it is not enough to look at the *letter* of the law, that its *"spirit"* must also be judicially involved.

at the ABA Convention on the overall problem of interpretation in 1989, Justice White decried the time-consuming task falling to the judiciary because of the so often prevalent linguistic ambiguities present in legislative language, observing: "The statute as is written . . . is what Congress enacted, not statements in hearings, not discussion of statutory terms contained in committee reports, and not statements on the floor."[104]

Fourteen. If the court does find that it must hold a law unconstitutional, it will usually try hard to confine the holding to that particular section of the statute which was successfully challenged on constitutional grounds— provided such a course of action is at all feasible. It would not be, of course, if the section at issue constituted the veritable heart of the legislation, in which case the Court would follow a well-established rule of statutory construction: if the various parts of a statute are inextricably connected to such degrees as to warrant the assumption that the legislature intended the law to function as a whole, then if some portions of the statute are unconstitutional the law must be treated as unconstitutional in its entirety.[105] "Sectionalized" unconstitutionality is known as *separability*—sometimes as *severability*[106]—for which Congress now customarily, and quite specifically, provides in its statutes, although it is not required by the courts to do so.[107] A typical separability clause, taken from the War Powers Resolution of 1973, reads:

> If any provision of this joint resolution or the application therof to any person or circumstance is held invalid, the remainder of the joint resolution and the application of such provision to any other person or circumstance shall not be affected thereby.

This not only serves to have those sections not affected by the Court's particular decision, but it may also act to preserve the law's entire structure for a test involving different litigants.

The series of decisions declaring portions of the Uniform Code of Military Justice Act of 1950 unconstitutional[108] are cases in point; certain powers delegated to the armed services under it are no longer valid, but the balance of the act stands and is enforced. On the other hand, although initially it was merely the "hot oil" provisions of the National Industry Recovery Act of 1933—standing apart from those provisions of the act dealing with codes of fair competition—that fell as an unconstitutional delegation of legislative power in January 1935,[109] four months later the codes, too, and with them the entire structure of the act, fell on similar grounds.[110]

104. As reported by *The Washington Post*, August 6, 1989, p. A7.

105. For example, see *Pollock v. Farmers' Loan and Trust Co.*, 158 U.S. 601 (1895).

106. A recent (1983) example is the *severability* of No. 244 (c)(2) of the Immigration and Naturalization Code, declaring the congressional veto (here by one house) unconstitutional (7:2), but also applying it (6:3) to *all* of the other similar 211 laws that contained one- or two-house vetoes (*Immigration and Naturalization Service v. Chadha*, 462 U.S. 919).

107. See Chief Justice Burger's opinion in *Tilton v. Richarson*, 403 U.S. 672 (1971), in which a portion of a federal statute was declared unconstitutional despite the acknowledged "absence of an express separability provision."

108. *United States ex rel Toth v. Quarles*, 350 U.S. 11 (1955); *Reid v. Covert* 354 U.S. 1 (1957); *Kinsella v. Singleton*, 361 U.S. 234 (1960), among others.

109. *Panama Refining Co. v. Ryan*, 293 U.S. 388.

110. *Schechter v. United States*, 295 U.S. 495.

Fifteen. A legislative enactment—or an executive action—may be unwise, unjust, unfair, undemocratic, injudicious, "if you like . . . even tyrannical,"[111] or simply stupid, but still be constitutional in the eyes of the Court. Much deference is thus paid to the legislature, and justly so under the American system of separation of powers and division of powers. In the clipped language of a Holmes opinion: "We fully understand . . . the very powerful argument that can be made against the wisdom of this legislation, but on that point we have no concern."[112] Justice Holmes once stated this constitutional and judicial philosophy in typically colorful fashion to the then sixty-one-year-old Justice Stone:

> Young man, about 75 years ago I learned that I was not God. And so, when the people . . . want to do something I can't find anything in the Constitution expressly forbidding them to do, I say, whether I like it or not, "Goddamit, let 'em do it."[113]

Or, as he said to John W. Davis on another occasion: "Of course I know, and every other sensible man knows, that the Sherman law [the Sherman Anti-Trust Act of 1890] is damned nonsense, but if my country wants to go to hell, I am here to help it."[114] James Wilson of Pennsylvania, one of the most influential Founding Fathers, had expressed similar sentiments during the Constitutional Convention of 1787: "Laws may be unjust, may be unwise, may be dangerous, may be destructive, and yet not be so unconstitutional as to justify the Judges in refusing to give them effect." His fellow Founding Father, George Mason of Virginia, seconded that view, utilizing even stronger adjectives: "[Laws] however unjust, oppressive, or pernicious."[115] And defending his position in McCulloch v. Maryland, John Marshall—combining judicial abstemiousness with judicial authority—lectured that the "peculiar circumstances of the moment may render a decision more or less wise, but cannot make it more or less constitutional."[116] The man who was appointed to the Holmes seat on the Court after Justice Cardozo's death in 1938, Justice Felix Frankfurter, continued to champion that philosophy of judicial self-restraint eloquently, repeatedly, and consistently. It was one he had articulated often, even prior to ascending the Court. For example, in a 1925 article, when he wrote, "Even the most rampant worshiper of judicial supremacy admits that wisdom and justice are not the tests of constitutionality."[117] On the Court, true to that philosophy, he thus dissented vigorously from the majority's declaration of uncon-

111. Justice Holmes, dissenting in *Lochner v. United States*, 198 U.S. 45 (1905).

112. *Noble State Bank v. Haskell*, 219 U.S. 575 (1910), opinion for the Court, at 580.

113. As quoted by Charles P. Curtis in his *Lions under the Throne* (Boston: Houghton Mifflin, 1947), p. 281.

114. As told by Francis Biddle, *Justice Holmes, Natural Law and the Supreme Court* (New York: Macmillan, 1961), p. 9. In the Holmes–Laski letters he put it somewhat differently: "If my fellow citizens want to go to Hell I will help them. It's my job." Mark De Wolfe Howe, ed., *The Holmes-Laski Letters, 1916–1935* (New York: Atheneum, 1963), p. 249.

115. Max Farrand, ed., *The Records of the Federal Convention* (New Haven: Yale University Press, 1936), 2, p. 73.

116. Gerald Gunther, ed., *John Marshall's Defense of McCulloch v. Maryland* (Stanford: Stanford University Press, 1969, pp. 190–91.

117. "Can the Supreme Court Guarantee Toleration?" 43 *New Republic* 85 (1925) at 87.

stitutionality of a section of the Immigration and Nationality Act of 1940 in *Trop v. Dulles:*

> It is not easy to stand aloof and allow want of wisdom to prevail, to disregard one's own strongly held view of what is wise in the conduct of affairs. But it is not the business of this Court to pronounce policy. It must observe a fastidious regard for limitations on its own power, and this precludes the Court's giving effect to its own notions of what is wise or politic. That self-restraint is of the essence in the observance of the judicial oath, for the Constitution has not authorized the judges to sit in judgment on the wisdom of what Congress and the Executive Branch do.[118]

But once again much, if not all, depends on how the Justices see the line between self-restraint, which they indubitably all recognize as an essential element in the judicial process, and *ultra vires* legislative and executive actions. If, in drawing this line, some Justices, on some issues, are prone to address themselves more to the judicial heart than the judicial mind, who is to say where and how the Founding Fathers of the Constitution of the United States would today distinguish between that document's heart and mind? They too were men, just as judges are men, "not disembodied spirits," in Justice Frankfurter's words; they are men who "respond to human situations . . . [who] do not reside in a vacuum." And his mentor, Holmes, believed that judges "should not be too rigidly bound to the tenets of judicial self-restraint in cases involving civil liberties."[119] Of course, even pedigreed champions of the latter may well disagree on the point in certain specific cases, as is intriguingly demonstrated by Justices Black and Douglas in the *Connecticut Birth Control case* of 1965.[120] There, speaking for the seven-man majority that held the state's anti-birth-control law unconstitutional on a host of grounds, Douglas insisted that "we do not sit [in rendering this decision] as a super-legislature to determine the wisdom, need, and propriety of laws that touch economic problems, businsess affairs, or social conditions. This law, however, operates directly on an intimate relation of husand and wife, and their physician's role in one aspect of that relation."[121] Black, however, dissenting together with his colleague Stewart, regarded the Court's action as one "based on subjective considerations of 'natural justice' [a formula that] is no less dangerous when used to enforce this Court's views about personal rights than those about economic rights."[122] Judges are men (and women). . . .

Sixteen. The Supreme Court has reiterated time and again that it *is not designed to serve as a check against inept, unwise, emotional unrepresentative legislators.* Chief Justice Waite put it well when he wrote in 1876 that for *"protection against abuses by legislatures the people must resort to the polls, not the courts."*[123] Some eighty years later, Justice Douglas reiterated this point of view forcefully: "Con-

118. 356 U.S. 86 (1958) at 120.
119. As quoted by Chief Justice Stone to Professor Clinton Rossiter, April 12, 1941, related by Alpheus T. Mason in *Harlan Fiske Stone: Pillar of the Law* (New York: The Viking Press, 1956), p. 516
120. *Griswold v. Connecticut*, 381 U.S. 479.
121. Ibid., at 482.
122. Ibid., at 522.
123. *Munn v. Illnois*, 94 U.S. 113, at 134 (italics supplied).

gress acting within its constitutional powers, has the final say on policy issues. If it acts unwisely the electorate can make a change."[124] This fundamental truth lies at the very core of the democratic process—a process that enables the people and their representatives at once to rise to soaring heights of wisdom and magnanimity and to descend to the depths of folly and pettiness. Yet that process, under law, proscribes *unconstitutional* action.

THE BULWARK

The Supreme Court of the United States of America—which Woodrow Wilson viewed as "the balance wheel of our whole constitutional system . . . a vehicle of the Nation's life . . ."[125]—may be perpetually steeped in controversy; it may not always have exercised all of its power, or exercised it wisely when it did; it may on occasion have gone well beyond its presumed functions; it may have deliberately avoided issues that might have proved to be potentially troublesome; it may not always have been able to make its decisions "stick"; and there may well be considerable room for improvement. No institution of government can be devised by human beings that will be satisfactory to all people at all times. The Court is much better at saying what the government may *not* do, or what it may do, than in prescribing what public policy the government ought to chart and how to go about doing it. Indeed, the Court should resolutely shun *prescriptive* policymaking.[126] It has quite enough to do in statutory and constitutional application and interpretation. To reiterate the second Justice Harlan's often-quoted admonition: "The Constitution is not a panacea for every blot upon the public welfare; nor should this Court, ordained as a judicial body, be thought of as a general haven for reform movements."[127] Paraphrasing Professor Freund, the question is not whether the Court can do everything, but whether it can do something. Of course, it can escape neither controversy nor criticism—nor should it. In Justice Holmes's oft-quoted words: "We are very quiet there, but it is the quiet of a storm center, as we all know."[128] As an institution at once legal, political, governmental, and human, the Court possesses both the assets and the liabilities that attend these descriptive characteristics.

Yet, when all is said and done, the Court, at the head of the U.S. judiciary, is not only the most fascinating, the most influential, and the most powerful judicial body in the world, it is also "the living voice of the Constitution,"[129] as Lord Bryce,

---

124. *Railway Employees' Department v. Hansen*, 351 U.S. 225 (1956).

125. *Constitutional Government in the United States* (New York: Columbia University Press, 1907), p. 142.

126. On this point see Alexander M. Bickel's *The Supreme Court and the Idea of Progress* (New York: Harper & Row, 1970); Raoul Berger, *Government by Judiciary: The Transformation of the Fourteenth Amendment* (Cambridge: Harvard University Press, 1977); and Sanford B. Gabin, *Judicial Review and the Rational Doubt Test* (Port Washington, NY: Kennikat Press, 1980).

127. *Reynolds v. Sims*, 377 U.S. 533 (1964), dissenting opinion, at 624.

128. As quoted by Max Lerner in his *The Mind and Faith of Justice Holmes* (Garden City, NY: Halcyon House, 1943), p. 388.

129. *The American Commonwealth* (New York: Macmillan, 1905), 1, p. 272.

who knew America well indeed, once phrased it. As such it is both arbiter and educator and, in essence, represents the sole solution short of anarchy under the American system of government as we know it. It acts, in the words of one commentator, "as the instrument of national moral values that have not been able to find other governmental expression"[130]—assuming, of course, that it functions within its authorized sphere of constitutional adjudication. In that role it operates "as the collective conscience of a sovereign people."[131] And, as Alexander Meiklejohn once observed, no other institution "is more deeply decisive in its effect upon our understanding of ourselves and our government."[132] It defines values and proclaims principles. It is a corrective force in our life.

Beyond that, moreover, the Supreme Court of the United States is the chief protector of the Constitution, of its great system of balances—as *United States v. Nixon* and *Immigration and Naturalization Service v. Chadha*, for example, proved again so tellingly in 1974 and 1983, respectively[133]—and of the peoples' liberties. It is the greatest institutional safeguard we possess. It may have retreated, even yielded to pressures now and then, but without its vigilance our liberties would scarcely have survived. Few have sounded this call more eloquently than did Justice Black in his memorable opinion for the Court in *Chambers v. Florida*:

> Under our constitutional system, courts stand against any winds that blow as havens of refuge for those who might otherwise suffer because they are helpless, weak, outnumbered, or because they are non-conforming victims of prejudice and public excitement. No higher duty, no more solemn responsibility, rests upon this Court, than that of translating into living law and maintaining this constitutional shield deliberately planned and inscribed for the benefit of every human being subject to our Constitution—of whatever race, creed, or persuasion.[134]

Within the limits of procedure and deference to the presumption of constitutionality of legislation, the Court—our "sober second thought," as Chief Justice Stone called it[135]—is the natural forum in our society for the individual and for the small group. The Court's essential function, as Chief Justice Warren told the Centennial Convocation of the New York School of Law, "is to act as the final arbiter of minority rights."[136] It thereby serves as a primary rather than an auxiliary check. In Justice Douglas's words: "The people should know that when filibusters occupy the forums, when oppressions are great, when the clash of authority between the individual and the State is severe, they can still get justice in the courts,"[137] assuming the existence of constitutional warrant therefor. It represents a power that so astute an observer of the American scene as Alexis de Tocqueville (Montesquieu's

130. Anthony Lewis, *The New York Times Magazine*, June 17, 1962, p. 28.
131. Judge J. Skelly Wright, "The Role of the Courts: Conscience of a Sovereign People," 29 *The Reporter* 5 (September 29, 1963).
132. *Free Speech and Its Relation to Self-Government* (New York: Harper & Brothers, 1948), p. 32.
133. 417 U.S. 683 and 462 U.S. 919, respectively.
134. 309 U.S. 227 (1940), at 241.
135. "The Common Law in the United States," 50 *Harvard Law Review* 25 (1936).
136. New York City, October 3, 1968.
137. *Bell v. Maryland*, 378 U.S. 226 (1964), concurring opinion, at 242–43.

student) viewed as "one of the most powerful barriers ever erected against tyranny of political assemblies."[138]

Thus, the Court must be prepared to say "no" to the government—as Madison, the father of the Bill of Rights, hoped fervently it would always do. There are many citizens—indeed, most citizens, once they have given the problem the careful thought it merits—who will feel far more secure in the knowledge of that guardianship, one generally characterized by common sense, than if it were primarily exercised by the far more easily pressured, more impulsive, and more emotion-charged legislative or executive branches. Far too easily do these two yield to the politically expedient and the popular, for they are close, indeed, to what Judge Learned Hand called "the pressure of public hysteria, public panic, and public greed." Hence—and again in Earl Warren's words—"The Court must always stand ready to advance the rights of . . . minority interests if the executive and the legislative branches falter—assuming, of course, the presence of constitutional or legal authority."[139] His Court did just that, moving dramatically from deference to the prerogatives of the other two branches and of the states to aggressive protection of the constitutional rights of the individual, as the Court perceived these, and it did so amid withering criticism from a host of diverse quarters, both lay and professional. In Judge Carl McGowan's trenchant observation: "The essence of judicial power is that it is a solvent of personal frictions, whether they grow out of the relationships of individuals to each other, or of the individual and the state. When the clash comes, it is the judicial power which must settle it, if a society is to be ordered by reason rather than by superior forces alone, which is the very negation of civilized living."[140]

The Court, which often has had to act as a "moral goad" to public panic and public greed, is neither engaged nor interested in a popularity contest: its function is not one of counting constituents. Should the time ever arrive when that is the Court's function, the supreme judicial tribunal will have lost its meaning. "[W]e have no constituency," mused Warren on the last day of his sixteen-year tenure as Chief Justice of the United States, just prior to swearing in his successor, Warren Earl Burger. "We serve no minority. We serve only the public interest as we see it, guided only by the Constitution and our own conscience."[141]

Even if a transfer of that guardianship to other institutions of government were theoretically desirable, which few thoughtful citizens believe, it would be politically impossible. "Do we desire constitutional questions," asked Charles Evans Hughes when off the bench, in his fine book on the Court, "to be determined by political assemblies and partisan division?"[142] The response must be a ringing "no!" In the 1955 Godkins Lectures, which he was preparing to deliver at Harvard Uni-

138. *Democracy in America* (New York: Doubleday, 1969), p. 104. He referred to the Court as "the boast of the Constitution."
139. As quoted in *The Philadelphia Inquirer,* October 4, 1968, p. 2.
140. Obituary, *The Washington Post,* December 25, 1987, p. A18.
141. As quoted in *The New York Times,* June 24, 1969, p. 24.
142. *The Supreme Court of the United States* (New York: Columbia University Press, 1928), p. 236.

versity when death intervened, Justice Jackson expressed this conviction eloquently and ably:

> The people have seemed to feel[143] that the Supreme Court, whatever its defects, is still the most detached, dispassionate, and trustworthy custodian that our system affords for the translation of abstract into concrete constitutional commands.[144]

And we may well agree with Thomas Reed Powell that the logic of American constitutional law is the common sense of the Supreme Court.

As a commentary on the point, that distinguished observer of Court and Constitution reported an incident that took place after the turn of the century in a debate on the floor of the U.S. Senate between Senators John C. Spooner of Wisconsin and "Pitchfork Ben" Tillman of South Carolina. At one juncture of the proceedings, Tillman exclaimed: "I am tired of hearing what the Supreme Court says. What I want to get at is the common sense of the matter." Rejoined Spooner: "I too am seeking the common sense of the matter. But, as for me, I prefer the common sense of the Supreme Court of the United States to that of the Senator from South Carolina."[145]

In the long run common sense has always served the Supreme Court of the United States well in its ceaseless striving, as a voice of reason, to maintain the blend of change and continuity which is the *sine qua non* for desirable stability in the governmental process of a democracy. In that role it will, because it must, live in history.

---

143. On this point see the interesting findings and reflections by Gregory Casey, "The Supreme Court and Myth: An Empirical Investigation," 8 *Law & Society* 385 (Spring 1974).
144. Jackson, op. cit., n. 4, p. 23. (The lectures were delivered by his son.)
145. "The Logic and Rhetoric of Constitutional Law," 15 *Journal of Philosophy, Psychology, and Scientific Method* 656 (1918).

APPENDIX A. MEMBERS OF THE SUPREME COURT OF THE UNITED STATES*

Name	Place of Birth	Year of Birth	State App't From	Appointed by President	(A) Judicial Oath Taken	Date Service Terminated	(B) Service Terminated By	Years of Service	Year of Death
Chief Justices									
Jay, John	N.Y.	1745	N.Y.	Washington	Oct. 19, 1789(a)	June 29, 1795	resigned	5	1829
Rutledge, John	S.C.	1739	S.C.	Washington	Aug. 12, 1795(C)	Dec. 15, 1795	rejected†	¾	1800
Ellsworth, Oliver	Conn.	1745	Conn.	Washington	Mar. 8, 1796	Dec. 15, 1800	resigned	4	1807
Marshall, John	Va.	1755	Va.	Adams, J.	Feb. 4, 1801	July 6, 1835	Death	34	1835
Taney, Roger Brooke	Md.	1777	Md.	Jackson	Mar. 28, 1836	Oct. 12, 1864	Death	28	1864
Chase, Salmon Portland	N.H.	1808	Ohio	Lincoln	Dec. 15, 1864	May 7, 1873	Death	8 ½	1873
Waite, Morrison Remick	Conn.	1816	Ohio	Grant	Mar. 4, 1874	Mar. 23, 1888	Death	14	1888
Fuller, Melville Weston	Maine	1833	Illinois	Cleveland	Oct. 8, 1888	July 4, 1910	Death	21	1910
White, Edward Douglass	La.	1845	La.	Taft	Dec. 19, 1910(C)	May 19, 1921	Death	10	1921
Taft, William Howard	Ohio	1857	Conn.	Harding	July 11, 1921	Feb. 3, 1930	retired	8	1930
Hughes, Charles Evans	N.Y.	1862	N.Y.	Hoover	Feb. 24, 1930(C)	June 30, 1941	RETIRED	11	1948
Stone, Harlan Fiske	N.H.	1872	N.Y.	Roosevelt, F.	July 3, 1941(C)	Apr. 22, 1946	Death	5	1946
Vinson, Frederick Moore	Ky.	1890	Ky.	Truman	June 24, 1946	Sept. 8, 1953	Death	7	1953
Warren, Earl	Calif.	1891	Calif.	Eisenhower	Oct. 5, 1953	June 23, 1969	RETIRED	15	1974
Burger, Warren Earl	Minn.	1907	Va.	Nixon	June 23, 1969	Sept. 26, 1986	RETIRED	17	
Rehnquist, William Hubbs	Wisc.	1924	Va.	Reagan	Sept. 26, 1986		RETIRED		
Associate Justices:									
Wilson, James	Scotland	1742	Penn.	Washington	Oct. 5, 1789(b)	Aug. 21, 1798	Death	8	1798
Blair, John	Va.	1732	Va.	Washington	Feb. 2, 1790(c)	Jan. 27, 1796	resigned	6	1800
Cushing, William	Mass.	1732	Mass.	Washington	Feb. 2, 1790(b)	Sept. 13, 1810	Death	20	1810
Rutledge, John	S.C.	1739	S.C.	Washington	Feb. 15, 1790(c)	Mar. 5, 1791	resigned	1	1800
Iredell, James	England	1751	N.C.	Washington	May 13, 1790(b)	Oct. 20, 1799	Death	9	1799
Johnson, Thomas	Md.	1732	Md.	Washington	Aug. 6, 1792(c)	Feb. 1, 1793	resigned	½	1819
Paterson, William	Ireland	1745	N.J.	Washington	Mar. 11, 1793(a)	Sept. 9, 1806	Death	13½	1806
Chase, Samuel	Md.	1741	Md.	Washington	Feb. 4, 1796	June 19, 1811	Death	15	1811
Washington, Bushrod	Va.	1762	Va.	Adams, J.	Feb. 4, 1799(c)	Nov. 26, 1829	Death	31	1829
Moore, Alfred	N.C.	1755	N.C.	Adams, J.	Aug. 9, 1800(c)	Jan. 26, 1804	resigned	3	1810

Name	State	Birth	President	Appointed	Terminated	Reason	Years	End
Johnson, William	S.C.	1771	Jefferson	May 7, 1804	Aug. 4, 1834	Death	30	1834
Livingston, Henry Brockholst	N.Y.	1757	Jefferson	Jan. 20, 1807	Mar. 18, 1823	Death	16	1823
Todd, Thomas	Va.	1765	Jefferson	May 4, 1807(a)	Feb. 7, 1826	Death	18	1826
Duvall, Gabriel	Md.	1752	Madison	Nov. 23, 1811(a)	Jan. 14, 1835	resigned	23	1844
Story, Joseph	Mass.	1779	Madison	Feb. 3, 1812(c)	Sept. 10, 1845	Death	33	1845
Thompson, Smith	N.Y.	1768	Monroe	Sept. 1, 1823(b)	Dec. 18, 1843	Death	20	1843
Trimble, Robert	Ky.	1777	Adams, J.Q.	June 16, 1826(a)	Aug. 25, 1828	Death	2	1828
McLean, John	Ohio	1785	Jackson	Jan. 11, 1830	Apr. 4, 1861	Death	31	1861
Baldwin, Henry	Conn.	1780	Jackson	Jan. 18, 1830	Apr. 21, 1844	Death	14	1844
Wayne, James Moore	Ga.	1790	Jackson	Jan. 14, 1835	July 5, 1867	Death	32	1867
Barbour, Philip Pendleton	Va.	1783	Jackson	May 12, 1836	Feb. 25, 1841	Death	4	1841
Catron, John	Tenn.	1786	Van Buren	May 1, 1837	May 30, 1865	Death	28	1865
McKinley, John	Ala.	1790	Van Buren	Jan. 9, 1838(c)	July 19, 1852	Death	14	1852
Daniel, Peter Vivian	Va.	1784	Van Buren	Jan. 10, 1842(c)	May 31, 1860	Death	18	1860
Nelson, Samuel	N.Y.	1792	Tyler	Feb. 27, 1845	Nov. 28, 1872	retired	27	1873
Woodbury, Levi	N.H.	1789	Polk	Sept. 23, 1845(b)	Sept. 4, 1851	Death	5	1851
Grier, Robert Cooper	Pa.	1794	Polk	Aug. 10, 1846	Jan. 31, 1870	retired	23	1870
Curtis, Benjamin Robbins	Mass.	1809	Fillmore	Oct. 10, 1851(b)	Sept. 30, 1857	resigned	5	1874
Campbell, John Archibald	Ala.	1811	Pierce	Apr. 11, 1853(c)	Apr. 30, 1861	resigned	8	1889
Clifford, Nathan	N.H.	1803	Buchanan	Jan. 21, 1858	July 25, 1881	Death	23	1881
Swayne, Noah Haynes	Ohio	1804	Lincoln	Jan. 21, 1862	Jan. 24, 1881	retired	18	1884
Miller, Samuel Freeman	Iowa	1816	Lincoln	July 21, 1862	Oct. 13, 1890	Death	28	1890
Davis, David	Ill.	1815	Lincoln	Dec. 10, 1862	Mar. 4, 1877	resigned	14	1886
Field, Stephen Johnson	Calif.	1816	Lincoln	May 20, 1863	Dec. 1, 1897	retired	34¾	1899
Strong, William	Pa.	1808	Grant	Mar. 14, 1870	Dec. 14, 1880	retired	10¾	1895
Bradley, Joseph P.	N.J.	1813	Grant	Mar. 23, 1870	Jan. 22, 1892	retired	21	1892
Hunt, Ward	N.Y.	1810	Grant	Dec. 9, 1873	Jan. 27, 1882	disabled	9	1886
Harlan, John Marshall	Ky.	1833	Hayes	Dec. 5, 1877	Oct. 14, 1911	Death	34	1911
Woods, William Burnham	Ga.	1824	Hayes	Jan. 5, 1881	May 14, 1887	Death	6 ½	1887
Matthews, Stanley	Ohio	1824	Garfield	May 17, 1881	Mar. 22, 1889	Death	7	1889
Gray, Horace	Mass.	1828	Arthur	Jan. 9, 1882	Sept. 15, 1902	Death	20	1902
Blatchford, Samuel	N.Y.	1820	Arthur	Apr. 3, 1882	July 7, 1893	Death	11	1893
Lamar, Lucius Quintus C.	Miss.	1825	Cleveland	Jan. 18, 1888	Jan. 23, 1893	Death	5	1893
Brewer, David Josiah	Asia Minor	1837	Harrison	Jan. 6, 1890	Mar. 28, 1910	Death	20	1910
Brown, Henry Billings	Mass.	1836	Harrison	Jan. 5, 1891	May 28, 1906	retired	15	1913
Shiras, George, Jr.	Pa.	1832	Harrison	Oct. 10, 1892	Feb. 23, 1903	retired	10	1924

Appendix A. (Continued)

Name	Place of Birth	Year of Birth	State App't From	Appointed by President	(A) Judicial Oath Taken	Date Service Terminated	(B) Service Terminated By	Years of Service	Year of Death
Jackson, Howell Edmunds	Tenn.	1832	Tenn.	Harrison	Mar. 4, 1893	Aug. 8, 1895	Death	2 ½	1895
White, Edward Douglass	La.	1845	La.	Cleveland	Mar. 12, 1894	Dec. 18, 1910	promoted	16	1921
Peckham, Rufus Wheeler	N.Y.	1838	N.Y.	Cleveland	Jan. 6, 1896	Oct. 24, 1909	Death	13	1909
McKenna, Joseph	Penn.	1843	Calif.	McKinley	Jan. 26, 1898	Jan. 5, 1925	retired	26	1926
Holmes, Oliver Wendell	Mass.	1841	Mass.	Roosevelt, T.	Dec. 8, 1902	Jan. 12, 1932	retired	29	1935
Day, William Rufus	Ohio	1849	Ohio	Roosevelt, T.	Mar. 2, 1903	Nov. 13, 1922	retired	19	1923
Moody, William Henry	Mass.	1853	Mass.	Roosevelt, T.	Dec. 17, 1906	Nov. 20, 1910	disabled	4	1917
Lurton, Horace Harmon	Ky.	1844	Tenn.	Taft	Jan. 3, 1910	July 12, 1914	Death	4 ½	1914
Hughes, Charles Evans	N.Y.	1862	N.Y.	Taft	Oct. 10, 1910	June 10, 1916	resigned	5	1948
Van Devanter, Willis	Ind.	1859	Wyo.	Taft	Jan. 3, 1911	June 2, 1937	RETIRED	26	1941
Lamar, Joseph Rucker	Ga.	1857	Ga.	Taft	Jan. 3, 1911	Jan. 2, 1916	Death	5	1916
Pitney, Mahlon	N.J.	1858	N.J.	Taft	Mar. 18, 1912	Dec. 31, 1922	disabled	10	1924
McReynolds, James Clark	Ky.	1862	Tenn.	Wilson	Oct. 12, 1914	Jan. 31, 1941	RETIRED	26	1946
Brandeis, Louis Dembitz	Ky.	1856	Mass.	Wilson	June 5, 1916	Feb. 13, 1939	RETIRED	22	1941
Clarke, John Hessin	Ohio	1857	Ohio	Wilson	Oct. 9, 1916	Sept. 18, 1922	resigned	5	1945
Sutherland, George	England	1862	Utah	Harding	Oct. 2, 1922	Jan. 17, 1938	RETIRED	15	1942
Butler, Pierce	Minn.	1866	Minn.	Harding	Jan. 2, 1923	Nov. 16, 1939	Death	16	1939
Sanford, Edward Terry	Tenn.	1865	Tenn.	Harding	Feb. 19, 1923	Mar. 8, 1930	Death	7	1930
Stone, Harlan Fiske	N.H.	1872	N.Y.	Coolidge	Mar. 2, 1925	July 2, 1941	promoted	16	1946
Roberts, Owen Josephus	Pa.	1875	Pa.	Hoover	June 2, 1930	July 31, 1945	RESIGNED	15	1955
Cardozo, Benjamin Nathan	N.Y.	1870	N.Y.	Hoover	Mar. 14, 1932	July 9, 1938	Death	6	1938
Black, Hugo Lafayette	Ala.	1886	Ala.	Roosevelt, F.	Aug. 19, 1937	Sept. 17, 1971	RETIRED	34	1971
Reed, Stanley Forman	Ky.	1884	Ky.	Roosevelt, F.	Jan. 31, 1938	Feb. 25, 1957	RETIRED	19	1980
Frankfurter, Felix	Austria	1882	Mass.	Roosevelt, F.	Jan. 30, 1939	Aug. 28, 1962	RETIRED	23	1965
Douglas, William Orville	Minn.	1898	Conn.	Roosevelt, F.	Apr. 17, 1939	Nov. 12, 1975	RETIRED	36½	1980
Murphy, Frank	Mich.	1890	Mich.	Roosevelt, F.	Feb. 5, 1940	July 19, 1949	Death	9	1949
Byrnes, James Francis	S.C.	1879	S.C.	Roosevelt, F.	July 8, 1941	Oct. 3, 1942	resigned	1	1972
Jackson, Robert Houghwout	Pa.	1892	N.Y.	Roosevelt, F.	July 11, 1941	Oct. 9, 1954	Death	13	1954
Rutledge, Wiley Blount	Ky.	1894	Iowa	Roosevelt, F.	Feb. 15, 1943	Sept. 10, 1949	Death	6 ½	1949
Burton, Harold Hitz	Mass.	1888	Ohio	Truman	Oct. 1, 1945	Oct. 13, 1958	RETIRED	13	1964
Clark, Thomas Campbell	Texas	1899	Texas	Truman	Aug. 24, 1949	June 12, 1967	RETIRED	18	1977

Name	State		Appointed by	Date	Status		
Minton, Sherman	Ind.	1890	Truman	Oct. 12, 1949	RETIRED	7	1965
Harlan, John Marshall	Ill.	1899	Eisenhower	Mar. 28, 1955	RETIRED	16	1971
Brennan, William Joseph, Jr.	N.J.	1906	Eisenhower	Oct. 16, 1956	RETIRED	34	
Whittaker, Charles Evans	Kansas	1901	Eisenhower	Mar. 25, 1957	DISABLED§	5	1973
Stewart, Potter	Ohio	1915	Eisenhower	Oct. 14, 1958	RETIRED	22¾	1985
White, Byron Raymond	Colo.	1917	Kennedy	Apr. 16, 1962			
Goldberg, Arthur Joseph	Ill.	1908	Kennedy	Oct. 1, 1962	Resigned	2 ¾	
Fortas, Abe	Tenn.	1910	Johnson, L.	Oct. 4, 1965	Resigned	3 ½	1982
Marshall, Thurgood	Md.	1908	Johnson, L.	Oct. 2, 1967	RETIRED	24	
Blackmun, Harry A.	Ill.	1908	Nixon	June 9, 1970			
Powell, Lewis Franklin, Jr.	Va.	1907	Nixon	Jan. 7, 1972	RETIRED	15½	
Rehnquist, William Hubbs	Wisc.	1924	Nixon	Jan. 7, 1972			
Stevens, John Paul	Ill.	1920	Ford	Dec. 19, 1972			
O'Connor, Sandra D.	Texas	1930	Reagan	Sept. 15, 1981			
Scalia, Antonin	N.J.	1936	Reagan	Sept. 26, 1986			
Kennedy, Anthony M.	Cal.	1936	Reagan	Feb. 18, 1988			
Souter, David H.	Mass.	1939	Bush	Oct. 9, 1990			
Thomas, Clarence	Ga.	1948	Bush	Oct. 23, 1991			

NOTES: The acceptance of the appointment and commission by the appointee, as evidenced by the taking of the prescribed oaths, is here implied; otherwise the individual is not carried on this list of the Members of the Court. Examples: Robert Hanson Harrison is not carried, as a letter from President Washington of February 9, 1790, states Harrison declined to serve. Neither is Edwin M. Stanton, who died before he could take the necessary steps toward becoming a member of the Court. Chief Justice Rutledge is included because he took his oaths, presided over the August term of 1795, and his name appears on two opinions of the Court for that term.

(A) The date a member of the Court took his judicial oath (the Judiciary Act provided "That the Justice of the Supreme Court, and the district judges, before they proceed to execute the duties of their respective offices, shall take the following oath . . .") is here used as the date of the beginning of his service, for, until that oath is taken, he or she is not vested with the prerogatives of the office. However, Senate confirmation may well have come earlier, for example, Bushrod Washington's (on December 20, 1798). Dates without lowercase-letter references are taken from the Minutes of the Court or from the original oath which is in the Clerk's file. The lowercase letter (a) denotes the date is from the Minutes of some other court, (b) from some other unquestionable authority that is questionable, and better authority would be appreciated.

(B) Explanation of terms used in identifying nature of termination of services:

1. A member of the Court of seventy or more years of age and of ten or more years of service who, pursuant to the Act of April 10, 1869, or subsequent acts, retired or resigned and continued to receive the salary which he was receiving when he retired or resigned, is here carried as "retired."

2. A member retiring since the Act of March 1, 1937 (50 Stat. 24) is granted the same privileges with regard to retiring, instead of resigning, that are granted to judges other than Justices of the Supreme Court. He may be assigned to perform such judicial duties as he is willing to undertake, and during the remainder of his lifetime continues to receive the salary of the office. Such member is here carried as "RETIRED."

3. A member of less than seventy years of age or having less than ten years of service, who resigned and who thereafter did not continue to draw pay based on his age or service, or who resigned before the Act of April 10, 1869, became effective, as Justice Duvall did, is here carried as "resigned."

4. A member of seventy or more years of age and ten or more years of service, resigning since the Act of March 1, 1937, who continues to receive the salary he was receiving when he resigned is here carried as "RESIGNED."

5. Justices Hunt, Moody, and Pitney, who retired under Special Acts, are here carried as "disabled."

6. A member retiring for disability under the general provisions of 28 U.S. Code 372 is here carried as "DISABLED."

(C) For Chief Justice's service as Associate Justice, see under the latter rubric.

*Adapted from a table revised by Frank M. Hepler, Marshal of the Supreme Court of the United States, 1972; revised 1985.

†Served under a recess appointment from August 12, 1795, to December 15, 1795.

§Resigned September 30, 1965.

APPENDIX B. TABLE OF SUCCESSION OF THE JUSTICES SHOWING YEARS OF ACTIVE

Judiciary Act of 1789 provided for a Chief Justice and 5 Associate Justices

Year	Chief Justices	John Rutledge 1789-1791	William Cushing 1789-1810	James Iredell 1790-1799	James Wilson 1789-1798	John Blair 1789-1796
1789 1790	John Jay 1789-1795	John Rutledge 1789-1791	William Cushing 1789-1810	James Iredell 1790-1799	James Wilson 1789-1798	John Blair 1789-1796
	John Rutledge 1795	Thomas Johnson 1791-1793				
	Oliver Ellsworth 1796-1799	William Paterson 1793-1806			Bushrod Washington 1798-1829	Samuel Chase 1796-1811
1800	John Marshall 1801-1835			Alfred Moore 1799-1804 William Johnson 1804-1834		
		Henry B. Livingston 1806-1823				
1810			Joseph Story 1811-1845			Gabriel Duval 1811-1836
1820		Smith Thompson 1823-1843				
1830					Henry Baldwin 1830-1844	
	Roger B. Taney 1836-1864			James M. Wayne 1835-1867		Philip P. Barbour 1836-1841
1840						Peter V. Daniel 1841-1860
		Samuel Nelson 1845-1872	Levi Woodbury 1846-1851		Robert C. Grier 1846-1870	
1850			Benjamin R. Curtis 1851-1857			
			Nathan Clifford 1858-1881			
1860						Samuel F. Miller 1862-1890
	Salmon P. Chase 1864-1873					
1870					William Strong 1870-1880	
	Morrison R. Waite 1874-1888	Ward Hunt 1872-1882				
1880		Samuel Blatchford 1882-1893	Horace Gray 1881-1902		William B. Woods 1880-1887	
	Melville W. Fuller 1888-1910				Lucius Q. C. Lamar 1888-1893	Henry B. Brown 1890-1906
1890		Edward D. White J 1894 CJ 1910-1921			Howell E. Jackson 1893-1895 Rufus W. Peckham 1895-1909	
1900			Oliver Wendell Holmes 1902-1932			William H. Moody 1906-1910
1910	Edward D. White 1910-1921	Willis Van Devanter 1910-1937			Horace H. Lurton 1909-1914	Joseph R. Lamar 1910-1916
					James C. McReynolds 1914-1941	Louis D. Brandeis 1916-1939
1920	William H. Taft 1921-1930					
1930	Charles E. Hughes 1930-1941	Hugo L. Black 1937-1971	Benjamin N. Cardozo 1932-1938 Felix Frankfurter 1939-1962			William O. Douglas 1939-1975
1940	Harlan F. Stone 1941-1946				James F. Byrnes 1941-1942 Wiley Rutledge 1943-1949 Sherman Minton 1949-1956	
1950	Fred M. Vinson 1946-1953					
	Earl Warren 1953-1969				William J. Brennan 1956-1990	
1960			Arthur J. Goldberg 1962-1965 Abe Fortas 1965-1969			
	Warren E. Burger 1969-1986	Lewis F. Powell, Jr. 1972-1987	Harry A. Blackmun 1970			
1970 1980						John Paul Stevens 1975
	William H. Rehnquist J 1986-	Anthony M. Kennedy 1988-			David H. Souter 1990-	
1990						

(Vertical note in James Iredell column: "Act of July 23, 1866, provided for reduction of the Court to 7 members as vacancies should occur")

*Adapted from a table revised by Frank M. Hepler, Marshal of the Supreme Court of the United States, 1972; revised 1985; revised 1992.

Vertical Act annotations (left to right across chart):

- Act of February 24, 1807, provided for increase of the Court to 7 members
- Act of March 3, 1837, provided for increase of the Court to 9 members
- Act of July 23, 1866, provided for reduction of the Court to 7 members as vacancies should occur
- Act of March 3, 1863, provided for increase of the Court to 10 members
- Act of July 23, 1866, provided for reduction of the Court to 7 members as vacancies should occur (Actually the Court fell to 8)
- Act of April 10, 1869, provided for increase of the Court to 9 members

Seat 1	Seat 2 (Catron)	Seat 3	Seat 4	Seat 5	Year
					1789 / 1790
					1800
Thomas Todd 1807-1826					1810
Robert Trimble 1826-1828					1820
John McLean 1829-1861					
	John Catron 1837-1865	John McKinley 1837-1852			1830
					1840
		John A. Campbell 1853-1861			1850
Noah H. Swayne 1862-1881		David Davis 1862-1877	Stephen J. Field 1863-1897		1860
				Joseph P. Bradley 1870-1892	1870
Stanley Matthews 1881-1889		John M. Harlan 1877-1911			1880
David J. Brewer 1889-1910				George Shiras, Jr. 1892-1903	1890
			Joseph McKenna 1898-1925	William R. Day 1903-1922	1900
Charles E. Hughes 1910-1916		Mahlon Pitney 1912-1922			1910
John H. Clarke 1916-1922					
George Sutherland 1922-1938		Edward T. Sanford 1923-1930	Harlan F. Stone 1925-1946	Pierce Butler 1922-1939	1920
		Owen J. Roberts 1930-1945			1930
Stanley F. Reed 1938-1957			Robert H. Jackson 1941-1954	Frank Murphy 1940-1949	1940
		Harold H. Burton 1945-1958		Tom C. Clark 1949-1967	1950
Charles E. Whittaker 1957-1962		Potter Stewart 1958-1981	John M. Harlan 1955-1971		
Byron R. White 1962				Thurgood Marshall 1967-1991	1960
			William H. Rehnquist 1972-1986		1970
		Sandra D. O'Connor 1981-			1980
			Antonin Scalia 1986-		
				Clarence Thomas 1991-	1990

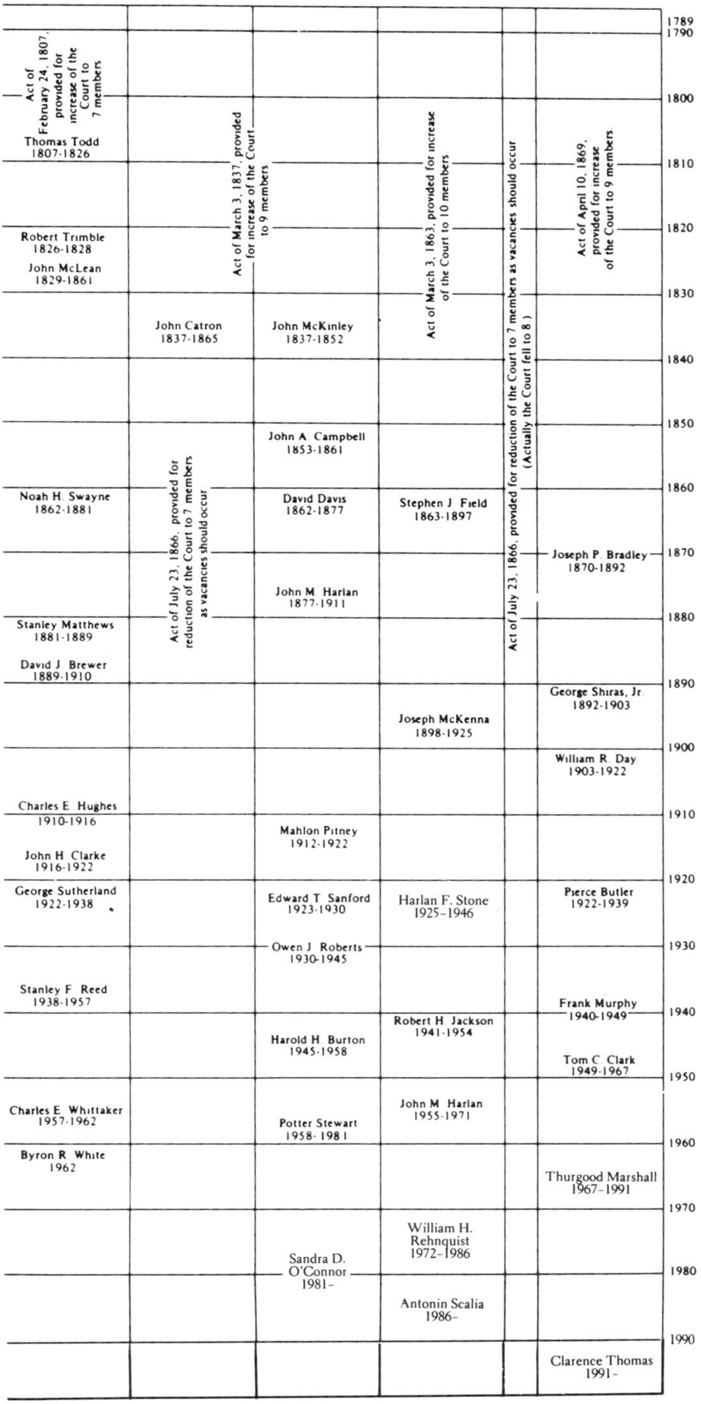

Bibliographical Note

It is a daunting task indeed to determine upon a relatively brief annotated bibliography, having utilized an ever-growing listing of works on the judicial process and civil rights and liberties that, after five editions of *The Judicial Process*, had numbered some seven thousand entries. As I have endeavored to explain in the preface to this edition, the task had simply become too unwieldy—and of questionable utility, given the ready availability of bibliographical source materials in our electronic age. Accordingly, my editor at Oxford University Press and I agreed that the erstwhile mammoth compendia should be replaced with the following annotations—much along the lines of the bibliographical note in my *Freedom and the Court*, 5th ed. (New York: Oxford University Press, 1988).

The nine chapters of this edition of *The Judicial Process* contain a host of footnoted references to major works in the field, all conveniently presented at the bottom of each page. Some of the following entries reflect those entries, while others are not mentioned in the chapters at issue. The listings that follow are arranged by chapter and are necessarily confined to a limited number of works—all of which, however, I regard as significant contributions to the literature.

CHAPTER 1: "INTRODUCTION: THE LAW AND THE COURTS"

A plethora of fundamental, seminal works exists and informs the introductory topic. Among them are C. K. Allen, *Law in the Making* (Oxford University Press, 1964), a seminal overview, as is H. L. A. Hart, *The Concept of Law* (Oxford University Press, 1961). For sheer majesty and beauty of both content and style, Benjamin N. Cardozo, *The Nature of the Judicial Process* (Yale University Press, 1921), and Oliver Wendell Holmes, Jr., *The Common Law* (Little, Brown, 1881) have no rivals. Their wisdom is as towering as it is transcendent. L. M. Friedman, *A History of American Law* (Simon & Schuster, 1986), presents a useful overview of the subject. So do A. T. von Mehren, *The Civil Law System* (Prentice-Hall, 1957), L. L. Fuller, *The Anatomy of Law* (Random House, 1969), F. H. Lawson, *The Rational Strength of English Law* (Stevens, 1951), John Chipman Gray, *The Nature and Sources of Law* (Columbia University, 1916), W. A. Robson, *Civilization and the Growth of Law* (Macmillan, 1935), and B. H. Levy, *Anglo-American Philosophy of Law* (Transaction, 1991).

CHAPTER 2: "STAFFING THE COURTS"

As the all but universal interest in appointments to the judiciary has cascaded, so have the publications dealing with that fascinating subject. A measure of that interest is the happily increasing number of judicial biographies that have become available. I have compiled a twenty-five-page listing of all judicial biographies published to date for the 106 past and present members of the Supreme Court of the United States, in alphabetical order, in the third edition of my *Justices & Presidents* (Oxford University Press, 1992). Among the important works that address the subject of either or both federal and state nominations and appointments are H. W. Chase, *Federal Judges: The Appointing Process* (University of Wisconsin Press, 1973), dealing with lower court jurists; J. P. A. Dawson, *A History of Lay Judges* (Little, Brown, 1960); L. Friedman and F. L. Israel, *The Justices of the United States Supreme Court, 1789–1969* (Chelsea & Bowker, 1969), a sometimes uneven but extremely useful and informative series of essays on the justices, penned by leading experts in the field); the Joint Center for Political Studies report, *Elected and Appointed Black Judges in the United States* (1987, et seq.); Stuart S. Nagel, *Comparing Elected and Appointed Judges* (Sage Publications, 1973); the National Legal Center for the Public Interest's compendium, *Judicial Selection: Merit, Ideology, and Politics* (1990); J. S. Schmidhauser, *Judges and Justices; The Federal Appellate Judiciary* (Little, Brown, 1978); C. E. Smith, *United States Magistrates in the Federal Courts: Subordinate Judges* (Praeger, 1990); and an old classic. A. T. Vanderbilt, *Judges and Jurors; Their Functions, Qualifications, and Selection* (Boston University Press, 1956). Three works on the impeachment and conviction of judges are R. Berger, *Impeachment: The Constitutional Problems* (Harvard University Press, 1973). W. T. Braithwaite, *Who Judges the Judges? A Study of Procedure for Removal and Retirement* (American Bar Foundation, 1971), and I. Brant, *Impeachment: Trials and Errors* (Knopf, 1972). The impeachment and convictions of three federal district court judges in the late 1980s prompted a flurry of scholarly and journalistic commentaries in the media.

CHAPTER 3: "COURTS, COURTROOMS, AND JURIES"

Again, a wealth of publications on the subject is available, ranging from lasting classics to contemporary treatments. Among the former are Max Radin, *The Law and You* (Mentor Books, 1948), James Marshall, *Law and Psychology in Conflict* (Doubleday & Co., 1969), and the wise, clairvoyant, insightful works by Jerome Frank, headed by his towering, still highly useful *Courts on Trial* (Princeton University, 1959). Among more recent treatments are S. Landsman, *The Adversary System: A Description and Defense* (American Enterprise Institute, 1984), W. V. McIntosh, *The Appeal of Civil Law: A Political-Economic Analysis of Litigation* (University of Illinois Press, 1989), D. W. Maynard, *Inside Plea Bargaining: The Language of Negotiation* (Congressional Quarterly Press, 1984), G. L. Wells and E. A. Loftus, *Eyewitness Testimony: Psychological Perspectives* (Cambridge University Press, 1984), and L. S. Wrightsman, C. E. Willis, and S. Kassin, *On the Witness Stand: Controversies in the Courtroom* (Sage Publications, 1987). The ever-controversial and live subject of juries continues to span a host of works. Noteworthy among more recent ones are J. Guinther, *The Jury in America* (Facts on File Publications, 1988), V. P. Hans and N. Vidmar, *Judging the Jury* (Plenum, 1986), R. Hastie, S. D. Penrod, and N. Pennington, *Inside the Jury* (Harvard University Press, 1987), B. Walter, *The Civil Juror* (Facts on File Publications, 1988), and S. Wishman, *Anatomy of a Jury: The System on Trial* (Random House, 1986). Text and footnotes of the chapter provide numerous references to apposite analyses and commentaries on both the grand and the trial jury.

CHAPTER 4: "COURTS AT HOME: I—THE LESSER TRIBUNALS"

The jurisdiction and organization of tribunals below the United States Supreme Court, at both the state and federal levels, properly evoke constant scholarly and popular attention. Noteworthy among contemporary studies are the following: A. Barak, *Judicial Discretion* (Yale University Press, 1989); J. Eisenstein, R. B. Flemming, and P. F. Nardulli, *The Contours of Justice: Communities and Their Courts* (Scott, Foresman, 1988); S. Goldman and C. M. Lamb, *Judicial Conflict and Consensus: Behavioral Studies of American Appellate Courts* (University of Kentucky Press, 1989); D. J. Meador, *American Courts* (West, 1991), a very useful explication of the system; C. Seron, *The Role of Magistrates in Federal District Courts* (Federal Judicial Center, 1983 and 1985); C. R. Swanson, Jr., and S. M. Talarico, *Court Administration: Issues and Response* (University of Georgia Press, 1988); and a trenchant case study by D. J. Barrow and T. G. Walker, *A Court Divided: The Fifth Circuit Court of Appeals and the Politics of Judicial Reform* (Yale University Press, 1988).

CHAPTER 5: "COURTS AT HOME: II—THE SUPREME COURT"

A veritable *embarras de richesse* exists in terms of publications on the highest tribunal in our land. I shall attempt to confine the following listings to the Court's *modus operandi* rather than to its jurisprudence, but some overlapping is patently unavoidable. Thus, it would be inadvisable to fail here to list such leading major histories of the Court and its work as John Beveridge's multivolume *The Life of John Marshall* (Houghton Mifflin, 1916); the magisterial, still not entirely completed, Oliver Wendell Holmes Devise, *History of the Supreme Court of the United States*, its many volumes authored by leading scholars, its initial financing coming from the great Justice's bequest (he left the bulk of his estate to the United States!) (Macmillan, 1971ff); Robert G. McCloskey's so readable compact history of the Court, *The American Supreme Court* (University of Chicago Press, 1960, brought up to date through the Warren Court by Martin Shapiro in 1971); Robert J. Steamer's *The Supreme Court in Crisis; A History of Conflict* (University of Massachusetts Press, 1971); and the still admirable history by Charles Warren, *The Supreme Court in United States History* (Little, Brown, 1922, 1926, and 1935). As to the myriad books on the Court's process, the following may be noted: L. C. Baum, *The Supreme Court* (Congressional Quarterly Books, 1991); J. E. Bond, *The Art of Judging* (Transaction, 1987); J. Brigham, *The Cult of the Court* (Temple University Press, 1987); G. Casper, *The Workload of the Supreme Court* (American Bar Foundation, 1976); the Congressional Quarterly's periodically published *Guide to the United States Supreme Court* (e.g., 1989, by Congressional Quarterly Books); S. Estreicher and J. Sexton, *Redefining the Supreme Court's Role: A The-*

ory of Managing the Federal Judicial Process (Yale University Press, 1986); the still engaging work by Paul A. Freund, The Supreme Court of the United States: Its Business, Purposes, and Performances (New American Library, 1961); another, still widely acclaimed classic, H. M. Hart and H. Wechsler, The Federal Courts and the Federal System (Foundation Press, 1988); ditto Charles Evans Hughes's own The Supreme Court of the United States (Columbia University Press, 1928); also Robert H. Jackson's The Supreme Court in the American System of Government (Harvard University Press, 1955); P. B. Kurland, The Supreme Court and the Judicial Function (University of Chicago Press, 1975); T. R. Marshall, Public Opinion and the Supreme Court (Unwyn Hyman, 1989); R. Neely, How Courts Govern America (Yale University Press, 1981); D. M. O'Brien, Storm Center: The Supreme Court in American Politics (Norton, 1992); Chief Justice William H. Rehnquist's timely explanation of the Court's procedures in his The Supreme Court: How It Was, How It Is (Morrow, 1987); S. R. Schlesinger, The United States Supreme Court: Fact, Evidence, and Law (University Press of America, 1983); J. R. Schmidhauser, The Supreme Court: Its Politics, Personalities, and Procedures (Holt, 1960); H. J. Spaeth and S. Brenner, Studies in United States Supreme Court Behavior (Garland, 1990); S. S. Ulmer, Supreme Court Policy Making and Constitutional Law (McGraw-Hill, 1986); S. L. Wasby, The Supreme Court in the Federal Judicial System (Nelson Hall, 1988); and E. Witt, The Supreme Court at Work (Congressional Quarterly Books, 1990).

CHAPTER 6: "COURTS ABROAD"

Although references to courts and judges and aspects of the judicial process generally may be found throughout the pages of this tome, chapter 6 is designed almost entirely to deal with the English and Welsh and French systems. Discussion of judicial review abroad will be found in chapter 7. The best work on the judicial system of England and Wales—Scotland operates under a different structure (see chapter 1)—is Richard M. Jackson's The Machinery of Justice in England, which he shepherded through seven editions, his most recent one appearing in 1977. In 1989 J. R. Spencer took over with the work's eighth edition (Cambridge University Press, 1989). The book does an excellent job of explicating the British judiciary in its contemporary mode. For a fine study of the English appellate process the best and most recent work is a comparative one: Robert J. Martineau, Appellate Justice in England and the United States; A Comparative Analysis (William S. Hein, 1990). E. C. Friesen and I. R. Scott discuss the criminal justice system in English Criminal Justice (University of Birmingham, 1977). Two well-known works on the Law Lords, Britain's highest judicial echelon, are Louis Blom-Cooper and Gavin Drewry, Final Appeal: A Study of the House of Lords in Its Judicial Capacity (Oxford University Press, 1972), and Alan Paterson, The Law Lords (University of Toronto Press, 1982). Judicial appointments are treated ably in Judicial Appointments (Her Majesty's Stationery Office, 1986). S. Lee analyzes jurists in Judging Judges (Faber and Faber, 1988). Among classic works on the British system that must be mentioned are E. C. S. Wade and G. Godfrey Phillips, Constitutional and Administrative Law, 9th ed., by A. W. Bradley (Longman, 1977), and J. A. G. Griffith, The

Politics of the Judiciary (Fontana, 1981). *The Economist* is a particularly good source for the current changes contemplated, and partly effected, in Britain's legal system.

For recent developments in the French judicial structure, which is also experiencing certain changes, see the third edition of William Safran's *The French Polity* (Longmans Books, 1991). No one knows more about the French administrative judicial system than Margherita Rendel, whose works, such as *The Administrative Function of the Conseil d'État* (Weidenfeld and Nicolson, 1970), are staples. Robert Boure and Patrick Mignard discuss endemic problems in *La Crise de l'Institution Judiciaire* (Bourgeois, 1977), as does Laurent Cohen-Tanugi in *Le Droit sans l'État* (Presses Universitaires de France, 1985). Hubert Pinsseau provides an overall view in *L'Organisation Judiciaire de la France* (Documentation Française, 1985). Alec Stone conveys timely insight in *The Birth of Judicial Politics in France: The Constitutional Council in Comparative Perspective* (Harvard University Press, 1992).

CHAPTER 7: "JUDICIAL REVIEW: I—THE SUPREME POWER"

A wealth of works are available on what is, indeed, the judiciary's ultimate and most awesome power. Although the chapter is replete with references to the staples and recent publications on judicial review, the following may serve to underscore the vitality of the basic issue. Thus, John Marshall's holding in *Marbury v. Madison* is never far from renewed and additional scholarly commentary in book form. Among the more recent are works that reexamine and reinterpret that famed decision, often providing diverse conclusions, e.g., Robert L. Clinton's *Marbury v. Madison and Judicial Review* (University Press of Kansas, 1989) and Leonard Levy's customarily assertive *Original Intent and the Framers' Constitution* (University of Chicago Press, 1988). There are, of course, the enduring, classic staples on judicial review, which will always serve as focal reference points. Thus, we have Edward S. Corwin's masterful *The Doctrine of Judicial Review* (Princeton University Press, 1914) and his seminal *The Establishment of Judicial Review* (Princeton University Press, 1930). There are Robert E. Cushman's *The Role of the Supreme Court in a Democratic Nation* (Public Affairs Committee, 1938) and Alpheus T. Mason's *The Supreme Court: Palladium of Freedom* (University of Michigan Press, 1962). Three other vital, frequently quoted major contributions are Thomas Reed Powell's *Vagaries and Varieties in Constitutional Interpretation* (Columbia University Press, 1956), R. Von Moschzisker's *Judicial Review of Legislation* (Da Capo Press, 1971), and Herbert Wechsler's *Principles, Politics, and Fundamental Law* (Harvard University Press, 1961). Among the many books penned before, during, and after the 1937 "Court-packing" controversy that address the underlying judicial review problem are D. Alfange, *The Supreme Court and the National Will* (Doubleday, Doran, 1937), L. B. Boudin, *Government by Judiciary* (Godwin, 1932), R. K. Carr, *Democracy and the Supreme Court* (University of Oklahoma Press, 1936), C. G. Haines, *A Government of Laws or a Government of Men* (University of California at Los Angeles Press, 1929), J. M. Henry, *Nine above the Law: Our Supreme Court* (Lewis, 1936), J. L. Lewinson, *Limiting*

Judicial Review (Parker, Staine and Braid, 1937), M. R. Senior, *The Power of Judicial Review with Respect to Congressional Legislation* (George Washington University Press, 1937), Charles Warren, *Congress, the Constitution, and the Supreme Court* (Little, Brown, 1935), and B. F. Wright, *The Growth of American Constitutional Law* (Reynal and Hitchcock, 1942). Many of the issues raised in these several works are still very much alive, and their pertinent analysts will be cited in chapter 8. But a few recent titles deserve mention here: A. R. Brewer-Carias, *Judicial Review in Comparative Law* (Cambridge University Press, 1989); Archibald Cox, *The Court and the Constitution* (Houghton Mifflin, 1987); P. R. Dimond, *The Supreme Court and Judicial Review: The Role of Provisional Review in a Democracy* (University of Michigan Press, 1989), which, along the lines of Louis Lusky's *By What Right? A Commentary on the Supreme Court's Right to Revise the Constitution* (Michie, 1975), suggests a type of "tentative" judicial review alongside "definitive" judicial review; G. J. Jacobsohn, *The Supreme Court and the Decline of Constitutional Aspiration* (Rowman & Littlefield, 1986); S. Levinson, *Constitutional Faith* (Princeton University Press, 1988); A. P. Melone, *Judicial Review and American Constitutional Democracy* (Iowa State University Press, 1988); R. F. Nagel, *Constitutonal Cultures: The Mentality and Cultures of Judicial Review* (University of California Press, 1989); S. Snowiss, *Judicial Review and the Law of the Constitution* (Yale University Press, 1990); J. M. Sosin, *The Aristocracy of the Long Robe: The Origin of Judicial Review in America* (Greenwood, 1989); and C. Wolfe, *The Rise of Modern Judicial Review: From Constitutional Interpretation to Judge-Made Law* (Basic Books, 1986).

CHAPTER 8: "JUDICIAL REVIEW: II—CONTROVERSY AND LIMITATIONS"

The overriding issue addressed in this chapter is, essentially, how to draw that elusive line between judicial "judging" and judicial "legislating," between "judge-found" and "judge-made" law, between "judicial activism" and "judicial restraint." A vast array of books that endeavor to deal with that vexatious and so fundamental problem of the Court's appropriate role has been published. Basically, the commentator–authors fall into three groups: (1) those who, like Justice William J. Brennan, Jr., quite candidly envisage an expansive, broadly "liberal" role for the judiciary, in general, and the Supreme Court, in particular; (2) those who, like Justice Lewis F. Powell, Jr., approach the matter from a "moderate" or "centrist" point of view; and (3) those who, like Justice Felix Frankfurter, are committed to an abstemious, deferential judicial role. I have attempted to characterize or catalogue the following works accordingly. In the first, the "aggressive judicial power exercise" group, belong these, among others, although some have certain limitations or reservations:

Lawrence H. Tribe, *Constitutional Choices* (Harvard University Press, 1985), a tenacious advocate, especially in the realm of civil rights and liberties; Arthur S. Miller, *Toward Increased Judicial Activism* (Greenwood, 1982), is a clarion call for unrestrained and unrestricted judicial power; Michael J. Perry, in *The Constitution, the Courts, and Human Rights* (Yale University Press, 1983) and *Morality,*

Politics, and Law (Oxford University Press, 1989) has few limits to the exercise of broad-gauged judicial exercise of power, again especially in the human rights realm; although Jesse H. Choper's *Judicial Review and the National Political Process* (University of Chicago Press, 1980) would place some thought-provoking limitations on the Court's authority in the horizons of federalism and the separation of powers, he offers none in those pertaining to civil rights and liberties; and Lief H. Carter's *Contemporary Constitutional Lawmaking: The Supreme Court and the Art of Politics* (Pergamon Press, 1985). The numerous journal and review articles by Paul Brest, Bernard Schwartz, Herman Schwartz, and Mark Tushnet manifest a similar jurisprudential posture.

Many well-known authors inform the second, the "moderate" or "centrist," group. Among them are the works of Alexander Bickel, the elegant and sophisticated scholar, led by one of his last works, *The Supreme Court and the Idea of Progress* (Yale Unviersity Press, 1978), which emphasizes the need to regard constitutional intepretation as a "joint enterprise" of all three branches of government, a view embraced affirmatively, with a special nod to the role of Congress, by John Agresto in his *The Supreme Court and Constitutional Democracy* (Cornell University Press, 1984). It goes without saying so that outstanding in this second group is the great Benjamin N. Cardozo, whose maginificent *The Nature of the Judicial Process* (Yale University Press, 1921) may well be the best among all works written on the subject in view of his measured, realistic insight and his beautiful, elegant pen. Others who have a place in this second category are the abovementioned (chapter 7) Paul R. Dimond and Louis Lusky, whose approach to the "line" is a reflectively cautious and quasi-abstemious one. Leslie Friedman Goldstein's carefully crafted *In Defense of the Text: Democracy and Constitutional Theory* (Rowman & Littlefield, 1992), emphasizes what she well describes as the logic of embracing "moderate textualism" with regard to the Court's responsibilities in terms of a written Constitution. And there is the so significant, albeit highly complex *Democracy and Distrust: A Theory of Judicial Review*, by James Hart Ely, who advocates *process* as the lodestar of judicial interpretative responsibility while counseling abstention from any forays into "substantive due process," e. g., abortion (Harvard University Press, 1980).

The third, and for these purposes last, group of commentators on the "line" constitute a coterie of eminent scholars who are dedicated to a highly deferential, abstemious judicial role, often, although not always, involving an embrace of the perceived obligations of "original intent," while nonetheless upholding the power of judicial review per se. They include the redoubtable nonagenarian Raoul Berger, whose *Government by Judiciary: The Transformation of the Fourteenth Amendment* (Harvard University Press, 1977) is a totally principled, uncompromising, stubborn adherence to original intent *qua* original intent; his follower Walter Berns's *Taking the Constitution Seriously* (Simon & Schuster, 1987); S. B. Gabin's *Judicial Review and the Reasonable Doubt Test* (Kennikat Press, 1980), an embrace of James Bradley Thayer's famed 1893 treatise, "The Origin and Scope of the American Doctrine of Constitutional Law" (7 *Harvard Law Review 129*), which became Felix Frankfurter's judicial process Bible; Gary L. McDowell's two thoughtful caveats, *Equity and the Constitution* (University of Chicago Press,

1982) and *Curbing the Courts: The Constitution and the Limits of Judicial Power* (Louisiana State University Press, 1988); Bernard H. Siegan's *The Supreme Court's Constitution: An Inquiry into Judicial Review and Its Impact on Society* (Transaction Books, 1987); and Christopher Wolfe's *Judicial Activism: Bulwark of Freedom or Precarious Security* (Brooks/Cole, 1991). A helpful collection of essays on most aspects of the issue is S. C. Halpern and C. M. Lamb's *Supreme Court Activism and Restraint* (Lexington, 1982); another is the symposium in 6 *Hastings Constitutional Law Quarterly* 2 1979 featuring Louis Lusky, Wallace Mendelson, K. C. Cerney, this author, Arthur S. Miller, Stanley I. Kutler, and a 110-page reply–commentary by Raoul Berger.

CHAPTER 9: "CODA: A REALISTIC BULWARK"

The final chapter is essentially an examination of the Court's self-perceived operative maxims of judicial self-restraint vis-à-vis the other, the political branches, of the government. What Alexander M. Bickel wisely termed the "passive virtues" in his *The Least Dangerous Branch: The Supreme Court at the Bar of Politics* (Bobbs-Merrill, 1962), these maxims had their initial formal elucidation in Justice Cardozo's concurring opinion in *Ashwander v. Tennessee Valley Authority*, 297 U.S. 288, in 1936, where he spelled out six of the most important. Both explicitly and implicitly students as well as experts on the judicial process have quite naturally addressed the overriding self-restraint problem, and their recognition of, and concern with, that crucial fact of judicial life and authority are all but necessarily present in all commentaries on the nature of the judicial function. A host of works are eminently citable, among them the following: Justice Robert H. Jackson's epitaph, *The Supreme Court in the American System of Government* (Harvard University Press, 1955); Gary L. McDowell's caveat to the Court in *Curbing the Courts: The Constitution and the Limits of Judicial Power* (Louisiana State University Press, 1988), especially chapter 6, "The Forms and Limits of Judicial Power"; the great Cardozo's own seminal treatise, *The Nature of the Judicial Process* (Yale University Press, 1921); Bickel's already severally mentioned *The Supreme Court and the Idea of Progress* (Harper & Row, 1970); Justice Hugo L. Black's touching valedictory, *A Constitutional Faith* (Knopf, 1968); and, indeed, the plethora of books cited under chapters 7 and 8, all of which, in one mode or another, come to grips with the problem of deference, of abstemiousness, of the advisability of, in Justice Frankfurter's memorable epigram, "when in doubt, don't."

One of the most contentious and most intriguing of the sixteen maxims of judicial self-restraint is the "political question" syndrome, discussed at some length in this chapter. The nature and attendant problems of this endemic "can of worms" have been of lasting interest to constitutional law scholars. They are treated expertly in such commentaries as those by Jack Peltason, *Federal Courts in the Political Process* (Doubleday, 1955); the towering Learned Hand in his thought-stimulating, troubling, small but truly significant *The Bill of Rights* (Harvard University Press, 1958); extensively and, at that period in history, significantly, by Charles C. Post in a full-length book, *The Supreme Court and Political Questions*

(Johns Hopkins University Press, 1936). The Court's momentous 6:2 decision in 1962, in *Baker v. Carr*, written by Justice Brennan, signaled a veritable flood of works in the reapportionment/redistricting realm. All inevitably deal with the political question maxim, one that the Court's ruling in *Baker v. Carr*, followed by Chief Justice Warren's opinion for his Court in *Reynolds v. Sims*, the lead case in a compendium of six, two years later, altered dramatically, with continuing reverberations for representative government, democracy, political power, and the nature of the judicial process.

I
General Subject Index

II
Name Index

III
Court Cases Index

408

WITHDRAWN